SHARON PACE grew up in Western and Central New York. She received a bachelor's degree from Georgetown University, a master's degree from Vanderbilt, and a PhD in Christianity and Judaism in Antiquity from the University of Notre Dame. Since 1983 Sharon has been a member of the theology faculty at Marquette University, where she teaches Bible, Judaica, and the freshman seminar "Introduction to Inquiry." The author of *The Old Greek Translation of Daniel 7–12*, *The Women of Genesis: from Sarah to Potiphar's Wife*, and the co-author of *Women's Stories*, Pace has also contributed to *The Anchor Bible Dictionary*; *The New Interpreter's Dictionary of the Bible*; *Studies in the Hebrew Bible, Qumran, and the Septuagint*; and *Biblica: The Bible Atlas*.

PROJECT EDITOR
R. SCOTT NASH
Mercer University
Macon, Georgia

OLD TESTAMENT GENERAL EDITOR
SAMUEL E. BALENTINE
Union Theological Seminary and
Presbyterian School of Christian Education
Richmond, Virginia

NEW TESTAMENT GENERAL EDITOR
R. ALAN CULPEPPER
McAfee School of Theology
Mercer University
Atlanta, Georgia

DANIEL

Smyth & Helwys Bible Commentary: Daniel

Publication Staff

President & CEO
Cecil P. Staton

Publisher & Executive Vice President
Lex Horton

Vice President, Production
Keith Gammons

Senior Editor
Mark K. McElroy

Book Editor
Leslie Andres

Graphic Designers
Wesley Crook
Dave Jones

Assistant Editors
Betsy Butler
Kelley F. Land

Smyth & Helwys Publishing, Inc.
6316 Peake Road
Macon, Georgia 31210-3960
1-800-747-3016
© 2008 by Smyth & Helwys Publishing
Printed in the United States of America.

The paper used in this publication meets the minimum
requirements of American National Standard for Information
Sciences—Permanence of Paper for Printed Library Materials.
ANSI Z39.48–1984 (alk. paper)

Library of Congress Cataloging-in-Publication Data

Pace, Sharon.
Daniel / by Sharon Pace.
p. cm.—(The Smyth & Helwys Bible commentary ; v. 17)
Includes bibliographical references and indexes.
ISBN 978-1-57312-074-6 (alk. paper)
1. Bible. O.T. Daniel—Commentaries. I. Title.
BS1555.53.P33 2008
224'.507—dc22
2008011733

SMYTH & HELWYS BIBLE COMMENTARY

DANIEL

SHARON PACE

SMYTH&HELWYS
PUBLISHING INCORPORATED • MACON, GEORGIA

ADVANCE PRAISE

"Sharon Pace has produced an excellent commentary on Daniel—not an easy task given the many ways in which this book has often been misused and abused. Readers will appreciate her careful attention to historical-critical questions about the text, her use of illustrative materials from the ancient Near Eastern world, her examples drawn from the history of interpretation of Daniel, and especially her insightful theological comments about the text. This commentary provides a good model of how to combine solid, critical exegesis of the biblical text with thoughtful application of ideas drawn from that exegesis."

Mitchell G. Reddish
Professor and Chair, Religious Studies
Stetson University

"Dr. Pace penetrates the manifold complexities of the Book of Daniel, providing the Babylonian, Persian, Greek, and Jewish historical background required to interpret it, as well as encyclopedic illustration of its archaeological, artistic, literary, and religious perspectives. She proves to be an experienced and insightful guide, decoding the text's miraculous stories and symbolic visions in an engagingly written exposition of its multi-layered message. Her commentary is ultimately a profound theological meditation on how, in a world historically filled with violence and suffering, we can seek hope."

Professor Eugene Ulrich
University of Notre Dame

"Imagination! Sharon Pace's thoughtful and enjoyable work on the stories of Daniel is honest historically but also useful religiously. A refreshing combination! By recognizing the faithful imaginative work of ancient Jewish storytellers and authors, Dr. Pace has written a work that will be welcomed by scholars, pastors, and laypersons alike."

James E. Bowley, Ph.D.
Chair, Department of Religious Studies
Associate Professor of Religious Studies
Millsaps College

"This commentary tackles a number of knotty issues in a lucid manner, without focusing only on historical explanations of the text or lodging itself in the apocalyptic speculation so dear to some commentators today. . . . She finds a sense of perduring strength in the struggle to envision a compassionate God, whose final gift to suffering people is a strong hope that the Divine One will ultimately transform the present experiences of exile for those who stand firm in trust. The most intriguing aspect of the commentary may be the "Connections" sections, which probe a wealth of Jewish and Christian responses to experiences of unexplained pain and suffering and places them in conversation with Daniel.

"As a result, Sharon Pace persuasively depicts Daniel as a word of hope for people suffering loss, opposition or oppression. Her counter-texts come either from inner-biblical processes of interpretation or from the history of the struggle with unaccountable evil, among Jews or Christians. It is highly recommended for students and pastors, and will also enrich the interpretive possibilities for scholars and students of religion and the Bible."

John C. Endres, S.J. Professor of Sacred Scripture (Old Testament),
Jesuit School of Theology at Berkeley and Graduate Theological Union

CONTENTS

DEDICATION

To Leah and Hannah

ABBREVIATIONS USED IN THIS COMMENTARY

Books of the Old Testament, Apocrypha, and New Testament are generally abbreviated in the Sidebars, parenthetical references, and notes according to the following system.

The Old Testament

Genesis	Gen
Exodus	Exod
Leviticus	Lev
Numbers	Num
Deuteronomy	Deut
Joshua	Josh
Judges	Judg
Ruth	Ruth
1–2 Samuel	1–2 Sam
1–2 Kings	1–2 Kgs
1–2 Chronicles	1–2 Chr
Ezra	Ezra
Nehemiah	Neh
Esther	Esth
Job	Job
Psalm (Psalms)	Ps (Pss)
Proverbs	Prov
Ecclesiastes	Eccl
or Qoheleth	Qoh
Song of Solomon	Song
or Song of Songs	Song
or Canticles	Cant
Isaiah	Isa
Jeremiah	Jer
Lamentations	Lam
Ezekiel	Ezek
Daniel	Dan
Hosea	Hos
Joel	Joel
Amos	Amos
Obadiah	Obad
Jonah	Jonah
Micah	Mic

Nahum	Nah
Habakkuk	Hab
Zephaniah	Zeph
Haggai	Hag
Zechariah	Zech
Malachi	Mal

The Apocrypha

1–2 Esdras	1–2 Esdr
Tobit	Tob
Judith	Jdt
Additions to Esther	Add Esth
Wisdom of Solomon	Wis
Ecclesiasticus or the Wisdom of Jesus Son of Sirach	Sir
Baruch	Bar
Epistle (or Letter) of Jeremiah	Ep Jer
Prayer of Azariah	Pr Azar
The Song of the Three Young Men	Sg Three
Daniel and Susanna	Sus
Daniel, Bel, and the Dragon	Bel
Prayer of Manasseh	Pr Man
1–4 Maccabees	1–4 Macc

The New Testament

Matthew	Matt
Mark	Mark
Luke	Luke
John	John
Acts	Acts
Romans	Rom
1–2 Corinthians	1–2 Cor
Galatians	Gal
Ephesians	Eph
Philippians	Phil
Colossians	Col
1–2 Thessalonians	1–2 Thess
1–2 Timothy	1–2 Tim
Titus	Titus
Philemon	Phlm
Hebrews	Heb
James	Jas
1–2 Peter	1–2 Pet
1–2–3 John	1–2–3 John
Jude	Jude
Revelation	Rev

Old Testament Pseudepigrapha

2 Baruch (Syriac Apocalypse)	*2 Bar.*
1 Enoch	*1 En.*
2 Enoch	*2 En.*
Jubilees	*Jub.*
Joseph and Aseneth	*Jos. Asen.*
Testament of Moses	*T. Mos.*

Dead Sea Scrolls and Related Texts

Hodayot or *Thanksgiving Hymns*	1QH
Pesher Habakkuk	1QpHab
Milḥamah or *War Scroll*	QM
Serek Hayaḥad or	1QS
Rule of the Community	
Prayer of Nabonidus	4QPrNab

Josephus

Against Apion	*Ag. Ap.*
Antiquities	*Ant.*
Jewish War	*J.W.*

Mishnah, Talmud, and Related Literature

Babylonian (Baylonian Talmud)	*b.*
ʿAbodah Zarah	ʿAbod. Zar.
Baba Batra	B. Bat.
Berakot	Ber.
Giṭṭin	Giṭ.
Ḥagigah	Ḥag.
mishnah	m.
Šabbat	Šabb.
Sanhedrin	Sanh.
Šebuʿot	Šebu.
Taʿanit	Taʿan.
Megillah	Meg.
Jerusalem (Jerusalem Talmud)	y.

Other Rabbinic Works

Genesis Rabbah	*Gen. Rab.*
Exodus Rabbah	*Exod. Rab.*
Leviticus Rabbah	*Lev. Rab.*
Numbers Rabbah	*Num. Rab.*
Deuteronomy Rabbah	*Deut. Rab.*

Song of Songs Rabbah	*Song. Rab.*
Lamentations Rabbah	*Lam. Rab.*
Mekilta	*Mek.*
Pesiqta Rabbati	*Pesiq. Rab.*

Other commonly used abbreviations include:

A. T.	author's translation
BCE	Before the Common Era
CE	the Common Era
C.	century
c.	*circa* (around "that time")
cf.	*confer* (compare)
ch.	chapter
chs.	chapters
comps.	compilers
d.	died
ed.	edition, edited by, or editor
eds.	editors
e.g.	*exempli gratia* (for example)
et al.	*et alia* (and others)
f./ff.	and the following (ones)
gen. ed.	general editor
ibid.	*ibidem* (in the same place)
i.e.	*id est* (that is)
lit.	literally
MT	Masoretic Text
n.d.	no date
n.p.	no place
OG	Old Greek
sg.	singular
trans.	translated by or translator(s)
vol(s).	volume(s)
v.	verse
vs.	*versus* (as opposed to or contrasted with)
vv.	verses

Selected additional works cited by abbreviation include the following. A complete listing of abbreviations can be referenced in *The SBL Handbook of Style* (Peabody, MA: Hendrikson, 1999):

AB	Anchor Bible
ABD	*Anchor Bible Dictionary*
ANET	*Ancient Near Eastern Texts Relating to the Old Testament*
AUSS	*Andrews University Seminary Studies*

BRev	*Bible Review*
CBQ	*Catholic Biblical Quarterly*
CBQMS	Catholic Biblical Quarterly, Monograph Series
EncJud	*Encyclopaedia Judaica*
ICC	International Critical Commentary
Int	*Interpretation: A Bible Commentay for Teaching and Preaching*
JB	Jerusalem Bible
JBL	*Journal of Biblical Literature*
JPS	Jewish Publication Society
JSOT	*Journal for the Study of the Old Testament*
JSOTSup	Journal for the Study of the Old Testament, Supplement Series
LXX	Septuagint
MT	Masoretic Text
NAB	New American Bible
NEB	New English Bible
NIB	The New Interpreter's Bible
NJPS	New JPS Translation (Tanakh)
NRSV	New Revised Standard Version
OTL	Old Testament Library
REB	Revised English Bible
SBLDS	Society of Biblical Literature, Dissertation Series
SJOT	*Scandinavian Journal of the Old Testament*
TDOT	*Theological Dictionary of the Old Testament*
VT	*Vetus Testamentum*
VTSup	Supplements to *Vetus Testamentum*
WBC	Word Biblical Commentary
ZAW	*Zeitschrift für alttestamentliche Wissenschaft*

AUTHOR'S PREFACE

In a world filled with horrific violence, suffering, pain, and endless sorrow, how does one find the courage to live with hope? Recognizing the infinite examples of innocent suffering, how can one believe in a compassionate God? These questions, which gnaw at modern humanity, are pondered and probed in the Hebrew Scriptures as well. Israel's struggle with these conundrums fills the pages of the Scriptures. Easy answers are never given, perhaps reflecting humanity's very experience. Although readers are probably most familiar with these agonizing questions as presented in the book of Job or in the Psalms, the book of Daniel offers a window into such essential reflections as well. It does so both through edifying stories that critique Israel's foreign overlords and through visions that imagine a completely different reality. The book of Daniel presents models of victories—both small and great—that lend dignity to everyday life under unpredictable and sometimes menacing rulers. It envisions a transformed future in which the entire world acknowledges the One God and a universal morality. It presents absolute confidence in this hope. This trust in the ultimate goodness of a just God does not mean, however, that the interim is easy. It is replete with great suffering. The experiences of Daniel and his companions as well as the content of Daniel's visions and his reaction to receiving them present a sobering scene. Facing fearsome ordeals, besieged by capricious and dangerous overlords, and powerlessness before rulers, Daniel and his companions stand against tyranny and with each other. Incapacitated by terrifying visions, Daniel nonetheless finds comfort in the compassionate divine presence.

The book of Daniel showcases these memories of a unique people—Israel—but it also transcends its specific time and place. This collection of stories and visions can comment on the experience of anyone or any group that finds itself weighed down by suffering. Clever designs by enterprising youths work quietly and subtly to defeat one much more powerful than they. Tested and threatened, Daniel never forgets to watch over his companions. Feeling the pain of a despairing community, the visions of the book offer an interpretation of history that is arresting in its expectation. It boldly declares, through the eyes of faith, that the suffering of the righteous matters, that God hears their voices, and that there is a divine plan for good.

It was determined long ago by the very foundations of God's creation: the evil of the present earthly kingdoms will end in dust. The kingdom of God will be ushered in because the universe follows a design in which wrongs are righted. With this confidence, Daniel—and hence all who hear the book's message—can live with courage.

During my years of studying this sometimes difficult book, I have been moved by these images of suffering, courage, and expectation. It is my hope that this commentary helps to unravel some of the quagmires that can veil the book's meaning. I am fortunate that throughout the process of writing, many colleagues and companions have aided me. My husband, Brian Sanborn, and my friends Harold Frolkis (of blessed memory) and Debra Alpert-Frolkis provided unending support. The work of Samuel Balentine, the Old Testament editor of the series, was incalculable. From the first submitted chapter to the last draft of the book, I have continued to learn from his insights. I am grateful to Ken Hoglund for his careful reading and for his suggestions for improvement. My biblical colleagues at Marquette University—Deirdre Dempsey, Julian Hills, William Kurz, Andrei Orlov, John Schmitt, Carol Stockhausen, and Kevin Sullivan—answered my many queries. Silviu Bunta offered sage commentary and invaluable editorial assistance. Michael Duffey, Mickey Mattox, Irfan Omar, Wanda Zemler-Cizewski, and Joseph Mueller kindly assisted me with questions on the history of interpretation. The chair of the department, John Laurance, aided me with university grant applications; I am grateful to Marquette for the summer faculty fellowship (2006) that I received to complete this work. I am fortunate to work in such a community of scholars who enhance my life.

SERIES PREFACE

The *Smyth & Helwys Bible Commentary* is a visually stimulating and user-friendly series that is as close to multimedia in print as possible. Written by accomplished scholars with all students of Scripture in mind, the primary goal of the *Smyth & Helwys Bible Commentary* is to make available serious, credible biblical scholarship in an accessible and less intimidating format.

Far too many Bible commentaries fall short of bridging the gap between the insights of biblical scholars and the needs of students of God's written word. In an unprecedented way, the *Smyth & Helwys Bible Commentary* brings insightful commentary to bear on the lives of contemporary Christians. Using a multimedia format, the volumes employ a stunning array of art, photographs, maps, and drawings to illustrate the truths of the Bible for a visual generation of believers.

The *Smyth & Helwys Bible Commentary* is built upon the idea that meaningful Bible study can occur when the insights of contemporary biblical scholars blend with sensitivity to the needs of lifelong students of Scripture. Some persons within local faith communities, however, struggle with potentially informative biblical scholarship for several reasons. Oftentimes, such scholarship is cast in technical language easily grasped by other scholars, but not by the general reader. For example, lengthy, technical discussions on every detail of a particular scriptural text can hinder the quest for a clear grasp of the whole. Also, the format for presenting scholarly insights has often been confusing to the general reader, rendering the work less than helpful. Unfortunately, responses to the hurdles of reading extensive commentaries have led some publishers to produce works for a general readership that merely skim the surface of the rich resources of biblical scholarship. This commentary series incorporates works of fine art in an accurate and scholarly manner, yet the format remains "user-friendly." An important facet is the presentation and explanation of images of art, which interpret the biblical material or illustrate how the biblical material has been understood and interpreted in the past. A visual generation of believers deserves a commentary series that contains not only the all-important textual commentary on Scripture, but images, photographs, maps, works of fine art, and drawings that bring the text to life.

The *Smyth & Helwys Bible Commentary* makes serious, credible biblical scholarship more accessible to a wider audience. Writers and editors alike present information in ways that encourage readers to gain a better understanding of the Bible. The editorial board has worked to develop a format that is useful and usable, informative and pleasing to the eye. Our writers are reputable scholars who participate in the community of faith and sense a calling to communicate the results of their scholarship to their faith community.

The *Smyth & Helwys Bible Commentary* addresses Christians and the larger church. While both respect for and sensitivity to the needs and contributions of other faith communities are reflected in the work of the series authors, the authors speak primarily to Christians. Thus the reader can note a confessional tone throughout the volumes. No particular "confession of faith" guides the authors, and diverse perspectives are observed in the various volumes. Each writer, though, brings to the biblical text the best scholarly tools available and expresses the results of their studies in commentary and visuals that assist readers seeking a word from the Lord for the church.

To accomplish this goal, writers in this series have drawn from numerous streams in the rich tradition of biblical interpretation. The basic focus is the biblical text itself, and considerable attention is given to the wording and structure of texts. Each particular text, however, is also considered in the light of the entire canon of Christian Scriptures. Beyond this, attention is given to the cultural context of the biblical writings. Information from archaeology, ancient history, geography, comparative literature, history of religions, politics, sociology, and even economics is used to illuminate the culture of the people who produced the Bible. In addition, the writers have drawn from the history of interpretation, not only as it is found in traditional commentary on the Bible but also in literature, theater, church history, and the visual arts. Finally, the *Commentary* on Scripture is joined with *Connections* to the world of the contemporary church. Here again, the writers draw on scholarship in many fields as well as relevant issues in the popular culture.

This wealth of information might easily overwhelm a reader if not presented in a "user-friendly" format. Thus the heavier discussions of detail and the treatments of other helpful topics are presented in special-interest boxes, or Sidebars, clearly connected to the passages under discussion so as not to interrupt the flow of the basic interpretation. The result is a commentary on Scripture that focuses on the theological significance of a text while also offering the reader a rich array of additional information related to the text and its interpretation.

An accompanying CD-ROM offers powerful searching and research tools. The commentary text, Sidebars, and visuals are all reproduced on a CD that is fully indexed and searchable. Pairing a text version with a digital resource is a distinctive feature of the *Smyth & Helwys Bible Commentary.*

Combining credible biblical scholarship, user-friendly study features, and sensitivity to the needs of a visually oriented generation of believers creates a unique and unprecedented type of commentary series. With insight from many of today's finest biblical scholars and a stunning visual format, it is our hope that the *Smyth & Helwys Bible Commentary* will be a welcome addition to the personal libraries of all students of Scripture.

The Editors

HOW TO USE
THIS COMMENTARY

The *Smyth & Helwys Bible Commentary* is written by accomplished biblical scholars with a wide array of readers in mind. Whether engaged in the study of Scripture in a church setting or in a college or seminary classroom, all students of the Bible will find a number of useful features throughout the commentary that are helpful for interpreting the Bible.

Basic Design of the Volumes

Each volume features an Introduction to a particular book of the Bible, providing a brief guide to information that is necessary for reading and interpreting the text: the historical setting, literary design, and theological significance. Each Introduction also includes a comprehensive outline of the particular book under study.

Each chapter of the commentary investigates the text according to logical divisions in a particular book of the Bible. Sometimes these divisions follow the traditional chapter segmentation, while at other times the textual units consist of sections of chapters or portions of more than one chapter. The divisions reflect the literary structure of a book and offer a guide for selecting passages that are useful in preaching and teaching.

An accompanying CD-ROM offers powerful searching and research tools. The commentary text, Sidebars, and visuals are all reproduced on a CD that is fully indexed and searchable. Pairing a text version with a digital resource also allows unprecedented flexibility and freedom for the reader. Carry the text version to locations you most enjoy doing research while knowing that the CD offers a portable alternative for travel from the office, church, classroom, and your home.

Commentary and Connections

As each chapter explores a textual unit, the discussion centers around two basic sections: *Commentary* and *Connections*. The analysis of a passage, including the details of its language, the history reflected in the text, and the literary forms found in the text, are the main focus of the *Commentary* section. The primary concern of the *Commentary* section is to explore the theological issues presented by the Scripture passage. *Connections* presents potential applications of the insights provided in the *Commentary* section. The *Connections* portion of each chapter considers what issues are relevant for teaching and suggests useful methods and resources. *Connections* also identifies themes suitable for sermon planning and suggests helpful approaches for preaching on the Scripture text.

Sidebars

The *Smyth & Helwys Bible Commentary* provides a unique hyperlink format that quickly guides the reader to additional insights. Since other more technical or supplementary information is vital for understanding a text and its implications, the volumes feature distinctive Sidebars, or special-interest boxes, that provide a wealth of information on such matters as:

• Historical information (such as chronological charts, lists of kings or rulers, maps, descriptions of monetary systems, descriptions of special groups, descriptions of archaeological sites or geographical settings).

• Graphic outlines of literary structure (including such items as poetry, chiasm, repetition, epistolary form).

• Definition or brief discussions of technical or theological terms and issues.

• Insightful quotations that are not integrated into the running text but are relevant to the passage under discussion.

• Notes on the history of interpretation (Augustine on the Good Samaritan, Luther on James, Stendahl on Romans, etc.).

• Line drawings, photographs, and other illustrations relevant for understanding the historical context or interpretive significance of the text.

• Presentation and discussion of works of fine art that have interpreted a Scripture passage.

Each Sidebar is printed in color and is referenced at the appropriate place in the *Commentary* or *Connections* section with a color-coded title that directs the reader to the relevant Sidebar. In addition, helpful icons appear in the Sidebars, which provide the reader with visual cues to the type of material that is explained in each Sidebar. Throughout the commentary, these four distinct hyperlinks provide useful links in an easily recognizable design.

AΩ

Alpha & Omega Language

This icon identifies the information as a language-based tool that offers further exploration of the Scripture selection. This could include syntactical information, word studies, popular or additional uses of the word(s) in question, additional contexts in which the term appears, and the history of the term's translation. All non-English terms are transliterated into the appropriate English characters.

Culture/Context

This icon introduces further comment on contextual or cultural details that shed light on the Scripture selection. Describing the place and time to which a Scripture passage refers is often vital to the task of biblical interpretation. Sidebar items introduced with this icon could include geographical, historical, political, social, topographical, or economic information. Here, the reader may find an excerpt of an ancient text or inscription that sheds light on the text. Or one may find a description of some element of ancient religion such as Baalism in Canaan or the Hero cult in the Mystery Religions of the Greco-Roman world.

Interpretation

Sidebars that appear under this icon serve a general interpretive function in terms of both historical and contemporary renderings. Under this heading, the reader might find a selection from classic or contemporary literature that illuminates the Scripture text or a significant quotation from a famous sermon that addresses the passage. Insights are drawn from various sources, including literature, worship, theater, church history, and sociology.

Additional Resources Study

Here, the reader finds a convenient list of useful resources for further investigation of the selected Scripture text, including books, journals, websites, special collections, organizations, and societies. Specialized discussions of works not often associated with biblical studies may also appear here.

Additional Features

Each volume also includes a basic Bibliography on the biblical book under study. Other bibliographies on selected issues are often included that point the reader to other helpful resources.

Notes at the end of each chapter provide full documentation of sources used and contain additional discussions of related matters.

Abbreviations used in each volume are explained in a list of abbreviations found after the Table of Contents.

Readers of the *Smyth & Helwys Bible Commentary* can regularly visit the Internet support site for news, information, updates, and enhancements to the series at **www.helwys.com/commentary**.

Several thorough indexes enable the reader to locate information quickly. These indexes include:

• An *Index of Sidebars* groups content from the special-interest boxes by category (maps, fine art, photographs, drawings, etc.).

• An *Index of Scriptures* lists citations to particular biblical texts.

• An *Index of Topics* lists alphabetically the major subjects, names, topics, and locations referenced or discussed in the volume.

• An *Index of Modern Authors* organizes contemporary authors whose works are cited in the volume.

INTRODUCTION

Surviving conquest, living as a people subject to powerful regimes, and enduring persecution and death constitute much of the tragic experience of Israel. The terrible reality of the Babylonian conquest of Judah and the reign of Babylon's successors over the Jewish people form the literary context for the narratives and visions of the book of Daniel. Reflecting on the great empires that vanquished and exiled the people of Israel as well as on the nations who are yet to come, the book of Daniel offers a picture of arresting faith. The horrendous sufferings that the nation endured prompt neither an abandonment of God, a capitulation to the successful conquerors, nor personal despair. Rather, the enigmatic book shows models for living imbued with hope and meaning. The courageous stories about Daniel's life in Babylon show a tenacious belief, despite terrible odds, that one individual's life can make a difference for good. Daniel's visions for the future display a resolute hope that God's sovereignty over all the earth, despite persecutions that defy description, inexorably will be manifest. From the depths of despair comes a faith that refuses to abandon the belief that the universe operates according to God's will—even though its unfolding cannot yet be seen.

An Overview of the Final Form of the Book

The first half of the book, namely Daniel 1–6, consists of a collection of narratives about Daniel and his friends Hananiah, Mishael, and Azariah, who bear captivity and tests of faith that demand the ultimate trial—martyrdom. Pressed to the brink, all endure their trials and, although willing to die rather than abandon their obligations to God, are miraculously spared multiple death threats from cruel regimes. Such accounts of the faithful belong to a genre of ancient Jewish literature that provides for the moral instruction of the members of the community. Along with books such as Esther, Judith, and Tobit, they are presented not as objective history, but as edification in the faith. [Esther, Judith, and Tobit] The stories of Daniel offer a model for ways to cope in exile, when daily life is highly unpredictable. At times honored, at other times derided, still at others persecuted, Daniel and his friends find dignity in their prayers and solidarity. Knowing that at any time their lives could be snuffed out

Hananiah, Mishael, and Azariah in the Fiery Furnace

This third century AD fresco located at the catacomb of Priscilla in Rome depicts the three youths in the fiery furnace in the pose of *orants*—figures with arms outstretched in prayer. Frequently used in early Christian art, the *orant* suggests either the soul, salvation, or the piety of the deceased. This painting may represent concerns for deliverance from persecution and the hope of resurrection. In the book of Daniel, the three are first introduced by their Hebrew names, Hananiah, Mishael, and Azariah, all of which praise the God of Israel. They mean, respectively, "The Lord has been gracious," "Who is what God is?" and "The Lord has helped." Nebuchadnezzar, however, renames them Shadrach, Meshach, and Abednego to honor his own gods (see below, ch. 1).

Shadrach, Meshach, and Abednego, the "Three Youths" in the "Fiery Furnace" of Nebuchadnezzar. Catacomb of Priscilla. Rome, Italy. (Credit: Erich Lessing/Art Resource, NY)

by the whim of a despot, they courageously stand up to threats. Never freed, their faith remains unshackled.

The second half of the book, Daniel 7–12, contains Daniel's first-person accounts of heavenly visions about the future and the celestial interpretations he receives. Guided by interpreting angels, Daniel learns that despite the earthly horrors of persecution by vicious regimes that seemingly remain unchecked, each action by every nation is seen and judged by God. The visions constitute an apocalypse, a genre of literature in which a pseudonymous author writes in the name of an ancient sage of Israel who receives a special revelation about the remote future (see below, [Daniel: An Historical Apocalypse]). Typically using symbols of beasts, cataclysms, and archetypal enemies, apocalypses present an unveiling of a fantastic future. This apocalyptic portrait usually contains an expected period of tumult, but is ultimately utopian. This is not to disparage the vision of the future as being absurd; rather, it is an idealized type. It is crucial to note that the purported distant time to come is actually a vision—or more accurately a hope—concerning the author's present. The vision of a world where evil itself is swallowed up and where a righteous God ensures justice is a world transformed and infused with God's goodness. It is a

Esther, Judith, and Tobit

The canonical book of Esther and the apocryphal books of Judith and Tobit (dated from the 3rd–2d century BC) all depict difficulties faced by Jewish communities under siege by foreign regimes. The threats may derive from malevolent officials who seek their deaths (Haman in the book of Esther), inept kings who fail to protect them against an enraged populace (Ahasuerus in Esther), direct assault by invading armies (Holofernes' troops in Judith), or from difficulties in keeping the commandments while under Gentile powers (Tobit). These texts provide a sense of pride to the powerless and encouragement for the beleaguered to follow commandments and customs.

world in which God's sovereignty is acknowledged by all and in which peace is instilled.

Although to a modern audience the technique of writing in the name of an ancient sage may appear fraudulent, it is important to note that it was a well-known practice in antiquity that was far from an attempt to deceive. Whatever these pseudonymous authors' motivation—a respect for the sage, an honoring of an ancient tradition, or a response to dangerous times—their goal was not prediction for prediction's sake, but was to present a theology about God's structure of the cosmos, an understanding of theodicy (the justice of God), and the place of humanity within the world. In other words, the apocalypticists, in the midst of their sufferings, search for meaning in the face of despondency. Such visions are cosmic, dealing with the place of nations in God's universal plan, the role of Israel, the transformation of the world itself, and reward and punishment for individuals and nation states.

In the book of Daniel, when despair reaches its height, the visions affirm that a compassionate God of justice will not abandon the earth to powers that relentlessly crush the innocent. Although only God knows the time, the *fact* of a just universe, a cosmos in which evil is punished and righteousness rewarded, is unshakably a part of Daniel's faith. The visions show that this beleaguered earth will indeed become a dwelling place for God and that God's plan for Israel remains intact. The visions show that even while in the midst of torments, God has a place for every tortured soul. Their lives have meaning. And for those who have seen only death, God promises an eternal reward, which no nation, however powerful, can ever deny. The combination of these two types of reflection, the narratives about everyday life in the Diaspora—Near Eastern lands in which Jews had lived since the Babylonian invasion—and visions that comment on the very nature of reality, present an understanding of what it means to be a person of faith when, at best, life is precarious, and, at worst, life seems hopeless.

Authorship and Dating

The authorship of the two major sections of the book of Daniel, the narratives of chapters 1–6 and the visions of chapters 7–12, first will be considered separately.

Daniel 1–6

Although the literary setting of the narratives of the book of Daniel is sixth century BC Babylon, the period of its authorship is most

Silver *tetradrachm* of Alexander the Great, mint of Amphipolis. 336–323 BC. The silver coins, with the head of Heracles on one side and a seated figure of Zeus on the other (as seen here), became one of the staple coinages of the Greek world. Inscription: "Alexandros." British Museum, London, Great Britain. (Credit: Erich Lessing/Art Resource, NY)

Alexander the Great

Minted during Alexander's reign, this silver *tetradrachm* shows the figure on Zeus seated on the throne. The name "Alexander" appears along one side of the coin's edge and "Zeus" along the other. This coin, which has the head of Herakles on the reverse, was one of the standards used throughout Alexander's empire.

Alexander the Great (356–323 BC), son of Philip of Macedon and Olympias, princess of Epirus, conquered the known world of the Greeks, incorporating all the lands of the Persian empire and extending the boundaries from Egypt in the west to India in the east. The influence of Alexander's Hellenistic culture continued long after his death. The establishment of Greek cities throughout his empire and the spread of the Greek language brought the treasures of literature, government, and philosophy to his conquered lands. Alexander, being open to the people of the Near East, included them in his government and accepted them in his personal relationships. Thus, the cultures and religions of the ancient Near East spread throughout his empire long after his death (see below, [Alexander the Great and the Divisions of the Hellenistic Empire], [Hellenism and Hellenization], and [Josephus on Alexander]).

likely the Persian period, namely between the rise of Cyrus (539 BC) to the conquest of Alexander the Great (d. 323 BC). It may be possible to extend this period to the early Hellenistic period, shortly after the time of Alexander, but clearly the book's perspective must pre-date the Maccabean period in which Jews revolted against the persecutions of Antiochus IV Epiphanes (ruled 175–164 BC). Various internal clues allow for this dating. The portrayal of the problems of Diaspora life corresponds with the portrayal of problems faced during Persian rule and during the early period of their Greek conquerors. Nebuchadnezzar (ruled 605–562 BC), no longer simply the wielder of God's punishment, becomes the perpetrator of unjust trials on the innocent, paralleling similar developments in other texts from this period.[1] The reference to Darius the Mede, while not historical, shows familiarity with the importance of the role of Media in wresting the empire away from Babylon and may be based upon the Persian emperors by that name. In addition, the stories contain many unique words that are of Persian origin (especially Dan 3) and presume the rise of Cyrus (Dan 6:28).

The stories of Daniel and of his fellow exiles Hananiah, Mishael, and Azariah are told in the third person, anonymously. Although Daniel is identified as a visionary in the latter half of the book, and although some later traditions recognize him as a prophet, he is not so distinguished in the narratives of chapters 1–6.[2] The author presents Daniel as a captive of noble Judean origins and as an interpreter of dreams and mysterious signs. He works both behind the

Cyrus

King Cyrus of Persia (559–530 BC) began his rule over a small kingdom in southeastern Iran. When invaded by King Astyages of Media—located in northwestern Iran—the victorious Cyrus extended the Persian kingdom to include eastern Iran and Anatolia, including the Lydian capital of Sardis. By 539 BC, Cyrus had conquered Babylon and obtained its colonies, including Yehud (Judah). Because of Cyrus's policies of repatriating the exiled Jews to their homeland, he is known as the Lord's "anointed" and God's "shepherd" (Isa 44:28; 45:1-4)—terms usually reserved for Davidic kings.

This column is from the king's Audience Palace in Pasargadae, Iran, the imperial city he founded.

Audience Palace of Cyrus the Great. Remains of columns. (Credit: SEF/Art Resource, NY)

scenes, enlisting officials for their help or outwitting them by clever action, and he unabashedly interprets the dreams and signs given to sovereigns that condemn their regimes. Both he and his friends are willing, when confronted with an ultimatum, to remain loyal to God and face martyrdom. They do, nonetheless, find deliverance and at times are promoted within governmental positions.

Although one can never know the intention of an author with certainty, the position taken in this commentary is that the characterization, plot, speech, and actions of Daniel, his companions, and the sovereigns and bureaucrats allow us to set the parameters of the concerns, faith, and worldview of this writer. The narratives show a passion for the preservation of a faith and culture besieged by untrustworthy overlords and their underlings who, although offering the material successes of a triumphant regime, might also—at a moment's notice—threaten their lives or their existence as a people set apart. Nebuchadnezzar, for example, both demands that Daniel become versed in the benchmarks of the Babylonian educational system and insists that Daniel eat the food prepared in his palace. These attempts at assimilation become tests of faith. Daniel and his companions must walk a

Nebuchadnezzar

This carved stone block lauds Nebuchadnezzar's building projects in the capital city of Babylon and in the nearby city of Borsippa. These projects glorified the chief Babylonian god, Marduk. Nebuchadnezzar's building projects were of immense proportions, using an estimated 15 million mud bricks.

The East India House Inscription. Neo-Babylonian dynasty. c. 604–562 BC. Stone block. (Credit: Todd Bolen/BiblePlaces.com)

tightrope between compromise and conviction. This they deftly do. In addition, the responses of the exiles become strategies for navigating the system. The account of Daniel's interpretation of Nebuchadnezzar's dream of the great tree (Dan 4), for example, suggests that Daniel's community feels the weight of poverty and is in need of redress by the king. The account of scheming courtiers shows that even when an overlord may feel personally amiable toward an exile, his impotence might threaten Jews as much as any decree by a hostile despot (Dan 3:8; 6:9 [6:10 MT]). The portrayal of Daniel and his companions' worship as providing a pretext for accusations reveals a climate of fear (Dan 3:12-15; 6:4-7 [6:5-8 MT]). The message is clear: tread carefully.

Such concerns are part and parcel of Diaspora Jewish life in the time of their Persian overlords. On the one hand, the Persians could help the Jews rebuild Jerusalem and its temple. On the other hand, a period of assistance readily could be exchanged for deprivation, with people taking mortgages to pay their taxes.[3] Jews had the freedom to serve the government as soldiers in their own military colony with their own temple, yet, when they request assistance after the local mob attacks their temple, their cries to Persian governors apparently fall on deaf ears. Like the ineffectual (and fictional or composite) Darius whose silence in face of his courtiers' demands threatens Daniel's very life, the actual Persian kings who ruled over the Diaspora community could be either hostile or benevolent. Artaxerxes, for example, who reacted unfavorably to Jews when Samarians spoke against the rebuilding of the temple, is shown to be volatile (Ezra 4:7-23). Living in an age when one king might support the building of the temple, yet another would capriciously stop it, taught Jews that life under Persian rule was never secure—that only the unexpected could be expected.

In this context, a host of stories from the Persian period shows that during such times of uncertainty, the community could often respond by turning inward, bonding with each other, and responding in solidarity. Like the heroes and heroines shown in Judith, Esther, and Tobit, the protagonist Daniel demonstrates acts of profound courage. With great personal risk, he defies Nebuchadnezzar's orders, inspiring his companions to stand up to the king, both alongside Daniel and on their own.

Thus, although the narratives of Daniel 1–6 show various ways to cope with the uncertainties of Babylonian or Median rule, the true message was originally for the Jewish Diaspora community under Persian rule or in the aftermath of the Persian fall to Alexander. The author does not propose to write an objective account of the historical Nebuchadnezzar, Belshazzar, or Darius; rather, the writer portrays a type of sovereign that existed both in Israel's past and that could be expected in the future. The kings of these stories, who are placed under divine scrutiny, become a cipher for Persian rulers who govern their subjects with both care and caprice. One day surrounded by opportunity, another by hazard, the author presents an unflappable Daniel who at once inspires his companions, controls Nebuchadnezzar's tirades, condemns Belshazzar's excesses, and showcases Darius's incompetence for all to see. Again, the concern is neither to provide a biography of Daniel nor to recount a history of his life at court. Rather, the historicity of the hero is bracketed; the author has other concerns. With this portrayal of the threatened, yet faithful servant of God, the author tells a story of victory. The vanquished become the victors; the exiles who live at the whims of powerful governments become the consummate champions who can outwit their conquerors because, ultimately, they are supported by the Judge of all.

Judith

This painting shows Judith preparing to slay Holofernes. In the book of Judith, Nebuchadnezzar plans to use his general Holofernes to annihilate the Jewish people, erasing even the dust of their footprints (Jdt 6:1-4). Judith rises to the challenge and prays for God's vindication. She states, "O Lord God of all might, look in this hour on the work of my hands for the exaltation of Jerusalem. Now indeed is the time to help your heritage and to carry out my design to destroy the enemies who have risen up against us" (Jdt 13:4-5).

This 2d century BC work is canonical in the Catholic, Orthodox, and Slavonic Bibles; it is part of the Apocrypha for Protestants and is referred to in medieval midrashim.

Alessandro Varotari (1588–1648). *Judith and the Maid*. (Credit: Cameraphoto/Art Resource, NY)

The approach in this commentary presumes that although the author of the narratives is *not* providing an eyewitness account, the history, memory, politics, religion, and experience of the community are part and parcel of the collection. The author sees the Persian Diaspora experience through a particular lens of interpretation that holds that the Babylonian emperor, Nebuchadnezzar, has become a paradigm for understanding the rulers of the community's own time. Although all monarchs' reigns are understood as making up part of God's plan for individual nations and for the world, their individual actions could be capricious and cruel. The memory of the Babylonian invasion of the temple and subsequent exile weighs upon the author as the challenges of Daniel and his friends are recounted. The community's experience—some as members of the Persian court and bureaucracy, others as impoverished laborers, some as confident in their faith, others doubting its efficacy—lies behind the presentation of Daniel's actions before sovereigns and his pleas for his fellow exiles. The author's trust in God provides a lens to see the Diaspora community's experience as one that can be difficult and dangerous, to be sure, but one that can be navigated by remaining loyal to the commandments and by faithful confidence that God has not abandoned them.

Although a Diaspora Persian setting (or early Hellenistic setting) for the authorship of Daniel 1–6 is most plausible, it is also important to note that the narratives both draw on more ancient traditions and show redactional elements of a later era. Examples of earlier traditions include the *Prayer of Nabonidus* and a possible earlier version of the account of the great statue (Dan 2). The Babylonian *Prayer of Nabonidus* gives an account of King Nabonidus of Babylon whose musings on his rooftop parallel the reflections of Nebuchadnezzar in the dream account of Daniel 4 (see below, [Prayer of Nabonidus]). The *Prayer of Nabonidus* contains a portrayal of Nabonidus's illness and confused mental state, which prompts his abandonment of the throne. This account may have influenced the narrative of Nebuchadnezzar's transformation into a beast as divine punishment; alternatively, the two accounts may both be unique developments of a common tradition.[4] In addition, as Ida Fröhlich has argued, Nebuchadnezzar's dream of the statue whose metal and clay elements represent four kingdoms that successively conquer the ancient Near East (Babylon, Media, Persia, and Greece) may originally have portrayed four successive kings of Babylon (see below, ch. 2).[5] When appropriate, this commentary includes a discussion of such contextual backgrounds.

After the death of Alexander, Jews in both the Diaspora and in Judah were governed by his successors, the Ptolemaic and Seleucid dynasts (see below, [Ptolemaic and Seleucid Rule] and [The Ptolemies and Seleucids]). Although it is not possible to know to what degree the tales of Daniel 1–6 were redacted during the later Hellenistic period, there is at least one place where a gloss is evident. Daniel 2:40-45 was inserted by an unknown hand that was familiar with the marriage alliances between the Ptolemies and Seleucids (see below, ch. 2). In addition, perhaps the insistence that all prayer be directed to Darius (Dan 6) was influenced by the claims to divinity that characterized Greek rule and reached its apex under Antiochus IV.

Daniel 7–12

Concerning the dating of Daniel 7–12, although the literary setting of the visions purports that Daniel received them during the exile, the symbols point to nations and specific rulers of the second century BC. This century was marked by the struggle for control over Judah by the Seleucids and Ptolemies. In particular, the worst times—the period of Antiochus IV—form the historical context for much of the visions (see chs. 7 and 8 below). Antiochus's reign was marked by the outlawing of Jewish practice, the desolation of the sanctuary, persecutions, and deaths of the innocent. The author presents the visions from the seer Daniel's perspective. While not historical, this technique casts the author's reflections about the sufferings of the community's present in light of the wisdom of the past. Since Daniel, as visionary, is presented as the same person who suffered under "the first Nebuchadnezzar," the message is clear: the community can endure the many subsequent Nebuchadnezzars who are to come—including Antiochus. In Daniel 7, the four beasts who battle each other and who confront the saints conform to the stereotyped depictions of four empires and a fifth—namely, four sequential empires who rule over Israel and the Diaspora and an ideal fifth kingdom that is made up of God's people. Daniel 8 focuses on the actions of the beast who represents Greece, paving the way for the predictive schema of Daniel 10–11 in which the particulars of the reigns of the northern king and southern king are delineated. The details about purported future conflicts between the unnamed king of the north and king of the south follow the historical details of the campaigns of the Ptolemaic and Seleucid empires, beginning with the reign of Ptolemy I of Egypt and Seleucus I of Syria. With the successive dynasts that followed, a fierce competition existed regarding the rule of Judah. This final vision becomes quite specific about the details of the reign of Antiochus—details that are known to us from other sources such as Maccabees and Josephus (see below, ch. 10). Campaigns of war, antipathies between kings, and internal politics of the Seleucid kingdom from the years 260–165 BC can be verified; however, the prediction about Antiochus's final days and his death do not correspond to other historical sources. Whereas the biblical text states that the king of the north will die in the holy land after his invasions toward the west and south, it is known that Antiochus died outside of the land while perusing targets in the eastern reaches of his empire. It appears that they are genuine prediction, as the author trusts that Antiochus's reign of terror will not last. In addition, the visions show no awareness of the successful

Maccabean revolt against Antiochus's successors and the subsequent rededication of the temple (see below, ch. 10). Finally, as Peter Ackroyd observes, Daniel 9 assumes a particular perspective on the exile, showing that it is no longer considered as a unique historical event. The exile is no longer linked only with punishment, but with a promise. It is interpreted to be a repeated condition that can be rectified only at the end of the age, a perspective that predominates in apocalyptic texts.[6] Therefore, most modern historical-critical scholars date the visions to some time shortly before Antiochus's death in 164 BC.

The visions of Daniel express a hope for a new age. In a time of political turmoil and persecutions, the book's hope for the future, in the main, comments on the author's present. The situation of the author's community is replete with difficulties. People feel distraught, but they also are committed to a life of obedience to God, as their faith anticipates restoration and the righting of the wrongs of a tormented world. The author, confident that God's faithful actions in the past rather than the corruption of the Hellenistic age better predict the future, anticipates a world that will reflect God's judgment and righteousness. At the same time, there is no pretense that one knows when these troubles will be righted. The author holds fast to the belief that although the sovereignty of God throughout the world is not manifest, it is, nonetheless, real. It would soon be seen and all nations would soon acknowledge it. Although God's face was hidden, all would proceed according to God's plan. Soon, every nation would see and accept divine law and God's judgment and would embrace God's will, even acknowledging Israel's special place in God's plan. The author anticipates cosmic changes, with a total repair and rebirth of the earth and of the human race. The visions show that all the earth is under the rule of God, whose judgment and grace breathe new life into the beleaguered, who are now judged and purified. The transformation of the earth is to be so extensive that even those who have undergone the ultimate sacrifice—martyrdom—will be resurrected (see below, [Martyrdom in Jewish Tradition] and [Resurrection, Martyrdom, and the Christian Hope]).

Sometime after the composition of the visions, the narratives about Daniel and his companions were attached, forming one book. The process is not clear. The visions are clearly linked, as all manifest a similar apocalyptic worldview and second-century BC context. Because Daniel 7 is written in Aramaic—yet Daniel 8–12 is composed in Hebrew—it is possible that Daniel 7 comes from a unique hand and was the first of the visions to be joined with the narratives. Although all the stories of Daniel 1–6 belong to the same narrative genre, portraying edifying tales of Diaspora life, Daniel 1 alone is written in Hebrew. Does this fact point to a unique author of Daniel 1? Yet, the narratives of Daniel 2–6 seem to presume the knowledge of Daniel 1. However the individual chapters came to be unified, the fact that these distinct genres and these two languages could be placed alongside one another tells us that the traditions associated with Daniel were extensive and that the author saw Daniel as both sage and visionary. [Aramaic and Hebrew in the Book of Daniel]

For all the differences in genre, tone, and content of Daniel 1–6 and Daniel 7–12, several features bind the two divisions of the book. The presence of Daniel himself draws them together. The visions are dated by noting the year in which a foreign king ruled, years that mark Daniel's service to the crown as presented earlier in the narratives. The portrayal of the four beasts of Daniel's first vision parallels the dream of Nebuchadnezzar's statue of the metals and clay, as both the beasts and the metals represent the four kingdoms that cause great suffering, but that also are followed by a kingdom of righteousness. For Jews who lived during the persecutions of Antiochus, the experiences of Daniel and his companions resonated strongly. The actions of Nebuchadnezzar and Darius, who, by design or incompetence, could sentence the exiles to horrible deaths, anticipate the situation of the pious who were mercilessly threatened. It can be seen that the stories of Daniel were similarly used by later generations in antiquity who suffered under cruel regimes. First Maccabees (early first century BC), 3 Maccabees (late first century BC), 4 Maccabees (first century AD), Hebrews, and Josephus all echo the heroic stories.[7]

The Textual History of the Book of Daniel

The extensiveness and influence of the many stories and visions about Daniel also are attested by the variants in the manuscript tradition of this book. A study of the Hebrew/Aramaic and Greek

---

Aramaic and Hebrew in the Book of Daniel

AΩ

| Hebrew | Aramaic | Hebrew |
| 1:1–2:4a | 2:4b–7:28 | 8:1–12:13 |

The Aramaic of the book of Daniel is classified as Imperial Aramaic, a Semitic international language used throughout the Near East from approximately 700–200 BC. Because the Hebrew sections contain more textual difficulties than the Aramaic sections, some scholars suggest that the entirety of the book of Daniel was originally written in Aramaic. Yet, the verses that are purportedly translated do not correspond to the formal features of the book (narrative in Dan 1–6 and vision in Dan 7–12), so the issue remains problematic. Concerning the correspondence of the Hebrew and Aramaic portions of the Masoretic text to the Qumran (Dead Sea) scrolls, Eugene Ulrich writes,

> The curious shift from Hebrew to Aramaic at 2:4a in the MT also is confirmed by the ancient manuscripts 1QDan[a] and 4QDan[a], and the shift from Aramaic back to Hebrew at 8:1 is confirmed by 4QDan[a] and 4QDan[b]; furthermore, all the extant fragments of all the Daniel manuscripts display the expected distribution of languages.

Eugene Ulrich, *The Dead Sea Scrolls and the Origins of the Bible*, Studies in the Dead Sea Scrolls and Related Literature (Grand Rapids MI/Cambridge UK: Eerdmans; Leiden/Boston/Köln: Brill, 1999), 150.

manuscripts of Daniel yields clues about its textual history. What did the earliest form of the book of Daniel look like? There are two witnesses, namely, the Hebrew/Aramaic text and the ancient Greek translation of an earlier Semitic *Vorlage* (prototype).

The Hebrew/Aramaic text is commonly known as the Masoretic Text (MT). It was fixed by a group of scribes known as the Masoretes between the seventh and tenth centuries AD, yet its earliest textual witnesses come from much earlier centuries. Eight manuscripts of the book of Daniel were discovered at Qumran (the Dead Sea Scrolls) in caves 1, 4, and 6. The Qumran texts of 4QDan[a] and 4QDan[b], which contain the largest proportion of Daniel verses, are dated to the first century BC and the first century AD, respectively.[8]

The Greek witnesses to the book of Daniel are known collectively as the Septuagint. More accurately, the earliest of the ancient Greek translations of Daniel is known as the Old Greek (OG), completed shortly after the composition of Daniel. The OG is known to us from the Hexapla of Origen—a multi-column translation in which Origen preserved this earliest Greek text (in critical editions, the OG of Daniel is also referred to by the siglum o' [the Greek letter *omicron*]). The Hexapla was compiled in the third century AD, but its origins go back to the late second or early first century BC.[9] In addition, Papyrus 967 (the Chester Beatty papyrus), a second-century AD manuscript discovered in Egypt, attests to the OG. Another important Greek textual witness is Theodotion, which dates from the second century AD. It was composed to bring the Greek into greater compliance with the developing Hebrew/Aramaic text (in critical editions the Theodotionic translation of Daniel is labeled θ' [the Greek letter *theta*]).

Although, for the most part, the OG and Masoretic text (MT) reflect the same *Vorlage* (prototype), the OG does present some unique readings. The greatest variation is found in Daniel 4–6, where it is best to understand that both the OG and MT point to parallel Hebrew/Aramaic editions, which existed simultaneously in the Jewish community and which can claim to be "original."[10] [Daniel 4–6] In addition, both the OG and Theodotion preserve additional poetry and narratives that are not present in the Masoretic text. These additions are *The Prayer of Azariah and the Song of the Three Young Men, Susanna,* and *Bel and the Dragon* (see below, [The Greek Additions to Daniel 3], [Bel and the Dragon], and [Susanna]). The very placement of the book of Daniel in two canonical locations—in the prophetic corpus of the Septuagint, but in the Writings of the Masoretic text—attests to its complicated history.

Daniel 4–6

In the main, the Old Greek (OG) and the Masoretic textual traditions witness to the same edition of the book of Daniel. However, great variation is seen in chs. 4–6 of Daniel. The variations do not follow a particular pattern. By analyzing the parallel verses of the OG and the Masoretic text (MT) of these chapters, Eugene Ulrich notes that *both* are secondary expansions of an original that no longer survives. Each expanded in a unique way. Ulrich concludes,

for rhetorical and dramatic effect beyond the edition preserved in the OG. The variant editions for chapter 4, in contrast, are signaled by the differing arrangements of various components and are confirmed by expansions in the OG, such as the expansion (perhaps a Babylonian astrological motif) of the sun and the moon dwelling in the great tree (4:8), and so forth. Thus, the double editions found in Daniel 4–6 are two different later editions of the story, both secondary, both expanding in different ways beyond a no-longer-extant form which lies behind both.

For example, for each of the three speeches in 5:10-12, 13-16, 17-23, the edition preserved in the MT greatly expands

Eugene Ulrich, *The Dead Sea Scrolls and the Origins of the Bible*, Studies in the Dead Sea Scrolls and Related Literature (Grand Rapids MI/Cambridge UK: Eerdmans; Leiden/Boston/Köln: Brill, 1999), 40–41.

Theological themes

(1) The belief in a just God who orders the universe according to a divine plan pervades the book of Daniel. This enduring faith, whether in times of capricious challenge or full-scale persecution, has important consequences for action as well. In the stories of Daniel and his companions, this perspective empowers the heroes to hold fast to the commandments. Their belief in the one God of Israel never wavers as they refuse to capitulate to the idols. Daniel's concern for his companions' welfare, his plea for the poor, his insistence for justice, his obedience to the food laws and to the obligations of prayer demonstrate that he fully abides by the covenant. In the visions, the unwavering belief in the God who designs the universe in order that the saints inherit the kingdom so predominates that even those who have died are included in God's reward. Finally, this tenet permeates the challenge that the author presents, "The wise among the people shall give understanding to many" (Dan 11:33; cf. 12:10). The original readers are encouraged

Daniel's Prayer

Edward Poynter. *Daniel's Prayer*. 1865. Relief print on paper, Tate Gallery, London, Great Britain. (Credit: Tate Gallery)

This 19th-century illustration by Edward Poynter shows Daniel in front of a window, praying toward Jerusalem. His obedience to God leaves him vulnerable to the authorities, as is suggested by the presence of the spying guard in the background (Dan 6:10).

to strengthen one another even when their very lives are threatened. The ones who hear and accept Daniel's message have a responsibility to others. They join the ranks of the wise of their nations' past—including the sage Daniel and his friends.

(2) Supporting this divine-centered outlook, additional themes include the particular perspective that Babylon, Media, Persia, and Greece are included in God's providential design and stand under divine judgment. Nebuchadnezzar is presented more as a type of ruler whose characteristics are repeated throughout Israel's history than as an individual. His arrogance and incompetence are repeated in the actions of many tyrants who will rule over the people of Israel. These include Belshazzar, Nebuchadnezzar's "son" (Dan 5); Darius the Mede (Dan 6); Antiochus IV, represented by the fourth beast (Dan 7) and the "little horn" (Dan 8); and the "king of the north" (Dan 11). Similarly, the exile that occurred when Babylon invaded Judah becomes a model for understanding the community's experience under Antiochus. Situations of humiliation, deprivation, and death are really the gateways to the world's inexorable path, designed by God, toward justice and peace. The task of the individual in such trying times is to look to the model of Daniel, who is both a displaced exile and a recipient of visions. As a child of the exile, Daniel prioritized his loyalty to the traditions and faith of his ancestors. From personal acts of piety such as obeying the dietary laws and offering required prayers, to the public refusal to bow to Nebuchadnezzar's idol, Daniel and his companions remained exemplary servants of God. As a visionary, Daniel's descent to the depths of anguish was followed by his disclosure of divine revelation that counseled his people to remain part of the wise—those whose unshakeable faith leads others by example. The author shows that nothing in human experience—from the past, the present, or the future—remains outside of the divine plan.

Continuing Importance for Jews and Christians

The book of Daniel continued to have an impact on both early Christian and Jewish tradition. In Christian interpretation, for example, references to the stone kingdom (Dan 2) and to the One like a Son of Man (Dan 7) were seen to refer to the church and to Christ. These interpretations are explored at length in chapters 2 and 7. The apocalyptic imagery of Daniel was reinterpreted in the book of Revelation as well; this association is particularly examined in the "Connections" section of chapter 7. In Jewish tradition, various references and imagery from the book of Daniel continued to appear in non-canonical writings (the pseudepigrapha) as well as in the midrashim (homiletic interpretations of Scripture) and in other Jewish holy writings, such as the Mishnah (a commentary on the Bible) and the Gemara (a commentary on the Mishnah—together the Mishnah and Gemara make up the Talmud). [The Talmud] Collectively, these writings, dated from the first to the sixth centuries AD—referred to as the works of "the rabbis" or "the sages"—often offer opinions about the motivations of characters, the ethical import of their actions, or the paradigmatic nature of the text for understanding history, psychology, or faith. Throughout the commentary, we note some of these interesting observations from antiquity, which, although usually not providing explanations about what the text meant for the community who originally read the text, provide examples of the living tradition of the text that continued to speak to generations. It is also true, however, that on occasion the ancient interpretations highlight a particular reading or interpretation that would have been relevant for the original readers. These are also noted.

In this commentary, examples of Christian and Jewish interpretation are given to show the continuing theological significance of Daniel for these two communities. Although some of the interpretations of the ancient Jewish commentators may strike the modern reader as fanciful, it is important to note the presuppositions of the ancient rabbis. As James Kugel explains, the biblical text was understood to be utterly intentional (that is, nothing was there by chance) and infinitely significant (symbols and events could have multiple referents). These tenets were buttressed by the view that the biblical text was of divine origin and cryptic. It cried out for interpretation on

The Talmud

The Talmud is the written form of the oral torah. This twenty-volume compendium of lore as well as law encompasses all aspects of Jewish life. It is composed of the six orders of the Mishnah together with its commentary, the Gemara. The "orders," or major topics of the Mishnah are (1) seeds (laws of agriculture); (2) appointed times (laws of shabbat and the festivals); (3) women (laws of marriage); (4) damages (business and criminal law); (5) sacred things (laws concerning sacrifice); and (6) purities (laws regarding purity in the temple). The Gemara expounds upon many—but not all—tractates (the subdivisions of the orders) of the Mishnah. There are two types of material in the Talmud, halakah and haggadah. The halakah contains the discussions on the proper observance of Jewish law and the debates of the various rabbis; the haggadah consists of stories about and homilies of the rabbis, commentary on the biblical text, philosophy, government, history, and folklore (including medicine). The Talmud continues to shape the identity and faith of Jews today. There are two Talmuds—one from Jerusalem, the other from Babylon. The Babylonian Talmud is the most complete and the one utilized in everyday learning among Jews today. It was compiled over the 3rd to the 6th centuries AD. As Adin Steinsaltz reflects,

> In many ways, the Talmud is the most important book in Jewish culture, the backbone of creativity and of national life. No other work has had a comparable influence on the theory and practice of Jewish life, shaping spiritual content and serving as a guide to conduct. The Jewish people have always been keenly aware that their continued survival and development depend on study of the Talmud. . . . At times, talmudic study has been prohibited [by those hostile to Judaism] because it was abundantly clear that a Jewish society that ceased to study this work had no real hope of survival.

Adin Steinsaltz, *The Essential Talmud*, trans. Chaya Galai (n.p.: Basic Books, 1976), 3.

many levels.[11] An examination of these interpretations shows, in the main, that early biblical interpretation was preoccupied with helping the reader make sense of a difficult world. They show a compassionate God who promises justice to those who suffer, who acts as judge of the universe, rewarding the just and punishing the wicked. They often speak of the importance of community and of loving one's neighbor. They debunk the importance of the treasures of the world and the attractions of their powerful conquerors. From the midrashim, for example, we learn that the early Jewish community understood that the interpretations of the cryptic references to the time of the end were known only to Jacob and to Daniel, both of whom never disclosed them. The lesson to be learned is that it is futile for anyone to seek to decipher this particular mystery. The trustworthiness of the visions of the end, and not their date, is what matters.

Readers today often find Daniel impenetrable. The visions' references to the time of the end seem to beg for decoding. Yet because the deciphering may seem so irrational, the text appears too far removed to be relevant for a scientific and skeptical age. Tabloids in the supermarket echo the language of Daniel (and Revelation) with outrageous predictions of Armageddon. The miraculous rescue of Daniel in the lions' den or the extraordinary deliverance of the youths in the fiery furnace may be off-putting by the very nature of their unreasonableness. But if we step back from the bizarre symbolism and the phenomena that defy nature, we might see that Daniel does not contain clues to be deciphered or litmus tests of belief in certain miracles. Rather, Daniel presents a way to look at the world—a way infused with hope and faith. The stance of the book acknowledges that the world is broken and that individuals and groups may be unjustly singled out—apparently without reason—for suffering. But the faith presented in this book is that things are not always what they seem. Daniel reminds us to consider that the world is created by a good and compassionate God who promises an end to suffering and a transformation of the world. In the meantime, while the waiting may seem interminable, the faithful will remain bound with God by acts—large and small—that defy cruelty and pain and hold fast to compassion and justice.

Armageddon

Credit: *Armageddon*, 1852 (oil on canvas) by Joseph Paul Pettit (1812–82). York Museums Trust (York Art Gallery), UK/ The Bridgeman Art Library. Nationality/copyright status: English/out of copyright.

This portrayal of Armageddon by Joseph Paul Pettit shows the cataclysms of the earth as it prepares to bring forth a new reality in which all nations are judged by God.

The book of Revelation contains a vision of a great climactic battle at the end of the world in which forces of good and evil confront each other (Rev 16:12-16). This apocalyptic scene is said to take place at "Armageddon"—probably a Greek transliteration of the Hebrew "Har Megiddo," or the hill of Megiddo. Although no hill or mountain of Megiddo is mentioned in the Hebrew Scriptures, Megiddo itself is identified as a city in both the Bible and in other ancient Near Eastern texts. Located in northern Israel—in the plain of Esdraelon—it was the place of crucial battles in ancient Israel. At Megiddo, Deborah and Barak routed Sisera's army (Judg 5:19), and Pharaoh Neco killed Josiah (2 Kgs 23:29). The book of Revelation anticipates the defeat of all the nations that defy God, namely, those that wreak torment upon the innocent and harbor injustice on earth. God is the mighty judge who judges all according to their deeds, punishing the wicked and rewarding the righteous. Upon God's victory, a new heaven and a new earth will be established in which justice prevails and in which evil terrorizes no more.

NOTES

[1] Peter Ackroyd, *The Chronicler in His Age* (JSOTSup 107; Sheffield: JSOT Press, 1991), 207–11.

[2] Matt 24:5; Josephus, *Ant*. 10.245. Note that both Greek versions of Daniel place the book within the prophetic corpus.

[3] Neh 5:4. See Peter Ackroyd, *The Chronicler in His Age*, 17.

[4] John Collins concludes that the Prayer of Nabonidus "is probably older than the 2d century BCE. The reminiscence of Nabonidus' stay at Tema suggests that the underlying tradition goes back to the eastern diaspora, wherever this particular work may have been composed" ("Nabonidus, Prayer of," *ABD* 4:977).

[5] Ida Fröhlich, *"Time and Times and Half a Time": Historical Consciousness in the Jewish Literature of the Persian and Hellenistic Eras* (Sheffield: Sheffield Academic Press, 1996).

[6] Peter Ackroyd, *The Chronicler in His Age*, 243.

[7] Donald Gowan, *Daniel* (Abingdon Old Testament Commentaries; Nashville: Abingdon, 2001), 14–15.

[8] Eugene Ulrich, *The Dead Sea Scrolls and the Origins of the Bible* (Studies in the Dead Sea Scrolls and Related Literature; Grand Rapids MI: Eerdmans, 1999), 150.

[9] Ibid., 210.

[10] Ibid., 42–44.

[11] James Kugel, *The Bible as It Was* (Cambridge MA: The Belknap Press of Harvard University Press, 1997).

DANIEL'S CAPTIVITY
IN BABYLON

Daniel 1:1-21

COMMENTARY

Introduction

The opening scene of Daniel introduces the first test of faithfulness encountered by Jewish youth under Babylonian captivity. The chapter begins with an interpretive reconstruction of Nebuchadnezzar's capture of Jerusalem, its temple treasures, and the exile of its people. As explained in the introduction, although the literary setting is Babylon, and although the stories may have roots that extend to the Babylonian period, they were composed in the Persian period, in the Diaspora. The author uses the period of the exile as a model for understanding the continuing problems that the Jewish people face while under foreign rule, far from the land of the temple and from Yehud—the name their captors gave to the former Judean

Map of the Babylonian Empire

Biblical Dietary Laws

"Kosher," which literally means "proper" or "correct," is used to describe various religious practices or objects. Concerning the dietary laws, "kosher" refers to food that both intrinsically and through preparation follows Jewish law. It is not possible to determine when this word was first used of dietary practices enumerated in the Hebrew Scriptures—laws that determine the types of beasts, fowl, and insects that are allowed or restricted and specify the way in which they are to be killed. Beasts are permitted or forbidden (impure) as categorized by physical structures, such as having cloven hooves or by being ruminants (Lev 11:3). Forbidden or permitted beasts, fowl, and insects are also identified by name in lists (Deut 14:4-5; Lev 11:20-23, 29-30). Blood and specific sinew can never be consumed (Lev 7:26; Gen 32:32). Meat from animals that are already dead (carcasses, Lev 11:39; Deut 14:21) or torn by beasts (Exod 22:30) is likewise forbidden. In addition, adult animals were not to be taken for slaughter at the same time with their young. For example, one was not to "boil a kid in its mother's milk" or take a mother bird and her chick simultaneously from the nest. Regarding fish, permissible species were defined as those having fins and scales (Lev 11:9; Deut 14:9).

Although vegetables and fruits are not categorized by pure and impure categories, in some cases they are restricted by ritual obligations. For example, grain was tithed and first fruits were to be offered to God as sacrifice before the remainder of the crop could be consumed (Lev 19:23-25; Deut 16:9-17). Similarly, there were sacral concerns for the Passover sacrifice and the consumption of leaven during the Passover period (Exod 12:8-15; Deut 16:2-8). The significance of the dietary laws is specified in Leviticus:

> You shall therefore make a distinction between the clean animal and the unclean, and between the unclean bird and the clean; you shall not bring abomination on yourselves by animal or by bird or by anything with which the ground teems, which I have set apart for you to hold unclean. You shall be holy to me; for I the LORD am holy, and I have separated you from the other peoples to be mine. (Lev 20:25-26)

As Baruch Levine shows, the importance of purity in dietary, sexual, and cultic laws were "all linked to the destiny of the Israelites as a people distinguished from other nations. . . . They offer a means by which individual Israelites and their families—the non-priests—may contribute to the attainment of holiness" (243–44). Particularly relevant to the test that Nebuchadnezzar gives to the young Daniel and his friends is this observation: "Underlying all the dietary regulations is a broad social objective: maintaining a distance between the Israelites and their neighbors, so that the former do not go astray after pagan religions" (244).

Baruch Levine, *Leviticus* (JPS Torah Commentary; Philadelphia: The Jewish Publication Society, 1989), 243–48.

---

kingdom. In these stories, King Nebuchadnezzar becomes the paradigm for the author's contemporary Persian overlords. The dilemmas of four youths who are no longer nobles at the Jerusalem court become a window for every person to understand their own troubles.

As the king's captive servants, Daniel and his three friends, Hananiah, Mishael, and Azariah, are forced to learn the Babylonian curricula and are provided only non-kosher food to eat. [Biblical Dietary Laws] These two trials challenge the youths' very identities. Their Babylonian education might affect the way they conceive the world, its meaningfulness, and the place of the God of Israel within it. The eating of non-kosher food would be a sure sign of their assimilation. These challenges are presented as important dramas; would these four exiles defy the king's orders or sin against the God of Israel? As the course of the story progresses through this chapter, the reader is reminded of the loss of the Judean kingdom, the might of Babylon, and the totalitarian regime of Nebuchadnezzar. Upon the chapter's conclusion, a paradigmatic reversal occurs. The youths indeed survive their first life-threatening test. Their cleverness and courage avert a death decree from Nebuchadnezzar, and Daniel and his friends' faithfulness to God's laws is ironically rewarded by advancement in the Babylonian court. The account ends with an important glimpse of the future: Babylonia's captivity of the people will end with the crushing defeat of the glory of Babylonia and the coming of the Persian emperor, Cyrus. Because the author is already living in Persian times, the might of the Persian Empire is itself implicitly challenged. Like Pharaoh in days of old or Nebuchadnezzar of recent memory, the days of Persian lords are not infinite, nor their power absolute, despite appearances to the contrary.

Daniel 1 begins with a reference to the fall of Jerusalem yet ends with an implicit allusion to the defeat of the once invincible conqueror. In between, we find a call to courage placed before four young adults, who respond with such fidelity that the story transcends its literary setting. It becomes relevant to all who are suffering political and religious persecution and domination. [Outline of Daniel 1]

Outline of Daniel 1

The Babylonian Conquest, 1:1-2
The Enslavement of Daniel and his Friends, 1:3-7
Daniel's Counter to His Captors, 1:8-17
Aftermath of the Educational Preparation, 1:18-21

The Babylonian Conquest, 1:1-2

The book of Daniel begins with a reference to a most ominous event in Jewish history: "In the third year of the reign of King Jehoiakim of Judah, King Nebuchadnezzar of Babylon came to Jerusalem and besieged it" (v. 1). This date is problematic, because Jerusalem actually was captured during the reign of Jehoiakim's son, Jehoiachin (597 BC). [The Dating of Nebuchadnezzar's Invasion according to the Book of Daniel] Nonetheless, the reference is to a formidable time—one of sobering consequences for the people of Jerusalem and Judah. It is the reality of the event of Nebuchadnezzar's capture of Jerusalem, and not the date in itself, that sets the stage for the beginning of the book. It evokes the powerlessness felt by the last kings of Judah—Jehoiakim, Jehoiachin, and Zedekiah—and the helplessness of the people. Although the exact year of the invasion is probably incorrect here, few would dispute the fact of the siege, the destruction by the despotic emperor Nebuchadnezzar, and the upheaval in the lives of the people. The long-term consequences of Nebuchadnezzar's siege profoundly affected the Jewish people. The loss of their territory, kingship, and temple service prompted many

The Dating of Nebuchadnezzar's Invasion according to the Book of Daniel

Dating crucial events to the year of a monarch serves not only a historical function, but a literary one as well. The historicity of the date *per se* is often not what is most important; rather, the historical impact and theological relevance of the event itself are what is crucial. Such references to key events, identified by a time in which a particular monarch reigned, often are used in the book of Daniel (2:1; 7:1; 8:1; 9:1; 10:1; 11:1). Daniel 1:1 begins with a reference to Nebuchadnezzar's invasion of Jerusalem during the third year of King Jehoiakim's reign (606 BC). Although Jehoiakim became Nebuchadnezzar's vassal, the historical accuracy of this reference is questioned because there is no other documentation that Nebuchadnezzar ever besieged Jerusalem during Jehoiakim's reign, which lasted from 609 to 598 BC. Some scholars suggest that the reference stems from confusion between the kings of Judah, as it can be verified that King Jehoiachin, son of Jehoiakim, was actually in power when Nebuchadnezzar destroyed the temple. Others argue that the reference to the third year of Jehoiakim's *reign* actually refers to the third year of his *rebellion* against Nebuchadnezzar. During that time, Jehoiakim died and was followed by his young son Jehoiachin (598 BC). Jehoiachin withstood the siege for only a few months, after which Nebuchadnezzar entered the temple. The author may simply be conflating the historical references and counting the early months of Jehoiachin's reign as the continuation of the third year of rebellion of his more famous father, Jehoiakim. Still other scholars suggest that "the third year" was chosen as part of a formalistic way of referring to a complete cycle of time. Although interpreters continue to debate this point, the significance of this verse stretches far beyond its historical verifiability. Indeed, the book of Daniel ends with a variation of this method that identifies events according to the date of a particular monarch. To frame the last vision of the book, the author marks the event with an unspecified future reference, "at that time" (12:1). No further temporal specificity is given to the reign of the Saints of the Most High, whose monarch is the God of Israel. This use of the reality of a monarch's reign as opposed to the exact date of one of the events in that governance is similarly reflected in a manuscript variant found in Daniel 7:1. In that verse, the Old Greek reads, "in the first year of King Belshazzar," whereas the Masoretic text reads, "in the third year of King Belshazzar."

John Collins, *Daniel: A Commentary on Daniel* (Hermeneia; Minneapolis: Fortress, 1993), 130–33. See also Shemaryahu Talmon, "Daniel," *The Literary Guide to the Bible*, ed. Robert Alter and Frank Kermode (Cambridge: Belknap, 1987), 347–49.

to continue to serve God by remaining faithful to the commandments that required neither living in the land of the promise, having a descendant of David on the throne, nor the temple services of the priests. Rather, a renewed emphasis on living a sacred life enabled Judaism to continue in a unique way. Unlike its surrounding neighbors, or its invincible conquerors, the tiny nation of Judah adapted and survived with its religious and cultural identity intact, even though it was in a foreign land surrounded by a dominant and wealthy civilization.

The readers originally addressed by the tales of Daniel 1–6 were probably familiar with other accounts of Babylon's invasion, such as this example from 2 Kings:

In the fifth month, on the seventh day of the month—which was the nineteenth year of King Nebuchadnezzar, king of Babylon—Nebuzaradan, the captain of the bodyguard, a servant of the king of Babylon, came to Jerusalem. He burned the house of the LORD, the king's house, and all the houses of Jerusalem; every great house he

The Capture of Jerusalem
Marc Chagall captures the enormity of the destruction of Jerusalem in this etching. The angel's presence is ominous, reflecting God's judgment as the city lay in flames. A crush of people is displaced as they exit the city in anguish, while one man extends his arms as though crying out. Note the deceased in the right-hand corner and the stooped king in the left.

Marc Chagall. Russian (1887–1985). The Capture of Jerusalem, 1957. Hand colored etching. 24 x 18" (61 x 45.7cm). Gift of Mr. and Mrs. Patrick Haggerty. Haggerty Museum of Art, Marquette University, Milwaukee, WI. 80.7.62

burned down. All the army of the Chaldeans who were with the captain of the guard broke down the walls around Jerusalem. Nebuzaradan the captain of the guard carried into exile the rest of the people who were left in the city and the deserters who had defected to the king of Babylon—all the rest of the population. But the captain of the guard left some of the poorest people of the land to be vinedressers and tillers of the soil. (2 Kgs 25:8-12) [Tisha B'Av]

At the time of Nebuchadnezzar's invasion, Israel had a four-hundred-year-old tradition of offering sacrifices in the Jerusalem temple. Because the fulfillment of sacrificial requirements demonstrated the people's obedience to God's law and their discharge of their responsibilities, the loss of these rituals was devastating. In addition, the offering of sacrifices was the primary way in which any individual connected with God not only on a daily basis, but also during some of life's most important and meaningful times. Expiatory sacrifices were used to reconcile God and people who were estranged because of sins; other temple sacrifices were completed to mark life-cycle events and religious holidays. Examples include the birth of a baby, the end of sickness, the deliverance from a life-threatening event, and celebrations recalling God's redemption, the giving of the Torah, and the life-sustaining harvest. The opening of the book of Daniel shows that this meeting of heaven and earth in the sacred space of Jerusalem's temple is no longer possible. Indeed, the holy objects now sit in the treasury of

Within the context of this sad history of defeat, Daniel sees a powerful example of God's activity. Nebuchadnezzar was successful only because the God of Israel gave him victory (1:2). Even the vessels of the holy temple were allowed by God to fall into Babylonian hands. The horror associated with the destruction of the very house of God is heightened by the fact that the vessels from the temple, used in the daily sacrifices, were captured and placed in the most humiliating of places, the treasury of Nebuchadnezzar's gods. Of all the devastation perpetrated by Nebuchadnezzar, it is this reference that is singled out by the opening words of Daniel.

This devastating image became part of Jewish consciousness. The Jewish holiday of *Tisha B'Av* (the ninth of Av) commemorates the destruction of the first and second temples by traditional mourning methods: fasting, prayer, and the reading of Scripture. According to Jewish teaching, both temples were destroyed on the ninth of the month of Av by Nebuchadnezzar and Titus, respectively. Other tragedies occurred on this day as well. According to rabbinic teaching, God forbade the generation of Israelites who came out of Egypt from entering the promised land; Rome crushed Bar Kokhba's independence movement and outlawed the practice of Judaism, and Hadrian barred Jews from living in Jerusalem. In addition, other acts of martyrdom and persecutions are remembered on this day, such as the deaths of holy rabbis who refused to commit idolatry, the massacres of Jewish villagers during the Crusades, and the martyrs of European pogroms.

The book of Lamentations, traditionally ascribed to Jeremiah, is read on *Tisha B'Av*. It captures the heartbreak of the destruction of Jerusalem:

How lonely sits the city that once was full of people!

How like a widow she has become, she that was great among the nations!

She that was a princess among the provinces has become a vassal.

She weeps bitterly in the night, with tears on her cheeks;

among all her lovers she has no one to comfort her;

all her friends have dealt treacherously with her, they have become her enemies.

Judah has gone into exile with suffering and hard servitude;

she lives now among the nations, and finds no resting place;

her pursuers have all overtaken her in the midst of her distress. (Lam 1:1-3)

Leo Trepp, *The Complete Book of Jewish Observance* (New York: Behrman House/Simon and Schuster, 1980), 206.

Babylon's gods, a sign of Israel's utter defeat. It is in keeping with the theological importance of the sacrificial system that the hope for the kingdom of God expressed in the visions of Daniel 7–12 includes key references to the rebuilding of Jerusalem and the reestablishment of sacrifices (8:13-14; 9:18, 24-25).

The exilic and post-exilic communities were familiar with Babylon's gods, myths, and its impressive temples. The most famous of the Babylonian gods was Marduk—named "Bel" (meaning "Lord") in the Bible—the champion of the Babylonian pantheon. According to the Babylonian myth *Enuma Elish*, Marduk created human beings from the blood of a defeated god in order to save the gods from the toils of labor. [The *Enuma Elish*] Other deities included Nabu, called Nebo in the Bible, the god of scribes and education; Shamash, the sun god; Nergal, the god of the dead; and Ishtar, the goddess of love. These deities captured the imagina-

---

The *Enuma Elish*

The *Enuma Elish*, or the Babylonian Epic of Creation (c. 1200 BC), gives an account of the origins of the gods, the world, the supremacy of Marduk, and the condition of humankind. It shows that the world is essentially chaotic, that most gods are capricious, and that their requirements to be served are so demanding that humans are crushed under such burdens. Indeed, human beings are created to serve the victorious gods after the vanquished ones lamented that the work was onerous, as shown in the following excerpt.

Blood I will mass and cause bones to be.
I will establish a savage, "man" shall be his name.

Verily, savage-man I will create.
He shall be charged with the service of the gods
That they might be at ease!
The ways of the gods I will artfully alter . . .
Out of [Kingu's] blood they fashioned mankind.
[Ea] imposed the service and let free the gods.
After Ea, the wise, had created mankind,
Had imposed upon it the service of the gods—
That work was beyond comprehension.

James B. Pritchard, ed., *Ancient Near Eastern Texts Relating to the Old Testament*, 3rd ed. with supplement (Princeton NJ: Princeton University Press, 1969), 68.

---

tion of exiles, who often mocked what they saw to be the pretensions of Babylonian power and materialism by disparaging the gods of Babylon. At the same time, their persistent references and echoes in biblical literature attest to the attraction they held for the captive people. A classic text comes from the prophet who speaks in Second Isaiah (Isaiah 40–55), who preached a message of hope to those who were allowed to return to their homeland after the Persian conquest of Babylon:

Bel bows down, Nebo stoops, their idols are on beasts and cattle;

These things you carry are loaded as burdens on weary animals.

They stoop, they bow down together; they cannot save the burden, but themselves go into captivity. . . .

Those who lavish gold from the purse, and weigh out silver in the scales—

they hire a goldsmith, who makes it into a god; then they fall down and worship! . . .

If one cries out to it, it does not answer or save anyone from trouble. (Isa 46:1-7)

Not only do we find biblical texts that mock the gods by name, but also the city of these gods, Babylon, is derided as a place of moral decadence. In Daniel 1:2, the word "Shinar" is identified as the new location of the captured vessels. "Shinar," a synonym of Babylon, is used pejoratively throughout the Hebrew Scriptures. It is the location of the arrogant building of the Tower of Babel (Gen 11:2) and the place of origin of one of the four kings who attacked Abraham (Gen 14:1).[1] In both the Former and the Latter Prophets, Shinar is infamous as the place of origin of a stolen luxury good

Judith and *Kashrut*

Like Daniel, Judith is of Judean nobility and becomes a captive of a purported Assyrian general, Holofernes, the right-hand man of an Assyrian emperor named Nebuchadnezzar (he is, of course, modeled on his famous Babylonian namesake). As is the case with Daniel, Judith's faith is tested when she is given the food items from the general's table. She refuses, however, saying, "I cannot partake of them, or it would be an offense: but I will have enough with the things I brought with me" (Jdt 12:2). When pressed a second time to eat from Holofernes' banquet, Judith eats only what her maid prepared for her, having the good fortune that Holofernes was too drunk to notice. The story derides Holofernes, showing him to be so inebriated that Judith is able to slay him, thus saving her people from annihilation. Both Judith and Daniel show that faithfulness and courage in spite of foreign attack will be rewarded by God's compassion.

that caused the downfall of Achan (Josh 7:21), the place of dispersion that requires God's rescue (Isa 11:11), and the place where Judah symbolically sends its sin (Zech 5:11). [Joshua, Achan, and the Mantel from Shinar] These connotations paint a sobering view of the exile as the book of Daniel begins. With this portrayal, we can easily imagine the people's quandary. How does the Diaspora community remain faithful to God and to their traditions when it seems that God has abandoned them in the face of such devastation? The books of Judith and Esther show similar struggles of the community in the Diaspora due to the imminent danger posed by tyrants and the long-term threat of assimilation. [Judith and *Kashrut*] Daniel 1:1-2 sets the stage for great questioning. The remainder of the book provides models of courage, fidelity, hope, and patience by illustration in story and vision.

The Enslavement of Daniel and his Friends, 1:3-7

Daniel 1:3-7 serves two purposes: to demonstrate that courage and faithfulness witness against the evil of a despotic ruler and to show that the God of Israel may endow his people with the wisdom and understanding to endure hardships and persecution. As do the biblical stories of Joseph and Esther, Daniel 1–6 portrays the adventures and trials of faithful Jews in a foreigner's court.[2] It is important to note that although the capture of Daniel and his compatriots, Hananiah, Mishael, and Azariah, as well as their arrival at Nebuchadnezzar's palace are not specified as slavery, these acts lead to, in effect, forced servitude. [Nebuchadnezzar's Palace] The captives have no choice but to consent to the king's demand that they work for him in the confines of the palace. In addition, they

serve under coercion, as the test of
their diet shows. The first command
that Nebuchadnezzar gives presses
them into his service. He has the
resources to accomplish this as is
indicated by the actions of
Ashpenaz. Ashpenaz is identified as
the palace master or captain of the
guard (*rab sārîsāyw*). This Hebrew
phrase has a broader connotation
than its translation into English, as
the word *sārîs* (guard) may also mean
"eunuch." ["Eunuch"—Tragic Connotations]
The very mention of such a captain

Nebuchadnezzar's Palace

The palace of Nebuchadnezzar showcased his wealth and success as an empire builder. Note the striding lions, symbol of the goddess Ishtar.

Façade of the Throne Hall from the Palace of Nebuchadnezzar II. 7th C. BC. Vorderasiatisches Museum, Staatliche Museen zu Berlin. Berlin, Germany. (Credit: Erich Lessing/Art Resource, NY)

underscores the climate of fear that Nebuchadnezzar instilled in his
foreign subjects. It is not certain whether Ashpenaz is to be seen as
a eunuch in this narrative, or simply as an ordinary official. In any
case, he is an effective enforcer of Nebuchadnezzar's commands.
[Ashpenaz and Potiphar]

The possible reference to Ashpenaz's mutilation contrasts with
the description of Daniel's appearance. Throughout the Bible, the
physical description of a character is often a clue to his or her personality. This description of Daniel as having no "physical defect"
and as being "handsome" helps to associate his personality with
virtue. The term for "physical defect" (*m'ûm*) may also refer to a
character flaw, as in Job 31:7. Not only is Daniel spared this, but
also he is "handsome to look at," a phrase that echoes descriptions

---

"Eunuch"—Tragic Connotations

The prophet Isaiah speaks in exile of a time when Jews in exile will suffer castration. To king Hezekiah, the prophet Isaiah pronounces:

Days are coming when all that is in your house, and that which your ancestors have stored up until this day, shall be carried to Babylon; nothing shall be left, says the Lord. Some of your own sons who are born to you shall be taken away; they shall be eunuchs in the palace of the king of Babylon. (Isa 39:6-7 = 2 Kgs 20:17-18)

On a similarly somber note, rabbinic commentators debate whether Daniel and his friends had been castrated. What a terrible fate for the sons of nobility of the tribe of Judah to leave no descendants! Not only would this be seen as a personal tragedy, but also as a national

scourge, since any future king or messiah would come from the line of Judah. Yet other rabbis argue that because Daniel was identified as being "without physical defect" (1:4), he was not, in fact, mutilated. These rabbinic interpretations demonstrate how connotations of words help to create parameters of possible interpretation in a text. The fear inflicted by the despotic Nebuchadnezzar and the shame and fear of being in exile is supported by the simple identification of a palace guard.

For an excellent discussion of the debates concerning whether or not Daniel was understood to be a eunuch, see Jay Braverman, *Jerome's Commentary on Daniel: A Study of Comparative Jewish and Christian Interpretation of the Hebrew Bible* (CBQMS 7; Washington DC: The Catholic Biblical Association, 1978), 66–68.

Ashpenaz and Potiphar

ΑΩ The name Ashpenaz is otherwise unknown, but his identification as the captain of the guard/eunuchs (*rab sārîs*), recalls two interesting references in Scripture. First, the word captain/eunuch is used of Potiphar, one of the foreign superiors who plays a key role in the life of Joseph. The story of Joseph's stay in Egypt (Gen 39–50) is linked with the narratives of Daniel in exile by many similarities of wording, setting, events, and themes. Potiphar, like Ashpenaz, is identified as *rab sārîs* (Gen 37:36; 39:1), and just as Joseph finds favor with Potiphar, so too does Daniel find that God allows him "to receive favor and compassion from the palace master" (Dan 1:9). Joseph faces a trial of endurance when he is imprisoned because of the false charge of attempted rape claimed by Potiphar's wife

(Gen 39:14-18). Imprisoned for this offense, Joseph paradoxically is appointed as Pharaoh's highest-ranking minister, paralleling Daniel's service in Nebuchadnezzar's palace (Gen 41:37-45). Although the accusation of Pharaoh's wife leads to Joseph's imprisonment, ultimately his release into Pharaoh's service allows him to interpret Pharaoh's troubling dreams about upcoming famine in Egypt. Similarly, the capture of Daniel leads to his service in Nebuchadnezzar's palace and the young sage's interpretation of Nebuchadnezzar's terrifying dreams. By linking these two stories with similar narrative detail, the author allows the reader to compare the ordeals of Daniel with those of Joseph. Both Joseph and Daniel begin their trials with a *sārîs* in a foreign land, both serve God, and both ultimately are vindicated.

---

of Israel's heroes and heroines of old. The favorite wife of Jacob, Rachel, is described as "beautiful in form and beautiful to look at" (Gen 29:17 A.T.; "graceful and beautiful," NRSV) as is her son Joseph (Gen 39:6 A.T.; "handsome and good looking," NRSV), the favorite son of Jacob. As the stereotypical association of beauty and strength with moral virtue may strike the modern reader as simplistic, the Bible also critiques such shallow associations. [Critiques of Emphasis on Appearance]

Despite these descriptions that cast Daniel and his friends in a positive light, the reader must wonder whether they could endure the kind of test that Nebuchadnezzar could arrange. The text emphasizes their youth and hints at their inexperience. Although words are available in biblical Hebrew that would unequivocally indicate that Daniel is an adolescent or young man, the author here employs the Hebrew word "*yĕlādîm,*" which usually means "children" or "boys" (v. 4) ("young men," NRSV). Their lack of years is contrasted, however, with their highly prized skills and virtues; they were "versed in every branch of wisdom, endowed with knowledge and insight, and competent to serve in the king's palace" (v. 4). Throughout the Hebrew Scriptures, these virtues are understood as endowing one not only with secular intelligence, but also with the insight to serve God and to keep the commandments. Wisdom helps one to discern God's presence and to avoid those attractions, vices, and disguised

---

Critiques of Emphasis on Appearance

In 1 Sam 16:6-7, we read that although the prophet Samuel misidentified Eliab as God's anointed because of his striking appearance, God reminded him that "the LORD does not see as mortals see; they look on the outward appearance, but the LORD looks on the heart" (1 Sam 16:7). Similarly, in Prov 31:30, in the testimony to the good wife, we find, "Charm is deceitful, and beauty is vain, but a woman who fears the LORD is to be praised." Nonetheless, the reference to Daniel's appearance would be particularly important to a Hellenistic audience, as Greek culture frequently associated beauty with virtue.

Louis H. Feldman, *Jew and Gentile in the Ancient World* (Princeton NJ: Princeton University Press, 1993), 249–51.

Daniel and Esther in the Bible and Talmud

As does the book of Daniel, the book of Esther portrays two Jews, Esther and Mordecai, at the palace of a foreign emperor, Ahasuerus of Persia, whose right-hand man, Haman, not only endangers the possibility of faithful practice of Jewish law, but also threatens the continued existence of the entire Jewish people in the Diaspora. As does Daniel, Esther and her cousin Mordecai face the dangers of powerful individuals like Haman, who suddenly can present life-threatening challenges, or like Ahasuerus, who acquiesces when Haman schemes. Just as Daniel was renamed Belteshazzar, Hadassah—the Jewish heroine—has the Persian name Esther, which probably honors the goddess Ishtar. Esther is brought to the court as queen because Ahasuerus's wife, Vashti, refuses to be obedient to her husband, the king. In the course of the narrative, Esther and Mordecai have their faith tested, and they turn to compliance, subterfuge, or defiance depending on the circumstances. Esther at first does not reveal her identity as a Jew, but after being counseled by Mordecai, who himself was unwilling to commit idolatry, Esther—identifying her heritage—risks her life to save her people and identifies her heritage (Esth 7:3-4). Michael Fox notes,

> Mordecai's command to Esther not to reveal her Jewishness shows him planning and waiting, his caution intimating an atmosphere of danger. The source of danger must be anti-Semitism, for otherwise public knowledge of Esther's Jewishness would not interfere with her usefulness to her people. The danger that will face them is thus not the unpredictable act of a spiteful individual, but a manifestation of an ever-present—but not universal—hostility, for which one must always be prepared.

Similarly, in the book of Daniel, courtiers and kings alike present terrible dangers to the hero and to his friends, as is shown in the tests of the worship of the statue (Dan 3) and of the proscription of prayer (Dan 6).

The Talmud links the books of Daniel and Esther by presenting parallels in Esther's and Daniel's behavior, by portraying the assistance that Daniel gives to Esther, and by showing a familial connection between Nebuchadnezzar and Vashti. R. Johanan argues that even though she was Ahasuerus's queen, Esther ate only kosher food, quoting the book of Daniel as being relevant not only to Daniel himself but also to Esther: "So the steward took away their food and gave them pulse" (*b. Meg.* 13a; Dan 1:11-14). When he was an old man under the service of the Persian court, Daniel provided assistance to Esther (*b. Meg.* 15a), as he is identified with the eunuch Hatach who brings Esther's messages to Mordecai (Esth 4:5, 6, 9, 10). Vashti, infamous as the daughter of Belshazzar (*b. Meg.* 12b), shares her ancestor's cruelty, for she forced Jewish women to work in the nude on the Sabbath (*b. Meg.* 12a).

Michael Fox, *Character and Ideology in the Book of Esther*, 2d ed. (Grand Rapids MI: Eerdmans, 2001), 32.

evils brought from a foreign culture. Similarly, great figures are portrayed as using their wisdom for noble purposes: Solomon is presented as presciently knowing the importance of prayer when the temple would no longer exist (1 Kgs 8:33-34); the virtuous woman is contrasted to the foreign temptress (Prov 5:8-23); and Mordecai's wisdom counsels Esther to save her people from annihilation (Esth 4:13-14). [Daniel and Esther in the Bible and Talmud] Joseph also used his wisdom for God's purposes to save both Israelites and Egyptians from famine, rather than for any self-aggrandizement (Gen 41:55-57). What would Daniel and his friends do in such difficult straits? Specifically, two proposed tasks serve to cut off Daniel and his friends from their heritage—studying Babylonian subjects and eating the king's food.

Because the youths continue their learning in the Babylonian palace instead of in the temple of Jerusalem, the author intimates that perhaps Daniel and his friends would compromise their way of life. They were to study for three years, a significant amount of time. Both Babylonian and Jewish curricula included scribal arts, lexicography, the study of natural phenomena, medicine, religious studies, economics, business, law, and government.[3] Nevertheless,

Babylonian Curricula and Magic

Literacy in Babylon was the purview of the scribal class, whose influence in the government and upon the common people was extensive. The excavations of Babylonian libraries have yielded texts of literature (epic, myth, prayer, and hymn), astrology, astronomy, mathematics, medicine, lexicography, historiography, and extispicy (the study of animal entrails in order to discern the messages of the gods). Much of Babylonian "education" was linked with the practice of magical arts. A. Kirk Grayson observes:

Almost anything could be a medium for divine messages, such as the shape of smoke from a fire, the configurations of oil poured upon water, the flight of birds, or the sudden appearance of a snake. The Babylonians, building upon a Sumerian tradition, developed the science (if we can call it that) of reading these signs into a very complex and comprehensive system. This system was carefully recorded on clay tablets and filed away in libraries for reference. One gains some idea of the importance of divination to Babylonians from the fact that of all the documents stored in Babylonian libraries, prognostic texts were the most numerous.

While the author of Dan 1 does not reveal any specifications of Babylonian curricula, references in the Hebrew Bible show disparagement of Babylon itself (see below, [Nebuchadnezzar in Ancient Jewish Sources], [The Tower of Babel in Rabbinic Sources], Portrayal of Babylon]) and its educated courtiers, such as its officials, sages, and diviners who are held accountable to God (Jer 50:35-36). Like the food test that comes from the context of Daniel's imposed instruction, the education itself becomes a test in this narrative. Although the teaching Daniel and his friends are to receive could be linked with either magic or with wisdom, this author makes clear at the end of the account that Daniel's education is linked only with wisdom. At the end of three years, instead of asking whether Daniel and his companions know the "literature and language of the Chaldeans" (Dan 1:4), the king asks whether they were versed in "wisdom and understanding" (1:20), virtues associated with the knowledge of God and the keeping of the commandments (Deut 4:6; 1 Kgs 4:29; Isa 11:2).

These lessons, however, were not taught by the palace officials but by the very God of Israel (Dan 1:17).

Daniel's polemic against the Babylonians' use of magic is similar to the portrayal of magic in the Torah, argues Jacob Milgrom. Unlike examples from the prophets, who sometimes perform signs or magic on their own, the Torah insists that any supernatural performance is actually a miracle that falls under God's purview (Exod 8:1-4 [7:26-29 MT]; 8:20-24 [8:16-20 MT]; 9:1-4, 13; Num 11:18-20; 16:16-17, 28-30). (The case of Joseph saying that he uses divination [Gen 44:5] may be used to justify the ruse against his brothers and not to prove that he valued independent engagement with magic.) Unlike foreign diviners who use magical formulas on their own with specific incantations in order to manipulate deities for their personal ends, leaders such as Moses perform signs and wonders to illustrate God's absolute sovereignty over the universe. Just as the Pentateuch and the book of Chronicles continually emphasize that "all miracles are performed by God," so too "in Daniel as well, we find miracles scrupulously attributed to God and punctuated by homiletic perorations of man's need to trust Him."

The portrayal of the court's magicians, sorcerers, enchanters, and Chaldeans (Dan 2:2) reveals Israel's critique of the misplaced values inherent in Babylonian structures. These courtiers, the wisest of Babylon, cannot divine Nebuchadnezzar's dream, and even the king suspects them. Daniel must announce to them that only *his* God can reveal mysteries (Dan 2:28). The very presence of the exile Daniel in a governmental institution that attempts to manipulate something as essential as Daniel's diet and education is suggestive of a polemic against the enticements of a powerful foreign culture. Such concerns would be relevant both in the Persian period, where the tales of Daniel 1–6 were written, or during the Hellenistic age when the tales reached their final form, as both periods presented challenges of assimilation for the Jewish people.

A. Kirk Grayson, "Mesopotamia, History of (Babylonia)," *ABD*, ed. David Noel Freedman (New York: Doubleday & Co., 1992), 4:775.

Jacob Milgrom, *Numbers*, JPS Torah Commentary (Philadelphia: Jewish Publication Society, 1990), 454–5.

the setting of the proposed education under Nebuchadnezzar's directive suggests that the outcome of the challenge presented to Daniel—to remain a member of a people "set apart"—could not be taken for granted. [Babylonian Curricula and Magic]

The account, however, turns to a more immediate problem before the results of the three-year training are given, creating suspense. The author presents a clever "test within a test" when Daniel and his friends are faced with their daily rations. The way in which the youths face the challenge of eating proper food serves to delay the results of the first trial, namely whether or not they accomplished the required learning to Nebuchadnezzar's satisfaction.

The problem of eating the king's food was a daily reminder to Daniel and his friends of the vigilance required to remain loyal to their religious obligations. Because the king's food and wine were not kosher, Daniel and his friends would be defiled. Although some interpreters argue that the issue of eating the king's food is not concerned with *kashrut* (keeping kosher), the very fact that Daniel states the food would "defile" him is an indication that he is concerned with spiritual purity and obedience to the food laws.[4] [Kashrut Today] Daniel's steadfastness regarding the food laws puts him in the tradition of Judith, Tobit, and the Maccabees, who also refuse their oppressor's food.[5]

During the occupation of Judah as well as throughout the Diaspora, *kashrut* takes on the further significance of obeying God's commands even while under foreign control and of bringing the holiness of the temple into one's home. A foreign government could easily legislate where subjects might live and work and could outlaw sacrificial services or public religious rites. In contrast, it would be difficult to regulate what foods a people will *not* consume or how a family infuses its table with holiness. Daniel and his friends acutely faced this challenge because their allotted food from the king was all they had access to. This consumption of the king's

Kashrut Today

The Jewish practice of keeping kosher has continued throughout history. Today's reasons, like those of biblical times and in antiquity, stem from the Torah itself: obeying God's laws and living a life of holiness. Two other reasons are often supplemented: personal discipline and reverence for life. The editors of the popular *The First Jewish Catalog* state,

> Kashrut is observed primarily as a mitzvah—commandment—from God, intended both for man's ritual purity and for the maintenance of a proper relationship between God and man. . . . We are engaged in determining boundaries for ourselves within which we regulate our lives. . . . The killing of an animal with flesh, blood, and life . . . is certainly weighty. It is proper and fitting to the dignity of man that he does not just kill and eat, but takes responsibility for his food—before God and before life itself.

The religious importance of *kashrut* is similarly echoed by Rabbi Leo Trepp who writes, "ultimately, the consumption of food is a 'religious' act. The symbolism of Kashrut invites us to be pure, inwardly and outwardly, in body and mind. The common meal is a form of worship, a communion: our choice of food should make it so."

Richard Siegel, Michael Strassfeld, and Sharon Strassfeld, eds. and comps., *The First Jewish Catalog* (Philadelphia: The Jewish Publication Society of America, n.d.), 18.

Leo Trepp, *The Complete Book of Jewish Observance* (New York: Behrman House/Simon and Schuster, 1980), 62.

I Think I Might Become a Vegetarian

"I Think I
might become a vegetarian"

"I THOUGHT meat came in
cellophane Packages."

"I Think I Might Become a Vegetarian," from Sharon Strassfeld and Michael Strassfeld, eds. and comps., *The Third Jewish Catalog* (Philadelphia: The Jewish Publication Society of America, 1980), 303.

This illustration underscores that people often forget that eating meat requires the shedding of blood.

food was to continue indefinitely, and their secular training was scheduled for three years, after which the assumption seems to have been that the youths would be indoctrinated and acculturated enough to serve the Babylonian king. These were the hopes of the oppressors.

It is only after the reader is informed that the exile has occurred that the identifications of the captives are given by name. These identifications are immediately followed by another act of attempted assimilation by the Babylonians. The totalitarian control that the king's court exercises over Daniel is evidenced in the renaming of Daniel and his friends. Throughout the Bible, renaming typically occurred to indicate that person's new status or function. [Renaming in the Bible] The renaming of Daniel and his friends potentially evidences a profound change. Each of their original Hebrew names is theophoric, that is, derived from one of the names of the God of Israel. Yet the Babylonian official gives them

---

Renaming in the Bible

Name changes in the Hebrew Bible occur in a variety of circumstances. For example, a monarch might take a throne name, as did King Solomon who used the name Jedidiah, meaning, "the LORD is my God" (2 Sam 12:25). God changed the name of the patriarch Abram to Abraham, meaning "father of many," indicating the importance of God's covenantal promises with him. Sometimes a name change signifies a particular role in the Gentile world. Hadassah is also named Esther (a probable reference to the goddess Ishtar, Esth 2:7), the name by which she is known as Persian royalty, and Pharaoh renames Joseph Zaphenath-paneah ("Riddle-solver," Gen 41:45) to signify his royal appointment in Egypt. Other occasions of renaming signify a negative change in circumstances. Daniel is renamed Belteshazzar by Nebuchadnezzar to honor the king's god. Naomi tells her friends to call her "Mara," meaning "bitter," because her loved ones have died (Ruth 1:20). Hosea's children are first named Jezreel, Lo-ruhamah, and Lo-ammi, meaning "God sows" (in a negative sense), "not pitied," and "not my people," but their names are later changed to Jezreel, Ruhamah, and Ammi, meaning "God sows" (in a positive sense), "pitied," and "my people," respectively, reflecting God's initial punishment but also subsequent salvation (Hos 1:4, 6, 9; 2:21-23). When first Pharaoh Neco and, later, Nebuchadnezzar placed the Judean monarchs Eliakim and Mattaniah on the throne, the foreign invaders signified their dominance by changing their names to Jehoiakim and Zedekiah (2 Kgs 23:34; 24:17).

Shemeryahu Talmon, "Daniel," in *The Literary Guide to the Bible*, ed. Robert Alter and Frank Kermode (Cambridge MA: The Belknap Press of Harvard University Press, 1987), 351.

names in honor of the gods of Babylon. These names are symbols not only of the oppressor's culture, but also of the very gods that the Babylonians believed granted them such power. Their name changes are as follows: Daniel, whose name means "El is my judge," is now called Belteshazzar, a name that honors the Babylonian deity Marduk (Bel). Ironically, Daniel's name also honors his future oppressor, Belshazzar, who appears in Daniel 5. The Hebrew names of Daniel's compatriots are Hananiah, which means "The LORD has been gracious"; "Mishael," meaning "Who is what God is?"; and Azariah, meaning "The LORD has helped." They are renamed Shadrach, Meshach, and Abednego, respectively (v. 7). "Shadrach" may mean "Command of Aku" (a Babylonian deity) or may be the author's purposeful

Nabu, Patron of Writing

This statue of a minor deity was found at a doorway of the Nabu Temple in Khorsabad, Iraq. Dating from the rule of the Assyrian emperor Sargon II (721–705 BC), it honors the god Nabu, the patron of writing and knowledge. The presence of the vase from which water flowed probably represents fertility.

Deity Holding a Flowing Vase. 721–705 BC. Gypsum. Courtesy of the Oriental Institute of the Univeristy of Chicago.

misspelling of the name of Marduk, written as such in order to mock the deity's name. "Meshach" means "Who is what Aku is?" or may be another derisive corruption of Marduk's name, and Abednego means "servant of Nabu."[6] Although the youths' new names represent an attempt by the conquerors to glorify Babylonian culture, the author's limited use of these names and the possibly deliberate misspellings provide the opportunity to ridicule the religion and values of the Babylonians. The youths have been captured, brought to a foreign land, enslaved for palace service, forced to be "re-acculturated" for three years, and renamed to honor the idols of despots and to symbolize their expected assimilation. Their survival requires tenacity under pressing challenges.

Daniel's Counter to His Captors, 1:8-17

Daniel 1:8-17 portrays a reversal of the Babylonians' control of Daniel and his friends. Rather than governing and assimilating the young men, the Babylonians themselves now face a test by Daniel.

The author shows that the God of Israel is far from being dominated by the gods of Babylon. Rather, God helps Daniel use his wisdom to defeat the Babylonians' attempts to crush his religious life by the imposition of their foreign study and dietary practices. Although Daniel's friends will have their own specific challenges to face (Dan 3), the text first turns to the hero and protagonist of the book, Daniel himself. Daniel's placement in the company of the three friends points to his special standing among them, as does the relating of his specific deeds before those of his companions.[7]

The author shows that Daniel had to marshal much personal courage in order to complete successfully this subversive act. "Daniel took to heart" (*wayyāśem dānîyēl ʿal-libbô*, A.T.; "Daniel resolved," NRSV) that he would "not defile" (*lōʾ yitgāʾāl*) himself (v. 8). The phrase "take to heart" indicates deepest sincerity concerning crucially important matters. For example, when Moses recites the entire covenant to the Israelites, he states they must "take to heart all the words that I am giving in witness against you today" (Deut 32:46). The word "defile" is used in the gravest matters of moral culpability. This term is used when Israel is accused of the sins of murder, injustice, lying, and iniquity (Isa 59:3) and to explain why certain returning exiles were excluded from the priesthood (Ezra 2:62). The reader thus finds that the first act on the part of the captive Daniel is one of subterfuge and defiance before the great Babylonian king who has the structures and bureaucracy to enforce his will.

Despite the power that the palace master, Ashpenaz, and his unnamed appointed guard have over Daniel and the youths, the author hints of Daniel's future victory. Instead of being the enforcer of Nebuchadnezzar's commands, the palace master himself now becomes an agent of God's fidelity as shown in the following verse: "now God allowed Daniel to receive *hesed* ("covenantal love"; "favor," NRSV) and *raḥămîm* (compassion) from the palace master" (v. 9, A.T.). These attributes of God, *hesed* and *raḥămîm*, are well-known indicators of God's covenantal loyalty to his people in their time of exile (cf. Jer 16:5; Hos 2:19 [2:21 MT]; Ps 103:4). They echo a similar grant of God's grace in the days of Joseph's trials in Egypt as the following text shows: "But the LORD was with Joseph and showed him steadfast love (*hesed*); he gave him favor (*raḥămîm*) in the sight of the chief jailer" (Gen 39:21).

The fear evidenced by Ashpenaz contrasts with the courage displayed by Daniel. Whereas the captain is terrified that the king will have his head when he sees that Daniel and the youths have deteriorated physically, Daniel finds another person to enlist for his cause. He proposes a test to a subordinate of the captain. This is a clever stratagem because the test seems harmless and because the subordinate is less powerful and perhaps less stringent. Daniel proposes that he and his compatriots eat only vegetables and drink only water for ten days in order to prove that there will be no physical ill effects. At the same time, a control group will be set up, as Daniel suggests that the condition of those who eat the king's food will be compared to his own and that of his companions. The appointed guard agrees that the test is acceptable. He can assume that ten days is too little time to inflict any major damage and that any ill effects could be remedied before Nebuchadnezzar inspects his subjects.

Although we never hear any conversation from Daniel's companions, it is important to note that Daniel includes them without hesitation when he sees that his own integrity concerning the food laws is challenged. The personalities of Hananiah, Mishael, and Azariah are not developed in this chapter, but their presence and their inclusion in Daniel's plan serve to provide a model of ethical behavior for the reader. [1 Maccabees and the Three Youths] Daniel's leadership and care for them are paradigmatic and indeed bear fruit as is seen in the courageous act of defiance shown by the three youths when they confront Nebuchadnezzar without benefit of Daniel's leadership in the subsequent narrative of the fiery furnace (Dan 3).

In contrast to the fear of the palace master, the guard does not feel threatened; indeed, when people are allowed to discover consequences by themselves, they can better accept that a policy should be changed. The following phrase highlights both the success of the test and God's providence: "they appeared better and fatter than all the young men who had been eating the royal rations" (v. 15). The phrase "they appeared" does not specify who sees them; rather, the implication is that the test makes the result clear to everyone. The stage is set, therefore, for the guard to continue to give them the food that does not violate God's commandments (v. 16). After Daniel survives his first test, God rewards him with further strength to remain steadfast and continues to protect him. The "favor and compassion" from the palace master (v. 9) now becomes "knowledge and skill in every aspect of literature and wisdom" (v. 17) as well as "insight into all visions and

1 Maccabees and the Three Youths

The books of Maccabees are important sources for understanding Antiochus's persecution of the Jews during the Seleucid period. In 1 Macc we find a prayer that lauds the faithfulness of Israel's ancestors. The stories of Daniel and the three young men are employed in a listing of Israel's heroes to counter the pressure to submit to a seemingly all-powerful surrounding culture:

Remember the deeds of the ancestors, which they did in their generations. . . . Hananiah, Azariah, and Mishael believed and were saved from the flame. Daniel, because of his innocence, was delivered from the mouth of the lions. And so observe, from generation to generation, that none of those who put their trust in him will lack strength. (1 Macc 2:51, 59-61)

dreams" (v. 17). These phrases have connotations of Babylonian learning and of Jewish wisdom. Daniel and his companions will have the secular knowledge to impress Nebuchadnezzar and to fulfill the dictates of their servitude, yet they will also have the religious wisdom to live a life of faithfulness to God.

For Jews who lived under Persian rule, in the Diaspora as well as in Yehud (occupied Judah), tension existed between living a life according to God's commandments and living a successful "secular" life. The demands of servitude placed before Daniel test his resolve to remain faithful to the commandments of obeying the food laws and remembering to care for one's neighbor as oneself (Lev 19:18). Daniel immediately sees the problem as one that affects not only himself, but also his companions. The solidarity Daniel shows with them bares fruit in the final scene, as not only are Daniel and his companions safe, but they also enjoy promotions within the government. They move from being captives, whose every move is watched, to being advisers and bureaucrats— yet in a land with limited rights and freedom. Here, the gifts God gives Daniel allow him to succeed in the Babylonian court as a skilled official.[8] Yet, questions remain. Would the community survive without being assimilated or without being continually harassed or threatened? The subsequent chapters of the narratives (Dan 2–6) show that the exiles must be continually vigilant.

Aftermath of the Educational Preparation, 1:18-21

At the end of the lengthy preparatory period, Daniel and his compatriots find that Nebuchadnezzar is still very much in charge. However, instead of the conqueror who pillages the temple and exiles Judean nobles, Nebuchadnezzar now sits as an evaluator of Daniel and his young friends. Would he find their education acceptable, or would he manifest irrationality in his judgment? Would the young men prosper within the limited autonomy of their confines in the Babylonian palace and bureaucracy? [Nebuchadnezzar in Ancient Jewish Sources] These questions had broader implications for the original audience of this text because, as reflected in the food test mentioned above, Nebuchadnezzar's evaluation echoed the long-term concerns of the exiles under foreign rule. Would these people remain loyal to God's commandments and yet be respected members of a foreign court? Would they remain in relative safety? Would the behavior of one person make a difference in the community?

In the last section of the chapter, the author delineates the Babylonian estimation of Daniel's importance. Nebuchadnezzar himself speaks with Daniel and the youths after their indoctrination period. Instead of directly reporting that Nebuchadnezzar is pleased with them, however, the author employs the passive voice to imply that all Babylonian evaluators find Daniel and his friends exceptional. Superlatives are used: "no one was found to compare with Daniel, Hananiah, Mishael, and Azariah" (v. 19). In the eyes of the Babylonians, it is the youths' merit and accomplishment that allows them to be stationed at the king's court. An additional reason accounts for their success—God has given them secular knowledge as well as spiritual insight (v. 17).

It is also noteworthy that Nebuchadnezzar himself judges Daniel and his companions with respect. Now the king himself finds that not only can these captives compare to his Babylonian diviners, but they also can surpass the Babylonian professionals in the practice of wisdom. This presentation of an implied contest between the diviners of Babylon and the captives recalls the competition between the magicians of Egypt and the skill of Moses and Aaron in the days of the exodus.[9] At that ominous time of enslavement and danger, Pharaoh was shown that the wisdom of the

> **Nebuchadnezzar in Ancient Jewish Sources**
>
> The Talmud records that Jews should bless and thank God for destroying the wicked Babylon and its tyrant Nebuchadnezzar and for saving Daniel from the lions' den and from the fiery furnace (*b. Ber.* 57b). The misery imposed by Nebuchadnezzar is likened to the sufferings under Pharaoh. Echoing Psalm 66:12, R. Hanina B. Papa says, "Thou hast caused men to ride over our heads, we went through fire and through water: through fire in the days of the wicked Nebuchadnezzar, and through water in the days of Pharaoh" (*b. Meg.* 11a).
>
> The midrashim present Nebuchadnezzar as an unrepentant idolater, yet for all his worldly power, he cannot stand up to the faith of Shadrach, Meshach, and Abednego, who refuse his demands of idol worship. In one text, Nebuchadnezzar accuses the Jews of having a long history of their own idol worship, while hypocritically refusing to worship his gods. The three confront the king, saying that they will only obey him in the requirement to pay taxes; they will not worship his gods: "You are our 'king' only as regards taxes . . . but in this matter of which you speak to us you are just 'Nebuchadnezzar' and your name is simply 'Nebuchadnezzar'" (*Lev. Rab.* 33:6).
>
> This pronouncement of the youths is similar to Jesus' words concerning whether people should pay taxes: "Give to the emperor the things that are the emperor's, and to God the things that are God's" (Mark 12:17). The three continue their bold response with a clever play on words with the name Nebuchadnezzar: "You and a dog are alike to us! O Nebuchadnezzar, bark (*nebah*) like a dog, swell (*nefah*) like a pitcher (*kad*), chirp (*nezar*) like a cricket (*zarzerah*)!" (*Lev. Rab.* 33:6).

Hebrews was greater than that of the Egyptians who esteemed themselves as the most advanced civilization on earth. Babylonians, too, see that it is the captives who outshine the wisest of the captors; using hyperbole, the author reports that Daniel and his friends were "ten times better" (v. 20). At the same time, the author disparages the traditional wisdom of the Babylonians by calling them "magicians and enchanters" (v. 20). The word for "magicians" (*ḥarṭummîm*) refers to those who have occult knowledge. It is used only of the magicians of Egypt and of Babylon in the Bible; it is never used of Israelites.[10] The word for "enchanters" (NRSV) or "astrologers" (*'aššāpîm*) is used only in the book of Daniel to refer to Babylonians (1:20 and 2:2). This specialized vocabulary may indi-

Pazuzu

The Demon Pazuzu. c. 800–600 BC. Bronze. Courtesy of the Oriental Institute of the Univeristy of Chicago.

This bronze statue from Iraq (c. 800–600 BC) represents the Assyrian and Babylonian deity Pazuzu, ruler of evil wind demons. Pazuzu fought against other threatening demons and was thus honored as a protector of childbirth.

cate that the wise were seen as an important class in Babylonian society; to be sure, the author believes so. The author, however, unmasks the Babylonians' preoccupation and anxiety regarding the future by mocking the multiplication of the categories of spiritual advisers whose purposes were well known.[11] Many scholars link the Babylonians' pervasive pessimism, fatalism, and hedonism to their lack of belief in an afterlife and to their belief in capricious and destructive deities.[12] Indeed, the Babylonians were famous for their insistent belief that their many gods left clues for understanding humanity's fate. By studying the flight patterns of birds, the entrails of sacrificed animals, and other natural phenomena, people could know the future and take action to avert any unfavorable or malicious plans of their gods.

The first chapter of Daniel closes with an important reference that is both indicative of God's continual care for Daniel and of the ultimate end of Babylon's might: "And Daniel continued there [in the king's court] until the first year of King Cyrus" (v. 21). This date informs the reader that almost a half a century has passed and Daniel has endured. Although he is still in the king's service, the success of his early years has allowed him to be considered a trusted adviser to Nebuchadnezzar and his successors. With the advent of the new emperor, Cyrus of Persia, who conquered Babylon and the lands under its control, dramatic changes would be introduced to the Jewish people.[13] The first year of Cyrus was actually the time of the end of the Babylonian Empire. On one level, this reference indicates the lengthy time that Daniel has persisted and the reward of a long life. At another level, it indicates that the status quo does not persist. The mighty Nebuchadnezzar, who could boast that he destroyed the Jerusalem temple, in turn had his own empire conquered by Cyrus, the emperor of Persia, who introduced a policy of repatriation to encourage stability among his many captive populations. [Cyrus's Policy of Repatriation] He allowed these various displaced peoples formerly under Babylonian control to return to their homelands. Jews could return to Judah. The prophet Second Isaiah celebrates this historic event, naming Cyrus as God's anointed (Isa 45:1). Yet the

Cyrus's Policy of Repatriation

Cyrus's decree is preserved in two locations in the Bible, in 2 Chr 36:21 and a longer version in Ezra 1:2-4:

Thus says King Cyrus of Persia: The LORD, the God of heaven, has given me all the kingdoms of the earth, and he has charged me to build him a house at Jerusalem in Judah. Any of those among you who are of his people— may their God be with them!—are now permitted to go up to Jerusalem in Judah, and rebuild the house of the LORD, the God of Israel—he is the God who is in Jerusalem; and let all survivors, in whatever place they reside, be assisted by the people of their place with silver and gold, with goods and with animals, besides freewill offerings for the house of God in Jerusalem.

For many Jews, the rebuilding of the temple was seen as a fulfillment of Jeremiah's prediction concerning the future of the temple, namely, that after its destruction, seventy years would pass before it would be rebuilt (Jer 29:10).

---

prophet's insistent encouragement of the exilic community to return to Judah shows its reluctance to do so. Many in the community have been in Babylon long enough to have heeded an earlier prophet's message. As Jeremiah states, "Build houses and live in them . . . seek the welfare of the city where I have sent you . . . for in its welfare you will find your welfare" (Jer 29:5-7). Daniel's brief reference to the time of Cyrus is given without any accolades, for life under Persian rule was still exile.

Although the specific political and cultural situations faced by the people under Babylonian, Persian, and Hellenistic governments were unique, life in all these environments was beset with similar problems. Jewish religion and culture was threatened by the whimsy or tyranny of foreign rule, by the attractions of the conquerors' wealth and power, and by internal disputes concerning the limits of accommodation. [Ezra–Nehemiah and Cyrus] The book of Daniel evidences the firm belief that the divine presence continues with God's people even when they are under foreign rule—whether in Yehud or in the Diaspora—and even when the place of God's dwelling lies in ruins or is compromised. The perspective shown in Daniel 1 is that individuals must be faithful and wise when threat-

Ezra–Nehemiah and Cyrus

The most important source for understanding Jewish concerns under Persian rule comes from the books of Ezra and Nehemiah. The book of Ezra credits God for prompting Cyrus's decree concerning Jewish return. In addition, Cyrus allows for the return of the holy items that Nebuchadnezzar had taken to the Babylonian temple. Even before the temple is rebuilt, the importance of sacrifices is seen by the returnees' immediate rebuilding of the altar, by the resumption of daily sacrifices, and by the institution of annual festivals. The rebuilding of the temple, however, was marked by strife. The Samarians, angered that their desire to participate was rebuffed, endangered the project by betraying returnees to the Persians, saying that illegal activities were occurring in the temple reconstruction, threatening Persian rule. These social problems were exacerbated by economic crises, onerous taxes, and high interest rates. In this difficult climate, religious leaders were appalled at the presence of numerous foreign marriages and lack of religious commitment. A concerted effort was made to rededicate the people to authentic religious practice, including Sabbath observance, obedience to agricultural laws, endogamy, and temple service. Ezra's prayer, describing life in the Persian satrapy of Judah, is poignant:

Here we are, slaves to this day—slaves in the land that you gave to our ancestors to enjoy its fruit and its good gifts. Its rich yield goes to the kings whom you have set over us because of our sins; they have power also over our bodies and over our livestock at their pleasure, and we are in great distress. (Neh 9:36-37)

ened. Sometimes, one could accommodate the whims of the dominant regime, as did Daniel when he studied Babylonian lessons. Nevertheless, at other times a stand must be taken, as when Daniel and his companions stood the test of the food laws. The courageous act of one youth resulted in supporting the faithfulness of three more. As we shall see in the examination of the visions, sometimes God delays in answering. As the final vision of the book of Daniel demonstrates, there is confidence that evil does not continue forever unabated; in the meantime, the victories have an eternal significance.

CONNECTIONS

One of the most memorable narratives from the Bible that critiques Babylonian mores is the story of the Tower of Babel (Gen 11:1-9). This account shows that when the human community gathers its technological resources, the result might not necessarily be for the good. [The Tower of Babel in Rabbinic Sources] The people use their unified strength and common language to separate themselves from a God they do not trust and to value success and security over compassion for one's fellow human being. The story's author shows that Babylon, which provided the literary setting of this story, embodies these values of success at any cost. Perhaps this story of the Tower of Babel mocks the impressive ziggurats, the pyramids that honored the Babylonian gods and functioned as a gateway to heaven. The awesome nature of these structures symbolizes the seemingly unlimited power of the Babylonian conquerors, who advanced their empire through the conquest and exile of peoples as well as by the imposition of Babylonian will.

In contrast to such impressive displays of wealth and power, the book of Daniel testifies to the

The Tower of Babel in Rabbinic Sources

The rabbinic commentaries concerning the story of the Tower of Babel built in the land of Shinar (another name for Babylon) heighten the biblical mockery of Babylon. Louis Ginzberg's masterful *Legends of the Jews*, a comprehensive collection of ancient Jewish sources, provides an excellent synopsis of the rabbinic teachings concerning this narrative. The tower was built by a rebel mob, which consisted of three groups of people: those who wanted to ascend to heaven to war with God, those who wanted to set up idols in heaven, and those who wanted to mutilate the righteous in heaven. They were punished, respectively, by being scattered throughout the earth, by being transformed into apes and phantoms, and by dying in battle. Their unconscionable brutality was also evidenced by their treatment of their fellows when the tower was under construction. If a man fell from the tower, no concern was shown. At the same time, if a brick were to fall, lamentation was made because the height of the tower required up to a year's time to climb to replace the brick. If a woman went into labor while making bricks for the tower's construction, she could not cease her work, and was required to immediately strap her child to her body after the birth and continue with the brick making.

See Louis Ginzberg, *Legends of the Jews*, trans. Henrietta Szold, 7 vols. (Philadelphia: The Jewish Publication Society of America, 1968), 1:179–81; for the discussion of original sources, see 5:201–206.

acts of courage by four captured youths. At first reading, the unqualified success of the weak against the strong may sound too much like a fairy tale to the modern reader, who is often plagued by doubt and skepticism. This *ennui*, which often characterizes the late twentieth and early twenty-first century, is well described by the Nobel laureate, Isaac Bashevis Singer, who writes, "not only has our generation lost faith in Providence but also in man himself, in his institutions and often in those who are nearest to him." Singer continues that our age is marked by lack of faith in God and disbelief in any system of

The Tower of Babel

Brueghel, Pieter the Elder. c. 1525–1569. *The Tower of Babel.* 1563. Oil on oakwood, Kunsthistorisches Museum, Vienna, Austria. (Credit: Erich Lessing/Art Resource, NY)

Inspired by the Colosseum, which, for Christians in the Middle Ages, was a symbol of the arrogance of the ancient world, Brueghel (1564–1638) presents an interpretation of humanity's hubris with this painting of the construction of the Tower of Babel. The massive size of the tower contrasts with the miniscule people and houses in the foreground, and its integrity is undermined by the haphazard construction and design.

reward and punishment. Although modern life is replete with technological advancement, much of humanity has pervasive feelings of loneliness, inferiority, and fear. Yet this son of Holocaust survivors holds that the writer's quest is a redemptive one: "in his own fashion he tries to solve the riddle of time and change, to find an answer to suffering, to reveal love in the very abyss of cruelty and injustice."[14] Thus, in his many moving stories of life in Eastern European Jewish ghettos, Singer reflects the passions, love, and faithful confidence that he experienced in his own parents' home. The Jews of the ghetto, in spite of persecutions and impoverishment, could find "pious joy, lust for life, longing for the Messiah, patience, and deep appreciation of human individuality . . . [and] gratitude for every day of life, every crumb of success, each encounter of love." The lives and stories of this Yiddish-speaking community can speak to all nationalities and faiths because they create "the idiom of the frightened and hopeful humanity."[15]

Daniel and his friends, like many people today, were also both frightened and hopeful. It is the task of the person of faith to remain hopeful even while experiencing the worst of human brutality, the ravages of nature, the incapacitation of illness and pain,

Isaac Bashevis Singer

The Yiddish novelist Isaac Bashevis Singer (1904–1991) was born in Poland to an observant Jewish family and moved to America in 1935 to escape Hitler's rise to power. His prolific legacy captures the lost world of Eastern European Jewish life and the trials and triumphs of American Jewish immigrants. His work is permeated with reflections on God, mysticism, and the spiritual world. Reflecting on the power of biblical stories, Singer finds that their emphasis on what people do, rather than what they think or feel, has an important lesson for humankind when facing modern dilemmas. Singer reflects,

> You are what you act. . . . The Almighty does not require good intentions. Deeds are what counts . . . . If you are in despair, act as though you believed. Faith will come afterward. . . . Although I've read other books and admire them, too, the Bible, the Talmud, the Torah, I admire even more so. They not only tell me a story but really tell me how to live and how to behave.

Richard Higgins, "At 80, Isaac Bashevis Singer Still Entertains and Instructs," *Boston Globe*, 9 November 1984.

Isaac Bashevis Singer (Credit: Harry Ransom Center, University of Texas, Austin)

the disappointment of failure, or the grief and loneliness that come from isolation and death. The human spirit often may be encouraged by the many stories of success that abound in our communities, if we are open to believing that they indeed exist. The scale of such victories varies. They may be individual, community, national, or global successes. An individual may find the courage to leave an abusive relationship, a community may keep open the alternative school whose budget was slashed, an oppressive regime may fall, a species on the brink of extinction might make strides in growth.

The author shows that Daniel believed it was possible to stay true to God's commandments despite Babylon's tyranny. This gave him the courage to confront those in power. Nevertheless, the faith that led him to persevere in his commitment to his food traditions did not deny him flexibility in other aspects of his life. Daniel found a way to remain a man of faith while he adapted to the constraints of living under another's regime. He was willing to speak out for himself and his compatriots and confronted the palace master. There is wisdom in knowing when to challenge, when to adapt, and when to keep silent. Daniel and his friends studied the Babylonian curriculum and served in the Babylonian court. Yet Daniel did so while implicitly critiquing a culture that supported a government committed to conquest and colonization. The narratives of the book of Daniel show that Babylon not only conquered Judah, desecrated its temple, and took exiles, but that it was ruled by a king who would sentence his own bureaucrats to death because they could not accede to his outrageous demands (Dan 2) and would crush the defiance of his subjects by torture (Dan 3; see the discussions of these topics below, chs. 2 and 3). [Portrayal of Babylon] Sometimes his faith was quiet; sometimes confrontational. His wisdom lay in knowing which path to choose as the occasions arose.

So too for ourselves. Sometimes the victories people achieve come from working within the status quo; sometimes they require defiance. All demand that hope dominate over despair. One's faith community can be a great source of strength when one faces individual, local, or global challenges. One's faith can provide the resources of stories, traditions, and examples of how God has responded to those in need in the past and how God might be understood today. It gives a context to challenge the values of the broader society and provides a framework for believing that change is possible, or it may provide a way to see that life can be meaningful even when difficulties are impossible to change. Others may have despaired that they had no choice but to obey Nebuchadnezzar or die. The author presents Daniel as a youth captured from Jerusalem. Presumably, he had seen the burning of his

---

Portrayal of Babylon

The portrayal of an arrogant Babylon that, despite its powers and riches, represents evil is not unique to the book of Daniel. Besides the account of the Tower of Babel (Gen 11:1-9) that showcases the pride of the people from the land of Shinar (examined above), the account of the fall of Judah to Babylon emphasizes the cruelty of its captors (2 Kgs 25), and the prophets Isaiah and Jeremiah detail its fall from the heights of success and power because of God's judgment (Isa 13:19; 14:4, 22; 21:9; 39:7; Jer 50–51). The following example from Jeremiah is representative:

A sword against the Chaldeans, says the LORD, and against the inhabitants of Babylon, and against her officials and her sages! A sword against the diviners, so that they may become fools! A sword against her warriors, so that they may be destroyed! A sword against her horses and against her chariots, and against all the foreign troops in her midst, so that they may become women! A sword against all her treasures, that they may be plundered! A drought against her waters, that they may be

dried up! For it is a land of images, and they go mad over idols. (Jer 50:35-38)

Babylon became a powerful symbol of evil for later generations of Jews and Christians, often used as a cipher for the ruthlessness of Rome, as shown in the following examples from *2 Baruch* and Revelation:

But the king of Babylon will arise who has now destroyed Zion, And he will boast over the people, And he will speak great things in his heart in the presence of the Most High. But he also shall fall at last. These are the black waters. (*2 Bar.* 67:7-8)

As she [Babylon] glorified herself and lived luxuriously, so
     give her a like measure of torment and grief.
Since in her heart she says, "I rule as a queen;
I am no widow, and I will never see grief,"
therefore her plagues will come in a single day—
     pestilence and mourning and famine—
and she will be burned with fire;
     for mighty is the Lord God who judges her.
     (Rev 18:7-8)

The Babylonian Ziggurat
This model of the Babylonian
Sanctuary of Marduk shows the
construction of a ziggurat, where
sacrifices to the gods were offered.
Such structures, whose summits
reached toward heaven, may have
been the inspiration of the biblical
account of the Tower of Babel.

Model of the Marduk Sanctuary at Babylon
with the "Tower of Babel" at the time of
Nebuchadnezzar II. 604–562 BC (model after
reconstruction by W. Andrae and G. Martiny,
1931). (Credit: Bildarchiv Preussischer
Kulturbesitz/Art Resource, NY)

beloved temple and the deaths of his countless family, friends, and
compatriots; he was a now part of a captive and subject people. It
would have been understandable if his spirit were broken. Instead,
Daniel saw things differently through the eyes of faith.

Although it is true that Daniel's success is outstanding, this first
chapter truly sets the stage for a more nuanced view of suffering in
the book as a whole. As the story continues, we find that the
despotic challenges to Daniel and his friends continue. Although
they successfully avoid death, Daniel later pleads, "O Lord, hear; O
Lord, forgive; O Lord, listen and act and do not delay!" (9:19). The
challenges to the community and to faith continue. The answer
from God is not a simplistic one. There is an assurance that the suffering will end, but the means and the time are cryptic. Daniel 1
shows that the same God who allowed Jehoiakim of Judah to be
captured by Nebuchadnezzar is the same God who gave knowledge, wisdom, and success to Daniel. Not all questions of theodicy
are explained here, but the parameters are set. There is only one
God, the creator of Nebuchadnezzar's victory as well as Daniel's
triumph. Daniel and his friends may not understand God's ways,
given the victory of such a cruel regime, but they have not lost their
faith that God's justice will prevail over the evil of this king. They
stand as witness against the powerful of the world who say, "Come,
let us build ourselves a city, and a tower with its top in the heavens,
and let us make a name for ourselves" (Gen 11:4). These young
captives rest confident that God scatters the latest builders of the
next Tower of Babel "over the face of all the earth" (Gen 11:9).

NOTES

[1] The midrashim preserve a tradition that the giant Nimrod (Gen 10:10) ruled over Shinar, where he punished Abraham's faithfulness to the one God by commanding that the patriarch be thrust into a fiery furnace (*Gen. Rab.* 38:13).

[2] John Collins, *Daniel, 1–2 Maccabees*, Old Testament Message (Wilmington DE: Michael Glazier, 1981), 1.

[3] A. Kirk Grayson, "Mesopotamia, History of (Babylonia)," *ABD*, ed. David Noel Freedman, 6 vols. (New York: Doubleday & Co., 1992), 4:771–77.

[4] Cf., for example, W. Sibley Towner, *Daniel* (Interpretation, a Bible Commentary for Teaching and Preaching; Atlanta: John Knox, 1984), 25. See also the judicious treatment of this issue in John Collins, *Daniel: A Commentary on the Book of Daniel* (Hermeneia; Minneapolis: Fortress, 1993), 141–43.

[5] Tob 1:10-11; 1 Macc 1:62-63; 2 Macc 5:27.

[6] Peter Coxon, "Shadrach, Meshach, Abednego," *ABD*, ed. David Noel Freedman (New York: Doubleday & Co., 1992), 5:1150.

[7] Shemeryahu Talmon explains that this is another example of the 3 plus 1 ancient Near Eastern pattern wherein a unit of three similar persons or events is "topped by a fourth of special standing and importance." See Shemeryahu Talmon, "Daniel," in *The Literary Guide to the Bible*, ed. Robert Alter and Frank Kermode (Cambridge MA: The Belknap Press of Harvard University Press, 1987), 347.

[8] It is important to note that Daniel did not seek any governmental position. Cf. Dana Nolan Fewell, *Circle of Sovereignty: Plotting Politics in the Book of Daniel* (Nashville: Abingdon, 1991), 126.

[9] Exod 7:8-13, 20-24; 8:5-7 [1-3 MT], 18-19 [14-15 MT].

[10] See Gen 41:8, 24; Exod 7:11; 7:22; 9:11; Dan 2:2.

[11] John E. Goldingay, *Daniel* (Word Biblical Themes; Dallas: Word Books, 1989), 35.

[12] Grayson, "Mesopotamia," 774–75.

[13] For a discussion of the impact Cyrus had on Jewish life and thought, see Ralph W. Klein, *Israel in Exile* (Overtures to Biblical Theology; Philadelphia: Fortress, 1979), 105–24.

[14] "Text of the Nobel Lecture by Isaac Bashevis Singer," *New York Times*, 8 December 1978, 1–4, <http://www.nytimes.com/books/98/01/25/home/singer-lecture.html> (14 July 2005).

[15] Ibid.

THE STONE DEFEATS THE STATUE

Daniel 2:1-49

COMMENTARY

In Daniel 1, the author shows that despite the demands of their Babylonian overlords, Daniel and his companions successfully maneuver the challenges of eating the king's food and studying Babylonian curricula. In Daniel 2, an even greater threat is issued against Daniel and his friends. Nebuchadnezzar has a troubling dream of a great statue, whose significance is opaque to him. He demands that his magicians not only interpret the dream, but also tell him the content—under penalty of death. Enraged at the inabilities of his officials, Nebuchadnezzar places all the wise under the death decree, not only the Chaldeans with whom he conversed directly, but also Daniel and his companions. Nevertheless, terror again yields to a dramatic reversal. Because of his faith in the God of Israel, Daniel not only saves himself and his companions but also protects all the Babylonian spiritual advisers as well. Unlike the king's attendants, Daniel is able to describe the portentous dream of an extraordinary statue and to give its interpretation—one that will indict the very king whom Daniel serves. As the chapter moves from the hostile

---

Mesopotamian Deity

This imprint of a cylinder seal from Iraq shows a Mesopotamian god, as determined by his horned helmet, standing atop a bull. To his side is a worshiper, followed by a goddess. Deities are often depicted with animal horns in Mesopotamian plaques, cylinder seals, and statues.

Cylinder seal and imprint. Paleo-Babylonian period. Haematite, Louvre, Paris, France. (Credit: Erich Lessing/Art Resource, NY)

The Diaspora

The Diaspora (from the Greek word for "dispersion") refers to the lands outside of Israel where Jews live. The first Diaspora communities in antiquity were in Egypt and in the lands of the Babylonian Empire. These communities increased during the Hellenistic and Roman empires because of forced exile, political difficulties, economic opportunities abroad, and proselytizing. Jews were allowed varying degrees of legal and religious autonomy in these regimes that permitted them to continue as a people. Spiritual and literary activity flourished in Diaspora communities, with the Septuagint (the Greek translation of the Scriptures) completed in Egypt and the Talmud in Babylon. Today the term still refers to the Jewish communities throughout the world outside of the modern state of Israel, established in 1948. The messianic hope in Judaism looks forward to the day when all Jews will be reunited in Israel, all the commandments can be fulfilled, peace will reign, and God will no longer suffer with the people in exile.

From the time of the Babylonian Diaspora, Judaism can be seen as a "world religion," as it is practiced by Jews throughout the world, irrespective of place. Jacob Neusner explains,

> Judaism has not limited itself to a single ethnic group or geographical area, but has been and still is an international and multiracial religion. . . . Judaism flourishes wherever Jews are located, and it is at once international—utopian, located in no special place—and multicultural, but also ethnic and locative—focused on single group, in a single place.

Menahem Stern, "Diaspora," *EncJud*, ed. Cecil Roth and Geoffrey Wigoder, 16 vols. (New York: Macmillan, 1971–1972), 6:7-19.

Jacob Neusner, *A Short History of Judaism: Three Meals, Three Epochs* (Minneapolis: Fortress, 1992), 5.

decree of the king to his promotion of Daniel and Daniel's friends, and finally to his acknowledgment of Daniel's God, the narrative underscores an important religious truth. The God who not only controls the universe, but also cares enough about human beings to communicate with them, limits the power of tyrants. God alone is truly "LORD of kings" (v. 47).

In the previous narrative, Daniel served as a model of faithfulness and wisdom as he outwitted Babylonian bureaucrats and kings, while yet living according to God's commandments. In Daniel 2, the author continues to encourage his audience with a story of Daniel's endurance. Daniel and his companions not only survive the king's order of execution, but they also are promoted within the government. The author thus emphasizes that even when outrageous threats to the exiles mark life in the Diaspora, an active God is still present. [The Diaspora] Just as the story in Daniel 1 underscores the continuing relevance of the sanctification of one's diet and the primacy of Jewish wisdom, so too does Daniel 2 encourage other important truths: faith in the efficacy of prayer, the power of the righteous behavior of one individual, and belief in the ultimate triumph of good over evil.

As is known from Daniel 1, the hero is identified as one of the nobles of Judah. [The Tribe of Judah] Although his youth at the time of his capture allows the reader to assume that he has little or no experience in the practice of government or in a position of authority, he provides an excellent contrast to the lack of leadership that characterized the last kings of Judah under whom the nation fell. Daniel's life in the Diaspora continues to evidence faithfulness to religious law, courage in the face of foreign tyranny, and leadership for those who look to him for guidance. His tests of loyalty come under the most difficult of circumstances, as a servant to a mercurial king. Daniel, nevertheless, turns out to be the kind of leader Israel and Judah's prophets have hoped for—one who shows faithfulness to God and demonstrates paradigmatic leadership for others. [Outline of Daniel 2]

Nebuchadnezzar Discloses his Anxiety, 2:1-4a

Nebuchadnezzar was known as one of the most successful Babylonian emperors. He engineered a brilliant campaign against the former lands of the Assyrians, assuming hegemony over all their territory. His own capital of Babylon, with its massive temple and palace and impressive processional way, inspired fear among his captives and awe among his subjects. The author builds upon this reputation, using it to further the portrayal of a mighty sovereign who, despite his power, must turn to the captive Daniel in his time of need. From Daniel 1, the reader knows that he prompts terror in the heart of the palace master, Ashpenaz, who fears for his life if he does not follow Nebuchadnezzar's instructions to the letter. It is striking, therefore, that it is this king who is plagued by nightmares and their consequent anxieties, finding no relief from his own expert attendants.

The dream occurs in "the second year of Nebuchadnezzar's reign" (v. 1). Some commentators see this date as a mistake, because Daniel 1 shows that the hero and his friends have been enslaved for three years before they have encountered Nebuchadnezzar. Others argue that the author understood this

The Tribe of Judah

According to Genesis, Jacob had 12 sons, each of whom became an eponymous ancestor of the 12 tribes of Israel. Judah was the fourth son of Jacob and Leah who surpassed his older brothers and was blessed as their "ruler" by Jacob. After Jeroboam's secession from the united kingdom established by David and Solomon, Judah (along with Benjamin) became the major tribe that made up the southern kingdom, which was also called by that name. While under Persian rule (539–333 BC), Judah was known as the colony of Yehud, leading to the Greco-Roman term "Judea."

Outline of Daniel 2

Nebuchadnezzar Discloses his Anxiety, 2:1-4a
A Debate on the Limits of Babylonian Power, 2:4b-11
Nebuchadnezzar's Decree of Death and Daniel's Meeting, 2:12-16
Request, Answer, Blessing, 2:17-23
Daniel's Encounter with Arioch and Nebuchadnezzar, 2:24-26
"A God in Heaven who Reveals Mysteries," 2:27-30
Daniel's Description of the Awesome Dream, 2:31-35
Daniel's Interpretation of the Dream, 2:36-45
Nebuchadnezzar's Response: Worship and Promotion of Daniel, 2:46-49

Tablet fragment

Nebuchadnezzar ruled for an exceptionally long period (605–562 BC). This Aramaic inscription comes from the 34th year of his reign.

Fragmented tablet with Aramaic inscription from the 34th year of the reign of Nabuchodonosor II, 566 BC. Terracotta, Louvre, Paris, France. (Credit: Erich Lessing/Art Resource, NY)

The Death of Zedekiah

Zedekiah, born Mattaniah, was set up on the throne of Judah as a puppet king by Nebuchadnezzar, after King Jehoiachin, his nephew, was taken captive. Zedekiah rebelled against Nebuchadnezzar, prompting his invasion of Jerusalem and the burning of temple and the city. Zedekiah suffered a terrible fate after escaping the siege. After the Babylonians killed his sons before his eyes, he was blinded and taken captive to Babylon (2 Kgs 24:18–25:17).

"second year" to refer not to the second year of Nebuchadnezzar's kingship, but to his direct control over Judah. The author thus presented Daniel as having been enslaved during the first deportation in 597 BC, a campaign that brought Babylonian hegemony to Judah, but not large-scale invasion and exile. Nebuchadnezzar's complete rule over Judah without the presence of Judean puppet kings occurred after the key events of the second deportation, the burning of the temple, and the death of Zedekiah, all of which took place after 587 BC. [The Death of Zedekiah]

To underscore the debilitating effects of Nebuchadnezzar's night-mares, the author not only refers to "dreams" in the plural but also states that Nebuchadnezzar's "spirit was troubled," and that his "sleep left him," indicating that he was affected both morning and night (v. 1). The reference to a plurality of dreams both indicates the dreams' significance and also provides important links to other texts. First, it points to Nebuchadnezzar's dream concerning the great tree in Daniel 4, which similarly foretells his downfall. Secondly, it recalls Joseph's interpretation that Pharaoh's multiple dreams indicated their certainty of actually occurring; indeed, the verb "was troubled" (*titpā'em*) is also used to describe Pharaoh's dis-quietude (Gen 41:8). The agitation the king feels is a preview of the sobering interpretation Daniel gives him, just as Joseph inter-preted Pharaoh's dreams of the upcoming famine. Joseph's dream interpretation ultimately led to a plan that saved his own people as well as the Egyptians from famine. Daniel's interpretation reveals that not only will Nebuchadnezzar fall, but also his unjust succes-sors will come to an end, to be followed by an infinitely better world (the relevance of the Joseph story is further explored in "Connections" below).

When Nebuchadnezzar seeks to explore the dreams' significance, he turns to all the people in the Babylonian establishment who are known for their wisdom and powers of interpretation. The terms "magicians" and "enchanters" are used in Daniel 1; now the list is expanded to include "sorcerers" (*mĕkaššĕpîm*) and "Chaldeans" (*kaśdîm*). These additional words point to the misplaced values of the Babylonians who multiply these preposterous governmental positions. The preponderance of this technical vocabulary under-scores the futility of prognostication that is based upon Babylonian gods and mocks the Babylonian religious hierarchy. This is the only usage of "sorcerer" in Daniel; the word is normally used of foreigners in the Hebrew Scriptures, pointing to the superstitions or idolatrous practices of other nations. Sorcery is associated with the "abhorrent practices of the Canaanites" including child sacrifice, the casting of spells, and necromancy (Deut 18:9-12). Such actions exploited marginalized peoples; they were thus forbidden and punishable by death. [Deuteronomy's Critique of Magic] The term "Chaldeans" refers to a class of people with a particular expertise in religious interpretation or astrology, rather than to an ethnic group, even though originally the word "Chaldea" indicated a unique people.[1]

[The Use of "Chaldeans" in Antiquity] Although the practices of the Chaldeans were considered by many Jews to be spiritually dangerous, the author holds that these customs are bankrupt; hence here the spiritualists are mocked for their inabilities. A similar critique is found in Second Isaiah, where Chaldea's sorceries, characterized by worthless astrological observations, cannot prevent Babylon's eventual ruin.[2] Indeed, in mocking Babylon's arrogance, the prophet illustrates Israel's polemic against the manipulations of the transcendent that foreign cults pretend to offer: "You are wearied with your many consultations; let those who study the heavens stand up and save you, those who gaze at the stars and at each new moon predict what shall befall you" (Isa 47:13).

These depictions of the many officials who are brought

The Goddess Gula

The Babylonian goddess Gula, patron of healing, was symbolized by a dog. Nebuchadnezzar placed statues of dogs, fashioned from bronze, silver, and gold, in the gates of the Gula temple in Babylon. It is also believed that such statues were used as defensive images to protect against disease.

Terracotta figure of a dog. Neo-Babylonian dynasty. Mesopotamia. 700–500 BC. British Museum. London, Great Britain. (Credit: Erich Lessing/Art Resource, NY)

Deuteronomy's Critique of Magic (Deut 18:9-15)

The number of technical terms in Deuteronomy associated with magic is extensive. There are augurs, soothsayers, and diviners (those who act as interpreters of physical items, patterns in nature, or the organs of sacrificed animals to predict the future); sorcerers and those who cast spells (those who practice magic either for self-defense or for malicious purposes); and necromancers (those who believe the spirits of the dead have privileged information about the future and can be consulted to obtain such knowledge). These practices are forbidden, but God does not leave Israel without sources of knowledge and comfort in times of fear, suffering, war, or disaster. God communicates through his prophets, according to Deuteronomy. Prophets act as God's mouthpiece, functioning solely on God's power and directive. It is not the case that these practices of magicians are condemned because the people doubt their efficacy. Rather, they are assailed because they deny that God is the master of the universe; they are an affront to his sovereignty and his will. As Jeffrey Tigay states,

> Magic is frequently predicated on the belief that there are powers independent of the gods, and even superior to them, that may be employed without their consent or even against their will. Even where magic is assumed to rely on divine assistance, the spells uttered by pagan magicians leave room for the impression that it is their own power, not the gods', that is operating. . . . The "science" of deciphering [information that diviners uncover] requires such extensive learning as to give the impression that the prognostication owes more to the diviner's wisdom than to divine revelation.

Jeffrey Tigay, *Deuteronomy* (JPS Torah Commentary; Philadelphia: The Jewish Publication Society, 1996), 173–74.

The Use of "Chaldeans" in Antiquity

In its original usage, Chaldea referred to a region at the head of the Persian Gulf, south of Babylonia, whose people migrated north. Merodach-Baladan II (8th century BC), united the Chaldean tribes and rose to power over Babylon (721 BC) while it was still under Assyrian hegemony. He is known from the Bible as the king who visited Hezekiah, probably to organize a campaign against Assyria (2 Kgs 20:12-19). The Chaldeans rose to power over an independent Babylon with the rise of Nabopolassar, Nebuchadnezzar's father, who ousted the Assyrians in 605 BC. Although the biblical polemic derides their expertise, Babylonians held these "Chaldeans" in the highest esteem, and other foreigners respected them as well. Ancient Greek historians referred to the class of Babylonian priests and wise men as Chaldeans, thus the name later came to be associated with Babylonia (Chaldea) and its peoples, as seen in biblical usage. One ancient historian who speaks of these Chaldeans is Diodorus Siculus (Diodorus of Sicily). This 1st-century BC historian of the Near East, India, and the Mediterranean, whose writings contain a mixture of fact and legend, writes,

> Now the Chaldeans, belonging as they do to the most ancient inhabitants of Babylonia . . . for being assigned to the service of the gods they spend their entire life in study, their greatest renown being in the field of astrology. But they occupy themselves largely with soothsaying as well. . . . [T]hey attempt to effect the averting of evil things and the fulfillment of the good. They are also skilled in soothsaying by the flight of birds, and they give out interpretations of both dreams and portents. (Diodorus Siculus, *Bibliotheca historica* 2.28.29)

John Collins, *Daniel: A Commentary on the Book of Daniel* (Hermeneia; Minneapolis: Fortress, 1993), 138–39.

Amélie Kuhrt, "Ancient Mesopotamia in Classical Greek and Hellenistic Thought," in *Civilizations of the Ancient Near East*, ed. Jack Sasson, 4 vols. (New York: Scribner, 1995), 1:55–65.

---

before Nebuchadnezzar present a fascinating scene that ironically uncovers the helplessness of such a putatively powerful empire. Although Nebuchadnezzar orders the experts to appear, he is not able to project a commanding presence. By a description of Nebuchadnezzar's own actions and by using his direct speech, the author portrays how troubled he is. Indeed, when Nebuchadnezzar refuses to tell the content of his dream, despite his advisers' seemingly reasonable pleas, his orders degenerate to the most outrageous commands that climax with the proposed massacre of his own subjects. [Mesopotamian Divine Revelation]

As a final observation on this section, we note that the Aramaic of the book begins at 2:4b and continues through Daniel 7:28. Many modern scholars propose that the Aramaic narratives of 2:4b-6:27 (2:4b-6:28 MT) reflect the *lingua franca* of the Diaspora community of Babylon and Persia. Daniel 1:1-24a is a later Hebrew introduction to the narratives, perhaps added by an author who was already acquainted with the visions found in 7-12, all of which—with the exception of Daniel 7—are written in Hebrew and had been appended to the narratives. It is also possible that Daniel 1 was originally written in Aramaic and was translated into Hebrew to reflect the literary setting of Daniel's youthful capture, or because it reflects traditionalist ideology.[3] Daniel 7, the only vision written in Aramaic, was probably the first of the visions to have been added to the tales. Thus, the Aramaic tales in chapters

Mesopotamian Divine Revelation

Jack Lawson details the commonalities in the wisdom traditions of Mesopotamia and Israel, arguing that both believe the source of wisdom, secrets, and other information about human destiny to be divine and that the very human capacity to know and interpret comes from God or the gods. Thus, he understands that Nebuchadnezzar is able to accept that Daniel's God is indeed a "revealer of mysteries," because his own religious tradition contains similar teachings. Lawson sees parallels between Daniel and the Mesopotamian mantics, interpreters of divine signs and omens, underscoring that Israel's polemic was never that the mantic practices of other nations were vacuous, but rather dangerous, idolatrous, or forbidden. The specialized nature of Mesopotamian divination attests to the dominance of this theology. Divination, the procuring of omens and their interpretation, comes from operational and magical methods, or "provoked and unprovoked communication." Examples of provoked divination include casting of lots, lecanomancy (observing the patterns of oil on water), libanomancy (observing the patterns of smoke), questions to a priest that could be answered affirmatively or negatively, and necromancy (calling up dead spirits). Unprovoked divination, where the gods themselves initiate messages, was found in "changes in natural phenomena: migrations of birds, monstrous human and animal births, astronomical phenomena, dreams . . . , as well as myriad everyday occurrences in people's lives." The author of Daniel was certainly familiar with these practices, and the Babylonian people, like Jewish contemporaries, believed in the divine source of these phenomena. It is also important to remember that Jews, nonetheless, took issue with some of the conclusions of their Mesopotamian counterparts, as is shown by the author of Daniel's portrayal of the ludicrous numbers of types of mantics who are incapable of responding to their king's request, and by the presentation of Nebuchadnezzar who cannot apparently distinguish between the interpreter Daniel and the God who directs his abilities.

Jack Lawson, "'The God Who Reveals Secrets,'" JSOT 74 (1997): 61–76.

2–6 and the first vision in Daniel 7 reflect their origins in the Diaspora communities of either Babylon or Persia, whereas chapters 8–12 probably reflect the continued use of the Hebrew language in Ptolemaic Palestine. Questions remain, but, to be sure, the final editor of Daniel 1–12 was comfortable with both languages. [The Use of Aramaic and Hebrew according to Traditional Sources]

A Debate on the Limits of Babylonian Power, 2:4b-11

The Chaldeans enter a debate with the tormented king. Their dialogue and actions reveal the author's concerns about the idolatry of the Babylonian religious leaders, the possible threat toward Daniel and other Jews prompted by their envy, and the capricious and tremendous political power of the king. The author explores the impact of Babylonian idolatry on the larger society, including the way in which those in power see the exiles. The author shows not only that Nebuchadnezzar himself has the necessary power to intimidate and massacre those who do not follow his every whim, but also that his own officials may turn on these captives when they feel threatened by their king as well.

At first, the king simply tells the Chaldeans that he is troubled by his dream (Dan 2:3). It is understandable that they ask him to tell

The Use of Aramaic and Hebrew according to Traditional Sources

In Judaism, Hebrew is considered "the holy tongue," a sacred language that God used to reveal the Torah. The Talmud relates that Aramaic was used for holy writing as well; Ezra translated the Torah into Aramaic, the Aramaic Targums were revealed by God, and a number of Aramaic words are used in the Torah, Prophets, and Writings. Hersh Goldwurm understands that Aramaic is used in Daniel not only because it was the language of the Jews in exile, but also because of the specific content of chapters 2–7. The majority of these chapters relates direct dialogue between Daniel and others or relates Daniel's spoken word about the content of his vision. For Goldwurm, the language reflects the authenticity of the events, yet remains appropriate for Scripture because of the accepted interpretation that it, too, is a holy language.

Hersh Goldwurm, *Daniel: A New Translation with a Commentary Anthologized from Talmudic, Midrashic and Rabbinic Sources*, The ArtScroll Tanach Series (New York: Mesorah Publications, 1979), 78–9.

them the nature of the dream, and then, presumably, they would interpret it. The king demands, however, that they first tell him what the dream itself is about. This request reveals the lack of trust that the king has for his own advisers. It also highlights the impossible nature of his demands, for even the master interpreter of dreams, Joseph, was first told the contents of Pharaoh's dreams (Gen 41:17-24). At the same time, because Daniel himself will ask for help from God when faced with the same conundrum, the author emphasizes the court officials' lack of faith in their gods as well as their gods' inherent weakness. When the Chaldeans insist on knowing the content of the dream, the king responds with an unconscionable pronouncement: his advisers must describe and interpret the dream or they will suffer a horrible death. On the one hand, Nebuchadnezzar's decree that they would be torn "limb from limb" heightens the drama of the account and makes Nebuchadnezzar appear as a murderous caricature.[4] On the other hand, if the Chaldeans are successful, they will be rewarded lavishly, although the degree of specificity of the reward pales in comparison with the details of the

Babylonian Governor in Prayer

This bas-relief from the palace of Nebuchadnezzar in Babylon (605–562 BC) shows the governor Shamash-ush-usar in prayer before the storm god, Adad, and the goddess of love and war, Ishtar. The exilic communities under Babylonian, Persian, and Greek rule were familiar with the extensive pantheons of their sovereigns. The author of Daniel portrays the sages of Babylon doubting that their gods will provide a revelation of the content of the king's dream (v. 11).

Shamash-ush-usur, governor of Suhi and Mari, praying to the gods Adad and Ishtar. 605–562 BC. Bas-relief from the palace of Nebuchadnezzar II. Babylon, Mesopotamia. Museum of Oriental Antiquities, Istanbul, Turkey. (Credit: Erich Lessing/Art Resource, NY)

punishment, which includes the destruction of their homes and the death of their families.

Nebuchadnezzar's statement that "this is a public decree" (v. 5) also underscores the fearsome nature of his demands. Once it is public, implementing the policy becomes a matter of pride for Nebuchadnezzar, who has every means of the state at his disposal to carry out his wishes. This phrase is reminiscent of the laws of the Medes and Persians, "which cannot be revoked," referred to in the book of Esther (Esth 1:19; 3:12-14; 8:8-14) and in the account of Daniel in the den of lions (Dan 6:8). With this reference, the author calls particular attention to the menacing nature of a state that would never retract the most outrageous decrees, even when they might undermine the very self-interest of the monarch. Presumably, if Nebuchadnezzar kills all the people who could interpret his dream, there will be no hope for him of ever having an answer.

The lack of judgment that characterizes this scene is also present in the response that the Chaldeans give the king. They believe they can reason with the unreasonable! They repeat their request to hear the content of the dream, but this time, the king's response omits any possibility of reward even if they in fact reveal the dream as well as the interpretation. Nebuchadnezzar displays his lack of trust of his advisers, saying that they are only trying to "gain time" (v. 8). The Chaldeans continue in their fruitless attempts at reasonable argumentation by adding a theological argument, yet their futile request actually underscores the author's denigration of their beliefs. The Chaldeans contend that their gods are so distant that even though they might know the content of people's dreams, they would never reveal it (v. 11). These exchanges between the Chaldeans and Nebuchadnezzar show that the gods revered by the most powerful emperor of the world are worthless when

Babylonian Protectors
This 9th century BC stone tablet from Sippar, Iraq, contains thirteen divine symbols intended to safeguard a royal land deed. The Babylonians believed that the actions of the monarch and the deities were inextricably linked.

Stone tablet of Nabu-apla-iddina. From Sippar, southern Iraq. Babylonian. c. 870 BC. British Museum, London, Great Britain. (Credit: Erich Lessing/Art Resource, NY)

called upon to assist human beings, even in the direst of circumstances. The author's portrayal of the impotence of the Babylonian gods is particularly ironic given that they are the protectors of an empire famous for its soothsayers.

Nebuchadnezzar's Decree of Death and Daniel's Meeting, 2:12-16

At this point, Nebuchadnezzar no longer waits to see whether the Chaldeans can respond to his demands. In ordering their execution, he now includes "all the wise of Babylon" (v. 12, A.T.; NRSV, "wise men"). The reference to "the wise" has not been used previously; rather, the deprecating terms "the magicians, the enchanters, the sorcerers, and the Chaldeans" have been employed (v. 2). Now, however, because Daniel may be implicitly included in this group of professional bureaucrats and religious experts, the more respectful term is appropriate. The king's decree is to be fulfilled imminently, and Daniel's life and the lives of his compatriots are potentially on the line. Nebuchadnezzar's order, nonetheless, remains ambiguous because whether it refers to all the indigenous wise ones of Babylon or to Babylon's conquered peoples as well is never specified. Because the text allows both possibilities by stating, "they looked for Daniel and his companions, to execute them" (v. 13), the subject as well as the motivation remains uncertain. Are those who are in charge of the execution acting on Nebuchadnezzar's orders, or are the native wise ones forcing Daniel to be included, revealing their animosity and jealousy concerning foreigners at the court? [Jews in Foreign Courts] The drama quickly escalates as the author introduces the possibility that the massacre has already begun. The present active of the verb *mitqaṭṭĕlîn* may actually be understood in two ways. The text in Daniel 2:13 may be translated either "the wise were about to be killed" or "as the wise were being killed." The seriousness of the first translation and the horror of the second add to the urgency of the need for a rescue.

The description of Daniel's encounter with the executioner, although reported laconically,

---

Jews in Foreign Courts

Joel Weinberg shows that the inclusion of foreigners within the Persian elite could elicit the latter's suspicion, envy, and retaliation, as is emphasized in the tales of Dan 1–6 and the book of Esther. These works share in common that the heroes, Daniel and Esther, consciously identify themselves as Jews, come to their positions without design, further the lot of their own people while at the same time helping the foreign monarch, and are judged positively because of their identification with their people. Weinberg concludes,

> This tension [of being a stranger among the international elite] was further aggravated by the atmosphere of suspicion and envy, rivalry and enmity that surrounded not only the fictitious heroes, the Jew at the court of a foreign king, but evidently was encountered also by the real, non-Persian members of the Persian political elite.

Although the literary setting of Dan 1–6 is Babylonian, the tales were probably first compiled during the Persian period and reflect the difficulties that Jews could face at any resurgence of fear and suspicion from the ruler, the elite, or even from the population at large.

Joel Weinberg, "The International Elite of the Achaemenid Empire: Reality and Fiction," *ZAW* 111 (1999): 608.

allows for intense, if brief suspense. Arioch's very name and title make him appear ominous. He is not only the "chief executioner," but also his name means "lion." Daniel's action recalls his unconventional approach to the palace guard (Dan 1), which ultimately resulted in his avoiding the king's selected food. Will he again be successful? In this instance, Daniel and his companions are already being sought out for execution. Others may already have been killed; thus, the reader can anticipate the fearsome results. Is Daniel's wisdom, described as "prudence and discretion" (v. 14), enough to protect him from the immediate actualization

of the death sentence? These virtues, indicative of Daniel's true wisdom, form a contrast with the empty preoccupations of the Chaldeans. Arioch, in fact, appears passive and does not fit the expectation of his ghastly profession. Neither arresting nor imprisoning nor killing Daniel, he appears to listen more to Daniel than to his own king. [Arioch in Jewish Sources]

Instead of taking action against Daniel, Arioch tells him what has happened. Underscoring Daniel's courage, the author immediately shows that Daniel proceeds to the king on his own. Surprisingly, the response of the king is unhurried. Neither executioner nor king kills Daniel; both are willing to wait before initiating the sentence. Daniel asks Nebuchadnezzar for time, confident that he will be able to reveal the dream and give its interpretation (v. 16). Although Nebuchadnezzar has earlier accused his own advisers of stalling, the author records no objection, suggesting not only Nebuchadnezzar's unpredictable nature, but also his possible agreement with Daniel. Before the reader knows the outcome of the king's allowance of time, the movement of the narrative slows in order to emphasize Daniel's request, God's answer, and Daniel's blessing.

Request, Answer, Blessing, 2:17-23

In between the impressive reversal that contrasts the beginning and end of this chapter, the author places a reference to the first of Daniel's visions (vv. 19-23). Although the vision itself is not described, it is clear that its occurrence allows Daniel to know and understand the specifics of Nebuchadnezzar's dream. Before this vision occurs, however, Daniel initiates prayer, requesting that God

God as the Revealer of Knowledge in the Hebrew Bible

Rāz, the Aramaic word for "mystery," is related to the concept of God's knowledge or providence that can be revealed to humanity. This knowledge of God, either concealed or not clearly understood, may be shown to certain individuals directly (Gen 17:1), by "the Spirit of the LORD" (2 Sam 23:2), through an angel (Gen 22:11; Num 22:23), through dreams (Gen 20:3), and through prophecy as shown in the following example:

> Surely the LORD God does nothing,
>   without revealing his secret
>   to his servants the prophets.
> (Amos 3:7; see also Isa 48:3; Jonah 1:1; Ezek 1:1; 2:2)

Sometimes mysteries relate a particular content regarding the end of the age that will be revealed at a later time, as is the case with the visions of the book of Daniel. They attest to the justice of God who is sure to reward the righteous, punish the wicked, and manifest the perfection of creation. H. M. Teeple explains,

> The Israelites believed that divine knowledge was needed to solve human problems; it provided laws for relations with God and among humans, rules for priestly ritual, and explanations of sin, injustice, and foreign domination. . . . In the eschatology (beliefs about the end of this age) in Daniel and later books, the secret, divine plan is that a new age will come, at which time the wicked will be punished, righteous Jews rewarded, and God will rule permanently over a perfect earth. . . . Even misfortunes fit God's purposes, for they purify the sufferers and ensure their inclusion among the happy righteous.

H. M. Teeple, "Mystery," in *Harper's Bible Dictionary*, ed. Paul Achtemeier (San Francisco: Harper & Row, 1985), 673.

---

reveal "the mystery" (*rāzā'*), and solicits his companions to join him (vv. 17-18). [God as the Revealer of Knowledge in the Hebrew Bible] The term "mystery" (*rāz*) appears to be used here in a technical sense, referring to crucially important information concerning God's plan for human history or for the end of days, determined from the foundations of creation and given by God (often by means of an angel) to an elected individual. All natural phenomena and historical events are part of the divine wisdom. This Persian loan-word is not found outside the book of Daniel in the Hebrew Bible, but is often found in the Dead Sea Scrolls to refer to cosmological, eschatological, or prophetic mysteries.[5] These texts indicate that the righteous will be vindicated at the end of days and that there are signs for these favored ones that justice is assured. Still, the righteous are warned that those without true wisdom will futilely attempt to provide an interpretation of signs they can never understand. Mysteries are comprehended only with God's help because God is the ultimate source of wisdom; they are meant to be understood only under the specific circumstances that God allows, and may be limited to a particular group of people. Although they often contain unsettling information about the suffering to come at the end of days, they also point to the ultimate righteousness of God, who determines that good supersedes evil, a design determined from God's plan of long ago.[6] [Examples from the Dead Sea Scrolls]

In this case, God gives the interpretation of the mystery only to an insider—Daniel. No Babylonian official is privy to the meaning

Examples from the Dead Sea Scrolls

The Qumran community, a sectarian group of Jews who took refuge in the Judean desert near the shore of the Dead Sea from approximately 130 BC to AD 70, believed it was imperative to live in strict holiness, separated from the larger community. Their copies of biblical and non-biblical texts, as well as their own writings, are important witnesses to the development of Jewish thought and to the context of nascent Christianity at the turn of the eras. The community members looked to their revered leader, "The Teacher of Righteousness," for instruction on how to understand the mysteries—God's predetermined plan for all nations, individuals, and creation itself, which was linked to the divine judgment at the end of days. Proper interpretation of events both past and present could yield discernment regarding what was truly important in life, helping the community stay on the path of truth despite their sufferings. The source of this understanding was understood to be God, as the Teacher of Righteousness himself states, "For you have uncovered my ear to wonderful mysteries" (1QH 1:22). Similarly, the *Pesher* to Habakkuk speaks of the Teacher of Righteousness as one "whom God caused to know all the mysteries of the words of His servants the prophets" (1QpHab 7:4-5). Both these texts indicate the Teacher's authority to instruct the group on the true meaning of God's plan for them, determined from the beginning of time. The following text shows how the individual can benefit from studying the mysteries:

> . . . and then thou shalt know truth and iniquity, wisdom [and foolish]ness thou shalt [recognize], every ac[t] in all their ways, together with their punishment(s) in all ages everlasting, and the punishment of eternity. (4Q417 [*Instruction*] 1 i, 6-8 [as cited in Collins])

Other examples attest to the belief that God determines all events—in both the physical and spiritual worlds—from the time of creation itself. See the following: Eph 1:9; 3:4; Col 4:3; *1 En.* 40–45; *2 En.* 22–29; *Jub.* 4:21; *T. Mos.* 3:13; 1QH 1:11-15, 21; 1QpHab 7:4-5; 1 QM 14:14; 1QS 3–4.

John Collins, "Sapiential Perspectives: Wisdom Literature in Light of the Dead Sea Scrolls," Sixth Orion International Symposium, 20–22 May 2001, Mt. Scopus Campus, Hebrew University of Jerusalem, <http://orion.mscc.huji.ac.il/symposiums/6th/collinsFullPaper.html> (11 February 2008).

See further, Bilhah Nitzan, "Education and Wisdom in the Dead Sea Scrolls in Light of their Background in Antiquity," Tenth Annual International Orion Symposium: New Perspectives on Old Texts, 9–11 January 2005, <http://orion.mscc.huji.ac.il/symposiums/10th/papers/nitzan.htm> (11 February 2008).

of the dream. Indeed, only after Nebuchadnezzar hears the content and interpretation of the dream does he also correctly call it a mystery (v. 47). This is not unexpected, because the Babylonian advisers do not believe it is possible for anyone ever to know the content of Nebuchadnezzar's dream. Nebuchadnezzar, on the other hand, does believe it is theoretically possible to understand the dream, but he taints his willingness to believe with his outrageous despotism. In this context, Daniel turns to God for help, while still remembering his companions. The manner of the revelation is mysterious—it occurred as "a vision of the night"—but no additional details are forthcoming (v. 19). God's providence and concern for Daniel, nonetheless, are indicated by its very disclosure.

Remaining in solidarity with his compatriots, Daniel immediately elicits their assistance. He instructs them to beseech God for mercy and for an explanation of the mystery (v. 18). The word sequence of the sentence underscores the urgency of the plea, as the word *raḥămîn* ("mercy") is placed first in the sentence, emphasizing the importance of God's role (v. 18). The specifics of their request

Alshich's Interpretation of Daniel's Concerns for His Companions

The 16th-century Torah scholar, Rabbi Moshe Alshich, emphasized the concern Daniel had for his companions as an example of his humility. He writes that Daniel reasoned as follows:

. . . that the dream was revealed to me—does not pertain to me alone, as we all joined together *to beg for mercy . . . that Daniel and his companions would not be put to death* (verse 18). It was not my righteousness, nor the merit of my forefathers which granted me this revelation. The merit of the four of us combined so that God saw our affliction and saved us from our enemy's sword. . . . Although I alone had the dream made known to me in a prophetic vision, this does not exalt me over my colleagues. It was only in my ancestors' merit that I was given the necessary preparedness for prophecy. But that merit is shared equally by my colleagues and myself.

R. Alshich lived what he saw in Daniel's constant inclusion of his colleagues. When his own community in Safed (Israel) was beset with disease and famine, he tirelessly traveled abroad to raise money for their survival.

Moshe Alshich, *The Book of Daniel: Shield of the Spirit: The Commentaries of Rashi and Rabbi Moshe Alshich on Sefer Daniel*, trans. Ravi Shahar (Alshich Tanach Series; Jerusalem: Feldheim, 1994), 80.

to God are not given; rather, the immediacy of God's response is indicated by the rapid movement in the narrative. By showing that Daniel includes his companions while praying, the author shows that effective leadership while under foreign rule requires the inclusion of one's colleagues in common pursuits for justice. [Alshich's Interpretation of Daniel's Concerns for his Companions] This presentation of Daniel and his companions shows that life under the regimes of tyrants should be characterized by concern for individuals in the community, faithful waiting in the context of prayer, and occasional acts of exceptional courage in the face of an unpredictable government. This close companionship between Daniel and his friends also provides a link to Daniel 3, where the three friends will assume the primary role of those whose faith is tested. It is also important to note who is *not* consulted at this point. Although all the Babylonian wise are included in the extermination decree, Daniel asks neither for their advice nor for their prayers. As a wise man himself, Daniel and the "Chaldeans" may be political bedfellows as far as the king is concerned, but the author portrays Daniel as one who knows that only the God of Israel can reveal the dream.

The author highlights the prayer itself by placing it as the poetic focal point in this prose chapter. G. T. M. Prinsloo argues that it serves four functions. First, it has the function of "foregrounding," which signals to the reader that something special occurs; secondly, it increases the tension in the account, because although the reader is told that Daniel has received the revelation of the dream, the reader must wait to hear about its content; thirdly, it delays the narrative; and fourthly, it gives the most important theological statement about God's wisdom and power precisely where the narrative is paused.[7] As an exile, Daniel is not able to offer a sacrifice in the temple, as it is now a distant memory, but he is able to approach God with words. Unlike Daniel's Babylonian counterparts who attempt to manipulate their gods, the author highlights this exile's response to God with blessing and prayer. [Blessings] Daniel's act of prayer, which is efficacious even without the act of an offering, becomes a model of hope, serving as a paradigm for the community whenever and wherever they may be under foreign rule and without their temple. By this depiction, the author recalls the hope expressed by the Deuteronomistic historian (the editor of the theology of history presented in the books of Joshua, Judges, Samuel, and Kings), who presents King Solomon's temple speech concerning prayer as follows:

> If they [the people] sin against you . . . and you are angry with them and give them to an enemy . . . yet if they . . . plead with you in the land of their captors . . . and pray to you toward their land . . . then hear in heaven your dwelling place their prayer and their plea. . . . Let your eyes be open to the plea of your servant, and to the plea of your people Israel, listening to them whenever they call to you. (1 Kgs 8:46-52)

This theology underscores that prayer can be efficacious anywhere, not only in the designated shrine of God. God's dwelling place is not only the temple; rather, it is heaven and earth.

Although the idea of the universal accessibility of God is common in the world's major religions today, it was not always the

---

Blessings

Blessings (*bĕrākôt*) are fixed formulae for prayers, usually found in the phrase, "Blessed are you O LORD . . . ." They indicate that God is the one to whom blessing is due and form the introduction to praise, thanksgiving, and petition. They are found in prayers that recognize God as the creator of the universe and of individual human beings, as the redeemer of Israel, the giver of Torah, the comforter of the bereaved, the healer of the sick, and the author of beauty and holiness. The blessing formula shows great consciousness of God's presence in all aspects of creation and human life, where all actions, when done according to God's will, are capable of bringing holiness into the world and meaningfulness in the life of the individual.

Baruch Levine, *Leviticus* (JPS Torah Commentary; Philadelphia: The Jewish Publication Society, 1989), 230–31.

The Importance of the Temple

The idea that God could be addressed in prayer beyond the physical space of the temple became increasingly important after the exile. Although the temple was destroyed and they were far from Jerusalem, Daniel and his companions are shown "seek[ing] mercy from the God of heaven," and offering praise to the God who revealed the mystery of Nebuchadnezzar's dream (2:17-23). This photograph shows a remnant of the wall, built by Herod the Great (37 BC–AD 4), that surrounded the second temple, destroyed by the Romans in AD 70. Known as the *Kotel* (Western Wall or Wailing Wall), today it is the holiest site in Judaism, inspiring prayer and pilgrimage.

Man and sons praying at western wall. (Credit: Todd Bolen/BiblePlaces.com)

case in antiquity. It is true that the Hebrew Scriptures have many examples of prayers and requests of God uttered by people throughout their territory, but the detail of the sacrificial system and the frequent insistence of its importance in Jerusalem highlight the essential place the temple had in Israel. The preponderance of shrines and temples in the ancient Near East similarly attests to the importance of holy physical space. Yet as Judaism developed in the Diaspora, the importance of prayer apart from the temple grew and was crucial after the destruction of the first and second temples. By underscoring the importance of Daniel's prayer in saving his life and the lives of his companions, the author confirms the possibility of the community's connection with God even when temple service is impossible. Daniel's prayer also shows that his people may continue to be linked with their ancestors even though they are distant from their land and its holiness. The prayer both refers to Israel's ancestors directly and employs the formal characteristics of a hymn of praise, a type of psalm well known to the audience from its long association with temple usage. Such prayers or hymns exalt the God who gives life, who redeems Israel, who protects and defends the sufferer and the innocent, and who ensures justice.

The prayer refers to the particular problem that Daniel and his community face from its ruler, to the way in which God responds to it through revelation, and explains why it is appropriate to offer gratitude and praise with confidence. Beginning with a call to offer praise to God—with the formula "blessed be the name of God"—it suggests a community setting, perhaps a liturgical context (see Pss 146–150). Throughout the Hebrew Scriptures, blessing may refer to the bequest of material prosperity, the passing on of a spiritual legacy, the gift of having descendants, and other proclamations of thanksgiving. In this present context of his difficulties, Daniel is portrayed as appreciating life itself as a gift from God, acknowledging God as its source. The expression "the name of God" (v. 20) is interesting here; it is most likely a circumlocution for God's personal name, which ceased to be pronounced sometime after the beginning of the exile, perhaps reflecting the community's belief in its profound holiness. [The Tetragrammaton] Daniel's reference to this blessing as being appropriate "from age to age" is an expression of the eternal nature of God, and it introduces the theme of God's sovereignty over time itself as well as

The Tetragrammaton

AΩ God's personal name is revealed to Moses at the burning bush as "YHWH," meaning "I am" (Exod 3:14). Because Hebrew is a consonantal language, the vocalization of this name is uncertain, although most philologists suggest it is "Y-a-h-w-e-h." The four consonants are known as the Tetragrammaton. Sometime after the exilic period, Jews ceased pronouncing the name; "the God of Heaven," or "Heaven" were common substitutes. In the New Revised Standard Version (and most others), Lord is used to indicate that the Tetragrammaton is in the Hebrew text. In Jewish practice today, the Tetragrammaton is never pronounced. In prayer, "Adonai" (Lord) is used.

God's complete transcendence.[8] The phrase, "He changes times and seasons" (v. 21), an expression found in parallel with "[he] deposes kings and sets up kings," indicates that earthly history is ultimately in God's control. As with other psalms of praise, the intent is not to petition God and then give thanks, but is to extol God's very nature as the one who determines history, provides revelation, and is the source of all wisdom and earthly power. The prayer indicates that God is a God of "wisdom and power" (v. 20), terms that point to the ultimate triumph of good over evil, as God's wisdom is linked with justice and following the commandments. In effect, these aspects of God not only provide deliverance in Daniel's particular situation before the irascible king Nebuchadnezzar, but also link the God of Daniel's present with the God of the ancestors (v. 23) and with the readers of the post-exilic community. The God who offered a covenant with Israel is the same one who determines history, even when a defeated and exiled Israel might have reason to believe otherwise. [*ḥokmĕtā'* and *gĕbûrĕtā'*]

ḥokmĕtā' and *gĕbûrĕtā'*

AΩ *ḥokmĕtā'* ([Hebrew, *ḥokmâ*] "wisdom") may refer to practical knowledge about the physical world, the skill of builders and artisans, judiciousness in government, proper ethical and virtuous conduct, reverence of God, following the Torah, or to the Torah itself. Its very source is God and is connected with God from creation. As the prayer in Jeremiah states, "It is he who made the earth by his power, who established the world by his wisdom, and by his understanding stretched out the heavens" (Jer 51:15). The book of Daniel also gives evidence of Israel's understanding of mantic wisdom, which attempts to predict and influence the future. On the one hand, the wisdom of Daniel allows him to understand and reveal the significance of dreams and mysterious writings on Belshazzar's wall. On the other hand, the mantic practices of the Babylonian magicians are mocked as being based upon their foolish trust in incompetent idols.

gĕbûrĕtā' ([Hebrew, *gĕbûrâ*] "power") refers to strength and authority. It may refer to physical, military, ethical, or spiritual strength. When used of God, it is associated with God's greatness and power in creation and redemption and is understood as the source of righteousness and justice.

H.-P. Müller, "*chākham*," *TDOT*, ed. G. Johannes Botterweck and Helmer Ringgren, trans. David Green (Grand Rapids MI: Eerdmans, 1980), 4:364–85.

H. Kosmala, "*gābhar*," *TDOT*, ed. G. Johannes Botterweck and Helmer Ringgren, trans. John T. Willis (Grand Rapids MI: Eerdmans, 1977), 2 (rev. ed.): 367–82.

The prayer continues with the acknowledgment that wisdom and knowledge are ultimately derived from God. Thus, it would be impossible, for example, for Daniel to have the arrogance of Nebuchadnezzar, even if the tables were reversed and Daniel were emperor. The ideal expressed here is similar to the one found throughout the Hebrew Scriptures: one builds a community of law, not monarchical fiat, because only God is the true king of Israel. Human action on earth must mirror the ways of a just God. Similarly, when the prayer acknowledges that God reveals "deep and hidden things," the text recalls the theology of Job:

He uncovers the deeps out of darkness,
and brings deep darkness to light.
He makes nations great, then destroys them;
he enlarges nations, then leads them away.
He strips understanding from the leaders of the earth,
and makes them wander in a pathless waste. (Job 12:22-24)

Job responds to the taunts of his friend who has earlier mocked him for questioning God's purpose for his suffering. Zophar has countered that the "deep things" of God can never be known (Job 11:7), yet Job holds fast to the knowledge that God's revelation of the unknown mysteries of the world is not only possible but is an essential part of justice itself. Job affirms that all earthly power remains under the watchful eye of God whose sovereignty supersedes earthly rulers. Placed within the context of the broader narrative of Daniel 2, this hymn shows that one specific event, the revelation to Daniel that spares his life and offers judgment to Nebuchadnezzar, has profound significance for the entire community. It asserts that God judges not only this one king, but *all* kings (v. 21). In addition, God "gives wisdom" not to Daniel alone, but to "the wise" (v. 21). This prayer reminds readers that there is a profound gulf between the Babylonian magicians and those who receive wisdom from the God of Israel. In the biblical tradition, references to wisdom are often linked with following the torah, that is, obeying God's instruction for living a life in accordance with God's will (Pss 1; 19; 119). Thus, the hymn may provide a model of opposition for an exilic community in which one must deal cautiously when making difficult choices or when forced to compromise. On the one hand, some might proceed like Daniel, standing up to the king. Others may act like Hananiah, Mishael, and Azariah, praying with quiet confidence. In a time when Israel could cry out "How long?" (12:6), this prayer of praise asserts, through the eyes of faith, that there is meaning in life, even when that meaning seems impossible to fathom.[9]

The particular wisdom Daniel receives during this crisis, namely the content of Nebuchadnezzar's dream, ultimately reflects this theology. The omniscient God knows the content and meaning of Nebuchadnezzar's dream, having both ordained its contents as well as the reality of history to which it points. Being the recipient of God's revelation, Daniel will now make known to Nebuchadnezzar that his kingdom is destined to end. God has other plans for the universe that go beyond Nebuchadnezzar's designs.

Daniel's Encounter with Arioch and Nebuchadnezzar, 2:24-26

Now that Daniel understands the dream, he approaches Arioch a second time. Some commentators argue that these verses seem to come from a distinct source because they present an alternative introduction of Arioch and Nebuchadnezzar. Instead of showing Daniel approaching the king on his own (vv. 14-16), the text refers to Arioch bringing Daniel to the king, with no reference to any earlier meeting.[10] Whether this scene reflects an independent source, it nevertheless is presented here sequentially and functions to provide a comparison of the two encounters. The differences between them add a new dimension to the portrait of these men. Now the king appears more disturbed, and Arioch acts more solicitously (v. 25). The author suggests that Nebuchadnezzar is unable to remember his previous meeting with Daniel, as he needs to be reintroduced to Daniel's origins and abilities. This time, Arioch himself escorts Daniel to Nebuchadnezzar with urgency, searching for an excuse not to carry out the order of execution. Nebuchadnezzar's inability to remember is reminiscent of the actions of King Ahasuerus who forgets that Mordecai saved his life (Esth 2:21-23; 6:1-3) and serves as a preview for the portrayal of Nebuchadnezzar in Daniel 4, where his memory appears quite fragmented. [Mordecai's Saving of Ahasuerus's Life] In both cases, the forgetfulness of the monarch ultimately contributes to the oppressors' inability to wipe out the Jewish people. In the case of Ahasuerus, his delay in responding to Mordecai's gracious act ultimately leads to Mordecai's promotion at a propitious time. Here, too, the apparent forgetfulness of Nebuchadnezzar allows him to consider Daniel at this crucially important time when life and death hang in the balance.

> **Mordecai's Saving of Ahasuerus's Life**
>
> In the book of Esther, the monarch Ahasuerus is portrayed as frequently neglecting, misunderstanding, or ignoring his subjects in a hapless fashion. When Mordecai saves his life by uncovering an assassination plot, the king is specifically told what Mordecai has done for him, and the event is recorded. Although Mordecai is ignored and not given the proper reward, it is all for the good. When Ahasuerus later reads about Mordecai's act and appropriately rewards him, the stage is set for the downfall of the book's villain, Haman, who plots the genocide of the Jews. Like Daniel, Mordecai becomes an official at the king's court; like Daniel, he, too, witnesses the whimsical nature of his people's rulers (Esth 2:19-23; 6:1-13).

When Arioch speaks to the king concerning Daniel's abilities, he makes a crucial omission, adding to the suspense of the scene. He tells Nebuchadnezzar that he has found an exile who can tell him the interpretation; he does not specify that he knows the content of his dream (v. 25). The reader must consider how the volatile Nebuchadnezzar will respond. Will the king listen to Daniel, or will he order an immediate execution to be implemented? Only after the author reminds the reader that Daniel is also called Belteshazzar—the Babylonian name that honors Marduk, given by the king himself—does Nebuchadnezzar begin to speak to him (v. 26). This name accentuates Daniel's subservient status, yet it is this same exile who will soon undermine Babylonian pretensions by announcing God's judgment against the kingdom. The honor that Nebuchadnezzar gives to his own god by the renaming of Daniel to Belteshazzar is undercut by the credit that Daniel gives to "the God in heaven who reveals mysteries" (v. 28).

"A God in Heaven who Reveals Mysteries," 2:27-30

Unlike the Babylonian sages, who argue that the gods dwell far from humans, the author shows that Daniel believes in a God who is intimately connected with the human community. This God reveals wisdom and mysteries whose very function is to serve the divine plan. The distance that separates Daniel from the other Babylonian sages is emphasized here by Daniel's distinctive demeanor before the king. He uses the term "mystery" twice (vv. 27-28) in his preliminary remarks to Nebuchadnezzar, stressing the special character of the king's dream and emphasizing that only God can reveal its meaning. Daniel carefully avoids crediting himself as being the source of the information, standing in the tradition of the righteous and successful dream-interpreter Joseph, who rose to prominence under similarly dire circumstances. Both Joseph and Daniel, one a prisoner in a foreign land and the other an exile, help their people within the confines of foreign control, far removed from their own traditions.

Marduk

A priest in prayer before the symbols for Marduk, chief god of Babylon, and Nabu, god of wisdom and writing. 7th–6th C. BC. Neo-Babylonian. Round seal, blue clay, Louvre, Paris, France. (Credit: Erich Lessing/Art Resource, NY)

By using self-effacing language so that the king will not see him as a threat, Daniel displays his skill in mollifying the king and preparing him to accept the interpretation (v. 30). When Nebuchadnezzar asks Daniel whether he can describe the dream and give the interpretation, Daniel never really answers the question. By using all four titles of the Babylonian spiritual advisers, Daniel highlights their ineffectiveness and redundancy, stating that no one can do what the king asks (v. 27). At first glance, Daniel sounds like the Babylonian diviners who precede him. Daniel, however, continues by emphasizing that only God can reveal mysteries and that God has particularly chosen Nebuchadnezzar as the recipient of this important dream (v. 30). Although the reader knows by Daniel's actions and character that he is in fact wiser than any of the advisers of Babylon, Daniel explains to Nebuchadnezzar that the revelation is given to him alone so that Nebuchadnezzar may understand God's plan, just as God designed. The narrative proceeds at a rapid pace, allowing for no interruptions on Nebuchadnezzar's part. In contrast to the first scenes of this chapter, wherein Nebuchadnezzar's conversation with the Chaldeans quickly degenerated into death threats, Daniel remains in control. The captured noble of Judah now becomes the quintessential wise one who leaves Nebuchadnezzar speechless before him.

Before Daniel details the import of the dream, he provides an overall focus; it is for "the end of days" (v. 28). The Hebrew equivalent of this phrase is also found in Daniel 10:14 to indicate the great struggle between Persia and Greece, and is used throughout the Hebrew Scriptures to refer to dramatic changes in world history and human experience; scholars disagree whether or not it is equivalent to the phrase, "the end times"—the belief that holds that God has designed distinct ages for humanity and that the present age is coming to a close.[11] Daniel's own age is characterized by the rule of kings who inflict great sufferings on his people, yet Daniel's reference to the successive kingdoms evidences a hope for a new age of peace and justice to come—one that is brought about when the despotic kingdoms of the earth confront God's reign. It cannot be determined to what degree the original author of Daniel 2 believed the reference was to a new world of supernatural and spiritual dimensions.

Daniel's Description of the Awesome Dream, 2:31-35

Daniel begins to describe the dream with formulaic language. The word "behold" (*ălû*) brings particular attention to what is described next and functions as a dramatic pause. Daniel reveals that the king's dream is about an awesome statue made of four metals and clay, twice described as "great" and "huge" (v. 31). Additional phrases indicate excess; "its brilliance [was] extraordinary . . . and its appearance was frightening" (v. 31). Various generations of readers in antiquity would have been familiar with the magnificent statues of their Assyrian, Babylonian, Persian, and Greek conquerors as attested in both artifact and written account. The Babylonians so revered their statues of gods that when threatened by the Persians, Nabonidus (555–539 BC), the last king of Babylon, protected them by forbidding their customary New Year procession. [The Roots of Nebuchadnezzar's Dream] Many statues were amalgamations of various animals of enormous proportions, constructed to inspire awe or terror. In the writings of the Greek historian Herodotus, for example, we find a description of a solid gold statue over twenty cubits in height.[12] [Herodotus on Babylonian Statues]

Although the specific use of four metals in a statue representing four kingdoms is not found outside Daniel in the Hebrew Bible, a similar image of four conquerors is found in Zechariah 1:18-21 [2:1-4 MT]. The text refers to four horns that "have scattered Judah, Israel, and Jerusalem" and that will be destroyed by four

The Roots of Nebuchadnezzar's Dream

Ida Fröhlich traces two possible Mesopotamian roots for the portrayal of Nebuchadnezzar's dream of the statue. One is the recognition, as reflected in early biblical texts, of the impotence of the gods who were supposed to provide protection against Assyrian attack on the northern kingdom of Israel. Such representations of impotent idols became more persuasive during the Babylonian exile and subsequent Persian rule (Isa 44:9-20; 46:5-9; Hos 8:5-6; Hab 2:18-20; The Prayer of Nabonidus [4QPrNab ar]; the book of Daniel itself; and Bel and the Dragon).

The second possibility, Fröhlich suggests, is the experience of the exilic community who witnessed the Persian invasion of Babylonian lands. Originally, argues Fröhlich, the statue was a symbol of four Babylonian kings, as opposed to successive kingdoms. The last king would have been Nabonidus, and the stone would represent the victory of the Persian Cyrus, echoing the themes of Second Isaiah. As Fröhlich points out, as the

Persian army advanced, Nabonidus directed that statues of Babylonian gods were to be transported to Babylon from other parts of the empire for safekeeping. When Jews saw his frenetic action, which was proven ineffective by the successful Persian invasion of Babylonia, they had more ammunition to verify the meaninglessness of idolatry; in essence they had "unequivocal proof of the impotence of the gods protecting the Babylonian state" (27). The annihilation of the statue in Nebuchadnezzar's dream, therefore, represented the fall of the Babylonian Empire and its gods.

Ida Fröhlich, *"Time and Times and Half a Time": Historical Consciousness in the Jewish Literature of the Persian and Hellenistic Eras* (JSPSup 19; Sheffield: Sheffield Academic Press, 1996), 26–27.

Ida Fröhlich, "Pesher, Apocalyptical Literature and Qumran," vol. 1 of *The Madrid Qumran Congress: Proceedings of the International Congress on the Dead Sea Scrolls, Madrid, 18–21 March, 1991*, ed. Julio Trebolle Barrera and Luis Vegas Montaner (STDJ 12; Leiden/New York: Brill; Madrid: Editorial Complutense, 1992), 295–305.

blacksmiths (instruments of God's destruction) in order that Jerusalem and the cities of Judah may be restored. Detailing the human skills of carpentry and smithery that had to be employed to construct a statue, the author expresses incomprehension that any artisan could then worship the work of his or her own hand.[13] Although direct and conscious borrowing cannot be proven, it is clear that the author of the dream employs the cultural paradigms of the time to color this narrative. John Collins shows that contemporary Persian literature includes the image of a four-branched tree made of the same four metals found in Daniel; perhaps, he suggests, the imagery comes from a common source.[14] [The *Bahman Yasht*] Also, the ancient historian Hesiod (eighth century BC) represents successive stages of history with four metals of

Herodotus on Babylonian Statues

The Babylonians had a reputation for representing their gods with great statues. The Greek historian Herodotus (484–425 BC) provides this report:

In the Babylonian temple there is another shrine below, where there is a great golden image of Zeus, sitting at a great golden table, and the footstool and the chair are also gold; the gold of the whole was said by the Chaldeans to be eight hundred talents' weight. Outside the temple is a golden altar. There is also another great altar, on which are sacrificed the full-grown of the flocks; only nurslings may be sacrificed on the golden altar, but on the greater altar the Chaldeans even offer a thousand talents' weight of frankincense yearly, when they keep the festival of this god; and in the days of Cyrus there was still in this sacred enclosure a statue of solid gold twenty feet high. I myself have not seen it, but I relate what is told by the Chaldeans. Darius son of Hystaspes proposed to take this statue but dared not; Xerxes his son took it, and killed the priest who warned him not to move the statue. Such is the furniture of this temple, and there are many private offerings besides. (*Histories* 1.183)

This excerpt shows how the Babylonians believed their king to rule by the permission of their god Marduk (here called by the name of the head of the Greek pantheon, Zeus) and how their Persian successors confirmed their conquest of Babylon by removing the statue that represented him.

declining worth, including gold, silver, bronze, and iron.[15]

The description of the statue takes the reader from its head to its foot, describing each part's composition. The descending order of the value of the metals is significant, for the image quickly changes from being awesome to being weak, because its feet—its foundations—are a mixture of iron and clay. The awesome quality of the dream increases with the presentation of the next stage: the weapon that destroys it is simple, yet has profound significance—a stone (*'eben*). In the Hebrew Scriptures, besides its various physical meanings, as natural stone, ore, precious stone, weapon, or weight, *'eben* is used symbolically as well to refer either to idols, who may be made of stone, or to the very God of Israel. Because this stone of Nebuchadnezzar's dream is "cut not from human hands" (v. 34), it has a supernatural sig-

> **The *Bahman Yasht***
>
> This Persian apocalyptic work, also called the *Zand-i Vohuman Yasn*, portrays the deity Ahura Mazda giving a symbolic dream to the seer Zoroaster. The vision includes the following description: "the root of a tree, on which were four branches, one golden, one of silver, one of steel, and one was mixed up with iron." Each branch represents a kingdom; the final kingdom is probably Greece, which will be destroyed. At the end of the millennium spoken of in this text, James VanderKam explains, "there will be a purification of creatures, resurrection, and the final material existence." This text dates from late antiquity (3rd–6th centuries AD), although its traditions may stretch back to c. 600 BC.
>
> James VanderKam, "Prophecy and Apocalyptics in the Ancient Near East" in *Civilizations of the Ancient Near East*, ed. Jack Sasson, 4 vols. (Peabody MA: Hendrickson, 2000), 3:2088.
>
> See further, Kenton Sparks, *Ancient Texts for the Study of the Hebrew Bible: A Guide to the Background Literature* (Peabody MA: Hendrickson, 2005), 247–48.

nificance. The reader can imagine that for Nebuchadnezzar the stone might be associated with his own gods, as they are for his successor, Belshazzar (Dan 5:4, 23). Jeremiah derides the idolaters among his own people "who say to a tree, 'You are my father,' and to a stone, 'You gave me birth'" (Jer 2:27), showing that Judeans, too, are lured by the gods represented by wood and stone idols. Yet, a stone could also refer to the "Rock of Israel" (Gen 49:24), on whom Jacob depends, and the "stone one strikes against; . . . a rock one stumbles over" (Isa 8:14), the God who comes in judgment. This stone defeats the great statue; indeed, it annihilates it. It is best, therefore, to understand it as symbolizing God's power, forming a dynamic contrast to the pretension of empires, symbolized by the statue. Yet, because its identification remains unspoken, the reader may surmise that Nebuchadnezzar is free to accept or reject its significance. Indeed, as will soon be made clear, Nebuchadnezzar remains completely unaware of the true meaning of Daniel's words.

The stone strikes the awesome statue at its most vulnerable part, that is, upon the feet. When the statue falls, its dissolution is total; even its strongest and most precious metals are totally obliterated. The stone that struck it is not only invincible, but it also increases to the point of becoming "a great mountain and filled the whole earth" (v. 35). This language is reminiscent of the words of this oracle, found in the books of the prophets Isaiah and Micah:

Map of the World, probably from Sippar, southern Iraq.
Babylonian. c. 700–500 BC. British Museum, London, Great
Britain. (Credit: © British Museum/Art Resource, NY)

In days to come
the mountain of the LORD's house
shall be established as the highest of the mountains,
and shall be raised above the hills;
all the nations shall stream to it.
Many peoples shall come and say,
"Come, let us go up to the mountain of the LORD,
to the house of the God of Jacob;
that he may teach us his ways
and that we may walk in his paths."
For out of Zion shall go forth instruction,
and the word of the LORD from Jerusalem.
He shall judge between the nations,
and shall arbitrate for many peoples;
they shall beat their swords into plowshares,
and their spears into pruning hooks;
Nation shall not lift up sword against nation,
neither shall they learn war any more. (Isa 2:2-
4=Mic 4:1-3)

Here, the mountain from which God's
instruction goes forth is Mt. Zion, the location
of the temple in Jerusalem. The oracle speaks of
a day in the future when God will judge all
nations and where justice will triumph. A profound hope is
expressed wherein all people will love God, seek out the LORD's
teachings, and live in peace. It is this vision that underpins Daniel's
interpretation of the dream, for the stone that defeats the statue
and fills the earth as a mountain similarly represents God's crushing
of the oppressive kingdoms of the earth, of which Babylon is only
the first. By the end of Daniel's recounting of the dream, no rem-
nants of the statue remain. Using the agricultural image of threshed
grain, Daniel continues that the wind dissipated all traces of the
statue. [Wind] The stone and the wind together, representing God's
judgment, ensure that Babylon's tyranny will be defeated.

In the course of the description, although Nebuchadnezzar is
duly warned, he does nothing to avert God's punishment. His
intransigence underscores his lack of judgment and previews his
second dream, when even after a specific warning he does not
repent and must endure a terrible punishment (Dan 4). Both
dreams serve to underscore that God's decree concerning the
empires is final. The mighty kings are only pawns in God's scheme.

Wind

AΩ Jews were familiar with the symbol of the wind representing the activity of God. The Aramaic *rûaḥ* (and its Hebrew equivalent), meaning "wind" or "spirit," may refer to the wind of nature or to the spirit of God. In Genesis, the "spirit of God" hovers over the waters of creation; in Exodus, the Sea of Reeds is drawn back by a "strong east wind" (Exod 14:21); Elijah's experience of theophany is preceded by the wind (1 Kgs 19:11); and God's presence in the heavens is accompanied by wind (Ps 104:3-4). The spirit of God may inspire the prophets (Num 27:18) and may refer to the divine presence (Ps 139:7). Here in Dan 2:35, the image of the wind scattering the dust of the statue like grain is reminiscent of the activity of God's judgment against Babylon and the redemption of the exiles expressed in Deutero-Isaiah. As John Goldingay shows,

. . . the major theme [of Daniel 2] is the contrast between the helplessness of the Babylonians' spiritual resources and the power and wisdom of the God of Israel to effect and to interpret history, and this is also a major theme of Isa 40–48 . . . [where] silver and gold, bronze and iron, end up useless as clay (40:19; 45:2; 41:25), crushed and blown away like chaff.

The nations' powers are likened to the grass that withers upon feeling the LORD's breath (Isa 40:7); similarly, God "takes up the isles like fine dust . . . [making] the rulers of the earth as nothing" (Isa 40:15, 23). No sooner than nations are planted and take root, then God, as creator of the universe "blows upon" them (Isa 40:24), returning "power to the faint" (Isa 40:29) and thus reversing the course of the earth's evil, preparing it for God's redemption.

John Goldingay, *Daniel* (WBC 30; Dallas: Word Publishing, 1989), 37.

Daniel's Interpretation of the Dream, 2:36-45

The author portrays a confident Daniel who does not need to wait for the king's acceptance of the description of the dream. Rather, Daniel moves immediately to the interpretation, detailing a schema of world history wherein the successive victories of four powerful empires are finally defeated by a fifth kingdom set up by God—one that can never be destroyed (v. 44). He begins with the language of protocol, acknowledging Nebuchadnezzar's power and authority, using superlatives that not only flatter the king, but serve at the same time to undermine his pretensions, for Nebuchadnezzar's "kingdom," "power," "might," and "glory" (v. 37) are ultimately derived from God alone. [Daniel's Laudatory Language] These descriptions serve two functions. On the one hand, the flattery contributes to Nebuchadnezzar's continuing trust of Daniel. At the same time, because Daniel repeats that Nebuchadnezzar's sovereignty is bequeathed by God, the author suggests that Nebuchadnezzar is obsessed with his own pride. Daniel addresses Nebuchadnezzar as "the king of kings," echoing Ezekiel's description of the same king whom God uses as a tool to effect providence (Ezek 26:7). The reference to Nebuchadnezzar's sovereignty over animals (the beasts of the field and

Daniel's Laudatory Language

In the Hebrew Scriptures, references to power, strength, kingdom, and glory are used of the sovereignty of God and may be given to humans only according to the Divine will. The following verses are representative:

Yours, O LORD, are the greatness, the power, the glory, the victory, and the majesty; for all that is in the heavens and on the earth is yours; yours is the kingdom, O LORD, and you are exalted as head above all. Riches and honor come from you, and you rule over all. In your hand are power and might; and it is in your hand to make great and to give strength to all. (1 Chron 29:11-12)

Similarly, see 2 Sam 22:33; Psalms 21:13; 62:7; 63:2; 65:6; 145:11; Isa 40:29; Rev 5:12.

Beasts of the Field and Birds of the Air

The phrases "beasts of the earth" and "birds of the air" are used in Genesis to indicate that the totality of God's creation is under his watchful command (Gen 1:30). Those who have sovereignty over the beasts do so only as determined by God. Thus, in Jeremiah we read:

It is I who by my great power and my outstretched arm have made the earth, with the people and animals that are on the earth, and I give it to whomever I please. Now I have given all these lands into the hand of King Nebuchadnezzar of Babylon, my servant, and I have given him even the wild animals of the field to serve him. (Jer 27:5-6)

In the book of Judith, the heroine confronts Holofernes, the Assyrian general of Nebuchadnezzar, with these words, thus gaining his confidence before slaying him:

By the life of Nebuchadnezzar, king of the whole earth, and by the power of him who has sent you to direct every living being! Not only do human beings serve him because of you, but also the animals of the field and the cattle and the birds of the air will live, because of your power, under Nebuchadnezzar and all his house. (Jdt 11:7; see also Dan 4:19-26 [4:16-23 MT])

birds of the air, vv. 36-38) as well can only be given by the Creator of all. [Beasts of the Field and Birds of the Air] With this, the author mocks the Babylonians for their confusion of earthly power with the omnipotence of God, the Creator of the universe and the determiner of all political success.

Daniel moves quickly over the second and third kingdoms, concentrating on the fourth. The image of iron is aptly employed to underscore the destructive actions of the fourth kingdom, as iron was known for its use in making military implements. In the days of David, for example, Israel was at a military disadvantage because it had no iron weapons (1 Sam 13:19-21); similarly, when the judge Deborah routed Israel's enemy Sisera, she faced 900 chariots of iron (Judg 4:3). It is in keeping with Israel's experience, therefore, that the destructive powers of the fourth kingdom are represented by the excessive actions of iron implements (v. 40). Immediately following this image of power, however, the author boldly interjects a remarkable image of weakness: the feet are made of iron mixed with clay. The fourth kingdom's power will not abide, even though it will attempt to strengthen itself by marriage alliances, which are also ultimately doomed to fail.[16]

Although the actions of the fourth kingdom are described, Daniel never reveals the identification of the statue's constituent parts other than equating the head of gold with Nebuchadnezzar. The author may have assumed that their identity was commonly understood by the reader, and the absence of specificity may reflect the continuing blindness of the king. Scholars identify these kingdoms in three main ways. One interpretation of the metals is that they represent the last four Babylonian kings; a second possibility is that they represent the kings or kingdoms of Babylon, Persia (or Media/Persia), and Greece; and a third position is that they represent the kings or kingdoms of Babylon, Media, Persia, and Greece.

The first position is represented by John Goldingay, who writes, "The statue represents the empire led by Nebuchadnezzar, and is thus confined to Babylonian kings. It is a single statue, a single empire, passed on from one king to another."[17] The second position, which culminates in the identification of the fourth kingdom with Rome, is an ancient one, as seen in the writing of Josephus and in rabbinic texts. This interpretation reflects the first century BC Jewish community's experience of the fall of the Greek subdivisions of the empire, namely, the Seleucids and Ptolemies, and the rise of Rome. As Montgomery states, "with the putting off of the fulfillment of the apocalyptic expectation of the consummation of the Kingdom of God, the interpretation simply proceeded to keep the prophecy up to date."[18]

There are many reasons why most modern scholars understand that in its present context, the text shows Greece to be the final kingdom. Whatever the origins of the original composition of this narrative, it was included in its present position by a final editor who joined the narratives of Daniel 1–6 with the visions of 7–12. Because of the specific references to the kingdom being weakened by marriage (v. 43), the most likely identification should be with the Seleucid rulers, that is, the heirs to the Hellenistic (Greek) empire established by Alexander the Great, but broken into three segments upon his death. The Seleucids, who ruled the Syrian province in which Judah was located, were continually engaged with the Ptolemies, additional heirs to Alexander's kingdom, who ruled the Egyptian division of the kingdom. Their association ranged from diplomacy to marriage alliances, to subterfuge, and to armed conflict. Examined in the light of Daniel 7–12, one finds that the final kingdom is consistently identified as Greece. The most compelling example is found in Daniel 10:20, where the man clothed in linen (an angel) speaks to Daniel in a vision stating, "now I must return to fight against the prince of Persia, and when I am through with him, the prince of Greece will come." Collins refers to this prince of Greece as "the latest gentile sovereignty acknowledged anywhere in the book."[19] This same angel reveals that the kingdom of Greece will be followed by the bellicose rule of "the king of the north" and "the king of the south" (Dan 11) whose details illustrate the antipathy between the Ptolemies and Seleucids. Similarly, the last beast of the vision of Daniel 8 is specified as the king of Greece, and its successive horns would then refer to the divisions of the Greek Empire after Alexander's death.[20] In the broader context of the entirety of Daniel 7–12, the references to the desecration of the temple, the persecutions of Jews, and inter-Jewish political struggles correspond to the period of the most infamous Seleucid king, Antiochus IV Epiphanes (ruled 175–163 BC). [Ptolemaic and Seleucid Rule]

Ptolemaic and Seleucid Rule

After the Babylonian defeat of Judah, the country of the Jewish people was ruled by the successive conquering empires of Persia and Greece. The rule of Alexander the Great over Mediterranean lands and the territory of the defeated Persian Empire (that included the region of Judah) was cut short by his untimely death and was fragmented among the four generals who inherited his territories. Two of these generals, Ptolemy I Soter (ruled 323–282 BC) and Seleucus I Nicator (ruled 312–281 BC) governed Egypt and Asia Minor, respectively. They and their dynastic successors, known as the Ptolemies and Seleucids, contended for the land that they called Phoenicia and Coele-Syria (which included Judah) from approximately 301–200 BC. In the book of Daniel, these times are recounted as the struggles between "the king of the north" and the "king of the south" (Dan 11:5-19). The Polemaic Kingdom retained its contested rule over Palestine until 200 BC, when Ptolemy V Epiphanes was defeated by Antiochus III the Great. The latter's successors reigned over the former lands of Phoenicia and Coele-Syria, which were probably divided into four territories known as Coele-Syria, Samaria (which included Judah/Judea), Idumea, and Phoenicia. The Seleucids ruled until c. 152 BC, when they lost control of most of the territory of Samaria and Judea to the final stages of the Jewish independence movement known as the Maccabean revolt (see below, ch. 10).

Daniel's interpretation climaxes with the description of what the kingdom of the stone symbolizes, namely, the final kingdom, or kingdom of God. As is common with apocalyptic literature, Daniel does not specify the identity of the kingdom that would never be destroyed. In terms of the literary setting, it would be most provocative for Nebuchadnezzar to hear that his conquered subjects of Judah would arise to prominence. Nevertheless, the reference would be obvious for the final editor's audience. When this kingdom destroys the other nations, it will have a victory previously unknown by any earthly kingdom, for it will "stand forever" (v. 44). This reference resounds with the theme of God's establishment of justice throughout the earth.

This concept of God's sovereignty occurs elsewhere in the Hebrew Scriptures, even though the phrase "kingdom of God" is not used. For example, in Psalm 45:6-7 [45:7-8 MT] we read, "Your throne, O God, endures forever and ever. Your royal scepter is a scepter of equity; you love righteousness and hate wickedness." This provides a capsule statement of the belief that God's rule is equated with justice, the key component of the kingdom of God. Any earthly power is only derivative of God's moral authority; thus, it must be just and show compassionate concern for those who are powerless. Hence, we find that Isaiah's description of the future Davidic king, who will rule with righteousness, is ultimately derivative of God's kingship:

His authority shall grow continually, and there shall be endless peace for the throne of David and his kingdom. He will establish and uphold it with justice and with righteousness from this time onward and forevermore. The zeal of the LORD of hosts will do this. (Isa 9:7)

Here too, the divine dimension of this final kingdom is underscored. The wielder of authority is none but God, who chooses the Davidic representative of that government on earth. The prophets express the hope that the future day of the Lord will come when oppressive earthly kingdoms cease and as Israel truly becomes a light of God's presence to all other nations: "On that day living waters shall flow out from Jerusalem. . . . And the LORD will become king over all the earth; on that day the LORD will be one and his name one" (Zech 14:8-9).

In Daniel 2 (as in Dan 7), the author expresses the hope for a kingdom on earth in which the powers of evil are defeated and Israel is allowed to serve God. Yet the vision for this future is not limited to the mundane world alone. The eschatological implications are developed in Daniel 12, with references to resurrection, reward, and punishment. In both Judaism and Christianity, there are similarities in the understanding the kingdom of God as both a heavenly and an earthly reality. In Christianity, the kingdom of God (or kingdom of heaven) is inaugurated in the person of Jesus and will reach total fruition with his second coming.[21]

The History of Interpretation of Daniel 2

The image of the idealized kingdom has been particularly important in the history of interpretation of Daniel 2. Gerhard Pfandl details the interpretations of "the Kingdom of God" in the writings of ancient and modern commentators by examining the identification of the fourth kingdom, the stone cut out without hands, and the stone smiting the image.[22] The

Illustration of Nebuchadnezzar's Dream

Book of Daniel. The statue with feet of clay (part 2). Treasures in the Royal Library, Copenhagen. Das Alte Testament deudsch. Die Propheten alle Deutsch. Das Newe Testament deutsch. Wittenberg: Michel Lotther and Hans Lufft, 1526–1532.

This illustration of the statue in Nebuchadnezzar's dream is found in a book that belonged to King Frederik II of Denmark (1559–1588). It contains parts of Luther's translations of the Bible. Of Nebuchadnezzar's dream, Luther writes, "For Christ is, as Daniel says, 'a stone which fills the whole earth; those who oppose Him will be ground to powder'" (*Luther's Works* 12:36).

Jewish historian Josephus, apparently referring to the narrative of Nebuchadnezzar's dream, writes that Daniel spoke of a future time when Rome would conquer Judah, revealing the meaning of the fourth kingdom. Josephus withholds the information about the destruction of the fourth kingdom, however, to avoid offending his Roman patrons (*Ant.* 10.208-210). The pseudepigraphic work *4 Ezra* (late first century AD) most probably identifies the fourth kingdom as Rome when, in the seer's dream, he is told, "the eagle which you saw coming up from the sea is the fourth kingdom which appeared in a vision to your brother Daniel" (*4 Ezra* 12:11). The Talmud also identifies the fourth kingdom as Rome (*b. ʿAbod. Zar.* 2b, *b. Šebu.* 6b) (for further discussion, see below, chapter 7).[23]

Several Christian fathers, including Irenaeus, Hippolytus, Origen, Eusebius, and Aphraates, equate the four kingdoms with Babylon, Medo-Persia, Greece, and Rome. A minority opinion, found in Porphyry, Ephraem Syrus, and Polychronius, identifies the fourth kingdom as Greece. Pfandl argues that the minority opinions were not generally accepted, as Cyril of Jerusalem identifies the equation of the fourth kingdom with Rome to be "the tradition of the Church's interpreters," and Jerome writes that the fourth kingdom, "which clearly refers to the Romans, is the iron empire which breaks in pieces and overcomes all others."[24]

Many of the early Christian fathers hold that "the stone cut out without hands" symbolized Jesus' incarnation. Justin Martyr argues that both the vision of the One like a Son of Man, which attests that Jesus is "not of human seed," and the account of the stone can be likened to the actions of "the will of the Father and God of all things, who brought Him [Christ] forth." This view is echoed by Jerome who writes, "a rock (namely, the Lord and Savior) was cut off without hands, that is, without copulation of human seed and by birth from a virgin's womb" (similarly Theodoret).[25] The "stone smiting the image," however, is not necessarily interpreted in the same way as "the stone cut off without hands." The stone that smites the statue could refer either to the first or to the second coming of Christ. Those who believed it to indicate the second coming include Irenaeus, who, after identifying Christ as the stone, says that He will "destroy temporal kingdoms, and introduce an eternal one, which is the resurrection of the just" (similarly, Hippolytus, Aphraates, and Theodoret).[26] Other early Christians interpreted the stone that struck the statue as a reference to the church, which began with Christ's first coming. Cyprian believed the stone that became a mountain "is the Bridegroom, having the Church as His bride, from whom children should be spiritually born."[27] Augustine argued that the stone was Christ and that his kingdom, which would gradually prevail, "is the Church, with which He has filled the whole face of the earth."[28] This interpretation of the stone as representing the first coming of Christ continued in the writings of the Venerable Bede, Luther, and Calvin. From the time of the post-reformation until the advent of historical-critical interpretations of the Bible, Christian interpreters commonly held that the visions of Daniel also were to be fulfilled with either the first or second coming of Christ, including the

coming of the One like a Son of Man (Dan 7) and the seventy
years of desolation (Dan 9).

Nebuchadnezzar's Response: Worship and Promotion of Daniel, 2:46-49

During Daniel's lengthy description of the dream and its interpretation, Nebuchadnezzar neither interrupts nor challenges him,
allowing the reader to weigh whether he understands and accepts what Daniel says. Although
he praises God, even elevating the God of Israel
over the gods of Babylon (v. 47), his skewed
understanding is quite arresting as he immediately "fell on his face, worshiped Daniel, and
commanded that a grain offering and incense be
offered to him" (v. 46). [Sacrifices]
Nebuchadnezzar is shown to be so completely
unaware of what it means to acknowledge
Daniel's God as "Lord of kings" that he worships Daniel, the sage who has reiterated that he
accomplishes nothing except with God's directive. Nebuchadnezzar compounds this
outrageous activity by offering sacrifices that
were normally brought only to the temple of
Jerusalem. With the temple destroyed, the outrageousness of such an action is even more
apparent. The author thus presents
Nebuchadnezzar as acknowledging the sovereignty of God with words while remaining
obtuse to its implications.

This description of Nebuchadnezzar as a confused tyrant whom one must approach
cautiously is consistent with the author's portrayal of the king throughout Daniel 1–4.
Nebuchadnezzar acknowledges God with his
lips, but the community should not let down its
guard; indeed, his worship of Daniel evidences a
bizarre understanding of the God of Israel.
Daniel's apparent silence in face of
Nebuchadnezzar's worship of him is perplexing—perhaps the author shows Daniel
being reticent to respond to a man whose unpredictability is life-threatening. Nonetheless, some

Sacrifices

The "grain offering and incense" that Nebuchadnezzar brought to Daniel refers to the *minḥâ* and the *nîḥōḥîn*, respectively—sacrifices given by the people to God in the temple. The grain offering was a preparation of semolina, olive oil, and frankincense. Part of this dough was completely burnt on the altar and the rest was cooked or baked to be eaten by the priests. The incense offering, which consisted of fragrant resins and spices, was either burned in censers or on the altar of incense (Exod 30:34-38; 40:26-27; Lev 10:1; 16:12-13; Num 16:17-18).

Because the incense offering was likened to the rising of prayer to God (Ezra 6:10; Ps 141:2; Luke 1:10), the author implies that Nebuchadnezzar's actions are particularly inappropriate. It is also noteworthy that Nebuchadnezzar "falls on his face" before Daniel (v. 46), as this response can be associated with a most holy sacrificial act. According to Leviticus, in the days of the wilderness, the act of sacrifice brought the Israelites close to God's very presence:

And Moses said, "This is the thing that the LORD commanded you to do, so that the glory of the LORD may appear to you" … Aaron lifted his hands towards the people and blessed them; and he came down after sacrificing the sin-offering, the burnt-offering, and the offering of well-being. Moses and Aaron entered the tent of meeting, and then came out and blessed the people; and the glory of the LORD appeared to all the people. Fire came out from the LORD and consumed the burnt offering and the fat on the altar; and when all the people saw it, they shouted and fell on their faces. (Lev 9:6, 22-24)

Gary Anderson, "Sacrifice and Sacrificial Offerings (OT)," *ABD*, ed. David Noel Freedman (New York: Doubleday & Co., 1992), 5:870–86.

Nebuchadnezzar's Honoring of Daniel in Rabbinic Interpretation

Some Jewish interpreters hold that Nebuchadnezzar indeed deified Daniel. One explanation holds that God ensured that Daniel was not thrown into the fiery furnace, because, as was known from the words of Moses, in generations past the Israelites were commanded to burn all idols (Deut 7:25); thus, as one of Nebuchadnezzar's "gods," he would have been burned (*Num. Rab.* 13:4). The Talmud relates that Daniel fled Babylon to avoid God's punishment for not protesting Nebuchadnezzar's act of deification; thus, he was absent when the friends were cast into the fiery furnace (*b. Sanh.* 93a). R. Shmuel ben Nissim Masnuth (AD 1190–1240) argues that because Daniel did not protest Nebuchadnezzar's prostration, he was punished by being thrown into the lions' den.

In contrast, others were embarrassed by the implication of the biblical text and insisted that Daniel did not accept Nebuchadnezzar's offerings (*Gen. Rab.* 96:5).

Hersh Goldwurm, *Daniel: A New Translation with a Commentary Anthologized from Talmudic, Midrashic and Rabbinic Sources* (ArtScroll Tanach Series; New York: Mesorah Publications, 1979), 110.

classical Jewish interpreters see a problem with Daniel's silence and suggest that he was punished by his suffering in the lions' den. [Nebuchadnezzar's Honoring of Daniel in Rabbinic Interpretation]

Nebuchadnezzar's last act in this chapter is to promote and reward Daniel. In keeping with the characterization of Nebuchadnezzar as a man of excess, the author shows that his advancement of Daniel is lavish, appointing him in both the political and religious sphere (v. 48). It is important to remember that Daniel's office is never something he seeks and that he uses neither overt acts nor clever subterfuge to obtain it.[29] Any political advancement, moreover, is never seen as an alternative to trusting in God's power. Daniel's concern is more immediate—to reveal the mystery to Nebuchadnezzar. While it is true that he will save himself, his companions, and the other Babylonians from death, his focus is not on rescue, but on declaring the righteousness of God.

In responding to his advancement, Daniel's first thought is to continue to protect his companions; thus he requests that the king appoint them as overseers. While some might argue that this, too, is simply an example of the quest for political power and its consequent personal rewards, it should be seen instead as the means to protect the broader community. The companions will be in a position to act in the same manner as Daniel. To be sure, this will not be the last of their tests.

Although Nebuchadnezzar is a ruler of immense power, this narrative demonstrates that ultimately he remains without understanding. Despite recognizing the superiority of the God of Israel and the interpretive wisdom of Daniel, Nebuchadnezzar's value system remains essentially the same. The disparagement of Nebuchadnezzar continues in the next chapter when the emperor builds a statue, even though he has just seen one annihilated in his dream. It, too, will be a catalyst to show that the God of Israel responds to injustice.

As we come to the end of this chapter, we find that Daniel has successfully endured his second ordeal with Nebuchadnezzar. Pleasing the king seemed impossible—how could anyone know the content of his dream? Nevertheless, Daniel, with God's help, accomplishes what the king demanded. His dream interpretation displays God's sovereignty over all the earth. He saved his life and those of his compatriots; moreover, he averted a massacre of the king's own people. Nevertheless, the fact of the exile has not changed. Nebuchadnezzar is still in power. The idolatrous sorcerers of Babylon yet exist. It is precisely in this climate of unpredictable danger that Daniel becomes a model of behavior under foreign rule. As the interpretation of the dream shows, the powerful, yet obtuse Nebuchadnezzar is destined to fall; thus, the community can have hope.

An important focus of recent scholarly commentaries on Daniel is the identification of the community responsible for the book in its present form. We will never know all the reasons why the final redactor of Daniel found it appropriate to link the specific stories about the named Babylonian and Median kings of 1–6 with the visions of the anonymous beasts of 7–12. This particular chapter, nonetheless, provides an important clue. Living under Nebuchadnezzar's rule was paradigmatic for understanding continuing Jewish existence under different circumstances. Depending on the specific circumstances, the same king may order a massacre or grant a pardon. Any given tyrant who seems invincible may actually stand on feet of clay. The author's vision offers hope to a sometimes jaded humanity. It is a hope that in the end, justice and peace will prevail over evil. Sometimes the triumphs are spectacular and miraculous, as they are in Daniel 3 when the companions walk through fire unscathed. At other times, a stubborn act of courage by a single individual may thwart a murderous design. Daniel's behavior underscores that hope should not be obliterated in the hearts of the readers.

CONNECTIONS

Throughout post-exilic history, Babylon and Nebuchadnezzar loomed large in Israel's imagination. Although Israel was only under Babylon's control for two or three generations, its symbolic force persisted for centuries. Babylon not only represented a fearsome and triumphant empire, but it also encapsulated the very power that challenged God's attributes of justice and mercy. In this chapter, we see how Israel confronts questions of theodicy. [Theodicy] How does God allow the injustice of earthly empires to continue? How do people trust that the world is under God's control when idolatrous despots are in power? When will suffering end?

One way that the book of Daniel addresses such questions is by portraying Daniel as one of Israel's faithful dream interpreters. The account of Daniel—the sage who is entrusted by God to be an interpreter of crucial dreams—finds parallels with the story of

---

Theodicy

Theodicy refers to the justice of God, a question considered in many texts of the Hebrew Scriptures. On the one hand, the God of Israel appears as a just judge, rewarding the innocent and punishing the guilty (Deut 11:13-25). Yet other texts lament the reality of the innocents who suffer without cause. Abraham's question could be repeated in every generation: "Far be it from you to do such a thing, to slay the righteous with the wicked, so that the righteous fare as the wicked! Far be that from you! Shall not the Judge of all the earth do what is just?" (Gen 18:25).

Throughout the exile, such questions took on a particular urgency. Various answers are offered. The Deuteronomists (the editors of Joshua, Judges, Samuel, Kings, and sections of Jeremiah) asserted that the collectivity of Israel suffered for the sins of its ancestors (2 Kgs 22:15-17; 23:27; 24:3-4). The book of Job, however, recognizes that a multitude of examples from life experience pose a profound challenge, as the sufferer Job, who endures unspeakable losses of family, prosperity, and health, is tormented by God. Job knows nothing he has done could account for this anguish. He asks,

> Did I not weep for those whose day was hard?
> Was not my soul grieved for the poor?
> But when I looked for good, evil came;
> and when I waited for light, darkness came. (Job 30:24-26)

Job asserts that he did nothing to deserve this suffering; he lived a righteous life, caring for the needy and pursuing the good (Job 30:24-26). Demanding a response from God, Job finds that God indeed replies—yet it is only a partial answer:

> Where were you when I laid the foundation of the earth?
> Tell me, if you have understanding.
> Who determined its measurements—surely you know!
> Or who stretched the line upon it?
> On what were its bases sunk,
> or who laid its cornerstone
> when the morning stars sang together
> and all the heavenly beings shouted for joy? (Job 38:4-7)

Job learns that the ways of God can never fully be known to humanity. Mysteriously, human beings are called to live with the fact that there are no sufficient answers.

Another approach echoes Job's position about the plight of the innocent and God's injustice, but has a different view of God's silence, as shown in Habakkuk:

> Your eyes are too pure to behold evil,
> and you cannot look on wrongdoing;
> why do you look on the treacherous,
> and are silent when the wicked swallow
> those more righteous than they? (Hab 1:13)

With this recognition, the author nonetheless holds that although the reason for suffering cannot be seen, it can nevertheless be asserted through the eyes of faith:

> For there is still a vision for the appointed time;
> it speaks of the end, and does not lie.
> If it seems to tarry, wait for it;
> it will surely come, it will not delay. (Hab 2:3)

Similar to the perspective shown in Habakkuk, in this narrative of Nebuchadnezzar's statue, Daniel reveals that the successive kingdoms and even the suffering they perpetrate are part of God's plan. This response, however, remains mysterious. Knowing that suffering is part of providence does not explain why it *necessarily* is part of providence. God is ultimately inscrutable. The mystery of suffering is not solved, but the parameters are set—God is still integral and essential, participating in the lives of individuals and in the world—even in suffering. Later in the book of Daniel, a new solution is presented: God rewards the martyrs with resurrection and punishes the wicked with eternal shame (Dan 12:2).

For more on the various responses to exile see Shaye Cohen, *From the Maccabees to the Mishnah* (Library of Early Christianity 7; Philadelphia: Westminster, 1987), 87–92.

Suffering: After the Pogrom

The suffering of Jews in exile and under the persecutions of Antiochus IV was, tragically, repeated throughout the millennia. Maurycy Minkowski (1881–1930) poignantly captures the trauma and despair of persecuted Jews left homeless after the pogroms in Bialystok and Siedlce, Poland (1905). Note the absence of adult men and the presence of the nursing mother that underscore the helplessness of the victimized community.

Maurycy Minkowski. 1881–1930. *After the Pogrom.* c. 1910. Oil on canvas, Gift of Lester S. Klein. Jewish Museum, New York. (Credit: Art Resource, NY)

Joseph (Gen 37–50). Both heroes are distinguished members of their people—Joseph the beloved adolescent son of Jacob, and Daniel a young nobleman of Judah. Both are brought to foreign lands against their will (Dan 1:3; Gen 37:27-28). Despite their lowly status as servant and prisoner under the control of superiors, Daniel and Joseph are sought by the sovereigns of Babylon and Egypt, respectively, to provide key dream interpretation (or to interpret the writing on the wall, as Daniel does for Belshazzar [Dan 5:16]) that eludes the best of the native interpreters (Dan 2:26; 4:18 [4:15 MT]; 5:8; Gen 41:25-36). Similar to Daniel who can interpret Nebuchadnezzar's dreams even when all the Babylonian interpreters cannot, so too can Joseph tell Pharaoh about the alarming future symbolized by his dreams of the emaciated cows eating the healthy cows and the withered stalks of grain eating their robust counterparts (Gen 41:25-36). The heroes are praised by their kings, given similar gifts that mark their status, and rise to higher positions of authority (Dan 2:49; 5:29; Gen 41:41, 45). Just as Nebuchadnezzar advances Daniel in a position of governmental service, Pharaoh makes Joseph second in charge in all of Egypt. It is true that Joseph experiences a more benign ruler, as Pharaoh allows Joseph to prevent the deaths that surely would have followed the famine. But these two faithful men, both exiles from their homeland, see God working through them. Their ability to interpret dreams is ancillary to their true gift: the ability to look at terrible things that happen to them or to their people and still see that they are part of God's plan for good. [Joseph's Ordeal] Daniel and Joseph both interpret two dreams about the future of their rulers' kingdoms (Dan 2:31-45; 4:20-27 [4:17-24 MT]; Gen 41:29-31).

Joseph's Ordeal

Joseph endured horrific suffering. Betrayed by his own brothers, he was sold as a slave. Falsely accused of attempted rape, he was imprisoned. Displaying his extraordinary ability to interpret dreams while in prison, he was forgotten. Eventually reconciled with his brothers, who continued to be consumed with guilt and fear, he offered them an extraordinary interpretation of his ordeal:

Do not be afraid! Am I in the place of God? Even though you intended to do harm to me, God intended it for good, in order to preserve a numerous people, as he is doing today. So have no fear; I myself will provide for you and your little ones. (Gen 50:19-20)

Daniel's explanation is used to teach Nebuchadnezzar about God's judgment (Dan 2:44; Dan 4:32 [4:29 MT]) and that of Joseph is used to save both the Egyptians and his own people (41:36; 50:20). Daniel and Joseph also share a corresponding faith. They similarly declare that their wisdom comes from God and that they serve a divine purpose (Dan 2:28; 4:24 [4:21 MT]; Gen 41:25, 28, 32). As Daniel states, the dream is "certain, and its interpretation trustworthy" (2:45). As this narrative was originally composed in the post-exilic period, it served to underscore that the injustice of Nebuchadnezzar and his successors is destined to be redressed. When the story was heard by the Hellenistic audience, it reassured the people that the tyranny of Antiochus would end, just as did the suffering imposed by the Babylonians, Medes, and Persians. There would be, moreover, additional reason to hope. This time the tyranny would be replaced by the reign of God.[30]

The dream that God gives to Nebuchadnezzar is a window to understand God's justice. Although it is Nebuchadnezzar who receives the dream, its message is for the interpreter—Daniel—and his grief-stricken community. The dream tells the reader that the world follows God's plan, precisely at a time when people may have every reason to doubt that history has any meaning. Even the tyrants exist because they serve God's will, and Nebuchadnezzar only has power over a defeated people because God permits it. As Israel looked back on its history, it saw that its destiny was still part of God's purpose, even when one empire and one trial followed another. The account of Nebuchadnezzar's dream and the revelation of its meaning to Daniel show that God's plan is available and evident to all who are willing to receive it. The message of the narrative to readers then and now is not only that justice is ensured in a world to come (Dan 12), but also that even here, in this physical, material world, God's plan is for good. For Daniel's readers today, the ability of the hero and his friends to endure by courage, wisdom, solidarity, prayer, and faithfulness can transcend time. Because the power of tyrants is ultimately one of fools who will not endure, the struggle to work for good is, this narrative proclaims, of incalculable value. [Dreams and Repentance]

Both before and after Daniel received the dream interpretation, he included his companions. He invited them to pray with him, even though God entrusted the interpretation to him alone. He did not manipulate the dream interpretation for personal gain; neither did he shirk from Nebuchadnezzar's appointment to governmental service. He used his position, rather, to include his companions in his newly appointed offices. Daniel provides a model of how to act in light of the faith that God is in control of history. The confidence that comes with the knowledge that God has a purpose for everything allows Daniel to think of others.

This, too, is the task of life in the modern world. In an age dominated by unfathomable horror, it may be difficult for many to believe that life is meaningful, that God has a purpose for humanity, and that death does not have the final say. Daniel's hope does not lie in becoming the next Nebuchadnezzar, but in trusting that all wisdom, all meaning, and all value come from God and not from earthly power. Although a world where justice rules is far from seen, this narrative holds that a vision of the end of suffering can serve as a powerful encouragement never to abandon striving for the betterment of the world. What Nebuchadnezzar should have done completely, namely acknowledge the sovereign God with full understanding of its implications, is the task for Daniel's readers. Complete answers to the questions of "why?" may not be given, but this account unequivocally states that even the most arrogant of rulers is under the watch of God. Whether we are challenged by privilege and success, as was Nebuchadnezzar, or by suffering, as were Joseph and Daniel, a continual reminder that

Dreams and Repentance

Just as modern psychological insight tells us that understanding dreams can be healing, the Talmud teaches that dreams can encourage repentance, for they are one of many ways that demonstrate that God's presence not only exists in the dramatic, but in the ordinary. Jewish tradition holds that prophecy ceased after the prophet Malachi, but that God's revelation continues, both through the study of Torah and in people's everyday lives. Because dreams are in the purview of the unconscious, they form an excellent bridge between the spiritual and physical worlds. Indeed, they are considered "one-sixtieth of prophecy" (*b. Ber.* 57b).

Dreams may provide the window to our deepest thoughts, prompt a new way of thinking, or may pose a challenge to our assumptions about our lives. As Judith Abrams writes,

Like Jacob in the Torah, with whom God communicated mostly through dreams, we tend to have our guard up. Like Jacob, we are often looking out for our best interests, trying to control our lives. It is difficult for God's messages to enter our consciousness while we hold this attitude. Therefore, God reaches out to us when we are more open, less defended—in sleep. (143)

In this context of recognizing God's presence in our everyday lives, the Talmud tells the story of Bar Hadaya, a dream interpreter who greedily uses his spiritual gifts to increase his own wealth, giving positive dream interpretations to those who could pay for them, but frightening interpretations to those who did not. Although he was given two occasions to repent, by his own avarice he put himself in a position to receive a capital sentence from the Roman authorities. As Abrams explains, the story teaches us, "when spiritual gifts are used in God's service, they elevate us in the most beautiful way. When they are directed toward earthy power or gain, they are destructive and unclean" (147).

Judith Abrams, *Prayer*, vol. 1 of *The Talmud for Beginners* (Northvale NJ: Jason Aronson, 1993), 142–51.

Joseph Reconciles with his Brothers

Francois Gerard (1770–1837). *Joseph Recognized by his Brothers*. Canvas. Musee des Beaux-Arts, Angers, France. (Credit: Erich Lessing/Art Resource, NY)

God is sovereign encourages people to live in confidence, never abandoning the quest to learn God's ways and to bring God's purposes to fruition on earth.

NOTES

[1] See Dan 5:30 and 9:1.

[2] Isa 47:5-13.

[3] See the discussion in Paul Redditt, *Daniel* (The New Century Bible Commentary; Sheffield: Sheffield Academic Press, 1999), 18–20.

[4] See also Dan 3:29.

[5] John Collins, *Daniel: A Commentary on the Book of Daniel* (Hermeneia; Minneapolis: Fortress, 1993), 159.

[6] Lawrence Schiffman, *Reclaiming the Dead Sea Scrolls* (The Anchor Bible Reference Library; New York: Doubleday & Co., 1995), 206–10.

[7] G. T. M. Prinsloo, "Two Poems in a Sea of Prose: the Content and Context of Daniel 2.20-23. and 6.27-28," JSOT 59 (1993): 93–108. See also P. M. Venter, "The Function of

Poetic Speech in the Narrative in Daniel 2," *Heervormde Teologiese Studies* 49 (1993): 1009–20.

[8] See the Hebrew equivalent in Ps 106:48.

[9] For a discussion on the significance of prayers of praise see Samuel Balentine, *Prayer in the Hebrew Bible* (Overtures to Biblical Theology; Minneapolis: Fortress, 1993), 199–224. Also, see below, ch. 9.

[10] Louis Hartman and Alexander Di Lella, *The Book of Daniel* (AB 23; Garden City NY: Doubleday & Co., 1978), 144–45.

[11] Num 24:14; Deut 4:30; 31:29; Isa 2:2; Jer 23:20; 30:24; 48:47; 49:39; Ezek 38:16; Hos 3:5. For further discussion see Norman Porteous, *Daniel: A Commentary* (OTL; Philadelphia: Westminster, 1965), 44.

[12] Herodotus, *Histories* 1.183; Collins, *Daniel*, 162.

[13] Similar to this text of Zechariah, Second Isaiah also mocks such activity (Isa 44:18-20).

[14] Collins, *Daniel*, 164.

[15] Hesiod, *Works and Days* 1.109; Collins, *Daniel*, 162.

[16] Indeed, after the divisions of the Greek Empire into the Ptolemaic and Seleucid regions, marriage alliances were attempted to strengthen their hegemony. See below, ch. 10.

[17] John Goldingay, *Daniel* (WBC 30; Dallas: Word Books, 1989), 57.

[18] James Montgomery, *A Critical and Exegetical Commentary on the Book of Daniel* (ICC 22; Edinburgh: T. & T. Clark, 1927), 62. See *b. 'Abod. Zar.* 2b and below, ch. 7.

[19] Collins, *Daniel*, 166.

[20] Montgomery, *A Critical and Exegetical Commentary*, 60.

[21] Richard Hiers, "Kingdom of God," in *Harper's Bible Dictionary*, ed. Paul Achtemeier (San Francisco: Harper & Row, 1985), 527–28.

[22] Gerhard Pfandl, "Interpretations of the Kingdom of God in Daniel 2:44," *AUSS* 34/2 (1996): 249–68.

[23] Ibid., 249–50.

[24] Ibid., 25.

[25] Ibid., 251–52.

[26] Ibid., 253.

[27] Ibid., 255, n. 22.

[28] Ibid., 256, n. 24.

[29] For a different interpretation see Dana Nolan Fewell, *Circle of Sovereignty: A Story of Stories in Daniel 1–6* (JSOTSup 72; Bible and Literature Series 20; Sheffield: Almond Press, 1988), 161.

[30] For more on the influence of the Joseph story on the book of Daniel, see Jan-Wim Wesselius, "Discontinuity, Congruence and the Making of the Hebrew Bible," *SJOT* 13 (1999): 24–77.

COURAGEOUS EXILES
CONFRONT A KING

Daniel 3:1-30

COMMENTARY

"*Plus ça change, plus c'est la même chose*" ("the more things change, the more they remain the same"). This famous French proverb well illustrates the situation of Daniel's fellow exiles in Babylon. They may outwit their Babylonian counterparts, and they may be protected by God's providence, but they continue to live under a whimsical and tyrannical king. Although this king can be mollified, his subjects must continue to walk a narrow line because his malevolence may appear suddenly. Daniel's fellows may even serve the Babylonian government, but they must constantly be aware that the people who hold power over them may strike out against them at any time. In this atmosphere of uncertainty, however, they are not to despair as their faithfulness provides truth and meaning in their existence that supersede any tyranny.

Daniel 3 tells the story of Nebuchadnezzar's fashioning of a golden statue and his command that all subjects worship it or be put to death. When governmental officials report that Shadrach, Meshach, and Abednego disobey the order, Nebuchadnezzar directly insists on their compliance. When they continue to refuse, he sentences them to death by burning in a fiery furnace. Miraculously, however, they are spared. In response, a changed Nebuchadnezzar issues a new decree that ostensibly protects them, and the story ends with an account of their promotion. Nevertheless, behind this simple story where there is a happy ending for Daniel's friends, the reader finds that Nebuchadnezzar's blindness remains. Never negating the decree that necessitates the worship of the statue, he issues an additional decree that the God of these three young men not be maligned. Because Nebuchadnezzar's original law, which began their frightful encounter, is still in effect, the author suggests that Nebuchadnezzar has no change of heart regarding his own gods or the policies of despotism that they enforce.

The Three Youths in the Fiery Furnace

This painting depicts Hananiah, Mishael, and Azariah with halos that represent sainthood. Note the outstretched arms of the angel, indicating divine protection. The Greek words in this painting read, "the three holy youths." In the Greek Orthodox tradition, the three youths, along with Daniel, are venerated as saints on December 17. The *kontakion* (hymn) especially dedicated to them reads, "An image made with hands you would not worship, O thrice-blessed three; but protected by the ineffable Essence you were glorified in your ordeal by fire. From the midst of the devouring flames you called upon God, crying: Hasten, O compassionate One, in Your mercy come to our aid, for if You will, You can." The story of the

Shadrach, Meshach, and Abednego, the Three Youths in the Fiery Furnace of Nebuchadnezzer. 11th C. BC. Mosaic, Monastery Church, Hosios Loukas, Greece. (Credit: Erich Lessing/Art Resource, NY)

fiery furnace is also read on one of the most festive liturgies of the year, namely, on the "Great Sabbath," which occurs on the Saturday before Easter. (I am grateful to Dr. Silviu Bunta for his assistance with this interpretation.)

This narrative shows that even when temporary safety exists and promotion occurs in foreign lands, long-term security is never certain. In the face of these lingering threats, the author reinforces the idea that what makes life truly valuable and worth living for the exilic community is not its own political advancement but its fidelity to God. The holding of power within the context of a foreign government is neither the goal of the people's existence nor the value they should hold most dear. Rather, willingness to obey God's commandments is the only principle that has ultimate significance. [Outline of Daniel 3]

The Requirement to Worship King Nebuchadnezzar's Statue, 3:1-7

This scene demonstrates that Nebuchadnezzar wields a heavy hand throughout his kingdom and attempts to exercise complete control over his subjects. The construction of the statue enables the king to flaunt his power and to demand total obedience from all who reside within his empire. [Dura—Translation and Tradition] Despite the control Nebuchadnezzar has over his subjects' lives, the author recognizes the emptiness of the king's arrogance, and thus mocks him and his institutions in various ways. We now examine the preposterous dimensions of the statue and the command to worship it; the overloaded lists of governmental officials, subjects, and musical instruments; and the proposed terrifying punishment for any disobedience. These depictions underscore Nebuchadnezzar's totalitarian rule, but also deride his lack of dignity and the ultimate futility of his plans, which are an affront to God. [The Use of the Epithet "King"]

The placement of this narrative as the sequel to the account of Nebuchadnezzar's dream of the statue made of four metals and clay allows for an appropriate comparison. In Daniel 2, the golden head of the statue in Nebuchadnezzar's dream symbolizes Babylon. In contrast to the three other metals of inferior quality found in that statue, as well as the foundation made of mixed clay and metal (2:32-33), the statue Nebuchadnezzar now constructs is entirely made of gold, suggesting Nebuchadnezzar's defiance. The sequence

---

Dura—Translation and Tradition

In Dan 3:1 the text states that Nebuchadnezzar erected his statue "on the plain of Dura in the province of Babylon." One interpretation holds that Dura is an unidentified place in Babylon, another that the reference is to a part of the city of Babylon. Some scholars hold that *"dûrā'"* refers not to a city but is an Akkadian loan-word for "wall"; hence the reference is to a region near the famous city wall built by Nebuchadnezzar. As Edward Cook states, "This prominent feature of ancient Babylon thus forms part of the local color of the narrative of Daniel; the author wishes us to imagine representatives of 'all peoples, nations, and tongues' (3:4) gathered to worship the golden image in the plain between the outer wall—the wall *par excellence*—and the city proper."

Ezekiel and The Valley of Life (Ezekiel and the dry bones restored to life). From the Story of Ezekiel. c. AD 239. Fresco, Synagogue, Dura Europos, Syria. (Credit: Art Resource, NY)

The midrashim and the Talmud preserve a tradition that Dura was the site where Ezekiel resurrected the dry bones. We read in *Song of Songs Rabbah*:

> Whence do we know that Ezekiel brought the dead to life . . . [on the day Hananiah, Mishael, and Azariah were delivered from the fiery furnace]? . . . R. Phinehas said: The same wind that blew down the image [of Nebuchadnezzar] brought the dead to life. (*Song. Rab.* 7:9, 1)

Henry Thompson notes that a fresco at the Dura-Europos synagogue (3rd C. AD), located in Syria, shows a painting of Ezekiel's vision and "may represent an early identification with the site and the story in Dan 3:1."

Edward M. Cook, "'In the Plain of the Wall' (Dan 3:1)," *JBL* 108 (1989): 115–16.

Henry O. Thompson, "Dura," *ABD*, ed. David Noel Freedman (New York: Doubleday & Co., 1992), 2:241.

The Use of the Epithet "King"

AΩ n the opening scene of Dan 3, "Nebuchadnezzar" is found with the royal title "king" (*hammelek*) four times in quick succession: 3:1, 3, 5, 7. This emphasis on Nebuchadnezzar's station contrasts the earthly king's power with that of the true king, "the King of heaven" (4:37 [4:34 MT]). The use of the title "king" continues throughout Dan 3 and 4, either alone or together with "Nebuchadnezzar." "(O) King," used alone, is found in 3:9, 10, 12, 13, 16, 17, 18, 22, 24, 28, 30; 4:19, 22, 23, 24 (*twice*), 27 [4:16, 19, 20, 21 (*twice*), 24 MT]. Besides the opening verses noted above, "(O) King Nebuchadnezzar" is found in the following: 3:9, 24; 4:1 (3:31 MT); 4:18, 28, 31 (4:15, 25, 28 MT). "(O) Nebuchadnezzar," used alone, is found in 3:3, 13, 14, 16, 19, 26, 28; 4:4, 33, 34, 37 (4:1, 30, 31, 34 MT).

of these two stories allows the reader to conclude that Nebuchadnezzar constructs this gold statue in the aftermath of the divine annihilation of the previous statue. Although the stories of Daniel 2 and 3 originally may have circulated as independent accounts, their current arrangement portrays a king who learns nothing from Daniel's dream interpretation. Previously, Nebuchadnezzar has threatened to kill all the wise of Babylon because they could not interpret his dream. Now, his insistence that everyone worship his statue likely threatens more people with death. This command, of course, has particularly grave consequences for Daniel's people.

The word used for statue (*ṣĕlēm*) is revealing, as it connotes not only "statue" but also "idol." It is possible to understand it as a representation of Nebuchadnezzar himself or of one of his gods, particularly Marduk or Nebo, the patrons of Babylon. The description of the statue is both impressive and unfathomable. [Colossal Statues in the Ancient World] Although the statue is made of gold, the description of its dimensions highlights its vulnerability—and Nebuchadnezzar's folly. The given dimensions, sixty cubits high by six cubits wide, correspond to approximately ninety feet by nine feet. For the readers of the Persian period, the height would make it the largest statue of the Mediterranean and the Near East at the time, and the width, to be sure, is greatly disproportionate to its height. These numbers illustrate the frequent use of symbolic numeration in ancient Near Eastern and biblical texts.[1] This enormous height is reminiscent of the outlandish gallows—fifty cubits high—constructed for the capital punishment of Mordecai, who similarly refused to bow to Haman. [Parallels between the Statue's Height and the Gallows Prepared for Mordecai] The height of the statue is the same as the width of the first temple and is exactly twice the first temple's height (1 Kgs 6:2). In addition, the statue is the same height as the second temple (Ezra 6:3). The choice of the width of the statue

Colossal Statues in the Ancient World

The ancient Greek historian Herodotus (b. 484 BC) speaks of several giant statues in Egypt and in Babylon. For example, he reports that the Egyptian King Sesostris constructed a fifty-foot statue of himself and his wife and a thirty-three-foot statue of his sons (*Histories* 2.110.1). He also records that the Babylonians have a tradition that a twenty-foot solid gold statue graced their temple before Xerxes conquered them. Their temple was replete with gold:

In the Babylonian temple there is another shrine below where there is a great golden image of Zeus, sitting at a great golden table, and the footstool and the chair are also gold; the gold of the whole was said by the Chaldeans to be eight hundred talents' weight. Outside the temple is a golden altar . . . on the greater altar the Chaldeans even offer a thousand talents weight of frankincense yearly. (*Histories* 1.183.1)

Such descriptions of the ostentatious display of foreign wealth surely influenced the Jewish depiction of Nebuchadnezzar's statue.

similarly recalls the width of the support beams of both the first and second temples (1 Kgs 6:6; Ezek 41:1). In addition to these interesting connotations of the statue's dimensions, the description of its gold recalls the biblical descriptions of the temple as well. According to the author of Chronicles—another composition of the Persian period—Solomon's use of gold in the construction of the vestibules, beams, holy of holies, upper chambers, and cherubim was unparalleled (2 Chr 3:4-10). These connotations suggest that the traditional association of gold with the holiness of God's temple is to be contrasted with the self-aggrandizing policies of Nebuchadnezzar.

Parallels Between the Statue's Height and the Gallows Prepared for Mordecai

The outrageous dimensions of the statue, which point to the debased values of Nebuchadnezzar, may be compared to the outlandish height of the gallows that the Persian courtier Haman prepared for the righteous Mordecai. Haman's wife and friends counsel him: "Let a gallows fifty cubits high be made, and in the morning tell the king to have Mordecai hanged upon it . . ." (Esth 5:14). Nevertheless, just as the three youths will be rescued from the fiery furnace and their very captors burned by the flames, so too does Haman suffer the intended fate of Mordecai: "so they hanged Haman on the gallows that he had prepared for Mordecai" (Esth 7:10).

The author continues to portray Nebuchadnezzar's far-reaching organization of the state as well as its inane nature by employing an inordinate list of his officials, subjects, and musical instruments. Seven types of representatives over the various populations are included: "the satraps, the prefects, and the governors, the counselors, the treasurers, the justices, the magistrates" (v. 3), as well as an additional comprehensive category, namely, "and all the officials of the provinces." Most of these are Persian terms, pointing to the Diaspora origins of the original story within the Persian Empire. The choice of seven terms indicates comprehensiveness, as this number is frequently used throughout the Hebrew Scriptures to indicate totality or a complete cycle of time. In addition, this list also implies that Nebuchadnezzar's hegemony is without limit, as these persons in leadership positions are expected not only to be in compliance themselves but also are required to ensure the obedience of their charges.

One of the references to the officials, namely, the "satraps" (*'ăḥašdarpĕnîn*) was well known to the exilic community of the Persian period; these regional administrators of the Persian Empire could exercise great control. [Persian Hegemony in Judah] The connotations of the word are now anachronistically projected onto their Babylonian predecessors. According to the book of Esther, it is these same satraps who are responsible for enforcing Haman's edict of genocide on the Persian Jewish populace. In that ominous text we find,

[A]n edict . . . was written to the king's satraps (*'ăḥašdarpĕnîn*) and to the governors over all the provinces and to the officials of all the

Map of Persian Empire

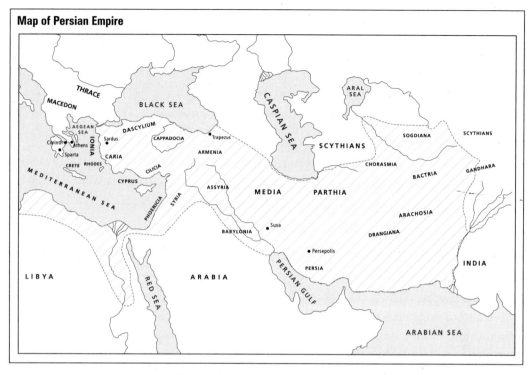

peoples, . . . giving orders to destroy, to kill, and to annihilate all Jews, young and old, women and children, in one day. (Esth 3:12-13)[2]

Similarly, the term for governor (*peḥāh*), another Persian word, has the potential to connote abuses of power. Once the Persians allowed the exiles to return to Judah, Jewish men were appointed as governors. Although the people were familiar with just governors,

---

Persian Hegemony in Judah

While under Persian rule, Jews could not proceed with the reconstruction of their temple without the approval of the Persian government. The Persian officials had the power to conscript laborers and soldiers, to enforce the empire's laws, and to collect taxes. During the governance of Zerubbabel, the Persian-appointed Jewish representative in Yehud (Judah), certain local persons objected to his plan for rebuilding the temple. When they accused Zerubbabel of treason against the Persian king Artaxerxes, Persian forces reacted quickly to the king's command that the putative Jewish rebellion be arrested. We read,

Then when the copy of King Artaxerxes' letter was read before Rehum and the scribe Shimshai and their associates, they hurried to the Jews in Jerusalem and by force and power made them cease. At that time the work on the house of God in Jerusalem stopped and was discontinued until the second year of the reign of King Darius of Persia. (Ezra 4:23-24)

Persian control was ubiquitous in the ordinary details of economic life as well. Although Persia allowed a certain amount of autonomy in order to lessen the chance of rebellion by its colonized people, the emperor had the final say, as is reflected in the book of Esther, when King Ahasuerus gives orders to Mordecai and Esther: "You may write as you please with regard to the Jews, in the name of the king, and seal it with the king's ring; for an edict written in the name of the king and sealed with the king's ring cannot be revoked" (Esth 8:8).

such as Nehemiah, they also had experienced abusive behavior from other appointees. In order to distance himself from the actions of his predecessors, Nehemiah offers this comparison:

> The former governors who were before me laid heavy burdens upon the people, and took food and wine from them, besides forty shekels of silver . . . yet with all this I did not demand the food allowance of the governor, because of the heavy burden of labor on the people. (Neh 5:15-18)

Although this quotation is apologetic, it points to the existence of economic and social hardships of the Jewish community under Persian rule. Thus, the use of these Persian terms in Daniel 3 helps to present a scene of intimidation. [Persian Warriors]

As Daniel 3:4 illustrates, the assembly of the various officials to worship the statue underscores that Nebuchadnezzar's dominion is absolute, requiring the submission of "all peoples, nations, and languages" within his empire. The reference to "peoples, nations, and languages" connotes intimidation when used of the orders of oppressors, as in the case of Kings Belshazzar (5:19) and Darius (6:25 [26 MT]). As is shown in Daniel 7:14, it is God alone who determines whom all peoples should serve. As the scene continues, the growing specificity of what Nebuchadnezzar demands reveals increasing danger. The author twice states that Nebuchadnezzar demands everyone's presence at the dedication of his statue (vv. 2-3). When the king's herald makes the official proclamation, he twice tells the people both to "fall down" and to "prostrate yourselves" (v. 5, A.T.) Both of these verbs are repeated to indicate the people's compliance (v. 7).

Because Daniel and his companions Hananiah, Mishael, and Azariah have already been introduced, the placement of this chapter allows the reader to speculate on the possible presence of Daniel and his companions at the dedication of this idol. In this scene, no particular nation is singled out for compliance to Nebuchadnezzar's ruling, and in fact, no reference to the location of either Daniel or the three has yet been given. If they

Persian Warriors

The formidable strength of the Persian army is depicted in this bas-relief from the staircase of the audience hall of Darius I. During the period of Persian rule, the Diaspora community was encouraged by the tales of the courage of Daniel and his friends who endured challenges from the Babylonians—the Persians' predecessors.

Persian warriors. Achaemenid period. Staircase of the Audience hall of Darius I. Persepolis, Iran. (Credit: SEF/Art Resource, NY

Ancient Instruments
These terracotta figures of musicians from Susa, Iran (14th–12th C. BC) illustrate the antiquity of various instruments and the importance of music in the ancient Near East.

Musicians playing the lute. 14th–12th C. BC.
Terracotta figurine, Susa, Iran. Louvre. Paris,
France. (Credit: Erich Lessing/Art Resource, NY)

indeed are present, how will they respond? Daniel has previously been identified as "the chief prefect" (2:48) over all the wise, and although his three fellow exiles were not given titles, they were, in fact, placed within governmental service. As members of all "peoples, nations, and languages," they, too, would be required to comply; yet their faith, to be sure, would require that they not. A narrative gap is introduced here whose suspense is heightened by the potentially misleading continuation of the account. At first reading, the following detail implies that everyone in the realm obeyed the intimidating order: "Therefore, as soon as all the peoples heard the sound of the horn, pipe, lyre, trigon, harp, drum, and entire musical ensemble, all the peoples, nations, and languages fell down and worshiped the golden statue that King Nebuchadnezzar had set up" (3:7).

Because this verse relates that *all* nations in fact comply, there is, at first, no reason to exclude Jewish obedience. In fact, this quotation repeats the same order of the list of peoples in compliance, the instruments sounded, and the content of Nebuchadnezzar's command in order to suggest that none dare to challenge the ruling. The author's delay in presenting the full account allows one to speculate that assimilation and loss of identity have occurred. Before further detail is given, the description of Nebuchadnezzar's excesses continues, allowing for the derision of his character as well as a more dramatic revelation of the youth's integrity.

The next set of royal extremes is found in the listing of the six instruments that will signify the commencement of the prostration before the statue. Except for the word "horn" (*qarnāʾ*) these specific instruments are not found elsewhere in the Hebrew Bible, and it is likely that three of the terms, lyre (*qatrôs*), trigon (*sabbĕkāʾ*), and drum (*sûmpōnyâ*), are Mesopotamian or Greek loanwords.[3] In addition, the term *mašrôqîtāʾ* (NRSV: pipe) may also mean "whistle" and sounds derisive here as potentially inappropriate in a collection of instruments. The linguistic strangeness of these terms, their overloaded listing, near-verbatim repetition (vv. 5, 7, 10, 15), and other usages in oppressive and idolatrous circumstances suggest the distance between Nebuchadnezzar's material culture and the spiritual heritage of the three young men. In this vein, it has been suggested that the instruments appear as a strange type of orchestra, further underscoring the bankruptcy of Nebuchadnezzar's civilization.[4] [Temple Music]

Temple Music

Overall, the description of these instruments stands in sharp contrast to the most familiar association of instruments in the Bible, namely, with temple worship. The Chronicler describes the music and instruments of the temple with awe and respect: "David also commanded the chiefs of the Levites to appoint their kindred as the singers to play on musical instruments, on harps and lyres and cymbals, to raise loud sounds of joy" (1 Chr 15:16). Similarly, "From the algum wood, the king made steps for the house of the LORD and for the king's house, lyres also and harps for the singers; there never was seen the like of them before in the land of Judah" (2 Chr 9:11).

The most fearsome aspect of Nebuchadnezzar's command is dramatically delayed until v. 6. All individuals must prostrate themselves before the statue lest they "immediately" be thrown into "a furnace of blazing fire." The use of the adverb "immediately" and the needless suffering of such a horrible death emphasize the terror of Nebuchadnezzar's command. In the Hebrew Bible, the image of fire is used of the testing of both the exile and of slavery in Egypt (Deut 4:20; Jer 11:4; Isa 48:10). Although Nebuchadnezzar proposes to use fire as an instrument of torture, the author shows that the flames become benign to the pious young men who are tested and survive. Like the lions who prove harmless to Daniel and attack only his accusers (Dan 6:24 [6:25 MT]), the fire destroys only those attendants loyal to Nebuchadnezzar. It is possible that the audience was already familiar with other stories of heroes who were rescued from similarly horrible fates. In the midrashim, the account of Abraham being thrown into Nimrod's fiery furnace may attest to a common tradition of representing a test by fire of a faithful hero from the hands of a despotic king. [Abraham in the Fiery Furnace]

Finally, we note that the content of Nebuchadnezzar's command, namely, a foreign government's requirement for Jews to commit idolatry, was a familiar theme to a Diaspora audience. Bowing to an idol or to another human being as a god was considered so offensive that it is one of the three most grievous sins singled out in early Jewish tradition: idolatry, sexual immorality, and murder.[5]

Abraham in the Fiery Furnace

One of the best-known midrashim concerning the obedience of Abraham is the account of his being thrown into the fiery furnace by King Nimrod of Babylon. Nimrod was incensed that Abraham disparaged his idols, paralleling Nebuchadnezzar's rage that the three would not honor his statue. Nimrod taunts Abraham to call upon his God to rescue him (*Gen. Rab.* 38:13), just as Nebuchadnezzar insists that no one could rescue his Jewish prisoners. The midrashim show specific parallels in these two acts of obedience. While discussing sacrifices, an analogy is made with the near-

sacrifices of Israel's heroes, including Abraham, and these three Jews: "[God] smelled the savour of the Patriarch Abraham ascending from the fiery furnace; He smelled the savour of Hananiah, Mishael, and Azariah ascending from the fiery furnace" (*Gen. Rab.* 34:9). After the test in the fiery furnace leaves the patriarch unscathed, Abraham states, "my sons are Hananiah, Mishael, and Azariah" (*Gen. Rab.* 39:3-5). These references show that the experiences of Abraham and the three young men become paradigmatic for the difficulties and tragedies of Jewish life in the Diaspora.

[Rabbinic Commentary on Idolatry] The best example of such a test is found in the book of Esther (Esth 3:2-4), where Mordecai refuses to bow to the murderous Haman. Although the act of bowing to a person is distinct from worshiping a statue, it is understood to be similarly offensive to God and threatening to the essence of what defines the Jewish people. Mordecai's refusal prompts Haman's retaliatory genocidal decree; yet Mordecai's character remains exemplary and heroic. [Idols and Value Systems]

Rabbinic Commentary on Idolatry

The Talmud considers that although idolatry was prevalent in the days of the first temple, it was no longer a temptation for Jews in the days of the second temple. Avoiding idolatry is seen as tantamount to obeying the commandments, practicing idolatry as denying them. The Talmud cites "various social and ethical" lapses as the equivalent to idolatry, including reciting prayers while intoxicated, succumbing to excessive anger, avoiding one's charitable obligations, or breaking a promise. It is interesting to note that the rabbis find the refusal of Hananiah, Mishael, and Azariah to worship the statue as one of two possible times in history in which the evil inclination toward idolatry definitively was rooted out (*Song. Rab.* 7:8 [The other is during the days of Mordecai and Esther.]). The Talmud uses the example of the three youths' refusal to worship the statue to illustrate the quintessential nature of the Jew as being one who denies idols (*b. Meg.* 13a).

Louis Isaac Rabinowitz, "Idolatry," *EncJud*, ed. Cecil Roth and Geoffrey Wigoder, 16 vols. (New York: Macmillan, 1971–72), 8:1235.

Defamation against a People and the Criminal Charges against Shadrach, Meshach, and Abednego, 3:8-12

The portrayal of events indicated in v. 7 is not challenged until v. 12; only then does the reader know for certain that it is *not* true that all people bowed. The author shifts the focus to the report of the Chaldean officials in order that the reader may hear the direct accusations of those officials who report the "crime" to the king (v. 8). As part of the Babylonian privileged classes, the Chaldeans were not only involved in the religious direction of the nation, but also were part of its government, as evidenced by their role in the kings' court (Dan 2). [The Chaldeans' Reputation] In Daniel 1 we saw that although Babylonian curricula and way of life would have formed an implicit threat to the captives, the officials were, in fact, outwitted. And although the Babylonian wise were rescued from Nebuchadnezzar's whimsical death decrees because of Daniel's dream interpretation, they now take steps directly to

Idols and Value Systems

 Idols represent the value systems that can be manipulated by humans. John Watts well expresses their significance:

As the swastika represented the Nationalist Socialist party, or the hammer and sickle represent Marxist communism, so specific idols represented ways of life for their adherents. . . . Bel and Nebo (Marduk) represented the political, social, military, and economic system that produced successful empires from the days of Hammurabi on. They were symbols of imperial privilege,

power, and wealth gained by violent seizure. They were also symbols of arrogance, pride, and unbridled ambition. . . . Babylon served YHWH's purpose well as a weapon to punish his people's sins. But otherwise there was no hope of "healing" or reforming Babylon's ruthless and tyrannical ways. Her idols—symbols of her greed, arrogance, and pride—contained no element capable of redemption or reformation.

John D. W. Watts, "Babylonian Idolatry in the Prophets as a False Socio-Economic System," in *Israel's Apostasy and Restoration: Essays in Honor of Roland K. Harrison*, ed. Avraham Gileadi (Grand Rapids MI: Baker Book House, 1988), 116–19.

---

threaten the lives of the exiles. The author calls attention to the sinister nature of the Chaldeans' accusations by the indication of their haste in bringing charges. This is accomplished by the use of the forceful phrase repeated in vv. 7 and 8, namely, "accordingly, at this time" (*kol-qŏbēl dĕnāh bēh-zimnāʾ*). Before the direct quotation of the Chaldeans' condemnatory words is given, however, the author assesses their speech, specifying that it is a deliberate attempt to defame the three and to have them murdered. Ominous words stand out: "Accordingly at this time certain Chaldeans came forward and denounced the Jews" (v. 8). [The Jew in the Court of the Foreign King] The phrase translated "denounce" (*ʾăkalû qarṣêhôn*) literally means "eat the pieces of." It is also found in Daniel 6:24 ("accuse," NRSV [v. 25 MT]) where it describes the actions of the officials who betray Daniel to Darius and finds its ironic culmination in the deaths of Daniel's accusers in the lions' den—the very place designated for Daniel's capital punishment (Dan 6).[6]

The uncertainty regarding exactly who is being charged is most telling. Because no qualifier limits the number or names of Jews who are denounced, a narrative gap is created that allows the possibility that all are endangered. Indeed, there are three possibilities for the object of the

The Chaldeans' Reputation

Throughout the neo-Babylonian Empire, the Chaldeans enjoyed a privileged position as the ruling class, and during the Persian and Hellenistic ages, they continued to be known as sages. Richard Hess remarks,

We may observe the later tradition of Merodach-Baladan, who was said to have maintained a garden of exotic plants supported by a contemporary list of 67 plants belonging to his garden and to have had an observatory in Babylonia for purposes of astronomy. . . . Further, the beginning of careful historical, economic, and astronomical record keeping in Babylon in 747 BCE, roughly coincides with the rise of Chaldean influence, two events which later traditions were to relate to one another. (887)

In the Bible, some texts use the term "Chaldeans" synonymously with "Babylonians" (2 Kgs 24:2; 25:4, 5, 10, 13; Jer 21:4; 22:25; 32:4-5, 24-25, 28-29). In the book of Daniel "the Chaldeans" are used in the sense of sages and advisers. John Goldingay suggests that the reputation of the Babylonian sages, who provided advice and protection for the king based on history, astrology, divination, and magic, may have provided the context for the portrayal of the Chaldeans in Daniel, as well for the diviners and sages (Isa 44:25; 47:13; and Esth 1:13. See also above, [Deuteronomy's Critique of Magic (Deut 18:9-15)]).

Richard Hess, "Chaldea," *ABD*, ed. David Noel Freedman (New York: Doubleday & Co., 1992), 1:886–87.

John E. Goldingay, *Daniel* (WBC 30; Dallas: Word Books, 1989), 16–17.

The Jew in the Court of the Foreign King

In his comparative study of texts that portray Jews in foreign governments in antiquity, Lawrence Wills argues that a unique feature of Dan 3 is the addition of religious persecution to the more common plot of antagonism among the kings' courtiers. Thus, there is "a more pointed critique of imperial institutions (whether of the Babylonian, Persian, or Hellenistic empires), with an increased tension in regard to the religious demands of the ruling society and the necessity of the hero to witness to Jewish piety."

Lawrence Wills, *The Jew in the Court of the Foreign King*, Harvard Dissertations in Religion (Minneapolis: Fortress, 1990), 86–87.

Chaldeans' charge. First, the author tells the reader that the Chaldeans "denounced the Jews" (v. 8), allowing for the possibility that all exiles in the empire are threatened by the accusation. Secondly, the Chaldeans specify "*certain Jews* whom you [Nebuchadnezzar] have appointed over the affairs of the province of Babylon" (v. 12, emphasis mine). This reference could, of course, include any number of Jews who were given positions of authority in the Babylonian government. Only as the last words in the sentence are read and all the details of the laws' requirements are given does the reader discover that only three specific individuals are meant: Shadrach, Meshach, and Abednego. This presentation prompts the reader to consider the insidious nature of prejudice. If one member of the community is singled out for his or her beliefs, all are at risk. No one can live under the pretense that he or she is safe while compatriots stand accused. This text parallels the following excerpt from the book of Esther, for when Esther at first protests to Mordecai that she is helpless to save her people, Mordecai accepts no excuses:

> Do not think that in the king's palace you will escape any more than all the other Jews. For if you keep silence at such a time as this, relief and deliverance will rise for the Jews from another quarter, but you and your father's family will perish. Who knows? Perhaps you have come to royal dignity for just such a time as this. (Esth 4:13-14)

As the Chaldeans specify their charges, the reader finds that not only are there three possibilities regarding who is included in these accusations (Jews, certain Jews, and finally the three), but also that even after it is clear that three individuals alone are threatened, it is still their identities as Jews that is more important than their individuality; the ethnicity and religion of the accused are given before their names. In addition, only their Babylonian names, earlier forced upon them by Nebuchadnezzar's palace master, are used (Dan 1:7). The reader may conclude that it is their otherness that the Chaldeans find so threatening. The Chaldeans try to link their very identity with their supposed disobedience in civil matters, a charge with which the Jewish people were familiar. Again Esther is illustrative, as the villain of the story, the murderous Haman, remarks to Ahasuerus, the king,

Esther

This painting shows Mordecai approaching Queen Esther, requesting that she defend her threatened people, condemned because of his refusal to bow to Haman. Just as the three young men respond fearlessly in face of Nebuchadnezzar's rage, Mordecai shows no hesitation when confronting Haman, and he convinces an initially apprehensive Esther to appeal to the king for mercy.

Aert van Gelder. 1645–1727. *Esther and Mordechai*. Oil on canvas, Museum of Fine Arts (Szepmuveszeti Muzeum), Budapest, Hungary. (Credit: Erich Lessing/Art Resource, NY)

There is a certain people scattered and separated among the peoples in all the provinces of your kingdom; their laws are different from those of every other people, and they do not keep the king's laws, so that it is not appropriate for the king to tolerate them. If it pleases the king, let a decree be issued for their destruction, and I will pay ten thousand talents of silver into the hands of those who have charge of the king's business, so that they may put it into the king's treasuries. (Esth 3:8-9)

This passage gives excellent insight into the roots of prejudice. Because the Jews are "different," Haman believes they cannot be trusted to be law-abiding, even though Mordecai actually saved King Ahasuerus from an assassination attempt. Because the author presents Shadrach, Meshach, and Abednego as administrators, one can assume they are responsible for upholding civil order. Yet the governmental rank and the privileges usually accorded with such positions do not matter in face of the king's preposterous demands. The author underscores that for the Chaldeans, these Jews' one act of refusal becomes a tripartite crime: "these pay no heed to you, O King. They do not serve your gods and they do not worship the golden statue that you have set up" (v. 12). [Royal Appeal to the Gods]

In addition, it is important to note that the Chaldeans repeat in detail all of the king's specifications concerning the inclusion of all peoples, the listing of the many instruments, and the exact punishment of the fiery kiln (vv. 10-11). Their haste and the detail with which they repeat the king's command make them appear eager to see the punishment meted out. They also give the king no choice

---

Royal Appeal to the Gods

Whether under Babylonian, Persian, or Seleucid rule, Jews were familiar with royal appeals to the gods for their support of the ruling dynast. A sample from a Babylonian stele of Nabonidus (555–539 BC) records:

> I had made [fabric] beautifully into garments befitting their godheads, for my lord Ea who increases my royal power, for Nebo, the administrator of all the upper and nether world, who lengthens the span of my life. . . . I am (also) a caretaker who brings large gifts to the great gods . . . (from) tokens of esteem (given) by kings, (from) the vast treasures which the prince Marduk has entrusted to me, (all) as perpetual . . . offerings for Bel, Nebo and Nergal, the great gods who love my rule and watch over my life. (*ANET*, 310–11)

Similarly, a foundation tablet from Persepolis (Iran) contains the following regarding the Persian king Xerxes (485–465 BC):

> Ahuramazda is the great god who gave (us) this earth, who gave (us) that sky . . . who made Xerxes, the king, (rule) the multitudes (as) only king, give alone orders to the other (kings). . . . Thus speaks king Xerxes: These are the countries—in addition to Persia—over which I am king under the "shadow" of Ahuramazda, over which I hold sway, which are bringing their tribute to me. . . .

> After I became king, there were (some) among these countries . . . which revolted (but) I crushed these countries, after Ahuramazda had given me his support. . . . (*ANET*, 316–17)

In the same way, the Seleucid king, Antiochus Soter (280–262 BC) appealed to his patron, Nebo:

> . . . may—upon your trustworthy command which cannot be made void—my days (on earth) be long, my years many, my throne firm, my rule lasting, under your lofty scepter which determines the borderline between the heaven and the nether world. May (only words of) favor be on your sacred lips with regard to me, and may I personally conquer (all) the countries from sunrise to sunset. . . . (*ANET*, 317)

The actions of the three young men of Dan 3 threaten Nebuchadnezzar himself, for by not serving the deities that sanction his rule, give him prosperity, and protect his very life, they denigrate the king's royal standing. The author shows that for Nebuchadnezzar, their refusal is not only a religious act; it is a thoroughly political one—namely disloyalty to the state.

James Pritchard, ed. *Ancient Near Eastern Texts Relating to the Old Testament*, 3rd ed. with supplement (Princeton NJ: Princeton University Press, 1969).

---

but to enforce his command, as their words are public and quote his very own decree.

Nebuchadnezzar's Direct Command as a Test of Totalitarian Control, 3:13-15

A multifaceted picture of Nebuchadnezzar is given in this text. On the one hand, he bristles with anger, yet on the other hand, he gives the three an additional opportunity to comply with his orders. Thus, his fearsome words and demeanor are juxtaposed with his pride, which gives his subjects another chance to comply. This presentation highlights Nebuchadnezzar's arrogance and at the same time denigrates his lust for power, for despite the king's command to worship the golden statue, his subjects will once more defy him. Two prepositional phrases punctuate his anger; Nebuchadnezzar is, literally, "in a rage" and "in a fury" ("in furious rage," NRSV, v. 13). The king poses questions to confirm their disobedience, but interestingly, does not repeat all three of the Chaldeans' accusa-

Tributaries

The Diaspora community in the Achaemenid period (553–330 BC) was quite familiar with the absolute fealty demanded by their Persian overlords. This bas-relief from Persepolis shows foreign tributaries bringing levies to Darius I (521 to 485/486 BC). The Persian Jewish community would have understood the stories about Nebuchadnezzar through the lens of their own experience.

Tributaries bringing gifts from their countries to the King. Achaemenid period. Relief from staircase. Audience hall of Darius I. Persepolis, Iran. (Credit: SEF/Art Resource, NY)

tions. Although he does include the charges that the exiles neither worshiped his god nor bowed to his statue, he omits the charge that they "paid no heed" (v. 12). Indeed, at the conclusion of this chapter we find that it is in fact the case that the three are promoted in governmental service. The author may have Nebuchadnezzar omit this charge here in order to underscore that as a Jew in Diaspora life, one may avoid idolatry while yet obeying the general rules of civil order demanded by the emperor. In addition, given that the king does not include this accusation, it is one to which they do not have to respond. Shadrach, Meshach, and Abednego *have in fact* obeyed Nebuchadnezzar's laws and took exception in this instance regarding idolatry alone. An unusual construction is used in v. 15 when Nebuchadnezzar proposes his second chance.[7] The conditional usage begins the sentence but is never completed. He states, "Now if you are ready when you hear the sound of the horn, pipe, lyre, trigon, harp, drum, and entire musical ensemble to fall down and worship the statue that I have made . . ." (v. 15). This sentence hints at the impossibility that the three would ever comply. Nebuchadnezzar continues to taunt the accused with a question he believes impossible to answer, saying, "who is the god who will rescue you out of my hands?" (v. 15). By this question, a contest is now set up, not between Nebuchadnezzar and the three exiles, but between Nebuchadnezzar and the God of Israel. It is one that Nebuchadnezzar cannot win.

The Fidelity of Shadrach, Meshach, and Abednego, 3:16-18

The fidelity of the three is immediately apparent with their response to the king, as is shown by the content of their speech.

Their solidarity for each other and courage are indicated by their single voice. They even have the temerity to address Nebuchadnezzar disrespectfully, calling him by his name without his title "king"; this is the very first time in the book that another addresses Nebuchadnezzar in this way. In their response, they shift the focus away from their own fate to the very will of God, stating, in effect, that their deaths are irrelevant. They will do the right thing and avoid committing idolatry irrespective of any intervention by God. The way they present God's potential response, moreover, is striking. Two ways of reading Daniel 3:17 conditionally are (1) "if our God whom we serve is able to deliver us from the furnace of blazing fire and out of your hand, O king, let him deliver us" and (2) "if our God whom we serve is able to deliver us from the furnace of blazing fire and out of your hand, O king, he will deliver us." However, it is also possible to read the sentence declaratively: "There is our God whom we serve; He is able to deliver us from the furnace of blazing fire and out of your hand, O king, he will deliver us." This ambiguity provides an excellent distinction between the perspective of any potential outsider and the insider. For Nebuchadnezzar, the question is a rhetorical one: which non-Babylonian god could possibly undermine his gods or challenge his power and thus rescue these captives? Yet for Daniel's companions, there is no ambiguity as to whether there is a saving God; neither is there any question that they will do the right thing, regardless of how God responds. God's freedom remains intact (v. 18) while the young men remain firm in their commitment to avoid worshiping Nebuchadnezzar's god, even though they know it is a capital offense. Like Esther, they conclude that doing the right thing, whether or not their lives are spared, is more important (Esth 4:16). [Judith]

Nebuchadnezzar's Response, 3:19-23

The author continues to present Nebuchadnezzar as a man of obscene excess. His anger and his orders are so outrageous that bystanders are inadvertently killed. Yet, in contrast to his rage, the three proceed without an additional word. The first example of Nebuchadnezzar's excesses is the description of his histrionic anger. The text literally states, "Nebuchadnezzar was filled with fury and the image of his face changed" (v. 19 A.T.). The word for "image" is the same used for the statue (*ṣĕlēm*) he constructed, linking his unrestrained rage with his own idolatry. The order to heat the furnace seven times its normal temperature makes him appear

Judith

The representation of Nebuchadnezzar as the quintessential tyrant continued in other Jewish texts. The example of Nebuchadnezzar from the book of Judith shows how his name became archetypical of any enemy of the Jewish people. This 2d century BC text (part of the Roman Catholic and Orthodox canons, and part of the Apocrypha for Protestants) also shows a hero/heroine who knows that acting faithfully when faced with the injustice of the state, regardless of whether God will provide rescue, is the right thing to do. Nebuchadnezzar, identified as the emperor of the Assyrian Empire, threatens the Jews of Bethulia in Judah. Judith's heroism saves her people from the onslaught of Nebuchadnezzar's general Holofernes. Her faith is reminiscent of Daniel's and that of his three companions who do not wait for proof of God's presence before they demonstrate their adherence to their traditions. All see meaning in their existence as faithful followers even in the most oppressive of times. The heroine Judith tells her compatriots who are ready to capitulate:

for if he [God] does not choose to help within these five days, he has power to protect us within any time he pleases, or even to destroy us in the presence of our enemies. Do not try to bind the purposes of the Lord our God; for God is not like a human being, to be threatened, nor like a mere mortal, to be won over by pleading. Therefore, while we wait for his deliverance, let us call upon him to help us, and he will hear our voice, if it pleases him. (Jdt 8:15-17)

Here Judith shows that faith in Divine Providence should be contingent neither upon security nor upon freedom. God has indeed been faithful to Israel's ancestors (7:28; 9:2), but ultimately God's will is unfathomable. Judith's community, like the three young men in the furnace, can hope for divine intervention, but cannot compel it. Both texts attest to the inscrutability of God.

For further information, see Daniel Harrington, *Invitation to the Apocrypha* (Grand Rapids MI: Eerdmans, 1999), 27–43.

---

maniacal—as though the increased heat would make a difference in the ability of the furnace to torment and kill his intended victims. Although the three have implied that they will be tested in the furnace and leave the decision of their fate up to God, Nebuchadnezzar acts as though he must fight to get them there. He calls the strongest guards to apprehend them, and he orders that they are to be bound, even though they have no weapons and no defenders. Ironically, these guards are defeated not by their captives, but by the very fire that was prepared to kill these captives and by Nebuchadnezzar's urging that the punishment be enacted quickly. The heat of the tremendous fire kills the king's strongest guards while the reader awaits the fate of the heroes. At this point, it has been demonstrated that God neither extinguished nor lessened the ferocity of the fire. If it killed the bystanders on the outside, what would it do to those within its confines?

Lion from Ishtar Gate

The Ishtar gate, built during the reign of Nebuchadnezzar, was the main entrance to Babylon. Nebuchadnezzar initiated several building projects in the capital city, including the restoration of the temple of Marduk and the construction of the king's palace. The palace, according to Herodotus, was the home of the famous "Hanging Gardens of Babylon."

Lion. Enameled tile and ceramic brick, from the Ishtar Gate, Babylon. Archeological Museum, Istanbul, Turkey. (Credit: Erich Lessing/Art Resource, NY)

The Binding of Isaac

This watercolor by Moshe Mizrachi, a Persian Jew who immigrated to Safed in the late 19th century, depicts the story of the Akedah, the binding of Isaac (Gen 22). The Hebrew inscription at the top of the painting reads, "Remember today, with mercy, the Binding of Isaac." On Rosh Hashanah, the Akedah is read as part of the High Holiday service.

In Jewish belief, divine mercy for Israel often is prompted when God remembers the Akedah. Indeed, the world itself stands because of the merit of Abraham or Isaac alone: "if there were no good deeds in Jacob then Isaac's deeds would suffice" (*Lev. Rab.* 36:5). Similarly, "so when the children of Isaac give way to transgressions . . . recollect for them the binding of their father Isaac and rise from the Throne of Judgment and betake Thee to the Throne of Mercy" (*Lev. Rab.* 29:9). In one midrash, Abraham proclaims to God, "my sons are Hananiah, Mishael, and Azariah" (*Gen. Rab.* 39:3); indeed, Abraham, Isaac, and the

Moshe Mizrachi. *The story of Abraham and Isaac, and of the Angel Halting the Sacrifice.* c. 1880. Painting from Safed, Palestine. Isaac Einhorn Collection. Tel Aviv, Israel. (Credit: Erich Lessing/Art Resource, NY)

three young men are seen as models of faith and obedience since they would rather choose death than disobedience.

See Shalom Spiegel, *The Last Trial*, trans. Judah Goldin (New York: Schocken, 1969; repr., Woodstock VT: Jewish Lights, 1993).

In contrast to the power wielded by Nebuchadnezzar, the men's subordination is indicated by the king's command "to bind" them and by the references to them being "bound" (vv. 20, 21, 23, 24 [the root *kpt* is used in each instance]). Indeed, they are restrained with their own clothing, highlighting the injustice of their impending doom. The author's frequent use of the root *kpt* in a short period may be a recollection of the binding of Isaac (Gen 22), the paradigmatic victim who suffers silently to do God's will. Such a depiction of Isaac was common in rabbinic times; perhaps this text shows knowledge of an early stage of this Akedah tradition. Rabbinic texts also use the root *kpt* to refer to Isaac's binding as well as to the binding of sacrificial animals.[8]

In keeping with the Jews' silence and willingness to be obedient unto death, none of their words are recorded as they are led to their punishment. Indeed, the reader is led to expect that the deaths will in fact occur.[9] Only one verb is used to describe their actions: they "fell down" (*nĕpalû*) into the furnace (v. 23). This verb can also mean to fall (die) in battle. It is interesting that the author uses the same word when Nebuchadnezzar himself says that the populace must "fall down" (in the sense of bow down and worship) to the statue (vv. 5, 6, 7, 10, 11, 15, 23). The contrast is striking; here the young men lie prostrate as devoted servants to God, not as paragons of obeisance to an outrageous king and his idol. The fallen and bound exiles now are poised to show the king the victory of God, as is presented in the next scene. [The Greek Additions to Daniel 3]

The Saving of the Jews and Nebuchadnezzar's Response, 3:24-28

A dramatic reversal of circumstances is evident in the next scene. The Jews are saved, yet the author shows this from the perspective

---

The Greek Additions to Daniel 3

The Greek versions of Daniel include three additions not found in the Masoretic Text, namely, the Prayer of Azariah and the Song of the Three Young Men, Susanna, and Bel and the Dragon. The Prayer of Azariah (vv. 1-22 [or vv. 24-45, following Dan 3:23] and the Song of the Three Young Men (vv. 23-68 [46-90]) are found between Dan 3:23 and 3:24, as one continuous text. Susanna is found in some Greek manuscripts before the book of Daniel and in others at the end; Bel and the Dragon is found after Dan 12:13. Today, these additions are considered as part of the Old Testament Apocrypha (in Protestant Bibles) or as part of the Deuterocanonical books (in Catholic and Orthodox Christian Bibles).

The identification of the original language (or languages) of the Prayer of Azariah and the Song of the Three Young Men is debated; it is possible that they reflect a Semitic original. The prayer and song (considered to be one addition) include Azariah's words of praise to God while he walks about in the fire (Pr Azar 1-22 [24-45]), a prose insert describing the angel's actions in stopping the flames (Sg Three 23-27 [46-50]), and the poetic praise of God by the three for their deliverance (Sg Three 28-68 [51-90]). Azariah's words evidence a theology of God's justice which holds that Israel suffers exile because of their sins, yet they express the hope that God will continue to show mercy, echoing similar hymns of praise (Pss 103; 136; 148). The Song of the Three Young Men concludes with the specific recognition that God delivered the three near-martyrs from death:

Bless the Lord, Hananiah, Azariah, and Mishael, sing praise to him and highly exalt him for ever; for he has rescued us from Hades and saved us from the power of death, and delivered us from the midst of the burning fiery furnace, from the midst of the fire he has delivered us. (Sg Three 66 [88])

In this composition we find another example of Nebuchadnezzar being presented as the embodiment of political evil: "You have handed us over to our enemies, lawless and hateful rebels, and to an unjust king, the most wicked in all the world" (Pr Azar 9 [32]). Some scholars (Collins, Hartman and Di Lella, Harrington) suggest that this reference is a cipher for Antiochus IV, the cruel Seleucid king who persecuted the Jewish people and whose reign forms the context of Daniel's visions (7–12).

John Collins, *Daniel: A Commentary on the Book of Daniel* (Hermeneia; Minneapolis: Fortress, 1993), 200.

Louis Hartman and Alexander Di Lella, "Daniel," *The New Jerome Biblical Commentary*, ed. Raymond Brown, Joseph Fitzmyer, and Roland Murphy (Englewood Cliffs NJ: Prentice Hall, 1990), 412.

Daniel Harrington, *Invitation to the Apocrypha* (Grand Rapids MI: Eerdmans 1999), 111–12.

For further study see these sources:
Randall Chesnutt and Judith Newman, "Prayers in the Apocrypha and Pseudepigrapha," in *Prayer from Alexander to Constantine: a Critical Anthology*, ed. Mark Kiley (New York: Routledge, 1997), 38–42.
Carey Moore, *Daniel, Esther, and Jeremiah: the Additions* (AB 44; Garden City NY: Doubleday & Co., 1977).
Carey Moore, "Daniel, Additions to," *ABD*, ed. David Noel Freedman, 6 vols. (New York: Doubleday & Co., 1992), 2:18–28.
Daniel Smith-Christopher "The Additions to Daniel," *NIB*, ed. Leander E. Keck, 12 vols. (Nashville: Abingdon, 2003), 7:153–94.
Marti Steussy, *Gardens in Babylon: Narrative and Faith in the Greek Legends of Daniel* (Society of Biblical Literature Dissertation Series 141; Atlanta: Scholars Press, 1993).

Israel's Redemption

God's promise of redemption for Israel is similarly reflected in this quotation from Isaiah: "When you pass through the waters, I will be with you; and through the rivers, they shall not overwhelm you; when you walk through fire you shall not be burned, and the flame shall not consume you" (Isa 43:2).

of the tyrant who sentenced them to their fate. The physical postures of both Nebuchadnezzar and Daniel's friends are changed, an angelic being appears, and the three come to no harm. [Israel's Redemption] The author shows that fidelity to God's commands is rewarded, and, at least in words, the foreign king comes to recognize the God of Israel. Nebuchadnezzar acknowledges that God was the savior of Shadrach, Meshach, and Abednego and promotes them; yet although he is mollified and the exiles are safe, his decrees remain despotic.

The words used to indicate Nebuchadnezzar's change of outlook are noteworthy. He is "astonished" (*tĕwah*, v. 24), a word that also connotes being alarmed or startled. In addition, the word usually translated "rose up quickly" (NRSV) (*bĕhitbĕhālâ*, v. 24) can also connote dismay and terror (Dan 5:9; 6:18 [6:19 MT]).[10] Before the saving outcome becomes clear, the amazed and frantic king asks a bizarre question. He requests a confirmation from his ministers that they indeed threw the three bound captives into the fire. When they assent, he contradicts them (vv. 24-25), relating that he sees his prisoners unbound and accompanied by an unknown fourth being. Not only are the three unharmed, but also the additional figure attracts special interest. Nebuchadnezzar literally remarks that the fourth "has the appearance of a son of the gods" (v. 25; "has the appearance of a god," NRSV). The choice of this phrase for Nebuchadnezzar is particularly appropriate given that it may be understood in two ways: either in a polytheistic sense, namely, as a divine being of a larger pantheon, or it may refer to an angel. For the idolatrous Nebuchadnezzar, the appropriate connotation would be the polytheistic sense; for the original reader, however, the phrase would indicate an angel. [Divine Beings] Later in the account, Nebuchadnezzar will recognize the rescuer as an angel; but for now, Nebuchadnezzar's astonished exclamation receives no response from his Babylonian attendants; they appear dumbfounded. The angel mysteriously disappears, perhaps because its role as the victims' protector is finished.

After this recognition, Nebuchadnezzar demands that his captives step out of the yet raging fire. Because they do not exit the kiln until they are summoned, they continue to belie the

Divine Beings

AΩ In Hebrew, the word "*bēn*," translated "son," means "member of the class/group." Hence, a "son of a prophet" refers to a prophet or a member of the prophetic guild; a "son of God" refers to a member of the Divine Council, or Heavenly Court wherein God makes judgments concerning the affairs of human beings. These divine beings or members of the Divine Council may act as God's messengers or agents (Ps 89:7 [89:8, MT]). They came to be equated with the "*mal'ākîm*," or "angels." There are several places where the Septuagint (LXX) makes this substitution. For example, for the Aramaic of Dan 3:25, the OG reads, "angel of God" for "son of God" (3:92 OG). Similar substitutions are found in the LXX of Gen 6:2, Deut 32:8 ("angels" for "sons of Israel"), and Job 1:6, 2:1, and 38:7.

Chaldeans' accusations that they disregard the king's laws. In contrast to Nebuchadnezzar's previous commanding words, however, the king now identifies the Jews not as his own subjects, but as "servants of the Most High God" (v. 26). When they step out, the reader is now privy to the perspective of the Babylonian attendants. They, like Nebuchadnezzar, see that the captives are not harmed, and the very clothing that was used to bind the prisoners now serves as testimony to their complete protection as "the fire had not had any power over the bodies of those men; the hair of their heads was not singed, their tunics were not harmed, and not even the smell of fire came from them" (v. 27). [Persian Clothing]

Although Nebuchadnezzar blesses God, his idolatry is still apparent, as evidenced by his word choice as well as by his subsequent decree. He thrice identifies God as the God of Shadrach, Meshach, and Abednego or as "their God," never really acknowledging the God of Israel as his own. This occurs despite the fact that he now correctly refers to God's "angel" and not to a "god" or "son of god" as their rescuer (v. 28). [Gabriel and the Three Youths] It is noteworthy that the same king who ordered the Jews' worship of the idol is now the one who praises the captives for their refusal to commit idolatry. The author uses four distinct phrases to impeach the king's praise. Nebuchadnezzar recognizes that the three "disobeyed the king's command," "yielded up their bodies," and refused either to "serve" or "worship" any god he could propose (v. 28). Their disobedience (lit., "change" [*sannîw*]) of the king's order, which was tantamount to defiance, is contrasted with the king's "change" of face (*'eštannî* [v. 19]) and the lack of "change" on their clothing (*šĕnô* [v. 27]) or bodies. The specific reference to "yielding up their bodies" is unique in

Persian Clothing

This silver statue of a Persian dignitary from the court of Artaxerxes I (464–424 BC) shows distinctive Persian dress.

Scholars note the possibility that the three terms that correspond to the list of the youths' clothing ("their tunics, their trousers, their hats, and their other garments" [Dan 3:21]) have Persian equivalents. The many Persian words in the Dan 1–6 point to a probable time of composition during the period of Persian rule of the former Babylonian captives.

John Collins, *Daniel: A Commentary on the Book of Daniel* (Hermeneia; Minneapolis: Fortress, 1993), 188–89.

Persian dignitary dressed in Persian trousers and Kyrbasia cap (dress of a Traveller). Silver statuette from the court of Artaxerxes I (464–424 BC). Vorderasiatisches Museum, Staatliche Museen zu Berlin, Berlin, Germany. (Credit: Erich Lessing/Art Resource, NY)

Gabriel and the Three Youths

Most rabbinic texts identify the angel who rescued the three youths with Gabriel, the same angel who appears in Dan 8:15-17 and 9:21. According to one tradition, Yorkami, the angel of hail, offered to quench the fire, but Gabriel emphasized that the miracle would be more arresting if he, the angel of fire, would protect the three while simultaneously increasing the heat outside of the furnace. The Talmud gives a moving presentation of the three men's worth by highlighting their nobility, even in face of Gabriel's intervention: "the three men made it possible for the angel to withstand the fire of the furnace, and not the reverse" (*y. Šabb.* 6). They represent the righteous of humankind who are even "greater than the angels"; thus Gabriel followed them as a disciple a master (*Pesiq. Rab.* 35:160b).

See Louis Ginzberg, *Legends of the Jews*, trans. Henrietta Szold, 7 vols. (Philadelphia: The Jewish Publication Society of America, 1968), 6:417–18.

the Hebrew Bible and seems particularly appropriate for this text. [Martyrdom in Jewish Tradition] Earlier, the three informed Nebuchadnezzar that they refused his command to "serve" (*pālĕḥîn*, v. 18) the idol that he had commanded they "worship" (*yisgud*, v. 6); now the same words are used in Nebuchadnezzar's blessing to express the fidelity of Shadrach, Meshach, and Abednego who did *not* serve and did *not* worship the idol (*lāʾ-yiplĕḥûn wĕlāʾ-yisgĕdûn*, v. 28). In Daniel 7, the seer's vision illustrates true service—all nations will "serve" the one like a Son of Man and all rulers will "serve" the everlasting kingdom (7:14, 27).

Nebuchadnezzar's Decree and Promotion of Shadrach, Meshach, and Abednego, 3:29-30

By not considering the possibility of rescinding his command, Nebuchadnezzar follows the pattern also seen in the account of the derided Ahasuerus of the book of Esther and also by King Darius in the book of Daniel. Instead, he issues a new decree that will put to death anyone who speaks "derisively" (*šālû*, NRSV "blasphemy") against the God of these Jews (v. 29). By this proclamation,

---

Martyrdom in Jewish Tradition

Scholars agree that Dan 3 and Dan 6 are the best examples of precursors to Jewish martyr accounts. They are not fully representative of the genre because, to be sure, the heroes do not die. One of the earliest examples of a developed martyr text in Jewish literature is 2 Macc 7. Seven sons and their mother courageously face torture and death rather than succumb to eating "unlawful swine's flesh" (2 Macc 7:1). Like the three Jewish men who refuse Nebuchadnezzar's commands, they resolutely tell Antiochus IV, "For we are ready to die rather than transgress the laws of our ancestors" (2 Macc 7:2). Martyrdom was seen as bearing witness to God's justice and providing testimony against the evil of tyrants. The Jewish martyrs show unflinching faith that God will ultimately triumph against such enemies. As the youngest brother of 2 Maccabees states to Antiochus, "For our brothers after enduring a brief suffering have drunk of ever-flowing life, under God's covenant; but you, by the judgment of God, will receive just punishment for your arrogance" (2 Macc 7:36). The reference to martyrs enjoying "ever-flowing life" finds a precursor in Dan 12:2, where we find that the faithful will rise to "everlasting life."

Early Jewish writings preserve variations of this story of the mother (called either Hannah, Miriam, or Nachtum) and seven sons, placing the account in the days of either Antiochus or in the days of the Roman emperors. One midrash makes the direct link between the suffering of Hananiah, Mishael, and Azariah with that of the mother Miriam and her seven sons in the time of Roman persecution. The emperor (most likely Hadrian, who persecuted Jews after the Bar Kokhba revolt), like Nebuchadnezzar, demands prostration to an idol. When the youngest son enters into a reproachful dialogue with the king, he retorts, "why does He not deliver you out of my hand in the same manner that He rescued Hananiah, Mishael and Azariah from the hands of Nebuchadnezzar?" The son responds, "Hananiah, Mishael, and Azariah were worthy men, and king Nebuchadnezzar was deserving that a miracle should be performed through him. You, however, are undeserving; and as for ourselves, our lives are forfeit to heaven" (*Lam. Rab.* 1:16, 50). Another midrash continues to make a link with the Akedah (binding of Isaac) tradition: When the mother embraces her youngest son before his death she implores him to relate her superior sacrifice to Abraham: "Thus says my mother, 'Do not preen yourself [on your righteousness], saying I built an altar and offered up my son, Isaac.' Behold, our mother built seven altars and offered up seven sons in one day, Yours was only a test, but mine was in earnest" (*Lam. Rab.* 1:16, 50. See also *b. Giṭ 57b* and *Pesiq. Rab.* 44:4).

Nebuchadnezzar does not, in fact, protect the Jewish people from any future charges that they are in defiance of the king's decree to worship the statue, and thus the potential despotism of such a capricious man and of "the Chaldeans" is still present. Additionally, now other individuals are potentially at risk of death if they do not comply. Nebuchadnezzar punctuates his new threat with the outrageous phrase used to describe the punishment for non-compliance. Concerning any perpetrator of

Cylinder of Nebuchadnezzar II, southern Iraq, Neo-Babylonian dynasty, 604–562 BC. British Museum, London, Great Britain. (Credit: Erich Lessing/Art Resource, NY)

derisive speech, Nebuchadnezzar declares: "[they] shall be torn limb from limb, and their houses laid in ruins" (v. 29); these are the same words used to threaten the Chaldeans when they could not interpret Nebuchadnezzar's dream (2:5), showing that Nebuchadnezzar remains tyrannical, even to his own people.[11] At the same time, however, the king does promote Hananiah, Mishael, and Azariah, assuring the reader that the young men are at least temporarily safe. As occurs at the end of Daniel 1 and Daniel 2, the threats to the heroes in the beginning of each tale can be contrasted with their promotions at each story's end. Those at risk because they were accused of not following the law now become responsible for continuing to enforce Babylonian law (v. 30). As we have seen, however, Nebuchadnezzar's tyranny continues, and terrible decrees fill his law books. Promotions do not mean that all is well in the Diaspora.

This is the last we hear of Daniel's three friends. Unlike tales of other heroes that include a reference to their future long-term security (such as Mordecai in Esth 10:2-3 and Daniel in Dan 6:28 [6:29 MT]), a narrative gap is created that prompts speculation about the future of Hananiah, Mishael, and Azariah. The fifteenth-century AD Jewish commentator Abarbanel understands that the three men still did not feel safe in Nebuchadnezzar's kingdom and left his jurisdiction. The narrative remains open-ended, thus enabling readers to imagine themselves in the same position as the three heroes, that is, with the experience or memory of a dangerous past, a temporarily safe present, but also an uncertain future. [The Fate of the Three Young Men]

The Fate of the Three Young Men

The Talmud considers various possibilities of the fate of the three youths: "Whither did the Rabbis [the three men] go? Rab said: They died through an evil eye; Samuel said: They drowned in the spittle; R. Johanan said: They went up to Palestine, married and begat sons and daughters" (*b. Sanh.* 93a). The evil eye refers to the awe or malice of other people or nations who were struck by the importance of the miracle. The spittle refers to the evil intentions of other nations.

CONNECTIONS

"You shall not make for yourselves an idol, whether in the form of anything that is in heaven above, or that is on the earth beneath, or that is in the water under the earth. You shall not bow down to them or worship them" (Exod 20:4-5). The biblical commandment to avoid idolatry is well known, yet for many who live in a secular culture it may seem irrelevant. The worshiping of idols, however, was never the mere worshiping of wood and stone, but rather the acceptance of values that were symbolized and justified by the religious, economic, and governmental ideals connected with it. The gods of Canaan, as Israel saw them, justified a system that valued economic prosperity over all other priorities. Although no one would question the necessity of insuring crops and fields, or the fertility of livestock and of the human population, Israel painfully learned that when they lost sight of the one God of Israel and worshiped Baal and Asherah, the Canaanite gods of fertility, they lost everything that truly mattered. Many human injustices and cruelties could be justified in the name of fertility and security. Could the Israelites ignore the plea of the widow and the cry of the orphan in order to secure their future? Israel's commandments taught that the priority of the dispossessed could never be abrogated. Could the king in Israel expropriate a farmer's land for his own protection against perceived threats, as did Ahab with Naboth (1 Kgs 21)? The prophet Elijah unequivocally condemned such a practice.

The biblical prohibition concerning idolatry may thus be likened to a condemnation of any regime that oppresses people as well as its supporters. In the Hebrew Scriptures, the practitioners of idolatry could be either native Israelites, foreigners who brought their attractive cults to Israel, or invaders who captured or exiled their subjects. It is against this background that the author constructs the account of Nebuchadnezzar's statue. Whether Nebuchadnezzar is presented as requiring the worship of the statue because it represents him, Babylon itself, or one of its gods, his intentions are clear: he demands the acceptance of his policies and way of life by all his subjects. The author presents Nebuchadnezzar as the head of an empire that was successful by any material, economic, or political standard. He conquered thousands of peoples around him, maintained a disciplined and fearless army, amassed great wealth by imposing tribute, and exiled the most skilled of the conquered peoples to his own land. The conquering, exiling, forced servitude,

Elijah

Israel could be as critical of its own kings as it was of its foreign oppressors. The prophet Elijah battled the injustices of the royal family in Samaria, including King Ahab and Queen Jezebel. This painting portrays Elijah's flight to the desert when he escaped from Jezebel's pursuit. The angel roused Elijah and gave him strength (cf. Dan 10:10). The first appearance of a celestial being in the book of Daniel occurs in this narrative of the three youths in the fiery furnace. Other heavenly beings appear throughout the book, offering interpretation and protection.

Godfrey Kneller. 1646–1723. *Elijah and the Angel.* Tate Gallery, London, Great Britain. (Credit: Tate Gallery, London/Art Resource, NY)

and crushing of other people's cultures was justified by Nebuchadnezzar's gods. In requiring the three Jews to worship his idol, he demands a tangible sign that they will not, in even the smallest way, refuse to bow down to his regime, extracting such public acceptance with no exceptions. He proposes death as the only alternative.

It might be easy for the modern reader to dismiss the importance of these three exiles because the caricature of the king, his bizarre excesses, and the grand proportions of the fiery furnace challenge our sense of reality. But the inclusion of their story in a biblical book canonical for Jews and Christians prompts us to search for its enduring message. It is difficult to know when this story of the three young men in the fiery furnace was first composed. One can see its relevance, however, in the various periods that have been proposed for its original composition and its inclusion in the final form of the book of Daniel. Babylonian hegemony did not last long after Babylon's invasion of Judah, but their Persian and Greek successors depended on Jewish submission in many governmental and cultural policies. The faithfulness of the Jews in standing up against idolatry served as courageous examples to remain obedient to God in a dominant and successful culture, whether it be in the time of the Babylonian conquest and its aftermath, in the time of the Persian Empire, or while under Greek rule.

It is not only under the rule of despots that such stories can encourage the human spirit. Although any given generation in a particular country may be spared the ravages of war and tyranny, examples of oppression, to be sure, frequently abound in any society. In every generation, each individual must decide whether to open his or her eyes to the oppression that occurs when a society "worships" domination and prosperity—a type of worship that leads to the silencing of the marginalized. It is often easier to obey orders and follow the ways of society than to critique it, just as all of Nebuchadnezzar's officials blindly bowed to the statue. Hananiah, Mishael, and Azariah refused to worship the idol—that is, they repudiated the status quo. As recipients of Israel's legacy, which never excluded economic and political life from God's judgment, they knew they could not participate in the injustice that the idol represented. We might imagine that such teachings as recorded in Psalm 72, for example, inspired them. This psalm encapsulates the role of the just king whose very source of justice is God, the One to whom all other nations should bow:

Persian Model Chariot
This extraordinary model chariot (Achaemenid Persian, 5th–4th C. BC), fashioned of gold, attests to the wealth Persia enjoyed after its conquest of Babylon.

Gold model chariot from the Oxus treasure. 5th–4th C. BC. Achaemenid Persian. From the region of Takht-i Kuwad, Tadjikistan. British Museum, London, Great Britain. (Credit: Erich Lessing/Art Resource, NY)

For he delivers the needy when they call,
    the poor and those who have no helper.
He has pity on the weak and the needy,
    and saves the lives of the needy.
From oppression and violence he redeems their life;
    and precious is their blood in his sight. (Ps 72:12-14)[12]

In saying "no" to the idol and to Nebuchadnezzar, the three attested to the king's injustice and expressed their faith that God's justice will necessarily come, in God's own time. [A Passion for Justice] By not cowering, they witnessed to possibilities of a community of justice.

In recent years, two Americans have spoken about how the story of Shadrach, Meshach, and Abednego resonated with them as they

A Passion for Justice

The tradition of Israel taught that faithfulness to God necessitates "a passion for justice" and a readiness to wait for the Lord's judgment upon all things. James Walsh explains the centrality of these two aspects of Israelite belief. If one neglects the pursuit of justice, God "is reduced to the status of the gods of the nations round about, a mere legitimator of an unjust status quo"; at the same time, if one "allows his own grievances to become central to his self-understanding . . . [one has] in effect embraced the spirit of self-absolutization and reliance on one's own power that is the well-spring of injustice. It is idolatry" (54). The willingness of the three young men to sacrifice their lives if necessary ultimately witnesses to their understanding that the world is designed with purpose and meaning by a just God who will defeat oppressive powers and the gods—or structures—that sustain them. Their act allows them to cooperate with God's plan for peace and justice.

The narratives of faithfulness found in Dan 1–6 culminate in the apocalyptic vision of Dan 7. Walsh explains:

The writer tries to communicate an understanding of what is happening to the people by imaging the future that will come out of present persecution, and he does this by going back to the foundational images of Israel's existence. [YHWH] will judge—indeed, has already passed judgment—and that judgment means destruction for the persecutor. It also means that dominion (*exousia*) and sovereignty are conferred on the faithful people. This outcome is assured: the judgment takes place in solemn session of the heavenly court; the human figure in whom the faithful see themselves and God's intentions for them has access to the judge of all. (55)

For Christians, the import of this vision continues in the New Testament where Jesus is shown to be the heir to the sovereignty of God. God offers to humanity the opportunity to participate in the transformation of the world,

Because he wishes to subject all things to the Son . . . this transformation of all things has to do with people having enough to eat and living in peace . . . and being happy. It has to do with freedom from oppression . . . [and] with what cannot be imagined except in general terms and by negation of the multiple ways human sinfulness devises to be destructive. (57–58)

James Walsh, "The Lordship of Yahweh; the Lordship of Jesus," in *Above Every Name: The Lordship of Christ and Social Systems*, ed. Thomas Clarke (Woodstock Studies 5; Ramsey NJ: Paulist Press, 1980), 35–65.

experienced racial prejudice and found the courage fight against it. The actor John Franklin Sawyer, who played a former slave in the film *Shadrach*, recalled his own experiences with racism in an interview with the *New York Times*. The movie *Shadrach*, based on the short story by William Styron, illustrates the profound influence a former slave's life of dignity and kindness in face of unbearable suffering had upon a boy in the American South. The making of the movie evoked John Sawyer's memories of his own experience as an African American in a land riddled with prejudice. The reporter writes,

Like Shadrach, Meshach and Abednego walking unscathed from Nebuchadnezzar's fiery furnace, John Sawyer believes he was spared and destined to achieve: teacher in the 1920's, Montgomery's lone black letter carrier in the 1930's, Navy seaman ("though they kept us on land") protesting military segregation in World War II, frustrated spectator during the Montgomery bus boycott in the 1950's and the civil rights era that followed, and an apparent anachronism insisting on gentleness at a time of raging incivility.[13]

Martin Luther King Jr.

Martin Luther King Jr., who championed nonviolent civil disobedience, wrote about the refusal of the three young men to worship the idol, seeing them as models of courage when faced with an unjust law. King explains,

> One who breaks an unjust law must do so openly, lovingly, and with a willingness to accept the penalty. I submit that an individual who breaks a law that conscience tells him is unjust and who willingly accepts the penalty of imprisonment in order to arouse the conscience of the community over its injustice, is in reality expressing the highest respect for law. . . . Of course, there is nothing new about this kind of civil disobedience. It was evidenced sublimely in the refusal of Shadrach, Meshach and Abednego to obey the laws of Nebuchadnezzar, on the ground that a higher moral law was at stake. It was practiced superbly by the early Christians, who were willing to face hungry lions and the excruciating pain of chopping blocks rather than submit to certain unjust laws of the Roman Empire.

(Credit: Barclay Burns)

Martin Luther King, Jr., "Letter from a Birmingham Jail," 16 April 1963, Historical Text Archive, <http://www.historicaltextarchive.com/sections.php?op=viewarticle&artid=40#> (14 July 2005).

John Sawyer protested against racism by his presence and quiet heroism over many decades. The victory given to the three heroes in Daniel 3 was dramatic; the ones we witness may indeed take decades of action on the part of many—both leaders and followers.

Similarly, Rev. Warren Ray Jr., pastor of the second Free Mission Baptist Church of New Orleans, found an inspirational parallel in both the courageous actions of Martin Luther King Jr. and of Shadrach, Meshach, and Abednego as he gave his sermon on the occasion of the thirteenth annual federal holiday honoring Dr. King's birthday. He states,

> Sometimes the problems are so subtle and some are so naïve that they say we don't have a problem . . . [but] all of us—white, black, women and men, heterosexual and homosexual, native-born and foreign-born—have a responsibility to help in the building of a new institution and a new society in which all men are really equal.[14]

Finding inspiration from the biblical story of Shadrach, Meshach, and Abednego's refusal to bow to Nebuchadnezzar's statue, Ray compared Dr. King's protests against governmental policy that segregated African Americans to the refusal of the three to bow to Nebuchadnezzar's laws. King's leadership in the boycott of Montgomery, Alabama's businesses led to the end of segregation on public buses and culminated in a national civil rights movement. Dr. King paid with his life. His legacy, like that of the three

Jews of the book of Daniel, however, is eternal. As one of Ray's colleagues, Rev. Zebadee Bridges, said at the same service,

> Today, politics is all about me . . . [but civil rights does not mean] . . . getting all you can . . . it means serving others, helping others get their rights, too. God has placed us here so that we can serve, and every one of us is responsible for one another.[15]

The heroism of the three men, their solidarity with each other, and their defiant refusal to capitulate to Nebuchadnezzar's demands can inspire anyone who recognizes and sympathizes with injustice, isolation, pain, and poverty in the human condition and who believes in the truth of this famous saying from the Mishnah: "In the place where there are no men, be a *mensch*" (*m. ʾAbot* 2:6).

NOTES

[1] John Collins, *Daniel: A Commentary on the Book of Daniel* (Hermeneia; Minneapolis: Fortress, 1993), 181.

[2] See also Esth 9:3 and Ezra 8:36. The term is used throughout Dan 6.

[3] For evidence of cultural contacts, including use of various musical instruments in both Mediterranean and Mesopotamian cultures, see T. C. Mitchell, "The Music of the Old Testament Reconsidered," *Palestine Exploration Quarterly* 124/2 (July–December 1992): 124–43; and Edwin M. Yamauchi, "Greece and Babylon Revisited," in *To Understand the Scriptures: Essays in Honor of William H. Shea*, ed. David Merling (Berrien Springs MI: Andrews University Press, 1997), 127–35.

[4] Ivor H. Jones, "Music and Musical Instruments, " *ABD*, ed. David Noel Freedman (New York: Doubleday & Co., 1992), 4:938–39.

[5] *b. Yoma* 9b.

[6] James Montgomery, A *Critical and Exegetical Commentary on the Book of Daniel* (ICC; Edinburgh: T & T Clark, 1927), 204.

[7] Collins, *Daniel*, 187.

[8] Marcus Jastrow, *A Dictionary of the Targumim, the Talmud Babli and Yerushalmi, and the Midrashic Literature* (New York: Traditional Press, n.d.), 662–63.

[9] Danna Nolan Fewell, *Circle of Sovereignty: A Story of Stories in Daniel 1–6* (JSOTSup 72; Bible and Literature Series 20; Sheffield: Almond Press, 1988), 77.

[10] John Goldingay, *Daniel* (WBC 30; Dallas: Word Books, 1989), 34, 66.

[11] Other commentators see the character of Nebuchadnezzar as more benign. See for example, James Montgomery, *Critical and Exegetical Commentary*, 89; P. R. Davies, "Reading Daniel Sociologically," in *The Book of Daniel in the Light of New Findings*, ed. A. S. van der Woude (Bibliotheca ephemeridum theologicarum lovaniensium 106; Leuven, Belgium: Leuven University Press, 1993), 358; and W. Sibley Towner, *Daniel* (*Int*; Atlanta: John Knox Press, 1984), 56–7.

[12] For discussion of Ps 72, see Moshe Weinfeld, *Social Justice in Ancient Israel and in the Ancient Near East* (Jerusalem: Magnes/Minneapolis: Fortress, 1995), 215–17.

[13] Paul Delaney, "Survivor of Many Tribulations, Including Stardom," *New York Times*, 27 September 1998, 2–11.

[14] Mark Schleifstein, "King's Dream Eludes Us Still, New Orleans Pastors Say," *New Orleans Times Picayune*, 18 January 1999, A-1.

[15] Ibid.

THE DREAM OF
THE GREAT TREE:
INTERPLAY OF
PERSPECTIVES

Daniel 4:1-37 (3:31–4:34 MT)

COMMENTARY

As seen in our examination of Daniel 3, the account of Nebuchadnezzar's response to God's rescue of the three youths in the fiery furnace indicated aspects of the king's bifurcated character. One the one hand, he praised the "God of Shadrach, Meshach, and Abednego"; on the other hand, Nebuchadnezzar continued his tyranny by decreeing that he would "tear to pieces" anyone who would speak derisively against their God, thus showing the emptiness of his understanding. This dual presentation invites questions about Nebuchadnezzar's future behavior. Will his praise of God translate into just behavior, or will his unpredictability continue to prove dangerous?

The account of Nebuchadnezzar's dream of the great tree (Dan 4) probes the nature of Nebuchadnezzar's character and explores God's concern for the just exercise of human power. By using this dream account as the last episode from Nebuchadnezzar's life, the author modulates the king's legacy. He is no longer the invincible conqueror; he is a subject to God's will. The last words Nebuchadnezzar speaks prove his subordination: "the Most High has sovereignty over the kingdom of mortals and gives it to whom he will" (4:25, 32 [4:22, 29 MT]). As we will show, however, this submission consists of Nebuchadnezzar's defeat, not of his transformation. With words, Nebuchadnezzar ultimately recognizes God's power over earthly sovereigns, but he remains blind to its implications. Indeed, Nebuchadnezzar's words and actions display a significant range of his ability to exercise power, but little change in his character. First a self-congratulatory emperor, he becomes a frightened man upon receiving the dream. The emperor who boasts of his great accomplishments loses not only his kingdom but also must leave his place in society itself. Upon completion of his exile, he rejoins the human community, praising "the Most High" and "the king of Heaven"; his recognition of God, nevertheless, is incomplete. His words of praise ultimately say more about Nebuchadnezzar himself than they do about the God of Israel. Remaining obsessed with power, Nebuchadnezzar proclaims that his sovereignty is greater than any experienced previously. Ultimately, the author uses this ambiguous presentation of Nebuchadnezzar to underscore that God is indeed the final victor over tyrants, and that Jewish life, even under the rule of foreign kings, would continue despite the sudden and unpredictable challenges to security and even to life itself.

Form Reveals Duplicity: The King's Letter vs. the Entire Narrative

The depiction of Nebuchadnezzar's cruelty, as presented in Daniel 3, prepares the reader to understand his arrogance and intransigence as shown in Daniel 4. It is possible that originally, distinct traditions of Nebuchadnezzar's dream and his punishment account for the multiple perspectives that now constitute Daniel 4. The Masoretic text and the Old Greek text of Daniel 4–6 differ substantially, and Daniel 4 has parallels with 4QPrayer of Nabonidus (4Q242) and with a fragment of Megasthenes (a Greek historian from Ionia who wrote c. 340–282 BC); this evidence suggests that Daniel 4–6 existed in earlier forms.[1] Some scholars have detailed a proposed original structure of Daniel 4; others evaluate its sources, but ultimately any definite reconstruction remains elusive.[2] It is more fruitful to explore the final form of Daniel 4, which appears purposely designed to showcase Nebuchadnezzar's pride, to underscore God's trustworthy revelation to the hero, and to emphasize God's sovereignty. [Prayer of Nabonidus]

The author constructs two accounts of Nebuchadnezzar's dream of the great tree. One presentation of the dream is given completely from Nebuchadnezzar's perspective in the form of a public letter, addressed to all his subjects. This letter consists of two broad sections: (1) Nebuchadnezzar's recitation of his dream, found in 4:1-18 = 3:31–4:15 MT (or, as explained below, 4:1-19a = 3:31–4:16a MT) and (2) Nebuchadnezzar's description of his restoration, found in 4:34-37 = 4:31-34 MT. Sandwiched between these two parts of the letter, another perspective is given in a lengthy narrative, which consists of two presentations: (a) Daniel's dream interpretation, found in 4:19-27 = 4:16-24 MT (or 4:19b-

Prayer of Nabonidus

The Prayer of Nabonidus (4Q242), a 1st century BC text from Qumran, speaks of the disease, exile (in Teima), prayers, and recovery of the Babylonian king Nabonidus, who is healed by God after consulting with an anonymous Jewish seer. In addition, Nabonidus is instructed to compose a letter, proclaiming his good news. These traditions share commonalities not only with Dan 4 but also with other Babylonian texts, namely, the Nabonidus Chronicle, the Verse Account of Nabonidus, and the Harran Inscriptions of Nabonidus (H2).

The Prayer of Nabonidus reads as follows:

The words of the p[ra]yer which Nabonidus, king of [Baby]lon, [the great] king, prayed [when he was smitten] with a bad disease by the decree of G[o]d in Teima. [I, Nabonidus, with a bad disease] was smitten for seven years and sin[ce G]od set [his face on me, he healed me] and as for my sin, he remitted it. A diviner (he was a Jew fr[om among the exiles) came to me and said]:

"Pro[cla]im and write to give honour and exal[tatio]n to the name of G[od Most High," and I wrote as follows]: "I was smitten by a b[ad] disease in Teima [by the decree of the Most High God]. For seven years [I] was praying [to] the gods of silver and gold [bronze, iron], wood, stone, clay, since [I thoug]ht that th[ey were] gods . . . ."

Scholars suggest that the author of Daniel was familiar with this prayer (either by oral tradition or by a written exemplar), but identified the seer as Daniel and used the name of the better-known king, Nebuchadnezzar.

John Collins, "Prayer of Nabonidus," in *Qumran Cave 4, XVII, Parabiblical Texts, Part 3*, ed. George Brooke et al. (Discoveries in the Judaean Desert 22; Oxford: Clarendon Press, 1996), 85–87.

Esther Eshel, "Possible Sources of the Book of Daniel," in *The Book of Daniel: Composition and Reception*, ed. John Collins and Peter Flint, 2 vols. (Supplements to Vetus Testamentum 83; Leiden: Brill, 2001), 2:387–94; Peter Flint, "The Daniel Tradition at Qumran," in *The Book of Daniel*, 2:329–67.

27 = 4:16b-24 MT as explained below) and (b) the author's description of the dream and the king's punishment, found in 4:28-33 = 4:25-30 MT.

This structure allows the author to construct two implied groups—the recipients of Nebuchadnezzar's letter alone and the readers of the entire account. The recipients of Nebuchadnezzar's letter alone receive a misleading view of a crucially important event in their sovereign's life. In contrast, the readers of the entire account see all perspectives of the dream: that of Nebuchadnezzar, that of Daniel, and that of the author of the entire account. A comparison of the information Nebuchadnezzar presents about himself in his letter to his subjects with the material known to the reader of the entire account underscores the king's inability to understand God's design. The author, who crafts all of these presentations, contrasts Nebuchadnezzar's self-importance and lack of understanding of his punishment with Daniel's superior wisdom. The readers of the entire account find not only a confirmation of the sovereignty of God but also are shown the importance of caring for one another. [Outline of Daniel 4] Because the author depicts Daniel as calling upon Nebuchadnezzar to repent by giving charity to the poor, this particular commandment is shown to be of great concern for our author—that the exiles in the Diaspora care for each other in face of oppression.

Outline of Daniel 4

 ### Nebuchadnezzar's recitation of his dream
Nebuchadnezzar's Epistolary Preface, 4:1-3 (3:31-33 MT)
Nebuchadnezzar's Request for Dream Interpretation, 4:4-9 (4:1-6 MT)
Nebuchadnezzar's Description of the Dream, 4:10-12 (4:7-9 MT)
Nebuchadnezzar's Account of the Watcher's Words, Dan 4:13-17 (4:10-14 MT)
Nebuchadnezzar's Second Request for Interpretation and Daniel's Reaction, 4:18 (4:15 MT)

Daniel's dream interpretation
Ambiguous words, 4:19a (4:16a MT)
Daniel's Cautious Response, 4:19b (4:16b MT)
Daniel's Description of the Dream and Its Significance, 4:20-26 (4:17-23 MT)
Call for Repentance, 4:27 (4:24 MT)

The author's description of the dream and of the king's punishment
The Author's Account of Nebuchadnezzar's Hubris and Heaven's Declaration of Punishment,
    Dan 4:28-30 (4:25-27 MT)
The Voice from Heaven, 4:31-32 (4:28-29 MT)
The Author's Description of Nebuchadnezzar's Punishment, 4:33 (4:30 MT)

Nebuchadnezzar's description of his restoration
The Completion of Nebuchadnezzar's Letter, 4:34-37 (4:31-34 MT)

Babylonian New Year

The akitu (New Year) festival was cele-
brated by Mesopotamia followers of
the god Marduk in the month of Nisan.
It included processions with statues,
declarations of faithfulness by the king,
offerings of prayer and sacrifice, and
rituals that predicted the future success
or failure of the regime. Its grandeur
reminded the exiles of their defeat, yet
Daniel shows

> that the Most High is sovereign
>   over the kingdom of mortals;
> he gives it to whom he will
>   and sets over it the lowliest of
>   human beings. (4:17 [14 MT])

Anonymous. Tablet inscribed with the New Year's
ritual in Babylon. Neo-Babylonian or Seleucid. 6th
or 3rd C. BC. Louvre, Paris, France.
(Credit: Erich Lessing/Art Resource, NY)

Nebuchadnezzar's Recitation of His Dream

Nebuchadnezzar's Epistolary Preface, 4:1-3 (3:31-33 MT)

At the outset of this section, Nebuchadnezzar begins with a "royal encyclical" or public letter to his subjects that reflects the typical form and standard greeting of such public documents attested in Hebrew and Aramaic.[3] [Hebrew and Aramaic Letters] John Collins summarizes some of the features of ancient public letters (epistles) that are echoed in Daniel 4.[4] The greeting identifies the writer first, before the recipients; two similar examples come from Ezra and 1 Maccabees: "Artaxerxes, King of Kings, to Ezra the priest" and "King Demetrius to the nation of the Jews, greetings" (Ezra 7:12; 1 Macc 10:18, 25). The identification of the recipients of many languages, "to all peoples, nations and languages," parallels the Persian multi-lingual Behistun inscription. This monumental relief, which details Darius's rise to power, contains Elamite, Akkadian, and Old Persian languages. Collins explains, "[its content] was allegedly circulated to all the provinces in the appropriate languages. . . . Parts of copies have been found

> **Hebrew and Aramaic Letters**
>
> AΩ Because few Hebrew and Aramaic letters are extant, and because letters in the Hebrew Bible may serve more as literary exemplars than as historical references, results of research are necessarily limited. This letter of Nebuchadnezzar to his subjects shares some formal features of Hebrew and Aramaic letters of antiquity. The stereotyped address, "to all the peoples, nations, and languages," identifies the recipients, and the initial greeting, "may your peace be multiplied," uses a form of *šlm* (peace), commonly found in Aramaic letters (see also Ezra 5:7 and 7:12). Although the identification of the sender is not always used, here it forms a primary place, thus emphasizing Nebuchadnezzar's importance as sovereign.
>
> D. Pardee, Paul Dion, and Stanley Stowers, "Letters," *ABD*, ed. David Noel Freedman, 6 vols. (New York: Doubleday & Co., 1992), 4:282–93.

in Akkadian at Babylon and in Aramaic in Egypt."[5] Similarly, the book of Esther speaks of circular letters that were sent in various languages (Esth 1:22; 3:12; 8:9), and the Old Greek (OG) of Daniel 4 specifies that Nebuchadnezzar "wrote a circular letter to all the nations in their individual places, and to countries and people of all languages" (4:34 OG). [The Use of Letters in the Book of Esther] After the writer and recipients are identified, salutations are expressed, and a summary statement is given: "The signs and wonders that the Most High God has worked for me I am pleased to recount" (4:2 [MT 3:32]). The well wishes (may you have abundant prosperity!) use a form of *šlm* (peace/prosperity), found also in Daniel 6:25 (6:26 MT), Ezra 4:17, and the summary statement is similarly echoed in Darius's letter (6:27 [6:28 MT]).

The phrase that Nebuchadnezzar uses to address his subjects, namely, "all peoples, nations, and languages," has ominous overtones because in all cases in the book of Daniel thus far, it has been used when the king's subjects are summoned to obey an arbitrary and despotic decree. Nebuchadnezzar's herald employs this phrase to demand that all subjects worship Nebuchadnezzar's statue on the

Behistun Inscription

Commemoration of the victory of Darius I over rebel kings. Achaemenid relief. Early 5th C. BC. (Credit: SEF/Art Resource, NY)

This early 5th C. BC monument from Behistun, Iran, contains both the multilingual inscription celebrating the victory of Darius I and a relief illustrating the king and his divine protector, Ahura Mazda.

pain of death (Dan 3:4-6); the author uses it to show that all (except Jews) were effectively compelled to bow to the idol (Dan 3:7); and Nebuchadnezzar himself responds with this phrase to threaten torture and death to his subjects who "spoke derisively" of the God of the three exiles (Dan 3:29 A.T.). Until the entirety of the missive is over, the reader (or hearer) of the letter as well as the reader of the entire narrative do not know whether Nebuchadnezzar will issue another death decree. [Nebuchadnezzar's Words—Retrospective or Proleptic? (Dan 4:1-3 [3:31-33 MT])]

The Use of Letters in the Book of Esther

Nebuchadnezzar's letter is unusual because it contains neither instruction nor request. It appears that he utilizes all the logistical resources of the empire to parade his pride. By showing his profligate usage of resources, the author may be deriding the famous communications system in Persia in order to emphasize the gulf between the values of Jews and their oppressors. This technique is exemplified in the book of Esther where, as Michael Fox states, "the state bureaucracy goes into urgent activity" whether it be to enforce a preposterous law, such as "declaring that every man should be master in his own house" (Esth 1:22) or to effect horrific evil, as is the case of the proposed annihilation of the Jewish people (Esth 3:13-15).

In contrast to their Persian overlords, the book of Esther shows Jews sending a missive for a very different purpose. Letters are employed to encourage people to remember their deliverance and celebrate Purim (Esth 9:21). Although the literary setting of Dan 4 is Babylon, references to the culture and government of Persia heavily influence the author. The postal system of Persia was famous in antiquity, as shown in this well-known quotation from Herodotus:

There is nothing mortal that is faster than the system the Persians have devised for sending messages. Apparently, they have horses and men posted at intervals along the route, the same number in total as the overall length in days of journey, with a fresh horse and rider for every day of travel. Whatever the conditions—it may be snowing, raining, blazing hot, or dark—they never fail to complete their assigned journey in the fastest possible time. (*Histories* 8.98)

Michael V. Fox, *Character and Ideology in the Book of Esther*, 2d ed. (Grand Rapids MI: William B. Eerdmans, 2001), 55.

Nebuchadnezzar's Words: Retrospective or Proleptic? Daniel 4:1-3 (3:31-33 MT)

In the Masoretic Text, these three verses are placed at the end of Dan 3, whereas in the English translations they are found at the beginning of Dan 4. These variations in the chapter divisions allow us to consider alternative contexts. Should Nebuchadnezzar's letter be seen as a response to the previous account of the men in the fiery furnace, or as a prospective commentary on a newly reported event? Coming from the Gentile king, these arresting words, reminiscent of God's saving activity in Egypt, immediately capture the reader's interest. If the phrase is retrospective, Nebuchadnezzar may be declaring that he will now draw implications from the drama of the Jews in the fiery furnace. Is it possible that the king sees the deliverance of these captured Jewish nobles, wrongly accused and then rescued by God's angel, as a sign of the saving activity of Israel's God? If the reference is prospective, however, other conclusions will have to be drawn, according to that context which is yet to be related.

As the text continues, it soon becomes clear that these epistolary words form a beginning, not an ending.

Nebuchadnezzar is not connecting God's signs and wonders with the rescue of the three Jewish men whom he condemned to torture and death. Rather, the letter previews a personal account that Nebuchadnezzar structures to emphasize his own accomplishments.

One rabbinic source, however, does consider that these words form the ending to the previous account of the three youth in the fiery furnace. Because of his cruelty, Nebuchadnezzar himself was burned by the flames as he sentenced his exiles to such a fate. Only because of God's mercy did he survive. We read:

> Whence do we know that Nebuchadnezzar became half burnt? R. Isaac said: From the fact that he said with his own mouth, *It hath seemed good unto me to declare the signs and wonders that God Most High hath wrought toward me.* ([Dan 3:] 32) *"He hath wrought toward me"*: that is, on my own person. (*Song. Rab.* 7:9, 1)

In this context, Nebuchadnezzar's words of praise mean that God delivered him from the fire.

See Hersh Goldwurm, *Daniel: A New Translation with a Commentary Anthologized from Talmudic, Midrashic and Rabbinic Sources* (ArtScroll Tanach Series; New York: Mesorah Publications, 1979), 132–33.

Nebuchadnezzar's own introduction to his words of praise cast doubt on whether he will give an unbiased telling. Because of the emphatic placement of the prepositions "for" and "to," his words may literally be translated, "the signs and wonders *for me* that the Most High God has done, it seemed good *to me* to declare" (4:2 [3:32 MT], A.T., emphasis added). Twice the reader is told that Nebuchadnezzar will give his own perspective on God's activity. Whereas for the readers of Nebuchadnezzar's letter, the king is simply praising "the Most High God," the readers of the entire account would have a broader context to judge his sincerity. This context includes the significance of the phrase "signs and wonders," the implications of God's sovereignty, and the inclusion of the upcoming narrative sections found outside the rubric of the letter to which only they are privy.

The reference to "signs and wonders" recalls Israel's redemption at the time of the Exodus. ["Signs" in Biblical Hebrew and Aramaic] It is ironic that Nebuchadnezzar's own words allow the reader to compare him to Pharaoh. Just as Pharaoh's cruelty and arrogance are vanquished by God, so too will Nebuchadnezzar be humbled. As God explains to Moses, "I will harden Pharaoh's heart, and I will multiply my signs and wonders in the land of Egypt. . . . The

---

"Signs" in Biblical Hebrew and Aramaic

AΩ The Hebrew *'ôt*, *'ōtôt*, or Aramaic *'āt*, *'ātîn* ("sign[s]") may be phenomena of nature, such as the luminaries of the heavens or the rainbow; events proclaimed in history, such as the plagues in Egypt and the subsequent exodus; or signs of religious ritual, such as circumcision, eating *maṣṣâ* (unleavened bread), and observing the Sabbath. Signs usually originate from the very design of God who is the source of their meaning and the one who gives humankind the capacity to understand them. As F. J. Helfmeyer states,

The function of a sign, like its outward form or substance, shows that its miraculous or striking nature is not what

matters, for the intention of a sign is not to terrify the onlooker, but to mediate an understanding or to motivate a kind of behavior. (*TDOT* 1:171)

The understanding required is that the LORD is God, that Israel must abide by the covenant, and that foreign rulers must recognize that God, and neither they nor their idols, determines what is right, for God holds nations accountable.

F. J. Helfmeyer, "'ōth," *TDOT*, ed. G. Johannes Botterweck and Helmer Ringgren, trans. John Willis, rev. ed. (Grand Rapids MI: William B. Eerdmans, 1975), 1:167–88.

Egyptians shall know that I am the LORD, when I stretch out my hand against Egypt and bring the Israelites out from among them" (Exod 7:3-5).

This text has an important place in the history of the tradition; the significance of these signs and wonders is connected with the community's continuing prosperity in the land (Jer 32:19-22), the importance of their obedience to the commandments (Deut 6:22-25), and their refusal to worship idols (see Deut 4:34-35; 6:22-25). It becomes apparent in the course of Daniel 4 that Nebuchadnezzar's actions have little to do with these values. Just as the phrase "signs and wonders" is associated with God's paradigmatic role in the past, so too do Nebuchadnezzar's references to God's "everlasting Kingdom" and to God's sovereignty that endures "from generation to generation" (4:3 [MT 3:33]) suggest God's justice. Yet, as the narratives in Daniel 1–3 have demonstrated, Nebuchadnezzar has never made the link between "signs and wonders" and divine justice. The reader has reason to doubt whether Nebuchadnezzar understands the meaning of his words, not only because he ignores their association with God's past relationship with Israel, but also because of the location of this dream narrative, which provides the conclusion to three previous stories about Nebuchadnezzar's actions as sovereign. When Daniel interprets Nebuchadnezzar's first dream of the statue, the king hears that the earthly kingdoms would not endure and that God's eternal kingdom would "stand forever" (Dan 2:44). Despite his praise of Daniel's God, however, Nebuchadnezzar proves by his subsequent actions (namely, the building of an idol and the proclamation that refusing to bow to it is punishable by a tortuous death) that he remains obtuse. Similarly, even though Nebuchadnezzar, upon witnessing the miracle, releases the Jews from the fiery furnace, he continues to issue outrageous decrees to his own people (3:29). It is only here in Daniel 4 that Nebuchadnezzar offers words of praise to God that are not accompanied by a death threat. Despite this apparent sign of spiritual awareness, however, he remains preoccupied with his own power and never refers to God's intervention that punished his arrogance.

Nebuchadnezzar's Request for Dream Interpretation, 4:4-9 (4:1-6 MT)

Through the form of the epistle, the reader first hears Nebuchadnezzar's recollection of the dream's visual content and his own version of the words of the dream's speakers. In Nebuchadnezzar's report of what happened to him, his very first comment calls attention to the ease and prosperity that he was enjoying (4:4 [4:1 MT]). Although Nebuchadnezzar uses such references to his wealth as an indication of his success as sovereign, the reader would be familiar with the tradition in the Hebrew Bible that holds that the riches of the wicked are destined for destruction. [Psalm 73—Questions of God's Justice] The statement, "I, Nebuchadnezzar, was living at ease in my home and prospering in my palace" (4:4 [4:1 MT]) previews the king's penultimate declarations in his letter, namely, "my majesty and splendor were restored to me for the glory of my kingdom," and "still more greatness was added to me" at the end of his ordeal (4:36 [4:33 MT]). This preoccupation with personal glory, which begins and ends Nebuchadnezzar's words, overshadows his acknowledgment of God's sovereignty and suggests that his wealth and achievements as emperor are his ultimate values.

Nebuchadnezzar's success, however, is about to be shaken to its foundations. The tremen-

Psalm 73—Questions of God's Justice

Psalm 73 is classified as a wisdom psalm—a poetic homily characterized by "concern with ordinary affairs such as piety at work . . . family life . . . the prosperity of the wicked . . . the transience of life . . . as well as God's knowledge of every detail of it."

This psalm reveals a struggle of faith; the psalmist desires to hold fast to a belief in a just God who infinitely cares for human beings even while witnessing the health and prosperity of enemies who oppress Israel and of those who act cruelly and without compassion. The psalmist reveals an inner struggle, but nonetheless concludes that God not only remains just, but also that only the righteous enjoy the presence of God:

> Indeed, those who are far from you will perish;
> you put an end to those who are false to you.
> But for me it is good to be near God;
> I have made the Lord God my refuge,
> to tell of all your works. (Ps 73:27-28)

S. E. Gillingham, *The Poems and Psalms of the Hebrew Bible* (Oxford Bible Series; New York: Oxford University Press, 1994), 228.

Babylonian Chronicles

Tablet with part of the Babylonian Chronicle. British Museum, London, Great Britain. (Credit: © British Museum/Art Resource, NY)

This Neo-Babylonian tablet from southern Iraq is part of a series that displays the summaries of key events in Babylon from 747–280 BC. Each entry begins with the identity and year of the king, stating his accomplishments.

dous effect of this dream that "frightened" and "terrified" him (4:5 [4:2 MT]) can be compared with that of his earlier dream of the golden statue, which "troubled him" and left him sleepless (2:1-2). Nevertheless, he repeats his earlier mistakes. Although the entirety of his royal entourage could not interpret his previous dream, and despite his earlier declaration that Daniel was of superior wisdom, he still calls for the same incompetent advisers to appear, even indicating all of their classifications, namely, "magicians, enchanters, Chaldeans, and diviners" (4:7 [4:4 MT]).

Nebuchadnezzar's Dream of the Great Tree

The dream of Nebuchadnezzar (Dan 4:11-12) is illustrated in this Mozarabic Bible of the 10th century AD. This illustration shows the tree laden with beautiful fruits and birds on its branches; a lion and ox, representing all the animals of the earth, are beneath it.

The Dream of Nebuchadnezzar: The Tree. Spanish. 10th C. Mozarabic Bible. Folio 319. S. Isidro el Real, Leon, Spain. (Credit: Giraudon/Art Resource, NY)

In addition, although his courtiers are unsuccessful at interpreting the dream, he makes no specific request for Daniel to come. He neither takes action to find him nor does he demand his presence, even though he responded to Daniel's earlier dream interpretation by treating him as a god (Dan 2:46). Indeed, Nebuchadnezzar's own words highlight his passivity when he reports that "at last" Daniel arrived (4:8 [4:5 MT]). This portrayal of Daniel's appearance without having been summoned can be seen as an indication of Daniel's distance from the king's advisers, his special status, and as a sign of God's providence.[6]

As Daniel stands before Nebuchadnezzar, the author reveals that the king continues to be entrenched in his own polytheistic world. He reminds the recipients of the letter that Daniel "was named Belteshazzar after the name of my god, and who is endowed with a spirit of the holy gods" (4:8 [4:5 MT]). For the Babylonian recipients of the king's letter, the name Belteshazzar symbolizes both Daniel's subjugation as well as the apparent triumph of the Babylonian god, Bel. In addition, they hear Nebuchadnezzar's self-praise within the expected context of their world—one filled with a multiplicity of divinities. For the audience of the entire account, however, the phrase "endowed with a spirit of the gods" can also be translated "endowed with a holy, divine spirit," a description in consonance with a monotheistic world. Similarly, in calling Daniel his "chief magician," Nebuchadnezzar displays his lack of understanding of Daniel's identity by referring to him as possessing a skill prized by the Babylonians, yet disdained by Jews. It is striking that although Nebuchadnezzar's report is retrospective, occurring *after* he had occasion to praise "the Most High God" (4:2 [3:32 MT]), he persists in these declarations. Hence, the author contrasts the idolatry of the conquerors, represented here by Nebuchadnezzar, with the fidelity to God displayed by the captives. [Chaldea: Land of Idols vs. Birthplace of Abraham]

By having Nebuchadnezzar use ambiguous wording to address Daniel, the author suggests that the king may expect both a description of his dream as well as its interpretation. Daniel 4:9 [4:6 MT] may be literally translated, "the vision of my dream which I saw, and its interpretation, tell me." His confused wording results in two possible connotations. Either Nebuchadnezzar appears bewildered, or his words recall his earlier rage directed against those who could not relate the content of his dream about the statue (2:12). The reader may wonder whether Nebuchadnezzar is going to repeat his threat to kill potential interpreters who cannot recount the dream. Although any potential for violence is quickly resolved, as the king does indeed begin his own description (4:10 [4:7 MT]), the author opens the possibility that Nebuchadnezzar's very request to Daniel is an indication of his confusion and his latent anger. Nebuchadnezzar's lack of understanding will continue to be manifest in the course of Daniel 4, as Daniel's repetition of the king's account of the dream will offer several correctives.

Nebuchadnezzar's Description of the Dream, 4:10-12 (4:7-9 MT)

As Nebuchadnezzar begins his description of the dream of the tree, he does not disclose its source. The author depicts the king as avoiding any reference to God, highlighting either the king's ignorance or his arrogance. The description of this grand tree reveals Nebuchadnezzar's complacency: the images appear to be those of power and success. Although some of its descriptive phrases will be

Chaldea: Land of Idols and Birthplace of Abraham

Just as Nebuchadnezzar and his magicians represent the practitioners of idolatry *par excellence*, so too, in Judaism, does Chaldea symbolize a land so associated with idolatry that God commanded the ancestors of Israel to abandon it. The midrashim contrast the Jewish belief in the one God *versus* Chaldean idolatry, showing, for example, how Abraham discovers the idea of the one God on his own despite his father's occupation as an idol maker. Abraham recognizes the folly of idolatry and tries to convince his father, Terah, that they are worthless. In a famous story, Abraham smashes all the idols in his father's shop, save for one, in whose arms he places a stick. When Terah angrily accuses Abraham of destroying them, Abraham replies to his father that the sole surviving statue had attacked the others in an argument concerning which of them should receive an offering. Not believing this to be possible, Terah says to his son, "have they then any knowledge!" Abraham responds, "Should not your ears listen to what your mouth is saying"—implying that Terah worships idols whom he believes have neither consciousness nor ability. (*Gen. Rab.* 38:13)

The Tree as Symbol

The symbol of the tree is used in various ways in the Hebrew Scriptures. Nebuchadnezzar's dream, which describes it as being located at the center of the earth, recalls the cosmic tree in Eden (Gen 2:9), cut off from humankind because of the sin in the garden (Gen 3:24); its height reaching to heaven is reminiscent of the Tower of Babel (Gen 11:1-9), symbol of human arrogance; and its destruction recalls the hewing of the great trees in Ezek 17 and 31, destroyed because they are a symbol of Babylon's hubris.

The link between this reference in Dan 4 and the image found in Ezek 31:1-18 prompts Walther Zimmerli to suggest that perhaps Dan 4 is dependent on the Ezekiel text.

The passage is directed at Pharaoh, who, like Nebuchadnezzar, is an embodiment of unjust powers that inflict suffering upon the people of Israel and whose rule and values so contradict Israel's ethics that he is described as challenging God himself. Pharaoh is likened to a huge tree, which, like the tree in Nebuchadnezzar's dream, becomes a place of safety and tranquility. It provides a home for "the birds of the air," and under its branches "all the beasts of the field" give birth. In both cases, the trees provide shade; in Ezekiel it is for all nations, whereas in Daniel it is for all the animals. In both cases, nonetheless, the image of the tree at the center of the world is suggestive of its political hegemony, whether it is expressed by nations or by animals.

Because of Pharaoh's arrogance, God decrees it will be "cut down," just as is the case in Dan 4. In an abrupt reversal, Pharaoh is subjected to a ruthless conqueror, and the use of his land as a haven for birds and beasts will end. Similarly, Nebuchadnezzar's reign will soon cease and the birds of the air and beasts of the field will no longer come under the branches of the tree that represents him. As Zimmerli states, "in this bold description of the world power, the prophetic word reveals how greatly and constantly all human power complexes and leaderships are at risk. . . ."

Walther Zimmerli, *Ezekiel II: A Commentary on the Book of the Prophet Ezekiel, Chapters 25–48*, trans. James Martin (Hermeneia; Philadelphia: Fortress, 1983), 153.

---

confirmed in Daniel's retelling, two phrases are distinct in Nebuchadnezzar's version. First, Nebuchadnezzar states that this tree is "at the center of the earth" (4:10 [4:7 MT]), indicating its essential importance. Secondly, the king relates, "its height was great" (4:10 [4:7 MT]), suggesting his particular preoccupation with its arresting appearance and magnitude. In addition, when stating, "in it was food for all" and "from it all flesh was fed" (4:12 [4:9 MT] A.T.), he emphasizes both the potential that the tree has for providing food as well as the actualization of providing sustenance. Below, Daniel's version will be examined further. [The Tree as Symbol]

Nebuchadnezzar's Account of the Watcher's Words, Dan 4:13-17 (10-14 MT)

Nebuchadnezzar's description of the watcher continues to mirror his confusion (4:14-17 [4:11-14 MT]). Nebuchadnezzar states, literally, "there was a watcher and a holy one coming down from heaven" (4:13 [4:10 MT]). "Holy one" (*qāddîš*) is usually understood epexegetically, that is, as an additional explanatory comment for "watcher"; hence the translation "a holy watcher" (NRSV).[7] If, however, the phrase "a watcher and a holy one" is understood as a plural subject, it is then followed by a singular verb, perhaps reflecting that Nebuchadnezzar himself is not certain of what he

Watchers

In the Second Temple period, "watcher" ('*aîr*) was a term used to refer either to angels or to fallen angels. In *1 Enoch*, the biblical account of "the sons of God [who] went in to the daughters of men" (Gen 6:1-4) is interpreted as referring to the sexual acts of the fallen watchers with women—unions that gave humanity a frightful legacy. These offspring, the giants of the antediluvian age, bring forbidden knowledge, evil, and violence into the world. They are held accountable by God and are eternally punished (*1 En.* 15:3-12; VanderKam, 123–30). Watchers, however, are also portrayed as fulfilling God's purposes and are called "the angels of the Lord" (*Jub.* 4:15; Sullivan, 213). According to *Jubilees*, before they were corrupted, they had been known as "[those who] descended on the earth, those who are named the Watchers, that they should instruct the children of men, and that they should do judgment and uprightness upon the earth" (*Jub.* 4:15-16). In the book of Daniel, the watchers are equated with the holy ones (4:13 [10 MT], 17 [14 MT], 23 [20 MT]) and are portrayed only as faithful messengers of God, similar to the description of the archangels in *1 Enoch* who are identified as "the holy angels who watch" (*1 En.* 20:1).

Kevin Sullivan, *Wrestling with Angels: A Study of the Relationship Between Angels and Humans in Ancient Jewish Literature and the New Testament* (Arbeiten zur Geschichte des antiken Judentums und des Urchristentums 55; Leiden: Brill, 2004), 213.

James VanderKam, *Enoch and the Growth of An Apocalyptic Tradition* (CBQMS 16; Washington DC: The Catholic Biblical Association of America, 1984), 123–28.

has seen.[8] "Watchers," "holy ones," and angels are found in similar Jewish texts of this period; they represent the celestial beings who are present in the assembly of God's heavenly court.[9] [Watchers] Because the beings often are understood to be part of a larger company, the watcher of v. 14 (v. 11 MT) may be addressing others; yet this seems to be unknown to the king. As he relates the watcher's account of the degrading alteration of the tree into the stump, Nebuchadnezzar quotes the speaker as follows: "Let him/it be bathed with the dew of heaven, and let his/its lot be with the animals of the field" (4:15b [4:12b MT]). [Dew of Heaven] These words allow for ambiguity, for Nebuchadnezzar does not specify whether the watcher refers to a tree or to a human being who is bathed with dew and who dwells with the animals. Surely the phrase "let his mind be changed from that of a human" in 4:16 (4:13 MT) refers to a man, but at what point the image found in v. 15b (v. 12b MT) should refer to a man is uncertain. Later, when Daniel does in fact recognize that the destruction of the tree represents the punishment of Nebuchadnezzar (4:25 [4:22 MT]), his superior wisdom is all the more apparent. It is Daniel alone who understands that just as the majesty of the mighty tree has been reduced to a remnant, the tree itself takes on the identity of the man, Nebuchadnezzar, whose mind is sentenced to be similarly degraded.

In describing the watcher's command to hew the tree, Nebuchadnezzar lessens the personal relevance of the act. The watchers and holy ones, according to Nebuchadnezzar, explain that the reason for the destruction is "in order that *all who live* [*ḥayyayyā*'] may know that the Most High is sovereign over the

Dew of Heaven

 In the semi-arid climate of Israel, the dew is essential for agriculture. In the Hebrew Bible, dew (*tal*) is a sign of blessing, something ubiquitous, or a symbol of that which is fleeting. For example, dew is a sign of blessing for Jacob, and its absence is a sign of Esau's tragic life and upcoming departure from his father and brother (Gen 27:39). Dew is likened to the blessings of a community that lives in harmony and peace (Ps 133:3). It may also be a sign of the inevitable: When David's loyal counselor Hushai gives deceptive advice to David's rebellious son Absalom, in order to allow David victory, Hushai states, "So we shall come upon him in whatever place he may be found, and we shall light on him as the dew falls on the ground; and he will not survive, nor will any of those with him" (2 Sam 17:12). Dew may also be used as a sign of something transient or unfaithful as found in the words of the prophet Hosea who remonstrates against Ephraim and Judah, "Your love is like a morning cloud,/like the dew that goes away early" (Hos 6:4).

As it is used of Nebuchadnezzar, the dew of heaven that bathes him is a sign of his animal-like state and his total dependence upon God. Like the animals that have no permanent shelter, when Nebuchadnezzar is separated from the human community, he has no way to escape the nightly dewfall.

Reference to dew also plays an important part in Israel's understanding of God's care for the human community. In Jewish daily prayers, God is thanked for the giving of rain from the time of *Shemini Atzeret* (the Eighth day of Assembly, which occurs at the end of *Sukkot* [Festival of Booths]) to Passover, and for dew from Passover to the next *Shemini Atzeret*.

Nissen Mangel, trans., *Siddur Tehillat Hashem: According to the Text of Rabbi Schneur Zalman of Liadi* (New York: Merkos L'Inyonei Chinuch, 1988), 51.

kingdom of mortals; he gives it to whom he will and sets over it the lowliest of human beings" (4:17 [4:14 MT], emphasis added). Saying that the dream's relevance is for all, Nebuchadnezzar's rendering shows no recognition that it, in fact, applies to him. As we shall see below (4:25 [22 MT]), Daniel's version specifically connects the reference to the king.

At the end of his account of the watcher's words, Nebuchadnezzar refers to God's placing of "the lowliest of human beings" (4:17 [4:14 MT]) as sovereign over the earth. This expression has an important history of usage, as it denotes the hope that God will ultimately ensure that righteousness and justice are provided on earth, even to those who have been marginalized and abused. Because Nebuchadnezzar never states in his letter that he is punished, one sees another aspect of his self-congratulatory presentation. For the king's subjects, it appears that Nebuchadnezzar is that "lowliest of human beings" who becomes great after receiving kingship from the Most High. Only the reader of the entire narrative knows that Nebuchadnezzar indeed has his kingship taken away and receives it back only after he is humbled.

Nebuchadnezzar's Second Request for Interpretation and Daniel's Reaction, 4:18 (4:15 MT)

In this section, the author contrasts Nebuchadnezzar's and Daniel's reactions to the dream. Nebuchadnezzar presumes that if he receives Daniel's interpretation, his terror will be lessened, but for Daniel, upon hearing this dream, an opportunity begins for him to be God's spokesman. As seen in Daniel 4:9 and 18 [4:6 and 15 MT], Nebuchadnezzar's requests for interpretation both precede and conclude his detailing of the dream. In both of these requests, Nebuchadnezzar's use of Daniel's imposed Babylonian name connotes the king's ultimate subjugation of his captive. Although Nebuchadnezzar's words continue to suggest his polytheistic outlook, as he repeats his view that Daniel possesses a spirit of the holy gods (*rûaḥ-ĕlāhîn qaddîšîn*, 4:18 [4:15 MT] A.T.), the author nonetheless underscores the king's recognition that Daniel's abilities are superior to that of his own courtiers.[10] This acknowledgment prepares the reader to appreciate Daniel's superior presentation of the dream.

Daniel's Dream Interpretation

Ambiguous Words, 4:19a (4:16a MT)

Before Daniel can respond to the king, the author continues to suggest Nebuchadnezzar's arrogance by the following phrase, whose speaker is ambiguous: "then Daniel, who was called Belteshazzar, was severely distressed for a while. His thoughts terrified him" (4:19a [4:16a MT]). These words can be read either as the last words that Nebuchadnezzar relates to his subjects in the first portion of his letter, or they may function as the author's introduction to Daniel's upcoming interpretation.

If the speaker is understood to be Nebuchadnezzar, this sentence would constitute his last reference to his dream within the rubric of his letter to his subjects. A narrative gap is thus created for the recipients of Nebuchadnezzar's letter whose information about Daniel is restricted; it is possible for them to conclude that, confronted with Nebuchadnezzar's request to interpret the dream, Daniel never responds. The recipients of the letter could surmise that either Nebuchadnezzar omits Daniel's response, or that Daniel remains speechless. In either case, the king allows Daniel's role to recede and his own to loom more importantly. [A Narrative Gap]

If the words are the author's introduction to Daniel's speech, however, they take on a different meaning, pointing to the significance of Daniel's role as Nebuchadnezzar's dream interpreter and to his need to speak in carefully constructed phrases as he confronts the king

A Narrative Gap

A narrative gap is an absence of information that interrupts the advancement of a story's plot. The effect of gaps prompts the reader to entertain various possibilities regarding the unconnected phases of the story. One way to underscore that Divine Providence is behind the developments of the plot is to use many gaps in the narrative. Yairah Amit explains, "the many-gapped scene structure . . . underlies the central role the author has assigned to God: God creates the circumstances, and God makes the tactics succeed."

Yairah Amit, *Reading Biblical Narrative: Literary Criticism and the Hebrew Bible* (Minneapolis: Fortress, 2001), 61.

Prophetic Response to Bringing God's Message

The protest, questioning, or fleeing of prophets is a common reaction upon first hearing God's word. Found within the context of the commissioning scene of the prophet, usually these responses are an indication of the prophets' acknowledgment of the seriousness of God's involvement within the lives of the people and form a contrast to the people's refusal to hear God's message. Inevitably, the true prophet receives assurance from God and is given a confirmation of his legitimacy. Examples of prophets who display fear and reluctance, only to be confirmed by God, are Moses, who protests that he is not a clear speaker (Exod 6:12); Jeremiah, who laments that he is but a youth (Jer 1:6); and Jonah, who endangers a shipload of innocents while attempting to flee God's command to preach (Jonah 1:3).

Although Daniel is not shown to experience visions until ch. 7, and although this scene is not classified as a call narrative, Daniel's reaction to the implications of Nebuchadnezzar's dreams is similar to those of other prophets who recognize the ominous implications of God's declarations—stupefied silence, terror, paralyzing fear, or sickness. Second Temple literature has further examples of the visionary who similarly becomes ill upon seeing visions of God's judgment that is to come in response to humanity's evil. Enoch, for example, falls into paralyzing grief upon experiencing a vision of the cataclysms of the world. He is reassured by his father who states, "rise and pray to the Lord of glory, for you are a man of faith . . ." (*1 En.* 83:8). Nebuchadnezzar takes the function here of providing assurance; Daniel, however, acknowledges that the interpretation comes from God (Dan 4:24 [4:21 MT]).

The components of the prophetic call narrative are delineated in Norman Habel, "The Form and Significance of the Call Narratives," *ZAW 77* (1965): 301–23.

with a difficult message. [Prophetic Response to Bringing God's Message] Indeed, Daniel's own reaction shows that he immediately understands the ominous implications for Nebuchadnezzar. Although Nebuchadnezzar apparently lessens Daniel's hesitation and enables him to speak (4:19b [4:16b MT]), the king nonetheless opens the door for himself to experience more anxiety since God's judgment against him is about to be given. At the same time, Daniel is shown to be solicitous and obedient to the king's demand for assistance by his immediate response. Although the king's subjects never are allowed to see this aspect of Daniel's character (as it is not included in the king's letter), the reader of the entire narrative knows that Daniel fulfills a courageous role by obeying the king's orders even under difficult circumstances.

The Prophet Daniel

The Prophet Daniel. 16th C. AD. Byzantine Museum, Athens, Greece. (Credit: Erich Lessing/Art Resource, NY)

This 16th C. AD Byzantine icon shows the prophet Daniel in the posture of an orant, in prayer. The elongated body expresses the connection between heaven and earth.

Daniel's Cautious Response, 4:19b (4:16b MT)

Daniel proceeds diplomatically, recounting the dream in such a way as to confirm Nebuchadnezzar's greatness while inexorably leading him to confront his own arrogance. Daniel's first words, "My lord, may the dream be for those who hate you, and its interpretation for your enemies!" (4:19b [4:16b MT]) are wisely chosen, as they may have different meanings for Nebuchadnezzar and for the reader of the entire account. As Nebuchadnezzar would hear it, the sentence could be understood positively, implying that anything unfortunate in the dream should occur for those who oppose him or his regime. For the reader of the entire account, Daniel's words may be read as a suggestion of Nebuchadnezzar's downfall and the advent of the next kingdom. In other words, what is bad news for Nebuchadnezzar is good news for his conquered peoples—for it is they who are his enemies. [The Rabbis' Interpretation of Nebuchadnezzar's "Enemies"]

Daniel's Description of the Dream and Its Significance, 4:20-26 (4:17-23 MT)

Daniel's description of the dream and its significance (Dan 4:20-26 [4:17-23 MT]) differs from that reported by Nebuchadnezzar, as shown by several alterations. Although Daniel must reveal the upcoming punishment of Nebuchadnezzar, he couches its terror by emphasizing its purpose, by showing it to be a prelude to restoration, and by giving the king an opportunity to repent. By the order in which he proceeds and by his carefully chosen statements, Daniel prepares Nebuchadnezzar to accept the truth of what this dream means, yet does not compromise the divine message.

Daniel's first task is to make Nebuchadnezzar understand that the dream directly critiques his behavior as sovereign. Although this dream may be relevant for all of his subjects, and indeed for all of humanity, Daniel solely applies it to Nebuchadnezzar's accountability. At first, Daniel confirms most of the positive imagery that Nebuchadnezzar has seen (4:20-21 [4:17-18 MT]), thus engaging the king's attention without provoking him. Nonetheless, there are significant changes in his presentation.

Although Daniel repeats one of Nebuchadnezzar's descriptions of the tree (4:20 [4:17 MT] parallels 4:11 [4:8 MT]), he avoids Nebuchadnezzar's initial declarations by never indicating that it

Rabbis' Interpretation of Nebuchadnezzar's "Enemies"

One Talmudic interpretation suggests that Nebuchadnezzar's "enemies" actually refer to God, and that Daniel thus expresses his hope that God's declaration of judgment upon Nebuchadnezzar comes true. The reason given for this interpretation is that Israel is the obvious choice for Nebuchadnezzar's enemy; how could Daniel curse Israel? Others suggest that the "enemies" refer to other non-Jewish enemies of Nebuchadnezzar. The medieval commentator Ibn Ezra (1089–1164), however, understands that Daniel was using a stock phrase of polite speech, and that Daniel neither implied any disrespect nor meant any harm to his own people. The midrashim, like the Talmud, understand God as Nebuchadnezzar's enemy, thus protecting the image of Daniel as one who would never wish harm on his own people. *Exodus Rabbah* explains that if one would interpret the verse literally, it could be understood that Daniel would have been speaking reproachfully of God:

> Can there be a greater enemy to him than God, whose Temple he [Nebuchadnezzar] destroyed and whose children he exiled? Moreover, Israel also were his enemies, and he [Daniel] was thus cursing them! But Daniel, however, directed his thoughts towards God and said, "Lord in heaven, cause this dream to come to this enemy of Thine." (*Exod. Rab.* 30:24)

See also A. J. Rosenberg, *Daniel, Ezra, Nehemiah* (Judaica Books of the Hagiographa—the Holy Writings; New York: Judaica Press, 1991), 39–40.

occupied center stage in the earth and by abbreviating the king's many references to its height (4:10 [4:7 MT]). These differences provide a less grandiose picture of Nebuchadnezzar's reign and heighten the king's arrogance. In addition, in Daniel's version of the dream, all the wild beasts *lived* (*tĕdûr*) under the tree (4:21 [4:18 MT]). Nebuchadnezzar's image was more pastoral: they *had shade* (*taṭlēl*) under it (4:12 [4:9 MT]), using for himself a term often associated with the protecting or comforting activity of God (Gen 19:8; Judg 9:15; Pss 17:8; 36:8). Whereas Nebuchadnezzar specified "from it all living beings were fed" (4:12 [4:9 MT]), Daniel states, "and food for all is in it" (4:21 [4:18 MT] A. T.). Daniel's perspective allows the reader to consider that although there was food for all in the tree's branches, the tree did not in fact provide for all, thus suggesting that Nebuchadnezzar squandered his chance to provide for the poor in his realm. The author shows that Daniel prepares Nebuchadnezzar to hear of his upcoming downfall and allows the reader to consider that the king's overstated recitation of the positive imagery of the tree was perhaps too self-congratulatory.

The author depicts Daniel as understanding that to speak about the king's grandeur and success will surely capture Nebuchadnezzar's attention. After Daniel completes his description of the dream, he dramatically announces, "it is you, O king" (4:22 [4:19 MT]). By declaring that the tree, at the pinnacle of its greatness, is representative of Nebuchadnezzar, Daniel thus leads him to accept the interpretation as true before he hears that the destruction of the tree also applies to him. Daniel continues with additional praise, confirming with his own unique words that Nebuchadnezzar has been extraordinarily successful (4:22 [4:19 MT]). Having captured Nebuchadnezzar's trust in his interpretation by appealing to his pride, Daniel's next task is to shift the king's focus to God's declaration of his end.

As Daniel proceeds to the more sobering images of Nebuchadnezzar's downfall, he first gives a shortened account of the description of the tree's destruction without immediately identifying the referent as being Nebuchadnezzar. The four verbs "cut down," "chop off," "strip off," and "scatter" (4:14 [4:11 MT]), which detailed the destruction of the tree in Nebuchadnezzar's version of the dream, are truncated: "cut down" and "destroy" (4:23 [4:20 MT]). In addition, Nebuchadnezzar's account of the animals' and birds' departure from the tree is not mentioned (4:14 [4:11 MT]). Perhaps Daniel's abbreviation of the graphic description of the tree's destruction is intended to prevent Nebuchadnezzar's tyrannical anger from flaring, or is intended to allow Daniel to

The Most High

It is appropriate that Daniel uses "the Most High" to refer to God when speaking to Nebuchadnezzar as it is typically used of God who directs the decisions of the Divine Council in passing judgment on the actions of humankind or upon other deities who support unjust policies on earth. An example of this usage is in Ps 82, whose opening scene shows a God who directs all powers in the universe to strive for justice:

> God has taken his place in the divine council;
> in the midst of the gods he holds judgment:
> "How long will you judge unjustly
> and show partiality to the wicked?
> Give justice to the weak and the orphan;
> maintain the right of the lowly and the destitute
> Rescue the weak and the needy;
> deliver them from the hand of the wicked." (Ps 82:1-4)

In recognizing the condemnation and judgment that God decrees against these exploitative deities, the psalmist declares:

> I say, "You are gods,
> children of the Most High, all of you;
> nevertheless, you shall die like mortals,
> and fall like any prince." (Ps 82:6-7)

When these powers have fallen, the psalmist can hope and trust that the God of Israel will rule the world with righteousness and concludes:

> Rise up, O God, judge the earth;
> for the nations belong to you! (Ps 82:8)

As Mitchell Dahood states,

> The psalmist prays God, once the pagan deities have been deposed, to govern the heathen nations himself, thus assuring an equitable governance of the universe and the stabilizing of the earth's foundations, presently threatened by the ignorance and the favoritism to the wicked of the heathen divinities.

Mitchell Dahood, *Psalms 51–100* (AB 17; Garden City NY: Doubleday & Co., 1968), 271. See also Pss 29:1-2; 77:13 [77:14, MT]; 89:6-9; 95:3; 96:4; 148:2.

---

avoid the king's consternation until he is further convinced of the truth of Daniel's words. Daniel quickly advances to the continuing presence of the stump, which symbolizes both Nebuchadnezzar's crushing defeat before God and his potential for restoration.

Daniel proceeds cautiously when giving the most condemnatory news to the king. Daniel's first introductory statement, "this is the interpretation" (4:24a [4:21a MT]), allows Nebuchadnezzar to recognize that Daniel is in compliance with the king's own request. The second introductory statement, "it is a decree of the Most High" (4:24b [4:21b MT]), appeals to an unassailable authority. [The Most High] In contrast to Nebuchadnezzar's own account of the watcher's words, where the king waited until the end before making any reference to God (4:17 [4:14 MT]), Daniel refers to the Most High before he speaks of the removal of Nebuchadnezzar from human society (4:24-25 [4:21-22 MT]).

As Daniel continues with the description of what is to happen to the nearly destroyed tree, the changes become more dramatic. The author has Daniel use two unique phrases, namely, "you shall be driven away from human society" and "you shall be made to eat grass like oxen" (4:25 [4:22 MT]). With these phrases, Daniel makes clear the divine intention of the dream, specifying how it affects Nebuchadnezzar directly. But because the subject of the sen-

The Ox who Acknowledges God

The use of the ox as a beast who acknowledges God is found in the midrashim. Each category of animal, namely, bird, beast, and wild beast, has its own "lord": the eagle, ox, and lion, respectively. Each of these animals appears on the heavenly throne, so that it may, as representative of an entire class of animals, know that it too is subject to God, the Lord of all creation. We find this telling statement:

The Holy One, blessed be He, took them and engraved them on the Throne of Glory, as it says, *The Lord hath established His throne in the heavens, and His kingdom ruleth over all* (Ps cIII, 19). The fact that He has established His throne above the lordly ones proves that "His kingdom ruleth over all." (*Song. Rab.* 3:10, 4; see also *Exod. Rab.* 23:13)

Thus, the image of Nebuchadnezzar behaving like an ox is particularly appropriate. Just as the ox, although superior to all beasts, acknowledges God as its master, so too must Nebuchadnezzar learn this lesson that it is God who determines his sovereignty (see also Isa 3:1).

tence is not specified, the author suggests that Nebuchadnezzar remains unaware that God determines his fate, contrasting Daniel's knowledge with Nebuchadnezzar's blindness.[11] The image of the ox is particularly appropriate for the defiant king. Oxen (*tôrîn*, Aramaic; *šĕwārîm*, Hebrew) are unique in that they are fit for sacrifice; yet although herbivorous, they have the potential for great violence. Special penalties are given to the owner of an ox that has been left uncontrolled and that has been known to gore humans (Exod 21:28-36). The image of God's battle with the primordial ox, akin to Leviathan or Behemoth, may also stand behind such an illustration.[12] [The Ox That Acknowledges God]

As Daniel continues his version of the length and purpose of punishment (4:25-26 [4:22-23 MT]), he omits the following phrases that were used previously in Nebuchadnezzar's version of the watcher's words: "let his mind be changed from that of a human, and let the mind of an animal be given to him" (4:16 [4:13 MT]) and "the Most High . . . sets over [the kingdom of mortals] the lowliest of human beings" (4:17 [4:14 MT]). By not repeating such devastating images, the author suggests that Daniel must continue to speak cautiously while yet indicating what the future holds for Nebuchadnezzar.

Turning to the final modifications in Daniel's version of the text, we note the unique words Daniel employs when speaking about Nebuchadnezzar's punishment. Unlike Nebuchadnezzar's account, which stated that the watcher's words applied to "all who live" (4:17 [4:14 MT]), Daniel personalizes the decree and states, "until *you* have learned that the Most High has sovereignty over the kingdom of mortals and gives it to whom he will . . . *Your kingdom* shall be re-established *for you* from the time that *you* learn that Heaven is sovereign" (4:25-26 [4:22-23 MT], emphasis added).

Daniel's final words concerning the interpretation of the dream emphasize its divine intent. The dream's message is indeed for Nebuchadnezzar—the one who believes there is no accountability for him even as he determines law and justice in Babylon.

Call for Repentance, 4:27 (4:24 MT)

In v. 27 (v. 24 MT), Daniel completes his words to Nebuchadnezzar with the most arresting of declarations. He speaks now like the prophets of old and calls upon Nebuchadnezzar to repent. He does not quote anything revealed in the dream; rather he appears to take the initiative. The content of the repentance is specific: "atone for your sins with righteousness, and your iniquities with mercy to the oppressed, so that your prosperity may be prolonged." As is reminiscent of many examples in the Hebrew Bible, repentance is shown not only by a reorientation of the heart, but also by obeying the commandments of God (Deut 30; 1 Kgs 8:47-60; Isa 58:6-9; Jer 3:11-14; Ezek 33:10-11; Hos 6:6; Mic 6:6-8). Daniel does not go so far as to say that the decree will be forever reversed, although he does not rule out this possibility. [Daniel's Call for Repentance] While the author gives no further specifications, it is true nonetheless that the reader finds that God's justice is confirmed and that the possibility of change remains open. What specifically is the content of "righteousness" and "mercy"? In the Hellenistic period it is clear that righteousness (justice, *ṣidqâ*) had the prime meaning of almsgiving.[13] Scholars debate whether that meaning was obvious in the Persian period, the time of the authorship of Daniel 1–6. Nevertheless, even in its earlier usage in the Hebrew Bible, it means caring for those in society whose needs are not being met. This can mean helping them monetarily or setting up the proper social structures to combat their plight. Often both are needed. Given that Daniel uses the word righteousness in parallel

Daniel's Call for Repentance

Like the prophets Jeremiah and Jonah, Daniel presents a future that will come to pass if Nebuchadnezzar persists in his cruelties; an alternative exists if there is radical change. Two extraordinary passages reveal that the possibility of change exists for both Jews and Gentiles. In the book of Jeremiah, the prophet gives the following declaration of the LORD to Judah:

> At one moment I may declare concerning a nation or kingdom, that I will pluck up and break down and destroy it, but if that nation, concerning which I have spoken, turns from its evil, I will change my mind about the disaster that I intended to bring on it. And at another moment I may declare concerning a nation or a kingdom that I will build and plant it, but if it does evil in my sight, not listening to my voice, then I will change my mind about the good that I had intended to do to it. (Jer 18:7-10)

A similar expression of hope for the capacity of humanity to change is found in the book of Jonah. After the prophet Jonah gives a hesitant proclamation of God's upcoming destruction, the king of Nineveh declares repentance and fasting for all humans and animals in his kingdom. He arrestingly states, "All shall turn from their evil ways and from the violence that is in their hands. Who knows? God may relent and change his mind; he may turn from his fierce anger, so that we do not perish" (Jonah 3:8-9).

As Norman Porteous underscores, the Hebrew Scriptures do not have a fatalistic view of humanity, and hence Daniel takes his own initiative in recommending to Nebuchadnezzar that he atone for his sins.

Norman Porteous, *Daniel* (OTL; Philadelphia: Westminster, 1962), 70.

Charity

In Jewish teaching, giving charity is a commandment or obligation, and the word for "charity" is the same as "justice" (*ṣĕdāqâ*). The king has a particular obligation to the poor, as is underscored by Daniel's appeal to Nebuchadnezzar.

Box for collecting alms. Spanish. c. 1319. (Credit: J. G. Berizzi. Musee du Judaisme. Paris, France. Réunion des Musées Nationaux/Art Resource, NY)

Almsgiving in the Book of Tobit

The book of Tobit, written between 225–175 BC (originally in Hebrew or Aramaic), provides another example of the importance of almsgiving in a community besieged by trial and adversity. Its value is comparable to sacrifice, it provides expiation from sin, and those who practice it are transformed. In this book, the wise Tobit encourages his son Tobias:

Revere the Lord all your days my son, and refuse to sin . . . give alms from your possessions, and do not let your eye begrudge the gift when you make it. Do not turn your face away from anyone who is poor, and the face of God will not be turned away from you. . . . For almsgiving delivers from death and keeps you from going into the Darkness. (Tob 4:5-10)

In a time when the everyday practices of Jewish life were under the control of hostile regimes, the practices outlined in Tobit remind the community that a life of purpose and hope, rooted in their faith, endures despite the reality of the Diaspora that could otherwise haunt and debilitate them. As Anathea Portier-Young concludes,

In this topsy-turvey foreign land, kings murder, demons destroy, neighbors deride. In the exile the Israelites can no longer seek God in the temple. Instead, they find God in the places of charity, in family, in community, in sacred writings (like the book of Tobit itself) that teach and give hope. Through these they are sustained and sustain one another. (26)

The book of Tobit, like the narratives of Daniel 1–6, portrays heroes who obey the food laws (Tob 1:10-11), offer prayers (3:11-15), care for their parents (4:3-4), seek wisdom (4:18-19), and rely on God and angels (6:18, 12:11-15). Both Tobit and Daniel show that such humble acts can repair a universe marred by sovereigns who defy the God who holds all accountable. Indeed, the book of Tobit shows the angel Raphael teaching Tobit and his son Tobias that almsgiving is a way to honor God, to avoid the lure of evil, and to enhance one's very life (Tob 12:6-10). Through the eyes of faith, such everyday acts can construct a purposeful existence. Following the commandments not only changes the dispositions of individuals, but can transform a world marred by cruelty and suffering into a world of endless possibility for blessing and renewal.

Anathea Portier-Young, "'Eyes to the Blind': A Dialogue between Tobit and Job," in *Intertextual Studies in Ben Sira and Tobit: Essays in Honor of Alexander Di Lella*, ed. Jeremy Corley and Vincent Skemp (CBQMS 38; Washington DC: The Catholic Biblical Association of America, 2005), 14–27.

---

with "mercy" (kindness, *mîḥan*), it appears that this broader interpretation of justice is implied.[14] [Almsgiving in the Book of Tobit]

Daniel disappears from the account at this point. Although Daniel has performed loyally for the king in giving the interpretation and preparing him to hear and understand its message, he receives neither reward nor acknowledgment from Nebuchadnezzar and never encounters him again. Daniel presents Nebuchadnezzar with the opportunity to repent, specifying the way it could be done; that he is met with silence prompts the reader to consider whether or not Nebuchadnezzar will ignore his advice.

The Author's Description of the Dream and of the King's Punishment

The Author's Account of Nebuchadnezzar's Hubris and Heaven's Declaration of Punishment, 4:28-30 (4:25-27 MT)

Because the description of Nebuchadnezzar's degrading punishment comes from the authoritative voice of the third person

Narrative Voices

The author of any narrative controls the way the reader receives information by constructing many voices, all of which present information with various levels of reliability. God's words, to be sure, are trustworthy, as are those of the storyteller (narrator) who is omniscient—that is, the storyteller can know the thoughts, feelings, motivations, and actions of the characters in the story. The reader must continually evaluate the words of Nebuchadnezzar and of Daniel, but the words of God and of the author (or of the storyteller, whom the author constructs) are presented as true. As Yairah Amit explains,

The biblical story-world [the world constructed by the author] assumes there are nonexplicit rules that say who is above suspicion and who may be misleading us, deliberately or otherwise. In this way, the reader knows when the information is reliable and can be trusted, and when it needs to be tested.

Amit's point is not that the narrative is history (although it may be presented by the author as true), but that the morals and values it upholds are expressed by the various perspectives of God's words, the storyteller's (narrator's) voice, and the characters' words and actions.

Yairah Amit, *Reading Biblical Narrative: Literary Criticism and the Hebrew Bible* (Minneapolis: Fortress, 2001), 94

---

narration (4:28-33 [4:25-30 MT]), the reader of the entire account has a trustworthy report about Nebuchadnezzar's intractable pride and God's demand for accountability. [Narrative Voices] The author's indication that twelve months have passed (v. 29 [v. 26 MT]) tells the reader that Nebuchadnezzar has had ample time to change. [Twelve Months as a Warning Period] Has Nebuchadnezzar repented and completed acts of righteousness or shown mercy to the poor? The text never specifies that he does. Rather than giving a direct answer, the narrative continues with a description of a singular action of the king and a record of his thoughts: he walks about the roof of his palace and, with great pride, considers the wealth and power of Babylon. The image here can be associated with ancient Near Eastern texts, which show that Nebuchadnezzar indeed had great reputation as a builder.[15] Given that the only description of Nebuchadnezzar's actions is one of arrogance,

Twelve Months as a Warning Period

A year's time can be used as the standard period for potential repentance or for the full measure of disaster. In the book of Esther, for example, the time interval from the choosing of "the lot" that determined the date of the annihilation of the Jews and the date of its implementation was one year (Esth 3:12-13). In rabbinic literature, the plagues inflicted upon Pharaoh and the Egyptians also lasted twelve months (*Exod. Rab.* 9:12; *Deut. Rab.* 7:9).

Building Decorations

Nebuchadnezzar's building projects in Babylon were made unforgettable not only by their massive proportions, but also by the beautiful blue tile, replete with decorations of plants and animals. Here is an example of a bull and of Mushussu, a mythological beast.

Bull and Mushussu, mythological animal with snake's neck and scales. From the Ishtar Gate, Babylon, Iraq. Vorderasiatisches Museum, Staatliche Museen zu Berlin, Berlin, Germany. (Credit: Erich Lessing/Art Resource, NY)

the author leads the reader to judge him unfavorably. If Nebuchadnezzar did indeed perform acts of charity during the twelve-month period, he either has not yet recognized God, or no longer acknowledges him. It is more likely that the silence encourages the reader to conclude that God has waited patiently, and now the time has arrived for the implementation of God's judgment. Indeed, Nebuchadnezzar's walking on the pinnacle of his palace in pride will soon be seen in stark contrast with his own statement that God humbles those who walk in pride (4:37 [4:34 MT]).

An examination of the boastful words that Nebuchadnezzar uses to note his accomplishments hints that he places himself close to God in importance. Such words as "mighty power" and "glorious majesty" (4:30 [4:27 MT]) are commonly used to refer to God's sovereignty over the universe. These words also form a preview to the very last words that Nebuchadnezzar will state before he disappears from the book (4:36 [4:33 MT]). With these final words, Nebuchadnezzar will repeat the aggrandizing self-understanding that was shown when he created the golden statue (Dan 3). The king could not be further from Daniel's declaration to show mercy to the poor.

Voice from Heaven, 4:31-32 (4:28-29 MT)

The author continues the third person account with a quotation from "a voice from heaven," which interrupts Nebuchadnezzar's speech and dramatically underscores God's judgment upon him. The words of the voice from heaven more closely recall Daniel's version of Nebuchadnezzar's dream than does the king's telling, thus upholding Daniel's position as an authentic interpreter of the dream, and hence, of God's plan. The most significant detail of the punishment, namely, Nebuchadnezzar's loss of kingship and departure from human society, is listed first. [A Voice from the Heavens] This voice from heaven, which appears even before Nebuchadnezzar finishes speaking, states, "You shall be driven away from human society" (4:32 [4:29 MT]), quoting Daniel's words (4:25 [4:22 MT]). Additional references that were unique in Daniel's telling (4:25 [4:22 MT]) are also echoed here, namely, the king's eating grass like oxen and knowing that the lesson of the Most High is designed for him (4:32 [4:29 MT]). It is interesting to note that from the perspective of the heavenly voice, no reference is made to any future restoration of the king. This in itself does not confirm that the author holds God has taken away the possibility, but it does show a more pressing concern—that God does hold all sovereigns accountable.

A Voice from the Heavens

In the Hebrew Scriptures, following the commandments is frequently referred to as obeying God's voice. Abraham obeys God's voice to sacrifice his son Isaac (Gen 22:2), the Israelites are cautioned that if they listen and obey God's word they will avoid punishments in the desert (Exod 15:26), and they learn that they will be God's treasured people if they keep the covenant (Exod 19:5). As God states to Jeremiah,

But this command I gave them, "obey my voice, and I will be your God, and you shall be my people; and walk only in the way that I command you, so that it may be well with you." Yet they did not obey or incline their ear, but in the stubbornness of their evil will, they walked in their own counsels, and looked backward rather than forward. From the day that your ancestors came out of the land of Egypt until this day, I have persistently sent all my servants the prophets to them, day after day; yet they did not listen to me, or pay attention, but they stiffened their necks. They did worse than their ancestors did. (Jer 7: 23-26)

In rabbinic tradition, the *bat qol* (lit., "daughter of a voice") may be defined as "a reverberating sound," or a voice from heaven that may "offer guidance in human affairs," and may be "regarded as a lower grade of prophecy."

The heavenly voice substitutes for prophecy, which ceased after the exile. As R. Abba states, "After the later prophets Haggai, Zechariah, and Malachi had died, the Holy Spirit departed from Israel, but they still availed themselves of the Bath Kol" (*b.* Yoma 9b).

The heavenly voice may also be used to announce reward and punishment. Hence, in the account of the martyrdom of Hananiah ben Teradyon, when the Roman executioner spares Hananiah additional torture and subsequently also perishes, a voice from heaven declares, "Hananiah and his executioner have both entered the World to Come" (*b.* 'Abod. Zar. 17b–18a), cited in Pearl, *Theology in Rabbinic Stories*, 50 (see also Mark 1:11 and Collins, *Daniel*, 230–31).

Judah Slotki, comp., *Midrash Rabbah: Index*, vol. 10 of *The Midrash Rabbah*, trans. and ed. H. Freedman and Maurice Simon, 3rd ed., 10 vols. (New York: Soncino Press, 1983), 1.

Chaim Pearl, *Theology in Rabbinic Stories* (Peabody MA: Hendrickson).

John J. Collins, *Daniel: A Commentary on the Book of Daniel* (Hermeneia; Minneapolis: Fortress, 1993).

The Author's Description of Nebuchadnezzar's Punishment, 4:33 (4:30 MT)

The last words of the third person account underscore the authority of God's word by a description of the simultaneous implementation of Nebuchadnezzar's punishment. Reflecting the order of Daniel's words as well as those of the heavenly voice, this description of Nebuchadnezzar's punishment confirms that its two key aspects are Nebuchadnezzar's separation from society and his complete degradation, shown by his animalistic behavior of eating grass as an ox. [Other Traditions about Nabonidus and Nebuchadnezzar] This perspective contains one unique description not disclosed earlier: "his hair grew as long as eagles' feathers and his nails became like birds' claws" (4:33 [4:30 MT]). In itself, the phrase does not appear to be an indication of the evil of the person so affected, as is seen in its benign usage in the tale of Ahiqar. [Ahiqar] Rather, it is indicative of the length of time passed and the degree of suffering endured. In the present context, this remarkable description provides a final picture of Nebuchadnezzar in his state of punishment, indicating his subjugation and humiliation by associating him with the very beasts he is amongst. In addition, it previews that a dramatic

Nebuchadnezzar's Punishment

William Blake. 1757–1827. *Nebuchadnezzar*. 1795/c. 1805. Color print finished in ink and watercolor on paper, Tate Gallery, London, Great Britain. (Credit: Tate Gallery/Art Resource, NY)

William Blake's imaginative interpretation of Nebuchadnezzar's punishment emphasizes the king's madness and degradation. The very posture of his muscular body appears as a beast. Note the claws on his feet, the deranged appearance, and the fallen tree in the background.

reversal is about to occur. Because this final confirmation of Nebuchadnezzar's degradation comes from the author, the reader can see that God indeed judges human sovereigns and is loyal to divine promises. [The Defeat of Injustice] All that has been previewed in the dream has been fulfilled.

Nebuchadnezzar's Description of His Restoration

The Completion of Nebuchadnezzar's Letter, 4:34-37 (4:31-34 MT)
After showing the reader of the entire account that God does indeed respond to Nebuchadnezzar's sin and arrogance, the author now returns to the king's letter to his subjects, presenting the second part, again in Nebuchadnezzar's words. By returning to the rubric of the letter, the author continues to contrast Nebuchadnezzar's report of his experience to his subjects with the one known to the reader of the entire account. With no data to fill in the gaps of interpretation, with no indication that

Other Traditions about Nabonidus and Nebuchadnezzar

Besides the Prayer of Nabonidus ([Prayer of Nabonidus]), other texts preserve traditions about both Nabonidus and Nebuchadnezzar that may have influenced this composition. The "Text from the Accession Year of Nabonidus to the Fall of Babylon" relates that Nabonidus stayed in Teima and improperly avoided the ceremonies and divine processions in Babylon where his presence would have been expected (*ANET*, 306).

An inscription of Nabonidus speaks of Nabonidus's failure to respond to a certain religious action directed against Marduk: "[he] did not raise his hand against the cult places of any of the great gods, but let his hair unkempt, slept on the floor (to express his pious desperation)" (*ANET*, 309). This depiction parallels the description of Nebuchadnezzar of Dan 4 who suffers as a beast.

Finally, certain Babylonian texts show a suppliant Nebuchadnezzar who appeals to Marduk:

O Marduk, my lord, do remember my deeds favorably as good [deeds], may (these) my good deeds be always before your mind (so that) my walking in Esagila and Ezida—which I love—may last to old age. May I (remain) always your legitimate governor (*šakanakku*), may I pull your yoke till (I am) sated with progeny, may my name be remembered in future (days) in a good sense, may my offspring rule forever over the black-headed. (*ANET*, 307)

Apparently, stories of both Nebuchadnezzar and Nabonidus have influenced Dan 4. It is possible that the author altered the presentation of these repentant kings with the more complex portrait of the Nebuchadnezzar of the book of Daniel—one who mouths words of praise to God, which, nonetheless are ambiguous and ultimately self-aggrandizing.

All texts translated by A. Leo Oppenheim and located in *ANET*, ed. James B. Pritchard, 3rd ed. with sup. (Princeton NJ: Princeton University Press, 1969).

Ahiqar

The book of *Ahiqar*, a 5th century BC Aramaic Jewish pseudepigraphical work from Egypt, tells the story of the man Ahiqar, the wise vizier to King Sennacherib. This wisdom tale, with its setting in the king's court, the portrayal of unfair accusations against its hero, and the hero's eventual triumph, offers comparisons with the book of Daniel. When Ahiqar is falsely imprisoned, the description of his suffering is analogous to that of Nebuchadnezzar's punishment:

And when the king [Sennacherib] looked at him, he saw him in a state of want, and that his hair had grown long like the wild beasts' and his nails like the claws of an eagle, and that his body was dirty with dust, and the color of his face had changed and faded and was now like ashes. (*Ahiqar* 4:26)

After the king of Egypt sees the righteous Ahiqar, who has been wrongly accused, in such a miserable state, he praises God for allowing him to discover the truth and restores Ahiqar to his authority, wealth, and freedom. Like Nebuchadnezzar, Ahiqar (Arabic version) trusts that he will succeed. He speaks to his king with these words of praise, "And I by the help of the Most High God and thy noble favour and the power of the king will build [a castle] for thee as thou desirest."

R. H. Charles, trans., "The Story of Aḥiḳar," in *Pseudepigrapha*, vol. 2 of *The Apocrypha and Pseudepigrapha of the Old Testament in English*, 2 vols. (Oxford: Clarendon Press, 1913; repr., 1976), 754, 758.

Nebuchadnezzar was ever addressed by Daniel or by the heavenly voice, and with no knowledge of Nebuchadnezzar's punishment, the king's subjects must rely on the only other information given to them: this final self-portrait by Nebuchadnezzar (4:34-37 [4:31-34 MT]). Only with this narrow portrayal can they judge his words. In contrast, the readers of the complete account, who see this continuation of the letter as the final portion of the entire narrative, have a larger context to evaluate Nebuchadnezzar's proclamation.

Nebuchadnezzar's voice continues with these words: "when that period was over" (4:34 [4:31 MT]). It is not clear, however, which "period" the king refers to. Surely it is possible that the reference is to his punishment, but because the punishment is depicted only in

The Defeat of Injustice

Several texts in the Hebrew Scriptures demonstrate that those evildoers who thwart justice and force people into deprivation will ultimately be defeated. Pss 10 and 37, for example, connect the theme of the cry to God for justice with a confirmation that the wicked of the earth will come to an end and that the oppressed will no longer suffer. Even though oppressors act confidently, secure in their belief that they may continue their cruel activities with impunity, God will hear those who suffer. As the Psalmist states,

The LORD is king forever and ever;
the nations shall perish from his land.
O LORD, you will hear the desire of the meek;
you will strengthen their heart, you will incline your ear
to do justice for the orphan and the oppressed,

so that those from earth may strike terror no more. (Ps 10:16-18)

This association of "doing" justice and righteousness is also linked in the Bible with the keeping of God's law and teachings. Ps 37:30-31 reads,

The mouths of the righteous utter wisdom,
and their tongues speak justice.
The law of their God is in their hearts;
their steps do not slip.

These words, far from being an expression of simplistic piety, reveal a striking faith. If one sees the world as mirroring justice, indeed if one sees God as being just, one will continually strive for such an outlook to become reality. This, too, is Daniel's hope.

the narrative portion, the addressees of the letter (his subjects) would not know this. The first portion of the letter concluded with either Nebuchadnezzar's request of Daniel (Belteshazzar) to provide interpretation (4:18 [4:15 MT] or with the statement that Daniel's "thoughts terrified him" (4:19a [4:16a MT]). Indeed, there is never any allusion to the events of his punishment in either the first portion of the letter or in the second part.

Because the king's letter to his subjects neither specifies Daniel's dream interpretation nor gives a description of his humiliation, it functions to suggest Nebuchadnezzar's self-serving nature. For those who hear only the letter, the image of Nebuchadnezzar remains completely respectable. Although he prefaces his doxologies with the introduction, "my reason returned to me" (4:34, 36 [4:31, 33 MT]), the phrase may simply imply that he no longer is afraid of the dream or that the dream is no longer an enigma to him. Both doxologies (4:34-35 [4:31-32 MT] and 4:37 [4:34 MT]) contain interesting features of contrast, connotation, and placement, and together they serve equally as a preface and conclusion to his statement concerning his own reign, thus calling particular attention to his self-designated importance.   [The Doxologies]

In both of Nebuchadnezzar's doxologies, the first and final statements about God provide an intriguing contrast. Just as the absence of Nebuchadnezzar's punishment in the context of his letter allows for an untarnished presentation of the king for those who hear only his perspective, the words of Nebuchadnezzar's doxologies take on unique connotations within the letter's conclusion. Nebuchadnezzar employs characteristic phrases from the Hebrew Bible to praise God, but because he uses them without their usual contexts, they take on new connotations, suggesting that God may act capriciously.

Immediately upon praising the Most High's kingdom, for example, Nebuchadnezzar states "all the inhabitants of the earth are accounted as nothing" (4:35 [4:32 MT]). Given that these words

---

The Doxologies

In the Hebrew Scriptures, a doxology is a liturgical poem or hymn that ends with a praise of God's name. Scholars believe that they usually have their provenance in temple liturgy, but they are also found in narrative, wisdom literature, and in the prophets as well. There are four doxologies in the Psalter, each concluding a collection of psalms and thus dividing the Psalter into five sections, perhaps corresponding to the five books of the Torah. Note the following two examples:

Blessed be the LORD, the God of Israel,
from everlasting to everlasting. Amen and Amen. (Ps 41:13 [41:14 MT])

Blessed be the LORD, the God of Israel
who alone does wondrous things.
Blessed be his glorious name forever;
may his glory fill the earth! Amen and Amen. (Ps 72:18-19)

The use of doxologies persisted after the close of the Hebrew Scriptures. Three examples from the New Testament are 2 Cor 1:3-5; Eph 1:3; and 1 Pet 1:3.

S. E. Gilingham, *The Poems and Psalms of the Hebrew Bible* (Oxford Bible Series; Oxford: Oxford University Press, 1994), 241–42.
Louis F. Hartman and Alexander A. Di Lella, *The Book of Daniel* (AB 23; Garden City NY: Doubleday & Co., 1978), 175.

are not placed in a broader context of God's care for humanity, they could imply that God is disdainful of human beings and of the earth's creatures. Within the broader context of the Hebrew Scriptures, however, one comprehends how these words are properly used to praise God, as seen in the following example from Isaiah:

> All the nations are as nothing before him;
> they are accounted by him as less than nothing and emptiness . . .
> The LORD is the everlasting God,
> the Creator of the ends of the earth.
> He does not faint or grow weary;
> his understanding is unsearchable.
> He gives power to the faint,
> and strengthens the powerless. (Isa 40:17; 28-29)

As this quotation shows, it is surely not the case that God despises his creation. Rather, God responds directly to those who, by their own evil, challenge his sovereignty; at the same time, God empowers the righteous. Similarly, Nebuchadnezzar's declaration that God "does what he wills with the host of heaven and the inhabitants of the earth," raises the possibility that God is whimsical. Yet Isaiah 24:21-23 gives us a more complete picture:

> On that day the LORD will punish
> the host of heaven in heaven,
> and on earth the kings of the earth.
> They will be gathered together
> like prisoners in a pit;
> they will be shut up in a prison,
> and after many days they will be punished.
> Then the moon will be abashed,
> and the sun ashamed;
> for the LORD of hosts will reign
> on Mount Zion and in Jerusalem,
> and before his elders he will manifest his glory.

This text makes clear that God's actions against heavenly and earthly opponents have cosmic implications. The earth itself will be transformed and God's kingship will become manifest on Mount Zion, the place whence the knowledge of God will become known to the entire world.

Finally, we note that Nebuchadnezzar's statement, "there is no one who can stay his hand or say to him, 'What are you doing?'" (4:35 [4:32 MT]), may connote that God's power defies justice.

This quotation is reminiscent of Job's complaint: "He snatches away; who can stop him? Who will say to him, 'What are you doing?'" (Job 9:12).

These problematic words are found within the context of Job's questioning of God's justice: "he destroys both the blameless and the wicked. When disaster brings sudden death, he mocks at the calamity of the innocent" (Job 9:22-23). Yet when one sees such challenging words in the book of Job, one has the entirety of Job's experience with which to judge them—experiences that include Job's eventual acceptance of the gulf that exists between God and humanity and his willingness to remain silent in face of the mysteries of the world's suffering. There is no comparable context for Nebuchadnezzar.

Before Nebuchadnezzar gives his final doxology, he repeats his statement concerning the return of his reason: "At that time my reason returned to me; and my majesty and splendor were restored to me for the glory of my kingdom. My counselors and my lords sought me out, I was re-established over my kingdom, and still more greatness was added to me" (4:36 [4:33 MT]). This time, however, he uses the occasion to introduce new laudatory references. These words of self-praise, located between the two doxologies, not only form a conclusion to the first doxology, but also temper the import of the second. As Nebuchadnezzar begins his final words of praise to "the King of Heaven," the glory he gives to himself has the disconcerting effect of deemphasizing the temporary nature of any kingship God bestows on human beings. By waiting to praise God until he heaps these narcissistic words upon himself, the final words of Nebuchadnezzar no longer are an unequivocal statement of a defeated king's submission to God; rather, their connotations allow for the skepticism about Nebuchadnezzar's own character to remain. The phrase, "and my majesty and splendor were restored to me for the glory of my kingdom" (4:36 [4:33 MT]), recalls an earlier scene of arrogance— namely, when Nebuchadnezzar spoke on the rooftop with these words regarding his building of Babylon: "and for my glorious majesty" (4:30 [4:27 MT]). Here, Nebuchadnezzar praises himself as much as he does God.

In one respect, the God of Israel does have the final victory over Nebuchadnezzar; this previously incorrigible enemy acknowledges God and even notes that God's sovereignty is equated with divine justice. God's control over the universe is especially underscored when his very enemy praises him.[16] Nebuchadnezzar speaks words that one would expect of Daniel: "for all his works are truth, and his ways are justice; and he is able to bring low those who walk in pride" (4:37 [4:34 MT]). For the first time, he refers to himself as "Nebuchadnezzar," without the title of "king." By addressing God as "the King of Heaven," he apparently acknowledges God's kingship. At the same time, Nebuchadnezzar's understanding remains incomplete. This is indicated not only by the connotations of the words employed, but also by Nebuchadnezzar's lack of any explicit identification of himself as the one who needed humbling. In addition, the abrupt ending of this chapter reports neither Nebuchadnezzar's continuing association with Daniel nor the passing on of his kingdom. [King of Heaven]

Although the impression given to the readers who know only of Nebuchadnezzar's letter severely limits their understanding of what God requires of rulers and how God responds to arrogance, for the readers of the entire account, God still has the final say. Nebuchadnezzar's last words, "he is able to bring low those who walk in pride" (4:37 [4:34 MT]), can be understood to refer to either Nebuchadnezzar's past or future humiliation, for the reader of the entire book would know that not only was Nebuchadnezzar punished, but also that his empire was conquered in fulfillment of God's plan.

The intriguing silence concerning Nebuchadnezzar's end ultimately may point to the ignominy of this king, who, in fact, disappears. Nebuchadnezzar's importance is reduced to a moral lesson. This chapter is clearly connected with the subsequent one, in which Daniel uses the account of Nebuchadnezzar's punishment as a paradigm for Belshazzar's own downfall. In the literary context of this book, Nebuchadnezzar is followed by his "son" Belshazzar with whom the kingdom of Babylon ends. Any restoration of Nebuchadnezzar, therefore, has only short-lived consequences. Nebuchadnezzar's letter, although structured as a decree to his own subjects with a restricted perspective, is, to be sure, a construct of the author who writes for the exilic community. With possible roots in Babylon, the story probably first circulated widely among

King of Heaven

AΩ The term "the God of Heaven" (Dan 2:18) became used frequently during the Persian period, perhaps, as Collins suggests, because of the celestial connotations of the God of Israel, who is creator of Heaven and Earth, and because the Persians also believed in a celestial god.

Sometime after the Maccabean era, scholars suggest, the appellation was avoided because of its similarity with the Greek term, "lord of heaven" (*ba'al šĕmayin, Zeus Ouranios*), a name that was derided by Jews with the substitution *šiqqûṣ šômēm* (appalling idol).

The unique usage here of "King of Heaven," which is tantamount to "God of Heaven," may have been chosen because it "has the advantage of emphasizing the theme of kingship in this context" (Collins, 232; see also 1 Esd 4:46).

It is also possible the author is able to suggest another connotation by the choice of this word. When Nebuchadnezzar speaks of God as "the King of Heaven," the name could mean either the God of Israel or a god of Babylon. The ambiguity of the king's sincerity is again suggested.

Louis Hartman and Alexander Di Lella, *The Book of Daniel* (AB 23; Garden City NY: Doubleday & Co., 1978), 139, 253.

John J. Collins, *Daniel: A Commentary on the Book of Daniel* (Hermeneia; Minneapolis: Fortress, 1993).

The Audience Hall of Darius I
The Audience Hall of Darius I (550–486 BC) and Xerxes I (485–465 BC) in Persepolis, Iran, bears witness to the great power and wealth of the Achaemenids. Note the lion attacking the bull and the impressive soldiers on this relief.

Reliefs of lion attacking bull and Persian guards. Achaemenid period. Audience Hall of Darius and Xerxes (Apadana), East Stairway, Persepolis, Iran. (Credit: Giraudon/Art Resource, NY)

Jews in Persia, where Nebuchadnezzar was interpreted through the lens of the community's experience with Persian overlords.

By showing how Nebuchadnezzar presented incomplete information to his own subjects, the Jewish audience of antiquity could contrast Nebuchadnezzar's limited self-disclosure with the full account that contained the trustworthy words of Daniel, the incontrovertible words of God, and the omniscient third-person narration. The readers of the author's day could see that although their own people had been subject to the consequences of Nebuchadnezzar's pride, they nonetheless survived, whereas Nebuchadnezzar's empire was vanquished. They are reminded that there is no king on which to rely but the true king, the God of Israel.

This portrayal of Nebuchadnezzar contrasts the supposed success, wealth, and power of the foreign overseer with the values and ethics of the Jewish people. The author of Daniel, far from portraying Nebuchadnezzar as benign, shows him to be inept, yet dangerous. Nebuchadnezzar's blindness has consequences: he is incapable of providing justice for his subjects and is portrayed as one who either wittingly or unwittingly brings danger to the Jewish people.[17] Jewish life in the Diaspora was indeed filled with insecurities and threat. As their irrational sovereign, Nebuchadnezzar would just as soon promote Jews in his service as he would sentence them to torturous deaths (Dan 3), insist upon their assimilation (Dan 1), or outlaw their faith (Dan 3). Indeed, Daniel's relationship with Nebuchadnezzar is particularly menacing because this sovereign represents an evil that is masked with familiarity. Stories of doltish kings show that despite their leaders' caprice, Jews secured protection and privileges with the help of their God, the legacy of their torah, and their own superior wits. There is another reason behind such stories of capricious rulers and their incompetent advisers.[18] In addition to the book of Daniel, other texts use the motif of the wise Jewish courtier to point out the injustice of the ruling culture and indict its politics. Citing 1 Esdras, which tells the story of the righteous Zerubbabel, Erich Gruen concludes, "The Jewish courtier, by hailing truth as the purveyor of justice, contrasts it with the injustice practiced by all elements of society—with explicit reference to the king among the perpetrators of injustice."[19]

Finally, even when Jews enjoyed a measure of peace and security under foreign rule, stories that underscore the cleverness of Jewish courtiers encouraged people to resist assimilation, a key to survival. For the Diaspora Jews in the Persian Empire who read this story, Gruen's remarks are most telling: "The Jews did indeed owe restoration and protections to the generosity of Persian rulers, a fact that could be made more palatable by having a Jew outwit rivals and take credit for determining the policy of the suzerain."[20]

We have seen that such a case is presented by the stories of Daniel and Nebuchadnezzar. Daniel serves as the wise Jew who knows that God is the source of his wisdom. He recognizes that Nebuchadnezzar is the perpetrator of terrible injustice and has the courage to speak out and demand that he change. By showing the ambiguity in Nebuchadnezzar's final self-serving words of praise, the author allows the reader to conclude that Nebuchadnezzar remains obtuse; nonetheless, God and hence Daniel's community are victors of the contest, as Nebuchadnezzar's last words yet attest. [Was Nebuchadnezzar Sincere? Rabbinic Skepticism]

Was Nebuchadnezzar Sincere? Rabbinic Skepticism

As shown in the midrashim, the rabbis were not swayed by Nebuchadnezzar's doxologies and saw them as hypocritical. To show this interpretation, they reverse the order of the doxologies. In comparing Nebuchadnezzar's words with those of Pharaoh (of the exodus) they argue,

So it always is with the wicked; as long as they are in trouble, they humiliate themselves, but as soon as the trouble passes, back they return to their perversity. Thus Nebuchadnezzar, when he was in trouble, praised God, as it says: *Now, I Nebuchadnezzar, praise and extol and honour the King of Heaven; for all His words are truth* (Dan. IV, 34), but as soon as he recovered his greatness, he began to boast: *The King spoke and said: Is not this great Babylon, which I have built for a royal dwelling-place, by the might of my power and for the glory of my majesty* (ib. 27). Pharaoh also did the same: for when he saw that THE RAIN AND THE HAIL AND THE THUNDERS WERE CEASED, HE SINNED YET MORE (IX, 34). (*Exod. Rab.* 12:7)

CONNECTIONS

Many Jewish and Christian community leaders today who fight against poverty find inspiration for their work from the values of the Hebrew Scriptures. Caring for the stranger, the orphan, and the

Maimonides on Charity

The great Jewish philosopher Maimonides presents an understanding of charity consisting of eight levels, as presented by Louis Jacobs:

1. A man gives, but is glum when he gives. This is the lowest degree of all.
2. A man gives with a cheerful countenance, but gives less than he should.
3. A man gives, but only when asked by the poor.
4. A man gives without having to be asked, but gives directly to the poor who know therefore to whom they are indebted, and he, too, knows whom he has benefited.
5. A man places his donation in a certain place and then turns his back so that he does not know which of the poor he has benefited, but the poor man knows to whom he is indebted.
6. A man throws the money into the house of a poor man. The poor man does not know to whom he is indebted but the donor knows whom he has benefited.
7. A man contributes anonymously to the charity fund that is then distributed to the poor. Here the poor man does not know to whom he is indebted, neither does the donor know whom he has benefited.
8. Highest of all is when money is given to prevent another from becoming poor, as by providing him with a job or by lending him money to tide him over a difficult period. There is no charity greater than this because it prevents poverty in the first instance.

Louis Jacobs, *The Book of Jewish Belief* (West Orange NJ: Behrman House, 1984), 185.

widow, three groups in Israelite society who had no advocate and who were chronically impoverished, was seen not as charity, or free giving from the heart, but as the fulfillment of the commandment to seek justice—an obligation that tolerated no excuses. [Maimonides on Charity]

This understanding of justice is rooted in the very nature of the God of Israel. God's creation mirrors God's justice; the order and harmony of the universe as well as God's subjugation of chaos and death establish divine justice over all creatures. God, moreover, is not only creator, but also the redeemer who frees the Israelites from slavery and who gives them the Torah, a paradigm for righteous behavior, justice, and holiness.

Israel teaches that Moses' laws called for both king and ordinary citizens to practice justice in all circumstances; similarly, the prophets demand it of king and commoner. As Israel looked to an ideal future, it expressed profound hopes that not only would its own nation be characterized by a perfect implementation of justice, but also that all peoples would love God and seek justice in a world of peace where even the animal kingdom no longer knows strife.

The content of social justice is aptly summarized by Moshe Weinfeld:

[It is associated with] *mercy and loving kindness* or . . . with the context of ameliorating the situation of the destitute . . . [they] cannot be aided by righteous judgments in court alone, but by the elimination of exploitation and oppression on the part of the oppressors.[21] [Justice in the Ancient Near East]

This understanding provided a mandate for acting in accordance with ideals, as governments and individuals alike were responsible for improving the lot of the destitute. The king was to provide just enactments and was to uphold just laws. The landowners and the upper classes were neither to exploit their workers nor enslave them for defaulting on debts. Individuals were obliged as well; care

Justice in the Ancient Near East

Israel's notions of social justice were rooted in the broader ancient Near Eastern context—it can be seen that some ideas were adopted and others critiqued and modified. The concept of *mīšarum* (righteousness), analogous to the justice and righteousness of Israelite society, was practiced by kings in Mesopotamia; it consisted of the liberation of slaves and the forgiveness of debt, declared by the fiat of the king in order to court favor with their subjects. An example of such declaration is as follows:

> The fields of the people of Babylon, belonging to them previously, which were robbed by enemy forces . . . the borders of which were forgotten and no borderstones were set up for them . . . he returned and gave over to the people of the *kidinnu* [symbol of divine protection], the people of Babylon and Borsippa, neglecting no one. He granted land to young and old alike . . . and gladdened their hearts. He placed his shadow over the people of the *kidinnu*, whoever they were; he gave them gifts and granted them estates. (Weinfeld, 108)

This text, which comes from a stele of Merodach Baladan (reigned 562–560 BC), provides an example of the privileges that Mesopotamian kings would grant to subjects of temple cities, a practice continued by Persian, Egyptian, and Greek sovereigns as well. Such grants would often occur upon their installation as sovereign or at other noteworthy occasions. Perhaps the author of Daniel further underscores his contempt of Nebuchadnezzar by suggesting that even when Nebuchadnezzar, upon his restoration, had the perfect opportunity to proclaim release or favor, he never did so.

For more on the study of *mīšarum* see Moshe Weinfeld, *Social Justice in Ancient Israel and in the Ancient Near East* (Minneapolis: Fortress, and Jerusalem: Magnes, 1995), 7–12, 16–21, 42–43, 48–49, 97–110.

needed to be provided for widows and orphans. Job understands this well when he states:

> If I have withheld anything that the poor desired,
> or have caused the eyes of the widow to fail,
> or have eaten my morsel alone,
> and the orphan has not eaten from it—
> for from my youth I reared the orphan like a father,
> and from my mother's womb I guided the widow—
> if I have seen anyone perish for lack of clothing,
> or a poor person without covering,
> whose loins have not blessed me,
> and who was not warmed with the fleece of my sheep;
> if I have raised my hand against the orphan,
> because I saw I had supporters at the gate;
> then let my shoulder blade fall from my shoulder,
> and let my arm be broken from its socket. (Job 31:16-22)

Daniel, too, underscores the priority of the needs of the poor by his words to Nebuchadnezzar. Of all the crimes that could have been singled out as examples of Nebuchadnezzar's cruelty to his subjects, the author chose to have Daniel condemn Nebuchadnezzar's neglect of the poor that existed within his kingdom. The author's portrayal of the kings' advisers as obtuse similarly indicts the hierarchy that supports Babylonian policies. Indeed, the Hebrew Scriptures have a long tradition of condemning oppressors for their virtual enslavement of people and for their abuse of the populace for narrow economic gain. In addition, the disregard that Nebuchadnezzar shows for God's holy city and that his son and successor Nabonidus has toward the sacrificial vessels constitute more evidence of Nebuchadnezzar's arrogance before God. The wealth of Babylon was unjust, Israel believed, because it came from the labor of subjugated peoples who had neither an advocate in their king nor any protection from a governmental system that had no accountability. In telling Nebuchadnezzar to do justice for the poor in order to show repentance, Daniel calls upon the king to adjust the economic policies under which his subject peoples work for the benefit of Nebuchadnezzar's empire. It is this lack of concern for the dignity, freedom, and religious practices of the community that prompted the author of the later chapters of Daniel to equate the tyranny of Antiochus with the cruelties of Nebuchadnezzar. The insight shared by both the narratives of Daniel 1–6 and the visions of Daniel 7–12 is that the quest for power and domination by foreign emperors not only compromises the religious and moral obligations of the Jews they have conquered, but also adds a severe burden of economic hardship upon all subjugated people.

It is impossible to know what the experience of poverty or slavery was for the author of our text. Although we cannot tell which percentage of Jews lived comfortably and which percentage were without means or sold into debt-slavery in periods of Babylonian, Persian, or Greek domination, we do find texts that say either implicitly or explicitly that such conditions were indeed problematic.

The records of the Marashu documents (455–403 BC) provide limited, yet important evidence concerning life in Babylonian lands conquered by Persia. These documents from Marashu, a household located within the city of Nippur (on the Chebar canal of the Euphrates), which earlier had been conquered by Nebuchadnezzar and had been used to settle exiles, speaks of the everyday lives of various ethnic groups. Because the ethnicity of these people can be identified from onomastics (the study of the origins of proper names), scholars have determined that at least 8 percent of the population was Jewish. In general, Persian society was composed of citizens, free classes without civic rights, semi-free, and slaves. Land was owned by the sovereign and was held by others only at his pleasure, in exchange for services and taxes. The semi-free worked on estates owned by the state, by temples, and by freemen. As M. Dandamayev explains, although the practices were not as ruthless as in Babylonian days, insolvent debtors could be arrested and imprisoned by the creditor.[22] Although some prospered, others suffered hardship or were threatened with the loss of liberty. There is attestation, for example, that one Jewish man had to replace his overseer for conscription. Another Jewish slave was ordered to make repairs on an irrigation canal or be responsible for ensuing damages. One Jewish woman was threatened with slavery if she had relations with a man before marriage.[23]

In the Hellenistic Period, Jews under Ptolemaic and Seleucid reign were semi-autonomous, yet there are indications of occasions of great difficulties. Steps taken by Ptolemy II Philadelphius to curb the rampant slave trade in Ptolemaic district of Syria-Palestine show that it was a serious problem. Free farmers were crushed with heavy burdens of taxes as the land was considered to be leased from the crown. If they could not pay, they could be sold as slaves.[24] Although the degree of historicity found in Esther, Tobit, and Maccabees has no consensus among scholars, nevertheless, their references to poverty and slavery assume such conditions to be possible. In the book of Esther, for example, upon telling Ahasuerus about Haman's proposal to have the Jewish people exterminated, Esther remarks, "If we had been sold merely as slaves, men and women, I would have held my peace" (Esth 7:4). Here the author appears to take for granted that such a fate for people was plausible. In addition, the marking of Purim (the holiday of the deliverance from annihilation at the hands of the Persians) by giving charity and by sending baskets of food both to friends and to the poor reflects the author's concern to support those who were in need (Esth 9:19, 22).

The book of Tobit extols the acts of feeding the hungry, clothing the naked, and burying the dead (Tob 1:16-17). Second Maccabees reports that in the days of Seleucid rule, Antiochus plundered the temple and had men killed and women and boys sold as slaves (2 Macc 5:24; see also 1 Macc 1:29-32). The author of 3 Maccabees, a book whose practices and descriptions of citizenry and slaves are much disputed, nevertheless paints the dire conditions of Jews as follows:

> [Ptolemy decreed] "all Jews shall be subjected to a registration involving poll tax and to the status of slaves. Those who object to this are to be taken by force and put to death; those who are registered are also to be branded on their bodies by fire with the ivy-leaf symbol of Dionysus, and they shall also be reduced to their former limited status." . . . Now some, however, with an obvious abhorrence of the price to be exacted for maintaining the religion of their city, readily

gave themselves up, since they expected to enhance their reputation by their future association with the king. But the majority acted firmly with a courageous spirit and did not abandon their religion; and by paying money in exchange for life they confidently attempted to save themselves from the registration. (3 Macc 2:28, 29, 31)

Although this account is not independently verified by any non-Jewish texts, it assumes that such a presentation was plausible. Apparently, the author wanted to show that freedom could come at a terrible price and that an unpredictable king could nullify a person's security at any time.

In our modern world, there are, fortunately, examples of tremendous self-sacrifice on the part of those who have gone to great lengths to assist those who suffer in poverty because of discrimination or lack of opportunities. Some challenge governments; others work behind the scenes. One such inspiring man was Leon Sullivan, an exceptional Christian minister of the twentieth century who not only helped the poor in his immediate circle, but who also started organizations that continue to help millions throughout the world. He showed extraordinary courage in the face of the discrimination he personally experienced and a drive to give others the tools to lift themselves up from the ravages of centuries of discrimination. His life belies the defeatist attitude that suggests that one person cannot make a difference.[25]

Leon Sullivan

Leon Sullivan. 1922–2001.

Leon Sullivan (1922–2001) first served as pastor for the Zion Baptist Church in Philadelphia. Even as a child he fought segregation and discrimination at the local drugstore counter that denied him service. In the 1950s, he helped to organize boycotts of businesses that refused to hire blacks. Not satisfied with these victories, he turned his energies into establishing agencies that would empower impoverished people by providing them with the skills necessary to advance in the labor force. In the 1960s he established the Opportunities Industrialization Center (OIC), a community-based organization that taught trade skills and more effective agricultural methods, and that developed partnerships with investors to provide seed money for black-owned businesses.

As the first black member of the board of General Motors, Rev. Sullivan set his sights beyond America and found multiple ways to help impoverished blacks of apartheid South Africa. He authored a code of conduct for businesses operating in South Africa, called "the Sullivan Principles." These principles were unprecedented at the time, calling for equal access to opportunities in the work force and housing opportunities, education, and advancement. When the government of South Africa delayed in dismantling apartheid, he called for the exit of American-owned businesses located there. In the 1990s his principles were expanded to address issues of economic disparity in a global economy, and, in an effort to improve human rights throughout the world, were supported by UN Secretary General Kofi Annan. U.S. Rep. Jack Kemp recalled that Rev. Sullivan believed he could make a difference by working behind the scenes and by believing that the Bible mandates people of faith to overcome evil with good. He stated,

> he's a role model because of his integrity, his commitment, his passion . . . we're talking about a man who has the vision, without which, the Bible says a nation perishes. He has a vision of that potential in all of us to do good and to be good. He sees every child as a child of God with a spark of divine talent and divine ability . . . he teaches all of us . . . never to give up, to see the good in people, to work for their highest ideals and to preach and practice, racial, ethnic and . . . I'm going to say religious tolerance and reconciliation. Those are great qualities.[26]

Rev. Sullivan saw the hopelessness and despair of people locked into poverty without the keys of education, mentoring, experience, or capital to ameliorate their condition. Rather than wait for governmental action, whether it be in Philadelphia or South Africa, Rev. Sullivan worked tirelessly to open agencies and secure funding to improve the lot of desperately poor people. His first "industrialization center," located in Philadelphia, now boasts an international network of forty-six educational and investment centers in seventeen countries of the world where millions of unskilled people now become trained and employed workers. While working behind the scenes, Rev. Sullivan also tirelessly pursued his vision that governments as well could be held to a higher standard of justice. His travels in apartheid South Africa personalized the experience of poverty and indignity that invigorated his quest. After being singled out and disrespectfully searched at a South African airport, he reflected,

> In 1974 I met with hundreds in South Africa, and I realized that apartheid was sinful. . . . When I was getting on the plane to go home, the police took me to a room and told me to remove my

clothes. A man with the biggest .45 I'd ever seen said, "we do to you what we have to." I stood there in my underwear, thinking, "I'm the head of the largest black church in Philadelphia and I'm on the board of directors of General Motors. When I get home, I'll do to you what I have to."[27]

It is that feeling of outrage and solidarity with those who experience injustice and poverty that many biblical texts address. The readers of the book of Daniel would know that despite Daniel's call for Nebuchadnezzar to repent and provide for the poor, foreign rulers, whether from Babylon, Persia, or Greece, could not be counted on to provide the proper care for the most marginalized in society. By calling upon Nebuchadnezzar to atone by assisting those in need, the author provides a paradigm not only for faith, but for action. For Daniel's readers today, the courage, vision, and sacrifices made by individuals like Rev. Sullivan allow us to see that it is possible to have hope for change. This trust in the ultimate goodness of humanity to work for social justice encouraged Daniel's disempowered community and can serve as a catalyst for people today to resist poverty and injustice as fervently as did this extraordinary man.

NOTES

[1] The work of Megasthenes is quoted in the writings of Abydenos (a Greek historian of the 2d or 3rd century AD), which, although lost, are preserved in Eusebius (c. AD 260–341 [*Praeparatio Evangelica* 9.41.456d–457b]). See Lawrence Wills, *The Jew in the Court of the Foreign King: Ancient Jewish Court Legends* (Harvard Dissertations in Religion 26; Minneapolis: Fortress 1990), 99–101.

[2] See John Collins, *Daniel: A Commentary on the Book of Daniel* (Hermeneia; Minneapolis: Fortress, 1993), 217–21; Esther Eshel, "Possible Sources of the Book of Daniel," in *The Book of Daniel: Composition and Reception*, ed. John Collins and Peter Flint, 2 vols. (Supplements to Vetus Testamentum 83; Leiden: Brill, 2001), 2:387–88; Ernst Haag, *Die Errettung Daniels aus der Löwengrube: Untersuchungen zum Ursprung der biblischen Danieltradition* (Stuttgarter Bibelstudien 110; Stuttgart: Verlag Katholisches Bibelwerk, 1983), 14–25; James Montgomery, *A Critical and Exegetical Commentary on The Book of Daniel* (ICC; Edinburgh: T. & T. Clark, 1927), 24–57; Wills, *The Jew in the Court of the Foreign King*, 87–121. For recent studies on the Old Greek of Dan 4, see Matthias Henze, *The Madness of King Nebuchadnezzar: The Ancient Near Eastern Origins and Early History of Interpretation of Daniel 4* (Supplements to the Journal for the Study of Judaism 61; Leiden: Brill, 1999) and T. J. Meadowcroft, *Aramaic Daniel and Greek Daniel: A Literary Comparison* (JSOTSup 198; Sheffield: Sheffield Academic Press, 1995).

[3] John Goldingay, *Daniel* (WBC 30; Dallas: Word Books, 1989), 82.

[4] Collins, *Daniel*, 208, 221, 232.

[5] Ibid., 221, and 221 n. 46. See also Edwin Yamauchi, *Persia and the Bible* (Grand Rapids MI: Baker Book House, 1996), 131–34.

[6] Montgomery, *A Critical and Exegetical Commentary*, 225.

[7] The *waw* is explicative (meaning, "that is"), Goldingay, *Daniel*, 122.

[8] Theodotion has the compound subject *eir kai hagios* (a watcher [transliteration] and a holy one). Montgomery, *A Critical and Exegetical Commentary*, 234.

[9] Collins, *Daniel*, 224–26.

[10] This expression can also be translated, "a holy, divine spirit."

[11] Such usages are found in the Qumran Aramaic fragments of *1 En.* 89 and 86, namely, 4Q206 En[e] ar4ii and 4Q207En[f] ar, respectively. See J. T. Milik, ed., *The Books of Enoch* (Oxford: Clarendon, 1976), 238, 244–45. See also Stephen Breck Reid, *Enoch and Daniel: A Form Critical and Sociological Study of Historical Apocalypses* (Berkeley CA: Bibal Press, 1989), 63.

[12] Ibid.

[13] Collins, *Daniel*, 230.

[14] Francis Brown, S. R. Driver, and C. A. Briggs, "*miḥan*," *Hebrew and English Lexicon of the Old Testament* (Oxford: Clarendon Press, 1962), 1093.

[15] Collins, *Daniel*, 230.

[16] W. Sibley Towner, "The Poetic Passages of Daniel 1–6," *CBQ* 31 (1969): 322–23.

[17] Daniel Smith-Christopher, "Prayers and Dreams: Power and Diaspora Identities in the Social Setting of the Daniel Tales," in *The Book of Daniel: Composition and Reception*, ed. John Collins and Peter Flint, 2 vols. (VTSup 83; Leiden: Brill, 2001), 1:285. Cf. Walter Brueggemann, "At the Mercy of Babylon: A Subversive Rereading of the Empire," *JBL* 110/1 (1991): 3–22, for a very different interpretation.

[18] The practice of deriding foreign kings has its precedent in the biblical portrayals of Pharaoh, Jeroboam, and Ahasuerus. This practice was particularly common in the Hellenistic period. See Erich Gruen, *Heritage and Hellenism: The Reinvention of Jewish Tradition* (Berkeley: University of California Press, 1998), 160–77.

[19] Gruen, *Heritage and Hellenism*, 167. The author cites 1 Esd 4:28-33, 36-37, 42.

[20] Gruen, *Heritage and Hellenism*, 166.

[21] Moshe Weinfeld, *Social Justice in Ancient Israel and in the Ancient Near East* (Jerusalem: Magnes Press; Minneapolis: Fortress Press, 1995), 7.

[22] M. Dandamayev, "The Diaspora" in *Introduction: The Persian Period*, vol. 1 of *The Cambridge History of Judaism*, ed. W. D. Davies and Louis Finkelstein (Cambridge: Cambridge University Press, 1984), 326–42.

[23] Dandamayev, "The Diaspora," 344–50. Also, Smith-Christopher, "Prayers and Dreams," 277–79.

[24] Henk Jagersma, *A History of Israel from Alexander the Great to Bar Kochba* (Philadelphia: Fortress, 1986), 25–26.

[25] "A Principled Man: Rev. Leon Sullivan," http://www.revleonsullivan.org/ indexf.htm> (18 October 2006).

[26] Ibid.

[27] Paul Lewis, "Leon Sullivan, 78, Dies; Fought Apartheid," *New York Times*, 26 April 2001 (Midwest edition), C-17.

THE HANDWRITING
ON THE WALL

Daniel 5:1-31

COMMENTARY

The narratives of Daniel 1–4 show that despite Nebuchadnezzar's lack of judgment and wisdom, he is particularly dangerous because he is so powerful. The author emphasizes the absurdity of his caricatured behavior, giving an unflattering portrait for a theological purpose; Nebuchadnezzar is doomed to fail because the world is under the control of a God who demands justice and will be victorious over tyrants. Nebuchadnezzar's power may allow him to harness the infrastructure of a mighty empire, but his character is the source of his undoing. His repentance is only tentative and limited, and although the king is reestablished, he falls shortly thereafter. The finality of Nebuchadnezzar's reign is indicated by the author's sequencing of chapters 4 and 5. As his successor appears, the reader soon recognizes that Nebuchadnezzar has disappeared. The end of this emperor who destroyed Judah, however, does not receive explicit commentary. Instead, the narrative now moves quickly to the end of his legacy and his very empire with the portrayal of the final act of the last Babylonian ruler, Nebuchadnezzar's son, Belshazzar. Daniel 5 portrays the successor and son of Nebuchadnezzar as a profligate ruler who learns nothing from God's response to his father's cruelty. In a stylized portrayal of a powerful, yet pathetic king, the author uses one episode from Belshazzar's life to illustrate that God's demand for justice supersedes any earthly ruler's quest for power. [Belshazzar in History]

Because Babylonian annals record that the historical Belshazzar was the son of Nabonidus, the biblical identification of Belshazzar as the son of Nebuchadnezzar has generated several hypotheses from modern biblical interpreters. The following have been offered: the biblical identification is simply an error on the part of the author; the supposed relationship between Belshazzar and Nebuchadnezzar was deliberately fashioned by the author in order to use available negative

Belshazzar in History

Unlike the book of Daniel, which identifies Belshazzar as the son of Nebuchadnezzar, Babylonian documents identify Belshazzar (556–539 BC) as the son of Nabonidus, the last emperor of Babylon, and his co-regent (see above, ch. 4). Nothing is said of Nabonidus in the Bible, although various biblical traditions about Nebuchadnezzar appear to be based upon him. Belshazzar began his co-regency because his father was absent from the seat of government for several years, when he went to Teima, in Arabia. Many scholars believe that Nabonidus's surprising move there was prompted by his neglect of the cult of Marduk and the subsequent unrest and deterioration of civil order. Others argue, however, that such negative portrayals of Nabonidus in the annals of antiquity were written by self-interested competitors and enemies. Whatever the cause of Babylon's domestic problems, Nabonidus had to face an even greater threat to his empire as Persia grew in domination and cast its eyes toward his lands, ultimately conquering Babylon. Although there is historical evidence that Nabonidus was spared death when the city was taken, Belshazzar's fate is uncertain.

See Edwin M. Yamauchi, *Persia and the Bible* (Grand Rapids MI: Baker Book House, 1996), 85–87.

Nabonidus

This stela probably represents the historical King Nabonidus (555–539 BC), who is clothed in the traditional royal dress and holds a type of standard used during religious ceremonies. Note the divine symbols of the moon-god, Sin (closest to the standard), the planet Venus of Ishtar, and the winged disc of the sun god Shamash.

Stela of King Nabonidus. Neo-Babylonian dynasty. 555–539 BC. British Museum, London, Great Britain. (Credit: © British Museum/Art Resource, NY)

information from the reign of Nabonidus to deprecate his supposed father Nebuchadnezzar; or the phrase "son of Nebuchadnezzar" may really mean "grandson of Nebuchadnezzar" or "successor to Nebuchadnezzar." The debate continues because Nabonidus was not related to Nebuchadnezzar, and it is not known how he ascended the throne. We should also consider that the author is expressing a relationship in kind, if not blood; the author casts Belshazzar in the light of his predecessor.[1] [Outline of Daniel 5]

Throughout this portrayal of Belshazzar's feast and Daniel's interpretation of the handwriting on the wall, the author recalls specific elements of the previous depictions of Nebuchadnezzar's reign and character. Belshazzar, like Nebuchadnezzar, has thousands at his bidding. Although he has unlimited resources, the interpretation of the mysterious handwriting on the wall eludes him until Daniel explains it. Just as Nebuchadnezzar depended on the Jewish exile to interpret what his own officials could not, so does Belshazzar remain stymied by a divine portent until Daniel arrives. To underscore further Belshazzar's humiliation at the end of his life and the weakness of the Babylonian Empire, the author shows that a woman, the queen, must inform Belshazzar of Daniel's ability to understand signs from heaven.

Unlike the previous scenes, where one incident of Nebuchadnezzar's oppression led to yet another, the pace quickens

in Daniel 5. Belshazzar has only one narrative devoted to him, and Daniel's interpretation of the upcoming end of the first kingdom is indeed closer at hand.
[Should Belshazzar Be Called "King"?]

Outline of Daniel 5

The Beginnings of the Feast, 5:1-4
The Writing on the Wall, 5:5-6
Belshazzar Appeals to the Wise Men, 5:7-9
The Information from the Queen, 5:10-12
Belshazzar's Words to Daniel, 5:13-16
Daniel's Interpretation of Belshazzar's Past, 5:17-24
Daniel's Condemnation of Belshazzar's Actions, 5:22-23
The Writing on the Wall, 5:24-28
The End of Belshazzar, 5:29-30

The Beginnings of the Feast, 5:1-4

By presenting a scene of opulence and profligate behavior, the author crafts the beginnings of an unexpected contrast. No reason is given for Belshazzar's feast, although scholars have suggested that the author may have been acquainted with traditions about a coronation ceremony, a New Year's or traditional festival, or a gathering that encouraged the Babylonians to resist the Persians as they faced an imminent attack.[2] The author paints a scene of infinite wealth and power in order to highlight Babylon's fall, for the lavish displays actually serve as the stage for God to announce the end of the kingdom of Babylon. Although Belshazzar has no apparent reason to sponsor the feast, God will soon infuse it with purpose—to precipitate Belshazzar's death.

The dramatic display of excess in this first scene sets the stage for Belshazzar's fall. Like similar portrayals of indulgence by emperors, the feast points to the hubris of the regime that is about to be defeated or whose designs will be outwitted (Jdt 1:16; Esth 1:3-7). Although there is no specific condemnation of the feast, it nevertheless highlights the king's pride. John Goldingay observes:

> The omen [of the handwriting on the wall] is provoked by an act of idolatrous sacrilege in a context of Bacchanalian excess. It is of manifestly supernatural origin and elicits the response appropriate to an announcement of divine judgment. . . . [Dan 5] begins with a scene that can be read as one of ostentation, decadence, carousing, coarseness, wantonness, and self-indulgence, a scene that might have been designed to illustrate the wisdom literature's warnings about power, sex, and drink. . . . From self-indul-

Should Belshazzar Be Called "King"?

Issues concerning the accuracy of the biblical references to Belshazzar as "king" are much debated. The Belshazzar known from history was acting regent when his father Nabonidus was away from the throne, but was never king in his own right. Thus, some exegetes have argued that the biblical appellation of him as "king" is inaccurate. Still others question whether he should be considered the last king of Babylon, because although we know the fate of Nabonidus, there is no evidence that Belshazzar was alive when Babylon was assaulted. The Greek historian Xenophon (d. c. 355 BC) reports that "the king" was overpowered and killed by Cyrus's forces, but the identity of this king is not stated and not all historians trust the accuracy of his report (*Cyropaedia* 5.2.1). Arguing from analogy, Alan Millard proposes that the title "king" does not need to be taken literally. He cites a statuary inscription that identifies a ruler of ancient Gozan as both "king" in Aramaic and as "governor" in Assyrian. He concludes that the reference to Belshazzar as "king" could have been used to describe his function as crown prince, with a precision of titles neither necessary nor relevant.

Other modern scholars see these concerns as misplaced. Lester Grabbe, for example, argues that the intention of the author is theologically motivated; hence the historicity is not verifiable.

Alan R. Millard "Daniel and Belshazzar in History," *Biblical Archaeology Review* 11/3 (May/June 1985): 73–78.

Lester Grabbe, "The Belshazzar of Daniel and the Belshazzar of History," *Andrews University Seminary Studies* 26 (Spring 1988): 59–66.

gence issued sacrilege and blasphemy; what was wrong with the banquet was not the thing itself but where it led.[3]

The initial focus of Belshazzar's banquet is hedonistic drinking; "he was drinking wine in the presence of the thousand" (v. 1). Indeed, Belshazzar confuses wisdom with pleasure, as indicated by the reference that he "took counsel" in wine (v. 2, A.T.). It is interesting to note that a midrash links Belshazzar's decision to use the temple vessels with his very destruction. With this act he practices the same "evil business" as does Pharaoh, Ahasuerus, and Haman (*Eccl. Rab.* 6:1). The flowing of alcohol indeed has its effects on Belshazzar. The author states that Belshazzar begins giving commands, literally, "while tasting the wine," in other words, "under the influence of the wine" (v. 2), suggesting that the king is drunk. [Insights from Classical Sources on the Portrayal of Belshazzar's Feasting] The spectacle of a drunken king adds to the drama of this scene, for it suggests that Belshazzar's ability to communicate what he sees may be impaired or that he may be more likely to issue an outrageous order. This image of Belshazzar's banquet finds its counterpart with the narrative of King Ahasuerus's feast in the book of Esther. In that account, the Persian king Ahasuerus appears both ridiculous and dangerous because his rule is capricious and totalitarian. After the Persian monarch feasts for seven days, he commands that

---

Insights from Classical Sources on the Portrayal of Belshazzar's Feasting

Herodotus and Xenophon, two Greek historians of antiquity, report that Babylon fell while its people were feasting during a holiday. This first quotation is from Herodotus (d. c. 425 BC):

Now if the Babylonians had known beforehand or learned what Cyrus was up to, they would have let the Persians enter the city and have destroyed them utterly; for then they would have shut all the gates that opened on the river and mounted the walls that ran along the river banks, and so caught their enemies in a trap. But as it was, the Persians took them unawares, and because of the great size of the city (those who dwell there say) those in the outer parts of it were overcome, but the inhabitants of the middle part knew nothing of it; all this time they were dancing and celebrating a holiday which happened to fall then, until they learned the truth only too well. (*Histories* 1.191)

This second quotation comes from the historian Xenophon (d. c. 355 BC):

At last the ditches were completed. Then, when he heard that a certain festival had come round in Babylon, during which all Babylon was accustomed to drink and revel all night long, Cyrus took a large number of men, just as soon as it was dark, and opened up the heads of the trenches at the river. . . . "My friends," said [Cyrus], "Let us, therefore, enter in with dauntless hearts, fearing nothing and remembering that those against whom we are now to march are the same men that we have repeatedly defeated, and that, too, when they were all drawn up in battle line with their allies at their side, and when they were all wide awake and sober and fully armed; whereas now we are going to fall upon them at a time when many of them are asleep, many drunk, and none of them in battle array. And when they find out that we are inside the walls, in their panic fright they will be much more helpless still than they are now." (*Cyropaedia* 7.5.15–20)

Although foreign nations were often portrayed negatively for the ancient historians' own polemical purposes, the theme of the Babylonians' hedonism provides an interesting context for the biblical author who emphasizes that the excessive banquet was an affront to God.

Queen Vashti be paraded for his guests. When she refuses, his anger is so roused that he agrees to the advice of his obsequious officials to dismiss her as queen and to harness the infrastructure of the empire in order to implement the inane decree that "every man should be master in his own house" (Esth 1:22). As we shall see, Belshazzar's depravity is exploited as comedy as well. Although he does not issue a fatuous decree, he is portrayed as physically losing his dignity. The similarities in these banquet scenes allow the reader to see the commonalities in both of these monarchs. Both portrayals depict rulers who abuse their populace and who live as though there were no accounting to the creator of the universe.

Besides including the telling descriptions of Belshazzar's actions regarding his feast, the author's sentence structure indicates that Belshazzar acts arrogantly. The first two sentences of this chapter, both of which have Belshazzar as subject, employ a less commonly used syntax that suggests something is amiss. Normally, Aramaic demands that the verb be placed ahead of the subject, but in two cases (vv. 1 and 2), the subject, i.e., Belshazzar, precedes the verbs "made" and "commanded." The particular attention drawn to the king as subject is appropriate, because now he uses his power to offend the God of Israel, demanding that the sacred vessels of the Jerusalem temple be used for his own sacrilegious purposes.

Although his order is not given in direct speech, the author reports that he commanded the vessels "that his father Nebuchadnezzar had taken out of the temple in Jerusalem" (v. 2) be brought to him. This remark suggests that although Nebuchadnezzar had indeed taken the holy vessels as booty, they had not yet been publicly debased. Belshazzar's command reveals an arrogance and contempt for the faith of the captives. According to Exodus, the temple vessels were made by Bezalel in the days of Moses; they were used in the service of the sanctuary, in accordance with the commandment of God to Moses: "Have them make me a sanctuary, so that I may dwell among them" (Exod 25:8). Exodus meticulously records that the people offered their own jewelry, metal, and precious materials for the construction of the sanctuary and its holy objects used in worship (Exod 25:1-7; 35:20-29). The book of Numbers similarly attests to the tradition of the vessels' importance: the initiation offering for the altar included silver and golden basins, dishes, and plates weighing hundreds of shekels (Num 7:84-86).[4] The holiness and importance of these objects were so precious that 2 Kings devotes a lengthy description to the abduction of the temple objects during Nebuchadnezzar's invasion (2 Kgs 25:13-17).

Wine

In the Hebrew Bible, wine is one of the components of a feast and its plentiful supply can be a sign of wealth. In addition, "the cup (of wine)" is a frequent reference to one's allotted fate or blessings. Wine can at times be perilous, however, as shown in these examples from Proverbs: "Wine is a mocker, strong drink a brawler, and whoever is led astray by it is not wise" (Prov 20:1). So, too, Prov 23:20: "Do not be among winebibbers, or among gluttonous eaters of meat; for the drunkard and the glutton will come to poverty, and drowsiness will clothe them with rags." This glass paste amphora, dated from the 4th–1st centuries BC, is representative of the containers used to hold wine.

Amphora from Israel. 330–60 BC. Glass paste, Haaretz Museum, Tel Aviv, Israel. (Credit: Erich Lessing/Art Resource, NY)

The barbaric nature of Belshazzar's request is heightened by several factors. First, the holy vessels are to be used for drinking the king's wine. Secondly, not only does Belshazzar himself debase them, but he also becomes the catalyst for the participation of others in the sacrilegious behavior, namely, "his lords, his royal consort, and his concubines" (v. 2, A.T.). The presence of these people, all royal possessions, presents another ostentatious show of power and wealth. It is interesting to note that that the word *šēgĕlāteh* (v. 2), used for the royal consort, comes from the root meaning "cohabit." It sometimes is translated as "queen," but here it is used in contradistinction to the true queen (*malkāʾ*) who will soon speak words of wisdom concerning Daniel (v. 10-12). Because the queen is not present here, the dignity of the wise words she soon speaks is heightened. When the king's command to bring the vessels is in fact carried out, the author brings a significant addition to the vessel's description. Instead of being defined as the ones "that his father Nebuchadnezzar had taken out of the temple in Jerusalem" (v. 2), they are now identified as the ones "that had been taken out of the temple, the house of God in Jerusalem" (v. 3). This description lessens Nebuchadnezzar's importance and underscores the rightful sovereignty of God. In addition, the Babylonians' sacrilegious behavior climaxes with the specification that the drinking was a catalyst for their idolatrous praises to their "gods of gold and silver, bronze, iron, wood and stone" (v. 4), words reminiscent of other prophets' and psalmists' condemnation of the futility of idolatry (Deut 29:17 [16 MT]; Pss 115:4; 135:15; Isa 2:20; 30:22; 31:7; Hos 8:4).

At the end of this first scene, the reader sees that Belshazzar and his entourage are ensconced in excess, mocking the God of Israel while they worship the idols that legitimate the injustices of the Babylonian Empire. The caricature is used to form the contrast with what is about to occur—the arresting revelation that the powerful and comfortable Belshazzar is about to meet God's judgment.

The Writing on the Wall, 5:5-6

The complacency and revelry of the banquet are suddenly interrupted in the next scene by the unaccountable appearance of a disembodied hand that writes on the wall of the banquet room. Without explanation, it disappears, leaving indecipherable words that alter the state of the king from enjoying his revelry to being awash in fear. This appearance of the portentous writing on the wall, Belshazzar's subsequent consternation, the inability of the astrologers to provide an interpretation, and the successful explanation by Daniel are reminiscent of the story of Nebuchadnezzar's dream of the great statue (Dan 2). In interpreting Nebuchadnezzar's dream, Daniel had declared that his kingdom would be crushed by a succession of others. Similarly, the mysterious writing declares that the corrupt kingdom of Belshazzar will soon come to an end. The supernatural origins and the importance of the writing on the wall are indicated by the description of how it occurred, by the unique grammatical features of its portrayal, and by Belshazzar's perception of the phenomenon. [The Writing on the Wall]

The scene is introduced by the adverbial phrase "at that hour," or "instantly" (v. 5; "immediately," NRSV). This phrase was used previously to express Nebuchadnezzar's rage that any noncompliance to his decree would be met with an instantaneous throwing of the violators into the fiery kiln (3:6 and 3:15), and to indicate that Nebuchadnezzar's arrogance was met by the simultaneous punishment of God (4:33 [4:30 MT]). So, too, does the word here indicate the striking power of the ultimate sovereign of the universe. The verb that describes the appearance of the fingers, "came forth" (*npq,* v.5), is the same verb used twice of the sacred vessels that Nebuchadnezzar made "to come forth" from the temple ("had taken," [NRSV] v. 2) and that Belshazzar made "to come forth" to the feast itself ("had been taken out," [NRSV] v. 3). The reference to the "fingers" recalls the very hand of God used to inscribe the tablets of the law. [The "Finger of God" in the Bible] The simultaneity of the appearance of the portentous sign with the event of Belshazzar's drinking from the vessels not only underscores the immediate

The Writing on the Wall

 The gripping description of the handwriting on the wall and Belshazzar's resulting fear are captured in Rembrandt's famous painting, *Belshazzar's Feast*. One rabbinic interpretation concerning why the words were impossible for the Chaldeans to read, namely, that the letters of the handwriting were written from top to bottom, instead of right to left, may be reflected in Rembrandt's work. The artist was well familiar with the Ashkenazic and Sephardic Jewish communities of the Netherlands, in whose neighborhoods he lived.

See Alan J. Millard, "Daniel and Belshazzar in History," *BAR* 11/3 (May/June 1985): 75.

Rembrandt van Rijn. 1606–1669. *Belshazzar's Feast*. National Gallery, London, Great Britain. (Credit: Art Resource, NY)

response by God, but also indicates that Belshazzar sees the actual *process* of writing and not simply the words alone. Although the reader will soon see that the words remain opaque to Belshazzar and to his professional interpreters, there is no question that the phenomenon itself was witnessed, as indicated by the reference to the king seeing the hand (*pas yĕdāʾ*) in the process of writing (v. 5b). In addition, the presence of the lampstand and the presumably white background of the plastered wall illumine the writing.

"The Finger of God" in the Bible

The phrase "finger of God" is found in descriptions of God's acts of redemption, revelation, and creation. When the magicians of Pharaoh are stymied in their attempts to reproduce the plague of gnats, they exclaim, "This is the finger of God!" (Exod 8:19 [8:15 MT]), recognizing that the sign is due neither to chance nor to the gods of Egypt. The authority, power, and holiness of the Decalogue itself are indicated by this description: "When God finished speaking with Moses on Mount Sinai, he gave him the two tablets of the covenant, tablets of stone, written with the finger of God" (Exod 31:18, cf. Deut 9:10). God's work in creation is reflected in the following: "When I look at your heavens, the work of your fingers, the moon and stars that you have established; what are human beings that you are mindful of them, mortals that you care for them?" (Ps 8:3 [8:4 MT]).

Thus, Belshazzar is not given a chance to think that the words came from a contender or from a traitor. Indeed, it is the method by which the words are given, and not the indecipherable words themselves, that elicits his reaction of great fear.

The description of Belshazzar's reaction to the event both emphasizes the gulf between God and humanity and maximizes the humiliation of the king. The first description, "the king's appearance changed" ("the king's face turned pale," NRSV), found three times in this chapter, is indicative of his great alarm. Not only does Belshazzar's witnessing of the hand prompt his striking response, but he also similarly experiences the fear anew when his sages are unable to read its writing (v. 9). This same alteration of countenance is what the queen first notices when she enters Belshazzar's banquet hall (v. 10).[5] It is interesting to note that the word that denotes "appearance" in this context (*zîwāyk*, v. 10) may also mean "splendor" or "brightness." It is used earlier in Daniel to indicate the brilliance of the statue that Nebuchadnezzar set up (2:31) as well as the importance of his own royalty (4:36 [4:33 MT]). Later in the book, the phrase "his appearance changed and his thoughts bewildered him" (7:28, A.T.) is used to describe Daniel's reaction upon seeing his vision of the four beasts. It signifies that the content of the revelation is of utmost importance, even altering the appearance of the beholder. Here, the image is deliberately comical, and Belshazzar is left stripped of any dignity. Verse 6 (A.T.) reads: "the belts [or "the joints/knots"] around his loins were loosed (from the root *šĕrā'*) and his knees struck one another." The word for "belts" or "joints" is in the plural, suggesting two possibilities. Perhaps the author implies that because his many fasteners cannot keep his clothing intact, his garments are unbound, and his consequent exposure is a sign of his humiliation. Alternatively, the verb "was loosed" which echoes Daniel's "untying knots" or "solving riddles" (vv. 12, 16 [from the root *šĕrā'*]), may indicate that Belshazzar lost control of his bowels, an equivalent disgrace that is suggestive of his upcoming defeat.[6] The verb "knocked" (*nāqĕšān*), used to indicate that one knee strikes the other, is rare in both Aramaic and biblical Hebrew, but in biblical Hebrew it is used in the context of striking with a weapon or with violence. The mighty Belshazzar has become the antithesis of a warrior. Whereas a soldier "girds his loins" for strength in battle, so now Belshazzar's loins are loosened; after seeing this sign he becomes the source of his own torment. [Belshazzar and Eglon]

Belshazzar Appeals to the Wise Men, 5:7-9

Despite Belshazzar's disgrace and bewilderment, he uses whatever strength he has left to cry out to three classes of soothsayers. His words recall those of Nebuchadnezzar to the Chaldeans when the latter demanded an interpretation of his mysterious dream. Belshazzar does not threaten to punish, however, but only to reward whoever will provide the correct interpretation.

Belshazzar and Eglon

The scene of the undoing of Belshazzar is reminiscent of the oppressive Canaanite king Eglon from the days of the heroic judges in Israel's past. The account of Eglon (Judg 3:15-30) shows that he, too, is humiliated by his loss of physical function before his death. Eglon, whose name suggests "fatted calf," is slain in the outhouse by the hero Ehud, while his guards are unaware that he is even threatened. When Eglon is stabbed, his death is described with the phrase, "and the dirt came out." The Hebrew of this phrase is uncertain but suggests the loss of control of his bowels (see Judg 3:22). In both of these stories of Belshazzar and Eglon, each oppressor of Israel falls to the judgment of God. For Eglon, Ehud is God's instrument, whereas Belshazzar's death comes either directly from God or from Darius as God's agent. Rabbinic interpretation similarly understands Belshazzar's humiliation to refer to the loss of bowel control. In the midrashim, Belshazzar's stomach cramps and a trip to the outhouse leads to his death (*Song. Rab.* 3:4, 2).

Purple Cloth

Cloth that was dyed purple was a luxury item in the ancient Near East, the fabric of royalty. In the Hebrew Bible, purple cloth is an item of booty prized by an enemy noblewoman (Judg 5:30), the color of Solomon's throne seat (Song 3:10), and the color of the fabrics used in the sanctuary and in the temple (Exod 25:4; 2 Chr 3:14). In the book of Esther, it is the color used in the palace decorations (Esth 1:6) and of the mantle given to Mordecai when he is honored by the king (Esth 8:15). The dye was obtained by the labor-intensive method of harvesting mollusks from the sea, specifically gastropods of the Mediterranean Muricidae family.

Roger S. Boraas, "Purple," *Harper's Bible Dictionary*, ed. Paul Achtemeier (San Francisco: Harper & Row, 1985), 844.

Mordecai's and Esther's Attempts to Save their People

The theme of a Jew who serves the government, but is, in effect, powerless alone to save his or her people, is also seen in the book of Esther. Neither Esther, who is queen, nor Mordecai, who is promoted to minister, can rescind "an edict written in the name of the king and sealed with the king's ring" (Esth 8:8). This decree contained orders "to destroy, to kill, and to annihilate all Jews, young and old, women and children" (Esth 3:13) on a single day. After Esther's pleas, Ahasuerus allows an additional law to be enacted that allows Jews to defend themselves (Esth 8:11-13). They are victorious, but not because the decree was ever disallowed.

His offer of purple clothing and a golden chain are the symbols of the ruling elite. [Purple Cloth] They were similarly offered to Daniel in the days of Nebuchadnezzar; they recall the ministry of Joseph in the days of Pharaoh and preview the political advancement of Mordecai (Esth 8:1-2). [Mordecai and Esther's Attempts to Save their People] Yet what exactly is offered to Daniel is ambiguous. It is unclear from the Aramaic whether Belshazzar offers the successful interpreter one-third of the kingdom, whether the interpreter would be the third ranking ruler of the kingdom, or whether he would rule as a member of a triumvirate. Other than the pronouncement of this office, there is no indication of what it actually entailed. Later, the author makes clear that it is, in fact, an empty gesture. Just as the power given to Daniel and to his compatriots (2:48) was ineffective in preventing Nebuchadnezzar from attempting to torture and kill the youths in the furnace, so the office given to Daniel fails to buttress him against the charges brought by Darius's aides (6:4-5 [6:5-6 MT]).

The author relates that the entirety of the kings' assembly of the wise attempts to solve the riddle. The steps leading to the king's encounter with them are puzzling. As he calls for them, he offers a reward for a successful interpretation even though they apparently are not yet present before him (vv. 7-8). Some commentators see this sequence as an example of the inadequate care on the part of the author or redactor, but it may also be a deliberate technique to suggest the king's confusion. The sight of the frightening omen causes Belshazzar not only to lose his decorum, but also his ability to think logically.[7]

Just as Nebuchadnezzar's sages need both to relate the dream and give its interpretation, yet are inadequate at even the first step, so failure is ensured when Belshazzar's entourage of the wise cannot even read the writing. It is striking that they are unable to do so, given that other places in the book of Daniel show the kings' courtiers to be skilled linguists. At the beginning of the book, Daniel and his friends were to be taught the languages of the Chaldeans, and in Daniel 3 and 6 we find that decrees are sent to every people throughout the Babylonian Empire in their respective languages. The author thus highlights the ineptitude of the king's sages who could not read the language even when it would soon be readily apparent to Daniel. The rabbis of antiquity suggest that the courtiers' consternation was prompted because a unique script was employed, because a code was used, or because the letters were out of their proper sequence or written vertically.[8] The author gives no suggestions of such descriptions; rather, the author makes it clear that the Babylonians' lack of ability shows that their famous skill of reading omens is bankrupt. God has the last say. The ineptitude of the wise has the same effect on the king as did the emergence of the words in the first place: his appearance changes and he is bewildered. The king who was engaged in a flurry of activity at his banquet for thousands is now paralyzed.

By juxtaposing the incompetence of the Babylonians with the wisdom of Daniel, the author recalls the contrast that was made between Daniel and the Babylonians who were called to interpret Nebuchadnezzar's dreams. Belshazzar, successor to Nebuchadnezzar, has failed to learn from the previous generation's arrogance. As the Babylonian empire is now poised to collapse, Daniel's audience under subsequent Persian rulers could perceive that their continuing difficulties under their own emperors are for a purpose that is in God's design.

Rhyton

A rhyton in the form of a goat, possibly an ibex. 5th–4th C. BC. (Credit: Werner Forman/Art Resource, NY)

The rhyton, a hornlike container used for drinking or pouring wine, was common in Mesopotamia. This exquisite 5th–4th C. BC gold vessel from the Achaemenid dynasty (Persia) displays a goat or ibex. Rhytons of precious metals would have been familiar objects among Babylonian and Persian royalty.

The Information from the Queen, 5:10-12

Surprisingly, it is the queen rather than the courtiers who serves to open Belshazzar's eyes concerning the writing on the wall. The text gives neither the identification of the queen's name nor her relationship to Belshazzar. She either could be Belshazzar's wife or the wife of the previous monarch (Nebuchadnezzar, according to the biblical chronology). [Adad-guppi, Mother of Nabonidus] Although the text does not state her identity, she is distinguished from the royal wives and concubines (vv. 2, 3) not only because a distinctive word for queen is employed (*malkāʾ*), which connotes "rulership" as opposed

Adad-guppi, Mother of Nabonidus

The Harran inscriptions preserve a stele regarding the hopes of Adad-guppi, the mother of Nabonidus (d. 545 BC), for restoring the proper cult of the Babylonian moon god. Because she had a significant influence upon Nabonidus, who obtained the throne by usurpation (having ousted Labashi-marduk, Nebuchadnezzar's grandson), some scholars suggest that traditions about her stand behind this portrait of Belshazzar's queen. The following text speaks of her importance:

> Sin, the king of all the gods, looked with favor upon me and called Nabonidus, my only son, whom I bore, to kingship and entrusted him with the kingship of Sumer and Akkad. . . . In a dream Sin, the king of all the gods, put his hands on me saying: "The gods will return on account of you! I will entrust your son, Nabonidus, with the divine residence of Harran; he will (re)build the temple Ehulhul and complete this task."

The historical Belshazzar, the son of Nabonidus, was the grandson of Adad-guppi. Israel also had examples from their own experience and literature of strong queen mothers. Bathsheba, for example, ensures that her son Solomon receives the throne from the ailing king David, even though David's son, Adonijah, is next in line. Here in Dan 5, it is possibly the queen's status as queen mother that allows her to play the role of the "female rebuker," as H. J. M. van Deventer argues. On the one hand, she holds the solution for the king to solve his troubling mystery, by informing him of Daniel. On the other hand, the author employs her to belittle Belshazzar as well.

A. Leo Oppenheim, trans., "The Mother of Nabonidus," in *ANET*, ed. James B. Pritchard, 3rd ed. with sup. (Princeton NJ: Princeton University Press, 1969), 561.

H. J. M. van Deventer, "Would the Actually 'Powerful' Please Stand?: The Role of the Queen (Mother) in Daniel 5," *Scriptura* 70 (1999): 241–51.

to concubinage, but also because the text relates that she apparently enters the king's presence for the first time during this banquet. Whereas the other women serve as props, representative of the king's power, she represents sagacity. Because of her prompting, Belshazzar has a chance of understanding the writing; if she did not appear, he might never know of Daniel. Her subordinate standing as a female monarch, moreover, underscores Belshazzar's inadequacy, as she comprehends what the king ought to know. This queen ultimately allows God's plan for Belshazzar's end to be clearly seen.

With forthright confidence this queen commands the king. Inexplicably, her words also serve to critique this monarch who shows such poor leadership in times of crises. Besides listing the many references to Daniel's specific skills, the queen twice mentions that Daniel has divine gifts (v. 11). Her first reference may be translated either "the spirit of the holy gods" or "the spirit of God" is with Daniel. Her second remark may be translated either the "wisdom of the gods" or the "Wisdom of God" is with Daniel. By leaving open these two possibilities of understanding the deity as either singular or plural, the author suggests that whereas one could presume that both Belshazzar and the queen believe in the idols of Babylon, Daniel is filled with the spirit of the one God of Israel.[9] The Jewish reader of antiquity could easily see that whereas the queen might not recognize that her words could refer to a monotheistic view of God, they easily hold that connotation.

The queen enters on her own accord, unlike the wise men who must be summoned. In contrast to her independence, Belshazzar appears weak, for she is obviously beyond his control. If the queen is his mother, she, unlike her son, remembers Daniel; if his wife, she has paid attention to the stories about the wisest interpreter in their midst. As does Nebuchadnezzar, who hears of Daniel from his underling, Arioch (Dan 2), so Belshazzar learns of Daniel's existence from his own subordinate. It is she who has better capacity to lead the empire, even though her gender does not give her the right of succession. [The Wise Queen vs. the Ineffective King]

The queen's multiple references both to Nebuchadnezzar's acquaintance with Daniel and to Daniel's many gifts dominate her speech. Her words both heighten Daniel's superiority and continue to cast doubt on Belshazzar's competence, for although Daniel's wisdom was famous in Nebuchadnezzar's day, even to the point of Daniel being promoted in Nebuchadnezzar's palace, Belshazzar has failed to consider him. The queen's speech is, on the surface, polite, but she continues to imply her consternation and exasperation. With her lengthy rendition of Daniel's talents, the reader must wonder how it could be that Belshazzar is unfamiliar with such an essential person. Indeed, the similarities of their names provide an ironic contrast. Daniel, whom Nebuchadnezzar called Belteshazzar, has a Babylonian name that differs from that of the king by only one additional medial syllable. Yet, the two are so different in character and faith. [Belshazzar in the Book of Baruch]

In contrast to Nebuchadnezzar, who not only welcomed Daniel to interpret his dream but also lauded his wisdom, Belshazzar appears reluctant to invite Daniel to come into his presence. The queen must give a detailed and convincing speech before Daniel ever is summoned; the author thus shows that the great impasse in Belshazzar's ability to understand God's revelation persists. Indeed, this implication that Belshazzar either lacks any awareness of Daniel or that he is reluctant to use him is presumed in various ancient sources. In the writings of Josephus, the queen "begged the king to send for him" (*Ant.* 10.238), and in the Old Greek, although the king knows he should send for someone when the

The Wise Queen vs. the Ineffective King

Athalya Brenner shows that the humiliation of the king functions to negate his sexuality and virility. Like other monarchs who are either feminized or impotent, the loosening of Belshazzar's loins previews his loss of power as a monarch. As Brenner states, "He is hit exactly in the organs he has employed in his orgiastic drinking feast; instead of having sexual intercourse with his concubines, he becomes impotent; instead of eating and drinking, he loses control and becomes incontinent" (239).

In contrast to the undignified and helpless king, the queen is portrayed as being wise and confident. By showing this woman, who can never attain the power of the king, as the only one who can correctly assess what needs to be done, the author discloses that the Babylonian men are inept rulers. Such use of sardonic humor may be one of the few avenues of an oppressed people to subvert a dominant culture.

Athalya Brenner, "Who's Afraid of Feminist Criticism?," in *Prophets and Daniel*, A Feminist Companion to the Bible, 2d ser. (London: Sheffield Academic Press, 2001), 228–44.

astrologers fail—it is the queen he summons, and not Daniel. In the Old Greek, the queen not only lists Daniel's many gifts, but also specifies, "he expounded exceedingly difficult interpretations for Nebuchadnezzar, your father" (v. 12 OG).[10] Just as these various features highlight Belshazzar's obtuseness, so too does the author mock the supposed wisdom of the Babylonian religious system, underscoring that wisdom comes from God. In addition, the author sets the stage to emphasize Daniel's courage. The sage must face this pathetic, yet powerful king, who has no apparent memory of Daniel's former faithful service to the crown.

Belshazzar's Words to Daniel, 5:13-16

In this section, Belshazzar's presence dominates, but his power and authority will soon be contrasted with the much longer description of Daniel's own response. The king's words consist of one possibly disparaging remark regarding Daniel's identity, and three demands: to read the writing, to provide the interpretation, and to serve in the kingdom. Before Daniel obeys, he inserts his own agenda: he counters the king's remark with a clever retort of his own. He details the evil of Belshazzar's past, and only then responds to Belshazzar's demands. [Babylon's Drunkenness] Daniel continues to act with courage, but before he has a chance to speak, Belshazzar preempts him. As we shall see, these words will also be his last.

Just as the queen's words showed that Belshazzar should have known about Daniel's ability, so now do Belshazzar's own words further point to his intransigence. The twofold meaning of his first words to Daniel provides the opportunity for the reader to see his blindness. On the one hand, the words may be translated indicatively: "so you are Daniel, one of the exiles of Judah, whom my father the king brought from Judah." On the other hand, they may be translated interrogatively: "are you Daniel, one of the exiles of

Judah, whom my father the king brought from Judah?" (v. 13). Indicatively, the statement emphasizes Daniel's marginalized identity as an unknown of a captive group. Belshazzar twice refers to Daniel's subordinate status—Daniel is an "exile of Judah" who came to Babylon because of Nebuchadnezzar's conquest and not on his own accord. Interrogatively, Belshazzar's questioning of Daniel's identity is striking because there is no reason given that would justify the need for the king's skepticism. Once Daniel is summoned, Belshazzar would have no reason to question his identity. This question can only be an indication of disparagement on the king's part. That Belshazzar

> **Babylon's Drunkenness**
> When the prophet Jeremiah speaks of the future fall of Babylon, he underscores that Babylon's cruel policies, flagrant waste, and arrogance against the God who granted them power are the cause of God's retribution. Jeremiah uses the imagery of the drunkenness of Babylon's captured lands to preview the end of the empire. The prophet states,
>
> for this is the time of the LORD's vengeance;
> he is repaying her what is due.
> Babylon was a golden cup in the LORD's hand,
> making all the earth drunken;
> the nations drank of her wine,
> and so the nations went mad.
> Suddenly Babylon has fallen and is shattered . . .
> Forsake her, and let each of us go
> to our own country;
> for her judgment has reached up to heaven
> and has been lifted up even to the skies. (Jer 51:6-9)

is not really seeking an answer to this question may be indicated by the fact that he never gives Daniel a chance to answer; indeed Daniel never responds to his condescending tone. Daniel's very first words to Belshazzar exploit the rhetorical structure of Belshazzar's own words (see below).

Belshazzar's second sentence similarly indicts him. He admits that he "has heard of" Daniel (v. 14; cf. v. 16). Although it is possible that Belshazzar is referring to the queen's discussion of Daniel, it is also possible to understand this phrase as an indication that Daniel's successful interpretations of Nebuchadnezzar's dreams were known to Belshazzar all along, but ignored in his own most obvious time of need. Yet, just as the author contrasts Daniel's wisdom with the Babylonian sages' inabilities in Nebuchadnezzar's day, so, too, will Daniel now outshine Belshazzar's associates. When Belshazzar reports to Daniel what he has heard about him, he inserts a telling change compared to the queen's report about him. Whereas the queen referred to Daniel's present ability (v. 12), Belshazzar speaks of Daniel's skills conditionally: "so, if you are able to read the writing and make known its interpretation to me . . ." (v. 16, AT). Besides revealing his skepticism, Belshazzar truncates the queen's words; the contrast between them points to Daniel's upcoming condemnation of the obdurate king. In addition, Belshazzar's own repetition of the unique phrase, "loosing of knots" (v. 16), recalls his earlier humiliation upon the loosening of his belts or the undoing of his bowels. Finally, Belshazzar offers Daniel the same rewards he offered his own astrologers (vv. 7, 16). These are the last recorded words of Belshazzar in the book. Although there will be one final act in which Belshazzar may possibly have participated, namely, the giving of gifts to Daniel, the passive construction leaves ambiguous whether or not Belshazzar actually participated (v. 29). Thus, these words of Belshazzar may indeed constitute his last act and his last words.

Daniel's Interpretation of Belshazzar's Past, 5:17-21

Daniel's presence and his words dominate the second half of this chapter. The lavish resources of Belshazzar, detailed in the first half of the chapter, prove to be no match for the judgment of God and for Daniel's interpretation of that judgment. Belshazzar now watches in stupefied silence as Daniel proceeds.

Daniel begins by detailing the shameful acts of Belshazzar's world of power, waste, and injustice [Babylon in Cyrus's Words] The author presents the possibility that Daniel does not wish to become a part of Belshazzar's world, and thus refuses to give an interpretation based on receiving Belshazzar's presents.[11] The contrast between the two men is well captured by the way in which Daniel echoes the king's words. Whereas Belshazzar said that Daniel should first read, then secondly give an interpretation, and thirdly participate in government, Daniel only claims that he will read and interpret (v. 17). Daniel's actions, however, do not proceed as he states. He delays the reading and interpretation in order to provide a detailed interpretation of the life of Belshazzar, one that, in fact, gives a fuller understanding of what the cryptic words on the wall mean.

Daniel's first words of address to Belshazzar provide an interesting double entendre. Earlier, Belshazzar's address to Daniel could be understood as a questioning of his identity (Are you Daniel?);

Babylon in Cyrus's Words

This mausoleum in Pasargadae, Iran, is believed to be the tomb of Cyrus. When Cyrus boasted about his defeat of Babylon, its captured emperor was easy prey for his verbal invective. Scholars dispute whether Cyrus's captive was Belshazzar or Nabonidus. One of Cyrus's cuneiform-inscribed cylinders records, "A weakling has been installed as the [ruler] of his country. . . . He interrupted in a fiendish way the regular offerings. . . . The worship of Marduk, the king of the gods, he [chang]ed into abomination."

Alan J. Millard, "Daniel and Belshazzar in History," *BAR* 11/3 (May/June 1985): 76.

Mausoleum of Cyrus II the Great. 559–529 BC. Parsargadae, Iran. (Credit: Scala/Art Resource, NY)

now, Daniel's words can be read not only as an evocative, namely, "O King" (NRSV), but also as an interrogative, "Are you the king?" (v. 18, A.T.). Just as Belshazzar did not give an opportunity to Daniel to respond, so, too, does Daniel swiftly move forward with his words. He provides another opportunity to denigrate Belshazzar as shown by the inverted syntax of the following sentence, translated literally: "God Most High gave kingship and greatness, and honor to Nebuchadnezzar, your father" (v. 18). Although the verb normally precedes the subject, here the subject comes first in order to emphasize the kingship of God and to emphasize that any earthly king rules only if God so wills. In addition, because the phrase begins with words of praise, Belshazzar could surmise that Daniel is referring to his own success—but Daniel withholds the name of the recipient of God's blessings until the end of the sentence, reserving it for Nebuchadnezzar, and not for the present king. Paralleling the queen who repeatedly referred to Nebuchadnezzar as Belshazzar's father, Daniel, too, underscores that Belshazzar, as Nebuchadnezzar's son, has a particular responsibility to learn from his father's mistakes.

Daniel's words to Belshazzar quickly become a history of Nebuchadnezzar's reign of terror. Several instances of his past cruelties are recalled. His first reference, that "all peoples, nations, and languages trembled before him," recalls the incident of the fiery furnace (Dan 3), where the same phrase indicates that all people were required to bow before Nebuchadnezzar's statue lest they be tortured and killed. The next reference is to the fate of those who lived and died at the whim of Nebuchadnezzar: "Whomever he wished, he killed, and whomever he wished, he gave life; whomever he wished, he raised up, and whomever he wished, he put down" (v. 19, A.T.). The evil of the king is made all the more striking by the repetition of the words, "whomever he wished," which indicate that the king's actions were based on his whims, and by the active and causative verbs ("he killed," "he gave life," "he raised up," "he put down"). The reader in antiquity would be very much aware of the arrogance of the king who ascribes to himself the attributes of God, for the Scriptures teach that it is God who determines life and death. The following example from Deuteronomy provides a telling reference:

See now that I, even I am he; there is no God besides me.
I kill and I make alive; I wound and I heal; and no one can deliver
    from my hand. (Deut 32:39)

After the worst of Nebuchadnezzar's reign has been recited, Daniel recounts the punishment that was given to him (vv. 20-21). He does so for one reason: to show Belshazzar that he bears special responsibility for understanding the significance of his father's punishment. [The Co-regency of Nabonidus and His Son] Daniel contrasts the *heart* of Nebuchadnezzar "that grew proud" (v. 20) with the detail that Belshazzar "did not humble" his *heart* (v. 22). Similarly, because Nebuchadnezzar endured his punishment "until he *knew* that the Most High God rules over the kingdom of men" (v. 21, A.T.), Daniel chastises Belshazzar for his arrogance, saying, "even though you *knew* all this" (v. 22). In recounting Nebuchadnezzar's punishment, Daniel does not stress Nebuchadnezzar's symbolic dream, but rather Nebuchadnezzar's actual experience itself, making it a preview to the upcoming downfall of Belshazzar. By comparing what Daniel said to Nebuchadnezzar when he interpreted his dream (Dan 4) to what Daniel says to Belshazzar concerning those same events, one finds that there are three interesting variations of detail. First, instead of saying that Nebuchadnezzar dwelt among the beasts (4:25 [4:22 MT]), Daniel states that his "heart was made like that of a beast" (v. 21), thereby further linking Nebuchadnezzar's pride (v. 20) with the opaque heart of Belshazzar (v. 22). Secondly, as opposed to the description that Nebuchadnezzar's dwelling was with wild animals (4:25 [4:22 MT]), Daniel states that "his dwelling was with wild asses," recalling perhaps the symbol of God's remarkable control over this untamed animal and the inability of human beings to comprehend God's ways (Job 39:5-8). Thirdly, in describing Nebuchadnezzar's offense against God, Daniel uses the word "rebel" (*lahăzādâ*, 5:20), a unique term not found in any of the previous descriptions of Nebuchadnezzar. This Aramaic word, and its similar Hebrew equivalent, is used to indicate a heinous, willful sin (Exod 18:11; Deut 1:43; 17:13; 18:20; Jer 50:29).[12] These three variations in Daniel's rec-

The Co-regency of Nabonidus and His Son

The difficulties of Nabonidus's reign are preserved in various Babylonian texts. The following excerpt is a polemical reference to his construction of an image of a deity, his appointment of his son (perhaps Belshazzar) as ruler in his absence, and his expedition in Tema (Teima).

(Nabonidus said): "I shall build a temple for him, I shall construct his (holy) seat,
I shall form its (first) brick (for) him, I shall establish firmly its foundation, . . .

(Yet) till I have achieved this, till I have obtained what is my desire,
I shall omit (all) festivals, I shall order (even) the New Year's Festival to cease!" . . .

After he obtained what he desired, a work of utter deceit,
Had built (this) abomination, a work of unholiness
—when the third year was about to begin—
He entrusted the "Camp" to his oldest (son), the first-born,
The troops everywhere in the country he ordered under his (command).

He let (everything) go, entrusted the kingship to him
And, himself, he started out for a long journey,
The (military) forces of Akkad marching with him;
He turned toward Tema (deep) in the west.

He started out the expedition on a path (leading) to a distant (region). When he arrived there,
He killed in battle the prince of Tema,
Slaughtered the flocks of those who dwell in the city (as well as) in the countryside,
And he, himself, took his residence in [Te]ma, the forces of Akkad [were also stationed] there.

A. Leo Oppenheim, trans., "Nabonidus and the Clergy of Babylon," in *ANET*, ed. James B. Pritchard, 3rd ed. with sup. (Princeton NJ: Princeton University Press, 1969), 313.

ollection of Nebuchadnezzar's transformation help to underscore the seriousness of the abuses of Nebuchadnezzar's reign. [Belshazzar in the Midrashim]

As Daniel prepares to specify Belshazzar's own malfeasance, he again uses the striking phrase, "whomever he will" (v. 21), but this time it is in reference to God's sovereignty regarding the rule of earthly kingdoms. Whereas the phrase "whomever he wished" dominated the description of the activity of Nebuchadnezzar, now Daniel ends his history lesson by underscoring that it is the Most High God who appoints "whomever he wishes" over the kingdoms of humanity. This reference forms a fitting conclusion to Daniel's recitation of the past, as it stresses that the designs of human beings, even those of the king of the mightiest empire, are subject to the approval of the God of the universe. Belshazzar is now primed to hear Daniel's words of condemnation about the specifics of his own life.

Belshazzar in the Midrashim

In the midrashim, Abraham's sacrifice of the heifer to God (Gen 15) is seen typologically as a preview of the sacrifice of the people Israel, caused by the heinous acts of Nebuchadnezzar, Evil-Merodach, and Belshazzar. In this sacrifice, the bird that Abraham placed on the altar symbolizes the Jewish people. The lesson gleaned by this interpretation is that "he who attempts to resist the wave is swept away by it, but he who bends before it is not swept away by it" (*Gen. Rab.* 44:15). In other words, because Judah succumbed to Babylon, the Jewish people suffered terribly but were not destroyed.

Daniel's Condemnation of Belshazzar's Actions, 5:22-23

Having completed his recitation and interpretation of Nebuchadnezzar's life, Daniel continues to preface his remarks concerning the interpretation of the writing by exposing the evil of Belshazzar's rule. Daniel describes Belshazzar's threefold affront against God. First, Belshazzar did not learn from his father's crimes and punishment; secondly, he placed himself above God, in effect saying that there was no one to whom he was responsible for his actions; and thirdly, he brought others into his depraved circle, influencing his compatriots to practice idolatry as well. Daniel thus effectively indicts the entirety of the Babylonian system. The arrogance of Belshazzar, his intransigence, and the wide-reaching scope of his corrupt regime are highlighted by the special resonance of language, recollections of previous phrases, and unique additions. We now examine his offenses.

First, Daniel refers to Belshazzar's kinship with Nebuchadnezzar.[13] As Nebuchadnezzar's son, he willfully squandered his responsibility to learn from his father's punishment. The sentence that reads "And you, Belshazzar his son, have not humbled your heart even though you knew all this!" (v. 22) could also be understood thusly: "Are you his son Belshazzar? You have not humbled your heart, even though you knew all this!" Daniel thus continues the double entendre with questions of identity that Belshazzar himself began when he first encountered Daniel (v. 13). The increased responsibility Belshazzar has held apparently points to the greater punishment he will face, for although Nebuchadnezzar was chastised, his kingdom continued. Now, under Belshazzar, it is about to vanish.

Secondly, we note that in referring to Belshazzar's own self-exaltation, Daniel laments that Belshazzar placed himself above "the Lord of Heaven" (v. 23). This appellation for God is reminiscent of the title "Lord of Kings" that Nebuchadnezzar used of God after Daniel's successful dream interpretation (2:47). The implicit comparison between the two rulers is appropriate here; although Nebuchadnezzar acknowledged God with words, he continued his cruelties (Dan 3) and never made effective repentance (Dan 4). Belshazzar, however, never once looked to any source but himself. Indeed, Daniel chastises him: "you exalted yourself" (v. 23; see also 4:36 [4:33 MT]). This word, which can potentially be used to praise God, is used by Belshazzar only for self-adulation.

Thirdly, Belshazzar enticed the people of his empire to commit idolatry, turning to idols that "do not see or hear or know" (v. 23). These words recall the specific tone and intent of a common biblical theme. We note the following example:

> Our God is in the heavens;
>   he does whatever he pleases.
> Their idols are silver and gold,
>   the work of human hands.
> They have mouths, but do not speak;
>   eyes, but do not see.

Idols

This seal shows two men praying—one before Sin, the moon god (who stands upon the crescent)—the other before Marduk, the head of the pantheon (represented by the dragon-like creature). The author of Dan 5 derides the Babylonian gods and the values they represent.

Seal depicting the moon god Sin standing on a crescent and receiving a prayer by the man standing before him. To the right another man prays before the mushrushu or sirrush, the symbol of Marduk, the chief of the Babylonian pantheon. (Credit: Werner Forman/Art Resource, NY)

They have ears, but do not hear;
   noses, but do not smell.
They have hands, but do not feel;
   feet, but do not walk;
   they make no sound in their throats.
Those who make them are like them;
   so are all who trust in them.
(Ps 115:3-8; see also Ps 135:15-18; Isa 40:18-20)

This text emphasizes the vacuousness of idols and the senseless futility of any belief in them. The might of Babylon is doomed because of the very religious and political system that supports it.

The final element of Daniel's critique uses a unique phrase, "the God in Whose hand is your soul" (v. 23, A.T.). The use of the word "hand" hearkens back to the hand that writes on the wall. The "hand of God" in biblical Hebrew and Aramaic is indicative of God's power and frequently is used to indicate God's victory over His enemies—the "haters of YHWH," who act with malice, greed, and aggrandizement. It is this same "hand" that wrote on the wall and that now exercises judgment. It is this hand that has power over Belshazzar's soul, or "very breath" (NRSV). The word used for soul, *nišmâ* (*nĕšāmâ*, Hebrew), is used for life itself throughout the Hebrew Scriptures. Second Isaiah provides an excellent reference; in speaking of God's servant the text states,

Thus says God, the LORD,
   who created the heavens and stretched them out,
   who spread out the earth and what comes from it,
who gives breath (*nĕšāmâ*) to the people upon it
   and spirit to those who walk in it:
I am the LORD, I have called you in righteousness,
   I have taken you by the hand and kept you. (Isa 42:5-6)

As this text shows, the God of Israel is creator of the universe and of individual life, demanding righteous living from his subjects and sustaining them only according to his will. Daniel reminds Belshazzar that God is the author of both his life (*nišmâ*) and his strength (v. 23). The hand of God controls all life, even that of the powerful, yet obtuse Belshazzar.

The Writing on the Wall, 5:24-28

Having completed his assessment of Belshazzar's crimes, Daniel now prepares to read the writing and give its interpretation.

Reminiscent of his earlier act in which he first described Nebuchadnezzar's dream and then gave the interpretation (Dan 4), Daniel now states the words written in Belshazzar's presence before giving their interpretation. There are many suggestions as to how to understand the words written on the wall. In v. 25, they are vocalized as nouns: *měnēʾ měnēʾ těqēl ûparsîn*; in vv. 26-28 they are understood as passive participles, with a play on words with the verbs "to number," "to weigh," and "to divide." If understood as nouns, the words themselves refer to standards of weight and measures. The first word, *měnēʾ*, is a unit of weight, namely, one-sixtieth of a talent in the Babylonian sexagesimal system. In a play on words, it is connected here to the Aramaic word "*mnh*," meaning to "count." Although it is used here twice in the MT, it is found only once in the Theodotionic text (see discussion in the introduction to this commentary), and hence some scholars see the second occurrence as a dittography.

Alternatively, others argue that the repetition is deliberate and is indicative of a particular symbolic pattern. [The Symbolic Use of Numbers] The second word, "*těqēl*" is equivalent to the Hebrew word "*šeqel*," a unit of monetary value, one-sixtieth of a mina. It is connected here in a play on words with the verb "*tql*" meaning "to weigh." The word "*ûparsîn*" is understood as a plural form of the word "*pěrēs*," a monetary unit meaning either half a shekel or half a mina. It forms a double play on words, with both "*prs*," meaning "to divide," and "Persia," the upcoming conqueror of Babylonian lands. These words all concern judgment: first, the judgment of Belshazzar's kingship; secondly, the judgment on Belshazzar personally; and thirdly, the specification of the next stage of God's plan for the world's empires. For the Jewish audience of the author's day, this language may have been understood in the context of the commandments concerning the need for just weights and measures. The economic and agricultural laws of Deuteronomy state, for example, "You shall have only a full and honest weight; you shall have only a full and honest measure, so that your days may be long in the land that the LORD your God is giving you. For all who do such things, all who act dishonestly,

---

Symbolic Use of Numbers

ΑΩ In a fascinating argument, Zdravko Stefanovic argues that the terms "*měnēʾ těqēl ûparsîn*" are indicative of three full measures and a partial unit fitting a pattern of "three and a fraction," found throughout the book of Daniel. In Dan 2, the three kingdoms and a fourth are represented by three metals (gold, silver, and bronze) plus a fourth that is *partly* iron and partly clay, hence another fraction. In both Dan 7:25 and Dan 12:7, the oppression of the beast and the suffering of the holy ones lasts for "a time, times and half a time" or "a time, times, and a half" (literal translation). These examples of three and a fraction highlight the inexorable development of God's plan definitively and suddenly to crush tyrants who oppose his will. Thus, the three and a fraction pattern that describes Belshazzar's rule on the very night that Belshazzar loses his kingdom in Dan 5 functions similarly to demonstrate "the progress and the end of the earthly powers which are commonly hostile to God" (202).

Zdravko Stefanovic, "The Presence of the *Three and a Fraction*: A Literary Figure in the Book of Daniel," in *To Understand the Scriptures: Essays in Honor of William H. Shea*, ed. David Merling (Berrien Springs MI: Andrews University Press, 1997), 199–204.

are abhorrent to the LORD your God" (Deut 25:15-16 see also Lev 19:35-36).

One scholar suggests that the author uses these three units of weight to symbolize Nebuchadnezzar, Nabonidus, and Belshazzar, with each successive Babylonian king equated with a decreasing monetary value, thus constructing an image of increasingly corrupt regimes.[14] Since it is the case, however, that Nabonidus is not included in the book of Daniel, this hypothesis remains unlikely. [A Theory about Libra] In the end, God's investigation and assessment of Belshazzar result in an inevitable judgment—God convicts and ends his oppressive rule.

The End of Belshazzar, 5:29-30

The last act of Belshazzar while still king hints that he already may be losing his authority. Although Belshazzar, like Nebuchadnezzar before him (2:48; 3:30), commands that Daniel be clothed with garments appropriate for his reward, it is ambiguous whether the king himself presents the clothing and chain of gold.[15] As did Joseph, the earlier interpreter of dreams and omens (Gen 41:42), Daniel receives the symbols of statecraft from Belshazzar's court. Unlike Pharaoh and Nebuchadnezzar, however, who directly present these signs of office to Joseph and Daniel, respectively, Belshazzar seems passive. The

Weights

This 9th C. BC Hittite funeral stele from Marash, Northern Syria, shows a merchant holding a pair of scales. A system of weights and measures was crucial for determining honest business practices. The author of Dan 5 uses the imagery of weighing to show that Belshazzar fails to meet God's standard.

Merchant carrying a pair of scales for weighing metals. 9th C. BC. Funeral stone stele. Late Hittite relief from Marash in Northern Syria. Louvre, Paris, France. (Credit: Erich Lessing/Art Resource, NY)

A Theory about Libra

Some scholars see that the phenomenon of handwriting on the wall in the book of Daniel to have its counterpart in the 6th century astrological practices of ancient Babylon. Al Wolters argues, for example, that the scales of justice implicit in Dan 5 correspond to the constellation Libra. Babylonian astrologers would have associated the words of the riddle in Dan 5 with weights and, in a broader context, scales—the representation of the constellation Libra. Wolters holds, in addition, that the annual rising of the constellation Libra occurred at the same time as the fall of Babylon, contributing to an appropriate context for this reference. The author of Daniel thus shows that it is God who judges the actions of earthly monarchs—and not the "stars" to which the Babylonians looked as a source of communication from their gods.

See Al Wolters, "An Allusion to Libra in Daniel 5," in *Die Rolle der Astronomie in den Kulturen Mesopotamiens, Beiträge zum 3. Grazer Morgenländischen Symposion (23.–27. September 1991)*, ed. Hannes Galter (Graz, Austria: rm-Druck & Verlagsgesellschaft, 1993), 292–306; see also, Al Wolters, "The Riddle of the Scales in Daniel 5," *HUCA* 62 (1991): 155–77.

Josephus's Portrayal of Belshazzar

Josephus identifies Belshazzar as another name for Nabonidus, perhaps because although the Bible portrays Belshazzar as the final king of Babylon, classical sources of his own day stated that Nabonidus was Babylon's last monarch. Indeed, Josephus quotes the historian Berossus who writes that Nabonidus fled Babylon while under Cyrus's attack, finding temporary refuge in Borsippa, yet later surrendered and was sent into exile (*Ag. Ap.* 1.152–158). Josephus, Louis Feldman argues, had to balance his concerns for his audiences while constructing his portrayal of Daniel. On the one hand, he needed to show to his imperial hosts that Jews were loyal and virtuous subjects and that he was deserving of royal patronage. On the other hand, Josephus believed that Daniel's prediction of the defeat of the fourth kingdom referred to the defeat of Rome and the triumph of Israel. Some changes that Josephus makes in his presentation of Belshazzar are as follows: Josephus has the Chaldean magicians appear and fail twice, thus highlighting Daniel's superior wisdom. When Belshazzar offers Daniel the symbols of rule, in Josephus's version, Daniel declines them with words that underscore that gifts of help are freely given, perhaps to counter the claim of Roman writers that Jews refused to help Gentiles. When addressing Belshazzar regarding Nebuchadnezzar's occasion of insanity, Daniel protects the king's image—he says he only had to eat the diet of a beast, not that he behaved as one. Josephus adds a striking detail to the motivation of Belshazzar's decision to honor Daniel, even though Daniel's words are testimony of God's condemnation of the king, as shown in the interpretation of the handwriting on the wall. Belshazzar concludes that Daniel was "good and just," and that the prophecy was independent of Daniel's own will; therefore he does not manifest any disrespect or subversion (*Ant.* 10.246). In this remark, Josephus, who saw many similarities between his own life and that of Daniel, reveals his hope that if any of his veiled references to the eventual fall of Rome were discovered, he will be judged with similar consideration.

Louis Feldman, *Josephus's Interpretation of the Bible* (Berkeley: University of California Press, 1998), 629–57.

portrayal of Belshazzar here demonstrates his foolish disregard of Daniel and suggests the king's incompetence in matters of state.

The final act of Belshazzar shows that although he expected that any reward for solving the riddle would be bestowed upon one of the Chaldean wise (v. 7), it instead goes to this unlikely captive, whom he dismissed. [Josephus's Portrayal of Belshazzar] Daniel's victory is symbolic of God's victory over tyrants; it is not about his victory for his own sake. Daniel neither sought nor savors it; in addition, he has no opportunity to rule effectively. Indeed, even the scene of the presentation of the gifts, although suggesting advancement, contains nothing to state unequivocally that Daniel is promoted, perhaps in keeping with Daniel's earlier refusal. In addition, it will be up to Darius to proclaim Daniel to be one of the three viziers after he comes to power. Thus, the author is able to suggest that Daniel finds this presentation of the symbols of authority to be empty gestures.

As the culmination to the loss of Belshazzar's power, the author specifies that Belshazzar was killed (v. 30). Because the death of the king is expressed in the passive voice, with no subject expressed, the identity of the one responsible for his death remains open. One possibility, given the context of the succession of empires (Dan 2), would be that the Medians or Persians killed Belshazzar. In terms of the literary presentation in the book, Darius the Mede, who is identified as Belshazzar's successor, would be a likely candidate. Indeed, rabbinic interpretation held that Belshazzar began to worry about his safety upon hearing Daniel's interpretation of the writing on the wall. In order to protect himself, he gave orders that if anyone were to appear in the palace, he should be slain, even if he were to say that he was the king himself. Nevertheless, Belshazzar left the palace to relieve himself. When he returned, his guards (none other than) Darius and Cyrus did not believe him when he identified himself as the king and thus slew him (*Song. Rab.* 3:4, 2). [Birth of Darius]

The other possibility to consider as the agent of Belshazzar's death is God, as it was God who did the weighing, reckoning, and judging. One could understand that God used Darius as his instrument. The author shows that world politics is not capricious, but rather follows the divine plan. The evil found in the policies and actions of human rulers will ultimately be judged by God.[16] Jews, far from being defined as only a captive people, must recognize that their wisdom, as exemplified in Daniel, is the only system that is true. Their understanding of the workings of empires and of the heavens is far more reliable than that of their overlords.

The division between Daniel 5 and 6 differs in the Aramaic and ancient Greek versions. In the Aramaic text, the chapter ends with the statement of Belshazzar's death (v. 30), whereas the Greek division concludes with the reference to Darius the Mede ascending the throne (5:31 [6:1 MT]). With the Aramaic text, the final point of this chapter is the finality of God's judgment against Babylon. With the Greek division, the reference to Darius's ascent to the

Birth of Darius

AΩ The sages calculate that the day of Darius's birth was the same day that Nebuchadnezzar entered and violated the sanctity of the temple. Thus, the individual who would bring about the subjugation of the Babylonian kingdom came to life on the same day that Israel's Babylonian enemy violated its most holy place, sixty-two years earlier (*b. Meg.* 11b). See also Hersh Goldwurm, *Daniel: A New Translation with a Commentary Anthologized from Talmudic, Midrashic, and Rabbinic Sources* (ArtScroll Tanach Series; New York: Mesorah Press, 1979), 175.

Babylonian Astronomical Tablet
This astronomical tablet from 7th C. BC Babylon charts the rising and setting of Venus. The narratives of Dan 1–6 deride the self-importance of the Chaldeans and their prognostications.

Astronomical tablet from Kish, recording the rising and settings of Venus from the first 6 years of the reign of the King of Babylon, 7th century (carved clay) by Ashmolean Museum, University of Oxford, UK/ The Bridgeman Art Library. Nationality/copyright status: out of copyright.

throne prepares the reader for the next act of the succession of world empires. Both divisions imply that the judgment against Babylon's evil is final and that God's plan for deliverance continues.

The reference to Darius the Mede, to whom Babylon falls, is a conundrum for scholars because, in fact, it was Cyrus the Persian who conquered Babylon. Moreover, although Mesopotamian history and the Bible both contain Persian rulers named Darius, neither preserves a record of any Median king by that name. It is not possible to equate definitively the biblical Darius with any other historical figure, although many persons have been proposed.[17] [Darius the Mede] The importance of Darius in the context of the book of Daniel is theological rather than historical. Just as the prophet Jeremiah speaks of a Median invasion to follow Babylonian rule (Jer 51:11), so now does this author see the prophecy fulfilled. The inexorable march of the four kingdoms thus continues.[18]

Darius the Mede

According to the book of Daniel, Darius was the Median emperor who conquered Babylon and ruled before the subsequent assent to power by Cyrus the Persian. The rabbis state that he ruled for one year after which the Persians came to power. Historical sources, however, do not give evidence for a rule of Babylon by an independent nation of Media. Media was conquered by Cyrus in 549 BC, and its capital, Ecbatana, became the summer residence of Cyrus, further complicating the separate identification of Media. The historical sources for our understanding of Media after its incorporation into the Persian Empire are sketchy, but it is interesting to note that the book of Esther speaks of the two nations in one breath; it refers to both the people and the law of "the Medes and the Persians" (1:18-19). Media apparently was an important administrative district for the Persian empire.

Although the historicity of this biblical Darius is difficult to ascertain, some scholars see Darius as the equivalent of Gobyras (also known as Ugbaru), Cyrus's general from Gutium (a region that may have included Media), who led the invasion of Babylon and who served as governor before Cyrus arrived. Other proposed solutions identify Darius as Cambyses, the son of Astyages (585–550 BC), the last king of Media before the Persian conquest and a relative of Cyrus (Cyrus was Astyages' grandson). Still other proposals include another son of Astyages, Cyaxares II, Cyrus himself, or Astyages himself. In response, other scholars see these solutions as attempts at harmonizing, pointing to the specificity of the name Darius and the lack of evidence that any ally or subordinate of Cyrus ever was called king or had a throne name. In addition, the existence of three Persian rulers with the name Darius may have influenced the representation of this biblical king.

John Collins, *Daniel* (Hermeneia; Minneapolis: Fortress Press, 1993), 30–32.

CONNECTIONS

The spirituality and drama of the narratives of Daniel have inspired artistic expression in the visual arts, drama, and music for hundreds of years. In the medieval period, Belshazzar was portrayed as an anti-Christ; in the Renaissance, dramatizations of Belshazzar's feast appealed to audiences because of their drama and mystery.[19] In vocal music, George Frederick Handel composed the oratorio *Belshazzar* in 1745, and Jean Sibelius composed *Belsazar's Gästabud* in 1906, which was used as incidental music for the drama by the Finnish-Swedish poet Jhalmar Procope and later rescored as an orchestral suite in 1907. Daniel 5 inspired the British composer, William Turner Walton (1902–1983), to write one of the most successful works of his career, *Belshazzar's Feast*. [Walton Bibliography] This oratorio for baritone solo, double mixed chorus, and orchestra was one of Walton's first to guarantee him a place as an honored contributor in

Walton Bibliography

The following is a bibliography of works about or by William Walton.

Avery, Kenneth. "William Walton." *Music and Letters* 28 (1947): 1–10.

Cooper, Martin. "The Unpredictable Walton." *The Listener* (25 July 1947): 146.

Craggs, Stewart R. *William Walton: A Source Book*. Aldershot, UK and Brookfield, VT: Scolar Press and Ashgate Publishing Company, 1992.

Howes, Frank. *The Music of William Walton*. London/New York/Toronto: Oxford University Press, 1965.

Johnson, Phil. "English Music's Enigma." *The Independent* 167/46 (7 March 2002): 10–11.

Jones, Arthur. "William Walton." *Musical America* 72 (February 1952): 18, 83.

Kennedy, Michael. *Portrait of Walton*. Oxford, New York: Oxford University Press, 1998.

Lambert, J. W. "Imp and Spectre: Conversation with Sir William Walton." *The Sunday Times*, 25 March 1962, pp. 38–39.

"Leeds Musical Festival: A Contrast of Religions—'Belshazzar's Feast' and Bach." *The Times*. London. 10 October 1931, p. 10. No author.

Lloyd, Stephen. *William Walton: Muse of Fire*. Woodbridge and Suffolk: The Boydell Press, 2001.

Palmer, Christopher. "Walton's Church Music." *Church Music* 3 (1973): 10–13.

Smith, Carolyn J. *William Walton: A Bio-Bibliography*. Westport CT and London: Greenwood Press, 1988.

Tierney, Neil. *William Walton: His Life and Music*. London: Robert Hale, 1984.

Walton, Susana. *William Walton: Behind the Façade*. Oxford/New York: Oxford University Press, 1988.

England's classical tradition. *Belshazzar's Feast* is still performed today; in 2003 performances were held in London (September 26); Milwaukee, Wisconsin (February 22–23); Rock Island, Illinois (April 6); and Charlotte, North Carolina (April 11–12).

Although commissioned for live broadcasting by the BBC, Walton's composition proved to require a larger chorus and instrumentation that went beyond their resources; thus, it premiered at the Leeds Festival Orchestra. The music was impressive for several reasons: its brass was dramatically prominent, its musical traditions diverse, including Jazz Age rhythms and unaccompanied voice reminiscent of the English choral repertoire, and the time signatures were continually alternating. [*Belshazzar's Feast*] Reviewers have remarked that the dissonance of the trombone in the beginning of the work underscores the ominous quality of Isaiah's prophecy, the low tones of the violas embody the lament of the exiles, the expressive trumpets and trombones represent the rage of the exiles, and the baritone soloist's and chorus's passion is resounded in the recitation of "If I forget thee, O Jerusalem," and "O daughter of Babylon, who art to be destroyed." The Babylonians' exultation of their gods utilizes mysterious percussion, evoking foreign deities, and the choral rendition of the

William Walton

William Walton. 1902–1983.

Belshazzar's Feast

The librettist, Osbert Sitwell, incorporated texts from Isa 39, Ps 139, Rev 18, and Dan 5 for Walton's *Belshazzar's Feast*. Dan 5 is echoed in the following:

In Babylon
Belshazzar the King made a great feast,
Made a feast to a thousand of his lords,
And drank wine before the thousand.
    Belshazzar, while he tasted the wine,
Commanded us to bring the gold and silver vessels:
Yea! the golden vessels, which his father,
Nebuchadnezzar,
Had taken out of the temple that was in Jerusalem.
    He commanded us to bring the golden vessels

Of the temple of the house of God,
That the King, his Princes, his wives,
And his concubines might drink therein . . .
    And in that same hour, as they feasted,
Came forth fingers of a man's hand
And the King saw
The part of the hand that wrote.
And this was the writing that was written:
"MENE, MENE, TEKEL UPHARSIN"
"Thou art weighed in the balance and found wanting."
In that night was Belshazzar the King slain
And his Kingdom divided.

Gary D. Cannon, *"Belshazzar's Feast* For Mixed Choir, Baritone Solo and Orchestra," *Sir William Walton*, U. M. (9 August 2006), <http://www.williamwalton.net/> (accessed 18 October 2006).

Babylonians' exultation that Belshazzar "live forever" cleverly connotes hysteria. An unaccompanied baritone soloist sounds God's judgment upon the king, whose death is proclaimed by the chorus's shouting. The final proclamations of joy are "rhythmically complex" and "increasingly frenetic," ending with a "thunderous reprise."[20]

The beauty and power of this work still move audiences today, but it is remarkable that when it was first produced, it became a tableau for biased critics to reflect their prejudice. The book of Daniel encourages all readers to stand up against injustice and to find courage when confronting evil. To find prejudice and dishonor in our own inclinations, to be sure, is much more difficult. Although the blatant prejudice of the following review might make it easy for readers to dismiss it as being unimaginable today, its publication in a well-known British newspaper and its echo in subsequent publications give us pause.

In 1931, the anonymous music critic of *The Times*, the prestigious London newspaper, contrasted the performances of Bach's *Mass in B Minor* and Walton's *Belshazzar's Feast* at the Leeds Musical Festival, on October 9 and 10, 1931. The critic uses the two compositions to contrast what are perceived to be examples of enlightened Christianity and primitive Judaism. Although the critic concludes that Walton "has produced a work of intense energy and complete sincerity . . . [that] could leave no one who heard it unmoved," he or she also describes the content of the work as displaying the vengeful designs of the exiles. The critic writes,

The psalm "By the Waters of Babylon" is set realistically. It begins in a mood of self pity, it culminates in a burning vengefulness. . . . Its diminuendo reasserts the pathetic note and balances the opening of the psalm, but the thought that Babylon "shall be found no more at all" would hold no pathos for these savage captives. . . . Again the baritone solo states the facts, "in that night was Belshazzar the king slain," the word is repeated in a choral shout, and a jubilant chorus of revenge accomplished makes a powerful finale.[21]

The music critic is confident that *Belshazzar's Feast* would never be performed by Britain's famous choirs:

Let not the Three Choirs of Worcester, Gloucester, and Hereford think that because this finale begins with "Sing aloud to God" and ends in antiphonal alleluias they may find here a suitable novelty for their Cathedrals. Belshazzar's Feast is stark Judaism from first to last. It culminates in ecstatic gloating over the fallen enemy, the utter negation of Christianity. Its power as a dramatic oratorio compels admiration, but it is no more a "sacred" oratorio than is Handel's on the same subject.

The critic's predictions proved correct for some time, for *Belshazzar's Feast* was not sung in these cathedrals until 1957.[22]

In contrasting this performance of Walton's work with the following day's performance (at the Leeds Festival) of Bach's *Mass in B Minor*, the music critic continues,

This morning we have returned to the Christian civilization with Bach's Mass in B minor. Dr. [Malcolm] Sargent's ability as a conductor was asserted in his grasp of the fact that the Mass in B minor is not a dramatic oratorio but an epic of devotion. . . . [Yet soloist] Mr. Dennis Noble was not altogether a happy choice for the "Et in Spiritum." The quality of his voice, just the right one for the barbarities of Belshazzar's Feast, is too coarse-grained for the serenity of Bach's confession of faith.[23]

This assessment seems to be assumed by another critic writing of *Belshazzar's Feast* in 1965:

The early part of the work is not merely dark, but bitter, and contrives to match the ferocious hate which lies just beneath the mournful surface of the text. The exact flavour of Jewish nationalism is caught alike in the harsh substance of the music and in the instrumental dress which it wears.[24]

This critic similarly concludes that "there is no suggestion of Christian sentiment anywhere, or indeed of edification, which has always been a defining element in oratorios."[25]

Finally, we note that as recently as 1984, a Walton biographer writes,

> The unfailing sense of drama running through Walton's score [of *Belshazzar's Feast*] from the first page to the last, the stark, simple imagery and the quality of the music itself make the work mighty and enduring. It expresses in a remarkable degree (especially as Walton was of completely Aryan origins) the fanaticism of the Jewish race and their implacable hatred of the Gentile oppressors.[26]

Clearly, such critics impose their own assumptions about the nature of Judaism and the ethical and moral superiority of Christianity upon these reviews. Walton was most interested in writing a dramatic score with compelling music; he chose the story of *Belshazzar's Feast* because it was recommended to him by his friend and patron Osbert Sitwell. Sitwell, who composed the lyrics, was convinced that the familiar story would appeal to a wide audience. I could find no evidence that it was either Sitwell's or Walton's aim to portray the Jewish exiles as vengeful. It is impossible, to be sure, to know what was in Walton's heart. On the one hand, Walton was welcomed in Israel in 1963 to conduct *Belshazzar's Feast*, sung in Hebrew, for Israel's July music festival held in Jerusalem, Haifa, and Tel Aviv.[27] On the other hand, it is troubling to read Walton's correspondence with his Jewish colleague, the pianist Harriet Cohen. In a letter dated to spring 1933, he writes an apology regarding an earlier letter—on which he drew a swastika—with these words: "I'm so sorry that I hurt you with my, what I thought harmless, if in somewhat bad taste, little joke & perhaps you will sometime both forgive & forget." He continues in the same letter, writing, "I think if you saw the 'refugees' here, you even might be inclined to side with the Nazis, for they are mostly all sleek, fat & clean ones, living in luxury in the best hotels!" At the end of the letter, he wrote, "Burn this."[28]

The comments of the music critics who see Walton's work as an example of Judaism's inferiority attest to the pervasiveness of prejudice in society, and specifically, of anti-Semitism. Walton's aims were primarily aesthetic: the biblical account of *Belshazzar's Feast* served as the backdrop for his innovative musical composition. Although it was not his main concern, one of his intentions seems to have been consonant with that of the author of Daniel: the identification of a part of society whose elevation of the values of prestige, power, and wealth needs to be examined. The music historian Byron Adams concludes that one of the intentions of the lyricist Sitwell was to challenge the mores of British upper-class society, and that Walton agreed with his perspective. As Adams states, the chorus of *Belshazzar's Feast* represented the Jewish exiles who react with the ferocious indignation of powerless outsiders forced to serve an oppressive society. Walton, himself a Lancastrian outsider at Oxford and in London, vividly contrasted the searing anguish of the Jewish slaves with a caricature of the garish ostentation of Belshazzar's court. Indeed, writes Adams, Walton, who came from a family of modest means, parodies Edward Elgar's "Pomp and Circumstance" in the oratorio so that the praise of Belshazzar's god, which symbolizes the decadence of Babylon, is cast "through a specific reference to an Edwardian musical style."[29] Indeed, all of Walton's works were known for their "certainty of touch, directness, and energy."[30]

The links made by the anonymous critic of *The Times* warn the reader that although one can use biblical stories for inspiration, others can also use them to perpetuate bias and the denigration of peoples. Modern biblical scholarship has not escaped the prejudice that is inherent in these presuppositions about the nature of Judaism. Much of twentieth-century biblical scholarship has been influenced by the seminal work of the European Lutheran biblical scholar, Julius Wellhausen (1844–1918), who reflects this bias in his evaluation of the sources of the Pentateuch.[31] Wellhausen argues that the Yahwistic and Elohistic histories (JE), the two earliest sources that make up the Pentateuch, correspond to an untainted form of ancient Israelite religion. These noble stories of early humanity and of Israel's patriarchs provided compelling narratives of a didactic nature, were closely attuned to God's presence in nature, celebrating a universal priesthood, and held that sacrifice could be offered to God in any location. These sources did not show a preoccupation with the law—a feature that predominated in later developments—which, Wellhausen believes, was marked by meaningless compulsivity. Wellhausen concludes that the development of the Pentateuch beyond JE was the beginning of its denigration. When the Deuteronomic (D) source was added, the period marked by the spontaneity of sacrifices was undone. Priesthood, no longer open to everyone, became the purview of the Levites. Wellhausen holds that the priestly insistence on following an exacting calendar and their requirement that sacrifice be offered at a particular place divorced the worship system from its natural roots, which he considers morally superior. As Jon Levenson states, "the connection with the soil and the rhythm of natural life has been dealt a severe blow" in Wellhausen's estimation.[32] In addition, because the D source included a written law for the first time in Israel's history, a substantial increase in the authoritarian nature of Israelite religion occurred. As the written law increased in importance, the spontaneous and therefore superior element of prophecy was diminished, further contributing to the decline of the golden age of the writings of J and E.[33]

Wellhausen concludes that the last contributor to the Pentateuch, the Priestly (P) source, was further preoccupied with the minutiae of the law, interpreted by a new "clerical caste."[34] With P, the Pentateuch teaches that the precise system of dates for sacrifice is fixed. Instead of being a dynamic faith, Israelite religion became concerned with following petty aspects of the law in order that people could feel justified that they were judged righteous before God. Judaism, therefore, developed not from the legacy of the JE source; rather, it is the child of P and thus is ultimately wanting. Wellhausen taught that Judaism grew from a petty, legalistic development of the Israelite religion and is thus preoccupied with rules and regulations. Christianity, in contrast, developed from the legacy of the prophets, who rightfully understood the depth of the earlier strands of the Pentateuch (JE) and critiqued the failures of the religion.

Many of the great European Christian biblical scholars following Wellhausen continued with this paradigm, often seeing the laws of the Torah as being completely divorced from anything of spiritual worth. Judaism's message of the joy of Torah and of the delight in serving God by keeping the commandments with the proper *kavanah* (intention), profoundly connecting God and humankind, remarkably, too often was completely ignored. For example, we note the following evaluation of Judaism from *The Theology of the Old Testament*, written by the German Protestant theologian Walther Eichrodt in 1933.[35] Eichrodt accepts the paradigm that held that with the advent of the priesthood in ancient Israel, the people fell away from the best of their earlier traditions. Priestly teachings, he argues,

> favoured an enhancing and entrenching of the outward apparatus of religion that had the strongest influence on religious thought and behaviour. The natural momentum of a richly developed cultic practice concentrated all reality of religion into the sphere of outward performance, the meritorious works of sacrifices, festivals, pilgrimages, fasting and so on. As a result the social and moral aspects of the divine demands were allowed to recede from men's attention. . . . The

religious values originally mediated by the covenant were falsified and the covenant concept itself became nothing more than a protective cover for irreligious self-seeking.[36]

Eichrodt continues that the love of God was replaced by the increased emphasis on the fear of God, which ultimately leaves Judaism bereft. He concludes,

> The essence of the Jewish religion of the Law may therefore be seen as a regulation of the God-Man relationship which exhausts itself in endless casuistry, and leaves the heart empty; which because of its exact knowledge of the heart of Man strives to incorporate even the lower motive as necessary, and yet at the same time seeks to restrain and combat unbridled desire for reward with the motive of love.[37]

Much has changed in the past decades in modern biblical scholarship, to be sure, and colleagueship occurs among modern interpreters of many faiths. To take one example, Professors Bruce D. Chilton and Jacob Neusner have written several books in collaboration that examine the theologies of both Judaism and Christianity. Such a project would have been inconceivable a half-century ago. In their book, *Classical Christianity and Rabbinic Judaism*, the authors discuss the legacy of the Tanakh (Bible, for Jews) and the Old Testament, noting the commonalties and differences between these two great faiths.[38] They show that both traditions approach questions of God and faith with elements of a common vocabulary, including creation, the human condition, grace, holiness, sin, and judgment. The authors respectfully address the unique elements of each tradition and the different ways in which the Tanakh/Old Testament is interpreted. For Judaism, the Torah is preeminent. The revelation at Sinai is the "antidote to the sinful human condition," and the holy community of the people Israel is the "medium for man's renewal," in which humanity strives to live ethically, awaiting the righting of the injustices of the world with God's judgment at the end of days.[39] For Christianity, the Prophetic Corpus of Scripture predominates, with the proclaimed Christ seen as the one who reconciles a fallen humanity back to God. With Christ comes the advent of the kingdom of God, open to all who share in Christ's redemptive sonship: "identifying with Christ means joining in the victory of life over death."[40]

As modern scholars increasingly show respect for and acknowledge the profound differences in religious traditions, we all become the beneficiaries of a more peaceful world. Knowing the past history—however uncomfortable—remains critical, as scholars, clerics, and people of faith and good will attempt to open paths of dialogue and healing. Awareness of presuppositions and prejudice is the first step toward change.

NOTES

[1] John Collins argues that "the type-role of the king was more important than the identity of the individual." See John Collins, *Daniel* (Hermeneia; Minneapolis: Fortress Press, 1993), 33.

[2] Paul Redditt, *Daniel* (New Century Bible; Sheffield: Sheffield Academic Press, 1999), 89–90.

[3] John Goldingay, *Daniel* (WBC 30; Dallas: Word Books, 1989), 103, 113.

[4] Jacob Milgrom, *Numbers* (JPS Torah Commentary; Philadelphia: The Jewish Publication Society, 1990), 54, 58. Milgrom shows that "the dedication offering" should rather be understood as "the initiation offering."

[5] It is also used of Daniel when he reacts to his first vision (Dan 7:28).

[6] Al Wolters, "'Untying the King's Knots': Physiology and Wordplay in Daniel 5," *JBL* 110/1 (1991): 118.

[7] Cf. Redditt, *Daniel*, 92.

[8] For the many suggestions, including possible codes and substitutions, see Hersh Goldwurm, *Daniel: A New Translation with a Commentary Anthologized from Talmudic, Midrashic, and Rabbinic Sources* (ArtScroll Tanach Series; New York: Mesorah Publications, 1979), 162–63.

[9] For the intentional ambivalence of the phrase, see Bob Becking, "'A Divine Spirit is in You': Notes on the Translation of the Phrase *rûaḥ ʾelahîn* in Dan 5, 14 and Related Texts," in *The Book of Daniel in the Light of New Findings*, ed. A. S. van der Woude (Bibliotheca ephemeridum theologicarum lovaniensium 106; Leuven: University Press, 1993), 515–19.

[10] All references to the Old Greek text of Daniel refer to the translation given in John Collins's *Daniel*.

[11] André LaCoque sees a parallel in the activity of Elisha, who also refuses payment for his help (2 Kgs 5:16). Both Elisha and Daniel thus make clear that their activities come from God; the sorcerers' powers are empty. See *Daniel in His Time* (Studies on Personalities of the Old Testament; Columbia SC: University of South Carolina Press, 1988), 184.

[12] Goldwurm, *Daniel*, 169.

[13] Danna Nolan Fewell shows how Belshazzar, compared to Nebuchadnezzar, was more intent on evil, arrogance, and lack of recognition of God by comparing the specifics of their words to those of Daniel. See Fewell, *Circle of Sovereignty: A Story of Stories in Daniel 1–6* (JSOTSup 72; Bible and Literature Series 20; Sheffield: Almond Press, 1988), 111–39.

[14] Collins, *Daniel*, 251, 252.

[15] Goldwurm, *Daniel*, 173. "And they clothed" can also be understood passively, namely, "Daniel was clothed."

[16] In the end, Belshazzar still apparently believes in his idols. That he dies is the point of this chapter. His death is not an automatic principle, argues W. Sibley Towner; but rather he is brought down because God decrees it. See Towner, *Daniel* (*Int*; Atlanta: John Knox, 1984), 77.

[17] James Montgomery, *A Critical and Exegetical Commentary on the Book of Daniel*, ICC (Edinburgh: T. & T. Clark, 1972), 65.

[18] Montgomery, *A Critical and Exegetical Commentary*, 63–65; Redditt, *Daniel*, 99–100.

[19] "Belshazzar," unsigned article, *EncJud*, ed. Cecil Roth and Geoffrey Wigoder, 16 vols. (New York: Macmillan, 1971–72), 4:449–450.

[20] Malcolm Hayes, "Belshazzar's Feast," bbc.co.uk (n.d.), <http://www.bbc.co.uk/proms/notes/walton_belshazzar.shtml#top> (10 February 2003).

[21] Author unknown, "Leeds Musical Festival: A Contrast of Religions—'Belshazzar's Feast' and Bach," *The Times* (London), 10 October 1931, 10.

[22] Michael Kennedy, *Portrait of Walton* (Oxford: Oxford University Press, 1998), 59.

[23] "Leeds Musical Festival," 10.

[24] Frank Howes, *The Music of William Walton* (London: Oxford University Press, 1965), 162.

[25] Ibid., 170.

[26] Neil Tierney, *William Walton: His Life and Music* (London: Robert Hale, 1984), 227.

[27] Stephen Lloyd, *William Walton: Muse of Fire* (Woodbridge and Suffolk: The Boydell Press, 2001), 240.

[28] Lloyd, *William Walton*, 131–32.

[29] Byron Adams, "William (Turner) Walton," *The New Grove Dictionary of Music Online*, ed. L. Macy (n.d.) <http://www.grovemusic.com> (5 February 2003).

[30] Lloyd, *William Walton*, 265.

[31] Jon Levenson, *The Hebrew Bible, the Old Testament, and Historical Criticism: Jews and Christians in Biblical Studies* (Louisville KY: Westminster/John Knox, 1993), 10–21.

[32] Levenson, *The Hebrew Bible*, 10.

[33] Joseph Blenkinsopp, *The Pentateuch: An Introduction to the First Five Books of the Bible* (Anchor Bible Reference Library; New York/London: Doubleday, 1992) 11.

[34] Blenkinsopp, *The Pentateuch*, 11–12.

[35] Walther Eichrodt, *Theology of the Old Testament*, trans. J. A. Baker, 2 vols. (Philadelphia: Westminster, 1961).

[36] Eichrodt, *Theology of the Old Testament*, vol. 1, 47.

[37] Ibid., vol. 2, 315.

[38] Bruce D. Chilton and Jacob Neusner, *Classical Christianity and Rabbinic Judaism: Comparing Theologies* (Grand Rapids MI: Baker Academic Press, 2004).

[39] Ibid., 38.

[40] Ibid., 39.

DANIEL DEFEATS THE LIONS

Daniel 6:1-28 (6:2-29 MT)

COMMENTARY

In Daniel 6 we come to the last of the narratives of the book of Daniel. Upon completion of this account of Daniel in the lions' den (lit., "pit"), the book turns to Daniel's visions; thus, this is the reader's last opportunity to examine the lessons of Daniel's experience in exile. Up to this point in the presentation of Daniel's life and in the lives of his companions, the author has shown that it is indeed possible to remain faithful to God despite the lures of a powerful material culture and the dangers that come from foreign kings. Although their policies have an impact on Jewish life, religion, and culture—some of which entail violence and the threat of death, others that encourage assimilation—the actions of Daniel and his friends prove that foreign oppression can be resisted by steadfastness, courage, and faith.

In Daniel 6, the author illustrates yet another menace. This time it is not a king who initiates the threat to life and security; rather, lesser government officials and bureaucrats are shown to be equally dangerous. In addition, the narrative shows that a weak, ineffective king—even a friendly one—can be as threatening as Nebuchadnezzar, for the power vacuum allows others to implement their own malevolent designs. Like the advisers to Nebuchadnezzar in Daniel 3, who remind the king that he must implement the decree that condemns to death anyone who fails to bow to the king's idol, Darius's officials goad the king to enforce a death penalty against Daniel on trumped-up charges. The chapter presents a unique picture of the officials because they are singularly powerful in the presence of a hapless monarch. [Outline of Daniel 6]

Scholars debate whether the narratives of Daniel 1–6 portray a relatively benign

Diaspora, which poses no immediate threat, or whether they portray a period of ever-present danger. Those who see less threatening circumstances emphasize that, because the king is shown as being sympathetic to Daniel, the narratives reflect a time when privileged classes of Jews, who were comfortable with the status quo, hoped to find advancement within governmental service and society.[1] A study by Daniel Smith-Christopher, however, emphasizes that the author of Daniel, far from being at ease with the government, underscores the dangers of Diaspora living. He concludes, "The Daniel tales teach that knowledge of Jewish identity as the people of [YHWH's] light and wisdom is the key not only to survival, but also to the eventual defeat of the Imperial rule of 'the nations' on earth."[2]

Although it is true that the king neither seeks the harm nor desires the suffering of Daniel, his impotence vis-à-vis his courtiers leaves Daniel completely unprotected and in danger of losing his life to the ravages of beasts. Daniel's position in governmental service holds no refuge for him. Thus, although King Darius is shown to like Daniel and to shudder at the thought of harming him, it is crucial to remember that Darius never challenges Daniel's accusers concerning their pretexts, even though he has several opportunities to do so. Furthermore, the king fails to challenge the law that a decree cannot be changed, nor does he offer another law to supersede it. This incompetence of the king is contrasted with the dominance of his officials, which cannot be underestimated.

This emphasis on the maneuverings of the courtiers details an insidious threat—one that comes from an individual's closest associates. These advisers of Darius initiate a test that no prayer be allowed to anyone but to Darius himself—an artificial test that would indeed be very strange in a polytheistic society wherein any perceived disrespect to the gods would be tantamount to a subversive act. In addition, because Persian royal ideology did not include the concept of divine kingship, the absurdity of the test is underscored. Nonetheless, Darius falls for the courtiers' scheme. Thus, in Daniel 6 the reader discovers that it is fruitless to put one's trust in the highest earthly authority, for even though King Darius shows respect and expresses concern for Daniel, he will not override the interpretation of the law given by his governmental advisers who have so obviously entrapped him. What the king feels about Daniel ultimately is irrelevant, but what he does or fails to do has consequences for life itself. Darius's powerlessness in face of his vicious governmental servants shows that no Jew can rely on the laws of overlords for protection in the face of local threats. The acquies-

Jews in the Persian Satrapy of Babylon

After the Persians defeated Babylonia in 539 BC, Jews continued to have a presence in Babylon. The Murashu documents from Nippur (455–403 BC), located on the Cheber canal of the Euphrates River (the same canal spoken of by Ezekiel), yield some important information concerning the continuation of distinctive Jewish life in what became the Persian satrapy of Babylon. A study of the Jewish names in these documents shows that most freemen had theophoric names of the God YHWH, even though their fathers had names reflecting Babylonian gods. As M. Dandamayev writes,

> Out of twenty persons whose names proclaim the graciousness of Yahweh (Hananiah, etc.), half had fathers whose given names invoked the favour of the idols of Babylon. Certainly, secular Babylonian names continued to be given to Jewish boys. Yet, a man called "peace of Babylon" . . . named his son "Who is mighty like Yahweh." (356)

This Jewish community of Nippur, instead of showing more adaptability to Babylonian ways by giving their children the names of their neighbors, shows their adherence to belief in YHWH alone. This theology is well represented in the post-exilic literature of Ezekiel and Second Isaiah. It is this devotion to strict monotheism that enabled the survival of the Jewish people who, unlike other conquered nations, did not disappear into the greater society. The Jews' dedication to their traditions, however, could prompt serious difficulties, as Dandamayev explains: "[they] appeared 'godless' to their neighbours. [Jews in the] Diaspora came to be a peculiar people, without parallel among the nations. For this reason the Jew was now a magnet attracting both the 'joiners' (Isa. 56:3) and the hate of those who, perhaps rightly [sic], cannot stand singularity" (358).

M. Dandamayev, "The Diaspora: Babylonia in the Persian Age," in *Introduction; The Persian Period*, ed. W.D. Davies and Louis Finkelstein (The Cambridge History of Judaism 1; Cambridge: Cambridge University Press, 1984), 356–58. See also Morton Smith, "Jewish Religious Life," in ibid., 222–23.

cence of the king to the proposed horrific action of his own servants only underscores the fact that no exiled person—not even a high-ranking governmental official—can feel totally at home in the Diaspora. Jews must always remember that a foreign king's failure to act, whether due to incompetence, benign neglect, or helplessness, may prove dangerous. The Jews' ultimate protector is God alone. [Jews in the Persian Satrapy of Babylon]

Daniel's Success and the King's Plan for Promotion, 6:1-3 (6:2-4 MT)

At the end of Daniel 5, Daniel's position in the government appears uncertain. Belshazzar gave Daniel the trappings of a governmental official and proclaimed that he would be one of the rulers of the realm (5:29). Yet with Belshazzar's death came a new nation as conqueror, and a new king, Darius. The references to the new regime and to the new divisions of territory create a gap for the reader, as a new government could portend danger for Daniel and his community. As Daniel 6 begins, it first appears that not only is Daniel safe under the new regime, but also that he does indeed continue successfully in governmental service. This time his position is not as an ad hoc interpreter in difficult situations; he serves permanently as an overseer in a complex and detailed divi-

Persian Administrative Districts

The Persian Empire was divided into administrative districts ruled by satraps who were responsible for levying taxes, drafting soldiers, and ensuring provincial order. The number of satrapies, however, as presented in the Bible and in classical writings is inconsistent. Whereas Herodotus states that during the reorganization of the empire by Darius I (522–486 BC) the empire was divided into 20 satrapies over 67 peoples and nations, the books of Daniel and Esther refer to 127 satrapies and 120 nations.

Darius I was famous for his administrative reorganization and improvements. After facing many serious rebellions to the Persian Empire upon taking the throne, he strengthened and extended his empire to include lands in India and Eastern Europe. His empire was larger than any previously attained in the ancient Near East, and his reign was famous for his construction of roads, an impressive postal system, and his reforming of laws. Ephraim Stern suggests that the upheavals stemming from the revolt in Babylon during the early part of Darius's reign, along with Darius's reorganization of the empire, prompted great movements of people, including that of the Jews to Judah. As Stern shows, Jews were encouraged to be repatriated "by Darius' new imperial organization. . . . Darius ordered that all obstacles placed in the way of the returning exiles by the enemies of Judah be removed."

Herodotus, *Histories* 3.89; John J. Collins, *Daniel* (Hermeneia; Minneapolis: Fortress Press, 1993), 264; Raymond Hammer, *The Book of Daniel* (The Cambridge Bible Commentary; Cambridge: Cambridge University Press, 1976), 68.

Ephraim Stern, "The Persian Empire and the Political and Social History of Palestine in the Persian Period," in *Introduction; The Persian Period*, ed. W. D. Davies and Louis Finkelstein (The Cambridge History of Judaism 1; Cambridge: Cambridge University Press, 1984), 72.

sion of bureaucratic power (v. 2 [v. 3 MT]). Darius is barely in place as emperor when he compartmentalizes his lands for the efficient running of governmental affairs. His first recorded act apparently affects Daniel for the good; of the 123 officials appointed (120 satraps plus three presidents), Daniel is one of the three highest ranking. [Persian Administrative Districts] Moreover, Darius soon plans to promote Daniel over all other officials; he will be second only to the king (v. 3 [v. 4 MT]). Thus, although the decline of Babylon and the advent of a new government present a host of unknowns for its subjugated peoples, the first administrative decision seems to hold promise for Daniel and, by extension, for his community. With Darius's proposal, all Jews scattered throughout former Babylonian lands now have Daniel as one of the overseers of their immediate superiors (vv. 1-2 [vv. 2-3 MT]). [Median Guards] It is all the more arresting, therefore, that the reader discovers that Daniel's appointment actually leads to more danger.

It is striking that Daniel's subordinates are quick to give "counsel" (*ṭaʿmāʾ*, "account," NRSV) to him and to his two colleagues (v. 2 [v. 3 MT]). Earlier in the narratives, it is Daniel who was in position to give dramatic counsel (Dan 2:14; "prudence," NRSV) to an official. Daniel persuaded Arioch to allow him to give a dream interpretation to the king rather than implement the decree to slay all the wise of Babylon. Although Daniel's past counsel persuaded an executioner to give pause to what he was doing, the advice of Daniel's subordinates, in contrast, is filled with jealousy. Ironically, the king's satraps are supposed to consult with Daniel in order to protect the king from "injury" (*nāziq*, v. 2 [v. 3 MT]), a word that may also connote treasonous acts; instead, they will ultimately cause much distress to the king by their false accusations. [The Use of *nāziq* in the Book of Ezra]

What uniquely characterizes Daniel in his new position is his "excellent spirit" (v. 3 [v. 4 MT]), a characteristic that the queen acknowledged when Belshazzar became disturbed by the hand-

Median Guards

The ancient kingdom of Media established a powerful empire in the 8th–6th centuries BC that included present-day northern Iran, Azerbaijan, Afghanistan, and Central Asia. Media became part of the Persian Empire when Cyrus the Great defeated the Median ruler, Astyages. As part of the Persian Empire, its soldiers served its king, Darius I, as shown in this bas-relief from Persepolis.

Median guards. Achaemenid period.
Relief from the stairway of the Tripylon. Persepolis, Iran.
(Credit: Bridgeman-Giraudon/Art Resource, NY)

writing on the wall (5:12). Used in conjunction with other descriptions of Daniel's special gifts, the phrase refers both to Daniel's intelligence and to his abilities in understanding signs and mysteries. In this instance, it highlights Daniel's superior skills when judged against his colleagues' in matters of state. Just as the queen noticed this character trait, so too is Darius similarly impressed.

By the end of v. 3 (v. 4 MT), it appears that the advent of Darius the Mede initiates a new chapter in the life of the Jews in exile—not because of his official policies or appointments, but because of the schemes of the king's own courtiers. Indeed, before the king can put his plan for the organization of his empire into effect, his own subordinates thwart him. By conspiring against Daniel, Darius's own viziers and satraps actually plot their treachery against the king himself. It is ironic that although these officials accuse Daniel of treason, it is they who unite in secret to undermine the king's wishes.

The Use of *nāziq* in the Book of Ezra

AΩ The book of Ezra relates that the Samarians, who opposed the rebuilding of the temple, argued that a newly built Jerusalem and temple would cause its own citizens to rebel. Using the word *nāziq* ("hurtful" or "cause harm"), they state that the rebuilding would undermine the king's ability to collect taxes and his ability to maintain public order:

You will discover in the annals that this is a rebellious city, hurtful (*nāziq*) to kings and provinces, and that sedition was stirred up in it from long ago. On that account this city was laid waste. We make known to the king that, if this city is rebuilt and its walls finished, you will then have no possession in the province Beyond the River. (Ezra 4:15-16; see also 6:13)

These words by officials in Samaria purport to show the Persians that Jews are disloyal to the crown and cannot be trusted because of their faith and their traditions.

The Officials' Conspiracy, 6:4-9 (6:5-10 MT)

The positive description of Daniel's success and the king's plans for his future immediately become the seeds for the conspiracy against Daniel (vv. 4-9 [vv. 5-10 MT]). [Bel and the Dragon] Although stymied by Daniel's righteous behavior, the officials cleverly have the king unwittingly condemn Daniel to death by the imposition of an arbi-

Bel and the Dragon

Bel and the Dragon (or Bel and the Snake), an apocryphal addition to Daniel, is found in both the Old Greek and Theodotion. The account of Bel and the Dragon, dated to the 1st or 2d century BC, preserves another tradition about Daniel being threatened by lions. As in the canonical book of Daniel, a test is proposed that would compromise Daniel's loyalty to God; he is commanded by the (unnamed) king to worship the great serpent that the Babylonians revered as a God. Daniel counters that he "will kill the serpent without sword or rod," thus proving it is not divine. Just as the narrative of Dan 6 shows a larger population (all the satraps and viziers) conspiring against Daniel, so too, upon hearing of Daniel's success, does the surrounding populace rise against him and demand that the king cast Daniel into the lions' pit. Similar to the account in Dan 6, the weak king of Bel and the Dragon readily capitulates to their demands. It is interesting to note that the OG version of Bel and the Dragon includes an ending to the narrative that parallels that of Dan 6. Dan 6:24 (6:25 MT) reads, "The king gave a command, and those who had accused Daniel were brought and thrown into the den of lions . . . ." Bel and the Dragon 31 has the following: "Those who plotted against the king were given over to them [the lions]." As in Dan 6, in Bel and the Dragon the king calls out to Daniel, acknowledges his God, and throws the accusers into the pit for the same death proposed for the innocent Daniel.

See Carey Moore, "Daniel, Additions to," *ABD*, ed. David Noel Freedman, 6 vols. (New York: Doubleday & Co., 1992), 2:18–28.

trary ruling to which he assents before he recognizes its consequences.

The following literal and highlighted translation of v. 4 (v. 5 MT) points out the repetition of key words:

Then the viziers and satraps sought to **find** <u>a ground of accusation</u> against Daniel concerning the kingdom; but any <u>ground of accusation</u> or *corruption* they were unable to **find** because Daniel was faithful—and any remissness or *corruption* could not be **found** in him.

This remarkable sentence introduces the conspiracy of Daniel's colleagues with the repetition of the words "find," "ground of accusation," and "corruption," as well as by the use of the words "faithful" and "remissness," each used once. The three-fold repetition of the word "find" (*šĕkaḥ*) calls attention to the tenacity of the officials' search for a way to accuse the innocent Daniel. The repeated word, "ground of accusation" (*ʿillâ*), suggests a "pretext" indicating that from the beginning, the colleagues knew there was nothing treasonous about Daniel's activity and that they would have to malign one of his acts in order to cast it in the light of their own sinister purposes. ["Finding" and "Seeking"] The word "corruption" (*šĕḥîtâ*) suggests a significant treasonous act, as it is the term Nebuchadnezzar himself used when he warned his astrologers that they must interpret his

"Finding" and "Seeking"

Bill T. Arnold argues that the play on words between "finding" and "seeking" (vv. 4, 11 [vv. 5, 12 MT]) is noteworthy. He states,

Daniel's enemies are seeking to *find* a fault in him (v. 5), but instead they *find* him *seeking* God (v. 12). . . . The irony here is that his enemies think they have found Daniel's weakness, but the narrator knows they have actually found his greatest strength. Indeed, it is his devotion to God that delivers him from the lions.

Bill T. Arnold, "Wordplay and Narrative Techniques in Daniel 5 and 6," *JBL* 112/3 (1993): 484.

dream or face the death penalty (Dan 2:5-9). These striking words show that the men who were once Daniel's colleagues now become tenacious accusers. They invest heavily in inventing trumped-up accusations with which to charge Daniel. Although they quickly learn that Daniel's loyalty and righteousness will make their conspiracy difficult, they will not be stopped. [Jerome's *Commentary on Daniel*]

The two words used singularly in v. 4 (v. 5 MT), "faithful" (*měhêman*) and "remissness" (*šālû*, "negligence," NRSV), echo other important usages found in the book of Daniel. In 2:45, Daniel remarks to Nebuchadnezzar that the interpretation of the dream is "faithful"; this same word is also used in 6:23 (6:24 MT) to underscore that Daniel "trusted in his God" while in the pit of lions, thereby showing his determination to complete his obligations to God despite dire circumstances. The singularity of the word "remissness" is appropriate, as it indicates a very serious transgression or a potentially treasonous offense. In Daniel 3:29, for example, Nebuchadnezzar uses this word to tell his populace that anyone who speaks "remissness" concerning the God of Daniel will be put to death, and in the book of Ezra, those who demand the cessation of the building of the temple and of the city of Jerusalem argue that such acts will prompt "remissness" ("hurt," NRSV) against the king (Ezra 4:22).

The author is careful to record the very words of the adversaries' conspiracy (v. 5 [v. 6 MT]). Because they can find nothing in matters of state against Daniel, they will proceed with charges on the basis of "the law (*dāt*) of his God." With such words, the satraps reveal their method of ensnaring Daniel: they will twist Daniel's religious obligations in order to make them appear threatening to the state. The term "law" (*dāt*) is used in the book of Daniel to indicate a verdict or decree that is unassailable. Nebuchadnezzar, for example, told his astrologers that if they did not interpret his dreams, "there would be one law for you"—the verdict of death (2:9, A.T.)—and it is found when the king decrees the massacre against the wise (2:13, 15). Thus, the use of the "law"

Jerome's *Commentary on Daniel*

Jerome (AD 331–420) left an incomparable legacy of translations and writings for the early church. His *Commentary on Daniel* confirms the antiquity of various rabbinic interpretations of the book. For example, in his remarks on Dan 6:4 (Vulgate, 6:5 MT), Jerome relates that there is a Jewish interpretation that holds Darius's aides were trying to accuse Daniel of sexual wrongdoing against the king's concubines, wives, or queen, but were stymied because Daniel was a eunuch. The tradition that Daniel was a eunuch, also attested in Jerome's commentary on 1:3, is similarly found in the Talmud (although there are also minority rabbinic opinions that he was not mutilated). Jerome counters the Jewish interpretation, offering a different argument, namely, that there indeed was nothing specific found in this "faithful man" upon which his accusers could cast suspicion. Although Jerome offers many rabbinic interpretations as examples of the "treasures of Hebrew erudition," he rejects this particular tradition with what Jay Braverman says is "his harshest invective against Jewish biblical interpretation" (82 n. 4). Jerome writes, "This [interpretation] was made by those [Jews] who make a practice of weaving long tales on the pretext of a single word." Jerome may have found this interpretation unacceptable, Braverman suggests, because he did not believe the tradition that Daniel was a eunuch.

Jay Braverman, *Jerome's Commentary on Daniel: A Study of Comparative Jewish and Christian Interpretations of the Hebrew Bible* (CBQMS 7; Washington DC: The Catholic University of America, 1978), 53–71, 81–83, 134–36.

dāt (law, religion)

AΩ Most interpreters understand the word *dāt*, usually translated either "law" or "religion," to be synonymous with the Hebrew word *tōrâ* (teaching), as is used of Ezra's study and doing of God's law (Ezra 7:10, 12, 14), or to *mišpāṭ* (judgment), usually found in contexts showing that God's teaching is tantamount to justice itself (Isa 42:4; 51;4). Norman Porteous remarks,

> If Daniel's religion had been a religiosity, it would not have provided the opportunity his enemies sought. . . . [The decree suggests] to the reader the *hybris* and intolerance of the hellenistic kings. This is perhaps the kind of mad decree that Antiochus Epiphanes in one of his less responsible moments might have issued.

This comment suggests the way in which the author of Dan 7–12 incorporated the narratives of Dan 1–6.

Norman W. Porteous, *Daniel* (OTL; Philadelphia: Westminster Press, 1965), 89.

of God is significant here because it forms a contrast to the laws of the kings. [*dāt* (law, religion)]

The conspirators maximize their prospects for success by gathering strength in numbers. Not only do they assemble to consider the plan amongst themselves, but they also appear as one unit before the king, calling particular attention to their solidarity in their proposal. Their intimidating show of unity serves to advance their duplicitous proposal (v. 7 [v. 8 MT]). Before they specify the content of their demands, they use words that lure Darius into assent. They state that they are requesting a confirmation of what the king already has in place. Their claim that they wish to "affirm" and "strengthen" what the king has already ruled makes it appear that they are loyal subjects and are proposing nothing new. Their specification that the proposal would have a time limit serves both to deride the Persian legal system by showing that its justice is corrupt and also develops the plot by facilitating the king's consent. Their demand that the king declare that whoever prays to any god other than to himself must be thrown into a pit (*gōb*) of lions is outrageous both because of what it requires and because of the horrifying consequences of disobedience. [Pit (*gōb*)] The Median and Persian peoples were known for worshiping many gods, and indeed were quite accommodating in including conquered people's deities in their own pantheon. [Ahura Mazda] With their statement, the author continues to mock the religious and moral values of the government whose directive would undercut the obligations of its own people to their gods. Even before the decree ensnares Daniel himself, it functions to underscore the sinister character of the officials who propose it, the cowardice of the king who agrees to it, and the fail-

Pit (*gōb*)

AΩ Although *gōb* is commonly translated as "den," it is also the word that indicates an underground pit or cistern, which could be used either as a prison or for water reserves. John Goldingay concludes that the image here is consonant with the Persians' unimaginable forms of horrible executions.

One of the most unforgettable scenes from the book of Jeremiah is that of the prophet, on the dictates of his opponents, being cast into a pit. Jeremiah argued that if the people submitted to Nebuchadnezzar's hegemony, they would be spared their lives. The rebels, however, expected to get help from Egypt in resisting Babylon. Similar to Darius's apparent helplessness in superseding the dictates of his counselors, King Zedekiah readily capitulates to the demands of his governmental officials who call for what they thought would be Jeremiah's slow and agonizing death in the pit. Ebed-melech, an Ethiopian palace official, had the courage to insist that the king release him and then directed the rescue operation, which proceeded by pulling Jeremiah up from the pit with ropes (Jer 38:6-13).

John E. Goldingay, *Daniel* (WBC 30; Dallas: Word Books, 1989), 128.

Ahura Mazda

Mary Boyce argues that Ahura Mazda, originally the name of a Persian deity, was later incorporated into the religious system of the prophet Zoroaster. Zoroaster taught that this god (whose name means "lord of wisdom") was the one supreme deity. Although he is omniscient, he is not omnipotent, as his power is challenged by the Evil Spirit, a reality that will continue until the Evil Spirit is defeated by Ahura Mazda at the end of time. Ahura Mazda sends various lesser gods to earth, the place where evil can be conquered. Zoroaster's teachings include the justice of God, a reward and punishment after death, a resurrection of the body, and a final cataclysmic battle led by a world savior.

Mary Boyce, "Zoroaster, Zoroastrianism"; "Ahura Mazda," *ABD*, ed. David Noel Freedman, 6 vols. (New York: Doubleday & Co., 1992), 6:1168–74; 1:124–25.

Two winged sphinxes topped by a winged disk; emblem of the god Ahura Mazda. 6th–5th C. BC. Achaemenid period. Enamelled brick panel, Susa, Iran. (Credit: Erich Lessing/Art Resource, NY)

ings of a government that employs its bureaucracy to intimidate its populace.

This proposal recalls earlier decrees in the book of Daniel that had similarly gruesome death penalties: namely, Nebuchadnezzar's command for all to worship the great statue he had set up under the pain of being killed in a fiery furnace as well as his edict that anyone who did not worship the God of Daniel would be torn from "limb to limb" (3:29). By including this account of yet another exceptional law and proposed execution, the author underscores the cruelty of an empire that rules through intimidation and fear, is rife with corruption and tainted by petty concerns, and blindsides its populace with extreme decrees. The author's audience in antiquity could readily contrast the world's esteem for the success and cultural advancements of powerful empires with their own values, which they believe are ethical and enduring because they come from the very will of a just God.

As the conspirators come to their conclusion, they speak not in requests but in demands. They repeat that the king must "establish the prohibition," but now they add a significant detail; he must "inscribe the writing" (v. 8 [v. 9 MT]). This ensures, they believe, that the ordinance could not be changed. The presupposition regarding the immutability of the laws of Media-Persia is attested not only in this narrative but also in the book of Esther.[3] In that account, Haman concludes that his own power is threatened because a single Jew, Mordecai, refuses to bow down to him. Just as

The Midrashim on Daniel 6

The midrashim include the following comments on Dan 6. The responses of praise to God by both Nebuchadnezzar and Darius, who saw the rescue of the three youths from the fiery furnace and of Daniel from the lions' den, respectively, show that both of these idol worshipers are made "to recognize God and praise him" (*Exod. Rab.* 15:6). Another text sees an additional parallel between the account of the rescue from the fiery furnace and the rescue from the lions' den. R. Huna, citing R. Joseph states,

> It was an angel that descended at that moment [when the den was sealed with a stone] and, assuming the likeness of a lion made of stone, sat down at the mouth of the pit. Hence it is written, *My God hath sent His angel, and hath shut the lion's mouths, and they have not hurt me.* (*Num. Rab.* 14:3)

Finally, one midrash notes that the lion is an important metaphor both for the tribe of Judah, of which Daniel was a member, and for the might of God. There is a text that cleverly links these symbols with the story of Daniel who is cast into the lions' den:

> Thus we have explained, *"By Judah God is known."* For what reason was Daniel saved from the lions? Because he offered prayer to the Holy One, blessed be He, who is described as a lion; as it is written, *They shall walk after the Lord, who shall roar like a lion* (Hos. XI, 10), and Daniel belonged to the tribe of Judah who was called a lion; for it says, *Judah is a lion's whelp* (Gen. XLIX, 9), and it also says, *Now among these were, of the children of Judah, Daniel,* etc. (Dan. I, 6). Let then the Lion come and deliver the lion from the mouth of the lion. Another exposition is that since he was like the lions, being himself a lion, he was therefore not injured (*Num. Rab.* 13:4).

Haman has an unsuspecting king, Ahasuerus, issue a decree of genocide against Jews, so too do the conspirators prompt an unwitting king to issue a decree that ensures Daniel's death. In addition, king Ahasuerus's claim that he cannot undo Haman's decree parallels Darius's helplessness when faced with Daniel's death. The authors of both Esther and Daniel use this theme of the law's supposed immutability to deride the policies of their successful overlords. Because it would be hard to imagine any empire successfully operating under such strictures, the fact that these impotent kings are so manipulated by their governmental assistants reveals an important concern of our author.[4] Even in the best circumstances, the exiles must be constantly vigilant. Any vacuum caused by kings who are either weak or willfully blind is indeed significant and potentially life-threatening.

Daniel's Response, 6:10 (6:11 MT)

The author temporarily interrupts the presentation of the conspirators' plan in order to underscore Daniel's response to the king's decree. It is striking because of its simplicity and profundity. The words used of Daniel's actions are "prayed and gave thanks." Daniel went home and "prayed and gave thanks" (*ûmĕṣallē ûmôdē*), expressing neither fear nor alarm (v. 10 [v. 11 MT]). [Midrashim on Daniel 6] It is interesting to note that when the author relates Daniel's activity, the words "make a request," previously employed in a technical sense by the conspirators to identify a crime against the state, are not found. Thus, Daniel's act does not, in fact, violate the decree of the courtiers who had stated that whoever "make[s] a request" ("prays," NRSV; v. 7 [v. 8 MT]) of anyone other than to the king. Thus, pointing to Daniel's innocence, the author avoids directly stating that Daniel did the one act that the king agreed to place under the interdict. In addition, by showing that Daniel's praying was consistent with what he had done in the past, the author indicates that just as Daniel previously was faithful to both God and king (v. 10

[v. 11 MT]), he remained so even after the conspirators set the trap.[5] [Lessons on Prayer]

The Advancement of the Conspirators' Plan, 6:11-13 (6:12-14 MT)

The satraps next lie in wait to catch Daniel in an activity that they can present as a crime. In a scene of intimidation, they gather strength for their plan by again assembling together before Darius and by portraying Daniel's act of prayer as a treasonous offense. The narrative's earlier description that Daniel prayed in a room with windows makes it possible that the men could claim that they witnessed this event (v. 11 [v. 12 MT]). [Identity in a Foreign Environment]

The officials' words to the king follow a clever strategy. They do not, at first, identify the offender or even state that a crime has been committed; rather, they only ask for confirmation of the king's sentence for such a crime. They repeat the content of the king's decision, and the king himself confirms that they are correct, while publicly proclaiming that these laws and their consequences cannot be altered. The king has firmly placed himself in a quagmire that cannot be readily undone.

Only when the king confirms the punishment (v. 12 [v. 13 MT]) do the conspirators refer to Daniel by name and allege that he has disobeyed the king's law (v. 13 [v. 14 MT]). To be sure, they know that Daniel is the king's favorite, and they rightly fear that he will not respond affirmatively to their request to enforce the death penalty. Although the king appointed Daniel as one of the three

Lessons on Prayer

The rabbis argue that this account of Daniel praying teaches that prayer should be conducted in a room that has windows because the sight of the sky, which is associated with God, encourages proper devotion. Similarly, the author of Tobit shows another occasion where an individual prays at a window. Sarah is described as follows: "At the same time, with hands outstretched toward the window, she prayed . . ." (Tob 3:11).

The rabbis also reason that, although the Torah requires that daily prayer be said, and yet does not specify the number of times prayer is to be offered, Daniel's actions demonstrate that such customs are pre-exilic. By rabbinic times, thrice-daily prayer became obligatory (*b. Ber.* 31a). Rabbinic tradition gives possible origins of thrice-daily prayers. One opinion is that Abraham, Isaac, and Jacob instituted the morning, afternoon, and evening prayers respectively. Another states that the prayers were instituted to correspond with the times of the daily sacrifices, but the persons who did this are unknown.

Hersh Goldwurm, *Daniel: A New Translation with a Commentary Anthologized from Talmudic, Midrashic, and Rabbinic Sources* (The ArtScroll Tanach Series; New York: Mesorah Publications, 1979), 180–82.

Identity in a Foreign Environment

The "otherness" of minorities sometimes prompts fears in the majority culture. Jews in Persian lands had to balance the need to adapt to the demands of the government and broader culture with the desire to retain their own distinctive traditions. Although some scholars condemn the "exclusivism" of Judaism under siege, Daniel L. Smith fittingly counters,

the ability of a group to reconstruct its identity is essential to its survival in a foreign cultural environment. . . . The pressures to worship other gods, to conform to the lifestyle of the conqueror and their values by necessity leads to a community of survivors. To be troubled by what appears to be "exclusivism" . . . is to misunderstand profoundly the nature of group solidarity and survival of minorities.

Daniel L. Smith, "The Politics of Ezra: Sociological Indicators of Postexilic Judaean Society," in *Second Temple Studies 1: Persian Period*, ed. Philip R.. Davies (JSOTSup 117; Sheffield: JSOT Press, 1991), 84.

presidents, his fellow satraps deny his rank and refer to him only as "one of the exiles of Judah" (v. 13 [v. 14 MT]). This phrase, which recalls Belshazzar's patronizing address, strips Daniel of his office and accomplishments and serves to distance him from his colleagues, who actually reveal their prejudice and hatred. In describing Daniel's offense, the conspirators state, "Daniel, who is of the exiles of Judah, has not paid heed to you, O King, or to the decree you have inscribed. Three times a day he offers his request" (*bāʿē bāʿûtēh*; "prays his prayer," NRSV; v. 13 [v. 14 MT]). With these words, the author shows that what Daniel actually *did* contrasts with what the conspirators report that they *saw*, demonstrating the mendacious nature of the allegations. Daniel did not, in fact, "offer his request," as they contend. Rather, the reader has already been shown that he "prayed and gave thanks" (v. 10 [v. 11 MT]). Because the officials have already recollected the interdict and its consequences, they do not need to specify that Daniel must now be put in the lions' pit, thereby avoiding putting into words what would be most distasteful to the king. Even though such specification is avoided, the fearsome implication is clear.

The author accomplishes another purpose by this presentation of the officials' demands and the king's response. Because Daniel will miraculously survive the lions' pit, the king ironically remains faithful to the contrived punishment that the conspirators demand, namely, that the perpetrator *be thrown* into the pit (vv. 7, 12 [vv. 8, 13 MT]). They assumed, to be sure, that Daniel would die there. God's victory is all the more highlighted, therefore, as the author shows that the contrived actions of the conspirators soon become the source of their undoing.

The Kings' Response to his Officials, 6:14-15 (6:15-16 MT)

The author reveals neither any verbal response of Darius nor any accounting of what the king thinks upon hearing the conspirators' statements. Would the king question the conspirators about what they saw or heard? This gap in information allows the reader to consider the lack of action on the part of the king. When the conspirators remind him of the immutability of the law, he fails to seize any opportunity to protect Daniel. He does not, for example, issue an additional decree (see below). The reader knows he was sorely troubled and "determined to save Daniel" (v. 14 [15 MT]), yet the ambiguity regarding his attempts allows the reader to consider that they may be disingenuous. In fact, the sycophantic officials' successful manipulation of the king underscores how dangerous the acts of the greater citizenry can be, especially in the absence of leadership. The description of the king's feelings about Daniel points to the narrator's true concern—to show the faithfulness of God in times of difficulty and the triumph of good over evil. Two of the words used to describe the king's wishes, namely, that he desired "to save" (*lĕšêzābûtēh*) and "to rescue" (*lĕhaṣṣālûtēh*) Daniel, are words normally associated with the activity of God. For example, these words are used to describe the actions of God who saved the three youths from the fiery furnace (Dan 3:17, 28, 29) and are used throughout Daniel 6 to indicate God's response to Daniel (vv. 16, 20, 27 [vv. 17, 21, 28 MT]). By showing a king who is ultimately powerless to rescue Daniel, the author actually highlights a saving act of the God of Israel.

The author continues to portray the king's weakness by showing that the event that stops Darius's ruminations is not any act of his own direction, but is, rather, the reappearance of the officials (v. 15 [v. 16 MT]). The author uses the verb *hargišû* (lit., "assembled around" or "surrounded") as well as an inverted syntax, in which the subject (the men) precedes the verb in order to show the intimidating nature of these conspirators (v. 15 [v. 16 MT]). The king can escape neither their dominance in policy, nor their physical presence, nor their horrific demands. The menacing words of these officials can be translated interrogatively: "Do you know, O King, that the law of Media and Persia . . . cannot be altered?" Here they appear to be questioning whether the king will follow the law, or if translated declaratively, it is they who are commanding the king: "Know, O King, that the law of Media and Persia . . . cannot be altered" (v. 15 [v. 16 MT]). The king immediately capitulates. Even if one accepts, for the purposes of this story, that "the laws of the Medes and Persians" were in fact considered immutable, one finds a possible alternative in other narratives of a similar time and place. For example, in the book of Esther, the king issues the additional decree that Jews could defend themselves on the day set aside for the pogrom established by Haman (Esth 8:9-14). In the tale of Susanna, the false witnesses are separated and questioned, revealing their lies (Sus 51-59). Here, we only have a statement about the king's feelings, not of his actions. He remains paralyzed.

Daniel in the Lions' Pit, 6:16-23 (6:17-24 MT)

In the following section, the author contrasts the imprisonment of Daniel in the pit and the king's confinement in his home.

Daniel's Acts of Lovingkindness

The homiletic work '*Abot de Rabbi Nathan* (4:5) preserves a moving story about the significance of Daniel's acts of lovingkindness. R. Yochanan ben Zakkai understands the words "your God whom you serve continually" (6:16 [6:17 MT]) to refer to Daniel's service of God during the exile. This service, or acts of kindness, included preparing brides for their weddings, making the dead ready for burial, giving alms to poor, and praying three times a day. Such service effected atonement in place of the sacrifices that had been offered in the days of the first temple.

Hersh Goldwurm, *Daniel: A New Translation with a Commentary Anthologized from Talmudic, Midrashic, and Rabbinic Sources* (The ArtScroll Tanach Series; New York: Mesorah Publications, 1979), 186.

Concerning the fearsome pit, much remains unspecified. We learn only that Daniel was thrown there; the agents who do this are not identified. Using the same word for "save" that was found in v. 14 (v. 15 MT), the king states that Daniel's God "must, may, or can rescue Daniel"—the verb may be translated in any of these ways.[6] In addition, it is interesting to note that in speaking to Daniel the king refers to Daniel's God as "the one whom you continually serve" (v. 16 [v. 17 MT, A. T.]). Although we cannot be certain how the idea of serving God was used in the time of the author, it could possibly mean sacrificial service, prayer, or doing acts of kindness and charity. [Daniel's Acts of Lovingkindness] In the rabbinic texts, the sages conclude that because there was no sacrificial service outside of the temple, the king's reference would most likely refer to Daniel's prayer and acts of kindness and charity. Whatever the connotations, the reader hears from the very lips of the foreign oppressor, who ultimately must take responsibility for sending Daniel to the lions, that Daniel's behavior is righteous. Daniel, however, does not speak; his silence heightens his innocence.

As the description of the sealing of the pit is given, the author continues with words of ambiguity that question the integrity of Darius, mock his pathetic weakness, and continue to underscore his ineffectiveness in protecting Daniel. The closing of the pit with the stone is described in the passive voice; we do not know who brought the stone or whether the king ever commanded it to be done (v. 17 [v. 18 MT]). Because the author expresses no specific motivation, there is more than one possibility for the significance of the king's sealing of the pit once the stone is brought. One possibility is to underscore the intimidation Darius feels from his nobles. By sealing the pit, he can prove that he will not attempt to rescue Daniel. At the same time, the sealing of the pit prevents the conspirators from tampering with it. If God will truly rescue Daniel from the lions' mouths, they will not have cause to kill Daniel by any other means, for the king will have fulfilled the obligatory punishment of throwing him to the beasts. The phrase, "so that nothing might be changed concerning Daniel" (v. 17 [v. 18 MT]), could refer either to the king's capitulation to insistent demands or to his hope that God would indeed rescue Daniel.

The author never details Daniel's experience in the aftermath of the sealing of the pit; rather, the focus turns to Darius himself. By this emphasis, the author shows that it is the king—and not Daniel—who is tormented. At the same time, the drama is heightened, for the hero's fate remains unknown. The motif of the king who can neither sleep nor eat when distressed is seen in other similar narratives—Nebuchadnezzar cannot sleep when he is unable to understand the meaning of his dreams (Dan 2:1), and, according to the book of Esther, King Ahasuerus cannot sleep in his palace due to an unspecified malaise (Esth 6:1-2). In all these cases, the monarchs' discomfort previews a drama that ultimately underscores the trustworthiness of a Jewish subject, for Nebuchadnezzar is prompted to rely on Daniel, and Ahasuerus finally discovers that Mordecai saved his life. Here, the king apparently endures a type of psychological torment, as he cannot sleep. While unable to sleep, he fasts and prays; it is striking that the king himself follows the piety of the righteous. By portraying the king in such a light, Daniel's victory over his conqueror seems assured. Apparently, the test was to continue until daybreak; by specifying the time and by indicating the haste with which the king proceeded, the author stresses that the king went to investigate as soon as possible, before dawn. The king's pathos is underscored by the description that "he cried out in a sad voice" (v. 20 [v. 21 MT] A.T.; "he cried out anxiously," NRSV). Daniel's survival will now be all the more stunning because of the emotional anguish of the one ultimately responsible. Daniel's response is delayed for one sentence, allowing the reader to consider whether Darius's sad voice was inaudible or whether Daniel delayed to respond. Only when the king specifies that Daniel is a "servant of the living God" (v. 20 [v. 21 MT]) does Daniel answer.

Daniel in the Lions' Den

This masterpiece of Rubens emphasizes Daniel's view of the heavens while in the midst of the lions that awake as the stone is rolled back from the pit. Note the evidence of earlier victims in the foreground.

Sir Peter Paul Rubens. *Daniel in the Lions' Den*. c. 1615. Oil on canvas, Ailsa Mellon Brice Fund, Image courtesy of the Board of Trustees, National Gallery of Art, Washington DC.

Daniel's first and last words of response consist of approbation to the king. His address, "O king, live forever," is, to be sure, a stock phrase, but it is probably used here as a sign of respect, just as Daniel used one as a sign of respect for Nebuchadnezzar. His final remark, "before you, O king, I have done no wrong" (v. 22 [v. 23 MT]), insists that his devotion to God never compromised his loyalty to his political sovereign. Daniel's rescue was miraculous, as an angel protected him (v. 22 [v. 23 MT]), just as an angel was present in the fiery furnace with Daniel's three companions (3:25). Paralleling God's deliverance of the Israelites from Egypt and God's salvation from Canaanite foes, the significance of the deliverance lies in the fact that the miracle shows God's victory over tyrants and affirms that the world is ultimately a place where good triumphs.

In order to underscore that God protected Daniel during his ordeal, the author uses the word "harm" three times in Daniel's response to the king and in the description of the immediate aftermath of Daniel's exit from the pit (vv. 22-23 [vv. 23-24 MT]). We hear him state that the lions "did not harm me" (v. 22 [v. 23 MT], A.T.; "would not hurt me," NRSV) just as Daniel did "no harm" (v. 22 [v. 23 MT] A.T.; "no wrong," NRSV) to the king. The narrator confirms Daniel's innocence in the next verse by repeating that "no harm" was found in him. The primary reason given for Daniel's deliverance, however, is not his innocence before the king, but his "merit" or "righteousness" (*zākû*; v. 22 [v. 23 MT]) before God, a concept linked with Daniel's "trust" (*hêmin*; v. 23 [v. 24 MT]). The closeness of these two ideas of righteousness and trust is reminiscent of an important verse in the Targums, the Aramaic translation of scripture: "And Abraham believed (*wěheˀěmin*) in these words of God and he reckoned it to him as righteousness" (Gen 15:6). In this reference, which comments on Abraham's completion of the covenant of circumcision, Abraham is shown to trust in God's word that his descendants would be as innumerable as the stars, even though at that time he had no child with Sarah. Just as Abraham believed when God's promise seemed impossible, so too does Daniel when his very life is threatened. [Calvin on Daniel]

Many scholars insist that because there is no direct Babylonian or Persian extra-biblical evidence that lions were ever kept in a pit or that

Calvin on Daniel

John Calvin, who was forced to leave his native France in 1535, derived inspiration from the book of Daniel as he faced opponents and persecution. In his *Commentary on Daniel*, he draws strength from the account of Daniel in the lion's den, stating, "Now, whatever we may fear, and whatever events await us, even if we become subject to a hundred deaths, we ought never to decline from the pure worship of God, since Daniel did not hesitate to submit to the worship of Israel's God."

Because unjust decrees themselves were tantamount to disobedience to God, Calvin believed in the use of civil disobedience in the face of unjust decrees from governmental officials.

John Calvin, *Commentaries on the Book of the Prophet Daniel*, trans. Thomas Myers, 2 vols. (Grand Rapids MI: Eerdmans, 1948), 1:353.

John G. Gammie, "A Journey Through Danielic Spaces," in *Interpreting the Prophets*, ed. James Luther Mays and Paul J. Achtemeier (Philadelphia: Fortress, 1987), 261–72.

humans were cast to them, no real drama such as Daniel's can be posited as the source of this narrative. In recent scholarship, explorations of metaphorical contexts predominate. John Collins suggests that biblical references to righteous individuals who are surrounded by lions that symbolically represent danger and suffering may have inspired this story.[7] Karel Van der Toorn finds a non-biblical symbolic usage of lions that may have prompted this story. In examining the Babylonian wisdom text "I will Praise the Lord of Wisdom" and similar letters, Van der Toorn argues that the portrayal of lions that torment an individual represents the malicious acts of courtiers who viciously compete against an innocent scholar. He concludes that the lions' pit "is the circle of his [the scholar's] former colleagues from which he has been ousted. . . . They have indeed turned into lions, eager now to devour him."[8] Because of the similarities of the setting at court, with Daniel also maligned by his colleagues, Van der Toorn argues that the metaphor of the pit of lions was mistakenly taken in a literal way by the author of Daniel. While recognizing that other biblical references to threats of lions (either metaphorical or literal) may also have contributed to the story, he argues that Daniel 6 is an example of metaphor taken literally.

As opposed to these metaphorical usages of lions, other biblical references that refer to actual lions are directly relevant. The account of Benaiah (2 Sam 23:20), like the account of Daniel in the lions' pit, includes an account of a hero's victory over a vicious beast in trying circumstances. This account may possibly have been well known enough for the author of 2 Samuel to make only passing reference to it:

> Benaiah son of Jehoiada was a valiant warrior [another reading: the son of Ish-hai] from Kabzeel, a doer of great deeds; he struck down two sons of Ariel [another reading: two lion-hearted men/two heroes] of Moab. He also went down and killed a lion in a pit on a day when snow had fallen. (2 Sam 23:20)

This account is particularly interesting because it shows that Benaiah's heroics were understood to include both bravery against Moabite foes as well as the slaying of a lion in a pit. The Hebrew text has uncertainties, including the possibility of reading "two [sons of] Ariel" or "two lion-hearted men/heroes." If the word translated "Ariel" (*ʾărîʾēl*) is a proper name (as the NRSV has it), it would be a theophoric name meaning "lioness of God." If it is a common noun, its translation is disputed, but it appears to come from the same root word for lion and could be translated "lion-hearted men." Either way, whether Benaiah slew two sons of Ariel ("lioness of God"), or whether he slew two lion-hearted men, the play on words between Ariel or "lion-hearted men" with lion (*'aryēh*) is clear, linking Benaiah's first heroic act with his second, namely, the slaying of the real lion in the pit.

In addition to this account of Benaiah's victories over the Moabites and with a lion, there are two other biblical texts that provide a context for understanding Daniel in the lions' pit, namely, David's reference to having killed a lion before his successful victory over the Philistine enemy, Goliath (1 Sam 17:34-37), and Samson's victory against the lion on the road before his encounter with the Philistines (Judg 14:5-9). Just as Benaiah, David, and Samson faced both lions as well as Moabite and Philistine enemies of Israel, so Daniel faces both the pit of lions and the Median/Persian enemies of Israel. Daniel's victory, unlike those of the previous heroes, does not come from his own hand, however, but from God. In keeping with the theme of God's defeat of the arrogant world powers, Daniel's victory in the lions' den previews God's crush of evil and brutality and paves a path for the kingdom of God.

Once Daniel has completed his ordeal in the pit of lions, earlier references to the king's actions become more significant. The reader has seen that neither the conspirators nor the king ever said that Daniel was to be put to death—rather he was to be thrown into the pit of lions. Because the king, in fact, has done this, the conspirators cannot accuse him of disobeying the law, which, they so forcibly argued, could neither be changed nor altered. They cannot now claim, for example, that he should face another death sentence, as that would compromise the unalterable law! The conspirators will have no choice but to accept Daniel's freedom.

Darius's Actions: A Death Sentence and a Missive, 6:24-28 (6:25-29 MT)

In contrast to the earlier portrayal of the passive and manipulated king, Darius finally is able to make his own commands. His first command is to bring Daniel out of the pit, followed by two additional decrees: he eliminates those who threaten him and sends a missive to all his subjects. Daniel's survival in the pit enables Darius to see that he need not be controlled by the acts of his subordinates, which are, in fact, treasonous. He punishes the conspirators and their families by throwing them into the same pit of lions intended for Daniel, suggesting the utter reversal of their schemes.

Public Executions and Public Letters

Daniel Smith evaluates the exilic and post-exilic evidence that contributes to the "politics of resistance" among Jews in Babylonian and Persian lands. The many references to confinement, public executions, public addresses, displays of power and of military might, renaming of captives, and desecrations (as opposed to destruction) of holy objects are examples of state control over captive populations. As Smith states, these acts show "a psychological intention beyond simply looting. The spiritual morale of the exiles in the light of such daily reminders that they are not home and that 'their god' appeared to have failed them" are theological problems that exilic writings, such as those of the prophets Second Isaiah and Ezekiel, must address (77). The references to the confinement and to the change of the names of Daniel and his companions when they first arrive in Babylon as well as to the attempted public executions of the righteous in the fiery furnace and in the lions' den also indicate that the spiritual well-being of the community is a concern

for the author of Dan 1–6 as well. In addition, although we have no direct evidence for chattel slavery, Babylonian and Persian documents show that large influxes of involuntarily transferred peoples were used to repopulate abandoned sites and to expand the empire by providing forced labor. Nebuchadnezzar himself, for example, boasts that he used foreign people in forced labor for the building of his temple. Any assessment of life in the exile will be piecemeal and ultimately speculative given the indirect nature of most of our evidence, but it is hard to image such stories of hardship, suffering, torture, and threat of death coming from benevolent and peaceful circumstances. The insistence on the validity of the praise and respect due to Daniel's God makes it most likely that such stories reflect a reality where the majority population dismissed the beliefs and values of this faith.

See Daniel L. Smith, "The Politics of Ezra: Sociological Indicators of Postexilic Judaean Society," in *Second Temple Studies 1: Persian Period*, ed. Philip R. Davies, (JSOTSup 117; Sheffield: JSOT Press, 1991), 73–97.

The intensity of this reversal is underscored by the description of their horrifying deaths (v. 24 [v. 25 MT]). The severity of the punishment mirrors the one given to the attendants who placed Daniel's three companions in the fiery furnace, for they were destroyed by the very flames that left the three youths unscathed. Both cases make clear that those who maliciously attempt to condemn the innocent to death will be doomed not only to failure, but to a horror worse than the one they propose. At the same time, the author does not present their deaths as something Daniel proposed or desired. It is Darius, a Median/Persian king, who enforces such a horrible punishment on his citizenry.

As the follow-up to the account of Daniel's vindication, the letter Darius sends to his subjects serves both to attribute Daniel's rescue to God in front of the entire populace and to show God's deliverance as paradigmatic. [Public Executions and Public Letters] God performed "signs and wonders" (*ʾotîn wĕtimhîn*; v. 27 [v. 28 MT]), language that recalls God's redemption of the Israelites out of Egypt (Exod 7:3; Deut 6:22; Isa 8:18; Neh 9:10). Despite appearances to the contrary, it is the God of Israel whose justice will ultimately triumph on this earth—not the capricious rule of governmental officials who can manipulate even a sympathetic king to inflict cruel punishment on the innocent. The God who delivered the Israelite people from the tyranny of the Egyptians is the same God who rescues Jews from the threats that come from living under the rule of foreign empires.

The sending of the letter is framed as a warning: the populace is told to "tremble" (*zāyĕʿîn*) and "fear" (*wĕdāḥălîn*) before the God of Daniel. These words are reminiscent of the reactions of the nations when they see the victories that God gave to the Israelites during the days of the conquest (Deut 2:25). Such victories have a theological content, as they are given by God to support justice over oppression. Similarly, the blessing contained in the letter functions as a sign of victory, showing that even the Gentile king will honor the God of Israel. Because of this declaration, it is actually Daniel who has triumphed. The author shows the community that whenever they may be pressured to conform to Gentile ways, both small and great, they should look to Daniel, who maintained the conviction that God's strength would see him through the most difficult of challenges.

As the ancient readers came to the end of Daniel 1–6, they were left with a certain impression of what life was like for their ancestors who had lived in the Diaspora in the days of three conquerors, Babylonia, Media, and Persia. Although the last statement, namely, "Daniel prospered in the days of Cyrus," may have been understood optimistically, it is also true that the overall impression of these tales was one of great caution. While it is true that all of the scenes of terrible danger in these stories have happy endings, their sheer frequency and the relentless repetition of such life-threatening situations prompted the reader of the author's own time to conclude that life in the Diaspora was never truly safe. The days of Nebuchadnezzar, Belshazzar, or Darius all were equally filled with idolaters who, because they created unspeakable conditions of suffering, were unworthy of respect. These emperors' enslavement and use of human persons, their horrific punishments, and their sorcery and profligacy were outrageous. Their evil did not stop with their greed; they were unpredictable and dangerous. Nevertheless, the

Cyrus the Great

Trilingual inscription: "I am Cyrus, King and Achaemenid . . ." in Persian, Elamite, and Babylonian. 6th C. BC. Pasargadae, Iran. (Credit: Art Resource, NY)

This inscription of Cyrus the Great from Pasargadae, Iran, is written in Persian, Elamite, and Babylonian. It attests to Cyrus's victories over many peoples and to the Persian use of documents and letters composed in more than one language.

Jews in the Persian Satrapy of Egypt

Although Jews benefited from a considerable amount of autonomy in religious affairs and practices in the Persian period, their experience was not consistent. In the Persian administrative district of Egypt, for example, there is evidence of an incident of retaliation against the Jewish temple of Elephantine, which was apparently spurred on by the local Egyptian priests and sanctioned by the Persian governor of the Egyptian administrative province. This temple was built in Egypt while under the rule of its pharaohs, but conquered while under the Persian emperor Cambyses in 525 BC. The Persians let the temple stand at first, but when threatened by local Egyptians, did nothing to stop the violence. Jews were powerless when locals decided to attack it. A letter from a certain Jedaniah, a leader of the Jewish community in Elephantine, to Begavahya (Bagohi), governor of the Persian province of Yehud (Judah), explains how their temple was destroyed and looted:

[The Egyptians with the other troops] came to the fortress of Elephantine with their implements, broke into that temple, demolished it to the ground, and the pillars of stone that were there—they smashed them . . . [and the] gateways of stone, built of hewn stone, that were in that temple, they demolished. And their standing doors and the pivots of those doors, (of) bronze, and the roof of wood of cedar . . . all (of these) with fire they burned. But the basins of gold and silver and the (other) things that were in that temple—all (of these) they took and made their own.

Jedaniah appealed to the Persian governor to have their temple rebuilt, but it was never restored.

Mary Boyce, "Persian Religion in the Achemenid Age," in *Introduction; The Persian Period*, ed. W. D. Davies and Louis Finkelstein (The Cambridge History of Judaism 1; Cambridge: Cambridge University Press, 1984), 301–302.

Bezalel Porten, "Settlement of Jews at Elephantine and Arameans at Syene," in *Judah and the Judeans in the Neo-Babylonian Period*, ed. By Oded Lipschits and Joseph Blenkinsopp (Winona Lake IN: Eisenbrauns, 2003), 451–56.

author appears to be pragmatic, showing that Jews can be faithful subjects. Repeatedly, Daniel is shown to be a loyal servant to the king. The author thus presents a nuanced examination of foreign laws that can be kept and foreign laws that should be abhorred. Even a sympathetic king might not be able to protect the community against those who hate and fear them—how much more so a king who despises them. For those in governmental service, the dangers that Daniel had faced reminded others living under foreign rule not to be complacent when things were going well and encouraged them to remain faithful to their traditions when threatened either overtly or through assimilation. The stories provided an unwavering faith that even the most serious of dangers could be met with deliverance. [Jews in the Persian Satrapy of Egypt]

CONNECTIONS

Centuries ago, these collections of stories found in Daniel 1–6 presented a model of hope to a community beset by questions essential to their survival. Although the earliest form of these narratives can be dated to the Jewish Diaspora under Persian rule, they were later incorporated into the entirety of the book of Daniel during the Hellenistic period. This final stage of redaction occurred in a time when Jews were again living in Judah, but under the unpredictable rule of the Seleucids, the dynasts who ruled after the conquest of Alexander the Great.

These stories of Daniel served to entertain; they either subtly or overtly mocked Gentile kings and their crushing bureaucracy, which, at any moment, could move from the inane to the murderous. In the days of Antiochus IV—a time of great uncertainty and eventually of persecution—these stories surely provided encouragement for those who cherished their faith and traditions. Keeping the food laws, worshiping according to the commandments, continuing the covenant of circumcision, providing for the poor, and speaking up for the accused all could entail considerable risk at any moment. Being a Jew under foreign rule—whether it be in the Diaspora under Babylon or Persia, or being in Judah under the Seleucids—was to live with constant uncertainty. A benign ruler could be followed by a murderous one; a period of peace could be followed by persecution and suffering.

In such uncertain times, further traditions about the young exile Daniel also found a forum in a unique way, namely, by the development of two additional stories in which he appears as a main character—"Bel and the Dragon" and "Susanna." In Bel and the Dragon, once again the foreign rulers are mocked and are outwitted by the humble Daniel.

In the story of Susanna, however, a different dimension of Jewish thought can be discerned. [Susanna] For even in the unpredictable times of living without any independent power, the Jewish community, nevertheless, did not only critique their foreign rulers. They also continued their long-standing biblical tradition of introspection. *Their own* values, leadership, and fidelity to God and the commandments were not immune from scrutiny. Erich Gruen presents a sterling analysis of the way in which the author of Susanna, an apocryphal addition to Daniel, applies the same critique of Gentile leadership to the community's own leaders. Far from restricting their critique of injustice to their foreign overlords, the Hellenistic Jewish community probed their own tradition and treatment of all members of

Daniel and Habakkuk

Angel carrying the prophet Habakkuk by his hair. 7th C. AD. Limestone bas-relief from the island of Thasos, Greece, Archaeological Museum, Istanbul, Turkey. (Credit: Erich Lessing/Art Resource, NY)

The story of Bel and the Dragon includes a tradition about the prophet Habakkuk being commanded to bring food to Daniel while he is in the pit of lions (see above, [Bel and the Dragon]). Protesting that he does not know how to travel to Babylon, an angel seizes Habakkuk by the hair and carries him to the mouth of the lions' pit. Habakkuk passes the meal to Daniel, who responds by thanking the God who has "not abandoned those who love you" (Bel 38). This 7th C. AD bas-relief depicts God's sending of the angel to Habakkuk.

Susanna

The narrative of Susanna, found as an addition to the canonical book of Daniel, was composed in approximately the 3rd century BC and reflects a Hellenistic Jewish community. It is unknown whether this account, preserved in two Greek texts (the Old Greek and the Theodotionic text), comes from an original Semitic *Vorlage* (prototype). For Catholics and Orthodox Christians, it is part of the biblical canon; for Protestants, it is found in the apocrypha. Jay Braverman has argued that the story of Susanna was apparently known in the Jewish community at the time of Jerome.

There are various theories concerning the origins of this story. Some see the catalyst to be the remark in Jer 29:29-33 that refers to the end of two false prophets, others, an argument between Sadducees and Pharisees concerning proper court procedures, others a secular folktale made relevant by adding a Jewish context.

Jay Braverman, *Jerome's Commentary on Daniel: A Study of Comparative Jewish and Christian Interpretations of the Hebrew Bible* (CBQMS 7; Washington DC: Catholic Biblical Association of America, 1978), 126–31.

Michal Dayagi Mendels, "Susanna, Book of," *ABD*, ed. David Noel Freedman, 6 vols. (New York: Doubleday & Co., 1992), 4:246.

their community. Gruen demonstrates how the story of Susanna shows that "inventive Jewish writers could hold even their fellow Jews up to scorn, a striking sign of the self-confidence of their communities."[9]

The story of Susanna tells the moving account of a married Jewish woman of considerable means who becomes the object of two judges' voyeurism. The story assumes that Jews have autonomous rights to judge one of their own in some matters—here the issues are adultery and bearing false witness. They give her an ultimatum: they will either force her to have sex with them or accuse her of committing adultery with an unspecified lover. Susanna chooses to submit to their lies, claiming, "I am completely trapped. For if I do this, it will mean death for me; if I do not, I cannot escape your hands. I choose not to do it; I will fall into your hands, rather than sin in the sight of the Lord" (Sus 22–23).

These elders apparently think they have a foolproof plan to ensure a capital sentence for Susanna because they can provide the required testimony of two witnesses. Although she has a wealthy husband, respected parents, hundreds of servants, and four children, no one questions the false testimony of these elders or takes steps to ensure that their words are honest. Perjury was a serious offense according to the law of Moses, and indeed any perpetrator would be subject to whatever punishment would have been imposed on the falsely accused (Deut 19:15-21). The turning point in the story comes when Susanna prays. Indeed, God hears the cry of the innocent, and the young Daniel is stirred to come to her defense. Even before he begins questioning the men, he knows they are guilty (perhaps God has revealed this to him), and he gathers proof that the elders are providing false testimony by questioning them separately, catching them in their lies. The community, happily, believes Daniel, and Susanna is saved.

Susannah Artwork
In this painting, the artist Frans Floris emphasizes the voyeurism of the elders as Susanna cowers.

Frans Floris. 1519–1570. *Susannah and the Elders*. Galleria Palatina, Palazzo Pitti, Florence, Italy. (Credit: Scala/Art Resource, NY)

This deceptively delightful detective story actually indicts the entire community. Everyone was silent—from Susanna's loved ones to all the people that passively stood by. George Brooke argues that this presentation of Susanna, the righteous woman in a garden who obeys God's commandments, provides an image of a reversal of Eve's behavior in the Garden of Eden. By showing Susanna's absolute faithfulness to God when she is threatened in her husband's garden, thus reversing Eve's disobedience in the garden of creation, the author shows that paradise can be here on earth, if only people obey God's laws: "this paradise is not distant, either temporally or spatially, but is available to all the righteous who obey the Law and keep the commandments in their own communities."[10]

The account of Susanna illustrates the importance of key legal procedures that must be pursued if there is to be justice and if an ideal community is to be created: witnesses must be properly cross-examined, perjurers must be punished according to what they intended to have done to their victim as the law of Moses specifies, and the community must guard against corruption among its leadership. This account targets both the lecherous elders as well as the uncritical community, which is far too quick to judge. With a clever plot, delightful word plays, and with the drama of a detective story, the audience is entertained yet challenged. How could it be that the community is duped so easily in a matter that involves condemning a woman to death? How could it be that they create a society wherein Susanna feels she must submit to this tragic choice? The story prompts the reader to have a healthy skepticism of its leaders and to be vigilant against community failings, especially when cloaked by the guise of hypocritical religious principles. By placing such a morally significant message in the form of a didactic tale with a happy ending, the author allows the introspection to occur with "a welcome sense of detachment," in an age of the many uncertainties associated with the overwhelming success of the ruling Hellenistic government and ethos.[11]

It is all the more arresting that Susanna is saved from the elders' plot given that she is female and powerless and that the only one who will speak in her defense is a youth.[12] The author thus shows that God responds to prayer and that any member in the community, no matter how marginalized, should take courage from her example and from the example of the young Daniel. It is clear that women and youth especially are encouraged in the face of injustice in this narrative. In addition, those who enjoy a higher status—the wealthy, men in positions of leadership—soberly are warned. If

they too will be on guard against injustice, the rewards are not only the protection of the innocent, but also the building of community according to God's plan and a taste of the ideal in the present. This kind of community could provide an island of righteousness even when a subject people may be ruled by others. [Susanna Bibliography for Further Reading]

Susanna shows that not only the justice system of their foreign overlords needs to be scrutinized. For as the story shows, Susanna is in danger equal to that of the three Jews who refuse to bow to Nebuchadnezzar's idol (Dan 3) and to that of Daniel who faces a pit of lions (Dan 6). Daniel's three companions, Daniel himself, and Susanna all faced challenges to their faith—the conspirators of Nebuchadnezzar's day tried to manipulate the three companions to commit idolatry, Daniel's governmental adversaries prodded him

Susanna Bibliography for Further Reading

Brenner, Athalya, ed., *A Feminist Companion to the Bible*. The Feminist Companion to the Bible 7. Edited by Athalya Brenner. Sheffield: Sheffield Academic Press, 1995.

Brooke, George J. "Susanna and Paradise Regained." In *Women in the Biblical Tradition*. Edited by George J. Brooke. Lewiston NY: Edwin Mellen Press, 1992. Pages 92–111.

Carroll, Michael P. "Myth, Methodology, and Transformation in the Old Testament: The Stories of Esther, Judith, and Susanna." *Studies in Religion* 12/3 (1983): 301–12.

Glancy, Jennifer A. "The Accused: Susanna and her Readers." *Journal for the Study of the Old Testament* 58 (1993): 103–116. Reprinted in *A Feminist Companion to Esther, Judith, and Susanna*. The Feminist Companion to the Bible 7. Edited by Athalya Brenner. Sheffield: Sheffield Academic Press, 1995. Pages 288–302.

———. "The Mistress-Slave Dialectic: Paradoxes of Slavery in Three LXX Narratives." JSOT 72 (1996): 71–87.

Moore, Carey A. "Susanna: A Case of Sexual Harassment in Ancient Babylon." *BR* 8 (1992): 21–29, 52.

———. *Daniel, Esther, and Jeremiah: The Additions*. AB 44. New York: Doubleday & Co., 1977.

Spolsky, Ellen, ed., *The Judgment of Susanna: Authority and Witness*. Atlanta: Scholars Press, 1996.

to neglect his obligation to pray, and the elders forced Susanna to choose between adultery (more accurately rape) or suffering death because of their false charges. That the tragic choice forced upon

"Nobody Need Wait a Single Moment"

This silkscreen by artist Erika Rothenberg depicts a pile of watches—reminiscent of the possessions confiscated by the Nazis before sending Jews to the death camps—alongside a quotation from the diary of Anne Frank: "Nobody Need Wait a Single Moment Before Starting to Improve the World." This graphic was commissioned by the Jewish Museum for the New Year 5754 (1994). Rosh Hashanah, the Jewish New Year, celebrates the birthday of the world and begins a period of reflection and repentance. Judaism considers that human beings are partners with God and must strive for the perfection of the world.

Erika Rothenberg. "Nobody Need Wait a Single Moment Before Starting to Improve the World" (quotation by Anne Frank). 1994. Silkscreen, (Credit: John Fletcher. The Jewish Museum. New York. Art Resource, NY)

Susanna was done by two of her own people, and indeed, community elders, is all the more striking. The author of Susanna is able to connect the passion for justice shown in the book of Daniel with love of God and of the community. The author of Susanna wants all to strive for that ideal of justice known in their own centuries-old traditions.

The self-confidence displayed by this author of Susanna continues a long-standing practice found in the Hebrew Scriptures. The stories of the ancestors of Israel, for example, do not hesitate to show the suffering that Sarah inflicted upon Hagar, the idolatry committed by newly freed Israelites, the narcissism of judges, the greed of kings, dishonest business practices, and the negligence of the widows and orphans by king and commoner alike. Israel bequeaths centuries of texts that call for constant vigilance, self-critique, and a posture that prevents complacency. What generation could not profit from such a stance?

NOTES

[1] W. Lee Humphreys, "A Life-Style for Diaspora: A Study of the Tales of Esther and Daniel," *JBL* 92/2 (1973): 211–23; Robert Wilson, "From Prophecy to Apocalyptic: Reflections on the shape of Israelite Religion," *Semeia* 21 (1981): 88; John Collins, *Daniel* (Hermeneia; Minneapolis: Fortress, 1993), 45–52. Collins argues that whereas Nebuchadnezzar is portrayed as being menacing, Darius is shown to be benevolent.

[2] Daniel Smith-Christopher, "Prayers and Dreams: Power and Diaspora Identities in the Social Setting of the Daniel Tales," in *The Book of Daniel: Composition and Reception*, ed. John Collins and Peter Flint, 2 vols. (VTSup; Leiden: Brill, 2001), 1:290.

[3] See Esth 1:19; 8:8 and *Diodorus Siculus* 17.30. See comments on the passage of Diodorus in John Goldingay, Daniel (WBC 30; Dallas TX: Word Publishing, 1989), 128.

[4] The issue is not so much that there really was such a law in Persian-ruled lands, but is used here to show the vulnerability of an ineffective king (Collins, *Daniel*, 268).

[5] Towner rightly points out that Daniel does not publicly defy the king's orders; nevertheless, his prayer is in effect an act of "civil disobedience." Although Daniel does not seek martyrdom, he is particularly apt to be noticed, reflecting the experience of Jews in the Diaspora who, no matter if they were in forced labor or in governmental service, would be similarly distinctive if they remained true to their faith (W. Sibley Towner, *Daniel* [Interpretation, a Bible Commentary for Teaching and Preaching; Atlanta: John Knox, 1984], 82–83).

[6] John Goldingay, *Daniel*, 21, 132.

[7] Collins, *Daniel*, 267.

[8] Karel van der Toorn, "In the Lions' Den: The Babylonian Background of a Biblical Motif," *CBQ* 60/4 (1998): 638.

[9] Erich Gruen, *Heritage and Hellenism: The Reinvention of Jewish Tradition* (Berkeley: University of California Press, 1998), 172.

[10] George J. Brooke, "Susanna and Paradise Regained," in *Women in the Biblical Tradition*, ed. George J. Brooke (Studies in Women and Religion 31; Lewiston NY: Edwin Mellen Press, 1992), 110–11.

[11] Gruen, *Heritage*, 176–77.

[12] Carey Moore, "Susanna: A Case of Sexual Harassment in Ancient Babylon," *BRev* 8 (June 1992): 21.

DANIEL'S VISION OF GOD'S JUDGMENT

Daniel 7:1-28

COMMENTARY

Introduction: Daniel 7–12

With chapters 7–12, the book of Daniel shifts from narratives to apocalyptic visions. No longer must Daniel and his companions respond to the whims of monarchs; rather, Daniel now becomes a recipient of mystifying and frightening visions that both reveal and conceal God's plan for the future. These visions confirm that suffering awaits the Jewish people, yet they also provide assurance that hope for the future and expectations of God's victory are not in vain.

Although Daniel's perplexity about the significance of his visions and dreams is addressed by an interpreting angel, he continues with disquietude and uncertainty even after the angel offers two interpretations. [Visions, Dreams, and Apocalyptic Imagery] Yet Daniel is never abandoned by the angel, who reassures him that vindication rests in God's hands. Although Daniel never knows the time of God's destruction of evil in the world, the angel's message is consistent: wait for the everlasting kingdom of the holy ones of the Most High. With this paradigm, the author presents a moving perspective of steadfastness, for despite terrible persecutions from their foreign oppressors and internal conflict within the community, the visions show that God has set up a universe where good triumphs. Having many fears and only limited knowledge, the ancient audience of the Hellenistic era is like Daniel, as they are encouraged to hope in God's ultimate plan, to pray, and to wait while continuing to live lives of holiness. In times of persecution and community upheaval, these acts become heroic and perhaps subversive. They are profoundly significant, because they serve as testimony to the God of Israel who demands justice.

Despite the differences between Daniel 1–6 and Daniel 7–12, the two sections have features in common. Both use Aramaic and

Visions, Dreams, and Apocalyptic Imagery

Visions and dreams are closely associated, as is indicated by the ease with which the Old Greek and Theodotionic versions of Daniel readily translate Daniel's statement, "The vision which I saw" with "the visions which I dreamt." Both of these phenomena relate experiences that defy the empirically verifiable world or go beyond normal human events; they are seen by an individual who shares what he or she has witnessed in sometimes unusual or highly symbolic language. The visionary or dreamer may have a glimpse into a purported spiritual world that is significant in the broader context of a literary work. Visions and dreams are often typical of apocalyptic literature; they may reveal secrets, warn of an impending judgment, explain history, or provide special instructions to the faithful in extreme circumstances. They usually employ imagery that is highly symbolic and often bizarre or disturbing, as this literature addresses times of great turmoil or suffering. Although some symbols have a one-to-one correspondence with a specific reality (such as the "little horn" representing Antiochus), they often are evocative of broader theological concepts such as God's judgment against evil, the struggle for justice on earth, and belief in a hopeful future even when all appears futile. As David S. Russell notes, such images in apocalyptic visions prompt the members of the community to consider their own participation in "'an alternative world' of spiritual forces where they themselves share in the victory of the divine forces of good over the demonic forces of evil" (196). By using these symbols in the context of the vision or dream, they participate in the authoritative experience of the visionary who has an incomparable closeness to God.

David S. Russell, "Apocalyptic Imagery as Political Cartoon?" in *After the Exile: Essays in Honour of Rex Mason*, ed. John Barton and David J. Reimer (Macon GA: Mercer University Press, 1996), 196–97. See also Adela Yarbro Collins, "Vision," *Harper's Bible Dictionary*, ed. Paul Achtemeier (San Francisco: Harper & Row, 1985) 1114–15.

Hebrew, symbolic dreams, time frames marked by sequential kings and interpreting angels, and both feature Daniel himself. Indeed, Daniel 1–6 becomes a paradigm to understand Daniel 7–12. The accounts of the capture of Daniel and his friends (Dan 1), the young men in the fiery furnace (Dan 3), and Daniel in the lions' den (Dan 6) all speak of grave dangers that Jews endure because of the violence, caprice, and idolatry of their captors. In addition, Nebuchadnezzar's dreams of the statue (Dan 2) and of the tree (Dan 4) as well as the account of Belshazzar's feast (Dan 5) all confirm the providential design of the defeat of unjust governments, a dominant theme of Daniel's visions in 7–12. Daniel and his compatriots remained loyal to their traditions and were delivered by God when in danger; similarly, the apocalyptic visions show that God will bring ultimate deliverance from the oppression of foreign regimes. Of all the parallels between Daniel 1–6 and 7–12, the dream of Nebuchadnezzar in Daniel 2 finds a particular resonance with Daniel's vision report in Daniel 7. Just as Nebuchadnezzar dreams of the metal statue that is made of four elements, ultimately vanquished by the supernatural stone, Daniel receives a vision about four beasts that are judged and defeated by God. Similarly, the emphasis placed on Nebuchadnezzar who ultimately becomes a beast (Dan 4) parallels the focus upon one particular creature, namely, the terrifying fourth beast that wages war against the holy ones of the Most High (Dan 7). This beast, however, will be annihilated and the saints will inherit God's kingdom, just as the statue is annihilated and the mountain fills the entire earth (Dan 2).

The genre of Daniel 7–12 is that of a historical apocalypse. An apocalypse, or unveiling, shows a special revelation to a seer or sage regarding a people's suffering or a community's crisis. Often revealed by a supernatural being, it includes an exhortation to remain faithful to God and to be loyal to the people's community and faith. It usually provides an account of the people's ultimate triumph and an end to suffering. Frequently, apocalypses include *ex eventu* prophecy and pseudonymity. [Daniel: A Historical Apocalypse] For example, although the literary setting of Daniel 7–12 is the time of the Babylonian exile, the modern scholarly consensus is that these chapters presuppose the successive empires of Babylon, Media, Persia, and Greece. The context for this judgment is found in the book of Daniel itself. The goat of Daniel 8, which shares a similar description to the beast of Daniel 7, is specified as referring to Greece. The battles between the king of the north and the king of the south (Dan 10 and 11) refer to the campaigns of the Ptolemaic and Seleucid armies, and the erection of the idol in the temple of Jerusalem points to the reign of Antiochus IV Epiphanes. Historians know that these events occurred during the period of Antiochus's political problems with the Ptolemies and his persecutions of Jews who kept their faith even as Jewish leadership collapsed under Seleucid hegemony. At the same time, the visions do not speak accurately of Antiochus's death, nor do they refer to the purification of the temple by the Maccabees (164 BC), the fighters who revolted against the Seleucids and who later established an independent state in the years 143–63 BC [The Maccabees] Thus, although the literary setting of Daniel 7–12 is shortly after the exile (c. 550 BC), historical critical scholarship sees the visions as coming from the time of Antiochus IV Epiphanes (175–164 BC). We discuss the historical context and the details of Antiochus's reign in subsequent chapters. [Alexander the Great and the Divisions of the Hellenistic Empire]

Other features of apocalypses include symbolic representations of the enemies of Israel, mysterious visions and dreams, fantastic journeys into the future, and descriptions of supernatural changes in

Daniel: A Historical Apocalypse

The consensus of modern historical-critical scholarship is that Daniel is representative of a historical apocalypse, wherein the great ages of empires are predicted, purportedly from the time of Daniel who was exiled during Nebuchadnezzar's onslaught on Jerusalem. In the literary framework of the book, Daniel becomes privy to the knowledge of subsequent kingdoms that will come, up to the time of the Seleucid king Antiochus IV, in whose reign the book was actually composed. Apocalypses often refer to the details of the oppressive reign of the author's time in symbolic language, predictive schemas of sequential kings and empires, *ex eventu* prophecies (prophecies after the fact), and "false" authorship (using the name of a pious sage) to underscore that even the most outrageous acts of cruelty are under the watchful plan of God, who will bring an end to suffering with great cosmological judgment wherein the wicked will be punished, the righteous rewarded, and the age of peace and prosperity established. The authors of apocalypses are typically pseudonymous, a common characteristic of Jewish writing in the Second Temple period. The convention was not an attempt at deception, but rather was a device that paid homage to what was understood to be the tradition of a particular sage, in whose debt the writer remained, and whose works were part of an ongoing dynamic community of interpretation.

The Maccabees

The Maccabees, or Hasmoneans, refer to Mattathias, his five sons, and descendants who provided the moral leadership and military prowess to fight against the abuses of Hellenism in the 2d and 1st centuries BC, and who established an independent Jewish state that endured from 164–63 BC. The catalyst for their revolt was Antiochus's setting up of the idol in the Jerusalem temple. After Judah the Maccabee purified the temple and removed the idol set up by Antiochus, the rebellion grew into guerrilla warfare, wherein the Jews successfully gained independence from their Syrian (Seleucid) overlords. After his death, Judah's brothers Jonathan and Simon provided leadership to continue the revolt. The Syrians recognized Simon as ruler, and although he was murdered, his descendants reigned until the invasion of Rome in 63 BC (from 63–37 BC, the Hasmoneans continued under Roman hegemony). In Dan 11:32-35, the author may refer to Judah's resistance to Antiochus (see below, ch. 10).

natural phenomena. These presentations usually climax in the triumph of the righteous and God's defeat of evil. Ultimately, although the reasons for evil and suffering are unknown, apocalypses typically show that the only proper faithful response is to understand that even these things fulfill God's purpose. No matter how incomprehensible, God revealed glimpses of such events to great sages of the past in order to give assurance that the suffering and evil in the world will not have the final say. God has so set up the universe that in the end, justice and righteousness will succeed and the world will be transformed to reflect their fruits. [The Roots of the Apocalyptic Genre]

Alexander the Great and the Divisions of the Hellenistic Empire

Alexander the Great (356–323 BC) not only ruled as king of the Greek city-states, but also defeated Persia to become emperor throughout the Mediterranean and Middle East. He successfully crushed resistance to his empire, destroyed the former Persian capital of Persepolis, and established his hegemony throughout Anatolia, Phoenicia, Palestine, Egypt, and Mesopotamia. Greek culture, language, and government stayed rooted in his empire long after his reign. Upon Alexander's death, the Hellenistic (Greek) Empire was divided among four generals: Ptolemy in Egypt, Seleucus in Syria and Babylon, Antigonus in Persia and Asia Minor, and Philip in Macedonia. Both the Egyptian province, ruled by Ptolemy and his successors ("the Ptolemies"), and the Syrian province, ruled by Seleucus and his successors ("the Seleucids"), vied for control of Palestine. The degree to which Jews should accommodate or eschew Hellenistic values was a major concern for many in antiquity. Although the ways in which Hellenism and Judaism influenced each other are debated, scholars agree that the interchange was profound as seen in economics, language, art and literature, social conventions, and the formulation of key philosophical and theological ideas.

Martha Himmelfarb argues that the influence of Hellenism upon Judaism was dialectical, with Judaism integrating particular Greek values with an eye to preserving traditional Jewish faith and culture as well. Thus, the commitment to Torah remained paramount, yet methods of interpretation, the dominance of Greek literary forms, and an increased emphasis on a belief in the afterlife all formed a part of an important interchange. In particular, the Jewish emphasis on the scribes as teachers and interpreters of Torah adapted the Greek emphasis on study as a means of obtaining wisdom and paved the way for the success of the Pharisees (a non-hereditary group) and rabbis as preservers of Judaism's traditions.

Martha Himmelfarb, "Elias Bickerman on Judaism and Hellenism," in *The Jewish Past Revisited: Reflections on Modern Jewish Historians*, ed. David N. Myers and David B. Ruderman (New Haven: Yale University Press, 1998), 199–211.

The Roots of the Apocalyptic Genre

The roots of the apocalyptic genre are found in the Hebrew Bible itself. Isa 24–27, sometimes referred to as a "mini-apocalypse," describes an awesome time of God's universal judgment. Nature itself responds to God's presence as "the earth dries up and withers . . . the heavens languish together with the earth" (Isa 24:4). Both the heavenly sphere and the earthly sphere come under God's scrutiny, as reflected in the "shame" of the moon and sun (Isa 24:23). It is a time when Israel is vindicated in the sight of its enemies as marked by the people's presence once again on Mt. Zion, enjoying a feast on the mountain where God's salvation is shown. Justice and peace are established, the wicked are punished, and all the righteous will worship God in Jerusalem (see also Zech 9:12, 14). These highly symbolic images are all seen in apocalyptic literature within the Hebrew Scriptures and develop on their own trajectories.

For understanding the book of Daniel, a particularly relevant example of early apocalyptic writing comes from the book of Zechariah. The book of Zechariah contains imagery of apocalyptic judgment including a sequence of enemies that attack Jerusalem, yet are defeated, the triumph of Israel's king, and the appearance of God in eschatological triumph who fights cosmic battles. It is a time when nature itself reveals the upheavals of God's judgment:

> On that day there shall not be either cold or frost. And there shall be continuous day (it is known to the Lord), not day and not night, for at evening time there shall be light. On that day living waters shall flow out from Jerusalem, half of them to the eastern sea and half of them to the western sea; it shall continue in summer as in winter. And the Lord will become king over all the earth; on that day the Lord will be one and his name one. (Zech 14:6-9)

The book of Zechariah reflects the difficult conditions the Jews faced after their return from Exile (539 BC). The visions in chs. 9–11 and 12–14 are dated to the 5th and 4th centuries BC, reflecting continuing disillusionment with those in leadership positions. In this book, God appears in triumph, fighting cosmic battles in which the enemies who attack Jerusalem are resoundingly defeated.

The degree to which the apocalyptic chapters in Daniel are seen to be in continuity with prophetic eschatology is much debated. Some interpreters see a sharp discontinuity between fully developed apocalypses such as Daniel and the prophetic texts that express hope for the end time, stressing that apocalypses are not only a unique form, but also are indicators of a distinct world outlook wherein nations' destinies have been established by God in advance. In addition, some scholars hold that the concept of resurrection, frequently found in apocalypses and directly expressed in Daniel 12:2, is not directly mentioned elsewhere in the Hebrew Scriptures. While it is true that apocalypses, by definition, contain a more elaborate, schematized view of a history determined by God, such a theology of history clearly has its roots in earlier texts in the Bible. In Genesis, for example, God tells Abraham that the Israelites will be slaves to Pharaoh for 400 years (Gen 15:13), and in Exodus, God hardens Pharaoh's heart so that God's plan for redemption can be fulfilled (Exod 10:27). In response to the argument that resurrection first appears in Daniel, we note that earlier texts also allow for hope of a continued presence with God after death, and they cannot simply be explained as only referring to Israel's national restoration (Isa 26:19 and Ezek 37:13; this issue is

Prophetic Eschatology and Apocalyptic Eschatology

 "Eschatology" refers to "the end times," or the final period of history as the world knows it. The prophets of the Hebrew Scriptures speak of a future redemption where all tribes of Israel will be restored, where evil oppressors will be overthrown, and where a just king will rule over Israel in peace. The degree to which the "end times" reflect a material or spiritual reality varies. For those scholars who stress the unique perspective between prophetic eschatology and apocalyptic eschatology, one determining factor is the locus of retribution. Are evildoers punished and the righteous rewarded in this world as we know it, or in the next? In addition, apocalypses, in drawing on the mythology of the ancient Near East for some of its symbolism, have more cosmological and supernatural imagery, more elaborate schemas of history or patterns of empires, and a stronger sense of the determinism of nations' actions.

studied in more depth below, in our examination of Dan 12:2). In other words, it is best to see the theological import of Daniel 7–12 on a continuum with roots of these ideas found in earlier biblical texts. All hold that the heavenly plane and the earthly plane impinge upon each other and are never beyond the watchful judgment of God. All expect that God will not allow evil emperors to have the last say on earth, and all wait with hope for the coming of Israel's restoration and vindication in an age of future peace. As do other apocalypses, the visions of Daniel 7–12 use symbols and metaphors to speak of unnamed tyrannical rulers who are to come in Daniel's future. The visions present a picture of the defeat of evil in the world and the triumph of God, but they remain mysterious, and the time of the defeat of the enemies of God is never known with certainty. [Prophetic Eschatology and Apocalyptic Eschatology]

Throughout Daniel 7 there are patterns of repetition. [Outline of Daniel 7] The content of the vision is given twice: first, Daniel reports it to the reader (vv. 1-8 [the four beasts] and 9-14 [the One like a Son of Man]) and secondly to the angel (vv. 19-22). The second telling contains some unique features that we examine

Outline of Daniel 7

Daniel's Vision of the Four Beasts, 7:1-8
Daniel's First Account of the Vision of the Ancient of Days and the One Like a Son of Man, 7:9-14
Daniel's First Reaction and First Request for Explanation, 7:15-16
The Angel's First Explanation, 7:17-18
Daniel's Second Account of the Vision and Request for Explanation, 7:19-22
The Angel's Second Explanation, 7:23-27
Daniel's Second Reaction, 7:28

below. The repetitive structure of this vision highlights the impact of the experience upon Daniel, given twice (vv. 15-16 and 28). The structure highlights the destructive power of the fourth beast, disproportionately described by Daniel (vv. 19-20), and the angel's promise of the ultimate vindication of the holy ones, patiently given twice (vv. 17-18 and 23-27). The fourth beast alone is revisited when Daniel frames his second request for explanation, and it alone is included of all the beasts when the angel

provides the second interpretation (vv. 23-26). This structure reflects that the first three beasts are ultimately inconsequential, a harbinger of the fate of the fourth beast. Nevertheless, Daniel's preoccupation with and singular reaction to the fourth beast provide a sympathetic portrait of the grief that the author's community experiences. Although the angel's interpretation demonstrates that the

Map of the Greek Empire

beast ultimately is annihilated, his patient response to an ever-fearful Daniel reflects the sympathy and understanding the author has for the community's suffering.

Daniel's Vision of the Four Beasts, 7:1-8

The urgency of Daniel's vision/dream is first indicated by its immediacy. With only the briefest of introductions, the author states what happened to Daniel: he "had a dream and visions of his head as he lay in bed" (v. 1). These phrases are reminiscent of Nebuchadnezzar's own dream that previewed his downfall as well as the exaltation of the righteous (2:1; 4:5 [4:2 MT]; 4:13 [4:10 MT]). The author suggests that if God could grant visions to Nebuchadnezzar that were true, how much more can the vision given to the faithful Daniel be trusted to come from God.

Paradoxically, Daniel's first vision both reveals and conceals. His dream is of four beasts, but their description defies reality, as they are hybrid creatures that do not correspond to anything known. [Hybrid Creatures] It is important to note that Daniel does not have a vision of an eagle, bear, and leopard, but of animals *like* an eagle, *like* a bear, and *like* a leopard. The three are each compared to a specific animal, yet each also has an anatomical feature that separates it from the prototype. The tentative nature of this description is reminiscent of the prophet Ezekiel's vision of the throne of God and the heavenly temple (Ezek 1:1-28). In that vision, the description of everything Ezekiel sees is analogous. Yet even such

Hybrid Creatures

Paul Porter considers the Mesopotamian context for the symbolic importance of hybrid creatures that have features normally associated with different species. Rather than being simply bizarre, they have an important history, coming from the imagery of a shepherd king or shepherd warrior who protects his people from the flocks of threatening beasts and predators. He argues that many relevant comparisons come from the *Summa izbu* series—texts from 1600–100 BC (from the Old Babylonian to the Seleucid period). The beasts of Dan 7 and 8 may also draw from a symbolic birth-omen tradition where creatures born with peculiar features represent the upcoming defeat or victory of their kings. Porter argues that by drawing on these symbols, the author of the visions in Dan 7 and 8 retrieves images from the broader culture that contain a rich field of references to express hope in God's upcoming deliverance.

Paul Porter, *Metaphors and Monsters: A Literary-Critical Study of Daniel 7 and 8* (Coniectanea Biblica: Old Testament Series 20; Uppsala: CWK Gleerup, 1983).

Griffins (or ram-headed sphinxes) between sacred trees. 7th C. BC. Syro-Phoenician ivory, Hadatu (Arslan Tash), Syria. (Credit: Giraudon/Art Resource, NY)

This 7th C. BC carved ivory relief from Hadatu, Syria, shows two griffins between sacred trees. Note the heads of rams, wings of eagles, and bodies of lions.

approximate language fails when the fourth beast appears, as it has no earthly counterpart. Daniel can only say that it is terrifying and horned. Instead, he turns to its actions.

It is appropriate, therefore, that the chapter opens with two references that point to the trustworthiness of Daniel's vision, even though it is an experience that cannot be fully articulated. By locating the scene "in the first year of Belshazzar," the time period closely contemporaneous with the events of Daniel 5, the author hints that Belshazzar did not endure. In addition, because the reader has been given the details of Daniel's life under Darius the Mede (Dan 6) and has learned that Daniel's career continued until the "days of Cyrus" (6:28 [6:29 MT]), the readers of the author's day could readily see that they lived in the time period of the fourth beast, Greece, and its little horn, namely, the tyrant Antiochus IV. There can be no question about the fate of the fourth beast; it too will come to an end by the power of God. [The Masoretic Reading of Daniel 7:1]

The vision begins by presenting a background that is reminiscent of a frequent image found in ancient Near Eastern and in biblical literature, namely, heavenly winds stirring up chaotic waters. In such texts, the creation of the world is inextricably tied with certain gods' triumphs over other deities of threatening seas, or, in the case of the Hebrew Bible, God's victory over such symbols of evil, suffering, and death (Pss 74:12-17; 89:9-11 [89:10-12 MT]). God's very creation of the universe is not only about the beginnings of the material world, but also about its order, pattern, and design, attesting to a benevolent God who cares that justice reigns. In the Psalms, God's creation is one where justice and goodness triumph over evil, suffering, and death. In Genesis, the world is the arena where the created order as well as the "times, seasons," and the day of rest (the Sabbath) mirror the order and justice in God's design. This ideal, to be sure, contrasts with the reality of Israel's history where chaos, suffering, and death reappear. God must defeat Sea to save the Israelites from their suffering in Egypt (Exod 15:1-18). The Israelites cross the Jordan "dry shod" in order to enter the promised land—a land fraught with danger nonetheless (Josh 3:14-17). Assyria conquers the northern kingdom (2 Kgs 18:9-11) and Babylon the southern (2 Kgs 25:9-11). Nonetheless, Sea is ultimately checked and put into its place, as God reminds Job (Job 38:8-11). In Daniel's dream, the chaotic waters are the source of the four beasts, which represent nations that inflict such terrible suffering. Scholars debate whether or not the "great sea" refers to the Mediterranean or to a mythological place; but clearly its symbolic referent as the source of the beasts is of the greatest import here.[1] [Tiamat and Yamm]

The descriptions of each of the first three beasts follow a similar pattern and build to the climactic description of the fourth beast. The physical appearance of each is first given, followed by a description of its status or power. The first appears to be involved in a struggle, the second beast follows a command to devour, and the third has an unspecified yet pervasive dominion. Most historical-critical exegetes interpret these first three beasts to represent Babylon, Media, and Persia, and the fourth beast as representing Greece, just as Nebuchadnezzar's dream of the statue had metals and clay that represented the same empires. Writers in antiquity were not uniform in their identification of the fourth beast; the

> **The Masoretic Reading of Daniel 7:1**
>
> The phrase "the beginning [or "head"] of the words, he said" is present in the Masoretic Text of 7:1, yet other textual evidence is not uniform. The Old Greek has the equivalent, yet Theodotion (θ') lacks it; 4QDan[b] does not appear to have enough room to contain these Aramaic words (see introduction above). Traditional Jewish interpretation holds that this phrase means that Daniel summarized the vision; some commentators believe that the words highlight the gulf that exists between Daniel's experience of the dream, his understanding of it, and any individual reader's potential for understanding it.
>
> Hersh Goldwurm, *Daniel: A Commentary Anthologized from Talmudic, Midrashic, and Rabbinic Sources* (The ArtScroll Tanach Series; New York: Mesorah Publications, 1979), 193.

Tiamat and Yamm

The symbolic imagery from the mythological literature of Canaan and Babylon provides the context for understanding Israel's "combat myth," a continuing theme in the Hebrew Scriptures wherein God subdues the forces of evil, suffering, and death. In the creation accounts from Babylon and Canaan, the heroic gods Marduk and Baal, respectively, triumph over the enemy gods Tiamat and Yamm (Sea) to bring about an ordered universe. In the texts of these two neighbors of Israel, the triumphant gods are assisted by the phenomena of nature that are portrayed as personified agents who defeat the chaos and death represented by the storm gods. Tiamat of the Babylonian myth *Enuma Elish*, represented by a sea monster of unfathomable size and power, crushes the younger gods who represent order and development. Because of Marduk's victory over Tiamat, the heavens and earth are created, as are the beginnings of civilization and people's responsibilities to the gods. Similarly, Yamm of the *Ras Shamra*

texts, represented by a monster so frightening that its lips stretch from heaven to earth, is capable of rendering speechless an entire assembly of gods. Because of Baal's victory, the heavens and the earth are fertile. Life continues and the victory over chaos and death supersedes the evil that threatened humanity.

Canaanite and Babylonian literature represented suffering and death as pervasive realities that are subdued by other awesome deities. Their very existence, nonetheless, is depicted by these fearsome displays of the anguish that would once again enter their world if their victorious gods are again to be crushed. In the book of Daniel, God's sovereignty is never compromised by the beasts from the sea; rather, God engages not in battle, but in ultimate judgment.

For the particular resonance of Dan 7 with Pss 8 and 89, see Paul Mosca, "Ugarit and Daniel 7: A Missing Link," *Biblica* 67/4 (1993), 496–517.

majority concluded it was Rome, others Greece.[2] [Early Identifications of the Fourth Beast with Rome]

Some of the more noteworthy features of these three beasts are now examined. The first beast, which resembles a lion, has wings that are like those of an eagle. In the Hebrew Scriptures, both animals are associated with power and strength. Although they can be imagined in a positive sense, as exemplified by the strength of the lion of Judah as a symbol of the nation, or the eagles' wings that serve as a metaphor for God's protective care, they are usually depicted as fearsome creatures or as symbols of attacking armies: "[The Chaldeans'] horses are swifter than leopards, more menacing than wolves at dusk; their horses charge. / Their horsemen come from far away; they fly like an eagle swift to devour" (Hab 1:8). In 7:4, the plucking of the lions' wings refers to the weakening of the Babylonian Empire and provides a paradigm to understand what will happen to the beasts that follow. This lion-like creature is also given a human heart, probably used here as a harbinger of its downfall. Some scholars interpret the giving of the human heart as a positive reference to the lessening of Babylon's evil, although this interpretation seems to go against the context, as the plucking of its wings is an obvious reference to its diminishment. In addition, this beast must stand on its hind legs—indicating that it must fight—but at the very moment it needs the most strength, a mere human heart is given to it. Although, in other contexts, the human heart could be an indication of greater capacity or cunning, it appears

Early Identifications of the Fourth Beast with Rome

There are attestations in both early Jewish and Christian writings that the fourth beast was identified as Rome. R. Hanina ben Pappa, when discussing God's judgment of the nations, states that Edom will be first to be questioned. He interprets Daniel's reference to the fourth beast, namely, "And he shall devour the whole earth and shall tread it down and break it in pieces" (Dan 7:28), to refer to Edom's cruelty. The Talmud continues, "R. Johanan says that this refers to Rome, whose power is known to the whole world" (*b. 'Abod. Zar.* 2b, *b. Šebu.* 6b). In 4 Ezra, an apocryphal work from c. AD 100, Ezra has a vision of an eagle representing "the kingdom which was seen in the vision of thy brother Daniel" (4 Ezra 12:11-12). The eagle here most likely indicates Rome.

Early Christian authors who identify the beast as Rome include John (the author of Revelation), Irenaeus, Hippolytus, Origen, Eusebius, Aphraates, Cyril of Jerusalem, Chrysostom, Jerome, and Theodoret. Their interpretations are similar to those given for Nebuchadnezzar's statue (Dan 2), where the stone, representing Christ, annihilates the statue, which symbolizes Rome, and fills the entire earth. These writers see the fourth beast as Rome, persecutor of the church, and defeated by the coming of the Messiah. Rowley states, "Christian interpreters are divided as to whether the prophecies were fulfilled in the birth of Christ, or whether they are to be fulfilled in the Second Advent, the latter view being by far the more widely held" (75).

Similar to the equation of the fourth beast with Rome is the identification of Esau/Edom with Rome. In 4 Ezra the seer inquires about the end of times, receiving this response: "For Esau is the end of the world, and Jacob is the beginning of it that followeth" (4 Ezra 6:9). Louis Feldman argues for two early equations of Esau/Edom with Rome in the Jerusalem Talmud and in Josephus. Rabbi Akiba homiletically interprets the biblical reference, "The voice is Jacob's voice, but the hands are the hands of Esau" (Gen 27:22) to mean that the suffering of Jacob (Israel) comes from persecutions inflicted by Esau (Rome) [*Gen. Rab.* 65:21]. Josephus writes of Esau's future great strength—one that would have "an agelong reputation"—a cipher for Rome (*Ant.* 1.275). Feldman also points out, however, that not all references to Rome in early Jewish texts are negative, as their jurisprudence often was understood to be just and fair.

For further information on the identification of Akiba as the earliest rabbi to make the equation between Esau and Rome and on the mixed review of Rome by Jews in antiquity, see Louis H. Feldman, *Jew and Gentile in the Ancient World: Attitudes and Interactions from Alexander to Justinian* (Princeton NJ: Princeton University Press, 1993) 102–106; 493–94 nn. 57–58.

H. H. Rowley, *Darius the Mede and the Four World Empires in the Book of Daniel*, (Cardiff: University of Wales, 1964), 73–77 (see also above, commentary for ch. 2, "The History of Interpretation of Daniel 2").

here to be the symbol that represents a *mere* human being—a mortal heart that will ultimately fail. In addition, because the passive voice is used to describe the giving of the human heart, the identity of the one who does this action is left in abeyance, engaging the reader's curiosity. Who is this unidentified commander who can pluck off the beasts' wings with ease? Because its defeat will soon be seen to be part of a greater pattern where evil is subdued and justice reigns, the reader can conclude it is God.

The second beast, the creature like a bear, is also ominous. In the Bible there are several references to ferocious bears. David must rescue his flocks from a bear (1 Sam 17:34-36), and bears destroy the taunters of Elisha (2 Kgs 2:24). This bear-like creature devours so fiercely that it has three ribs in its mouth. The number three is often used in the Hebrew Bible to indicate completeness or wholeness, and the idea of the beast with meat in its mouth is reminiscent of the frightful description of the foreign nations' assault on Israel as described by the prophet Amos. Amos speaks of the day when God, like a shepherd, will have to respond to the attacked flock, rescuing "two legs or a piece of an ear" (Amos 3:12). The description that the bear was "raised up on one side" is confusing; perhaps the suggestion that it was "half crouching" (NEB) is best.[3] Thus, when the unidentified voice says, "arise, devour much flesh," the image is of a fully erect bear-like creature, ready to lunge forward with the capacity of great destruction. As with the first beast, the identity of the commander is not specified, again pointing to the hidden design of God.

Leopard

Rampant leopard. 17th C. BC. Ivory figurine, National Museum, Aleppo, Syria. (Credit: Erich Lessing/Art Resource, NY)

This ivory carving (from Syria) attests to the presence of leopards in the ancient Near East.

The third beast, like the first, appears as a combination of a ferocious feline and a birdlike predator. It is described as being like a leopard with four wings. In the Hebrew Bible, the leopard is known for its speed, fierceness, and its distinctive spots. In Hosea, for example, it is used in poetic parallelism with "lioness" to describe a powerful God who will bring future wrath upon the Assyrians (Hos 13:8). Here, its depiction of having four heads and pairs of wings is particularly fearsome. It is striking to read that this beast is given "dominion" (power, rule), a term normally used to refer to God's sovereignty. Here its usage by an enemy of Israel is reminiscent of Jeremiah 5:6: "a leopard is watching against their cities; everyone who goes out of them shall be torn in pieces."

Whereas the first three beasts are introduced with the brief phrases, "then as I watched" (v. 4), "and behold" (v. 5, A.T.), and "as I watched" (v. 6), the introduction to the fourth is lengthy and explicit: "after this I saw in the night visions and behold" (v. 7), calling attention to Daniel's special preoccupation with this beast. It is so different from the first three that there is no animal with which it can be compared. To underscore its viciousness, three adjectives are used in quick succession: "terrifying and dreadful and exceedingly strong" (v. 7). Daniel's first concrete description of the fourth beast is concerned solely with teeth and horns. The specification of the iron composition of its teeth allows the reader to associate its power with war and destruction. [Iron Weapons in the Hebrew Bible]

The actions of this fourth beast are reported in greater detail than those of its predecessors. Three active verbs, "devour," "broke in pieces," and "stamped" (v. 7), under-score its ability to obliterate everything it attacks. The word "broke in pieces" (*maddĕqâ*) was used of the stone that destroyed the statue (2:34, 45) and of the lions that killed Daniel's accusers and their families (6:24 [6:25 MT]). The fourth beast differs from the others not only because of its activity, initiated without a commanding voice, but also because of its horns, which take on a significance of their own; indeed, the very focus of this chapter is on the "little horn" who ultimately battles God's saints. First, however, the author makes quick reference to the ten horns and the three that are torn away to make room for the little horn. Their destruction is reported in the passive voice—they are uprooted by an unknown hand. The author continually invites the reader to con-sider God's providence in the demise of kings and empires. Like the beasts themselves, the three horns represent kings or kingdoms. Because they are all impotent in front of the little horn, the author shows that the little horn represents a heretofore-unknown power, which has already

Iron Weapons in the Hebrew Bible

Although iron can be associated with implements of peace, as is the case of the lost axe, which is used to fell trees for housing (2 Kgs 6:1-7), it is more often associated with the powerful implements of war. In the days of the judges, for example, Israel was continually beleaguered by the Philistines, in part because of the Philistines' superior military, replete with "chariots of iron." For example, King Jabin, who oppressed Israel for 20 years, had "900 chariots of iron" (Judg 4:3). The most famous reference to the importance of iron as an implement of war is found in this statement of its transformation in the future: "they shall beat their swords into plowshares, and their spears into pruning hooks; nation shall not lift up sword against nation, neither shall they learn war any more" (Isa 2:4=Mic 4:3). These words continue to inspire world leaders today.

In October 1998, UN Secretary General Kofi Annan gave an address to the special commemorative meeting of the General Assembly, marking the fiftieth anniversary of United Nations peacekeeping forces, wherein he recalled, 1,500 troops lost their lives in the 49 peacekeeping missions undertaken by the UN. While recognizing that the UN's mission was not to end war, but rather to prevent or delay conflict, these prophetic words from Isaiah and Micah inspire Annan, who states, "[the words of Isaiah] will never be more than an ideal for humanity. If, in our service as United Nations peacekeepers, we can help make that ideal more true than false, more promising than distant, more able to protect the innocent than embolden the guilty, we will have done our part."

"Fifty Years of United Nations Peacekeeping Has Helped Pave Road to Peace, Secretary-General Tells Special Commemorative Meeting of Assembly," *Press Release SG/SM/6732 PKO/74* (6 October 1998), <http://www.un.org/News/Press/docs/1998/19981006.sgsm6732.html> (18 October 2006).

subdued its contemporaries. Readers have speculated about the identities of the ten and the three horns associated with it for gen-erations. Some scholars understand that the ten horns symbolize the Greek predecessors to Antiochus, beginning with Alexander. Alternatively, if one begins with the head of the Seleucid dynasty, then there are seven predecessors to Antiochus, and the final three horns would refer to Antiochus's contemporaries who vied for the throne. [Examples of Identifications of the Ten Horns]

As the focus changes from the ten horns to the one horn that uproots the last three, the author cleverly deprecates it even before its temporary victory is described. It is "little" and appears as a car-icature, having eyes and a mouth (v. 8). Even the syntax of the sentence reflects its ultimate insignificance. The text reads literally,

Examples of Identifications of the Ten Horns

The following are representative interpretations for the identities of the horns. If one starts with Alexander the Great, the ten predecessors of Antiochus IV are Alexander, Philip, Alexander IV, Seleucus I, Antiochus I, Antiochus II, Seleucus II, Seleucus III, Antiochus III, and Seleucus IV. For those who list seven predecessors before the "three horns," the list begins with Seleucus I and ends with Seleucus IV. Suggestions for the final three horns include three of the following four contemporaries known to history as those who attempted to claim the throne: the two sons of Seleucus IV (Antiochus IV's immediate predecessor and brother), namely, Antiochus and Demetrius; Heliodorus (the prime minister of Seleucus IV), an intended usurper who perhaps murdered Seleucus IV and who supported Seleucus's son Antiochus with whom he hoped to rule; and Ptolemy VI Philometor (a Seleucid on his mother's side), ruler of Egypt who also could claim rule over Palestine.

Scholars propose that Antiochus IV was able to pass over the sons of Seleucus IV (Antiochus and Demetrius), even though they were closer heirs in line to the throne. Demetrius served time in Rome as a hostage, and Antiochus (son of Seleucus IV)—who indeed had served with Antiochus IV as co-regent—was killed, perhaps even by Antiochus IV himself. Heliodorus had hoped to rule with Antiochus, son of Seleucus; some scholars say he too was murdered by Antiochus IV.

From antiquity to the present, there have been a wide range of interpretations regarding the ten horns. Most traditional Jewish scholarship, following Rashi (Rabbi Shlomo Yitzhaqi, a renowned 11th-century commentator on the Bible and Talmud), equates the ten horns with the Roman emperors who ruled before the destruction of the second temple. Other Jewish commentators identify them as ten subsequent Roman subdivisions of the empire or with Arab or Christian conquerors of Europe. Christian authors have proposed a wide variety of possibilities, from Roman emperors to subsequent European kings in nations that were formed from previous Roman territory, to various popes, to the successors of Mohammed, to kingdoms not yet created.

John Goldingay, *Daniel* (WBC 30; Dallas: Word Books, 1989), 179.
Hersh Goldwurm, *Daniel: A New Translation with a Commentary Anthologized from Talmudic, Midrashic, and Rabbinic Sources* (The ArtScroll Tanach Series; New York: Mesorah Publications, 1979), 201.
H. H. Rowley, *Daius the Mede and the Four World Empires in the Book of Daniel* (Cardiff: University of Wales, 1964), 76–85.

"a mouth speaking big" (v. 8). In other words, this sentence ends with an adjective ("big") but has no noun accompanying it. It is understood to mean "arrogantly" (i.e., the horn speaks arrogant words), as is the case in 7:11. This is a fair reading, but we should also note that the absence of the noun is an appropriate indication of the ultimate weakness of this horn that challenges God with such pride. Its words will ultimately mean nothing, and it will be cut off, just as the incomplete syntax suggests.

Daniel's First Account of the Vision of an Ancient of Days and the One like a Son of Man, 7:9-14

Although the reader might expect to hear the content of the horn's words, Daniel's vision abruptly leads to another scene, namely, the majestic appearance of "an Ancient of Days" (7:9; "the Ancient of Days," 7:13) in the heavenly court. This interruption serves to heighten the importance of the sovereign of the universe and to lessen the significance of the beast and horn whose frightening power is, in truth, only temporary. The abrupt change in perspective is a preview to the reality that Daniel's vision proposes: as terrorizing as the fourth beast is, its end will be equally horrific. It will be destroyed and no trace of its existence will remain. ["Four" as the Maximum Number of Grievances God Will Endure]

The phrase "as I watched" (v. 9) indicates that this scene is a continuation of Daniel's vision, and the scene itself reveals the vision's most important aspect: the court of the Ancient of Days, the destruction of the beast, and the establishment of the perpetual kingdom of the One like a Son of Man. This scene of the appearance of an Ancient of Days and the coming of the One like a Son of Man is also set apart by the poetic language used to describe it (vv. 9-10 and 13-14). The destruction of the beast is recounted in vv. 11-12, between the references to the Ancient of Days and the One like the Son of Man. This structure reflects that the beast is surrounded by heavenly forces that he cannot challenge. The author thus shows that God's decrees in heaven cannot be challenged on earth, even by the most powerful of emperors.

The description of the judgment scene is rich in symbolism. The righteousness of God and his sovereignty over the beasts and the evil they represent are indicated by (a) the presence of the thrones; (b) the appearance of an Ancient of Days; (c) His description of having white raiment and hair like wool; (d) the fiery flames and wheels of fire that accompany him and his throne; (e) the myriad attendants; and (f) the opening of the books. Each of these references has an extensive symbolic history in biblical literature. This portrait yields an unforgettable picture of the God of judgment who has no equal. We now turn to each of these symbols.

(A) the presence of the thrones
The first feature that Daniel identifies in this scene of judgment is the heavenly thrones. In the Hebrew Scriptures, thrones are indicative of the seat of power (judgment) of either God or, less frequently, of earthly rulers (see Ps 122:5). God does not, to be sure, always judge in Israel's favor. God's presence in the divine council may be used to test Israel, as in the case of King Ahab or Job, or to render judgment against Israel, as in the case of Isaiah's throne scene (Isa 6:1-13; see also Job 1:6; 1 Kgs 22:19; Ps 82).[4] In this scene, the ownership of the thrones remains a mystery. The ambiguous phrase reads either "thrones were set up," or "thrones were cast down," since the verb *rĕmîv* can be interpreted as coming

"Four" as the Maximum Number of Grievances that God Will Endure

In the book of Amos, the prophet uses the phrase "for three transgressions and for four I will not revoke the punishment" to indict both foreign nations for their cruelty and Israel for its acts of injustice. Daniel's reference to the three beasts and a fourth outrageous beast seems to use the numbers in a similarly suggestive fashion, as the fourth beast provokes God's actions for judgment; the number four appears as a sum after which God's patience is exhausted.

See Herbert Marks, "The Twelve Prophets," in *The Literary Guide to the Bible*, ed. Robert Alter and Frank Kermode (Cambridge: Belknap, 1987), 207–33.

Judgment in the Divine Assembly

Ancient Israel's view that each nation has its own god or divine patron in the council, but only the LORD, God of Israel, is ultimately in charge, is expressed in Ps 82:

God has taken his place in the divine council; in the midst of the gods he holds judgment: "How long will you judge unjustly and show partiality to the wicked? . . ." I say, "You are gods, children of the Most High, all of you; nevertheless, you shall die like mortals, and fall like any prince." Rise up, O God, judge the earth; for all the nations belong to you! (Ps 82:1-2, 6-8)

This extraordinary psalm's understanding of the transcendent world is indebted to Canaanite mythology in which the patriarch El is surrounded by members of the heavenly council. In Israel's earliest history, the sons of the Most High may have been understood to refer to other divinities; by the time of Daniel, they most likely were understood to refer to the angels or to divine patrons of other nations.

from either the verb *rum*, meaning "to set up," or *rwm*, meaning "to cast down." The ambiguity remains until the end of v. 14, allowing the reader to sense the insecurity of the future. Will the beasts remain powerful, or will they be defeated? Although the reader soon finds that one throne remains and is occupied by the Ancient of Days, it is not immediately apparent who occupies the other. Only at the end of v. 14 does it becomes apparent that God prepares the other throne for the One like a Son of Man.

Once it is known that the Ancient of Days does indeed come to the throne, it is important to note that although God's judgment takes place in heaven, its significance is found on the earthly plane. [Judgment in the Divine Assembly] Thus in Jeremiah we find the following expression of God's judgment in the future:

And I will bring upon Elam the four winds from the four quarters of heaven . . .
    and I will *set my throne* in Elam, and destroy their king and officials. . . . But in the latter days I will restore the fortunes of Elam, says the Lord. (Jer 49:36-39, emphasis added)

The setting up of God's throne in Elam, a province of Persia, refers to God's judgment concerning Babylonian captivity and Persian hegemony. The author of Daniel similarly trusts that God will now judge Antiochus and his contemporaries who are persecuting the Jewish people (see also Joel 3:12 [4:12 MT]; Ps 96:10).

(B) the appearance of the Ancient of Days

In the Hebrew Bible, the title "Ancient of Days" is used only here, yet several similar phrases are used to indicate that God is beyond the boundaries of time.

El Enthroned

The Canaanites believed that El, the chief god of the divine assembly, was enthroned in the heavens. This bas-relief from Ugarit (Ras Shamra), Syria, shows a suppliant appealing to El, seated on his throne.

El, father of the gods, and an orant. Late middle Syrian period. Bas-relief on a serpentine stele from the acropolis at Ugarit (Ras Shamra), Syria. National Museum, Aleppo, Syria. (Credit: Erich Lessing/Art Resource, NY)

God is the one who exists "from ever-lasting" (Pss 90:2; 93:2); God is "the first and the last" (Isa 41:4; 44:6); God's "years have no end" (Ps 102:26-28); and "the number of his years is past searching out" (Job 36:26). These phrases show that God is beyond human categories and is the One for whom limits cannot be envisaged. God's providential design will be neither challenged nor abridged.

The central debate concerning this imagery in historical-critical circles is whether or not the origin of this symbol can be traced to the Canaanite portrayal of the patriarch El, who is described in Ugaritic texts as the "father of years." El is portrayed as having a gray beard, which is a manifestation of his wisdom, and he sits in the divine council as judge of the heavenly assembly. As John Collins points out, these Canaanite myths form a broad tradition upon which our author may have drawn.[5] Whatever the origins of the symbol, the image was significant to second- and first-century Jews as shown by its usage in the book of Enoch. [1 Enoch] This first biblical image of the Ancient of Days begins a trajectory that is found in other Jewish non-canonical texts and in early Christian writings. For example, in the book of Matthew, the author uses a heavenly scene of judgment to assess the righteousness of peoples:

> When the Son of Man comes in his glory, and all the angels with him, then he will sit on the throne of his glory. All the nations will be gathered before him, and he will separate people one from another as a shepherd separates the sheep from the goats. (Matt 25:31-32; see also Matt 19:28; Rev 1:13-14)

In the heavenly judgment, doing acts of kindness, feeding the poor, including the stranger, and caring for the sick are rewarded with eternal life (Matt 25:31-46). [Christian Usage of the One Who Comes as "An Ancient of Days"]

The Ancient of Days

This imaginative representation of God the Creator by William Blake (1757–1827) combines imagery of the Ancient of Days from Dan 7:9, 13, and 22 with that of Wisdom from Proverbs 8:22-23, 27-30. The Creator, represented as an old man with "hair like wool," reaches toward earth from the fiery cloud. Note the beams of light from his hands are fashioned as an architect's compass.

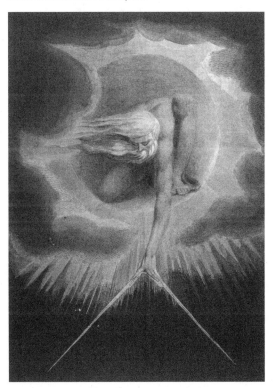

William Blake. 1757–1827. "The Ancient of Days." Frontispiece to Blake's *Europe: A Prophecy.* (Credit: The Pierpont Morgan Library/Art Resource, NY)

1 Enoch

1 Enoch, a Jewish apocalyptic work dated to the 3rd century BC–1st century AD, contains imagery similar to that found in Dan 7, including references to the Ancient of Days and the Son of Man. The following quotation is illustrative:

> And there I saw One who had a head of days,
> And His head was white like wool,
> And with Him was another being whose countenance had the appearance of a man,
> And his face was full of graciousness, like one of the holy angels.
> And I asked the angel who went with me and showed me all the hidden things, concerning that Son of Man, who he was, and whence he was, (and) why he went with the Head of Days? And he answered and said unto me:
> This is the son of Man who hath righteousness,
> With whom dwelleth righteousness,
> And who revealeth all the treasures of that which is hidden,
> Because the Lord of Spirits hath chosen him,
> And whose lot hath the preeminence before the Lord of Spirits in uprightness for ever.

> And this Son of Man whom thou hast seen
> Shall raise up the kings and the mighty from their seats,
> [And the strong from their thrones]
> And shall loosen the reins of the strong,
> And break the teeth of the sinners. (*1 En.* 46:1-4)

The book of Enoch shows the patriarch and seer, Enoch himself, undertaking heavenly journeys where the secrets of the heavens are revealed, confirming that there will be a judgment to come in which God rewards the righteous and punishes the wicked. The Son of Man, also called "the Messiah," "the Righteous One," and "The Elect One," is present with God in a heavenly court scene and is given the authority to exercise judgment against the wicked. Still, it is God, sovereign above all, who opens the books of the living before his entire council (*1 En.* 47:3), demanding a reckoning from evildoers. Later in *1 Enoch*, Enoch himself is identified as the Son of Man who, while seeing myriad angels and the Ancient of Days himself, receives a promise of peace as he becomes a protector and deliverer of the righteous (*1 En.* 71).

(C) white raiment and hair of wool

The whiteness of both snow and wool is associated with purity, or absence of sin, as seen in this telling verse from Isaiah: "If your sins be as scarlet, they shall be made as white as snow; and if they be red as crimson, they shall be white as wool" (Isa 1:18; see also Ps 51:7

Christian Usage of the One Who Comes as "An Ancient of Days"

In early Christian interpretation, imagery of the One who arrived as "An Ancient of Days" (literal translation) and the One like a Son of Man are linked. Daniel's vision of An Ancient of Days highlights God's acts of judgment and the bequest of power to the One like a Son of Man. In the New Testament, Jesus, the Son of Man, receives authority from God (Luke 1:32), exercises it upon earth (Mark 2:10; Luke 1:32), and bequeaths it to others (Matt 19:28-29). As Son of Man, Jesus has authority to forgive sins and to reward those who follow him with eternal life. In the book of Revelation, the authority as well as the appearance of the One who appears as An Ancient of Days are joined in this image of the Son of Man:

> I saw the one like the Son of Man, clothed with a long robe and with a golden sash across his chest. His head and his hair were white as white wool, white as snow, his eyes were like a flame of fire, his feet were like burnished bronze, refined as in a furnace, and his voice was like the sound of many waters. (Rev 1:13-15)

In this scene, Christ appears as the eschatological judge. The link between the One like a Son of Man and the One who appears as An Ancient of Days suggests that the early Christian community believed they met God in the glorified Christ (see also Rev 3:21). John thus comforts the Christian community with the message that Christ has conquered death and its hold upon the earth. As judge of all nations and churches, the people can hope that their struggles against Rome are not in vain. (See below, [The Equation of the One Like a Son of Man with the Messiah].)

[51:9 MT]). White clothing, reflecting light or luminosity, is also used of God, as seen in the following text:

> You are clothed with honor and majesty,
>> wrapped in light as with a garment. You stretch out the heavens
> like a tent,
>> you set the beams of your chambers upon the waters,
> you make the clouds your chariot,
>> you ride on the wings of the wind,
> you make the winds your messengers,
>> fire and flame your ministers. (Ps 104:1-4)

This psalm is particularly interesting for our study of this scene because it shows how the image of the robed, sovereign God is attended by ministers of fire and is serviced by a chariot of clouds. Second Esdras, an apocalyptic work of the first century AD, also uses garments to indicate God's reward to the righteous at the end of days:

> Those who have departed from the shadow of this age have received glorious garments from the Lord. Take again your full number, O Zion, and conclude the list of your people who are clothed in white, who have fulfilled the law of the Lord. The number of your children whom you desired is full; beseech the Lord's power that your people, who have been called from the beginning, may be made holy. (2 Esd 2:39-41; see also Matt 28:3; Mark 9:3)

(D) fiery flames, wheels of fire
The phrases "his throne was fiery flames," "its wheels were burning fire," and "a stream of fire issued and flowed out from his presence" (vv. 9-10) give a powerful three-fold impression of the awe-inspiring surroundings of the enthroned Ancient of Days. In the Hebrew Scriptures, fire can be used as a vehicle of judgment or destruction, but it also can be a sign of God's presence and of authority in the physical world. God's accompaniment by fire or streams of fire is a common element throughout the Hebrew Scriptures and in early Jewish literature. In the Torah, God's presence is depicted as a smoking firepot (Gen 15:17), a burning bush (Exod 3:2-4), a mountain that quakes and smokes (Exod 19:18), and a pillar of fire that leads Israel in the wilderness (Exod 14:24; 40:34-38). These are all images of guidance, protection, and God's loyalty to the covenant. The images of cloud and fire associated with God are often inseparable. In the days of the wilderness wan-

Israelites in the Wilderness
This fresco, from the school of Raphael (1483–1520), depicts God's presence in a pillar of cloud among the Israelites in the wilderness.

The Pillar of Smoke. From the Story of Moses. Fresco, Logge, Vatican Palace, Vatican State. (Credit: Scala/Art Resource, NY)

derings, the cloud that covered the tabernacle had "the appearance of fire. It was always so: the cloud covered it by day and the appearance of fire by night" (Num 9:15 [MT lacks "by day"]). As is seen in the book of Exodus, the mere presence of the pillar of fire disperses the Egyptian army: "At the morning watch the LORD in the pillar of fire and cloud looked down upon the Egyptian army, and threw the Egyptian army into a panic" (Exod 14:24). Fire may also be associated with God's judgment: the Israelites are warned not to forget the covenantal obligations because "the LORD your God, is a consuming fire, a jealous God" (Deut 4:24; similarly, Ps 18:8 [18:9 MT]).

In the book of Ezekiel, the prophet has a vision of God on the throne that is surrounded by cherubim who move by means of fantastic wheels. The wheels are also the repositories for the heavenly fire that is used in the temple (Ezek 10:2). Ezekiel uses many references to flames, fire, and wheels to present a scene of judgment against Israel, which climaxes in the departure of God's presence from the temple. In addition, we note that God ascends Mt. Sinai "with mighty chariotry, twice ten thousand" (Ps 68:17 [68:18 MT]). [Fire and Theophany]

(E) myriad attendants
In the Hebrew Bible, "myriads" ("thousands") can refer either to Israel's armies, to the heavenly armies who fight on God's behalf for Israel, or to the innumerable divine chariots that attend God in the heavens. In the book of Numbers, we find that "thousands," meaning Israel's soldiers, fight against the Midianites, as God commanded. The war with Midian becomes a symbol of resisting evil, as the expression "Day of Midian," comes to mean (Isa 9:4). In addition, the innumerable hosts of heaven, the "thousand thou-

Fire and Theophany

The Hebrew Bible often represents God's presence through theophany, magnificent features of nature such as fire, smoke, wind, lightning, and storms. God is certainly never limited to these phenomena, but they serve to heighten the divine presence and actions at crucial times. The most striking example of a theophany that uses fire is the giving of the Torah on Mt. Sinai. The mountain itself is described as "wrapped in smoke, because the LORD had descended upon it in fire; the smoke went up like the smoke of a kiln, while the whole mountain shook violently" (Exod 19:18). God is revealed at this time in order to give the Israelites the covenant at Sinai, the laws and instructions for living a righteous and holy life. As Moses appears before God on the mountain, "the appearance of the glory of the LORD was like a devouring fire on the top of the mountain" (Exod 24:17). The Israelites are redeemed, that is, are freed from slavery and oppression, in order that they become "a kingdom of priests and a holy nation" (Exod 19:6), a people who agree to follow God's covenant. As they prepare to enter the holy land, God commands them to construct a sanctuary, so, God states, "that I may dwell among them" (Exod 25:8). God's association with fire continues in the sanctuary with the daily burnt offering, the burning of incense, and the lighting of the menorah.

sands" and "myriads of myriads" (heavenly armies), are also found in the book of Numbers, where they signify God's protection of Israel:

> Whenever the ark set out, Moses would say, "Arise, O LORD, let your enemies be scattered, and your foes flee before you." And whenever it came to rest, he would say, "return, O LORD of the ten thousand thousands of Israel." (Num 10:35)

God's presence among the Israelites in the wilderness was especially apparent in the ark of the covenant. As the vision of Daniel 7 progresses, the fear that has so permeated Daniel's vision gives way to hope. As the ark represented God's presence and protection in the days of the wilderness, now God's seat in judgment allows for the end of the suffering.

(F) the opening of the books

When the reader arrives at v. 10b, it is clear that the Ancient of Days does not sit in the heavenly assembly to present a test, but to render a judgment. In order to proceed, "the books" are opened. In the Hebrew Bible, the heavenly books (or "record," Ps 56:8 [56:9 MT]) record the deeds and character of individuals—both good and evil. The phrase also refers to the document in which the names of evildoers are blotted out (Exod 32:33; Pss 40:7 [40:8 MT]; 69:28 [69:29 MT]; 139:16). A well-known example is Moses' intercession to prevent the death of the innocent when God threatens to wipe out the idolatrous Israelites: "So Moses returned to the LORD and said . . . 'if you will only forgive their sin—but if not, blot me out of the book that you have written.' But the LORD said to Moses, 'Whoever has sinned against me will I strike out of

"Books" in Judaism and Christianity

As Mitchell Reddish delineates, two images of heavenly books are found in Jewish and Christian writings, the book of humanity's deeds and the book of life. The record of deeds shows that humanity's actions are scrutinized, rewarded, and punished in the apocalyptic divine judgment (Dan 7:10; Mal 3:16; 2 Esd 6:20; *1 En*. 47:3; 81:1-4; 89:61-77; 90:17, 20; 98:7-8; *2 Bar*. 24:1). The book of life, first used in Exodus when Moses intercedes for the Israelites (Exod 32:32-33) and used in Daniel to mark those who are redeemed, represents a compendium of those who share in God's salvation (Luke 10:20; Phil 4:3; Heb 12:23; Rev 3:5; 13:8; 17:8; 20:12, 15; 21:27). The imagery in the following texts from *1 Enoch* and Revelation illustrate these uses.

In the book of *1 Enoch*, Enoch relates that the angel Uriel tells him,

> Observe, Enoch, these heavenly tablets,
> And read what is written thereon,
> And mark every individual fact.

Enoch responds,

And I observed the heavenly tablets, and read everything which was written (thereon) and understood everything, and read the book of all the deeds of mankind, and of all the children of flesh that shall be upon the earth to the remotest generations. (*1 En*. 81:1-2)

In Revelation, John relates this vision:

Then I saw a great white throne and the one who sat on it; the earth and the heaven fled from his presence, and no place was found for them. And I saw the dead, great and small, standing before the throne, and books were opened. Also another book was opened, the book of life. And the dead were judged according to their works, as recorded in the books. And the sea gave up the dead that were in it, Death and Hades gave up the dead that were in them, and all were judged according to what they had done. Then Death and Hades were thrown into the lake of fire. This is the second death, the lake of fire; and anyone whose name was not found written in the book of life was thrown into the lake of fire. (Rev 20:12-15; see also Luke 10:20; Phil 4:3; Rev 21:27; *m. 'Abot* 2:1)

Mitchell Reddish, *Revelation* (Smyth and Helwys Bible Commentary; Macon GA: Smyth & Helwys, 2001) 389–90. Also, see below, [The Book of Truth (Daniel 10:21)].

---

my book'" (Exod 32:32-33). Being written in the book means to live, and the punishment—or not being in the book—means death. In other instances, God uses the heavenly books to take note of the righteous who will be rewarded when God comes in judgment on the earth (Isa 4:3; Mal 3:16-18; Dan 12:1). ["Books" in Judaism and Christianity]

With the scene thus painted, the history of God's sovereignty over the world and the divine pursuit of justice now prepare the reader to find that the tormenting fourth beast will not endure; its body is burned. Although its incineration recalls the images of fire surrounding the heavenly throne, the director of this punishment is yet unnamed as the activity occurs in the passive voice (v. 11). It at first may be surprising that the author does not use the active voice here to describe the beast's death, but this is consistent with the author's emphasis in the next scene, in which the reader sees the drama of the holy ones receiving the kingdom.

It is only after the fourth beast is destroyed that the final fate of the other three beasts is mentioned (v. 12). Their deaths are presented as being incidental to the fate of the fourth beast, underscoring that their end is inevitable and is an intrinsic part of God's plan. Although one might first suspect that the destruction of the beast would bring Daniel's vision to a close, the scene shifts to a preview of what is most significant. The fourth beast's end breaks the pattern of one oppressive kingdom following another. Now, an entirely new kingdom of God's choosing follows.

For the first time in this vision, a kingdom is not represented by a beast. Instead, a mysterious "One like a Son of Man" appears, approaches the Ancient of Days, receives dominion over the earth, and all serve him (vv. 13-14). The scene is described in poetic language, linking it with the verses devoted to the arrival of the Ancient of Days and separating it from the description of the fourth beast, which immediately precedes it.

The success of the dominion of the One like a Son of Man is indicated by several factors. First, it is the Ancient of Days who establishes that dominion, recalling the proclamation to Nebuchadnezzar that God sets up kingdoms and destroys them. Secondly, both the conferral of power and the subjugation of peoples are each expressed three times with the words "dominion, honor, and kingship"—a description reminiscent of earlier usages from the time of Nebuchadnezzar's life (Dan 4:22 [4:19 MT]; 4:26 [4:23 MT]; 4:30 [4:27 MT]). Thirdly, the eternal quality of this kingdom and its success are also indicated in three different ways: his dominion is "everlasting," it will never "pass," and his kingship will never "be destroyed" (v. 14). The author thus shows that the justice God establishes with the kingdom of the saints will exist eternally.

The majority of historical-critical interpreters understand the Aramaic phrase "Son of Man" to mean "a human being," according to the Semitic idiom in which "son of" means "a member of the class/group." In Ezekiel, the Hebrew equivalent is used of the prophet himself, where it emphasizes the prophet's humanity in contrast to God's sovereignty. Nevertheless, in Daniel we do not find "a Son of Man," but rather the comparative "One like a Son of Man," allowing for a broader range of interpretation.[6] First, it is important to note his function. This "One like a Son of Man" serves an important transcendent role, coming with the clouds and being present at the court of heavenly judgment in order to receive the kingdom on behalf of the holy ones (vv. 18, 25, 27). These holy ones, or saints, are God's faithful people, who are persecuted by an oppressive foreign government. This "One like a Son of Man" stands in contrast to the beasts as the ideal human being who does as God wills and helps to establish God's kingdom, according to the justice that God intends. He is portrayed as the antithesis to the wicked beasts that have ruled over their own unjust kingdoms and have persecuted innocent subjects.

The specific way in which the "One like a Son of Man" is understood by modern historical-critical scholars varies greatly. For some, he is an unnamed symbolic figure representing Israel—either a faithful group within Israel, or the entire people. This interpretation is based on internal evidence, since in subsequent verses the Ancient of Days is said to give the kingdom to "the holy ones of the Most High" (vv. 18, 21), and "to the people of the holy ones of the Most High" (v. 27). These "holy ones" are understood to be celestial beings, and the "*people* of the holy ones" are their counterparts on earth—that is, the faithful ones of the community. The "One like a Son of Man" is equated with them, just as each beast represents a nation.[7] Others argue that he is a particular figure: the angel Michael or Gabriel; a Davidic king or the messiah; Daniel himself; Judah Maccabee; a high priest; or a heavenly figure whose identity is not known.[8] John Collins argues that the "One like a Son of Man" represents the angel Michael, based upon the similar references to angels in the book of Daniel itself (8:15; 10:5; 12:1) and because of the description in Daniel 7 that he is the advocate and protector of the "people of the holy ones of the Most High."[9] No argument has won consensus. It is clear that the author underscores that God ensures that the suffering community is not forgotten. God will bring about his victory through this mysterious agent—whether celestial or human, collective or singular, is never specified. [The Equation of the One Like a Son of Man with the Messiah]

Daniel's First Reaction and First Request for Explanation, 7:15-16

In contrast to Nebuchadnezzar, who either was enraged or paralyzed until he found interpretations for his own dreams, Daniel's reaction is multifaceted. For all his uneasiness, he has the courage to approach one of the angels, here identified as one of the "standing ones." [Angels as Guides to Interpretation in Joseph and Asenath] Daniel's overture is not rebuffed. Because this famous interpreter of dreams now needs an interpretation, the author shows that this vision has a most powerful significance.

The Angel's First Explanation, 7:17-18

The angel's statement quickly passes over what is ultimately insignificant—the kingdoms represented by the four beasts. This omission of the beasts piques the reader's interest, and Daniel's relentless pursuit of understanding their significance may showcase

The Equation of the One Like a Son of Man with the Messiah

In antiquity, many Jews and Christians equated the One like a Son of Man with the messiah. In its root meaning, "messiah," or anointed one, was the king of Israel, selected with God's approval and anointed with oil by a prophet to rule his people with righteousness. In the prophets, the hope is expressed for a future descendant of King David who would be extraordinarily capable of bringing people to God and who would establish justice and peace. Thus, for Jews, the messiah is a descendant of the line of David, fully human, who rescues Israel from its enemies and who redeems the exiles from among the nations, bringing them back to the land of Israel, as promised to Abraham. The messiah is king over all of Israel and leads the people in fulfilling the commandments so that the entire world is filled with the knowledge of God. The messiah's coming also brings about a new age wherein the righteous are resurrected and the world is filled with peace, prosperity, and the absence of suffering.

For the rabbis who lived during the Roman persecutions, it is not difficult to understand why they would interpret the predictions concerning the end of the fourth beast to refer to the end of Roman persecution. In discussing the future reign of the messiah, the rabbis note that his reign will encompass all the earth, including sea and land. They find two relevant texts from Daniel, from the image of the One like a Son of Man coming with the clouds and from the stone not cut from human hands (Dan 2:35):

> How do we know that he [the messiah] will hold sway on land? Because it is written, . . . Behold, there came with the clouds of heaven one like unto a son of man . . . and there was given unto him dominion . . . that all the peoples . . . should serve him; . . . And the stone that smote the image became a great mountain, and filled the whole earth. (*Num. Rab.* 13:14)

For Christians, the messianic age, as in Judaism, also shares the expectations of peace, justice, and the resurrection the dead. Christian theology is distinct, however, in its understanding of the messiah as the preexistent son of God, equal to the Father, fully human and fully divine, who redeems humankind from sin. The phrase "Son of Man" is used as a title for Jesus throughout the New Testament. In the book of Mark, for example, the vision of Daniel becomes the paradigm for understanding Jesus as Messiah: "Jesus said, 'I am'; and 'you will see the Son of Man seated at the right hand of the Power,' and 'coming with the clouds of heaven'" (Mark 14:62). Here the author of Mark uses quotations from Exod 3:14, Ps 110:1, and Dan 7:13-14 to show that the authority, power, and divinity of Jesus will not be defeated. Although the Son of Man must suffer, he will come on earth again in triumph.

---

the author's concern about the insecurities of the age. The angel has a different focus, namely, upon the "holy ones . . . of the Most High" who receive "the kingdom forever—forever and ever" (v. 18). By placing these words in the angel's mouth, the author accents the ultimate significance of the vision. By stating that these holy ones "receive" the kingship, the connection is made that kingship is indeed in God's purview and is God's alone to bequeath. God's kingship is different from the kingship of the nations; it is passionately consumed with providing justice. [The Kings' Establishment of Justice in the Hebrew Scriptures] It is now given to the One like a Son of Man, and, as the angel

Angels as Guides to Interpretation in Joseph and Asenath

In Second Temple literature, angels often appear as guides to heavenly journeys, interpreters of dreams and mysteries, and messengers of comfort to those who are perplexed or who are suffering. In the book "Joseph and Asenath," a Jewish apocryphal romance dated from 1st century BC–1st century AD, an angel appears to the heroine as a man, but with supernatural elements of lightning and fire. He announces an end to her suffering and God's acceptance of her repentance. Her marriage to Joseph will occur soon, but more importantly, she becomes a symbol of the refuge other proselytes will find in the God of Israel. An angel also explains the spiritual significance of the mysteries that she witnesses and of her consumption of the honeycomb that he provides to sustain her (*Jos. Asen.* 14–16).

The Kings' Establishment of Justice in the Hebrew Scriptures

Israel's institution of kingship was to reflect a passionate concern for justice, reflecting the divine will. In a world where the nations were preoccupied with security, fertility, and power, exploitation could easily be justified, even to the point of slavery. Israel is to have a different vision, where concern for the orphan and widow supersedes the quest for power and security. It is to be a society where no one is excused from the prioritization of doing what is right for those in need, especially not the king. Apocalyptic writings encourage readers to hold fast to this vision, even in despairing times as God ensures that their suffering will end. God promises not only an end to their suffering but also reconstitutes them as a people. As James Walsh states, they will be:

Not a shadow people, not a people by sufferance of foreign rulers, or living out their identity in the interstices of dual citizenship: they will be the people—the political entity—[YHWH] long ago purposed to form, and which [YHWH] again and again redeems (buys back) from the hand of the oppressor, at a great price.

The Ancient of Days arrives with the authority to grant "judgment" (*mišpāṭ*, din). To say that God has *mišpāṭ* means that one cedes one's decisions about what is right and wrong to God. A profound faith is expressed—that good will prevail over evil and that the holy ones will prevail. These holy ones do not take thrones by force. Rather, they inherit them from God; there can be no question about their legitimacy.

James P. M. Walsh, *The Mighty from their Thrones: Power in the Biblical Tradition* (Overtures to Biblical Theology; Philadelphia: Fortress, 1987), 146.

explains, to all the people represented by the holy ones. The final phrase used to explain the endurance of this kingdom, "forever—forever and ever," is appropriately repetitious.

The angel's explanation leaves many questions wanting and is never as specific as Daniel would like. In this, the author portrays the situation of the community living under Antiochus's regime. In times of suffering and fear, people are desperate for understanding. Any lessening of the dread for the future becomes precious. The angel's response makes clear that God's promise will ensure a righteous world and that the holy ones are held dear to God. Nonetheless, the response also reveals that the specifics of God's plan can never be completely known. Truth is revealed in a vision, but it is not completely understood. This parallels Daniel's life experience—the tremendous sorrow, fear, and upheaval that he experiences are seen in a context of a faith that lives with uncertainty and mystery in the face of suffering. Yet this faith refuses to divorce the experience from the trust that God's world of ultimate justice will endure. In the meantime, being one of the holy ones serves as a model of faith and behavior. If the holy ones receive the kingdom, surely one can cast his or her lot with this group.

The meaning of the phrase "holy ones of the Most High," which may also be translated as "the high holy ones," is disputed. Some scholars see these holy ones as representing the collectivity of Israel, either the earthly Israel, or the deceased who are now with God in heaven. For some, they are heavenly beings of an unspecified type. Others identify them as angels. The immediate context of this

The Angel Michael

This woodcut of Albrecht Duerer (1471–1528) shows the angel Michael fighting the Dragon, interpreting Rev 12:7-9:

And war broke out in heaven; Michael and his angels fought against the dragon. The dragon and his angels fought back, but they were defeated, and there was no longer any place for them in heaven. The great dragon was thrown down, that ancient serpent, who is called the Devil and Satan, the deceiver of the whole world—he was thrown down to the earth, and his angels were thrown down with him.

Albrecht Duerer. 1471–1528. *St. Michael Fighting the Dragon*. Bibliothèque Nationale, Paris, France. (Credit: Giraudon/Art Resource, NY)

chapter, however, shows that the author moves easily from the term "holy ones of the Most High" to "people of the holy ones of the Most High" (v. 27). In other words, if these holy ones of the Most High represent angelic beings, they also have their human counterparts on earth, namely, the faithful of Israel. Thus, the heavenly scene wherein the One like a Son of Man and the Saints of the Most High receive the kingdom is a prototype of what the author expects on earth: an age where the people of Israel enjoy God's kingdom and its consequent benefits of a peaceful world. The language, rooted in ancient traditions reflected in the Hebrew Bible, remains metaphorical, allusive, and multivalent. We turn to the following examples.

When the phrase "holy ones" means celestial beings in the Hebrew Bible, they appear as members of God's heavenly council who praise the divine handiwork and testify to God's control of the

Leviathan

This embroidery by Hannah Rivka Hermann of Jerusalem shows Leviathan surrounding the Cave of Machpelah, the burial site of the Patriarchs and Matriarchs of Israel. In Jewish writings, God slays Leviathan and prepares a messianic banquet for the righteous (*b. B. Bat.* 74b–75a). Thus, far from being threatened by the power of evil, chaos, and death that Leviathan represents, the ancestors of Israel will be the first to join in the eschatological banquet, testifying to the faith in God's triumph over evil and the salvation of the righteous in the world to come.

Hannah Rivka Hermann. Sabbath cloth. Depicts Leviathan, a biblical beast, surrounding the central cave of Machpelah. Israel Museum, Jerusalem, Israel. (Credit: Erich Lessing/Art Resource, NY)

universe and God's utter subduing of chaos:

Let the heavens praise your wonders, O LORD, your faithfulness in the assembly of the holy ones. . . . You rule the raging of the sea; when its waves rise, you still them. You crushed Rahab like a carcass; you scattered your enemies with your mighty arm. The heavens are yours, the earth also is yours; the world and all that is in it—you have founded them. . . . Righteousness and justice are the foundation of your throne; steadfast love and faithfulness go before you. (Ps 89:5, 9-12, 14 [89:6, 10-13, 15 MT])

This psalm shows the connection between the holy ones' praise of God's handiwork and the setting up of creation where chaos and suffering, personified as the sea monster Leviathan or Rahab, cannot dominate over God's justice and covenantal loyalty. The psalm continues to extol the faithfulness of King David, whom God allows to be victorious over the Sea (v. 25 [v. 26 MT]), thus restoring God's righteousness and justice on earth. The role of these holy ones is to provide testimony to God's setting up the world as a place where faith is not in vain.

"Holy ones" can also refer to human beings. Psalm 34:9 (34:10 MT) serves as an example: "O fear the LORD, you his holy ones, for those who fear him have no want." Most interpreters understand "holy ones" to mean human beings, here, with the psalm showing how readily these holy ones can be close to the divine. These holy ones, who acknowledge God's sovereignty and do not resist his will, ultimately find refuge in him: "the angel of the LORD encamps around those who fear him, and delivers them" (v. 7 [v. 8 MT]).

Similar to this usage of "holy ones," there are several places in the Hebrew Scriptures where Israel is called "holy," or "a holy nation." Throughout the Bible, "holy nation" is often found to refer to Israelites, and individuals continually are reminded "to be holy." [Israel's Covenantal Holiness] Being holy, or set apart, has a particular obligation: it requires covenant—the social, religious, ethical, and ritual legislation that defines the people's relationship to God and to the community. These values cover every aspect of life in community, including agricultural practices, business ethics, the judicial system, personal integrity and behavior, worship, sacrifice, eating, drinking, and sexual behavior. To be holy requires following these commandments and avoiding the ways of other nations. Because earthly kingship is to be a mirror of covenantal living, the angel's message in Daniel proclaims that what was known in the past remains true despite the conquests on the international scene that subjugated Israel to a foreign power. Despite the consequent indignities and persecutions, people's lives could still be permeated with holiness.

Thus, by portraying a scene where faithful holy ones receive the kingdom, the author may be integrating both these images of "holy ones" in heaven and "holy ones on earth." This especially seems to be the case when we consider that the phrase "holy ones" readily becomes "the people of the holy ones" in v. 27. With this fluid identification, images of both heavenly and human beings are among the conquered or persecuted and serve as witnesses for hope.

Israel's Covenantal Holiness

In the book of Exodus, the Israelites become a kingdom of priests and a holy nation because they assented to the covenant (Exod 24:3, 7). In Jewish interpretation, it is underscored that the Israelites at Sinai agreed to obey even before they heard; this emphasizes their trust in God and their willingness to follow him. It is because of their willingness to live by the values and laws of the covenant that they become a kingdom of priests and a holy nation (Deut 7:6; 26:19).

Daniel's Second Account of the Vision and Request for Explanation, 7:19-22

Following the reassurances of the angel, Daniel continues to express his bewilderment. The first explanation by the angel is insufficient for Daniel, and, like other patriarchs and prophets before him who express their confusion upon encountering an angel, he must ask his question again. The repetition both underscores his near-paralyzing fear and provides a model of the proper response for his people. [Similarities with Patriarchs and Prophets] Daniel's repetition of the description of the beast provides new details. The beast has claws of copper, its special horn is greater than all the others, and it wages war against the holy ones. Daniel's words give voice to the lingering fear and doubt of his audience. Was the angel's explanation

Norman Habel, "The Form and Significance of the Call Narratives," *ZAW* 77 (1965): 297–323.

Similarities with Patriarchs and Prophets

Daniel's response to the vision resembles that of the patriarchs and prophets of old. Abraham hesitates when God offers him a covenant (Gen 17:17-18); Moses hesitates when commanded to speak to his people and to confront Pharaoh (Exod 3:11, 13). Similarly, several of the prophets, when called by God to do their mission, protest that they are inadequate before they marshal the courage to carry forward as messengers of God's will and judgment. Isaiah, for example, laments, "Woe is me! I am lost, for I am a man of unclean lips, and I live among a people of unclean lips; yet my eyes have seen the King, the LORD of hosts!" (Isa 6:5). Similarly, Jeremiah retreats with these words, "Ah, LORD God! Truly I do not know how to speak, for I am only a boy" (Jer 1:6). God encourages both prophets, setting aside their fears.

enough? Even though the angel's first explanation confirmed that the holy ones had received the kingdom, Daniel continues to focus on the fourth beast. Nonetheless, when Daniel articulates his question, he actually recognizes that the Ancient of Days stopped the activity of the fourth beast. He states, "As I looked, this horn made war with the holy ones and was prevailing over them, until the Ancient One came; then judgment was given for the holy ones of the Most High . . . and the time arrived when the holy ones gained possession of the kingdom" (vv. 21-22). Even though Daniel sees this, he still cannot understand the significance, as he awaits the further assurance of the angel.

Perhaps the author used Daniel's shift in focus to provide a model for the original audience. Only when he repeats what he saw in the vision does he begin to understand it properly. Waiting with faith involves shifting one's focus away from preoccupation with either the beast or little horn to consideration of the holy ones who will receive the kingdom. The author appears to counsel the community members that despite the indignities of foreign rule, they must strive, even in suffering, to build their lives with dignity and holiness.

Daniel's insistent questioning invites the angel to give a second interpretation that serves both to give greater assurance to Daniel and to confirm that the vision is true. Providing a second interpretation is a technique similar to the doubling of the vision found in other biblical accounts. As in the Joseph narratives and in the book of Esther, dreams and significant events come in pairs, signifying God's hand, and may witness to the close proximity of the event. Joseph tells Pharaoh that his dreams "are one and the same" (Gen 41:25), Nebuchadnezzar has two dreams, and Daniel's insistence for further explanation allows the angel patiently to give confirmation. The answer provided is still symbolic and incomplete, but the very fact that the angel is willing to address Daniel a second time with specific, yet mysterious content, must serve as assurance enough.

The Angel's Second Explanation, 7:23-27

Because the angel responds with even more detail and never admonishes Daniel, the seer's fear is portrayed as being understandable. Specifying that the final horn is "different from the former ones" (v. 24), the angel suggests that this horn, although able to uproot its predecessors, no longer crushes or humbles the holy ones. Although it "wears out" the holy ones (v. 25), speaking words against God, its power over them is temporary. Before we hear of the beast's defeat, the angel relates more information regarding the havoc it accomplishes. It "attempts to change times and seasons," a scourge that lasts literally for "time, times and half a time" (v. 25, A.T.). "Times and seasons" represent all the religious markings of time, including the time for daily prayer and sacrifice, the observance of the Sabbath, the honoring of festivals, and the agricultural and economic practices of the sabbatical year and the jubilee. They are so fundamental to the marking of what makes life holy and meaningful that they are part of the very foundation of the world. Thus, when the little horn tries to change "the law," the covenant between God and Israel, he attacks what forms the heart of their relationship. [Sacred Time in Israel]

Sacred Time in Israel

The Sabbath marks the Creator's authority over the world and creation's utter dependence upon God. A day marked by rest and devotion, in the times of the first and second temple it also included additional sacrifices above the daily requirement. Festival times included pilgrimages of Sukkot (Booths), Pesach (Passover), and Shavuot (Weeks), where God's protection of the Israelites in the wilderness, deliverance from oppression in Egypt, and the receiving of the Torah were marked by special sacrifices in Jerusalem. These markings of time into sacred periods characterize the close relationship between God and the Jewish people.

Some commentators say that the author represents the period of the little horn's success as being equivalent to three and a half years, based on the interpretation that "time, times, and half a year" (literally translated, v. 25) refers to "a year, two years, and half a year." However, the equation of the word "time" with "year" is not certain. There is no definite article before the word *'iddān*, and nowhere else in the Hebrew Bible does the Hebrew equivalent have the specific meaning of "a year." It is possible that this language is poetic and points to an unspecified period. Its doubling and its halving may also be indicative of its symbolic and unspecified nature, which underscores the inability of the human community to know with certainty when the time of oppression will end.

Although Daniel's last question was a request for further explanation about the fourth beast alone, the angel instead turns again to the victory of the holy ones. The angel's final words confirm Daniel's observations that "judgment" was given and that "dominion" was taken away from the fourth beast (v. 26; cf. v. 10). In addition, the angel confirms that the holy ones receive "kingship," echoing his own words (v. 17) as well as Daniel's (v. 21), and repeats that the "kingship" of the One like a Son of Man is tantamount to kingship of "the people of the holy ones." Finally, for the first time in this vision we find the words "kingdoms" and "kingdom." We have seen "kingship" earlier; the author adds a distinct image by drawing attention to the transformation of the world. Before it was said that the One like a Son of Man and the holy ones received "kingship" (vv. 13, 17, 21). Now the final reference by the angel to kingship underscores the reversal of the all-encompassing powers of the previous earthly kingdoms. Once the people of the holy ones of the Most High have received their kingdom, it becomes perfectly clear that all other earthly rulers "shall serve and obey them" (v. 27).

These repetitions highlight Daniel's journey into understanding and trusting his vision. Daniel was most preoccupied by what was terrifying in his dream and not by what was reassuring or victorious. Thus, the angel ends on a note that addresses Daniel's apprehension. The angel does not offer any new information, nor is a specific time frame ever given for God's alteration of the world. Nevertheless, by underscoring that the world is truly affected by God's judgment, the angel gives Daniel some modest hope. It is a positive thing to hear that the "beast was burned with fire" (v. 11); the image, however, remains symbolic, resisting any easy identification with an earthly response of violence. To say that all dominions serve the people of the holy ones of the Most High is to confirm the reversal that God promised of old—that the mighty ones of this earth who oppress the weak will fall. All the readers of Daniel's vision can know that as they remain faithful to what makes Israel holy, they can hope in the words of Hannah, their heroine of old:

> My heart exults in the LORD; My strength is exalted in my God.
> My mouth derides my enemies, because I rejoice in my victory . . .
> The bows of the mighty are broken, but the feeble gird on strength.
> Those who were full have hired themselves out for bread,
>   but those who were hungry are fat with spoil. . . .
> He raises up the poor from the dust;
>   he lifts the needy from the ash heap,
> to make them sit with princes
>   and inherit a seat of honor . . .
> The LORD! His adversaries shall be shattered;
>   the Most High will thunder in heaven.
> The LORD will judge the ends of the earth;
>   he will give strength to his king,
>   and exalt the power of his anointed. (1 Sam 2:1-10)

In this text, Hannah recognizes that those who use their wealth and power to trample the weak are the enemies of the Most High. God responds to their arrogance by making the world just—by making it a place where once again those who love God and keep the commandments find peace.

Daniel's Second Reaction, 7:28

Although mystery still pervades, now that Daniel twice has articulated the vision and has appealed for explanations, he can conclude the report of this vision. The second description of Daniel's demeanor (v. 28) continues to showcase his fear, highlighting the effect on him personally. Moses' face was altered by his encounter with God (Exod 34:29, 30, 35); similarly, Daniel's face changes, becoming pale, upon encountering this vision. [*zîw* (countenance)] He has the courage, however, to have "kept the matter in my mind" (v. 28), a phrase that links this vision to the one following in Daniel 8.

When people are suffering, it is natural to ask, "How long?" With Daniel's vision, an answer is given, but it is clothed in mystery. It is heartening to know that evil does not endure, despite humanity's fear. The answer, although enigmatic, is honest. The time of the beast's reign cannot be calculated. It is a poetic answer: "time," doubled as well as halved. The symmetry of the answer suggests that there is still order in the universe and that God's sovereignty ensures that justice will endure. The inability to decipher the end with any exactitude is reiterated by Daniel's closing statement. He remains frightened and guards the matter in his heart (v. 28).

zîw (countenance)

AΩ Upon experiencing this vision, Daniel is forever changed. He relates, "Here the account ends. As for me, Daniel, my thoughts greatly terrified me, and my face turned pale; but I kept the matter in my mind" (7:28). *zîw*, the word translated "face," may also mean "countenance" or "splendor." Elsewhere in Daniel, it is used to indicate an equally dramatic event, namely, the transformation of Nebuchadnezzar's countenance back to being human after his punishment as a beast was completed (4:36 [4:33 MT]). Similarly, *zîw* is employed for the countenance of the statue that features in Nebuchadnezzar's dream (2:31). The conclusion of Dan 7 invites the reader to consider that a significant transformation occurred in the person Daniel. Perhaps that transformation empowers him to endure the difficulties he faces, providing a model for the original audience who face daily peril from their oppressors.

The themes in Daniel 7 serve as a microcosm for the rest of the book. In the subsequent visions, we find that God privileges Daniel to understand that the future for Israel will contain much suffering at the hands of four kingdoms, but that ultimately the world as he experiences it will not endure. God's judgment prevails, evil will be eradicated, and the world will be complete with God's justice as sovereign.

If readers look for a complete understanding of the symbolic language in these visions, they will be disappointed. For more than two thousand years, Jewish and Christian interpreters have sought to understand the specifics of the symbols, with many interpreters seeing the final evil kingdom occurring in their own time. But this vision shows that waiting involves shifting the focus from considering the beast to considering the holy ones. It is they who will receive the kingdom. The question to ask, therefore, is not which nation is the beast. It is, rather, how does a person remain one of the holy ones? Or, perhaps, what does it mean to be holy?

CONNECTIONS

Because of the book of Daniel's immense evocative power to elicit hope among the faithful in times of suffering, its images of the heavens, God's judgment, and future reward often serve as symbols in other texts, both in Jewish and in Christian writings. One of the most well known of these texts is the book of Revelation, the paradigmatic Christian apocalypse. Written in the first century AD, this work uses much symbolic imagery from the book of Daniel as it presents its vision of God's victory over the evils of Rome and the vindication of Christians who suffer in its pervasive grip.

The consensus of most New Testament scholars is that the book of Revelation was composed in response to the powerful rule of Rome. Although in past centuries of Christian tradition, the social context was considered to be the systematic and widespread state-sanctioned persecutions of Christians under Domitian (AD 81–96), many scholars today hold there is not enough evidence to support this conclusion. Nevertheless, because the book speaks about the persecution of an individual Antipas, and possibly others (Rev 6:9-11; 11:7; 20:4),[10] modern interpreters do hold that the book reflects a difficult time in the Christian community that knew of the sufferings of individuals under Roman hegemony. Even if the persecutions were not rampant and were not part of a state policy, the sufferings of individual Christians led to the belief that the future would be filled with even more trauma. The perspective, indeed, comes from an author who knows and represents the conditions that caused the suffering or death of fellow Christians. Whether those deaths came from statewide policy or from the isolated responses of local Roman officials is immaterial. John portrays the mindset of the community members who have experienced the derision, misunderstanding, prejudice, and distrust of the Roman majority. Some were exiled or killed; others lost economic, social, or political clout.

Persecution of Christians under Nero

One of the most well-known passages from antiquity that attests to Roman persecutions of Christians is from Tacitus's *Annals*. Tacitus (c. AD 55–117) reports that after the devastating fires in Rome, Nero (AD 54–68) found a scapegoat in the Christians. Although Tacitus shows sympathy for the inhumanity of the torture inflicted upon them, the prejudice against them was so entrenched that he could say the following:

> But all human efforts, all the lavish gifts of the emperor, and the propitiations of the gods, did not banish the sinister belief that the conflagration was the result of an order. Consequently, to get rid of the report, Nero fastened the guilt and inflicted the most exquisite tortures on a class hated for their abominations, called Christians by the populace. Christus, from whom the name had its origin, suffered the extreme penalty during the reign of Tiberius at the hands of one of our procurators, Pontius Pilatus, and a most mischievous superstition, thus checked for the moment, again broke out not only in Judaea, the first source of the evil, but even in Rome, where all things hideous and shameful from every part of the world find their centre and become popular. Accordingly, an arrest was first made of all who pleaded guilty; then, upon their information, an immense multitude was convicted, not so much of the crime of firing the city, as of hatred against mankind. Mockery of every sort was added to their deaths. Covered with the skins of beasts, they were torn by dogs and perished, or were nailed to crosses, or were doomed to the flames and burnt, to serve as a nightly illumination, when daylight had expired. Nero offered his gardens for the

Bust of Emperor Nero. Reigned AD 54–68. Uffizi. Florence, Italy. (Credit: Scala/Art Resource, NY)

spectacle, and was exhibiting a show in the circus, while he mingled with the people in the dress of a charioteer or stood aloft on a car. Hence, even for criminals who deserved extreme and exemplary punishment, there arose a feeling of compassion; for it was not, as it seemed, for the public good, but to glut one man's cruelty, that they were being destroyed. (*Annals* 15.44.5)

The author of Revelation, who identifies himself as "John," is otherwise unknown, yet his identification of Rome with "Babylon" and his apparent references to the legends of the coming again to life of the deceased despot Nero (Rev 13:3; 17:10-11), a belief held during the last three decades of the first century, is suggestive of a time frame between AD 68–100. This John knew of the death of a certain Antipas of Smyrna, and possibly that of others. He writes, "Yet you are holding fast to my name, and you did not deny your faith in me even in the days of Antipas my witness, my faithful one, who was killed among you, where Satan lives" (Rev 2:13). John encourages the Christians of Smyrna to remain faithful to their commitments to their church, even though they experience deprivation and possible imprisonment for refusing to participate in the cult of the emperor (Rev 2:9-11). Christians were accused by Romans of being subversive if they did not pay homage to Roman gods or to the emperor himself. Their refusal to sacrifice to other gods was considered a serious threat to the state, and they could be punished by the authority of local governors. The pressures to conform to the broader Roman culture and share in its values were constant. The author's admonitions against listening to false prophets are most likely an indication of his plea to be rigorous against accommodation to the majority practices of Roman subjects. John addresses these concerns in his letters to seven churches of Asia Minor. In his edicts, he often refers to their patience or endurance (Rev 2:2-3, 19), yet admonishes them to refrain from participation in local practices such as eating forbidden foods sacrificed to idols and "fornication" (Rev 2:14), or, as collectively expressed, "the deep things of Satan" (2:24). This vision exhorts the community to remain steadfast, believing that God's justice will triumph completely over Rome's evil.

In relating his vision, John uses various motifs that show his familiarity with the Hebrew Bible and with the book of Daniel in particular. The ultimate triumph of God's goodness and the reign of the Son of God are represented by the vision of the destruction of the beast, which represents the antichrist. The description of the beast is reminiscent of the fourth beast of Daniel's vision. We note the following descriptions:

> When they [the prophetic witnesses] have finished their testimony, the beast that comes up from the bottomless pit will make war on them and conquer them and kill them. . . . (Rev 11:7)

> And I saw a beast rising out of the sea, having ten horns and seven heads; and on its horns were ten diadems, and on its heads were blasphemous names. And the beast that I saw was like a leopard, its feet were like a bear's and its mouth was like a lion's mouth. And the dragon gave it his power and his throne and great authority. (Rev 13:1-2)

> But the angel said to me, "Why are you so amazed? I will tell you the mystery of the woman [Babylon=Rome], and of the beast with seven heads and ten horns that carries her. The beast that you saw was, and is not, and is about to ascend from the bottomless pit and go to destruction. (Rev 17:7-8)

These descriptions of the beast combine elements of the four beasts in Daniel 7 as well as unique features. In Revelation, the sea of Daniel 7 is described as a bottomless pit; its beast has seven heads, representing the Seven Hills of Rome or perhaps seven distinct rulers; its ten horns symbolize the hegemonic extent of Roman power. This fearsome picture, nonetheless, does not have the final say, because of the certainty of the kingdom of God (Rev 1:6; 5:10; 21:1; 22:5), Christ's coming (Rev 1:7; 3:11; 4:5; 19:11-16; 22:7), the New Jerusalem (Rev 3:12; 21:2, 10), God's judgment (Rev 6:10; 16:6-7; 18:8; 19:2), and the resurrection (Rev 20:4-6, 12-13). The final judgment scene of Revelation is reminiscent of Daniel 7 and Daniel 12:

> Then I saw a great white throne and the one who sat on it; the earth and the heaven fled from his presence, and no place was found for them. And I saw the dead, great and small, standing before the throne, and the books were opened. Also another book was opened, the book of life. And the dead were judged according to their works, as recorded in the books. And the sea gave up the dead that were in it, Death and Hades gave up the dead that were in them, and all were judged according to what they had done. Then Death and Hades were thrown into the lake of fire. This is the second death, the lake of fire; and anyone whose name was not found written in the book of life was thrown into the lake of fire. (Rev 20:11-15)

The books of Revelation and Daniel both served as faithful witnesses when their authors' communities faced powerlessness and persecution. As Mitchell Reddish writes,

> John has a different perspective on the world than most of the people of his day. He sees it as a world that has turned its back on God, that has followed its own desires, that has allowed evil to run rampant throughout society. A part of the function of the Apocalypse and especially its visions of judgment and destruction is to convince its readers to change, to repent, in order that they might avoid such calamities.[11]

The metaphoric language of the book of Revelation that both conceals and reveals reminds the community then and now that life has meaning, value, and infinite significance in the eyes of God. This is true even when earthly powers of cruelty and injustice are beyond description and understanding. John's approach is reminiscent of the author of Daniel, who eschews the attractions of the powerful government and culture of Antiochus and who provides a model of prayer and concern for the community. John challenges his readers not to underscore their sorrow, but to channel their suffering into a resolve of absolute fidelity. [The Beast Rising from the Sea]

The Beast Rising from the Sea

In the book of Revelation, John combines the features of the four beasts of Dan 7 into one horrific beast that arises from the Sea in order to defy God. The beast represents Rome and its emperors, whose powers—like those of Nebuchadnezzar and Antiochus IV—the world finds attractive. John shows that the beast, or Rome, is merely an instrument of Satan; it will persecute the Christians, but in the end will be defeated by the triumphant Christ.

This fresco from the Baptistery of Padua, Italy, by Giusto de Menabuoi (1349–1390), illustrates the seven-headed beast of Revelation.

Giusto de Menabuoi. 1349–1390. *The Beast Rising from the Sea*. Scene from the Apocalypse. 1360–1370. Fresco, Baptistery, Padua, Italy. (Credit: Alinari/Art Resource, NY)

NOTES

[1] John Goldingay, *Daniel* (WBC 30; Dallas: Word Books, 1989), 160–61.

[2] John Collins, *A Commentary on the Book of Daniel* (Hermeneia; Minneapolis: Fortress, 1993), 312. H. H. Rowley, *Darius the Mede and the Four World Empires in the Book of Daniel* (Cardiff: University of Wales, 1964), 70–137.

[3] Rene Peter-Contesse and John Ellington, *A Handbook on the Book of Daniel* (New York: United Bible Societies, 1993), 181–82.

[4] Norman Porteous, *Daniel: A Commentary* (OTL; Philadelphia: Westminster, 1965), 107–108.

[5] Collins, *Daniel*, 290–91.

[6] Goldingay, *Daniel*, 167–72.

[7] Louis Hartman and Alexander Di Lella, *The Book of Daniel* (AB 23; Garden City NY: Doubleday & Co., 1978), 218–19.

[8] These arguments are summarized in Collins, *Daniel*, 308–10, and Paul Redditt, *Daniel* (New Century Bible; Sheffield: Sheffield Academic Press, 1999), 127.

[9] Collins, *Daniel*, 305–306.

[10] David Aune, "Revelation," *Harper's Bible Commentary*, ed. James Mays (San Francisco: Harper & Row, 1988), 1306.

[11] Mitchell Reddish, *Revelation* (Smyth and Helwys Bible Commentary; Macon GA: Smyth & Helwys, 2001), 189.

A COMFORTING VISION

Daniel 8:1-27

COMMENTARY

There are many occasions in the Hebrew Scriptures in which repetition is an indication of truth. Verbal repetition, for example, may indicate that a person fulfills commands or dictates. The repetition of events or the presentation of a parallel scene may attest to their importance. The sequence of Pharaoh's comparable dreams about seven emaciated cows that consume seven robust cows and seven withered stalks that consume seven vigorous ones (Gen 41:25-32) proves to Joseph that Pharaoh's dreams point to events that truly are about to occur. Similarly, the vision of Daniel 8 repeats the information found in Daniel 7. Both confirm that the four kingdoms responsible for Israel's exile are part of God's plan, that the power they exercise is temporary, and that even the cruelest of tyrants, Antiochus IV (Epiphanes), will be subject to God's judgment. In addition, both present a window into a world where faith and hope are sustained by images of heavenly beings, identified yet mysterious times, and the trustworthiness of apocalyptic visions.

The emphasis in Daniel 8 is on the sufferings Antiochus imposes on the Jewish people, with a particular emphasis on his devastating edicts concerning Jewish worship. [Outline of Daniel 8] Although Antiochus first won the hearts and minds of some of the Jewish people who willingly accepted some Greek customs, the situation changed after Antiochus's fear of dissent and desire for control prompted him to outlaw key practices such as circumcision, the observance of *kashrut*, the offering of the daily sacrifice, keeping the Sabbath, and the possession of Torah scrolls. [Hellenism and Hellenization] If this were not enough, he also committed a great sacrilege by invading the temple and instituting the worship of foreign gods. Refusal to comply was met with death. All of the

Outline of Daniel 8

Daniel's Vision of the Ram and the Goat, 8:1-12

The Angels' Conversation, 8:13-14

Gabriel's Appearance and Address to Daniel, 8:15-26

Daniel's Response to the Vision, 8:27

Hellenism and Hellenization

"Hellenism" refers to the social, political, religious, literary, and cultural values of Greece, the Greek Empire, and its later successors—Rome and the Byzantine Empire—which ruled over the Mediterranean, Middle East, and western Asia. "Hellenization" refers to the absorption and adaptation of Greek values by peoples who lived under its rule and influence. Hellenistic influences on Judaism in the 2d century BC are evident in the material culture, community organizational structure, literary styles, and use of the Greek language. The degree to which Jews integrated these elements is very much debated. Were elements of Hellenistic culture and values adopted in such a way that essentially compromised unique Jewish beliefs, or were aspects of the ruling culture integrated in a manner that allowed Judaism's distinct way of life

to remain intact? These very questions are reflected in much of Judaism's Second Temple literature. The Books of Maccabees, our best source for understanding Antiochus's impact on Judaism, show that many Jews themselves believed that adapting to Hellenistic institutions was desirous and possible. Only when Antiochus responded with totalitarian control did the community's resistance strongly mobilize. As Lee Levine concludes, "Generally speaking, the ability to relate positively to outside influences was in direct correlation to a sense of security and self-confidence. When threatened, the pendulum swung toward self-absorption and self-protection; when secure, the reaction tended to be more responsive."

Lee Levine, *Judaism and Hellenism in Antiquity: Conflict or Confluence* (The Samuel and Althea Stroum Lectures in Jewish Studies; Seattle: University of Washington Press, 1998), 183.

visions of Daniel 7–12 have these terrible days as their context. Because Daniel 11 speaks of the various wars of "the king of the north and the king of the south" that can be specifically linked with Antiochus's campaigns against the Ptolemies, yet, at the same time, predicts details of his death that are inaccurate, the dating of the authorship of the book of Daniel is quite specific—to 166–165 BC, the time in which the atrocities existed, when the temple was still operating under Antiochus's dictates and the tyrant was not yet dead.[1]

Daniel's Vision of the Ram and the Goat, 8:1-12

With the beginning of Daniel 8, the text returns to Hebrew, which continues until the end of the book.[2] Because the more poetic and cryptic Daniel 7 is composed in Aramaic, it is possible that Daniel 8 originally was written to explain the meaning of the earlier vision to a Hebrew-speaking audience. The use of Hebrew also may serve as a sign of hope, for now Daniel returns to the language of his youth, the language of his freedom. In Daniel 8, Daniel's vision of the rise and fall of four kingdoms is set in the time of the third or final year of King Belshazzar, the last king of Babylon. Just as Daniel is shown to have witnessed the end of Babylon with the humiliation of Belshazzar, so now does the vision portend the end of the reign of the cruelest of Greek tyrants, Antiochus IV.

The author identifies Susa as the location of Daniel's vision. Susa, an administrative seat of the Persian Empire (Neh 1:1), would likely have been identified by the Hellenistic audience as the capital that no longer ruled them. In addition, they were probably familiar with Susa as the location of the victory over the murderous plot of Haman (Esth 9:12-15). The specification of Susa as being in the province of Elam may have helped the audience of antiquity locate the capital that no longer ruled them, as well as recall the biblical pronouncements against it. References to Elam are found in all the major prophets; it is a nation that attacks Babylon as well as Judah, yet it is also crushed by God (Isa 22:6; Jer 25:25; 49:34-39; Ezek 32:24).

In addition, Daniel identifies the location by specifying that he was "at the Ulai river" or "at the Ulai gate" (*ʿal-ʾûbal ʾûlāy*), a problematic phrase with varying translations, since *ʾûbal* occurs only here in the Hebrew Bible. Some

Map of the Seleucid Empire

translators equate *ʾûbal* with the Hebrew *ywbl*, meaning "river." Others, however, understand that *ʾûbal* derives from the Akkadian *abullu*, meaning "city-gate." If the reference is to "city-gate," a location of civic importance is indicated, as the "city-gate" was a public gathering place where transactions were made and juridical procedures took place.[3] If "river" is indicated, the Ulai may be equated with the River Eulaeus or with one of the canals in the region; the scene would recall such visionary or dream experiences as those of Pharaoh near the Nile and those of Ezekiel by the river Chebar (Ezek 1:3).

The vision consists of a symbolic presentation of history, where, echoing the use of the four beasts of Daniel 7 and the four metals and clay of Daniel 2, the author presents the four sequential empires that ruled over Israel since the exile. Daniel first perceives a ram with two horns, a symbol of the Medo-Persian Empire, as the angel indicates; the longer of the two horns indicates Persia, which absorbed Media into its empire. The author identifies three directions of Persia's conquest—westward, northward, and southward—the extent of the Persian Empire most familiar to Jews. As they were keenly aware, Persia subdued all nations who were engaged with it; hence the author's comment that all other animals were conquered. In rapid sequence, Daniel's vision yields continually surprising results.

The first surprise of the vision is that there is yet one animal that can vanquish the heretofore invincible ram, namely, the goat that charges from the west. The power of this animal, which the angel later identifies as Greece, is underscored by the way in which it advances, its savage force, its rage, and its ability to break the ram's horns. Daniel says the ram travels with such awesome force that it moves "without touching the ground" (v. 5). Commentators rightly note that similar language is used of the Persian emperor Cyrus in the book of Isaiah (Isa 41:3); thus, the author links the domination of the Greek Empire and its founder, Alexander the Great, with that of Alexander's vanquished nemesis, the Persian Darius III. A pathetic picture emerges when the ram, which conquered all other animals, is left utterly powerless with none to defend it. Indeed, although the Persian Empire was magnificent in its power and wealth, the Greek Empire displayed even greater military strength, financial resources, extent of conquest, and hegemony over civilization and culture. [The Voice of the Conquered]

Despite the stunning power of the goat, the second surprise of Daniel's vision is that it, too, is weakened. At the very "height of its power," its mighty horn is broken, replaced by four others—representing the premature death of the young Alexander and the rise of the four subdivisions of his empire, consisting of Macedonia and Greece; Asia Minor; Syria, Babylonia, and eastern provinces; and Egypt. The author of 1 Maccabees suggests that although Alexander's reign was stunning, Alexander knew, even while he lay dying, that the empire would not survive. Hence, the text shows Alexander himself dividing up his territory (1 Macc 1:5-7). The focus of Daniel's vision quickly turns to what is dis-

The Voice of the Conquered

Norman Porteous underscores that the author of the book of Daniel illustrates the perspective of the conquered. Although Hellenistic civilization brought unity and progress, Porteous remarks,

there were other values which the world, then as now, desperately needed and which were in danger of being lost. It may well be that it was only by an extreme attitude of opposition to the dominant civilization that in that particular crisis of history these values could be conserved. But perhaps the most important lesson that can be learned from this chapter of the Book of Daniel is that those who represent a dominant and, it may be, a noble civilization should try to see themselves as others see them and to realize that there are things which, in the sight of God, may be of more value than culture.

Norman Porteous, *Daniel* (OTL; Philadelphia: Westminster, 1965), 124.

paragingly called "the little horn," a reference to Antiochus IV, of the Seleucid division of Alexander's empire. The locations of Antiochus's campaigns are indicated by direction of the little horn's growth—"toward the south" and "toward the east," symbolizing Egypt and Parthia, respectively (v. 9). Yet in order to indicate the little horn's attacks against Jerusalem or Judah, the author chooses a unique expression. It proceeds toward "the beautiful land" (lit., "the beauty" [*haṣṣebî*], which can also be translated "the fairest of cities"). This reference echoes God's own words in referring to the land of the promise, as is found in Ezekiel, Jeremiah, and Malachi (Ezek 20:6, 15; Jer 3:19; Mal 3:12). It is apparently a favorite of the author (it is used again in Dan 11:16, 41, and 45), for it is clearly associated with covenantal overtones. At a time when the community sees its holy land abused, the language is a hopeful reminder of God's promises. [The Beautiful Land (*ṣbî*)]

In describing the goat's attack, the language remains mythological—he attacks the "host" and the "stars," references that could either refer to the celestial beings who dwell with God, or to other deities whom the goat (Antiochus IV) attempts to supersede. If the author intends the terms to reflect celestial beings such as angels, then this language suggests that Antiochus's campaigns are an affront to God, as "hosts" and "stars" often represent the transcendent servants who fight alongside God when God brings deliverance. In the famous battle of Deborah and Barak, for example, "the stars fought from heaven, from their courses they fought against Sisera" (Judg 5:20). If, however, the terms refer to other deities, the description reflects Antiochus's belief in a polytheistic world—one in which, according to Jewish perspective, he will fall like any other idol. It is possible that the myth of the Day Star and Son of Dawn forms the background for this image. In Isaiah 14:12-15, the poet speaks of the fall of the Canaanite deities Helal (Day Star) and Shahar (Dawn), who in the past attempted to supersede the Most High, but now have fallen. In the book of Isaiah, the ancient Canaanite references are used of the arrogant king of Babylon; so, too, in this case do they form an appropriate commentary on the arrogance of Antiochus. Norman Porteous

Antiochus IV Epiphanes

Tetradrachm (silver coin) of Antiochus IV Epiphanes (175–163 BC), Seleucidan king of Syria who, by his imposition of Greek law and customs in Judea, caused the Macabeean Revolt (167 BC). Israel Museum (IDAM), Jerusalem, Israel. (Credit: Erich Lessing/Art Resource, NY)

The Beautiful Land (*ṣbî*)

AΩ In the book of Ezekiel, God recounts the history of salvation to the prophet, remarking that the Israelites were taken out of Egypt and into "the most glorious of all lands" (Ezek 20:6). Recalling the tender connection between God and Israel, God remarks that Israel's land is "the most beautiful heritage of all the nations" (Jer 3:19).

suggests that this same passage is also behind another reference to Antiochus in 2 Maccabees, where Antiochus's painful and ultimately deadly disease is described:[4]

> Because of his intolerable stench no one was able to carry the man who a little while before had thought that he could touch the stars of heaven. Then it was that, broken in spirit, he began to lose much of his arrogance and to come to his senses under the scourge of God, for he was tortured with pain every moment. And when he could not endure his own stench, he uttered these words, "It is right to be subject to God; mortals should not think that they are equal to God." (2 Macc 9:10-12)

Although this author's primary purpose is to showcase the justified suffering of Antiochus and his ultimate self-abnegation before God, the almost casual reference to his hubris—that he could "touch the stars"—makes quite plausible the thesis that Isaiah 14:12-15 stands behind the text.[5]

The author seems careful to relate that the goat's actions against the "prince of the host" are restricted to its assault against the burnt offering and the overthrowing of the sanctuary; the author avoids suggesting that the goat actually assaulted the prince himself. Although possibilities for the identification of the prince include Onias III, the legitimate high priest, or the angel Michael, most commentators are in general agreement that this prince of the host is indeed God. [Onias III] Although the prince is never assaulted, the author represents Antiochus's affront against God by showing that the goat attacks the regular burnt offering. This offering, or *tāmîd*, was outlawed by Antiochus, along with the observance of Shabbat and festivals. Antiochus not only proscribed the *tāmîd*, but also built idolatrous altars on the very site of the holy altar and instituted sacrifices of forbidden animals. Because sacrifices were offered at the very place where heaven and earth met—the temple—effecting reconciliation between God and humanity, this loss was devastating. First Maccabees shows that Antiochus manipulated the entirety of the state's infrastructure to maximize his oppression, using letters and messengers to relay his edicts and the deployment of soldiers to enforce them (1 Macc 1:41-50). To emphasize further the eternal effects of this disaster, the author states that "truth" itself was assaulted. Some interpreters suggest that the "cast[ing of] truth to the ground" is a specific reference to the fact that Antiochus physically desecrated Torah scrolls and made their possession a capital crime (1 Macc 1:56-57).

Onias III

Onias III inherited the office of the high priest about 190 BC, succeeding his father Simon II, of the family of Jehoiada, a descendant of Zadok. His family line of priests was known as the Oniads. He was opposed by Simon (the brother of Menelaus and Lysimachus) from the priestly clan Balga (Bilgah), who, along with another priestly family, the Tobiads, competed with the Oniad family to control the priesthood. The author of 2 Maccabees sees the ousting of Onias III as the catalyst for the success of the Jewish "Hellenizers"—those who wanted their fellows to engage in the practices of Greek culture.

These tensions among the priestly families began even before the rise of Antiochus IV. When Antiochus's predecessor, Seleucus IV (187–175 BC), sent his minister Heliodoros to collect taxes from the temple treasuries, violence erupted, and Heliodoros was close to death. According to 2 Maccabees, Onias saved him by prayer and sacrifice, proving the triumph of God's sovereignty. Yet the upstart Simon used these events as an excuse to attack Onias (2 Macc 4:1-2) with the result that Onias brought his case to King Seleucus himself, who was in Antioch.

The accounts of Onias after his travels to Antioch differ. According to 2 Maccabees, when Onias arrived, he discovered that Heliodorus had murdered Seleucus, allowing Antiochus IV to ascend to the throne. Onias became an exile in Antioch, while Onias's brother Jason, a proponent of Hellenization, succeeded him as high priest. Under Jason, a significant number of Jews received privileges for adopting the ways of the state. The author of 2 Maccabees even reports that Jason sent sacrificial money to offer sacrifices to the god Hercules (2 Macc 4:19). After three years as high priest, Jason was ousted by Simon's brother Menelaus, who obtained his position by bribery (and who consequently raided temple funds), setting the stage for riots by outraged fellow Jews. This same Menelaus had the government official Andronicus lure Onias out of his place of sanctuary in Daphne and murdered him. Although Josephus has one report that agrees with this account from 2 Maccabees 4 (*Ant.* 12.237), he also records that Onias never stayed in Antioch and that he founded a temple in Egypt (*J.W.* 1.33; 7.423).

Uriel Rappaport, "Onias," *ABD*, ed. David Noel Freedman, 6 vols. (New York: Doubleday & Co., 1992), 5:23–24.

Jonathan Goldstein, *II Maccabees* (AB 41A; New York: Doubleday, 1983), 201.

The last thing Daniel sees in this section of his vision is the continuing success of the little horn. The picture is bleak, reflecting the sense of fear that the author's original audience must have experienced. [Persecutions according to the Book of Jubilees] It is the author's next task to reveal why the readers could hope, for at the nadir of Daniel's visual experience, the voices of the holy ones will make all the difference.

The Angels' Conversation, 8:13-14

Daniel is not only given the privilege of seeing this vision; he also hears a message of hope with the words of the holy ones. They, too, appear to be as disturbed by the scene of the goat's terror as is Daniel. It is this terrible arrogance before God that prompts one of holy ones, or angels, to express his grief to another, asking the plaintive cry, "how long?" [How Long?] His remarks about the goat's assaults echo the earlier references to the offering, the sanctuary, and the host. One phrase is distinct, namely, the "transgression that makes desolate" (*happeša' šōmēm*), which occurs here alone. This

Circumcision

By outlawing circumcision, Antiochus IV forbade the tangible sign of the covenant between God and the Jewish people. The covenant of circumcision ceremony is still performed today on the eighth day after a boy's birth. This swaddling cloth was made in the early 20th century for ceremonial use.

Wimpel (swaddling cloth used in the circumcision ceremony). 1966. Collection of Robert Weyl, Strasbourg, France. (Credit: Erich Lessing/Art Resource, NY)

phrase, equivalent to the "abomination that makes desolate" (Dan 9:27; 11:31; 12:11), refers to the altar or cult that Antiochus set up either to his god Zeus or to the local god, Baal Shamayim. John Goldingay argues that the term *happeša' šōmēm* appears to deride the title of the god "Baal of the Heavens" because *šmm*, "desolation," varies from *šmym* (heavens) by only one letter and because *happeša'* (transgression) replaces "Baal."[6] The author of

Persecutions according to the Book of *Jubilees*

 The book of *Jubilees* (mid-2d century BC) also presents reflections on the persecutions that occurred in the times of Antiochus:

And a great punishment shall befall the deeds of this generation from the Lord, and He will give them over to the sword and to judgment and to captivity, and to be plundered and devoured. And He will wake up against them the sinners of the Gentiles, who have neither mercy nor compassion, and who shall respect the person of none, neither old nor young, nor any one, for they are more wicked and strong to do evil than all the children of men.

And they shall use violence against Israel and transgression against Jacob,
And much blood shall be shed upon the earth,
And there shall be none to gather and none to bury. In those days they shall cry aloud,
And call and pray that they may be saved from the hand of the sinners, the Gentiles;
But none shall be saved. And the heads of the children shall be white with grey hair,
And a child of three weeks shall appear old like a man of one hundred years,
And their stature shall be destroyed by tribulation and oppression. *(Jub. 23:22-25)*

Like the books of Maccabees, *Jubilees* also holds that Jews who accommodated to the Hellenistic culture opened the door for Antiochus's devastating edicts. The author of Jubilees calls upon the community to repent by strictly adhering to the commandments and to avoid any of the lures of Hellenistic culture. John Endres concludes that the text "represents an inner-Jewish tendency which appears unwilling to effect the compromise with hellenistic culture, especially on the issues of circumcision, dietary regulations, intermarriage with Gentiles, incorrect celebration of Jewish festivals (based on a variant calendar), and profanation of Jewish sacrificial worship."

John Endres, *Biblical Interpretation in the Book of Jubilees* (CBQMS 18; Washington DC: The Catholic Biblical Association of America, 1987), 248.

2 Maccabees identifies the sacrilege as the temple of Zeus Olympius (2 Macc 6:2); Zeus and Baal were chief gods of the Greeks and Syrians, respectively. All these actions to which the angels refer point to the worst of the retaliatory measures that Antiochus inflicted upon the Jewish people, crushing their freedom of worship and devastating their morale. We now examine the historical context as primarily attested in the books of Maccabees.

In 169 BC, Antiochus had abandoned his campaign against the Ptolemies of Egypt, and, upon returning to Jerusalem, felt particularly threatened from the internal disputes among Jews in Jerusalem that occurred in his absence. First Maccabees records,

> **How Long?**
>
> AΩ The Hebrew *'ad mātay* (how long) is often used as a refrain of petition in prayer and lament in which the petitioner articulates his or her distress directly to God. Here, Daniel hears the words of one angel to another before the angel Gabriel assists him and speaks to him, similar to the prophet Zechariah who hears a communication between God and an angel that precedes his own experience of hearing the angel's address: "Then the angel of the LORD said, 'O LORD of hosts, how long will you withhold mercy from Jerusalem and the cities of Judah, with which you have been angry these seventy years?'" (Zech 1:12).

> He went up against Israel and came to Jerusalem with a strong force. He arrogantly entered the sanctuary and took the golden altar, the lampstand for the light, and all its utensils. He took also the table for the bread of the Presence, the cups for drink offerings, the bowls, the golden censers, the curtain, the crowns, and the gold decoration on the front of the temple; he stripped it all off. He took the silver and the gold, and the costly vessels; he took also the hidden treasure that he found. (1 Macc 1:20-23)

Antiochus's experience in Egypt is alluded to in Daniel 11; those events are explored below (ch. 10). The likely context for Daniel 8 includes the disputes between the high priests Jason and Menelaus, the response of pious Jews, the attack on Jews by Antiochus's commander Apollonius, the imposition of an enormous tax burden upon the Jewish populace, and arresting decrees concerning the proscription of Jewish practices, including the outlawing of Torah observance, the imposition of idolatrous cults, and subsequent persecutions and martyrdom upon those who dared defy his edicts.

From the beginnings of Antiochus's reign, the office of high priest was in turmoil. Because Jews were given limited

Zeus

This 2d C. BC marble head of Zeus from Aigeira, Greece, is representative of the types of statues of the gods familiar throughout the Hellenistic world.

Zeus. Colossal marble head from Aigeira. 2d C. BC. National Archaeological Museum, Athens, Greece. (Credit: Erich Lessing/Art Resource, NY)

Jason and Heracles

The high priest Jason, appointed by Antiochus IV, was sympathetic to the king's Hellenizing agenda, even sending delegates to Tyre to honor Heracles. The author of 2 Maccabees reports that although the envoys attended, they did not use the money for sacrifice (2 Macc 4:18-20). This 2d C. BC bronze statuette from Ephesus, Turkey, depicts Heracles fighting a centaur.

Heracles fighting a centaur. 2d half of 2d C. BC. Bronze statuette, Ephesus, Turkey. Kunsthistorisches Museum, Vienna, Austria. (Credit: Erich Lessing/Art Resource, NY)

autonomy under their various Hellenistic rulers, the high priest not only acted as a religious ruler, but wielded important political power as well. Early in Antiochus's rule, the priest Jason bribed the king in order to become high priest, forcing out his own brother, Onias III. Jason apparently represented the opinions of some Jerusalemites who believed that the best way to adapt to their new overlord was through accommodation. First Maccabees reports, "In those days certain renegades came out from Israel and misled many, saying, 'Let us go and make a covenant with the Gentiles around us, for since we separated from them many disasters have come upon us'" (1 Macc 1:11). Under the leadership of Jason, various commandments were abandoned, and some men even tried to surgically disguise their circumcisions. Key customs of Hellenistic life were willingly adopted by Jews of Jerusalem, including the building of a gymnasium—even before Antiochus imposed other, more threatening customs by force. The author of 1 Maccabees concludes that this attempt of appeasement and adaptation was tantamount to a betrayal, commenting that such persons "sold themselves to do evil" (1 Macc 1:15).

Jason was soon to discover that "what goes around comes around," when Antiochus replaced him as high priest with Menelaus, whose bribe was even higher than his own. Menelaus

Gymnasium

The gymnasium, represented on this 6th C. BC amphora, was the location of the athletic and intellectual education of young males, beginning at either puberty or at the age of eighteen. It was an important rite of passage for young men who met their civic obligations there, for it was the prerequisite for citizenship and acceptance into the upper levels of society.

Andokides (painter). Wrestling Scene in the Gymnasium. c. 525 BC. Antikensammlung, Staatliche museen zu Berlin, Berlin, Germany. (Credit: Bildarchiv Preussischer Kulturbesitz/Art Resource, NY)

had his own financial difficulties and could not live up to his promise of payment to Antiochus. Along with his brother Lysimachus, Menelaus stole temple revenue to pay his obligations. Rioting ensued and Jewish elders tried to exact justice through the judicial system, but Menelaus remained in power by another bribe. [Menelaus] The disarray reached a climax when Jason, upon hearing a false rumor of Antiochus's death, returned to Jerusalem to attempt to oust Menelaus and to recapture his position as high priest, resulting in terrible civil unrest. The author of 2 Maccabees laments the deaths of Jews by a fellow Jew: "Jason kept relentlessly slaughtering his compatriots, not realizing that success at the cost of one's kindred is the greatest misfortune, but imagining that he was setting up trophies of victory over enemies and not over compatriots" (2 Macc 5:6-7). Jason not only was unsuccessful and met an ignominious death, but also set the stage for Antiochus's revenge. Believing that the entirety of the Jerusalem populace was rebelling against him upon his return from Egypt, he crushed the Jews with merciless assault. The report in 2 Maccabees is chilling:

> **Menelaus**
>
> Menelaus raised the revenues he owed Antiochus by several unpopular and disastrous means. He increased the tribute paid to the king that required an approximate doubling of the taxes owed by the populace; he sold temple vessels and gold objects, and confiscated the temple treasury.
>
> Otto Mørkholm, "Antiochus IV," *The Hellenistic Age*, ed. W. D. Davies and Louis Finkelstein (Cambridge History of Judaism 2; London: Cambridge University Press, 1989), 281–83.

[Antiochus] commanded his soldiers to cut down relentlessly everyone they met and to kill those who went into their houses. Then there was massacre of young and old, destruction of boys, women, and children, and slaughter of young girls and infants. Within the total of three days eighty thousand were destroyed, forty thousand in hand-to-hand fighting, and as many were sold into slavery as were killed. (2 Macc 5:12-14)

Such retaliatory measures were, sadly, not a one-time event. Approximately two years later, Antiochus sent his army commander to retaliate against pious Jews:

[Antiochus commanded Apollonius] to kill all the grown men and to sell the women and boys as slaves. When this man arrived in Jerusalem, he pretended to be peaceably disposed and waited until the holy Sabbath day; then finding the Jews not at work, he ordered his troops to parade under arms. He put to the sword all those who came out to see them, then rushed into the city with his armed warriors and killed great numbers of people. (2 Macc 5:24-26)

After these horrors, Antiochus continued his assault against Jews by making any practice or acknowledgment of their faith a capital offense and by polluting the temple, dedicating it to a foreign god. The holiest place in Judaism now became the location of forbidden offerings and festivals to pagan gods, a practice that began in December of 167 BC and lasted until December of 164 BC.

Sacrifices to Foreign Deities

It is likely that the reason Antiochus tried to force the foreign cultic practices on Jews was in order to make them more like the other conquered peoples of the Seleucid Empire and to eliminate two important Jewish religious practices that the Greeks found objectionable and unreasonable—their uncompromising monotheism and their refusal to allow images.

Jonathan Goldstein, *1 Maccabees* (AB 41; NewYork: Doubleday & Co., 1976), 142–43, 222.

[Sacrifices to Foreign Deities] Such outlawing of Judaism spread throughout Antiochus's territory (2 Macc 5:7). It is precisely during these most oppressive years that the book of Daniel was compiled and that the "transgression that makes desolate" (Dan 8:13) was forever inscribed in Jewish memory.

In the context of the vision, the angel's plaintive cry, "how long?" stands out. By underscoring the angel's struggle to understand, the author lends legitimacy to the same question that haunts the readers. Yet, the cryptic answer resides only among angels, for it is not Daniel who is told "two thousand three hundred evenings and mornings [literally, "evening morning"]; then the sanctuary shall be restored to its rightful state" (8:14); rather, it is one angel who answers another. While it is true that Daniel hears these words, their mysterious nature is confirmed by the equally non-specific response that Gabriel gives to Daniel later in this vision (v. 26). No consensus can be found in either ancient or in modern commentaries concerning the significance of this puzzling expression of time. Because the *tāmîd* was offered twice a day, one interpretation holds that the 2,300 evenings and mornings refers to 1,150 days, approximating the "time, times, and half a time" of Daniel 7, which in turn is understood to refer to three and a half years. Others hold that the 2,300 evenings and mornings refer to 2,300 days, which closely approximates the seven years of desolation referred to in 9:27. It is also possible that the number has a strictly symbolic significance; for example *1 Enoch* 90:5 states that twenty-three of the seventy shepherds who are assigned to protect the Jews during the exile are specifically assigned to the Hellenistic period.[7]

Although the period of the desecration remains ambiguous, what is confirmed is that the sanctuary "will be restored to its rightful state" (*wĕniṣdaq*). This verb, from the root *ṣdq* (to be just/righteous), means "to be vindicated." As James Montgomery states, "[the sanctuary] will be restored to its rights."[8] Because it is God alone who determines ultimate justice, the angels not only confirm that the discouraging vision has another development yet to be seen, but also that the vindication will be part of God's setting the world right. This most important part of Daniel's vision remains a mystery; unlike the vision in Daniel 7, there is no unveiling of the horn's defeat or of the glorification of the faithful. Daniel, like the author's audience of antiquity, must have faith in the unseen.

Gabriel's Appearance and Address to Daniel, 8:15-26

In the next scene, Daniel reports that he "had seen the vision," indicating that it is over. God's revelation continues to Daniel in an increasingly reliable form, however, as he is privileged to have the angel Gabriel appear to him with an interpretation of the vision. This interpretation is divided into three parts. The first, vv. 19-22, quickly lists the first four kingdoms; the second, vv. 23-25, gives a more detailed and poetic account of the little horn; and in the third, v. 26, Gabriel explains the implications of the vision for Daniel personally.

Daniel's first response to having experienced the vision was literally to "seek understanding" (v. 15). Because the word *bqš* ("seek") can connote a quest for finding God or can mean to draw close to God, the author's description underscores Daniel's fidelity and sincerity. Furthermore, the use of the word "understanding" (*bînâ*) contrasts Daniel's attempt to comprehend with the comment that "no one understood" (*ʾên mēbîn*) at the end of the chapter (v. 27). Although it is surprising that Daniel, who could interpret the most difficult of dreams, cannot understand the vision, the appearance

The Angel Gabriel

This painting by Francesco Botticini (1446–1497) shows the hero Tobias guided by the angels Raphael, Michael, and Gabriel.

In the Second Temple period, one finds increasing emphasis on angels and archangels who are presented as forming a hierarchy. Individually named angels include Michael and Gabriel, first attested in Daniel; Uriel, found in 4 Ezra; and Raphael, who features in Tobit. The name Gabriel is a play on words with the Hebrew *gbr*, meaning "man" or "warrior." The author of *1 Enoch* portrays him as one of the angels who plead with God to address the world's evils, and the author of Luke shows Gabriel to be the one who announces to Mary that she will give birth to Jesus (*1 En.* 9:1-11; Luke 1:19).

Francesco Botticini. 1446–1497. *Tobias and the three archangels*. Uffizi. Florence, Italy. (Credit: Alinari/Art Resource, NY)

of the angel at this difficult time allows the audience to see that he is privileged and that his vision report is authoritative. The text reads, literally, "and behold! [*wĕhinnēh*] someone like a man was standing next to me" (v. 15 A.T.). The author heightens the awesome quality of this revelation by using the interjection, "and behold!" while the mysterious description of what he sees (someone *like* a man) allows the reader to understand that Daniel's experience defies words. Although the voice was human, the speaker is not. Daniel hears the angel's voice at a river ("by the Ulai"), paralleling the final vision of the angels who speak at "the banks of the river" (12:5). Both visions confirm that Antiochus's cruelty signifies that a new age, in which such kingdoms no longer defy God, indeed will arrive.

In the history of interpretation, scholars have understood the speaker to be either Michael or God. This unspecified speaker addresses the being standing before Daniel and, in effect, also identifies him: "Gabriel, make this man understand the vision" (v. 16 A.T.), using the same root for understand (*byn*) as Daniel spoke earlier (v. 15). The word for "man" (lit., "this one" [*hallāz*]) in v. 16 is unusual. It contrasts with the earlier usages of the noun for "man" or "one like a man" that referred to Gabriel and to the mysterious voice. The now identified angel immediately complies with the command, but Daniel's response does not imply that he is comforted; rather, he feels terror and falls prostrate (see also Dan 10:9). [Angels' Appearances] Responding in terror to the presence of the holy indicates the profundity of the event, and falling prostrate, an action one does before kings, acknowledges God's sovereignty. When Gabriel does speak (v. 17), he exactly repeats the verb "understand" (*hābēn*) that the voice earlier commanded him, showing his obedience. Gabriel states, "understand, son of man, that the vision is for the time of the end" (v. 17). Here, the author emphasizes that the reader must similarly understand Daniel's words, for although the angel's words are intended for Daniel's distant future, it is a time in which the author's original reader now resides. The appellation for Daniel, "son of man" (*ben-ʾādām*), is reminiscent of God's address to the prophet Ezekiel that emphasized the prophet's distance from the ineffable God. The

Angels' Appearances

Reflecting the awesome nature of the appearance of an angel, the recipient of the vision often shows both reverence and fear. In the book of Numbers, for example, Balaam falls to the ground in the presence of the angel, even before the angel's presence is fully revealed (Num 22:31). Ornan's sons hide in fear when an angel appears to their father (1 Chr 21:20), and in the book of Tobit the angel Raphael appears to Tobit and Tobias, who fearfully fall prostrate. The angel Raphael responds, "Do not be afraid; peace be with you. Bless God forevermore" (Tob 12:16-17). The detailing of these persons' fear highlights the angels' awesome appearance, the importance of their revelation, and the gulf of inequality that exists between angels and humans (see also Matt 28:2-5 and Acts 10:3-4).

Kevin Sullivan, *Wrestling with Angels: A Study of the Relationship between Angels and Humans in Ancient Jewish Literature and the New Testament* (Arbeiten zur Geschichte des antiken Judentums und des Urchristentums 55; Leiden: Brill, 2004), 32.

"time of the end" most likely indicates the end of the miseries inflicted by the little horn, Antiochus.

Gabriel barely completes these words when Daniel relates, "I fell into a trance" (*nirdamtî*) and again (?) falls to the ground (v. 18). This trance, or deep sleep, is the same that fell upon Adam when God made Eve, indicating overwhelming unconsciousness.[9] The angel shows compassion and sympathy for Daniel, who is undone by the power of this awesome revelation, and helps him to stand— a sign of strengthening him. His first word to Daniel is the command, "listen," which begins his brief summary of the symbols of the first four kingdoms, confirming that they are for "the period of wrath" or "the appointed time of the end." As Montgomery explains, with these phrases, similarly to "the latter days," of the prophets, "a fixed term is given for the consummation of the 'age,' which has been counted in days [the 2,300 evenings and mornings of vv. 13-14]. . . . What the 'end' is appears from 9:26, [it is] 'his end,' *i.e.*, Antiochus's . . . the later *nuance* of the end of time and the ushering in of eternity . . . is not to be found here."[10]

Indeed, Gabriel's focus turns to the "king of bold countenance" who arrives "when transgressions have reached their full measure" (v. 23), reminiscent of the suffering Abraham's descendants endured because, as God informs the patriarch, "the iniquity of the Amorites is not yet complete" (Gen 15:16). These "transgressions" are references to the cruelties of the nations who have oppressed Israel as they ruled over it. Even though the series of ruling kingdoms is part of God's plan, the author still holds the nations morally accountable and expects God to respond to their inhumanity.

The apex of the injustice lies with this last king who comes from the four horns. [Polybius] The author paints an increasingly fearsome portrait of this ruler, first portraying his character, secondly, his actions against humanity, and thirdly, his attack against God himself. His "bold countenance" underscores his arrogance; his "skill in intrigue" (v. 23), his prodigious energy for inflicting cruelty. He uses his power to "cause fearful destruction" (v. 24) and "make deceit prosper" (v. 25), referring to the despicable crushing of "social institutions as well as concrete things."[11] This king defeats three identified groups of people, namely, "the powerful,"

Polybius

Although the Greek historian and contemporary of Antiochus IV, Polybius (c. 200–118 BC), does not speak of Antiochus's treatment of Jews, he does detail his bizarre, profligate, and outlandish behavior, recording that his epithet was "Epimanes" or "madman":

Epimanes (the Madman), would sometimes steal from the court, avoiding his attendants, and appear roaming wildly about in any chance part of the city with one or two companions. . . . Whenever he found any young men carousing together he would come to the place without giving notice, with fife and band, like a rout of revelers, and often by his unexpected appearance cause the guests to rise and run away. . . . This conduct was very embarrassing to respectable people, some of whom regarded him as a good natured easy-going man, and others as a madman. . . . In regard to public sacrifices and the honours paid to the gods, he surpassed all his predecessors on the throne; as witness the Olympieium at Athens and the statues placed round the altar at Delos. (*Histories* 26.1)

Dionysus

The author of 2 Maccabees notes that not only were the practices of Judaism outlawed and a pagan cult established in Jerusalem, but also that persecutions were instituted outside of Jerusalem and Judah, and that Jews were also compelled to participate in the festival of Dionysus where they were forced to eat of the god's sacrifices. The worship of Dionysus, the Greek god of ecstasy, wine, vegetation, and rebirth, is well attested in the Hellenistic world. Features of Dionysian worship would have been abhorrent to Jews as sexual symbolism, secret initiation rites, sacrifice, and communion with the god were included. The ivy wreath that was associated with Dionysus is identified in 2 Maccabees. The following passage is remarkable, as it shows that the refusal to worship was a capital offense:

> On the monthly celebration of the king's birthday, the Jews were taken, under bitter constraint, to partake of the sacrifices; and when a festival of Dionysus was celebrated, they were compelled to wear wreaths of ivy and to walk in the procession in honor of Dionysus . . . a decree was issued to the neighboring Greek cities that they should adopt the same policy toward the Jews and make them partake of the sacrifices and should kill those who did not choose to change over to Greek customs. (2 Macc 6:7-9)

In these terrible times, mothers and their babies were paraded and hurled to their deaths, the faithful were burned alive, and the pious went into hiding (2 Macc 6:1-6). Although some of these tales of martyrdom are judged by some interpreters to have legendary elements, the suffering was, to be sure, of such enormous impact that an untrained guerrilla force, the Maccabees, rose up in revolt and eventually defeated the Seleucid army. Those who suffered in these times are remembered in Christian tradition as part of the heroes and heroines of faith, as seen in Hebrews 11:35-38. The author of Hebrews holds that the fullness of their reward in heaven came about with Christ's saving acts—a reward that those who are faithful to him yet will share.

Myles Bourke, "The Epistle to the Hebrews," *New Jerome Biblical Commentary*, ed. Raymond Brown, Joseph Fitzmyer, and Roland Murphy (Englewood Cliffs NJ: Prentice-Hall, 1990), 940.

Dionysos. Archaeological Museum, Eleusis, Greece. (Credit: Alinari/Art Resource, NY)

"the people of the holy ones" (v. 24), and "the many" (v. 25). Although most scholars are in agreement that the last two groups refer to Jews, "the powerful" possibly refers to Jews or to defeated Gentiles. To indicate that the worst of Antiochus's reign of terror came without any preview, the author states that this was all done "without warning" (v. 25). Only after this bleak portrait comes to its conclusion does the author add even greater sorrowful news: this king "shall even rise up against the Prince of princes" (v. 25), here clearly God.

Throughout this vision, Gabriel does not give a glimpse of any human victory, and he speaks only vaguely about Antiochus being defeated. Although the details of victory are withheld, the fact of victory is assured. Echoing the climax that Daniel himself spoke to King Nebuchadnezzar in interpreting his dream of the statue, the author assures Daniel with these words: "He shall be broken, and not by human hands" (v. 25). Some scholars hold that this reference hints of the ignoble and horrible death that the author of 2 Maccabees 9 believed to have been inflicted by God; more likely it indicates the author's unwavering faith in the unseen, reflecting the confidence that just as Jews endured the oppression of Nebuchadnezzar who also met his defeat, so too would Jews be relieved of such indescribable sufferings as they endured during the last years of Antiochus.

Gabriel's final words confirm that the vision is true, underscoring the veracity of Daniel's words. Daniel is told to "seal up the vision, for it refers to many days from now" (v. 26). With this *vaticinium ex eventu* (prophecy after the fact), the author shows that what Daniel was shown to have perceived in the days of Belshazzar was indeed relevant for the time of Antiochus. The word for "seal" may also mean "confuse"; some interpreters hold that this suggests that although Daniel was privy to understand when the end would occur, it was a divine command that he not reveal this to others, for it was only to be understood by those who lived through the injustices of Antiochus.

Daniel's Response to the Vision, 8:27

At first, Daniel is overwhelmed upon experiencing this vision, yet he also evidences courage in the face of the unknown. He states, "so I, Daniel, was overcome and lay sick for some days" (v. 27). Although these terms portray gripping emotions, Daniel returns to his position, namely, to "the king's business." Indeed, he "arose" from his terrible state that he might attend to his job and the business of living.[12]

Reflecting on what he has experienced, Daniel remarks (literally), "and there was no understanding" (*wĕʾên mēbîn* [v. 27]). These words imply either "no one understood it [the vision]" *or* "(I) did not understand it." The nuance of this last phrase shows that the task of understanding is incumbent on both Daniel and his community. It had been Gabriel's task to have Daniel understand the vision. Did either Gabriel fail in his teaching or Daniel fail in his understanding? The author shows that what Daniel was able to grasp was *partial* understanding. This, too, is the lot of the author's audience. The vision of Daniel 8, like that of Daniel 7, does not ultimately address the holy ones' discussion of "how long?" The time of the oppression and injustice is not known, but it is *certain* that it will come to an end. The promise is vouchsafed by the God who reveals his plan to Daniel and who sends his angel to comfort and guide him. For the faithful to whom this text was first addressed, continuing with their task of living the best they could in face of sorrow and fear is modeled here in Daniel's response. They would remember, too, that in the time frame of Daniel's vision, the third year of King Belshazzar was the last year of that generation's suffering under Babylon. God's veiled, yet assured promise would have to be enough.

CONNECTIONS

In the terrible times of Antiochus, Israel lost the ability to offer sacrifices. Daniel laments the cessation of the *tāmîd* with plaintive words (Dan 8:11-13. See also 9:27; 11:31; 12:11). The *tāmîd*, which literally means "continuous" or "daily," is part of the technical language of sacrifice, referring to the twice daily offerings of a yearling lamb.[13] In other biblical texts it is known as the *'olat/'olâ tāmîd* ("the daily burnt offering," [Exod 29:42, Num 28:3, 6]). The portrait of Daniel as one extremely aggrieved reflects the sorrow of the author's community. While the author writes in an era when sacrifices ceased, subsequent generations of readers of Daniel saw the Roman destruction of the temple itself. How could these communities adapt to such a loss of the *tāmîd* and the temple? An examination of the Bible and the midrashim shows that spiritual, moral, and ethical values were gleaned from this ancient rite while the community hoped for the restoration of the temple.

The Bible explains that the perpetual burnt offering consisted of a yearling lamb that was completely burnt upon the altar, forming "a pleasing odor to the LORD" (Exod 29:41; Num 28:8).[14] Performed at the entrance to the tent of meeting, the sacrifice was the place where the God of Israel promises to dwell and where the people will recognize the divine presence (Exod 29:45-46). Although sacrifices are commanded, and the people show their obedience to God in performing them, the offerings are ultimately inscrutable, for God does not *need* them (Pss 50:7-15; 51:16-17 [51:18-19 MT]). Jacob Milgrom argues that sacrificial offerings taught reverence for life. The sacrifice of well-being (*šĕlāmîm*), for example, in which the meat of the animal was eaten and its blood poured upon the altar, showed that the shedding of animal blood was taken very seriously. Eating meat was never a casual act; God,

The Roman Forum
This relief from the Arch of Titus shows the emperor carrying the spoils of the temple, including the menorah and ark of the covenant, in a triumphal procession.

The Roman Forum. Relief from the Arch of Titus showing the emperor Titus after the destruction of Jerusalem in AD 70. Spoils from the temple of Jerusalem, including the seven-branched candlestick, are carried in the triumphal procession. Arch of Titus, Rome, Italy. (Credit: Werner Forman/Art Resource, NY)

the author of all life, was owed the animal's life force. If animal blood were shed under such exacting circumstances, how much more so would be the shedding of the blood of human beings! The demands of sacrifice showed the community that, as creatures, all are subject to God's will.[15]

In the midrashim, a number of stories depict sacrifice as a sign of the people's obedience and their courage to speak out against injustice. In addition, God's institution of the rite and the divine acceptance of sacrifice underscore the transformative power of forgiveness and the role of God's justice in the world.

In the past, bringing sacrifice was performed by the righteous, who recognized God as the author of right and wrong. Adam and Noah brought sacrifices, fulfilling God's will. Abraham, Isaac, and Jacob did so as well, even before they were required. Their offerings, done in anticipation of the commandments regarding sacrifice, are connected with their unfailing willingness to keep *all* of the commandments; thus, God responded to them with "complete love" *(Lev. Rab.* 2:10*)*. The very elements of the sacrifice give evidence that God is a just judge. The fire of the sacrifice served as a harbinger of the punishment of the wicked—Pharaoh, Sennacherib, and Nebuchadnezzar are among those punished by fire for their refusal to live by God's laws. Such divine judgment in the past continues as a sign of God's anticipated righteous judgment against any evil nation that inflicts cruelty (*Lev. Rab.* 7:6). God not only punishes the wicked, but also institutes the rite of sacrifice as the means for humanity to atone for their transgressions and to be reconciled. The same spirit of divine graciousness still exists, for God will bring gifts to the righteous in the world to come. The table of the sacrificial loaves of bread will be replaced in heaven by a banquet for the just (*Num. Rab.* 21:21). Similarly, the fire that burnt in the past will become a fire of protection for those who suffer in this world.[16]

The procedures of the sacrificial rite and the daily requirements also taught important ethical lessons. The way Aaron carried the materials of the sacrifice indicated "that pride has no place with God" (*Num. Rab.* 4:20). The insistence that sacrifice unfailingly be offered at specific times also prompted stirrings of conscience. By neglecting to unlock the temple, Solomon delayed in performing his sacrificial duties and prevented others from fulfilling theirs. Bathsheba does not hesitate to reprimand her son—even when others are afraid to approach the monarch. Admonishing Solomon, she recalls her vow to "have a son diligent and learned in Torah [in order to keep the commandments]." Indeed, the essential role of the king is to carry out the will of God! (*Num. Rab.* 10:4; *Lev. Rab.* 12:5).

As the authors of the midrashim reflect on the loss of such an important means to bring God and humanity together, they conclude that God accepts two equivalent substitutes for sacrifice, namely, prayer and the meditation on God's revelation. Daily prayer and the study of torah—God's teaching—become crucially important in the formation of one's faith and values (*Lev. Rab.* 7:3). Thus, the patriarchs themselves are seen not only as the practitioners of sacrifices (*Lev. Rab.* 2:10), but also as the initiators of prayer services. Abraham, Isaac, and Jacob instituted the morning, afternoon, and evening services, respectively. Thus, daily prayer services are specifically identified as corresponding to the daily offerings (*Gen. Rab.* 68:9).

For our own age, these words of the psalmist are still relevant:

I call upon you, O LORD; come quickly to me;
give ear to my voice when I call to you.
Let my prayer be counted as incense before you,
and the lifting up of my hands as an evening sacrifice. (Ps 141:1-2)

NOTES

[1] Lester Grabbe, *Judaism from Cyrus to Hadrian* (Minneapolis: Fortress, 1992), 226.

[2] The Daniel scrolls from Qumran confirm the change from Hebrew to Aramaic in 2:4 and the change back from Aramaic to Hebrew in 8:1. See Eugene Ulrich, "The Text of Daniel in the Qumran Scrolls," in *The Book of Daniel: Composition and Reception*, ed. John J. Collins and Peter W. Flint, 2 vols. (Leiden: Brill, 2001), 2:579.

[3] Norman Porteous, *Daniel* (OTL; Philadelphia: Westminster, 1965), 120.

[4] Ibid., 125.

[5] John Collins, *Daniel: A Commentary on the Book of Daniel* (Hermeneia; Minneapolis: Fortress, 1993), 332–33.

[6] John Goldingay, *Daniel* (WBC 30; Dallas: Word Books, 1989), 212.

[7] Ibid., 213.

[8] James Montgomery, *A Critical and Exegetical Commentary on the Book of Daniel* (ICC; Edinburgh: T. & T. Clark, 1927), 343.

[9] W. Sibley Towner, *Daniel* (*Int*; Atlanta: John Knox, 1984), 124.

[10] Montgomery, *A Critical and Exegetical Commentary*, 346.

[11] Ibid., 350.

[12] Judah Slotki, *Daniel, Ezra, Nehemiah,* rev. 2d ed. by Ephraim Oratz (Soncino Books of the Bible; London: Soncino, 1951, rev. ed. 1992), 71, n. 27.

[13] In the Bible the word *"tāmîd"* is used in other contexts as well. For example, the bread of the presence must be placed before God continuously, the menorah is to burn perpetually, and the incense is to burn always. For a full explanation of the usage of this word, see K.-M. Beyse, *"tāmîḏ" TDOT*, ed. G. Johannes Botterweck, Helmer Ringgren, and Heinz-Josef Fabry, trans. David E. Green (Grand Rapids MI: Eerdmans, 2006), 15:690-94.

[14] As Naham Sarna explains, this phrase denotes a specialized vocabulary [*Exodus* (The JPS Torah Commentary; Philadelphia and New York: The Jewish Publication Society, 1991), 191–92]. Scholars differ on whether the book of Daniel uses the term *"tāmîd"* as does early rabbinic literature, meaning the twice-daily mandatory offerings of a lamb, accompanied by a grain offering. An equivalence is seen by Sarna, Jacob Milgrom, and John Collins. See Sarna (as cited above); Jacob Milgrom, *Numbers* (The JPS Torah Commentary; New York: The Jewish Publication Society, 1990), 486–88; and John Collins, *Daniel: A Commentary on the Book of Daniel* (Hemeneia; Minneapolis: Fortress, 1993), 333–34. Alternatively, John Goldingay suggests it refers to the entirety of the sacrificial system. See Daniel (WBC 30; Dallas: Word Books, 1989), 211.

[15] Jacob Milgrom, *Leviticus: A Book of Ritual and Ethics* (A Continental Commentary; Minneapolis: Fortress, 2004), 14–16. See also [Sacrifices] and [*minḥâ*].

[16] *Leviticus Rabbah* 7.6 explains that the people of Israel, "who are despised and lowly in this world, will be comforted by means of fire, as it is said, *For I, saith the Lord, will be unto her a wall of fire round about, and I will be the glory in the midst of her* (Zech. II, 9 [=Zech 2:5 Eng])."

DANIEL'S PRAYER

Daniel 9:1-27

COMMENTARY

Prophecy, prayer, vision, and interpretation combine powerfully in Daniel 9 to present a somber, yet hopeful view of life for the exiles. The worst of times, whether they stem from exile in Babylon, as presented by the literary setting, or from the persecutions under Antiochus, as indicated by the historical context, ultimately will yield a future in which people once again can live in peace and fulfill the commandments according to the covenant with God. The vision in Daniel 9 portrays a future in which the temple would once again stand as a beacon of the reconciliation between God and humanity, a place where God would dwell on earth.

Daniel 9 is made up of three main parts—Daniel's consideration of Jeremiah's prophecy concerning the exile, Daniel's prayer, and Gabriel's interpretation of the seventy weeks [Outline of Daniel 9] Throughout these sections there is a unifying theme: trust in God's righteousness despite defeat and suffering. Thus, the author depicts the current trials of the community by drawing parallels with the suffering of earlier generations who endured the exile. Moreover, the author shows that the time of Antiochus's terror has been determined by God to come to an end, as proven by the words of Jeremiah that now address the community's situation in a new way. The meaning of the past has continuing significance for the author's present.

Outline of Daniel 9
Daniel's Consideration of Jeremiah's Prophecy, 9:1-2
Introduction to Daniel's Prayer, 9:3-4a
Daniel's Prayer: Confession, 9:4b-14
Daniel's Prayer: Supplication, 9:15-19
Daniel's Individual Supplication and Gabriel's Appearance, 9:20-23
Gabriel's Message, 9:24-27

Daniel's Consideration of Jeremiah's Prophecy, 9:1-2

Paralleling Daniel 7 and Daniel 8, which begin by identifying the year of the king under whom Daniel served (the first and third year of Belshazzar), Daniel 9 begins by marking the first year of Darius.

Jeremiah

The catalyst for the vision of Dan 9 is the seer's comment, "I, Daniel, perceived in the books the number of years that, according to the word of the LORD to the prophet Jeremiah, must be fulfilled for the devastation of Jerusalem, namely, seventy years" (Dan 9:2). Here, the artist Marc Chagall depicts the prophet Jeremiah praying for the city of Jerusalem, while an angel gives comfort.

Marc Chagall. 1887–1985. *The Prophet Jeremiah*. 1968. (Credit: ©2008 Artists Rights Society (ARS), New York/ADAGP, Paris)

Thus, this vision is linked with the narrative of Daniel 6, which also is set during the time of these otherwise unknown kings. This identification is significant because in the literary context of the book of Daniel, the vision occurs at a time when the Babylonian Empire has been conquered by the Medes, here marked by the first year of its king. This change in regime forms the context of Daniel's meditations; now the seer struggles between hoping in the prophet Jeremiah's words, which predicted that Babylon's rule would be limited, and fearing the apparent postponement of the redemption. Because under the reign of Darius prayer was proscribed and because the punishment for disobedience was being thrown to the lions (Dan 6), the identification of the reign of this same king in Daniel 9 forms an unsettling picture. In addition, even though the change in regime also marks the end of the reign of Babylon, Israel yet finds itself in exile.

Jeremiah (640–586 BC) prophesied throughout the reigns of Jehoiakim (609/608–598/597 BC), Jehoiachin (December 598 or January 597–March 597 BC), and Zedekiah (597–587 BC) of Judah, the kings vanquished by Babylon. Jeremiah witnessed not only the devastation of Judah, but also two deportations of his people (597 BC and 587 BC). [Deportations] Despite Judah's crushing defeat, Jeremiah saw a future for his people and predicted that Babylon's power would last seventy years, as shown in the following texts:

> This whole land shall become a ruin and a waste, and these nations shall serve the king of Babylon seventy years. Then after seventy years are completed, I will punish the king of Babylon and that nation, the

Deportations

As Babylonians conquered Judah in the 6th century BC, the population endured not only war and famine, but also at least two and possibly three deportations. The first deportation occurred in 597 BC when King Jehoiachin of Judah surrendered and was exiled along with thousands of nobles, governmental officials, and artisans. The number of exiled persons is difficult to determine. The account in 2 Kings speaks of the "10 thousand captives" (2 Kgs 24:14), the "7 thousand men of valor," and the "1000 artisans and smiths" (2 Kgs 24:16) who are exiled, along with other identifiable groups. It is not clear whether these numbers are a portion of a greater list. The historical Jeremiah reckons the first deportation as displacing 3,023 Judeans, a number that apparently does not include women and children (Jer 52:28).

As tragic as the first deportation was perceived to have been, the second was prompted by an arresting depiction of the desperation of the final siege of Jerusalem. As is recorded in 2 Kings, "all the rest of the population . . . [except] some of the poorest people of the land" were "carried into exile" (2 Kgs 25:11-12). This account does not reckon the number of people, although Jeremiah speaks of 832 men (Jer 52:29). Jeremiah also refers to a third, otherwise unknown deportation of 745 men (Jer 52:30). Although modern biblical scholars debate whether the deportations had a profound or slight impact on the subsequent number and composition of the Babylonian-ruled Jewish population, the interpretation by the author of 2 Kings reveals that these deportations were understood in some circles to have had a long-term devastating impact, along with the loss of Davidic kingship, the destruction of the temple, and the fall of Jerusalem. Nevertheless, this understanding would eventually yield a new dedication to the return and rebuilding of life in Judah.

See B. Oded, "Judah and the Exile," in *Israelite and Judaean History*, ed. J. H. Hayes and J. M. Miller (Philadelphia: Westminster Press, 1997), 435–88. Cf. Paolo Sacchi, *The History of the Second Temple Period* (JSOTSup 285; Sheffield: Sheffield Academic Press, 2000), 46–68.

land of the Chaldeans, for their iniquity, says the LORD, making the land an everlasting waste. (Jer 25:11-12)

For thus says the LORD: Only when Babylon's seventy years are completed will I visit you, and I will fulfill to you my promise and bring you back to this place. For surely I know the plans I have for you, says the LORD, plans for your welfare and not for harm, to give you a future with hope. Then when you call upon me and come and pray to me, I will hear you. When you search for me, you will find me; if you seek me with all your heart, I will let you find me, says the LORD, and I will restore your fortunes and gather you from all the nations and all the places where I have driven you, says the LORD, and I will bring you back to the place from which I sent you into exile. (Jer 29:10-14)

Daniel relates that he "perceived in the books" (v. 2) the content of Jeremiah's words, namely, that the completion of Jerusalem's devastation would be seventy years. "The books" may indicate that the book of Jeremiah was considered Scripture at this time, may refer to the prophetic corpus, or may refer to the individual letters of Jeremiah.[1] During the period of Antiochus's reign, Jeremiah's words would have prompted consternation—how could the restoration be delayed for centuries when the prophet's words assured a limited exile? Although the people were physically in the land of Judah and although the temple had been rebuilt under the rule of the

Jeremiah's Letter to the Exiles

Jeremiah's letter to the exiles in Babylon encouraged them to make their peace with living under subjugation, yet to hope for a future restoration for the community (Jer 29:1-23). Individually, the people were not to give up their faith or culture; they were to continue with the mundane acts of constructing homes, getting married, raising families. Yet, they were also to remain Jews and hope for a future restoration, if not for them personally, then for their people. Exile would be limited to "70 years," wrote Jeremiah, after which time Babylon itself would be conquered and the people would return to their holy city and temple.

In Dan 9, the exile Daniel is left with a dilemma. Given that Darius the Mede ascended the throne and Babylon was conquered, were the 70 years completed? Was the oppression of his people over? Would his people return to Jerusalem, restore the temple and their sacrificial system? The reinterpretation of the prophecy offers new hope.

Persians, the daily degradations and oppression of Jews under the Seleucids made the question all the more urgent. [Jeremiah's Letter to the Exiles]

It is noteworthy that the author encapsulates Daniel's description of the exile as the "desolations [NRSV: devastation] of Jerusalem" (v. 2). The word for "desolations" (*ḥorbôt*) has the connotation of "waste places," as is seen in this text from the book of Isaiah. Here, the speaker pours out an urgent plea to God for a restoration not only of Judah, but, specifically, of the temple:

Yet, O LORD, you are our Father; we are the clay, and you are our potter; we are all the work of your hand. Do not be exceedingly angry, O LORD, and do not remember iniquity forever. Now consider, we are all your people. Your holy cities have become a wilderness, Zion has become a wilderness, Jerusalem a desolation. Our holy and beautiful house, where our ancestors praised you, has been burned by fire, and all our pleasant places have become ruins (*ḥorbâ*). After all this, will you restrain yourself, O LORD? Will you keep silent, and punish us so severely? (Isa 64:8-12 [64:7-11 MT]) [*ḥorbôt*]

By focusing on the city instead of, say, the Judean army, the deaths of civilians, the deportations, or other tragedies of war, the author of Daniel turns to the city that is inextricably connected with the temple—the place of God's dwelling on earth. This portrait emphasizes not only the physical devastation, but also the spiritual loss. Nonetheless, because the restoration of the temple serves as a symbol of the redemption of the Jewish people, and because the temple represents the connection of God and the people that even victorious armies cannot subdue, the author underscores a statement of faith that transcends material defeat.

ḥorbôt

ḥorbôt refers to desolations, or ruins, of cities, land, temple, or dwellings. It is frequently used of Jerusalem and Judah in the context of God exercising judgment, as is exemplified by this passage from Ezekiel: "I will lay your town in ruins; you shall become a desolation, and you shall know that I am the LORD" (Ezek 35:4). These same places of desolation are also associated with God's deliverance: "For the LORD will comfort Zion; he will comfort all her waste places, and will make her wilderness like Eden, her desert like the garden of the LORD; joy and gladness will be found in her, thanksgiving and the voice of song" (Isa 51:3).

Introduction to Daniel's Prayer, 9:3-4a

The introduction to Daniel's prayer expresses resolve, faith, and quest for understanding. Daniel "set[s] his face to the Lord God" (v. 3, A.T.), addressing God with a demeanor of determination and with sincerity. It is possible that this phrase implies he prays toward Jerusalem, as he is shown to have done previously (Dan 6:11 [6:12 MT]). This is the third time in the book of Daniel that the hero prays. On the first occasion (2:20-23), Daniel expresses his thanksgiving after God reveals the interpretation of Nebuchadnezzar's dream, thus allowing him and his companions to escape a certain death. On the second occasion, Daniel prays as is his custom, yet faces death because prayer has been proscribed by Darius (6:11 [6:12 MT]). Thus, the author of Daniel continues to portray both the possibility of communication between God and the visionary as well as the gravity of Daniel's situation, for prayer earlier had served as Daniel's response to death itself. Here, Daniel's concern is even greater—it is for the very existence of an entire people. Daniel resolved, literally, "to seek [*lĕbaqqēš*] prayer and supplication" (v. 3). The word for "seek" is often used in biblical Hebrew to refer to a person's act of prayer (2 Sam 12:16; 21:1; Pss 24:6; 27:8; 105:3; Hos 5:15). Surely, it is not the case that the author portrays Daniel demanding an interpretation regarding the seventy weeks. Rather, as is the case when Daniel continues his daily prayer even when threatened with death, the commitment to prayer is unequivocal.

The piety of the hero and the gravity of the community's situation are underscored by showing that Daniel uses fasting, sackcloth, and ashes as tangible signs of repentance and supplication as he begins his prayer. As expressed in the Torah, on Yom Kippur fasting is associated with the "affliction of one's soul," in which the atonement from sin is effected. In addition, fasting may mark the prelude to a revelatory or ecstatic event, a preparation for battle, an act of petition, or may indicate mourning.[2] The sackcloth and ashes express both Daniel's sincerity and grief, as similar usages in the Hebrew Bible show (Job 2:12; Ezra 9:3).

Daniel's final introductory words relate that he "made confession" (*'etwaddeh,* v. 4). In the Hebrew Bible, the *hitpa'el* form of the verb *ydh* occurs ten times; six times in the Writings, in the context of prayer, and four times in the Torah, with reference to Yom Kippur.[3] [*ydh*] The tone of this prayer in Daniel 9 makes possible an appropriate link

---

ydh

AΩ The *hitpa'el* of *ydh*, which means "to reveal oneself" is used in the context of confessing sin (Ezra 10:1, Neh 9:3). In the book of Leviticus, *ydh* is used in the following passage, which details a crucial part of the Yom Kippur ceremony:

> Then Aaron shall lay both his hands on the head of the live goat, and confess over it all the iniquities of the people of Israel and all their transgressions, all their sins, putting them on the head of the goat, and sending it away into the wilderness by means of someone designated for the task. (Lev 16:21)

In ancient Israel, as in other ancient cultures, sin was understood as an "external force that had clung to them"; therefore, it was deemed necessary to take these tangible steps to rid the community of its palpable effects. Once the sins were no longer concealed, or were confessed, they could be thus exorcised.

Baruch Levine, *Leviticus* (JPS Torah Commentary; Philadelphia: Jewish Publication Society, 1989), 106.

with the usage of "confess" as is found in the Yom Kippur ceremony. This ancient ritual requires that the high priest make atonement for the sanctuary (tabernacle), for the altar of sacrifice, for himself, and for the people. The book of Leviticus lists instructions for Aaron:

> [Aaron] shall lay both his hands on the head of the live goat, and confess over it all the iniquities of the people of Israel, and all their transgressions, all their sins, putting them on the head of the goat, and sending it away into the wilderness by means of someone designated for the task. The goat shall bear on itself all their iniquities to a barren region: and the goat shall be set free in the wilderness. (Lev 16:21-22)

Because Daniel is shown to be living in the exile, the author may be suggesting that even when sacrifice and ritual are denied the Jewish people, as they surely were in the days of Antiochus's worst repression, prayer and confession for the individual and community are still possible.

Daniel's Prayer, 9:4b-19

Three reasons are often cited by scholars who argue that Daniel's prayer is an addition to Daniel 9. The prefatory words in v. 4b and the conclusion in v. 21 repeat the content of v. 3 and v. 20, respectively, indicating editorial splicing; the material in vv. 20-27 follows v. 3 in both theme and style, as the material before and after the prayer all deal with the content of the seventy weeks; and the unique theology and diction of the prayer itself, which stress confession and petition with Deuteronomic language, stand alone when compared to the rest of the book.[4] [Deuteronomic Language] Other scholars emphasize that the use of known prayers in any given author's composition is common and that even if the theology of the prayer seems distinct, the author clearly believed it was compatible with the narrative or vision in which it was incorporated.[5] The inclusion of this prayer does not necessarily provide a contradiction to other aspects of the theology of the book of Daniel, but, rather, provides a model of coping and response in times of spiritual and physical loss when great uncertainty, doubt, and corresponding fear weigh with such enormity.

In recent studies, Mark Boda investigates the unique character of penitential prayers of Israel during Persian occupation (Ezra 9, Neh 9) and discusses the parallels with Daniel 9.[6] He shows that key aspects of the penitential prayer are the emotional depiction of the

Deuteronomic Language

One of the consenses of historical-critical studies is that the books of Joshua, Judges, Samuel, and Kings were redacted during the Babylonian exile by an editor who believed the sufferings were a result of Israel's failure to live up to the covenantal demands, as expressed in the book of Deuteronomy. A particular structure and vocabulary, representative of this theology, not only permeates these biblical books (the so-called Deuteronomistic history) but also marks the redactions of other biblical books outside this corpus. The Deuteronomic language of the prayer of Dan 9 includes the following phrases, as listed by Mark Boda:

"Lord, great and awesome God, keeping covenant and steadfast love" (v. 4)

"by [your servants] the prophets" (v. 10, literally "by the hand of [your servants] the prophets")

A list of leaders, such as prophets, kings, princes, ancestors, all the people of the land, officials, ancestors (vv. 6-8)

A specific content of confession: "we have sinned, we have done evil, we have done wrong" (v. 5; see 1 Kgs 8:47)

Boda argues that other unique vocabularies have influenced this prayer as well. For example, the underscoring of the justice of God has roots in the language of Ezekiel, and the combination of using both "the curse" and "the oath" reflects Priestly language. (Priestly language [P] refers to the exilic redactor of the Pentateuch, or the associated school, whose members were particularly interested in matters of holiness and the preservation of a Torah-based community.) The influences of these Ezekielian and Priestly traditions led to what is typical of second temple penitential prayers, namely, a lesser emphasis on the cries of the community and a renewed appeal to the covenantal traditions. This shift was crucial for the post-exilic community who returned to Jerusalem under the aegis of the Persian government. This community, who lived in the Persian colony of Yehud, the name given to the conquered land of Judah by their overlords, struggled to survive, to preserve their faith, and to cling to hope.

Mark Boda, *Praying the Tradition* (Beihefte zur Zeitschrift für die alttestamentliche Wissenschaft 277; Berlin: Walter de Gruyter, 1999), 43–46; 62–64; 71–73

distress of the community, a request for God's acknowledgment of their suffering (which may include a request for alleviation or intervention), confession of sin (both past and present), and a particular theological orientation that acknowledges the "awesome greatness of God," God's faithful grace, covenantal fidelity, and righteousness. Throughout the penitential prayers, there is emphasis on the justice of God and on the importance of Torah.[7] Boda continues that unlike the lament—the precursor to this prayer—the penitential prayer lessens the emphasis on the cries of the people and highlights their sins and failures to live up to the covenant. There is greater stress on the justice of God's response to their sins and the ensuing punishment. Because of this, there is a renewed emphasis on the responsibilities of the group, who then respond to the grace of God and take the opportunity to beseech God to reverse their plight.[8] These elements appear throughout the prayer of Daniel 9 and are referred to in the analysis below.

Overall, the prayer has two main divisions: the confession, the admission of sin and responsibility (vv. 4-14); and supplication, the plea for God's help (vv.15-19). [Structure of Daniel's Prayer] Both sections show an alternating pattern of praise and acknowledgment of sin. The confession concludes with the punishment the people have experienced, and the supplication ends with a plea for forgiveness.

The confession admits that the community did not live up to the obligations of the covenant and hence are now suffering the consequences of their failure. The supplication pleads with God to show mercy—not because it is deserved, but simply because God is compassionate. Each stanza includes praises of God's characteristics, followed by an admission of sin. The sins are specified as disobedience to the covenant and a rejection of God's servants. The personal tone of the prayer is highlighted by the frequent references to God, indicated either by the tetragrammaton (YHWH [vv. 4, 8, 10, 13, 14]), "God" (a form of *'ĕlōhîm* [vv. 4 *bis*, 9, 11, 13, 14]), "Lord" (*'ădōnāy* [vv. 4, 7, 9]), and the frequent second person singular references (*your* commandments, *your* ordinances [v. 5], *your* servants, *your* name [v. 6], *your* teaching, *your* voice [v. 11]). [Names of God] The depth of the communal guilt is portrayed by the frequent usage of the first person plural (*we* have sinned, *we* have done wrong, *we* have acted wickedly, *we* have done evil, *we* have rebelled [v. 5], *we* have not listened [vv. 6, 10]).

Daniel's Prayer: Confession, 9:4b-14

Throughout the confession, Daniel recalls key terms from the Torah and the Prophets that have distinct associations concerning the nature of the covenant between God and Israel, the mercy and compassion of God, and the consistent failures on the part of the people. Before Daniel begins his confession, he first offers praise, underscoring God's covenantal nature: "Ah, Lord, great and awesome God, keeping covenant and steadfast love with those who love you and keep your commandments" (v. 4). These words recall God's bequest of the commandments at Mt. Sinai (Exod 19:5; 20:5-6), the exhortations of Moses to the Israelites to obey God's commandments (Deut 7:9; 26:18), and Jeremiah's words regarding the justice of God (Jer 32:18). These texts read as follows:

Names of God

AΩ In Dan 9, three names of God are used: YHWH (LORD), *'ădōnāy* (my Lord), and *'ĕlōhîm* (God). YHWH, considered the most holy appellation, is God's own self-revelation, given first to Moses (Exod 3:15). Its mysterious meaning, "I am who am," both reveals and conceals, indicating that God both responds to the suffering of the slaves in Egypt and yet transcends human ability to define God. *'ădōnāy* is a title of respect and honor; it does not necessarily connote divinity, although it is used frequently for God. Sometime after the exile, the pronunciation of YHWH ceased and was substituted orally with *'ădōnāy*, just as the Septuagint uses the equivalent *kyrios* when it translates YHWH. *'ĕlōhîm*, which may denote either "gods" or "God," is most often used for the God of Israel in the Hebrew Bible.

It is interesting that the prayer in Dan 9 uses all three of these titles for God. Perhaps it reflects a long history of usage of this prayer or a particularly broad theological background.

Potsherd (ostracon), probably from a cultic vessel, with inscription in Hebrew. Studium Biblicum Franciscanum, Jerusalem, Israel. (Credit: Erich Lessing/Art Resource, NY)

This ostracon includes the personal name of the God of Israel.

Now therefore, if you obey my voice and keep my covenant, you shall be my treasured possession out of all the peoples. (Exod 19:5)

You shall not bow down to them or worship them [idols]; for I the LORD your God am a jealous God, punishing children for the iniquity of parents, to the third and the fourth generation of those who reject me, but showing steadfast love to the thousandth generation of those who love me and keep my commandments. (Exod 20:5-6)

Today the LORD has obtained your agreement: to be his treasured people, as he promised you, and to keep his commandments. (Deut 26:18; see also 7:9)

You show steadfast love to the thousandth generation, but repay the guilt of parents into the laps of their children after them, O great and mighty God whose name is the LORD of hosts. (Jer 32:18)

All of these texts emphasize God's loyalty to the covenant as well as God's righteousness—if one generation lives by a code of injustice, subsequent generations will suffer. The texts confirm that the suffering of Daniel's community is not the result of a cruel, uncaring God, but rather is the consequence of free choice. This stance parallels other penitential prayers of the Second Temple period (Ezra 9, Neh 9), which include a marked decrease in portraying the "disciplinary side of God" and an increase in acknowledging responsibility.[9] The poignant words of the prayer stress the various ways in which the community has failed to live up to their obligations. It is noteworthy that all the references to people's failings are in the third person plural— no one is singled out for particular culpability above his or her neighbor, nor does anyone escape judgment. When Daniel's community is specified, the circles of reference include everyone: "the people of Judah, the inhabitants of Jerusalem, and all Israel, those who are near and those who are far away" (v. 7). Indeed, the results of the people's disobedience can be felt not only forward to the next generation, but backwards in time, to those who came before: "Open shame, O LORD, falls on us, our kings, our officials, *and our ancestors*, because we have sinned against you" (v. 8, emphasis added). With these outcries, the prayer expresses the depths of their overwhelming grief. [Daniel in the *Machzor*]

After establishing what Israel has done, the author emphasizes what they failed to do—they neglected the prophets whom God had sent (v. 10). Underscoring the righteousness of God, Daniel acknowledges that the prophets addressed all levels of their community, kings, officials, and ancestors, yet all spurned them. Thus he can summarize with the rhythmic: "*lĕkā ʾădōnāy haṣṣĕdāqâ wĕlānû bōšet happānîm*" ("to you, Lord, is righteousness; but to us, shamefacedness" [v. 7, A.T.]).

The confession continues to emphasize God's characteristics, namely, "mercy and forgiveness" (v. 9, cf. Exod 34:6). Admission of fault is given using language characteristic of the Deuteronomic tradition, as the people have rebelled and ignored the prophets, Moses, and the judges (NRSV: "rulers," vv. 10-12).[10] Communal guilt is highlighted by the use of first person plural: *we* have sinned (v. 11), *we* have not entreated (v. 13), *our* kings, *our* princes, *our* ancestors (v. 6), *our* rulers (v. 12), *our* iniquities (v. 13). Daniel emphasizes that they were repeatedly taught what would be the consequences of their sin—"the curse and the oath written in the law of Moses, the servant of God" (v. 11). The phrase "curse and

Daniel in the *Machzor*

The *machzor* (the prayer book) for Yom Kippur includes a quotation from Daniel's prayer (Dan 9:18-19) in the evening, morning, and afternoon services. Yom Kippur, ordained since biblical times as a religious holiday for the forgiveness of sin, continues today as the holiest day in the Jewish calendar. The prayer reads,

Give ear, my God, and hear; open your eyes and behold our desolate places and the city upon which Your Name is proclaimed, for it is not on account of our own righteousness that we offer our supplications before You, but because of Your abounding mercies. My Lord, hear; my Lord, pardon; my Lord, hearken and take action, do not delay, for Your own sake, my God, for Your Name is proclaimed over Your city and Your people.

Nissen Mangel, trans., *Machzor for Yom Kippur* (New York: Merkos L'Inyonei Chinuch, 1994), 45, 55, 136, 201.

oath" echoes the language of Deuteronomy (28:15-46; 29:12, 14 [11, 13 MT]); the curse refers to the terrible consequences that will occur if the people do not abide by the commandments and by the oath to the covenant itself. [The Oath and Curse] Appeal to the importance of the past is presented here by the references to "the book of the law of Moses," used in the context of exhortations to obey the covenant (cf. Josh 8:31, 34-35; 1 Kgs 2:3), and the reference to Moses as "servant" points to his particularly esteemed position as the recipient of God's word and of the covenant itself. ["Moses, the Servant of God"]

Daniel twice underscores that even with their sin, the people had opportunities for reconciliation, yet, he laments, they still did not turn to God or turn away from their sin. The author indicates the crushing pervasiveness of the defeat of Jerusalem by the three-fold reference to "calamity" (*rāʿâ*, vv. 12, 13, 14) and by the use of the verb "watch" (*šqd*) to show that God has long since decided on the fate of Jerusalem because of sin. The book of Jeremiah shows a similar usage in the form of a play on words, for when Jeremiah sees a vision of a branch of an almond tree—in Hebrew *šāqēd*—God proclaims, "You have seen well, for I am watching—*šōqēd*—over my word to perform it" (Jer 1:12). The great evil or calamity that God brings against Jerusalem also echoes the words of Jeremiah, who proclaimed that the Babylonian invasion occurred because of God's decree in response to the people's refusal to obey the commandments: "Therefore, thus says the LORD, the God of hosts, the God of Israel: I am going to bring on Judah and on all the inhabitants of Jerusalem every disaster (*rāʿâ*) that I have pronounced against them; because I have spoken to them and they have not listened, I have called to them and they have not answered" (Jer 35:17; see also 36:31). With these references the author has presented an unwavering image of the people's confession. It is not, to be sure, a compendium of guilt alone; rather, it forms a statement of responsibility and

Oath and Curse

AΩ The expression "oath and curse" is rooted in the covenantal language of Deuteronomy. The covenant God made with the people, to be their God, to have them as a treasured people, and for the people to keep God's commandments, was sworn by God's very oath, both with present and subsequent generations (Deut 29:12, 14). The curse refers to the dire consequences of breaking the covenant: war and defeat, the wasting of land, the loss of fertility, illness, and captivity (Deut 28:16-68). This prayer evidences great hope, because even though these traumas have befallen Jerusalem, the author has the courage to yet ask God to respond. As Norman Porteous states, "Just as in the Book of Lamentations hope breaks forth from the depths of the disaster, as soon as the justice of God's judgment is fully admitted, so here the belated act of confession leads to renewal of hope" (*Daniel* [OTL; Philadelphia: Westminster, 1965], 138).

"Moses, the Servant of God"

AΩ Like its counterpart, "the servant of the LORD," the phrase "the servant of God" indicates that Moses acts as God's trusted and loyal representative and spokesman. It underscores the esteem in which he is held by the author and appeals to the covenant made at Sinai. This title is reserved for individuals, leaders, as well as for Israel collectively, including Abraham, Moses, Joshua, Caleb, David, the prophets, Israel, and the righteous—all in the context of leadership, covenantal fidelity, and self-sacrifice.

Jeffrey Tigay, *Deuteronomy* (JPS Torah Commentary; Philadelphia: The Jewish Publication Society, 1996), 337, 412 n.13.

sincerity. With this confirmed, the author can now express the community's request of God.

Daniel's Prayer: Supplication, 9:15-19

Having completed the confession, the author next indicates the change in focus of the second part of the prayer, the supplication (vv. 15-19), by the interjection of the words "and now" (vv. 15 and 17). Having accepted responsibility for not living up to the covenantal ideal, the petitioner now asks God to acknowledge the straits of the community. The petitioner hopes God will respond with righteousness and mercy, recalling the prayer's earlier words of praise (vv. 16, 18). Boda shows that these elements are constitutive of other penitential prayers, identifying them as the "divine recognition of distress" and a "divine modification in disposition."[11] The outcry is made all the more poignant by the use of "God," or "Lord God," fifteen times in these five verses. God's loyalty to the covenant is again implied, but with a unique focus. The God who previously rescued Israel from slavery in Egypt is now called upon to spare the suffering of Jerusalem. [Exodus] The redemption from Egypt was understood to have a particular theological content: Israel's freedom was not for the fulfillment of personal desire but was given in order that the people would become servants of God, living according to the covenantal teachings in the land of the promise where the earth could become a dwelling place for God. This theology of the holiness of the land and the temple is implied with the Deuteronomic phrases: "made your name renowned" and "the city that bears your name" (v. 18). Similarly, the plea to God to spare Jerusalem was not for its material or physical primacy, but because it was the location of the temple, now the "desolated sanctuary" (v. 17). The prayer poignantly leads to a crescendo of outcries: "O Lord, hear; O Lord, forgive; O Lord, listen and act and do not delay! For your own sake, O my God, because your city and your people bear your name!" (v. 19)

This climax uses five verbs in the imperative, and four interjections, making for a palpable cry. The final statement, which expresses the petitioner's reason for the plea, appeals to the very nature of God—God is the one who made the covenant with this

Exodus

The exodus, the redemption from Egypt, shows God's compassion for those who suffered, the exercise of just judgment upon the Egyptians, and God's bequest of freedom upon the Israelites for a specific purpose: so that they could become servants of God by keeping the commandments. God's deliverance of the Israelites from slavery in Egypt becomes the paradigm for future deliverance from exile and foreign oppression (Pss 19:14 [15 MT]; 25:22; 106:10; Isa 41:14; 43:1-4; 44:21-22, 24-28; Hos 13:14). When Second Isaiah proclaims that God redeems the exiles in Babylon, bringing them back to Judah, God's previous redemption in Egypt is cited (Isa 51:9-11; see also Isa 43:14-21; 48:20-21). In addition, redemption itself is associated with God's defeat of chaos during creation, thus linking these two essential characteristics of the God of Israel: creator and redeemer.

Solomon's Prayer

This 19th C. AD oleograph illustrates Solomon's prayer at the dedication of the temple.

Daniel's ardent plea echoes the words of Solomon's temple dedication speech, a poignant reminder of Israel's emphasis on repentance:

> Regard your servant's prayer and his plea, O LORD my God, heeding the cry and the prayer that your servant prays to you today; that your eyes may be open night and day toward this house, the place of which you said, "My name shall be there," that you may heed the prayer that your servant prays toward this place. Hear the plea of your servant and of your people Israel when they pray toward this place; O hear in heaven your dwelling place; heed and forgive. (1 Kgs 8:28-30)

Most modern scholars date this prayer to the Deuteronomist (6th century BC) and to the post-exilic Deuteronomistic redaction (5th century BC). The emphasis on God's willingness to listen to prayer and to accept sincere repentance, thus offering hope to a suffering people, underscores the author's trust in the sacredness of the temple and Jerusalem and in the infinite faithfulness of God.

Solomon's prayer at the consecration of the Temple, II Chronicles VI. c. AD 1870. (Credit: Image Select/Art Resource, NY)

particular people and chose Jerusalem and its temple as a unique resting place for divine holiness. The author highlights that God is ultimately the initiator of this covenant by the use of four second person suffixes in this last sentence that refer back to God (*your* sake, *your* city, *your* people, *your* name [v. 19]).

This prayer recalls some of Israel's great petitioners of the past, including Solomon, Hezekiah, and Jeremiah. King Solomon, who, like Daniel, identified himself as God's servant, marked the completion of the first temple with a dedication prayer that spoke of a time to come when exiles would pray *toward* the temple, asking for God's forgiveness (1 Kgs 8:28-30). When faced with Sennacherib's impending invasion, King Hezekiah of Judah used similar words to express his plea to God (2 Kgs 19:16-19) while praying in the temple. Jeremiah's prayer upon buying a field at Anathoth especially reveals the significance of Daniel's prayer. As a sign of his confidence in the future, Jeremiah redeems his cousin's field (despite the Babylonians' invasion), yet perhaps second-guessing his decision, he pours out his lament to God. As does Daniel, Jeremiah calls attention to the God who redeemed Israel from Egypt, a God who had "made yourself a name that continues to this very day" (Jer 32:20), and confesses the failures of the community in covenantal terms. Because of these sins, Jerusalem has suffered; yet this is not the last word. God responds and promises:

> See, I am going to gather them from all the lands to which I drove them in my anger and my wrath and in great indignation; I will bring them back to this place, and I will settle them in safety. They shall be my people, and I will be their God. I will give them one heart and one way, that they may fear me for all time, for their own good and the good of their children after them. I will make an everlasting covenant with them, never to draw back from doing good to them; and I will put the fear of me in their hearts, so that they may not turn from me. I will rejoice in doing good to them, and I will plant them in this land in faithfulness, with all my heart and all my soul. (Jer 32:37-41)

Just as Jeremiah believed in God's ultimate mercy and faithfulness to the covenant, so too did the author of Daniel. This author, however, had a problem that Jeremiah never had to face. How could the years of exile, promised to be limited to seventy, last so interminably? Surely the return of Jews to Judah under the policy of Cyrus of Persia could not be considered the end of exile, when at the time of the author's writing, the worst of Antiochus's oppression was so extensive that the temple had been, in effect, expropriated for another god! Thus, Daniel's prayer, set in the time of exile, truly becomes the prayer for the community of the author's day who sees a defiled temple that, in essence, belongs to the new Nebuchadnezzar—Antiochus.

Daniel's Individual Supplication and Gabriel's Appearance, 9:20-23

Just as God responded to Jeremiah's request (Jer 32:26-44), Daniel is privileged to receive a response from the angel Gabriel. Before this encounter is specified, however, the author draws attention to the importance of Daniel's intercessory role by the emphasis on his individual supplication (vv. 20, 21). Paul Redditt argues that in contrast to the portrait of Daniel seen in earlier chapters in the book, the prayer is the first time where Daniel confesses his sinfulness. The author inserts this prayer, therefore, to underscore the community's need to repent and to explain why God has not yet intervened. The author presents Daniel's confession as a model for what the community themselves must do—"turn fervently to God and confess its sinfulness."[12] Although the portrait of the confessing Daniel is unique, the earlier depiction of Daniel's humility, faith, and concern for his people allows the author to expand his paradigmatic role.

As is common in apocalyptic texts, an angel appears as God's spokesman. Gabriel (whose name means "man of God"), who was earlier introduced in the book of Daniel as having "the appearance of a man" (8:15), again appears as a man, thus linking the two visions. The author pauses to state that Daniel was "yet speaking," highlighting the connection between prayer and revelation. At the same time, it is clear that Daniel's prayer does not necessitate that Gabriel appear, as the angel states that a "word," or divine decree, was "sent forth" from the very beginning of Daniel's supplication. There is a textual problem in v. 21, allowing for two possible readings; either Gabriel came "swiftly" or "wearily." [Gabriel's Approach] It is significant that Gabriel arrives at the "time of the evening offering," as this suggests that just as God accepted the sacrifice of the Israelites when the temple was still standing, so too would Daniel's prayer be accepted. For the readers of Antiochus's day, the text indicates that prayer can still be acceptable even when Antiochus had proscribed certain rites and polluted the temple. Prayer transcends temple. [*minḥâ*]

Daniel soon learns that the revelation requires willingness on his part to see that Jeremiah's words may have another level of meaning. The author emphasizes that Daniel must be open to the words of the angel by the use of the terms "wisdom" (v. 22), "understand/understanding" (vv. 22, 23, 25), and "consider" (v. 23). The readers of the second century BC find that they, too, are in a similar position; like Daniel, they must see that the words are timeless and have new levels of meaning.

Gabriel Artwork

This 16th C. AD Russian icon of Gabriel expresses the link between God and humankind.

The Archangel Gabriel. Russian School. 16th C. AD. (Credit: R. G. Ojeda. Louvre, Paris, France. Réunion des Musées Nationaux/Art Resource, NY)

Gabriel's Approach

AΩ A textual difficulty in v. 21 allows for two possible readings. Either Gabriel approached Daniel "wearily" (*y'p*) or "in flight" (*'ûp*). Some commentators reject the idea that Gabriel would be described as being weary, yet "in flight" is a difficult reading as well because in the Hebrew Bible angels are not described as having wings. It is indeed the case that the heavenly creatures cherubim and seraphim (the supernatural guardians of the LORD's throne) are described as being winged (Exod 25:18-20; Isa 6:2), but angels, if described, are simply depicted as men. This text may, therefore, preserve the earliest equation of angels with the other winged heavenly creatures. Otherwise, the earliest text that shows winged angels is the *Similitudes of Enoch* 61:1 (c. 1st century BC).

John Collins, *Daniel: A Commentary on the Book of Daniel* (Hermeneia; Minneapolis: Fortress, 1993), 352.

Gabriel's Message, 9:24-27

The angel Gabriel offers Daniel a new interpretation of Jeremiah's words, showing a distinct understanding of the time required for the suffering of the exile. Although this new interpretation is given,

minḥâ

AΩ *minḥâ* may mean "cereal [grain] offering" or gift, usually in the context of a gift offered to the temple. As grain was an important economic commodity in Israel, it was a common gift to the priests in the temple. The cereal offering was a prepared mixture of fine flour, oil, and frankincense, shaped into loaves or wafers. It was presented at the altar along with the twice-daily burnt offering of a lamb (the *tāmîd*). Except for a small portion of dough that was completely burnt, solidifying the connection between God and the one presenting the offering, the flour mixture was cooked and was eaten by the priests. There is also some suggestion in later texts, including Dan 9:21, that perhaps the evening offering consisted of the grain offering alone (2 Kgs 16:15). According to the Talmud, the sacrifices in the Second Temple period were highly ritualized, accompanied by petitions, blessings, and scriptural readings.

In Jewish interpretation, sacrifice is understood as a way to approach God, showing humanity's dependence upon and obedience to God who is willing to accept humanity's offerings and forgive sin. After the destruction of the second temple (AD 70), the daily prayers are seen as a substitute for sacrifice, with an emphasis on the common spirituality between sacrifice and prayer. As H. H. Donin writes,

And since the times for prayer were synchronized with the biblically fixed times for the sacrificial offerings, the spiritual link between the two was strengthened. Faithful to a spirit in Judaism that was always striving for greater spirituality in man's relationship with God, one sage, Rabbi Elazar, declared rather unequivocally that "prayer is superior to sacrifices" (Berakhot 32b); and others taught that "if one is humble of spirit, the Torah credits him with having brought every offering to God" (Sanhedrin 43b).

Joseph Dan, "Sacrifice," *EncJud*, ed. Cecil Roth and Geoffrey Wigoder, 16 vols. (New York: Macmillan, 1971–72), 14:607–12.

Hayim Halevy Donin, *To Pray as a Jew* (New York: Basic Books, 1980), 11–12.

the cryptic words and phrases as well as the presentation as vision leave a veil of mystery. In contrast to Daniel's consideration of seventy *years*, the angel says that "seventy *weeks* are decreed" (v. 24). [Seventy Weeks in Traditional Jewish Interpretation] Commentators differ regarding the meaning of this cryptic phrase. Most understand that seventy weeks mean "seventy weeks of years," that is, seventy times seven—hence 490 years, with the time commencing sometime during the exile and ending sometime after the period of Antiochus. Possibilities for the beginning of the 490 years include 605 BC, when Judah capitulated to the Babylonian Empire; 597 BC, the date of the first deportation; 587 BC, the date of the destruction of the temple and the second deportation; 539 BC, the date of Cyrus's conquest of Babylon; or 517 BC, the date of the completion of the second temple.[13] This understanding of Jeremiah's prophecy (Jer 25:12) may be based upon the language of Leviticus (Lev 25:1-7; 26:31-35, 43), which suggests that the land will be desolate for seventy years to atone for the abuses of profaning the Sabbaths—abuses that lasted 490 years.[14] Because Leviticus 26 ends with an expectation that repentance will prompt God's mercy, this prayer in Daniel may well serve as a call to the community not to lose faith. [Leviticus 26] Other scholars understand both seventy and seven as symbolic numbers—seventy the symbolic number of years (a lifetime) of exile and seven the symbolic number for completion or multiplication. Jeremiah and the book of Chronicles refer to

Seventy Weeks in Traditional Jewish Interpretation

The sages understand that Darius began his reign just as the 70 years of Babylonian dominance of which Jeremiah spoke were completed. They understand that from the time Nebuchadnezzar conquered Jehoiakim (the beginning of the exile), until the end of his successors' (Evil Merodach and Belshazzar) reigns there were a total of 70 years. Although Belshazzar knew of the prophecy of 70 years, they argue, he mistakenly calculated that the years were completed. When he concluded that he was safely ensconced in power, he arrogantly concluded that God would not honor Jeremiah's prophecy that Babylon would come to its end. Hence, Belshazzar lacked no scruples in drinking from the temple vessels. This interpretation underscores Belshazzar's flagrant arrogance. Hersh Goldwurm explains that the sages

see this seemingly casual act of desecration as a meticulously calculated and premeditated act on the part of Belshazzar. . . . [When he concluded] that the seventy years had passed without the divinely promised return of the Jews . . . he felt that the Chaldean royal house had

finally triumphed over the God of the Jews, and therefore proceeded to desecrate the vessels of the temple without fear of retribution.

The 7 x 70, or 490 years, was understood by Rashi and Ibn Ezra to refer to the period from the destruction of the first temple by the Babylonians to the destruction of the second temple by Rome. The first period of 70 years refers to Babylonian exile itself and the remaining 420 years to the Second Temple period. Thus, various Roman references are understood to be indicated by the final week. The anointed one who is "cut off" (v. 26) may be King Agrippa II; the "people of a prince" (v. 26), who come to destroy Jerusalem, are understood to be the Roman army of Vespasian; the "desolations" refer to Titus's destruction of the city; and the detestable things (v. 27) refer to the idol Hadrian had set up in the temple.

Hersh Goldwurm, *Daniel: A New Translation with a Commentary Anthologized from Talmudic, Midrashic, and Rabbinic Sources* (ArtScroll Tanach Series; New York: Mesorah, 1979), 157–59. See also *b. Meg.* 11b.

Judah Slotki, *Daniel, Ezra, Nehemiah*, rev. ed., ed. Ephraim Oratz (London: Soncino, 1992), 77–79.

seventy years of exile, and seven is the number of times sin can be repaid. Thus, John Goldingay writes, "[the reference to 490 years] is not chronology but chronography: a stylized scheme of history used to interpret historical data rather than arising from them, comparable to cosmology, arithmology and genealogy as these appear in writing such as the OT."[15] Despite these differences in understanding whether the author of Daniel gives symbolic or specific demarcations of time, most modern commentators understand that a portion of the author's references did, in fact, apply to the period of Antiochus's persecution. We now turn to some of the most important features and symbols of this vision.

The angel divides the seventy weeks into four periods of importance: seven weeks, sixty-two weeks, one week, and half of the one week. Before the angel details the four periods,

Leviticus 26

Michael Fishbane shows that the prayer of Dan 9 reinterprets the prophecy of Jeremiah's 70 years (Jer 25:9-12) as well as the requirements of praying for the remission of sins and the cessation of sabbatical cycles, including the desolation of the sanctuary and of their land (Lev 26). Just as the author of Leviticus admonishes the community that if they confess their sins God will forgive them and the desolation of the land, so too does Daniel's prayer follow the same sequence. Because of this interpretation of Jeremiah's prophecy and of the admonitions of Lev 26, Fishbane concludes, "The key purpose of Daniel's prayer was not solely to suggest that old curses had been fulfilled. It was also to emphasize the more hopeful side of Lev 26, which announced the repentance that could terminate the severe decree."

Michael Fishbane, *Biblical Interpretation in Ancient Israel* (Oxford: Clarendon, 1985), 488–89.

he expresses the overall significance of the "seventy weeks" (or "seventy sevens") in the capsule statement of v. 24: the end of sin and suffering ("to finish the transgression, to put an end to sin, and to atone for iniquity"), and the presence of holiness on earth ("to bring in everlasting righteousness, to seal both vision and prophet, and to anoint a most holy place"). The emphasis on the cessation of sin, as John Collins states, is "the idea that evil must run its course until the appointed time"—an apocalyptic image found also in Daniel 12:4.[16] The phrase "to seal both vision and prophet" indicates the trustworthiness of the meaning of the vision, as affixing one's seal to a document was done by someone in authority to attest to its validity.[17] Hence, this image adds to the authority of the vision, even though its mysterious nature is undeniable. The "everlasting righteousness" harkens back to God's righteousness (v. 7), and the anointing of a most holy place refers to the temple, which, as seen in Daniel 8:13-14, has been desecrated. Just as the holy objects of the sanctuary were anointed when the sacrificial system was codified, so too would the temple and the holy objects once again be dedicated for worship when the period of defilement by Israel's conquerors was over. Because the audience of Antiochus's time knew of the emperor's proscription of sacrifice, which was the very vehicle of atonement, and because the length of exile and its suffering seemed interminable to the community, this verse serves as an important harbinger of hope. The members of the community were encouraged to remember that the covenantal promises were eternal.

The first period of time, identified as seven weeks, reflects the Babylonian exile, when Jerusalem was destroyed, the temple razed, and its services ended. Various people have been suggested for the "anointed prince," a term that can refer to either political or spiritual leaders, as both kings and priests were anointed. Possibilities include Cyrus, the Persian emperor who allowed Jews to return to Judah; Zerubbabel, the governor of Judah under Persian rule; or

Seals

Seals, small pieces of stone or baked clay etched with engravings, were used to imprint writing and designs on wet clay or wax. Shaped in the form of cylinders or stamps, their distinctive marks include representations of gods, animals, and common objects. They were affixed to documents and goods, attesting to the object's authenticity or providing a signature. They may also have been used as amulets. This 6th century BC stone seal shows a farmer reaping with a sickle.

Seal showing a man harvesting with a sickle. 6th C. BC. Reuben & Edith Hecht Collection, Haifa University, Haifa, Israel. (Credit: Erich Lessing/Art Resource, NY)

Joshua, the first high priest of the restored temple.[18] [Cyrus, Zerubbabel, and Joshua the High Priest]

The majority of the angel's explanation is devoted to the second era, or sixty-two weeks, characterized by multiple references to turmoil. Although the rebuilding of Jerusalem was welcomed news, and although the description of the reconstruction of its "street and moat" may be an indication of the extent of its reconstruction, there could be no rejoicing in this rebuilding, as the description is tempered by the adversative phrase, "but in a troubled time" (v. 25).[19] The reference to the cutting off of "an anointed one" most likely refers to the anointed high priest Onias III, who was ousted by Jason and later murdered on the orders of Menelaus (2 Macc 4:34-38).[20] Mostly likely, the "prince to come," whose troops "destroy the city and the sanctuary," refers to Antiochus (2 Macc 4–5), and the reference to the soldiers who attack the sanctuary may refer to Antiochus's massacres and plundering of the temple upon his return from a campaign in Egypt in 169 BC, or to his second assault on the temple in 167 BC (1 Macc 1:29-35).[21] But just as quickly as his violence is noted, so too is his end: it comes "with a flood," an apparent reference to God's defeat of Israel's adversaries.[22]

The revelations concerning the final week are devoted to the specifics of this prince who makes "a strong covenant with many," a reference to the Hellenizers who supported Antiochus's attempts to incorporate Greek cultural values into Jewish practices (1 Macc 1:1-11).[23] The cessation of sacrifice is the least cryptic reference in the angel's explanation, referring to the worst days of Antiochus's persecutions and proscription of Jewish practice. The "abomination that desolates" (v. 27; cf. 8:13) indicates the idol or idolatrous altar that Antiochus set up in the temple, yet the last words of the explanation make certain that its time is limited. The passive construction of the phrase, "until the decreed end is poured out upon the desolator" (v. 27) underscores the author's view that God's victory is determined in advance, just as the ages of the four sequential kingdoms were determined. [The Decreed End] Because the angel's explanation ends abruptly, with no indication of his departure or of Daniel's response, this decreed end remains the final image of the vision. The reader is left with this image of the ultimate defeat of evil (Antiochus); at the same time, the lack of any

Cyrus, Zerubbabel, and Joshua the High Priest

Cyrus II (ruled 539–530 BC), the emperor of Persia whose policy of repatriation allowed Jews to return to Judah, was praised by Second Isaiah as the Lord's anointed (Isa 45:1-3). Various roles are ascribed to Zerubbabel, a descendant of David. He is named as a recipient who (along with Joshua) received the prophet Haggai's word to rebuild the temple, the leader of a group of returnees, and the governor of Judah (Hag 1:1, Ezra 2:2; 3:2, 8; 4:2, 3). Joshua the High Priest served at the time of the beginning of the construction of the second temple (Hag 1-2; Zech 3:1-9; 6:11).

The Decreed End

AΩ The phrase "decreed end" (*kālâ wĕneḥĕrāṣâ*) is reminiscent of language found in Isaiah that stresses that despite the horror of invasions and defeat, God is yet in charge of history: "Destruction is decreed, overflowing with righteousness. For the LORD God of hosts will make a full end, as decreed, in all the earth" (Isa 10:22-23; see also 28:22).

This "decreed end" will be "poured out" (*tittak*)—a verb that connotes God exercising judgment: "Therefore, thus says the LORD God: My anger and my wrath shall be poured out on this place, on human beings and animals, on the trees of the field and the fruit of the ground: it will burn and not be quenched" (Jer 7:20; see also 42:18; 44:6).

Judah Slotki, *Daniel, Ezra, Nehemiah*, rev. ed., ed. Ephraim Oratz (Soncino Books of the Bible; London: Soncino, 1992), 79.

James A. Montgomery, *A Critical and Exegetical Commentary on the Book of Daniel*, (ICC; Edinburgh: T. & T. Clark, 1927), 365.

statement of rejoicing is typical of apocalyptic literature, reflecting the entrenched difficulties of the besieged community.

CONNECTIONS

Daniel's prayer reflects the deep-seated belief that God has created a world in which the deeds of humankind are seen by a righteous God who ensures that justice will have the final say. Israel's teachings and traditions had well prepared the author of Daniel to express this confidence in the purposefulness of God's creation, despite the frustrations, sufferings, and disappointments of protracted foreign rule. The cornerstones of Daniel's prayer, namely, the righteousness of God, God's willingness to listen to petition, and the continuing significance of the temple—even when it is held captive—attest to essential truths. Despite the loss of the sacrificial system and the subjugation by an often cruel regime, the prayer shows confidence in God's faithfulness and expresses trust in the ability of the community to live holy, just, and purposeful lives. This confidence in the importance of the temple and the continuing relationship between God and the people in the time of the Antiochan assault previews the same continuing significance of the ideal temple even after the second temple was destroyed by the Romans.

The holiness of the temple and the intimacy it affords God and humanity have their roots in the tabernacle traditions of Sinai. The tabernacle, the precursor to the temple, was a tangible sign that God's purpose for Israel was not only to be found in its settlement of the land, but also in the sanctification of the people and their communion with God, as occurred in its sacred space. There the world could truly become a dwelling place for God. The service of the tabernacle offered the divine eternal presence. At the tabernacle, the people experienced the idealized form of what the world could be—a place of God's immanent presence, a place where the goodness and purpose of creation could be experienced, and a place where the community's commitment to following God's commandments was proclaimed. It was also a place of divine forgiveness—where God accepted atoning sacrifices and where the community could be reconciled with God and with each other.

In ancient Israel, the priests served the sanctuary (and later, the temple) in order to assist the entire congregation to be "a kingdom of priests and a holy nation"—a people bound by the covenant to live as God intends. The building of this transformed world was to take place not only in the present, but in the idealized future. This eschatological ideal would be a world filled with justice, where people would be respected as the living image of God, would willingly do God's bidding, and would live in harmony with the created world, in peace. In addition to the priests, who retain the distinction of ministering to the LORD in prayer and sacrifice, the people have a role in the divine service as well. Psalm 101:6, for example, shows that whoever is faithful, keeping the commandments, ministers to God (Ps 101:6). The eschatological hope for all people is that when foreigners keep the commandments, they, too, please God with their ministry (Isa 56:6). Not only foreign individuals, but also their kings and even their flocks will be accepted as sacrifice and thus "minister to God" (Isa 60:7, 10). The theology of the temple continued the ideal of the tabernacle. Instead of the portable shrine, God's presence would be found in the holy abode of God in the holy city of Jerusalem. As Jon Levenson states: "The temple is the world as it ought to be. It is a world in which God's reign is unthreatened, and his justice is manifest, in which life is peaceful and every Israelite is without blemish."[24] From the temple, God's blessings and grace would go forth not only to Israel, but to the entire world.

Daniel's prayer, set in the exilic period bereft of the temple, served as a model of faith not only during the era of Antiochus, but also previews a crucial rabbinic teaching presented in the aftermath of the destruction of the second temple. The literary setting of Daniel's prayer, the exile, was a time when the first temple lay in ruins, and the historical setting of the prayer, the years of the Antiochan persecutions, both reveal a striking faith: the intimacy and constancy of the people's relationship with God endure even when sacrifice and the temple no longer exist. The obedience to the commandments, living a life of pursuing justice, and doing good deeds are inherently holy and meaningful. This spiritual reality is not destroyed by the absence of the holy space of the temple.

These beliefs became a crucially important feature in Judaism during the first through fifth centuries AD. After the destruction of the second temple, the sacrificial system ceased, thousands of Jews were killed or sold into slavery, and Jews were barred from living in Jerusalem. Yet the loss of an institution as important as the temple did not end the belief in the permanent connection between God and the Jewish people, whose lives were infused with the holiness that was so apparent within the temple walls. This holiness now moved from the temple to the home and community, where everyday actions afforded the faithful the opportunity to live in the manner of a priest. Specific examples include the holiness of the family table, where the keeping of the dietary laws and the recitation of blessings mirrored the sacrifices of the temple; the keeping of the Sabbath, where Israel could imitate God's own action; the holiness of marriage, where the following of the laws of family purity ensured that procreation was sacred; the careful compliance with ethical business and agricultural law which ensured justice; and the giving of charity, where all members of the community cared for the poorest among them. These practices, to be sure, did not begin only when the second temple was destroyed, but they received a new emphasis, showing that the truth of the temple, the place whence God's teachings would go forth, transcended the temple's materiality. The temple provided the paradigm that the world could become perfect as the place of God's dwelling. Judaism's emphasis on living a holy life by following the commandments in all things, both "spiritual" and "material" shows that these two worlds of transcendence and imminence can become one. [Everyday Holiness]

In Christian teaching as well, the significance of the temple and its model of holiness continue. Thomas Dozeman shows how the Christian faith similarly gives guidelines "to recognize the progression of holiness from the sanctuary into the larger world."[25] Once, the Israelite priest served as the mediator of God's holiness to the community at large; now the ordained minister or priest leads the way for Christians to bring the experience of the holiness of the sacraments and of worship into the broader world. The priests of old exercised leadership and authority in offering sacrifice and prayer, in management and protection of the sanctuary, and in teaching and healing. All of these acts served to bind the people with God and to help them to remain God's people "set apart." The legacy of these teachings about the mediation of the priests, the holiness of the sanctuary, and the covenantal response of the people of Israel serve the Christian community as well. The Gospel of Mark shows, for example, that the proclamation of Jesus is "about the descent of holiness into our world," and Hebrews presents Jesus as the high

Everyday Holiness

Jacob Neusner details the way in which the roots of the rabbinic emphasis on holiness are found in the biblical presentation of the temple cult:

Israel, which was holy, ate holy food, reproduced itself in accord with the laws of holiness, and conducted all of its affairs, both affairs of state and the business of the table and the land, in accord with the demands of holiness. . . . So the Torah stood for life, and the covenant with the Lord would guarantee life and the way of life required sanctification in the here and now of the natural world.

Jacob Neusner, *An Introduction to Judaism* (Louisville KY: Westminster/John Knox, 1991), 154.

priest who mediates "this holiness through his priestly vocation" (Heb 4:14-5:10).[26] In the church, both the ordained ministers, who perform the sacraments, and the laity, who share in the priesthood of Christ, serve as a beacon for its ethical mission. Dozeman concludes,

We will know that holiness is infiltrating our larger world when we are purged of malice and envy (1 Pet 2), when we live and interact with others through love, not hate (1 Pet 3), and, especially, when we willingly absorb violence through suffering as an antidote to the contagion of sin (1 Pet 4).[27] [1 Peter]

In forming concerned communities that complete acts of righteousness, people become partners with God in the repair and redemption of the world. The legacy of the sanctuary and temple, the holiest of spaces on earth, continues to represent the hope for a future transformed earth, here and in the world to come.

1 Peter

Richard Nelson provides an excellent analysis of the social location and purpose of 1 Peter. He concludes,

[The readers of 1 Peter] are to understand and reevaluate the present in terms of the Christ story, their own biography of salvation, the will of God, and the prospect of coming judgment. What was true of chosen Israel is now true of them . . . they are being formed into a priesthood typified by Spirit, life, and holiness. As a body of priests, they are challenged with the priestly responsibilities of proclamation and sacrifice. . . . Neither ritual prerogatives nor individual privileges are in view, but the shared election, holiness, and responsibilities of the whole people of God.

Richard Nelson, *Raising Up a Faithful Priest: Community and Priesthood in Biblical Theology* (Louisville KY: Westminster/John Knox, 1993), 168.

NOTES

[1] Gerald Wilson, "The Prayer of Daniel 9: Reflection on Jeremiah 29," JSOT 48 (1990): 91–99.

[2] John Muddiman, "Fast, Fasting," *ABD*, ed. David Noel Freedman, 6 vols. (New York: Doubleday & Co., 1992), 2:773–76.

[3] Francis Brown, S. R. Driver, and C. A. Briggs, *"ydh," Hebrew and English Lexicon of the Old Testament* (Oxford: Clarendon Press, 1962), 392.

[4] Louis Hartman and Alexander Di Lella, *The Book of Daniel* (AB 23; Garden City NY: Doubleday, 1978), 244–45. See also Louis Ginsberg, *Studies in Daniel* (Texts and Studies of the Jewish Theological Seminary of America; New York: The Jewish Theological Seminary of America, 1948), 33.

[5] John Collins, *Daniel: A Commentary on the Book of Daniel* (Hermeneia; Minneapolis: Fortress, 1993), 347–48; Paul Redditt, "Daniel 9: Its Structure and Meaning," *CBQ* 62 (2002): 236–49.

[6] Mark Boda, "The Priceless Gain of Penitence: From Communal Lament to Penitential Prayer in the 'Exilic' Liturgy of Israel," *Horizons in Biblical Theology* 25 (2003): 51–75; Boda, *Praying the Tradition: The Origin and Use of Tradition in Nehemiah 9* (Beihefte zur Zeitschrift für die alttestamentliche Wissenschaft 277; Berlin: Walter de Gruyter, 1999). For additional studies on the origin and function of penitential prayer, see *The Origins of Penitential Prayer in Second Temple Judaism*, vol. 1 of *Seeking the Favor of God*, Mark Boda, Daniel Falk, and Rodney Werline, eds. (SBLEJL 21),

Atlanta/Leiden: Society of Biblical Literature/Brill, 2006, and *The Development of Penitential Prayer in Second Temple Judaism*, vol. 2 of *Seeking the Favor of God*, Mark Boda, Daniel Falk, and Rodney Werline, eds. (SBLEJL 22), Atlanta/Leiden: Society of Biblical Literature/Brill, 2007.

[7] Boda, "The Priceless Gain," 52–56.

[8] Ibid.; Boda, *Praying the Tradition*, 41.

[9] Boda, *Praying the Tradition*, 54.

[10] See [Deuteronomic Language].

[11] Boda, "The Priceless Gain," 53.

[12] Redditt, "Daniel 9: Its Structure and Meaning," 244, 249.

[13] John Goldingay, *Daniel* (WBC 30; Dallas: Word Books 1989), 231.

[14] Ibid., 231.

[15] Ibid., 257.

[16] John Collins, *Daniel*, 354.

[17] Paul Redditt, *Daniel* (New Century Bible Commentary; Sheffield England: Sheffield Academic Press, 1999), 161.

[18] Hartman and Di Lella, *Daniel*, 251.

[19] James Montgomery, *The Book of Daniel* (ICC; Edinburgh: T. & T. Clark), 380.

[20] Donald Gowan, *Daniel* (Abingdon Old Testament Commentaries; Nashville: Abingdon, 2001), 135. See our discussion in ch. 8.

[21] Hartman and Di Lella, *Daniel*, 252.

[22] See Nahum 1:8. Judah Slotki, *Daniel, Ezra, Nehemiah*, rev. ed. by Ephraim Oratz (Soncino Books of the Bible; London: Soncino Press, 1992), 79.

[23] John Collins, *Daniel*, 357.

[24] Jon Levenson, "The Jerusalem Temple," in *Jewish Spirituality: From the Bible to the Middle Ages*, ed. Arthur Green (World Spirituality 13; New York: Crossroad, 1994), 53.

[25] Thomas Dozeman, "The Priestly Vocation," *Int* 59/2 (2005): 128.

[26] Ibid., 127.

[27] Ibid., 128.

AN ETERNAL HOPE

Daniel 10:1–12:13

COMMENTARY

The previous visions of the book of Daniel reflect the community's preoccupations with the terrible sufferings it has experienced because of the rise of Antiochus IV, his persecutions, the destruction of holy sacrificial rites, and the prohibition of everyday Jewish practice. These visions shed light on why such horrors were occurring, for with all their impenetrable unknowns, they too are part of God's plan for Israel. God allows Daniel to see the very throne room of heaven and to hear conversations of angels in order to shed light in such times of extreme distress, persecution, and sorrow.

Daniel's final vision, concerning conflicting kingdoms (Daniel 10:1–12:13), is the last he receives. It confirms that history's epochs are designed by God and that Antiochus's ascendancy is actually a harbinger of the defeat of the sequence of oppressive kingdoms. Ultimately showing that good triumphs and that the holy people of faith will receive God's kingdom, its details of the territorial advances and political posturing of the Seleucid and Ptolemaic kingdoms underscore that even in the minute details of political life, God's plan for justice in the world unfolds inexorably. The specifics of the successes and failures of so many leaders show that no avenue of history can take priority over God's design; no human action, in the final scheme of things, has definitive power or significance. Moreover, God's plan for humanity and justice in the world has a further dimension for, as the vision shows, God's final judgment and resurrection of the righteous forge an eternal hope.

[Outline of Daniel 10:1–12:13]

Prelude to the Vision, 10:1-4

Daniel relates that his vision occurs in "the third year of King Cyrus," recalling the earlier identification of his governmental service, which lasted to the first year of Cyrus's reign (Dan 6:28 [6:29 MT]). Placing the vision in the period of Cyrus reminds the reader of the end of Persia's precursors, Babylon and Media, thus forming an appropriate background for the content of the vision. Just as Babylon and Media's great wealth and power could not stop God's plan for their downfall, so too will Persia's rule, the venue of the seer's day, and the Seleucid kingdom, the very setting of the composition of this vision, come to their demise.

Before the reader hears Daniel's own words, the author of the vision establishes its truth (10:1). This confirmation serves to underscore the authority of the revelation as well as the solace it can give during the difficult times the community faces. The vision is identified as concerning a great "conflict" (*ṣābāʾ*, v. 1), a term that can refer to a heavenly army, to war, or to a time of service. The choice of this word suggests that the author shares with Second Isaiah a sympathetic portrayal of the community's plight: "Speak tenderly to Jerusalem, and cry to her that she has served her term [*ṣābāʾ*], that her penalty is paid, that she has received from the LORD's hand double for all her sins" (Isa 40:2).

As does Second Isaiah, the author of the vision shifts the focus from the sins that prompted exile to the confirmation that the end of suffering is at hand. Various references in this prelude to the vision recall elements of Daniel's life as an exile and at the same time portray the community's life experience as analogous to the prophet's own. Daniel's slave name, Belteshazzar, given to him by Nebuchadnezzar, is used once again (10:1). Although the description of Daniel's life at the time of this vision is brief, it is stark and sad. Switching to the first person, the author shows in Daniel's own words that he was "mourning for three weeks" (10:2). The reason for the mourning is not specified, adding to the mystery of the scene and drawing the reader's sympathy to Daniel's feeling of sorrow. [Mourning Customs] Indeed, the term used here for "mourning" (*mitʾabbēl*) is reminiscent of the lament for Jerusalem (Isa 66:10), appropriate both for the exile Daniel as well as for the readers who lived through Antiochus's desecra-

Mourning Customs

In the Hebrew Bible, personal mourning in response to the death of a relative is marked by the following: the wearing of sackcloth, rending one's garments (Gen 37:34), refraining from self-anointing (Isa 61:3), donning of ashes, shaving one's head (Job 1:20) or cutting one's hair (Mic 1:16). Not all presentations in the Hebrew Bible are identical, however, and certain practices referred to in one text may be forbidden in another (Lev 19:27-28). It is interesting to note that in speaking of the devastation of Jerusalem, Jeremiah states, "No one shall break bread for the mourner, to offer comfort for the dead; nor shall anyone give them the cup of consolation to drink for their fathers or their mothers" (Jer 16:7). Perhaps Daniel's actions of abstaining from bread and wine indicate that he cannot be comforted. Times of national catastrophe are also marked by mourning practices, such as fasting and rending of garments; for example, Mordecai fasts upon learning of Haman's murderous designs (Esth 4:3).

L. Schiffman, "Mourning Rites," *Harper's Bible Dictionary*, ed. Paul Achtemeier (San Francisco: Harper & Row, 1985), 661–62.

tions of Jerusalem and its temple. Indeed, as 1 Maccabees reports, Antiochus's proscription of Sabbath observance and the offering of sacrifices devastated Jerusalem and its people:

> Her sanctuary became desolate like a desert;
> her feasts were turned into mourning,
> her sabbaths into a reproach,
> her honor into contempt. (1 Macc 1:39)

Daniel's period of mourning is marked by elements often associated with the preparation of a vision, namely, fasting and the refraining from anointing. These actions recollect Daniel's experience as a newly captured servant in Nebuchadnezzar's palace when the king proposed that Daniel eat the king's food. In that instance, Daniel's refusal to eat led to his triumph over the king's looming threat that he disavow his faith. Here, Daniel's fasting and self-affliction prepare him to receive the vision, which, in turn, allows him to endure his trials. Daniel explains that his fasting continued for three weeks during the first month, that is, the month of Nisan. Daniel's refusal to eat any "rich food" or, literally, "bread of pleasantness" (10:3) occurs in the period of the Passover, whose hallmark is the "bread of affliction."[1] By linking Daniel's mourning with the Passover, the author suggests that perhaps only another redemption, as powerful as God's victory over Pharaoh during the exodus, would end these forbidding times. Indeed, Daniel's self-imposed test appears as a unique Passover that will climax in the promise given at the end of this vision, namely, that "many of those who sleep in the dust of the earth shall awake, some to everlasting life" (12:2). [The Month of Nisan]

The Month of Nisan

Nisan, previously known as Aviv, was the first month of the calendar, falling in March–April. In the book of Esther, the month of Nisan—a time when Jews should be preparing for or celebrating the Passover—proved to be most ominous. During that month, the villain Haman cast the lot to determine which day would be most propitious for his proposed genocide of Jews. The lot fell on the 15th of Adar, the twelfth month. The people had a year to wait to see what would happen with this horrific plan (Esth 3:7).

The setting of Daniel's vision is located on the "the Great River," here equated with the "Tigris" (10:4), recalling visions of other heroes whose dramas occurred at a river, thus highlighting the significance of his experience.[2] Parallel settings include Jacob at the Jabbok (Gen 32:24-32), Ezekiel at the Cheber (Ezek 1:1), and Daniel himself at the Ulai (Dan 8:2). The allusion to Ezekiel's experience is most suggestive here, as Daniel will soon use symbols that are also employed by Ezekiel in recounting his heavenly vision.

The Man Clothed in Linen: Description and Response, 10:5-10

The author indicates the drama and importance of the revelation by portraying the extraordinary features of the man clothed in

I Was by the Great River Hidekel

Partly funded by his artwork based on biblical themes, William J. Blackmon (b. 1921), a Milwaukee, Wisconsin, social justice advocate and artist, opened a self-help agency and food pantry. His paintings illustrate not only his commitment to preach the importance of keeping the command-

William J. Blackmon. *The Great River Hidekel*. (Photo courtesy of Paul Phelps)

ments, but also show a deeply felt compassion for the plight of impoverished and struggling African Americans. This painting is based on Daniel's vision by the river (Dan 10:4).

linen, the trembling of Daniel's associates, and Daniel's own personal reaction. The imagery used for the man clothed in linen identifies him as an angel. Ezekiel's visions of heavenly beings as well as the descriptions of holy objects for the sanctuary provide the sources for most of the visual imagery for this heavenly being. Linen and gold are used to describe the clothing and belt that adorn him, followed by analogous descriptions of beryl, lightning, flaming torches, and polished bronze for his appearance (10:5-6). Linen is the fabric worn by Israelite priests as well as by God's heavenly executioners in Ezekiel's vision (Exod 28:42; Ezek 9:11). A unique phrase for gold is found here—the "gold" (*kĕtĕm*) of Uphaz. The more common word for gold, *zāhāv*, is used in a similar expression in Jeremiah 10:9, where the "gold (*zāhāv*) of Uphaz" refers to the purest gold of the wealthy nations that flaunt their riches before God. Unlike Jeremiah, however, who uses the term to scold the nations, the author of Daniel underscores the preciousness of the metal with this unusual phrase. Beryl, which may correspond to topaz or aquamarine, is one of the stones found in the breastplate of Aaron, and it is also used to describe the color of the wheels of the heavenly creatures in Ezekiel (Exod 28:20; Ezek 1:16). For the use of lightning and flaming torches, Ezekiel provides the best context:

> In the middle of the living creatures there was something that looked like burning coals of fire, like torches moving to and fro among the living creatures; the fire was bright, and lightning issued from the fire. The living creatures darted to and fro, like a flash of lightning. (Ezek 1:13-14)

Similarly, just as Daniel's heavenly visitor has "arms and legs like the gleam of burnished bronze" (10:5), so too do Ezekiel's heavenly beings have "[feet that] sparkled like burnished bronze" (Ezek 1:7). In addition, descriptions of bronze objects are found in the listings of various holy objects in the tabernacle, including the altar, laver, utensils, and mirrors. The use of this imagery, clearly associated with the heavenly beings of Ezekiel and with the holiest of objects of the sanctuary, creates an awesome scene that portends its revelatory significance. This one clothed in linen joins the other angels in the book of Daniel who are sent to explain to Daniel the mysteries of current suffering as well as to offer future hope.

Beside the description that appeals to the sense of sight, the auditory reference adds to the comprehensiveness of the experience. Daniel hears a voice "like the roar of a multitude" (10:6), a description that parallels this account from Ezekiel: "When they [the cherubim] moved, I heard the sound of their wings like the sound of mighty waters, like the thunder of the Almighty, a sound of tumult like the sound of an army; when they stopped, they let down their wings" (Ezek 1:24). [The Sound of Revelation] These words capture the ominous nature of what is ultimately an indescribable scene.

Once the visual and auditory descriptions have been given, the reader next sees the reaction of others who are now mentioned for the first time. Even though these unnamed persons who accompany Daniel did not see the vision, it was so awesome that it prompted them to flee and hide. Daniel's own courage is underscored by this detail, for if these companions who did not even witness the vision have fled in fear, how much more terrifying is the appearance of the angel to Daniel. Indeed, Daniel's own response is described with terms that not only connote dread, but also death (10:8). Daniel's falling into a trance recalls his earlier experience (8:18) as well as the ecstatic phenomena of others who receive crucially important revelations, including Abraham (Gen 15:12), Balaam (Num 24:4, 16), and Ezekiel (Ezek 1:28; 3:15, 26). Daniel's plight is addressed neither with additional awesome sights nor arresting sounds, but from the realm of touch; Daniel feels "a hand" (10:10) rousing him. The identity of the one to whom the hand belongs is not specified, adding to the mystery of the experi-

---

The Sound of Revelation

John's vision of the Son of Man includes this description of the sound of his voice, similar to Ezekiel's description of the sound of the heavenly beings: "his feet were like burnished bronze, refined as in a furnace, and his voice was like the sound of many waters" (Rev 1:15). In addition to these images of heavenly beings in Ezekiel and the Son of Man, Ps 29 depicts the God of Israel as having a voice that defies description.

> The voice of the LORD flashes forth flames of fire.
> The voice of the LORD shakes the wilderness; the LORD shakes the wilderness of Kadesh.
> The voice of the LORD causes the oaks to whirl, and strips the forest bare; and in his temple all say, "Glory!" (Ps 29:7-9; see also Exod 19:19; Deut 5:22-26 [5:18-22 MT])

Daniel's trembling reaction as well as the compassionate reassurance of the angel parallel the caring assistance that the angel Uriel gives to the seer in 2 Esdras (end of 1st century AD). The text reads:

"At that time people shall hope but not obtain; they shall labor, but their ways shall not prosper. These are the signs that I am permitted to tell you, and if you pray again, and weep as you do now, and fast for seven days, you shall hear yet greater things than these." Then I woke up, and my body shuddered violently, and my soul was so troubled that it fainted. But the angel who had come and talked with me held me and strengthened me and set me on my feet. (2 Esdr 5:12-15)

As is Daniel, the seer of 2 Esdras is sorely distressed over what has happened to his people. He fasts and mourns, prays and weeps, trembles and faints, but, like Daniel, he is comforted by the angel sent by the God who compassionately responds to his grief. Despite the mysteriousness of the one who comforts and addresses Daniel, what is unambiguous is that this heavenly visitor directly addresses Daniel's suffering, attesting that God has not abandoned him in his fear. The revelation that Daniel is about to witness will give meaning to the community's experience of the frightful events of their past and present.

ence, although the context suggests it is the man clothed in linen (10:5). Scholars debate whether this heavenly figure is best understood as unidentified, or whether it should be equated with either God or with Gabriel.[3] Because this "man clothed in linen" still appears to be the antecedent for the one who was "sent" (10:11) and "the one in human form" (10:16-18), it does not seem possible that God is indicated, as these phrases would be inappropriate. Although identification with Gabriel is possible because of his presence in the immediately preceding vision (9:21), the man clothed in linen does appear again at the end of this vision, called by the same appellation (12:6). Therefore, it seems best to see the identification as deliberately mysterious. [The Angel Uriel in 2 Esdras]

The Exchange between the Heavenly Visitor and Daniel, 10:11–11:1

The man clothed in linen affords Daniel what the vision will provide to the community: confirmation that God loves him just as God hears the cry of the people. The heavenly visitor first makes clear that his words of reassurance ultimately come from God, stating to Daniel, "For I have now been sent to you" (10:11). The exchange between Daniel and the angel revolves around the following repeated images: the celestial touch, which allows Daniel to stand (10:11, 16, 18) and to speak (10:17, 19); the words of the angel who gives a message of comfort (10:11, 12, 19) and of purpose ("pay attention" [10:11]; "understand" [10:12, 14]); the threat from the Prince of Persia and the Prince of Greece (10:13, 20); and the introduction to Michael (10:13, 21). During this exchange, Daniel finds courage, moving from his silent paralysis to his expression of fear, to his willingness to listen. Once Daniel states that he will listen, the angel confirms that his are words of truth.

The encounter with the angel continues to be so overwhelming that Daniel falls a second time (10:15) and is again strengthened by the angel (10:16), repeating the action found in v. 10. This time, the angel touches Daniel's lips, allowing the prophet to be strengthened for the difficult task of delivering God's message (cf. Isa 6:6). Upon receiving the angel's touch, Daniel is able to stand, yet he still trembles. Daniel is now composed enough to speak; his words, however, are solely words of defeat: "My lord, because of the vision such pains [literally, "my pains"] have come upon me that I retain no strength. How can my lord's servant talk with my lord? For I am shaking, no strength remains in me, and no breath is left in me" (10:16-17). With these brief words, Daniel twice relates that he is powerless. [Response to a Vision] The reference to "my pains" (*ṣîray*) is particularly poignant, as it is used both of a woman in labor (1 Sam 4:19) and of Isaiah's response to a vision:

Response to a Vision

This image of an extreme physical response in the face of revelation is also found in the book of Acts. While on the road to Damascus, Saul has a vision of Jesus, rendering him totally helpless: "Saul got up from the ground, and though his eyes were open, he could see nothing; so they [the fellow travelers] led him by the hand and brought him into Damascus. For three days he was without sight, and neither ate nor drank" (Acts 9:8-9; see also 22:11).

> Therefore my loins are filled with anguish; pangs [*ṣîrîm*] have seized me, like the pangs of a woman in labor; I am bowed down so that I cannot hear, I am dismayed so that I cannot see. My mind reels, horror has appalled me; the twilight I longed for has been turned for me into trembling. (Isa 21:3-4)[4]

Just as Isaiah's anguish is followed by horror, trembling, and the loss of his physical senses, so, too, do Daniel's references to "shaking" and having "no breath" provide a harrowing scene. Because he questions why the angel deigns to speak to one who is so crushed by fear, Daniel's upcoming words of courage are all the more arresting (10:19).

Throughout this encounter, the man clothed in linen continues his compassionate response to Daniel by his touch and by his words. Because he confirms that God hears Daniel's words, the scene is similar to the vision in Daniel 9, in which God responded to Daniel's prayer with the words of the angel Gabriel. The heavenly visitor's announcement to Daniel, "do not fear" (10:12, 19), is reminiscent of words of reassurance found in visions, oracles of salvation, or in a priest's response to a person's lament.[5] [Raphael's Reassurance in the Book of Tobit] When these words are spoken the second time (10:19), coupled with the phrase, "be strong and courageous," God's reassurance to Joshua is recalled: "I hereby command you: Be strong and courageous; do not be frightened or

Raphael's Reassurance in the Book of Tobit

The angel Raphael, whose name means "God heals," provides great comfort to Tobit and Tobias, who, like Daniel, are overwhelmed by seeing an angel: "'I am Raphael, one of the seven angels who stand ready and enter before the glory of the Lord.' The two of them were shaken; they fell face down, for they were afraid. But he said to them, 'Do not be afraid; peace be with you. Bless God forevermore'" (Tob 12:15-17).

To Humble and to Afflict Oneself

AΩ As James Montgomery shows, the verb "to humble oneself" (*lĕhitʿannôt*; Dan 10:12) is found in poetic parallelism with "deny oneself" in Ezra and is used as a technical term to refer to fasting. The following texts are relevant: "Then I proclaimed a fast there, at the river Ahava, that we might deny ourselves [*lĕhitʿannôt*] before our God, to seek from him a safe journey for ourselves, our children, and all our possessions" (Ezra 8:21). In Leviticus, it is used of the fast on Yom Kippur: "This shall be a statute to you forever: In the seventh month, on the tenth day of the month, you shall deny yourselves [*tĕʿannû*] and shall do no work, neither the citizen nor the alien who resides among you" (Lev 16:29).

James Montgomery, *A Critical and Exegetical Commentary on The Book of Daniel* (ICC; Edinburgh: T. & T. Clark, 1927), 411.

dismayed, for the LORD your God is with you wherever you go" (Josh 1:9; see also Deut 20:1; Josh 11:6). Indeed, the allusion to Joshua is particularly appropriate here, as the terror caused by Antiochus is reminiscent of that faced by Joshua's people in generations past.

Daniel's role becomes clear in this exchange—he is to "understand" (10:11 [NRSV "pay attention"]; 10:14) the angel's presentation regarding "the end of days" (10:14). This imperative (understand) was similarly used by Gabriel when he explained earlier visions to Daniel (8:17; 9:23), but only in this instance does the heavenly visitor also command Daniel "to humble yourself," a verb that has technical connotations of repentance. [To Humble and to Afflict Oneself] Although it is difficult to determine all the connotation of the "end of days" (Dan 2:28; 8:17, 19; 12:4, 9, 13), the scholarly consensus holds that the vision refers primarily to the period of the end of Antiochus that is to be followed by the reign of "the people of the holy ones of the Most High" (Dan 7:27). It is especially important that Daniel pay heed to the angel's words because he is not offering any quick resolution to Daniel's grief; there are yet many sorrows to come.

This man clothed in linen presents an extraordinary image of the enemies of Israel with his explanation of his delay. The "prince of the kingdom of Persia," who fights against him, is so powerful that even this awesome heavenly being needed the assistance of "Michael, one of the chief princes" (10:13). His explanation continues to present a sympathetic picture of the community's suffering, for if an angel needs assistance, how much more so do mere human beings. Commentators understand this prince of the

The Four Archangels

Francesco Borromini. 1559–1667. *The four archangels Michael, Gabriel, Rapael, and Uriel on the steeple.* S. Andrea Delle Fratte, Rome, Italy. (Credit: Erich Lessing/Art Resource, NY)

A reference to the four archangels of Israel is found in *1 En.* 40; each stands on one of the four sides of the throne of God. In Jewish and Christian texts they function as messengers of God, guardian angels, interpreters of visions, revealers of divine secrets, healers, and miracle workers.

kingdom of Persia to be either the patron angel of Persia or its earthly ruler. The belief that each nation has its own divine patron is reflected in the following biblical texts:

> When the Most High apportioned the nations, when he divided humankind, he fixed the boundaries of the peoples according to the number of the gods; the LORD's own portion was his people, Jacob his allotted share. (Deut 32:8-9)[6]

> God has taken his place in the divine council;
>   in the midst of the gods he holds judgment:
> "How long will you judge unjustly
>   and show partiality to the wicked?"
> I say, "You are gods,
>   children of the Most High, all of you;
> nevertheless, you shall die like mortals,
>   and fall like any prince." (Ps 82:1-2, 6-7)

These texts attest to the belief that God divided up the world into nations, each with its own deity, later identified as an angel. The LORD was Israel's own protector and ultimately all other deities were seen as subordinate (Ps 82). In this vision, the angel Michael has a unique protective role for Israel, defending it when the prince of Persia attacks. [The Angel Michael] Despite Michael's role, no contradiction or competition is seen with God's own, as all history, all meaning, and all eternity are unequivocally under God's control. This theology is similarly represented in 2 Maccabees where, although Antiochus or his nation is not represented by a heavenly patron, Israel is indeed defended by divine troops:

> About this time Antiochus made his second invasion of Egypt. And it happened that, for almost forty days, there appeared over all the city golden-clad cavalry charging through the air, in companies fully armed with lances and drawn swords—troops of cavalry drawn up, attacks and counter-attacks made on this side and on that, brandishing of shields, massing of spears, hurling of missiles, the

The Angel Michael

This is the first time that the angel Michael, whose name means, "Who is like God?" is identified in the Hebrew Scriptures. The way in which the author of the vision refers to him without further explanation shows that the community is already well familiar with this angel; he is simply identified as "one of the chief princes" (10:13). As the guardian of Israel, the angel Michael's role is to protect God's people and to triumph over evil so that justice and peace can reign unencumbered. Just as Michael contends with the divine princes of Persia and Greece, so too does he slay the dragon (Rev 12:7), contend with devil for the body of Moses (Jude 9), and fight against the prince of wickedness. The Qumran text, *The War Scroll*, is illustrative:

> This is the day appointed for the defeat and overthrow of the prince of the kingdom of wickedness, and he will send eternal succour to the company of his redeemed by the might of the princely angel of the kingdom of Michael. With everlasting light he will enlighten with joy (the children) of Israel; peace and blessing shall be with the company of God. He will raise up the kingdom of Michael in the midst of the gods, and the realm of Israel in the midst of all flesh. (1QM 17.5ff, as quoted in Rowland)

Christopher Rowland, *The Open Heaven* (New York: Crossroad, 1982), 89.

Celestial Warfare

Deut 32:8, Ps 82, and 2 Macc 5:1-4 are but a sampling of texts from the Hebrew Bible and from Second Temple literature that include references to the role of angels in celestial warfare. Of these texts Raymond Hammer writes, "This is another way of asserting that the ultimate destiny of nations is determined not upon earth, but in heaven. The development of monotheistic thinking led to substitution of 'angels' for the earlier reference to 'deities' [Deut 32:8]." In Israel's oldest literature, God acts as divine warrior in order to bring justice on earth by defeating Israel's enemies. The enemies whom God destroys are typically tyrants whose worldview supports the usage of people as means to cruel ends, such as Pharaoh, who enslaved the Hebrews; King Jabin, who oppressed Israel for twenty years; and the king of Midian, who destroyed Israel's land and produce (Exod 15:3-11; Judg 5:4-5; 7:22).

God's enemies are also represented cosmically by Sea and by the sea monster known as Rahab or Leviathan (Job 26:12-13; 38:8-11; Pss 74:12-17; 89:9-10 [89:10-11 MT]; 77:16-20 [77:17-21 MT]; 104:5-9; Isa 51:9-11). God's contests are sometimes supported by the heavenly host (deities), stars, or angels (Exod 32:34; 33:2; Josh 5:14; Judg 5:20; 2 Kgs 19:35). Hammer correctly notes here that after the exile the beings who accompany God as warrior or who act on God's behalf are more commonly presented as messengers or angels, than as other deities. In this way, Israel denied other nations' gods any validity (2 Macc 3:26 [where "young man" is a circumlocution for "angel"]; 2 Macc 15:22; 3 Macc 6:18; 4 Macc 4:10; Rev 12:7).

Raymond Hammer, *Daniel* (The Cambridge Bible Commentary; Cambridge: Cambridge University Press, 1976), 103.

flash of golden trappings, and armor of all kinds. Therefore everyone prayed that the apparition might prove to have been a good omen. (2 Macc 5:1-4) [Celestial Warfare]

Despite the ominous heavenly scene portrayed at the beginning of Daniel's vision, the message for the seer is so crucial that this unnamed heavenly visitor leaves Michael alone to withstand the Prince of Persia while he seeks out his charge to reassure him. Indeed, only after receiving multiple assurances from the heavenly visitor is Daniel finally ready to hear the message. Recalling the words the priest Eli instructed the young Samuel to say upon receiving a vision (1 Sam 3:9), Daniel confirms, "Let my lord speak, for you have strengthened me" (10:19). With this expression Daniel has embarked upon the journey that his community also must take; he is ready to listen to God's plan. [The Book of Truth (Daniel 10:21)]

History from the Persians to the Seleucids, 11:2-45

The need to understand the suffering and the subjugation of a powerless people as well as the desire to make sense of the unchecked powers of empires are combined in this scene to present an interpretation of history that transforms a bleak worldview into one of hope. After the man clothed in linen teaches Daniel that his task is to trust the truth of his words, he proceeds with a detailed recitation of the political actions of various kings who have ruled the Jewish people from the time of Persian ascendancy, to the

---

The Book of Truth (Daniel 10:21)

The presentation in Dan 10 underscores the patience of the angel who addresses and assists Daniel multiple times as well as the mercy of the God who responds to Daniel's plight. God sends the angel, who was already battling a foe of Israel, in order to comfort Daniel. Although the angel's message for the future is sobering, it is, ultimately, one of truth and assurance, as the angel says to Daniel, "But I am to tell you what is inscribed in the book of truth" (10:21). Sometimes the heavenly books refer to decisions regarding reward and punishment (see above, ch. 7 commentary and ["Books" in Judaism and Christianity]). In addition, divine books may refer to the record of God's plan for the universe, as is the case here. This reference to an angel's explanation of the book of truth is similar to the usage of the "heavenly tablets" found in *1 Enoch*. Enoch speaks of the vision of the world's history that he has received from the angels: "According to that which was revealed to me from the heavenly vision, that which I have learned from the words of the holy angels, and understood from the heavenly tablets" (*1 En.* 93:2). The tablets explain that the history of the world is replete with injustice and suffering, occurring in epochs called "weeks," that will be completed with God's intervention.

> Then after that in the ninth week the righteous judgment shall be revealed to the whole world. All the deeds of the sinners shall depart from upon the whole earth, and be written off for eternal destruction; and all people shall direct their sight to the path of uprightness.
> Then, after this matter, on the tenth week in the seventh part, there shall be the eternal judgment; and it shall be executed by the angels of the eternal heaven—the great (judgment) which emanates from all of the angels. The first heaven shall depart and pass away; a new heaven shall appear, and all the powers of heaven shall shine forever sevenfold.
> Then after that there shall be many weeks without number forever; it shall be (a time) of goodness and righteousness, and sin shall no more be heard of forever. (*1 En.* 91:14-17)

In this text, the phrase "be written off for eternal destruction" implies the existence of heavenly books that serve as a witness for an eschatological judgment.

---

advent of Greece, and finally to the quarrelling subdivisions of Alexander's great empire, the Ptolemies and Seleucids. The angel gives particular attention to the tyrant who wreaks havoc in the author's own day—Antiochus IV Epiphanes. From the time of the ancient writer Porphyry (c. AD 232–305), this "king of the north," who is the main focus of this revelation, has been identified as Antiochus Epiphanes, the same Seleucid king who set up the desolating sacrilege in the temple and who persecuted Jews. This tyrant is also equated with the fourth beast of Daniel 7, the little horn of Daniel 8, and the one who invades the temple of Daniel 9. The consensus of modern historical-critical scholarship is that the interpretation of history found in Daniel 11:2-39 constitutes a *vaticinium ex eventu*, or prophecy after the fact. The prediction of Antiochus's end in 11:40-45, however, turns to genuine prophecy, as the references to the king become vague and unsubstantiated, the prediction about his death has elements that do not conform to what is known from history, and the vision does not allude to the removal of the desolating sacrilege from the temple that occurred in December of 164 BC.

For modern audiences, the idea of presenting history as a prophecy after the fact by a pseudonymous author who adopts the

Pseudonymous Writing

Various reasons have been proposed for the phenomenon of pseudonymous authorship. Perhaps pseudonymity protected writers who composed in dangerous times, or it reflected the personal understanding of authors—namely, that they wrote in the tradition of a respected sage. It may also have served as a technique to gain respect and belief in the work. In Dan 12:4, the angel tells Daniel to "keep the words secret and the book sealed until the time of the end," similar to the instructions given to Enoch and Moses in the pseudonymous writings *1 Enoch* and the *Testament of Moses* (*1 En.* 1:4; *T. Mos.* 1:16-18). Such pronouncements account for the hiding of the message until a later propitious time and express the belief that history truly unfolds according to the design of God, despite historical circumstances that belie God's presence.

name of a sage may seem strange, misleading, or false. [Pseudonymous Writing] It is important to recognize, nonetheless, that these apocalypses, which present an interpretation of history in the form of a revelation from an angel, are frequently attested in Second Temple literature and were apparently an accepted form within the community. [Apocalypse: A Definition] It would be impossible to know how literally or figuratively people understood this appearance of the heavenly visitor to a human being, but the truth of the vision transcends any empirical referent: the long period of suffering is destined by God for a greater purpose. The people are capable of enduring their turmoil, pain, and doubt through the eyes of faith—a faith that is buttressed by knowing that every battle of the dominating empires, every political intrigue, every advance on the temple, even every sacrilege is seen by God. Ultimately, what appears to be so powerful and unstoppable is only fleeting, for all the empires that have subdued Israel or that oppress it will be judged by God.

The Predecessors to Antiochus IV, 11:2-20

After a brief reference to Persian emperors and to the fall of its empire to Alexander the Great, the angel offers an extensive inter-

---

Apocalypse: A Definition

An apocalypse is a type of literature in which current suffering is addressed by a revelation from God and is mediated through a human being via spiritual means, such as dreams, visions, and otherworldly journeys. The highly symbolic revelation is often interpreted by an angel. It offers a glimpse of the future where injustice and evil are addressed by a God who rewards the righteous and punishes or annihilates the guilty. · Despite the sometime fearsome and perplexing images found in apocalypses, they ultimately provide a message of hope for a future void of the terrible burdens faced in the present. The upcoming judgment of God is one that will bring the restoration of Israel and a world filled with peace, justice, and the knowledge of God.

The definition of "apocalypse," which is widely employed by modern scholars, finds this consensus:

A genre of revelatory literature with a narrative framework, in which a revelation is mediated by an otherworldly being to a human recipient, disclosing a transcendent reality which is both temporal, insofar as it envisages eschatological salvation, and spatial insofar as it involves another, supernatural world. . . . [It serves] to interpret present, earthly circumstances in light of the supernatural world and of the future, and to influence both the understanding and the behavior of the audience by means of divine authority.

John Collins, "Introduction: Towards the Morphology of a Genre," in *Apocalypse: The Morphology of a Genre*, ed. J.J. Collins (*Semeia* 14; Missoula: Scholars Press, 1979), 1–20, and Adela Yarbro Collins, "Introduction: Early Christian Apocalypticism," *Semeia* 36 (1986): 7, as quoted in John Collins, *Daniel: A Commentary on the Book of Daniel* (Hermeneia; Minneapolis: Fortress, 1993), 54.

pretation of the political tensions and intrigues of Alexander's successors, the Ptolemaic and Seleucid regimes. In the first section of this interpretive historical rendering (11:2-20), the angel pays particular attention to Antiochus III, the predecessor of the tyrant Antiochus IV. The reign of Antiochus III the Great solidified Seleucid rule in Coele-Syria, the province that included Judah. Because Antiochus III is the precursor to Antiochus IV, the author has a particular interest in his advance to power and in the way in which the aggrandizement of his own reign previewed the cruelties of his successor. Modern scholars' ability to decipher most of the details of this vision is based on our knowledge of classical antiquity as provided by Jewish, Christian, and Roman authors, including the writings of 1 and 2 Maccabees (2d century BC), Polybius (200–118 BC), Diodorus Siculus (80–20 BC), Livy (64 BC–AD 17), Josephus (AD 37–100), Porphyry (c. AD 232–305), and Jerome (AD 340–420).[7]

Because the time of the vision is set during the reign of Cyrus, the recitation of history appropriately begins with a reference to the remaining Persian monarchs who rule after Cyrus and who antedate the rise of Alexander the Great (11:2). Perhaps the author is indicating the Persian kings identified in the Bible, namely, Cyrus, Darius, Xerxes (the biblical Ahasuerus), and Artaxerxes I, who are mentioned in the books of Ezra and Nehemiah (Ezra 4:5-7; Neh 12:22). Because the author does not provide a comprehensive listing of all Persian monarchs from Cyrus to Darius III, the king who fell to Alexander, many scholars conclude that the angel refers to "three more kings" and "the fourth" in order to isolate the individual Persian rulers who fought famous battles with the Greeks.[8]
[Persian Monarchs from the Advent of Cyrus to the Fall of the Empire to Alexander]
It is also possible that these references to the "three" and "the fourth" are used as a literary device that shows God's intervention in human affairs to be prompted by three trials, followed by a decisive judgment.

More important than the accuracy of the names of these kings is the point that all the wealth and resources of Persia could not stop its fall to Greece and to its "warrior king" (11:3), Alexander. [Josephus on Alexander] The author quickly indicates that despite Alexander's success, his legacy was shameful because he did not leave the empire to "his posterity" and because his lands were "uprooted" (11:4), indications of the failure of Alexander's heirs, Philip

Persian Monarchs from the Advent of Cyrus to the Fall of the Empire to Alexander

Cyrus 559–530 BC
Cambyses 530–522 BC
Darius 522–486 BC
Xerxes 486–465 BC
Artaxerxes 464–424 BC
Darius II 423–405 BC
Artaxerxes II 404–359 BC
Artaxerxes III 358–338 BC
Arses 337–336 BC
Darius III 335–330 BC

Josephus on Alexander

Josephus (1st century AD Jewish historian) reports that when Alexander besieged Tyre, a contingent of 8,000 Samaritans, under the guidance of their leader Sanballat, met the famous conqueror and asked that they be allowed to build a temple on Mt. Gerizim (*Ant.* 11.321–339). Alexander demanded in return that they hand over the Jews and Jerusalem, but Jaddus, the high priest of the Samaritans, claimed he could not do so on account of his loyalty to Darius. While Alexander was proceeding to Jerusalem, Jaddus went ahead to try to calm the Jews, saying he had seen in a dream that Jerusalem would not be destroyed. When Alexander saw Jaddus he astonishingly bowed down to him. When his soldiers asked him why, Alexander

responded that Jaddus was the one who appeared to him in a dream, assuring him that he would be victorious over Persia. Alexander then entered the Jerusalem temple and offered sacrifice to the God of Israel. The Talmud preserves a similar story, but important features differ (*b. Yoma* 69a). The Samaritans ask Alexander's permission to destroy the Jerusalem temple, to which he agrees. Upon Alexander's arrival in Jerusalem, it is the high priest of Jerusalem, Simon the Just, to whom Alexander bows down, saying that he recognized Simon to be the one who appeared in his battles, guiding him to victory. Thus, the temple was spared.

Abraham Schalit, "Alexander the Great," *EncJud*, ed. Cecil Roth and Geoffrey Wigoder, 16 vols. (New York: Macmillan, 1971–72), 2:578–79.

Arrhidaeus (the illegitimate son of Alexander's father Philip II) and Alexander IV (Alexander's posthumous son born to Roxana), to inherit his vast lands. The four divisions of the empire, indicated by the four winds of heaven (the directions of the compass), were originally separated by Alexander's generals as follows: Greece and Macedonia to Cassander, Thrace to Lysimmachus, Babylonia and Northern Syria to Antigonus (later replaced by Seleucus I), and Egypt and southern Syria (including Palestine) to Ptolemy I Soter. Collectively, these rulers are known as the Diadochi. The various wars and shifting boundaries amongst these rulers and their successors are alluded to throughout the vision, allowing the angel to contrast Alexander's hubris with his failure. The one who took "action as he pleases" (11:3) is now marked by the absence of an intact legacy; Alexander's bequest is only the continuous warfare between the Ptolemies and Seleucids, which next occupies the angel's interpretation.

[The Ptolemies and Seleucids]

Throughout the account of the rulers who follow Alexander, the "king of the south" refers to one of the Ptolemies and "king of the north" refers to one

Map of the Lands of the Diadochi

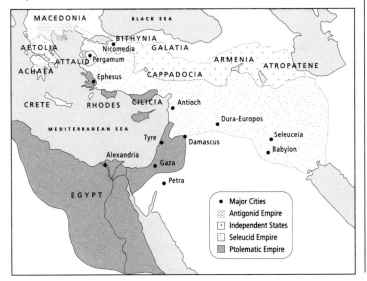

of the Seleucids. The vision initially refers to Ptolemy I Soter (305–282 BC) and to Seleucus I (311–281 BC), whose relationship with the former was initially as a commander ("one of his officers," 11:5). Seleucus I lost Babylonian territory to Antigonus and later fought as an ally of Ptolemy against Antigonus's son Demetrius. After the defeat of Demetrius at Gaza (312 BC), Seleucus I recaptured Babylon and regained even more territory than he had originally lost from Antigonus, thus ruling "a realm greater than his [Ptolemy's] own realm" (11:5). Despite these alliances, Seleucus I became a rival with Ptolemy for rule over Judah. With this depiction of the first Ptolemaic and Seleucid kings, the author sets the groundwork for showcasing their competition and the continual shifting of borders.

The author next discusses the political maneuvering between Ptolemy II Philadelphus (284–246 BC) and Antiochus II Theos (261–246 BC). By offering his daughter Berenice in marriage (11:6), Ptolemy II attempted to forge an alliance with Antiochus II. In order to accept this offer, Antiochus II had to divorce his then-current wife Laodice, setting the stage for her murderous revenge. After

> **The Ptolemies and Seleucids**
>
>
> *The Ptolemies*
> Ptolemy I Soter (305–282 BC)
> Ptolemy II Philadelphus (284–246 BC)
> Ptolemy III Euergetes I (246–222 BC)
> Ptolemy IV Philopator (222–204 BC)
> Ptolemy V Epiphanes (204–180 BC)
> Ptolemy VI Philometor (180–145 BC)
> Ptolemy VII Neos Philopator (never reigned)
> Ptolemy VIII Euergetes II [Physcon] (170–163 BC and 145–116 BC)
>
> *The Seleucids*
> Seleucus I Nicator (311–281 BC)
> Antiochus I Soter (281–261 BC)
> Antiochus II Theos (261–246 BC)
> Seleucus II Callinicus (246–225 BC)
> Seleucus III Ceraunus [or Soter] (225–223 BC)
> Antiochus III the Great (223–187 BC)
> Seleucus IV Philopator (187–175 BC)
> Antiochus IV Epiphanes (175–164 BC)
> Antiochus V Eupator (164–162 BC)
> Demetrius I Soter (161–150 BC)

Ptolemy I Soter and Seleucus I

Tetradrachm of Pharaoh Ptolemy I Soter. Israel Museum (IDAM), Jerusalem, Israel. (Credit: Erich Lessing/Art Resource, NY)

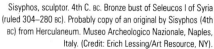

Sisyphos, sculptor. 4th C. BC. Bronze bust of Seleucos I of Syria (ruled 304–280 BC). Probably copy of an original by Sisyphos (4th BC) from Herculaneum. Museo Archeologico Nazionale, Naples, Italy. (Credit: Erich Lessing/Art Resource, NY).

Ptolemy II

Museo Gregoriano Egizio. Vatican Museums, Vatican State. (Credit: Scala/Art Resource, NY)

These three sculptures show an unknown princess, Arsinoe II, and Ptolemy II.

Antiochus II had died, Laodice had Berenice, her attendants, and Berenice's two sons killed (11:6), thus ensuring that her (Laodice's) own sons by Antiochus II could be heirs to the throne. After the murder of Berenice, Ptolemy III Euergetes I (246–221 BC), the son of Ptolemy II and the brother of Berenice ("a branch from her roots," 11:6), avenged his sister's death by killing Laodice. He successfully campaigned in Seleucia and Antioch, the territory of the new Seleucid king, namely, Laodice's son Seleucus II ("the king of the north"). In addition, Ptolemy III invaded other regions of upper Asia, but for unknown reasons, he returned to Egypt without retaining control over his newly captured lands. Nonetheless, "the spoils of war" that he captured (11:8), including the statues that had been taken during previous Persian incursions by Cambyses (525 BC), brought such significant wealth to Egypt that he became known as Euergetes, "the benefactor." Euergetes' occasions of conflict with Seleucus II were not over, however, as he later attempted to steal Ptolemaic lands during a two-year campaign (11:9) that only yielded loss of life (242–240 BC).

The sons of Seleucus II, namely Seleucus III (227–223 BC) and Antiochus III (223–187 BC), followed their father in succession, undeterred by his lack of success in breaking Egypt's hold on Judah and southern Syria (11:10). Because Seleucus III was murdered after only four years of rule, the vision next describes the battles between Antiochus III and Ptolemy IV Philopator (11:10-19) in which Antiochus III hoped to wrest Judah from Egyptian control. The attempt would prove to take years. In 217 BC, Ptolemy IV Philopator fiercely resisted the attack of Antiochus III upon his (Philopator's) fortress city of Raphia ("his [Philopator's] fortress," 11:10), and the Seleucid king lost thousands of troops. [Polybius on Raphia] Although Philopator was the unequivocal victor, he lost the opportunity to capitalize on his success and returned to Egypt with no additional Seleucid lands; hence the comment "he [Philopator] shall not prevail" (11:12). This defeat did not crush the ambitions of Antiochus III, however, who led other highly successful campaigns in Asia Minor and in Persia (during the years 217–204 BC) emboldening him to set his sights on Judah again.

When Ptolemy IV died (203 BC), Egypt faced the problem of being ruled by a child king, Ptolemy V, and his regent Agathocles. With these propitious circumstances for the Seleucids, Antiochus III attacked Egypt again (11:13), where he faced the Egyptian general Scopas along with Philip V of Macedon, who was allied with the Ptolemies. The strife in Egypt and among Jews alluded to in 11:14 is difficult to decipher. Based on the account of Polybius, some modern commentators conclude that there were domestic problems on two fronts—one with the Egyptian populace engaged in insurgent activity against the rule of Agathocles and the other with either pro-Seleucid or pro-Egyptian Jews sowing the seeds for internal strife ("the lawless among your own people" [11:14]).[9] In these troubling times, Antiochus III defeated Scopas in 199 BC at Paneas (also known as Caesarea Philippi or Banyas). Scopas attempted to find refuge at the Egyptian fortress in Sidon, but was vanquished when famine forced him to surrender a year later (11:15). Now the dream of Antiochus III the Great to control Coele-Syria had come true.

The phrase the angel uses to describe the victories of Antiochus the Great, namely, that he "shall take the actions he pleases" (11:16), is also used of Alexander and of Antiochus IV Epiphanes (11:3, 36), thus suggesting that his campaigns are an affront to God. Of these three kings, Collins states, "in each case, prides goes before a fall."[10] The "position [of Antiochus the Great] in the beautiful land" (11:16) is a reference to the Seleucid victory in the land of Israel (Dan 8:9; 11:41; Jer 3:19; *1 En.* 89:40; 90:20). The detail that "all of it shall be in his power" (11:16) sounds an ominous note about his rule. As is the case with the other emperors portrayed

---

Polybius on Raphia

The Greek historian Polybius (c. 200–118 BC) presents an arresting account of the battle at Raphia between Ptolemy and Antiochus:

By the beginning of spring Antiochus and Ptolemy had completed their preparations and were determined on deciding the fate of the Syrian expedition by a battle. Now Ptolemy started from Alexandria with an army of seventy thousand foot, five thousand horse, and seventy-three elephants, and Antiochus, on learning of his advance, concentrated his forces. . . . The whole army of Antiochus consisted of sixty-two thousand foot, six thousand horse, and a hundred and two elephants. (*Histories* 5.79)

Antiochus III

Head of Antiochus III the Great of Syria (223–187 BC). Marble, Louvre, Paris, France. (Credit: Erich Lessing/Art Resource, NY)

Antiochus the Great in Josephus

Josephus details the sufferings of the Jewish people caused by the wars of Antiochus the Great against Ptolemy Philopator and Ptolemy Epiphanes, stating,

> When Antiochus the Great reigned over Asia it was the lot of the Jews to undergo great hardships through the devastation of their land, as did also the inhabitants of Coele-Syria. For while he was at war with Ptolemy Philopator and with his son Ptolemy, surnamed Epiphanes, they had to suffer, and whether he was victorious or defeated, to experience the same fate; so that they were in no way different from a storm-tossed ship which is beset on either side by heavy seas, finding themselves crushed between the successes of Antiochus and the adverse turn of his fortunes. (*Ant.* 12.129–130)

After Antiochus the Great took possession of Judah, he recognized that the loss of life, expulsions, presence of the Egyptian garrison, and heavy taxes took a terrible toll. But because the people welcomed his arrival, and because he finally recognized that his policies had dire consequences, Antiochus granted them various privileges. He gave money for sacrificial provisions, freedom to live according to their own ancestral laws, remission of taxes for temple officials, and forgiveness or reduction of taxes for the rebuilding of their great losses. In addition, he bestowed freedom to those who had been captured and took measures to ensure that only clean animals be brought into Jerusalem (*Ant.* 12.134–146).

The authenticity of these magnanimous reports is debated, but it is important to note that the author of Daniel does not include any of these more positive traditions of Antiochus the Great, as his focus is on the arrogance of all empires that bring evil and suffering into the world, and especially on this predecessor of Antiochus IV.

---

in the book of Daniel, the intransigent evil of this king leads inexorably to his end. [Antiochus the Great in Josephus]

After Antiochus the Great solidified his conquests, he hoped to obtain a treaty with Egypt rather than invade it, fearing that any incursion would prompt Rome to ally itself with his nemesis. Thus, he arranged that his daughter Cleopatra marry Ptolemy V Epiphanes, hoping she would keep the Egyptian king on a course favorable to his own interests. Cleopatra, however, proved to be more loyal to Egypt than to the land of her birth; thus the author can say that giving "the woman in marriage" will not "be to his advantage" (11:17). The author of the vision thus draws a parallel between both attempted marriage alliances—that of Ptolemy II who hoped to use his daughter Berenice to forge an alliance with Antiochus II and that of Antiochus the Great who attempted to use Cleopatra to make an alliance with Ptolemy V. Both were futile.

The desire of Antiochus III the Great to continue his success by conquering the lands of the Diadochi proved to be the beginning of his end. He continued his incursions into the coastal cities of Asia Minor, which were under Egypt's control, and to the Thracian Chersonese (the modern Turkish Gallipoli Peninsula), poised to invade Greece. Despite Rome's warnings to desist, he fought for a year but was defeated at Thermopylae in 191 BC. His disgrace continued when a year later he lost his lands in Asia Minor to Rome as well, being resoundingly defeated at the battle of Magnesia. The reference to "a commander" who "put[s] an end to his insolence" (11:18) apparently refers to the Roman officer Lucius Cornelius

Elymais

There are two traditions associated with two distinct Seleucid kings at the temple of Elam or Elymais, a province in Persia. First, Antiochus III plundered the temple of Bel (Baal) there in order to fund the enormous penalties he owed to Rome after losing battles in Asia Minor. The Roman author Justin (end of 2d–beginning of 3rd century AD) records,

> Meanwhile, in Syria, King Antiochus had been defeated by the Romans and subjected to a heavy tribute as a condition of peace. Forced by financial difficulties, or else motivated by greed, he now entertained hopes that, under the pretext of his obligation to pay the tribute, he would be the more easily forgiven for sacrilege, and so he took an army and made an attack at night on the temple of Jupiter of Elymais. When news of this got out, the local people rushed to the scene and Antiochus was killed, along with his entire force. (*Epitome of the Philippic History of Trogus* 32.2)

Second, Antiochus IV, according to Josephus, also went to the temple of Elymais in order to seize its great cache of money and weapons. Yet, this raid led to his end:

> As those within the city, however, were not dismayed either by his attack or by the siege, but stoutly held out against him, his hopes were dashed; for they drove him off from the city, and went out against him in pursuit, so that he had to come to Babylon as a fugitive, and lost many of his army. (*Ant.* 12.355)

Shortly afterward, Antiochus IV fell ill and died. Josephus reports that the historian Polybius recorded that the local populace said his illness was due to his insult to the temple at Elymais; nevertheless, in Josephus's view, Antiochus himself admitted that his pain and impending death was due to his earlier assault on the temple in Jerusalem (*Ant.* 12.354–359).

Scipio (Asiaticus), who arranged for the terms of surrender upon the defeat of Antiochus the Great. Being required to pay excessive tribute and penalties to Rome, Antiochus went to Elymais ("his own land," 11:19) in order to take treasure from the temple of Bel to pay his debt. There, he was murdered. [Elymais]

Seleucus IV Philopator (187–175 BC), son of Antiochus III, succeeded his father to the throne. Still under heavy tribute from Rome, the vision's reference to Philopator's sending of "an official for the glory of the kingdom" (11:20) may refer, in general, to his many demands for taxes to meet his obligations, or, specifically, to his sending of Heliodorus, the finance minister, to the temple in Jerusalem in order to raid its treasuries. Heliodorus's attempt was disastrous; although the exact circumstances of his failure to take temple funds are unknown, 2 Maccabees preserves a tradition that he was miraculously prevented from plundering the temple. Thus, the heavenly interpreter states, "but within a few days he [Seleucus IV Philopator] shall be broken" (11:20), which refers either to the relatively few years of his reign, compared with his father, or to Heliodorus's aborted attempt to abscond with the temple's wealth. The death of Seleucus IV was as humiliating as the events of his reign, for he was murdered by conspirators who were led by the same Heliodorus. Seleucus's young son, another Antiochus, inherited the throne, but the boy was outflanked first by Heliodorus, and next by Antiochus IV, who became king.

Heliodorus

Raphael (Raffaello Sanzio). 1483–1520. *Heliodorus being driven out of the temple*. Stanze di Raffaello, Vatican Palace, Vatican State. (Credit: Scala/Art Resource, NY)

This painting by Raphael (1483–1520) shows Heliodorus being driven out of the temple.

Second Maccabees gives the miraculous account of the subduing of Heliodorus. Note the heavenly warrior and the "young men," or angels, who bring divine justice:

> But when he [Heliodorus] arrived at the treasury with his bodyguard, then and there the Sovereign of spirits and of all authority caused so great a manifestation that all who had been so bold as to accompany him were astounded by the power of God, and became faint with terror. For there appeared to them a magnificently caparisoned horse, with a rider of frightening mien; it rushed furiously at Heliodorus and struck at him with its front hoofs. Its rider was seen to have armor and weapons of gold. Two young men also appeared to him, remarkably strong, gloriously beautiful and splendidly dressed, who stood on either side of him and flogged him continuously, inflicting many blows on him. When he suddenly fell to the ground and deep darkness came over him, his men took him up, put him on a stretcher, and carried him away—this man who had just entered the aforesaid treasury with a great retinue and all his bodyguard but was now unable to help himself. They recognized clearly the sovereign power of God. (2 Macc 3:24-28)

Antiochus IV, 11:21-45

Having portrayed all of Seleucid and Ptolemaic history to have been filled with armed conflict, failed alliances, hubris, family squabbling, conspiracy, and murder, the angel has established the pattern that will now be repeated: the terrible times of Antiochus IV Epiphanes. Despite the even greater conflict to come, the angel assures Daniel that these horrific times are surely known by God and are destined for an ignominious end. The interpretation given in Daniel 11:21-45 shows that the events that mark Antiochus Epiphanes' reign hearken back to his predecessors, for his wars against and negotiations with Ptolemy VI Philometor (180–145 BC), his attacks on Jews, and his pollution of the temple are all consonant with the actions of previous Seleucids and Ptolemies. Moreover, his profligacy, arrogance, and cruelty reach a nadir not previously seen among Judah's occupiers. Despite the horrors he inflicts upon innocent people, the author expresses confidence that these terrible times, too, shall end.

The account in Daniel 11:21-24 provides an overview of Antiochus Epiphanes' shameful seizure of the throne and the characteristics of his rule. His ascent to the throne was suspect among many, for upon the death of Seleucus IV, one of Seleucus's own sons should have succeeded him to the throne. Yet because one of the sons of Seleucus IV, Demetrius, was held hostage in Rome (as an exchange for Antiochus IV who was previously held captive) and because his other son was very young, Heliodorus believed himself to be in position to exercise power through the latter as regent. Heliodorus was no match for Antiochus IV, however, who, backed by King Eumenes II of Pergamum (Asia Minor), came into Judah with his troops; hence, the author represents the kingship of Antiochus IV as illegitimate (11:21). In contrast to his Greek appellation, "Epiphanes," meaning "God manifest," the author calls Antiochus IV "contemptible"; others would call him "Epimanes," a word play meaning "madman" (Polybius, *Histories* 26). The vision quickly establishes that Antiochus's reign will be marked by violence and suffering. The particular injury to the community is marked by his harming of "the prince of the covenant" (11:22). This allusion is to Onias III, the high priest, whom Antiochus IV ousted from office in order to appoint Jason, another priest (and Onias's brother), who had bribed the king with funds and promise of additional support (175 BC). [The Portrayal of Jason in 2 Maccabees] Later, Jason was outbid by Menelaus, a man so incensed when he heard that Onias had protested his theft of objects from the temple that he had Onias murdered (170 BC). The reference to "an alliance" (11:23) is obscure, yet Antiochus's profligacy is well known from the classical sources, as he used the wealth he gained from foreign temples and treasuries to build loyalties and patronage. [The Character of Antiochus] Antiochus's eventual downfall is assured, nonetheless, for these self-important campaigns will last "only for a time" (11:24).

The account in Daniel 11:25-39 continues to detail Antiochus's reign. The violence and loss of life that punctuated his rule are underscored by the many references to the conflict between Antiochus IV and Ptolemy VI Philometor, the "king of the north," and the "king of the south," respectively. Prompted by the bad advice of his officials ("those who eat of the royal rations," 11:26), the young Ptolemy VI attempted to regain Judah and Coele-Syria from Antiochus beginning in 173 BC (11:25-26), but was readily stopped on his own soil, where Antiochus successfully asserted his rule over Egypt for a time. Antiochus IV and Ptolemy VI entered into negotiations at Memphis, which the author identifies as "sit[ting] at one table and exchang[ing] lies" (11:27), where, feigning friendship, Antiochus solidified his power. Tensions remained particularly high in Alexandria, however, where Antiochus was not accepted as king, and where Ptolemy VII, the younger brother of Ptolemy VI, asserted his rights for the throne. Antiochus then attempted to restore Ptolemy VI as ruler in Alexandria, expecting to be able to continue his control of him, but was unsuccessful in ousting Ptolemy VII.

In 169 BC, Antiochus IV left Egypt but kept the fortress he had won in Pelusium for future assaults. Indeed, in 168 BC ("at the time appointed," 11:29) the Seleucid king invaded Egypt again, this time facing the united front of Ptolemy VI and Ptolemy VII, who had reconciled and had become co-regents. This campaign would not end in Antiochus's victory; hence the author's remark that "it shall not be as it was before" (11:29). Gaius Popillius Laenas, the Roman consul who aided the Ptolemies, drove Antiochus out of Egypt in humiliation. The

Romans, or "Kittim" (11:30), had become the most powerful force in the Mediterranean after their defeat of King Perseus of Macedonia, thus Antiochus knew he had no other choice but to depart from Egypt when Popillius Laenas insisted. [The Kittim] With the references to both of these campaigns of Antiochus IV against Egypt, the author stresses that neither victory nor defeat is of any ultimate consequence. Despite the impressive strength of Antiochus, God has determined that all of the king's deeds have only a temporary impact and "there remains an end at the time appointed" (11:27).

Ptolemy VI Philometor

Gold ring. Ptolemy VI Philometor (?) in Egyptian double-crowned headdress. 2d C. BC. Hellenistic. (Credit: H. Lewandowski. Louvre, Paris, France. Réunion des Musées Nationaux/Art Resource, NY)

The author shows that these wars between the "king of the north" and the "king of the south" had particularly ominous consequences for Jews, as life in Jerusalem became worse for the people of "the holy covenant" when Antiochus IV "return[ed] to his own land" (11:28). Internal problems in Jerusalem may have contributed to Antiochus's hurried return. Hearing a rumor of Antiochus's death, Jason, who had lost the office of high priest to Menelaus, attempted to regain his position and murdered many of Menelaus's supporters. Learning of this disturbance, which ultimately threatened Antiochus's own power (as he feared Jason would support an Egyptian government over his own), the king returned to Jerusalem with a vengeance, quashed Jason's attempt, reinstated Menelaus, attacked the temple itself, and plundered its wealth (2 Macc 5:5-21; 1 Macc 1:20-24; see the discussion in ch. 8). Although it is not certain whether Antiochus invaded the temple only once (169 BC) or on a second occasion as well (168 BC), this vision appears to refer to two different occasions. Antiochus was not necessarily present in Jerusalem the second time, as "forces sent by him shall occupy and profane the temple and fortress" (11:31); nevertheless, the author presents all attacks on the community as stemming from Antiochus's direction. An additional reason why Jews found Antiochus's policies to be such an affront to God was because he established a garrison (the "Akra," 1 Macc 1:33) in

The Kittim

AΩ "Kittim" may refer to Cyprus or to any lands west of the Mediterranean island. In the book of Numbers the foreign prophet Balaam, who was hired by Israel's enemy Balak to utter curses against it, is directed by God to bless the fledgling nation. Balaam predicts that Israel's enemies will perish when "ships shall come from Kittim" (Num 24:24). Daniel uses the term here for the Romans, as does the Pesher to Habakkuk (a commentary on the book of Habakkuk from Qumran) to remind the reader that the words of the prophets of old are being fulfilled.

Temple Inscription

 This Greek inscription (c. 3rd C. BC– 1st C. AD) was placed just outside the inner precinct of the Jerusalem Temple. It forbids foreigners from entering under punishment of death, reading, "No outsider shall enter the protective enclosure around the sanctuary. And whoever is caught will only have himself to blame for the ensuing death." In Acts 21:28 Paul is accused of bringing a Gentile, Trophimus (an Ephesian), into this area and is arrested.

K. C. Hanson, "The Jerusalem Temple Warning Inscription," n.p., <http://www.kchanson.com/ANCDOCS/greek/temple warning.html> (5 February 2007).

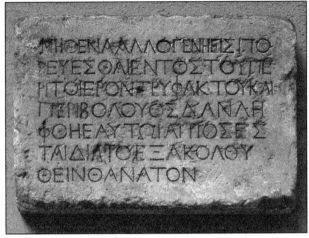

Interdiction for non-Jews to enter the Inner Sanctum of the temple in Jerusalem. Greek inscription from the outer wall of the temple. 3rd C. BC–1st C. AD. Plaster cast, Museo della Civilta Romana, Rome, Italy. (Credit: Erich Lessing/Art Resource, NY)

the temple precincts (11:31, 38). This "stronghold" provided troops to oversee the city and temple. These soldiers well could have restricted access to the temple only to those they approved— including Gentiles—who were forbidden by Jewish law to enter beyond the outer courtyard. [Temple Inscription] Because 2 Maccabees shows the successor of Antiochus IV, namely, his son Antiochus V Eupator, returning the control of temple access to Jews and giving them freedom to practice their own laws and customs, it is probable that admission was indeed controlled by the fortress in the days of his father. [The Letter of King Antiochus V]

The author places the worst of the persecutions as having occurred after Antiochus's second arrival to Jerusalem. The description found in Daniel 11:30-36 refers to the temple desecrations, including the setting up of foreign cults ("the abomination that makes desolate" [11:31]), violent assaults and murder, and subsequent enslavement ("they shall fall by sword and flame, and suffer captivity and plunder," [11:33]). First Maccabees describes these terrible times as follows:

The Letter of King Antiochus V

 According to 2 Maccabees, the king's letter states the following:

King Antiochus [V] to his brother Lysias, greetings. Now that our father [Antiochus IV] has gone on to the gods, we desire that the subjects of the kingdom be undisturbed in caring for their own affairs. We have heard that the Jews do not consent to our father's change to Greek customs, but prefer their own way of living and ask that their own customs be allowed them. Accordingly, since we choose that this nation also should be free from disturbance, our decision is that their temple be restored to them and that they shall live according to the customs of their ancestors. (2 Macc 11:22-25)

Two years later the king sent to the cities of Judah a chief collector of tribute, and he came to Jerusalem with a large force. Deceitfully he spoke peaceable words to them, and they believed him; but he suddenly fell upon the city, dealt it a severe blow, and destroyed many people of Israel. He plundered the city, burned it with fire, and tore down its houses and its surrounding walls. They took captive the women and children, and seized the livestock. Then they fortified the city of David with a great strong wall and strong towers, and it became their citadel. (1 Macc 1:29-33)

The collector who enforced such a program is not identified here, although he is identified as Apollonius in 2 Maccabees 5:24.

[1 Maccabees and Community Conflict]

In addition to detailing the crimes of Antiochus, the vision also underscores the shameful practices of the community members who did not resist the king's assaults and his attempts at eliminating Judaism. The author derides them as those who will forsake and violate the "holy covenant" (11:30) and who are "seduce[d] with intrigue" (11:32). As Hartman and Di Lella say, "the ordinary Jew was confused by the tumultuous events he had to live through and was undecided whether he should go along with Hellenization as even some of the high priests had done. With fidelity to the covenant would come the test of 'sword and flames,' exile and loss of property."[11] During these times of cruel choices and ethical crises, some Jews tried to follow a course of appeasement or tried to embrace enthusiastically aspects of the Hellenistic government and culture that they believed did not go against Jewish law. Once Antiochus's tyrannical program began, however, there was no escape. The author of the vision indicates the overwhelming nature

---

1 Maccabees and Community Conflict

As does the book of Daniel, 1 Maccabees refers to disagreement within the Jewish community regarding how to respond to their Hellenistic rulers. Some felt that the best way to save their lives was to capitulate to Antiochus's demands that they adopt as many Greek ways as feasible, to appoint leaders who were sympathetic to the king's demands that all his subjects be united in religion, custom, and outlook, and to abandon any particularity. Although scholars question whether the perspective shown in Maccabees truly represents Antiochus's religious expectations of his subjects—as surely he himself accepted many gods—it was apparently an accepted notion among many Jews that their emperor was violently opposed to *their* God.

Then the king wrote to his whole kingdom that all should be one people, and that all should give up their particular customs. All the Gentiles accepted the command of the king. Many even from Israel gladly adopted his religion; they sacrificed to idols and profaned the sabbath. And the king sent letters by messengers to Jerusalem and the towns of Judah; he directed them to follow customs strange to the land, to forbid burnt-offerings and sacrifices and drink offerings in the sanctuary, to profane sabbaths and festivals, to defile the sanctuary and the priests, to build altars and sacred precincts and shrines for idols, to sacrifice swine and other unclean animals, and to leave their sons uncircumcised. They were to make themselves abominable by everything unclean and profane, so that they would forget the law and change all the ordinances. (1 Macc 1:41-49)

These declarations—outlawing the observance of sacred times, proscribing circumcision, the very the sign of the covenant itself, outlawing sacrifice and demanding offering to foreign gods, attacked the very essence of Judaism. 1 Maccabees also records that refusal to comply, or even the mere possession of the book of the law, was a "crime" punishable by death (1 Macc 1:54-61).

of these decrees and their affront to God by the description of Antiochus as one who "acts as he pleases" (11:36).

The vision not only shows that Antiochus ravaged the country with war and subjected Jews to the tragic choice of assimilation or death, but also portrays this tyrant as having been so arrogant that he believed himself to be a god (11:36). Antiochus's attachment to the idea of deification of kings seems to have been taken to the extreme, as demonstrated by the epithet used in his coins, "Epiphanes" ("God manifest"). These claims, to be sure, would have been contemptible for a Jewish audience. The author of the vision devotes a relatively lengthy section to Antiochus's hubris (11:36-39), including not only an exposé on his self-adulation and on his effrontery to God, but also on his disrespect for his own gods (11:37-39). This abandonment of "the gods of his ancestors" (11:37) reflects more the author's contempt of Antiochus than the neglect of Antiochus's local gods. Classical sources confirm that there were many gods represented at the traditional festivals during Antiochus's day, and extant coins show both images of Zeus and of Apollo.[12] Similarly, the reference to Antiochus's abandonment of "the god beloved by women" (11:37), identified by most scholars as Tammuz or Adonis, may be included here to underscore contempt of local sensibilities. [Tammuz and Adonis]

In response to these indignities and acts of violence, the angel explains to Daniel that his community must "stand firm" and "take action" (11:32). These words do not unequivocally indicate whether their resistance was passive or armed, an issue that scholars debate. Armed resistance did begin as one response to these terrible times, and, indeed, some scholars argue that the "little help" the wise receive (11:34) refers to the armed resistance of the Maccabees, the leaders of a rebel group who eventually defeated the Seleucids. [The "Little Help"] The reference is vague, however, and may well refer to any assistance that other faithful individuals lent in the face of the overwhelming might of Antiochus IV and not necessarily to the Maccabees. The focus of this vision is neither on armed resistance nor on a response of pacifism. Rather, it is being among "the wise" that shows loyalty and faith to God and to the commandments (11:33, 35; 12:3, 10). Concretely, this means refusing to comply with the demands of the state that compromise

---

Tammuz and Adonis

In Sumerian mythology, the deity Dumuzi (Tammuz, Hebrew) was the god of the harvest and the lover of the goddess Inanna (later Ishtar), who bitterly mourned his loss and traveled to the depths of the underworld to retrieve him, but instead was imprisoned until Ea, the god of Wisdom, orchestrated their release. While imprisoned, the earth was desolate and even the gods were in mourning. The book of Ezekiel reflects the Babylonian practice of "weeping for Tammuz" (Ezek 8:14) as the prophet laments that the community has taken up this idolatrous practice as well as the related worship of Adonis, another dying and rising god who is coupled with a goddess—in this case Aphrodite or Persephone.

Richard J. Clifford, "Tammuz," *Harper's Bible Dictionary*, ed. Paul Achtemeier (San Francisco: Harper & Row, 1985), 1017.

The "Little Help"

AΩ From antiquity, interpreters have speculated on the identity of the "little help" (Dan 11:34). According to Jerome, Porphyry believed the phrase to refer to Mattathias and his son Judah (called "the Maccabee"—meaning "the hammer"), the first Maccabean martyrs. The Maccabees comprised this religious family and their followers who opposed Hellenistic practices. They employed guerrilla tactics to fight the armies of Antiochus IV and successfully pressured Antiochus V to remove the idolatrous cults from the Jerusalem temple. Under the leadership of Jonathan, Judah's brother, they later ousted the Seleucids from power in Judea (166–160 BC) and set up an independent dynastic state. The roots of the revolt began with the acquiescence and, in some circles, the enthusiastic embrace of Hellenistic practices by Jews who had been encouraged by the usurper high priests Jason and Menelaus. These priests had challenged Jewish law and disregarded Jewish prohibitions in order to buttress Hellenistic institutions. When Antiochus IV, prompted by his defeat in Egypt and his rage against the attempt of Jason's supporters to oust Menelaus, began his persecutions of Jews, the pious Mattathias and his sons began an armed revolt not only against the king but also against other Jews who had abandoned their faith in favor of Greek religion and philosophy. Crucial victories against the Samaritan governor Apollonius and the commander Seron eventually led to the crushing losses of the Seleucid army under the leadership of Lysias and his commanders Nicanor and Gorgias. The Maccabees were able to recapture Jerusalem, oust the Jewish aristocrats who supported the Hellenization of the city, and rededicate the temple. Lysias, in the name of Antiochus IV, rescinded the persecutions, but the problems with the priesthood prompted the continuation of Maccabean opposition. Insurgencies continued in the days of the Seleucid kings Antiochus V and Demetrius I, eventually leading to a battle between Judah and Bacchides, Demetrius's commander. Judah died in battle, but with the rise of Jonathan as leader and the continuing weakening of the Seleucid Empire, the Maccabees (or Hasmoneans) established an independent state that lasted until 37 BC, succumbing to the ascendancy of Rome.

Uriel Rappaport, "Maccabean Revolt," *ABD*, ed. David Noel Freedman, 6 vols. (New York: Doubleday & Co., 1992), 4:433–39.

the commandments, even on the pain of death (11:35), and being courageous enough to teach others to remain faithful as well. This final vision shows that times were so intolerable that resistance through martyrdom might constitute the only righteous stance in such unimaginable circumstances. [The Wise (*maśkîlîm*)]

Given this bleakest of portraits, why should Daniel not despair? The author shows that these terrors are known by God and exist only in the appointed time—one that is surely limited. Antiochus's despotism is no different from that of the preceding kingdoms; just as Babylon, Media, Persia, and Greece have fallen, so too will the empire of the new Nebuchadnezzar, namely, Antiochus IV. When this day arrives, however, a radical change will occur, for instead of one kingdom following yet another, it will be the time of the end (12:4). Indeed, the author ends the account of Antiochus by speaking of a time when he will be no more.

From vv. 40-45, the *ex eventu* prophecy regarding the "king of the north" turns to general statements about what will happen to Antiochus and to his regime. Antiochus's past is the best prediction of his future, including another war with the king of the south and further incursions into the northeastern-most boundaries of the

The Wise (*maśkîlîm*)

AΩ The references to "the wise" (*maśkîlîm*) in Daniel who have a distinctive role in leading "the many" and who are identified as those who will be resurrected have led some modern scholars to posit the existence of a distinct group within Judaism of that name. This group was remembered for their teaching and their willingness to suffer and die for their faith, but otherwise any distinguishing beliefs remain unknown. Some scholars identify the *maśkîlîm* with the *ḥasîdîm*, the pious Jews who joined the Maccabees in the resistance movements, refusing to fight on the Sabbath and enduring martyrdom during the time of Antiochus's

persecutions. John Collins, however, rightly points out the problematic nature of this identification, as the book of Daniel shows the *maśkîlîm* neither to be active resistance fighters nor supporters of the Maccabees. Rather, the book of Daniel portrays the *maśkîlîm* as concerned with the heavenly mysteries and with speculation about the end times, unlike the books of Maccabees that evidence no connection of the *ḥasîdîm* with such concerns. In Maccabees, they await every opportunity to remain faithful to their traditions by following the law and not by armed struggle.

John Collins, *Daniel: A Commentary on the Book of Daniel* (Hermeneia; Minneapolis: Fortress, 1993), 66–69.

Seleucid kingdom (11:44). The author presents imagery from several enemies whose significance became so important in Israel's tradition that they came to symbolize any tyrannical power that oppressed it. Past Egyptian and Assyrian advances against Israel are recalled with the phrase "pass through like a flood" (Dan 11:40; cf. Dan 11:10; Isa 8:8; and Jer 46:8); and the phrase "stretch out the hand" (Dan 11:42) is used of the invading Babylonians (Ezek 30:25). [Israel's Enemies in the Book of Jeremiah] Throughout the Hebrew Bible these images also are used of God, who definitively ends the ascendancy of Egypt, Assyria, and Babylon. In the book of Exodus, for example, God states, "So I will stretch out my hand and strike Egypt with all my wonders that I will perform in it; after that he [Pharaoh] will let you go" (Exod 3:20; see also Exod 7:5; Isa 31:3; Ezek 35:3; Zeph 1:4; 2:13). The imagery of God's coming like a flood against the enemies of Israel is shown as follows: "So those in the west shall fear the name of the LORD, and those in the east, his glory; for he will come like a pent-up stream that the wind of the LORD drives on" (Isa 59:19, cf. Gen 7:17-24). With such imagery, it becomes clear that Antiochus's actions will continue to be outrageous until his very end. The author continues to display the arrogance and idolatry of this despot and the particular suffering of Israel by contrasting the "tens of thousands" of deaths of those he kills in "the beautiful land" (Judah) with other classic enemies of God (and Israel) who survive at first, "for Edom and Moab and the main part of the Ammonites shall escape from his power" (11:41). Antiochus's final

Israel's Enemies in the Book of Jeremiah

Antiochus's end will be no different from that of Israel's earlier foes, as shown in the book of Jeremiah:

Egypt rises like the Nile, like rivers whose waters surge. It said, Let me rise, let me cover the earth, let me destroy cities and their inhabitants. Advance, O horses, and dash madly, O chariots! Let the warriors go forth: Ethiopia and Put who carry the shield, the Ludim, who draw the bow. That day is the day of the LORD God of hosts, a day of retribution, to gain vindication from his foes. (Jer 46:8-10; see also Isa 20:4)

victory before his definitive fall is shown to be analogous to those of Egyptians, Assyrians, and Babylonians in generations past, who spread abroad as a flood or river, increased their armies with foreign troops, and appeared unstoppable. What all these nations have in common, however, is that they are subdued by God's incomparable attack.

The predictions of Antiochus's final actions, which will be marked by his "bring[ing of] ruin and complete destruction to many," take the king away from Egypt and locate him at the opposite end of the Seleucid Empire, for they occur after hearing reports from "the east and the north" (11:44). The reference to Antiochus's pitching his tent between the coast and the "beautiful holy mountain," which refers to Mount Zion, may indicate that the author understands that Antiochus's final battle will take place in the land of Israel, for it is there he will "come to his end" (11:45). [10.38 War Scroll] Despite all the schemes and alliances that characterized Antiochus's tenure, the vision shows that he will be left utterly alone to perish in an ignominious death, as there will be "no one to help him" (11:45). Many scholars conclude that the date of the composition of the book of Daniel can be determined by these remarks of Antiochus's last days. Because this campaign in Egypt is not attested elsewhere, and because it is known that Antiochus died not in the land of Israel but rather in the eastern reaches of his empire, the date of composition is fixed sometime after the advent of the persecutions but before Antiochus's death (164 BC). [Believers' Response to Visions of the Future]

The War Scroll

The *War Scroll* (1st century BC–1st century AD), portrays a great eschatological battle at the end of days between the Sons of Light and the Sons of Darkness:

> And on the day on which the Kittim fall, there will be a battle and savage destruction before the God of Israel, for this will be the day determined by Him since ancient times for the war of extermination against the sons of darkness. On this (day), the assembly of the gods and the congregation of men shall confront each other for great destructions. The sons of light and the lot of darkness shall battle together for God's might, between the roar of a huge multitude and the shout of gods and of men, on the day of the calamity. (1QM 1:9-11)

As this representative text shows, the *War Scroll* has many features that echo Daniel, including battles, angels who fight for God, armies of nations (including the Kittim and the king of the north), and an expected day of anguish. In addition, just as the book of Daniel emphasizes the futility of Antiochus's power by stating that his end will occur with "none to help him" (Dan 11:45), so too does the *War Scroll* say that, "rule of the Kittim will come to an end, wickedness having been defeated, with no remnant remaining" (1QM 1:6).

Translations from Florentino Garcia Marinez and Eibert J.C. Tigchelaar, eds., *The Dead Sea Scrolls, Study Edition*, vol. 1, 1Q1-4Q273 (Grand Rapids MI: William B. Eerdmans Publishing Co., 1997).

Reassurance and Resurrection, 12:1-7

In these bleakest of times, the author turns to the final consummation—a time that is characterized by such trauma as the world has never known (12:1). Nonetheless, such an age is also marked by a hope that can never be abrogated—the promise of the resurrection of the righteous. [Terminology: Resurrection, Immortality, and the Afterlife] The

Believers' Response to Visions of the Future

Although ancient readers of this vision would have seen that the details of the prediction of Antiochus's death were not completely correct, they could nonetheless trust in the essential truth of the vision. As Paul Redditt writes,

What matters is that new programs for the future address the real needs of the readers: for example, the need to know that God rules; virtue will be rewarded; a new day will dawn (if not now, sooner or later); and they are on the right track. The book of Daniel as a whole and in its individual narratives meets just those needs, and this last vision is no exception. In its concluding vision, the book also looked ahead to the fall of Antiochus while he was at the height of his power. That was no small achievement; it got the essence of the future correct.

For centuries, Jews and Christians have continued to find hope in the visions of Daniel. This vision proclaims that Antiochus IV will not prevail. The imaginative representation of this tyrant, and indeed, of all the despots in the book of Daniel, make it possible for believers to see that whenever the innocent are terrorized, God has set up the world so that justice will prevail. Nebuchadnezzar, no less than Antiochus, came to his end—so too any despot who defies the "Ancient of Days" (Dan 7:13), for all earthly power is derivative of God's own authority.

Paul Redditt, *Daniel* (New Century Bible Commentary; Sheffield, England: Sheffield Academic Press, 1999), 189.

presentation of the woes of the earth at the time of God's judgment upon the nations is characteristic of apocalyptic literature and has its roots in prophetic texts. The book of Joel, for example, states that on the day when God judges the nations for their shedding of innocent blood, "The sun and the moon are darkened, and the stars withdraw their shining. The LORD roars from Zion, and utters his voice from Jerusalem, and the heavens and the earth shake" (Joel 3:15-16). In the book of Daniel, such times are characterized by a new reality, "a time of anguish (ṣārâ), such as has never occurred since nations first came into existence" (12:1). These words recall both Jeremiah's description of God's restoration of the land of Israel to the exiles as well as Joel's descriptions of the Day of the Lord:

Alas! that day is so great there is none like it; it is a time of distress [ṣārâ] for Jacob; yet he shall be rescued from it. (Jer 30:7)

A day of darkness and gloom, a day of clouds and thick darkness! Like blackness spread upon the mountains a great and powerful army comes; their like has never been from of old, nor will be again after them in ages to come. (Joel 2:2)

The angel reminds Daniel that he does not stand alone at such terrifying times, because Israel's patron and defender, the angel Michael, protects the people as God exercises judgment. God takes special notice of "everyone who is found written in the book" (12:1), that is, of all the righteous (7:10; 10:21).[13] They will be "delivered," not only from war, violence, or suffering, but from death as well; this

Terminology: Resurrection, Immortality, and the Afterlife

AΩ As attested in Second Temple literature, "resurrection," or the restoration of the life of the body after death, may be linked with immortality (the eternal existence of the soul) and the afterlife (personal existence in the world to come, or 'ôlām habbā') , or may be used independently. In the first centuries AD, Jewish teaching came to the consensus that both body and soul, inseparably, would be judged by God for either punishment or reward at the end of days, which would be marked by the age of the messiah who brings peace and justice into the world, where all will know God.

Daniel Boyarin and Seymour Siegel, "Resurrection," *EncJud*, ed. Cecil Roth and Geoffrey Wigoder, 16 vols. (New York: Macmillan, 1971–72), 14:95–103; and no author, "Afterlife," *EncJud*, 2:335–39.

The Rewards for Sacrifice

In Dan 12:2-3, the "many who sleep in the dust of the earth" are paralleled with "those who are wise," linking the earlier description of the self-sacrifice of the wise (*maśkîlîm*, 11:35) with their eschatological reward. This connection stresses that the tasks of modeling and teaching righteous actions are not forgotten by God, even though the time of suffering is undetermined. In addition, most scholars interpret the reference that the righteous will be "like the stars forever" as indicating their reward among the angels, or heavenly host in heaven (Collins, Montgomery, Wright). In the book of Daniel, the martyrs, equated with the wise, are said to "shine like the brightness of the sky . . . like the stars forever and ever" (12:3). N. T. Wright argues that the reference to the use of stars here is symbolic:

The righteous, the wise, will not so much be transformed into beings of light, as set in authority in the world . . . the resurrection is not so much a resuscitation in which the dead will return to life much as they knew it before. They will be raised to a state of glory in the world for which the best parallel or comparison is the status of stars, moon, and sun within the created order.

Here, Wright argues that the poetic language surely points to an unspecified transcendent reality, although some scholars hold that Dan 12:1-3 reflects a belief that the *maśkîlîm* would be transformed into actual stars, which are understood to be the equivalent of angels (Segal). With this reward, they would take their place among the heavenly host as exalted beings.

N. T. Wright, *The Resurrection of the Son of God* (Christian Origins and the Question of God 3; Minneapolis: Fortress, 2003), 113.
Alan Segal, *Life after Death* (New York: Doubleday & Co., 2004), 265–66.
John Collins, *Daniel: A Commentary on the Book of Daniel* (Hermeneia; Minneapolis: Fortress, 1993), 393–94.
James Montgomery, *A Critical and Exegetical Commentary on The Book of Daniel* (ICC; Edinburgh: T. & T. Clark, 1927), 472–73.

reward applies not only to those who currently suffer, but also to the righteous who have already died (12:2). This resurrection will not be followed by another oppressive kingdom, but by the kingdom of the saints. Just as Daniel 2 speaks of the final kingdom that fills the whole earth, and Daniel 7 speaks of the kingdom of the saints that will last forever, here the angel remarks that "the shattering of the power of the holy people comes to an end" (12:7), confirming that the terrible persecutions will usher in the fulfillment of God's promises.

With the description of the vindication of the righteous we find the first indisputable reference to resurrection in the Hebrew Bible:

Many of those who sleep in the dust of the earth shall awake [*yāqîṣû*] some to everlasting life, and some to shame and everlasting contempt. Those who are wise shall shine like the brightness of the sky, and those who lead many to righteousness, like the stars forever and ever (12:2-3). [The Rewards for Sacrifice]

This text unequivocally indicates that the just will be rewarded with an eschatological resurrection. On this scholars agree; other concepts later associated with resurrection, however, are not specified. Christopher Rowland writes,

Daniel has nothing to say about the last assize [judgment] and the coming of the messiah. Virtually nothing is said [in the book of Daniel] about the character of the new age, except for the prediction of resurrection . . . [and] the messianic woes which were to become such an important feature of Jewish eschatology are only hinted at in Daniel 12:1f.[14]

In Jewish literature, the term "resurrection" (*tḥyt hmtym*) does not appear until the Rabbinic period,[15] yet several verbs are used in the Hebrew Bible that refer to God's granting of life once again for those who have died. Leonard Greenspoon lists them as follows: *ḥyh*, "to live"; *qwm*, "to stand up"; *hqyṣ*, "to wake up"; *šwb*, "to come back"; and *ṣyṣ*, "to sprout forth."[16] The raising up of the dead whose "sleep" separates them from the fullness of life has its roots in several other texts from the Hebrew Bible, examined below.

There is great disagreement among scholars regarding how ancient Israel conceived of the concepts of resurrection and immortality. There are several texts that allow for the *possibility* of these ideas *in some form*, but any equation with the beliefs expressed in Jewish texts from the late Second Temple period and beyond or in early Christian writings defies consensus. Nevertheless, because such texts show hope for a generous God's continuation of the life of the nation or of the lives of individuals, they readily become part of the legacy of later interpretations that show the resurrection of the body to be a reward for the righteous during the *eschaton*, or end times. [Eschatology]

In order to appreciate fully the context of the expression in Daniel 12:2, it is helpful to consider the connotations and association of the texts that form its conceptual antecedents. An examination of Isaiah 26:19, 66:24, and Ezekiel 37:12-14 is particularly useful.

First, Isaiah 26:19:

> Your dead shall live, their corpses shall rise. O dwellers in the dust, awake and sing for joy! For your dew is a radiant dew, and the earth will give birth to those long dead.

The context of this verse in the book of Isaiah is the devastation brought upon Israel by its enemies—the ones who are excluded from the promise of life given to those who have died. The image

---

Eschatology

Eschatology, the study of "last things" or "end times," represents a worldview that is frequently attested in Second Temple literature and in early Christian writings. It holds that the present world, with all its sin and violence, will be transformed to a radically new reality in which God directly acts to ensure righteousness by definitively subduing evil. This theology took root and flourished in times of Greek and later Roman hegemony over the Mediterranean, among both Jews and Christians. Foreign oppression and persecutions, economic hardship, and the perceived faithlessness of members of the group sparked texts that imagine a powerful eschatological transformation of the world. The apparent shattering of ultimate values is understood actually to make sense in the predetermined plan of God, whose own authority ensures that injustice in the world necessarily will be righted in the future. As evidenced in such texts as *1 Enoch*, 2 Maccabees, 4 Maccabees, Wisdom of Solomon, and 2 Baruch, this recompense may include the resurrection of the body or immortality and eternal life for the righteous.

George Nicklesburg, "Eschatology, Early Jewish," *ABD*, ed. David Noel Freedman, 6 vols. (New York: Doubleday & Co., 1992), 2:579–93; and Nicklesburg, "Resurrection, Early Judaism and Christianity," *ABD*, 5:684–91.

of the "radiant dew" and the earth itself giving birth shows the association of the God who creates the world with the One who promises reward for the righteous as recompense for their suffering. Just as nature comes back to life after desolation, so too does this imagery show that life is restored to dead individuals, but whether or not the reference means more than the restoration of the nation of Israel remains controversial.[17]

Second, Isaiah 66:24,

> And they shall go out and look at the dead bodies of the people who have rebelled against me; for their worm shall not die, their fire shall not be quenched, and they shall be an abhorrence [*dērā'ôn*] to all flesh."

Here the prophet speaks of God's judgment against the nations. The book of Daniel's unique reference to the resurrection of the wicked for "everlasting shame" (Dan 12:2b) has its roots in this text of Third Isaiah where the rare word *dērā'ôn* finds its only other usage in the Hebrew Scriptures. Just as the righteous are rewarded, so too does Third Isaiah confirm that divine justice ensures the wicked will be judged by God as well. [Others Restored to Life]

Third, Ezekiel 37:12-14:

> Therefore prophesy, and say to them, Thus says the LORD God: "I am going to open your graves, and bring you up from your graves, O my people; and I will bring you back to the land of Israel. And you shall know that I am the LORD, when I open your graves, and bring you up from your graves, O my people. I will put my spirit within you, and you shall live, and I will place you on your own soil; then you shall know that I, the LORD, have spoken and will act," says the LORD.

Ezekiel's famous description of the dry bones attests to a belief in the restoration of Israel, and the intimate depiction of God's care for those in the grave allows for the possible interpretation of individual resurrection for the exiles. The very manner in which the book of Daniel refers to resurrection, without a detailed defense or explanation, may imply that the readers do not need to be convinced. In addition, there are Jewish texts outside the Bible, contemporaneous with Daniel, that show the belief to have been assumed in some circles. While it is true that early Judaism was divided on the issue, with the Sadducees, for example, denying its existence and the Pharisees holding it as a crucial tenet, Daniel anticipates the idea reflected in 2 Maccabees. [Pharisees and Sadducees]

Others Restored to Life

Some interpreters associate resurrection with other texts in the Hebrew Bible. In the Elijah and Elisha narratives, for example, the prophets restore to life two cherished sons of distressed women. The son of the widow of Zarephath was raised by Elijah (1 Kgs 17:17-24) as was the boy of the unnamed wealthy woman (2 Kgs 4:32-37). Although these children were not buried, the texts unequivocally state that they were indeed dead, and the prophets restored them to life once again. To be sure, these children were not restored to *everlasting* life, but their association with Elijah, who was taken to heaven and did not die, and with Elisha, whose very bones restored another man to life (2 Kgs 13:20-21), prompts some scholars to conclude that the author understood that a continuation of this life (the boys) or a continued presence with God (Elijah) was possible for some. Another Northern Israelite text, Hos 6, shows the prophet speaking disparagingly of shameful Israelites who brazenly defy God, confident nonetheless that God will restore them to life after death:

Come, let us return to the LORD; for it is he who has torn, and he will heal us; he has struck down, and he will bind us up. After two days he will revive us; on the third day he will raise us up, that we may live before him. Let us know, let us press on to know the LORD; his appearing is as sure as the dawn; he will come to us like the showers, like the spring rains that water the earth. (Hos 6:1-3; see Greenspoon, "The Origin of the Idea of Resurrection," 308)

Although Hosea quotes these statements only to prove the Israelites' hypocrisy, it is not the people's idea of God's raising them up that is offensive; rather, it is their behavior and manipulation of God. Leonard Greenspoon offers these and other texts from the Hebrew Scriptures to argue that biblical texts earlier than Daniel do evidence belief in resurrection. They are rooted in the understanding of God as the Divine Warrior who restores both the languishing earth and his people to life. In defeating his enemies, God uses the weaponry of nature, restoring its very essence and Israel itself to life, while ensuring that justice is done to those who have brought injustice and death.

Leonard Greenspoon, "The Origin of the Idea of Resurrection," in *Traditions in Transformation: Turning Points in Biblical Faith*, ed. Baruch Halpern and Jon Levenson (Winona Lake IN: Eisenbrauns, 1981), 247–321.

The second of the seven sons of the faithful woman, who is about to be martyred, confronts Antiochus, saying, "You accursed wretch, you dismiss us from this present life, but the King of the universe will raise us up to an everlasting renewal of life, because we have died for his laws" (2 Macc 7:9). Here the main point is to portray the faithful Jews' willingness to remain loyal to the covenant; thus the references to resurrection ("raise us up") and to immortality ("everlasting") are assumed rather than argued.

The community addressed by the book of Daniel is confronted with the unjust suffering and deaths of their compatriots as well as

Pharisees and Sadducees

The Pharisees and Sadducees were two of the perhaps many groups of Jewish leadership during the latter part of second temple Judaism. The Pharisees believed in not only the written but also the oral Torah, and as such are the spiritual ancestors of the *tannaim* and *amoraim*—the rabbis of the Mishnah and Talmud. The Sadducees were the stricter interpreters of the Torah, not allowing for the contemporary updates and applications that were characteristic of the oral Torah. Priests and servants of the temple, they disappeared after its destruction, and no independent writings from Sadducees survive. Josephus comments:

[The Pharisees] believe that souls have the power to survive death and that there are rewards and punishments under the earth for those who have led lives of virtue or vice: eternal imprisonment is the lot of evil souls, while the good souls receive an easy passage to a new life . . . the Sadducees hold that the soul perishes along with the body. (*Ant.* 18.14–18; see also *J.W.* 2.164; Matt 22:23; Mark 12:18; Luke 20:27; Acts 23:8)

the very demise of their traditions and community identity. In this context, the angel speaks to Daniel of God's ultimate justice with the promise of resurrection for both the righteous, who are vindicated, and the unjust, who are shamed. With this depiction, the vision offers a hope for the future where suffering is no more and where the wrongs of the earth are righted by a God whose power is not only sufficient to stop a tyrant, but also can effect justice beyond the grave. [Wisdom of Solomon]

Daniel's Questions and the Angel's Response, 12:8-13

Continuing the account of his vision, Daniel relates that he sees two additional divine beings—one on each side of the river. Similar to the scene of 8:13-14, Daniel hears an angelic conversation. One of the angels poses a question to the man clothed in linen—the very question presumably Daniel himself dares not ask: "How long until the end that is hidden?" (12:8, A.T.). In Daniel's earlier vision of the ram and the goat, a similar question was

The Doubt: "Can These Drying Bones Live?"

Henry Alexander Bowler. 1824–1903. *The Doubt: "Can These Drying Bones Live?"* Exhibited 1855. Tate Gallery, London, Great Britain. (Credit: Art Resource, NY)

Henry Bowler's *The Doubt: "Can These Drying Bones Live?"* (Ezek 37:3) shows a butterfly, a symbol of the resurrection, on a skull along with a headstone that reads *"resurgam"* (I shall rise again). The presence of the exposed grave and the woman's reflective posture, however, intimate uncertainty.

posed by one of the angels: "For how long is this vision concerning the regular burnt offering, the transgression that makes desolate, and the giving over of the sanctuary and host to be trampled?" (8:13). The man clothed in linen shrouds his answer with images of both awe and mystery. Gesturing toward heaven before he speaks, he swears "By the One Who Lives Forever" that the interval of waiting for the fruition of the vision would be "time, times, and half" (12:7, A.T.).[18] It is noteworthy that the appellation for God in this exchange uniquely contrasts the limited period of earthly suffering with the infinity of the Being who transcends time itself (see also 7:25). The heavenly gestures of the man clothed in linen, namely, the lifting of "his right hand" and "his left hand," anticipate the reversal of the fragmentation of the power or "'hand' [*yād*] of the holy people" (12:7, A.T.). Nonetheless, no exact specification of the date of that reversal is forthcoming, for although "time, times, and half" *may* mean three and a half years, its poetic expres-

The Wisdom of Solomon

The belief in the immortality of the righteous and the punishment of the wicked is also reflected in Wisdom of Solomon, an apocryphal text that dates from the 3rd century BC–1st century AD. The following text is representative:

But the souls of the righteous are in the hand of God,
and no torment will ever touch them.
In the eyes of the foolish they seemed to have died,
and their departure was thought to be a disaster,
and their going from us to be their destruction;
but they are at peace.
For though in the sight of others they were punished,
their hope is full of immortality.
Having been disciplined a little, they will receive great
good,
because God tested them and found them worthy of
himself;
like gold in the furnace he tried them,
and like a sacrificial burnt offering he accepted them.
In the time of their visitation they will shine forth,
and will run like sparks through the stubble.
They will govern nations and rule over peoples,
and the Lord will reign over them forever.
Those who trust in him will understand truth,
and the faithful will abide with him in love,
because grace and mercy are upon his holy ones,
and he watches over his elect.

But the ungodly will be punished as their reasoning
deserves,
those who disregarded the righteous
and rebelled against the Lord;
for those who despise wisdom and instruction are
miserable.

Their hope is vain, their labors are unprofitable,
and their works are useless. (Wis 3:1-11)

This text, extant in Greek, probably comes from a Hebrew or Aramaic original and reflects the concerns of the diaspora community in Egypt, including the use of Greek philosophical concepts and a polemic against Egyptian religion. Daniel Harrington explains that immortality is offered not as an entitlement or as part of the inherent nature of an immortal soul, but rather as a gift from God. In this way, the Wisdom of Solomon presents a theology similar to the book of Daniel's understanding that resurrection is a reward for the righteous. This "hope of immortality," Harrington explains,

gives purpose and direction to human ethical activity, since eternal life with God is the reward for righteous living. It also provides a solution to the problem of innocent suffering. God's justice is deferred until the time of death and/or the last judgment. The sufferings that the righteous undergo in the present serve as a test of their virtue and/or as a source of discipline by which they are brought back to the way of righteousness. (60–61)

As is the case in Daniel, the righteous, who have suffered before their deaths, will be vindicated when they will "shine forth" (Dan 12:3), ruling the nations as partners with God (Dan 7:27). The ethical acts performed by righteous persons are not forgotten by the God of justice.

Daniel Harrington, *Invitation to the Apocrypha* (Grand Rapids MI: Eerdmans, 1999) 55, 60–61.

sion is also open-ended. In other words, the man clothed in linen provides assurance *that* the suffering will cease, but the obscurity of the time line prevents any assurance of *when* the suffering will end.

Daniel's response to hearing this exchange is to ask the angel another question (12:8), thus underscoring that the vision can only be partially understood. Although the angel responds and addresses Daniel's questions, mystery remains. His response emphasizes one command that is given twice: "Go!" (12:9, 13). This imperative does not answer Daniel's question; rather, it redirects what he is to do. Couched between this double command is the angel's patient response, explaining that the world will yet be divided into the wise who purify and those who are wicked. Only with this division confirmed and the ultimate secrecy underscored does the man in linen return to the question of time. The context is limited to the end of

Antiochus's perversions of the temple sacrifice, its purification, and its eventual resumption (12:11). This alone he addresses, giving two responses, namely, 1,290 and 1,335 days. If the "time, times and half a time" of 12:7 (also 7:25) are understood to be three and a half years, then the 1,290 and 1,335 days express two periods slightly longer. Some scholars see the references to 1,290 and 1,335 as two separate corrections to the first prediction of three and a half years, added by two different emendators who lived through the three and a half years of the Antiochan persecutions without seeing the restoration of the temple. Others propose that the two additional time references are intended to represent unspecified stages of a new era of victory after the persecutions, reasoning that a listing of three contradictory dates so closely in one document would defy reason.

With the second usage of the word "go!" the author indicates Daniel's upcoming death; Daniel now approaches his "rest" (12:13). His death is now placed in the context of rising again—the main theme of the final scene of this vision. Indeed, just as Michael will arise (*ya'ămōd*) at the final deliverance (12:1), so too, the angel announces to Daniel, "you shall rise [*ta'ămōd*] for your reward [literally, "lot"] at the end of days" (12:13). [Lot (*gôrāl*)] With this remark, the angel confirms that the just will experience their final recompense of resurrection, whether or not they live to see the triumph of God's kingdom on the earth. For they, like Daniel, have the same task—to be one of the righteous, to face life with courage in the face of protracted suffering, and to be confident that all wrongs will be righted, both on earth and after death.

CONNECTIONS

The final vision in the book of Daniel interweaves an interpretation of history with a future hope in which God's mercy and justice permeate not only worldly experience but also the transcendent reality to which the vision points. Daniel's vision begins with reference to Persian rule and ends with the hope of everlasting life. Within this sweep one finds a microcosm of the community's suffering and hope. Looking back on Israel's experience, Daniel sees that the overwhelming power and control that empires have evidenced are not outside God's purview. What the world sees as success is, on a more profound level, only the petty squabbles of ignorant and arrogant rulers who will not escape God's judgment. Israel's lessons of old—that the God of the covenant is a God who created a world where good triumphs over evil—are affirmed. Victory is assured both on earth as well as in a reality that can only be hinted at—a reality in which human beings become linked with the transcendent beyond the grave. [The World to Come]

The past century as well as our current one are replete with images of overwhelming violence and near annihilations of peoples. Daniel's cry, "how long?" can be repeated by millions of individuals who have lived through persecutions, war, and genocide. How can it be, for example, that as Hitler reflected on other nations' acts of genocide, he remarked to his inner circle, "It was knowingly and lightheartedly that Genghis Khan sent thousands of women and children to their deaths. History sees in him only the founder of a state. . . . *Who today still speaks of the [Ottoman] massacre of the Armenians?*"[19] These chilling words haunt not only Armenians, but also Jews, Roma (gypsies), Cambodians, Rwandans, and Bosnian Serbs whose inconceivable horrific experiences are repeated as the world debates whether the slaughter of the Sudanese in the twenty-first century should be classified as genocide. There are no sufficient answers to account for such suffering. How can humanity hope for the triumph of good over evil when there is so much overwhelming evidence to the contrary?

The community originally addressed in the visions of Daniel 7–12 never witnessed the end of their people's suffering. Nevertheless, this veil of mystery did not prevent the author of the vision from affirming with the eyes of faith that God's creation

The World to Come

The Mishnah (AD 200) teaches that Jews should believe in the world to come, or afterlife, and should understand that this promise is taught in the Bible itself. One is not to speculate on its characteristics, however, as illustrated by the following text, "The [subject of] forbidden relations may not be expounded in the presence of three nor the work of creation in the presence of two nor [the work of] the chariot in the presence of one, unless he is a sage and understands of his own knowledge" (*m. Ḥag.* 2:1).

This discussion lists three subjects that require much caution: forbidden sexual relations, creation, and "the chariot"—a reference to the heavenly visions of the divine throne seen by the prophet Ezekiel, representing the mysteries of heaven itself. The resurrection is associated with the afterlife as is shown in this well-known Mishnaic teaching:

> All Israel have a portion in the World to Come, for it is written, "Thy people are all righteous; they shall inherit the land for ever, the branch of my planting, the work of my hands, that I may be glorified." [Isa 60:21] But the following have no portion therein: he who maintains that resurrection is not a biblical doctrine, the Torah was not divinely revealed, and an *epikoros* [skeptic]. (m. Sanh. 10:1)

Although in its original context in the book of Isaiah the quotation referred to the national restoration of the people, in the Mishnah's interpretation, the bequest of the land lies in the eschatological future and hence is a proof of resurrection and of the world to come. R. Simai similarly saw proof of the resurrection in the Torah itself:

> How do we know that the resurrection of the dead can be derived from the Torah? From the verse, "I also established My covenant with them [i.e., Abraham, Isaac and Jacob], to give them the land of Canaan" (Exod. 6,4), "To you" is not written but "to them." Hence, resurrection of the dead can be derived form the Torah. (*b. Sanh.* 90b, quoted in Levenson, 308)

Here R. Simai understands that God told Moses that the covenantal promise given to Abraham, Isaac, and Jacob was not yet fully realized. Since these patriarchs were already dead, God would fulfill the promise to them after they would be resurrected. In Jewish thought the resurrection of the dead is associated with the final redemption, of which the exodus is a foretaste. In commenting on the Torah's presentation of the exodus, Rabbi Judah Ha-Nasi similarly argues that the opening verse of the Song of the Sea (the song of thanksgiving recited after the crossing of the Red Sea) should be read as "Then Moses *will sing* [to the LORD]" rather than "Moses *sang* [to the LORD]" (Exod 15:1; *Mek.*, Shirata 1). Moses' words of praise cannot be given until he is resurrected from the dead and experiences the final redemption. As Jon Levenson explains, this interpretation

> celebrates an even greater redemption [than the exodus], and even greater vindication, and an even greater and more miraculous passage: the redemption of the dead, the vindication of the righteous, and the passage from death to life. The exodus has become a prototype of ultimate redemption, and historical liberation has become a partial but proleptic experience of eschatological redemption, a token, perhaps *the* token of things to come . . . so long as human beings are subject to death, they are not altogether free: Resurrection is the final and ultimate liberation. (307–308)

Jon Levenson, "The Resurrection of the Dead and the Construction of Personal Identity in Ancient Israel," in *Congress Volume: Basel 2001*, ed. A. Lemaire (VTSup 92; Leiden: Brill, 2002), 305–22.

continues under providential watch. An answer that only partially addresses Daniel's questions must suffice. This vision shows that the seer accepts the angel's hand to arise from the ground and comprehends that God does not abandon the world to the ravages of evil. For the book's powerless readers, the message of this vision is two-fold. Justice in this world will come, because God's very self demands it. Meaning and purpose in life can yet be gleaned. For those who died in anguish, God's covenantal loyalty ensures that they, too, are not forgotten. Although the future reality is never detailed, Daniel receives with quiet confidence the angel's message

Resurrection, Martyrdom, and the Christian Hope

In the book of Daniel, bodily resurrection allowed for God's righting of wrongs perpetrated on earth. Although innocent martyrs were murdered, their lives were not sacrificed in vain. As Alan Segal states, "Foreign invaders had killed the faithful saints of Israel. Resurrection of the body gave transcendent worth to the death of the martyrs by stating that God would make good on his covenantal promises to reward the righteous and punish the iniquitous."

Similarly, for the first Christians, Jesus' martyrdom heralded the commencement of God's fulfillment of the promise made to Daniel and to Israel. For early Christians, the mysterious identity of the One like a Son of Man was revealed to be Jesus, and the end of evil on earth, as revealed in Daniel's visions, was now at hand. The resurrection of the righteous, promised by the angel to Daniel, was now confirmed by the very death and resurrection of Jesus. With Jesus' resurrection came the climax of Israel's history and the beginnings of a new world where the messianic kingdom of God knows no death (1 Cor 15:20-28), where heaven and earth are united (Rev 20–22), and where Jesus would come again to judge the sinners and the righteous.

Alan Segal, *Life after Death* (New York: Doubleday & Co., 2004), 394.

N. T. Wright, *The New Testament and the People of God* (Christian Origins and the Question of God 1; London: SPCK, 1992), 459–64.

that the righteous will rise to everlasting life. For those who have literally gotten away with murder, there will be a cosmic punishment as well. Justice and mercy continue to define Daniel's God. [Resurrection, Martyrdom, and the Christian Hope]

With the temple occupied and the ability to offer atoning sacrifices denied them, the community sees that God has not abandoned the heirs to the covenant. The vision shows that Daniel finds meaning as he waits with quiet confidence and learns from the angel that the wise, who encourage the community, are models of righteousness. Meaning lies not in deciphering the cryptic references to the end, but in acknowledging the very mysteriousness of the revelation. The vision and its interpretation from the angel show that God's plan for the world will not be trampled by beasts. Although the promise of justice is cloaked in mystery, the vision shows that a new age will indeed come, that it is on course, and that it will culminate in the absolute end of the world's tyrants. And this is not all, for the individuals who have suffered will find that God remembers them as well; they will find an eternal reward.

It is this ability to live in faith and confidence, knowing that God has every deed on earth measured, that provides the powerful message of Daniel. God gives humanity a directive of hope, but never a full disclosure. The sending of the angel to a beleaguered Daniel and the very fact of the revelation show God's compassion and faithfulness. With this, the community is given the message to "pay attention" and "be strong." Although Jews are a small and insignificant people in the eyes of the Seleucids and in the broader world, the truth of history is that cruel empires do not last, that the only real power belongs to God, that suffering will end, and that righteous people will be rewarded by an infinitely compassionate God.

In this final vision, Daniel learns that his task is to be one of the wise (the *maśkîlîm*)—to be one who acts in accordance with God's structuring of the world for good (12:10). The wise are able to see the patterns that others do not, namely, that God is at work in human history, bringing the world and its injustices into subjection to God's righteousness. They evidence a world perspective where the teachings of Jewish wisdom are paramount. This wisdom is open to receiving visions and special understanding to endure hardships and even persecutions, confident that a radical transformation of the world is at hand. The author of the apocalyptic chapters of Daniel 7–12, therefore, felt that the model of behavior presented by Daniel and his companions in Daniel 1–6 was most appropriate and encouraging. Their behavior as young exiles fit the *maśkîlîm*'s paradigm of the proper response to oppressive behavior. Sometimes, a courageous word is necessary, and faithful waiting must continue. The faithful must hold firm in their expectation of the righteous intervention of God, which will effect true change on earth. Those who understand this are the wise teachers (11:33; 12:3) who lead others by their example, teaching lessons in faithfulness, ever hopeful that doing the right thing is not forgotten by the LORD who subjects all to the divine will and to an eschatological judgment.[20]

It is this hope that allows humanity to come out of the worst of its horrors to struggle for good. The tireless efforts of individuals who work for peace and justice give humanity pause so that it neither despairs nor falls into a numb disregard for evil. The millions of individuals who have seen their families slaughtered yet have continued to live their lives with courage and hope bear witness. The book of Daniel shows that it is possible for the human spirit to continue the search for meaning in the midst of the unfathomable. [Wisdom and Apocalyptic]

The response of ordinary men and women who act with extraordinary courage and tenacity encourages us to see that Daniel's hope was not an illusion. The author of the visions lived in a world replete with personal challenges that continually assaulted faith itself and with oppression and violence that plagued the community. [The *maśkîlîm* and the Suffering Servant] Rather than retreat from that world, the angel reminds Daniel to continue to act in that same world by remaining loyal to the faith of his ancestors. By doing so, Daniel finds that the best path to take in the midst of his suffering is to refuse to retreat. With this he finds that his humble purpose is to act as a witness against unchecked evil—for it will never have final authority, neither in the material nor in the transcendent world.

For many modern people who read the book of Daniel, there are a host of obstacles to overcome. The narratives in 1–6 seem like fairy tales, with the miraculous deliverances assured after the first

Wisdom and Apocalyptic

Both Wisdom Literature and apocalyptic reflect two worldviews found in the Second Temple period concerning revelation and the mysteries of the universe. The Wisdom tradition stresses that much knowledge can be gleaned from the natural world, created by God, as well as from revealed sources. Both of these sources contain the imprint of God's hand. Wisdom teaches practical knowledge—how to best avoid debt, disease, and worry; how to pursue knowledge and learning; and how to be righteous, modest, and pious. It is based upon knowledge available to the entire community, found both in the common experience of the world (Proverbs, Ecclesiastes), from a consideration of innocent suffering (Job), and from the wisdom revealed in the religious sphere (Ben Sira).

The apocalyptic tradition, however, underscores that revelation comes directly from heaven—in cryptic form—and is given to a seer and/or a select few. This knowledge is special and specific, presenting a predetermined revelation that is relevant for the end of days, and not for the mundane aspects of everyday life (Dan 11:40–12:3). It has a particular relevance for individuals as opposed to the group, as it is concerned with reward and punishment after death. Its disclosures instruct those privy to the revelation to live in accordance with God's demands. Without God's unique revelation, the world and the goal of creation would remain ever impenetrable.

Although the visions of the book of Daniel call upon the seer to be one of the wise, they are not representative of wisdom teachings in the classic sense. Rather, they form an apocalypse, concerned with the unique revelation determined by God from the foundation of the world, given to Daniel, and interpreted by angels. Although this unique heavenly disclosure is given to a special person and requires divine beings to understand it, the author also expected that any reader of the day could have access to the mystery if only he or she would be open to receiving it.

It is important to remember that although Wisdom and Apocalyptic reflect distinct locales for the origin of revelation, they are not incompatible. The manifest world (which is God's creation) as well as the specific revelations to prophets and seers manifest God's plan for humankind. God's ways are not completely understood, but the search to understand them can yield either practical knowledge, such as the youth Daniel experienced (Dan 1–6), or can provide an idealized hope, which serves, in effect, as encouragement. Daniel finds meaning in being a model of righteousness and solace, as he hopes for a world in which God's justice is no longer concealed.

See John Collins, *Wisdom in the Hellensitic Age* (OTL; Louisville KY: Westminster/John Knox Press, 1997).

narrative. The imagery in the visions of 7–12 seems bizarre and the highly symbolic language sometimes impenetrable. An even greater challenge to the modern reader may be the book's history of interpretation. The fantastic beasts have been identified in ways that seem inane to the modern reader—with caliphs, popes, and communist leaders, interpreters have projected their own fears onto the tableau of Daniel's symbolism. Yet Daniel and his companions' aspirations, as expressed in the stories, and the revelations Daniel experiences, as detailed in the visions, attest to the capacity of human beings to strive for

The *maśkîlîm* and the Suffering Servant

Michael Fishbane argues that the author of the book of Daniel portrays the *maśkîlîm* as the spiritual heirs of the "suffering servant" of the book of Isaiah who act as the "vindicators of the many" (12:3) by their acts of teaching and martyrdom. Just as the servant suffered yet prospered and was glorified (Isa 53:11-12), so too would the suffering of the *maśkîlîm* be rewarded with eternal life (Dan 12:2). Because of this equation, the final vision of the book of Daniel includes echoes of the promise of resurrection (Isa 26:19) as well as of eternal punishment (Isa 66:24) in order "to reinforce confidence in divine vindication at the final end, whose fulfillment was forecast of old, and now [was] believed to be an imminent reality."

Michael Fishbane, *Biblical Interpretation in Ancient Israel* (Oxford: Clarendon Press; New York: Oxford University Press, 1985), 493.

justice and for good in a world where evil is a tenacious competitor. The stories show that it is possible to believe that might does not always win, and the visions demonstrate that even when evil reaches ascendancy, a radical reversal can occur. Ultimately, even those who have suffered the unfathomable will be vindicated. The testimony of the book of Daniel to the resurrection can only be grasped through the eyes of faith, but for those who embrace it, the belief not only provides solace but motivation never to tire of the quest for ultimate values of kindness, justice, and hope. For the hope of resurrection, immortality, and the last judgment ultimately reflects what we value most and how we make sense of a world when everything seems shattered.

NOTES

[1] Raymond Hammer, *The Book of Daniel* (Cambridge Bible Commentary 41; London: Cambridge University Press, 1976), 102.

[2] "The Great River" may also be equated with the Euphrates (Deut 1:7; 11:24 and Dan 10:4, Syriac).

[3] André LaCocque argues that the being possibly represents God; see *The Book of Daniel*, trans. David Pellauer (Atlanta: John Knox Press, 1979), 20. The following scholars argue that he possibly represents Gabriel: Norman Porteous, *Daniel: A Commentary* (OTL; Philadelphia: Westminster, 1965), 152; Kevin Sullivan, *Wrestling with Angels* (Arbeiten zur Geschichte des antiken Judentums und des Urchristentums; Leiden: Brill, 2004), 61–63; Paul Redditt, *Daniel* (The New Century Bible Commentary; Sheffield, England: Sheffield Academic Press, 1999), 169–71. Others note that the angel remains unidentified: James Montgomery, *A Critical and Exegetical Commentary on the Book of Daniel* (ICC; Edinburgh: T. & T. Clark, 1927), 404; John Collins, *Daniel* (Hermeneia; Minneapolis: Fortress, 1993), 373; John Goldingay, *Daniel* (WBC; Dallas: Word Books, 1989), 290.

[4] Collins, *Daniel*, 375.

[5] Gen 15:1; 21:17; 26:24; Lam 3:52-57; Tob 12:17; Luke 1:13, 30. Louis Hartman and Alexander Di Lella, *The Book of Daniel* (AB 23; Garden City NY: Doubleday, 1978), 281.

[6] The reading "number of the gods" (*bny ʾlhym*) is supported by 4QDeutʲ and by the Septuagint. See Emanuel Tov, *Textual Criticism of the Hebrew Bible* (Minneapolis: Fortress, 1992), 269.

[7] Collins, *Daniel*, 371–404.

[8] Hartman and Di Lella, *The Book of Daniel*, 287–88; Montgomery, *A Critical and Exegetical Commentary*, 423; Collins, *Daniel*, 377.

[9] Hartman and Di Lella, *The Book of Daniel*, 291–92; Goldingay, Daniel, 297.

[10] Collins, *Daniel*, 380.

[11] Hartman and Di Lella, *The Book of Daniel*, 299–300.

[12] Collins, *Daniel*, 387.

[13] For discussion of the heavenly books see ["Books" in Judaism and Christianity] and [The Book of Truth (Daniel 10:21)].

[14] Christopher Rowland, *The Open Heaven* (New York: Crossroad, 1982), 12.

[15] Leonard Greenspoon, "The Origin of the Idea of Resurrection," in *Traditions in Transformation: Turning Points in Biblical Faith*, ed. Baruch Halpern and Jon Levenson (Winona Lake IN: Eisenbrauns, 1981), 253.

[16] Ibid., 254.

[17] Ibid., 285.

[18] See discussion above, Dan 7:23-27.

[19] Samantha Power, *"A Problem from Hell": America and the Age of Genocide* (New York: Basic Books, 2002), 23.

[20] Collins, *Daniel*, 66–67.

BIBLIOGRAPHY

Abrams, Judith Z. *The Talmud for Beginners*. 2 vols. Northvale NJ: Jason Aronson, 1993.

Ackroyd, Peter R. *The Chronicler in His Age*. Journal for the Study of the Old Testament Supplement Series 107. Sheffield: Sheffield Academic Press, 1991.

"Afterlife." Editorial staff. In vol. 2 of *Encyclopaedia Judaica*. Edited by Cecil Roth. 16 vols. New York: MacMillan, 1971. 335–39.

Arnold, Bill T. "Wordplay and Narrative Techniques in Daniel 5 and 6." *Journal of Biblical Literature* 112/3 (1993): 479–85.

Balentine, Samuel E. *Prayer in the Hebrew Bible: The Drama of Divine-Human Dialogue*. Overtures to Biblical Theology. Minneapolis: Fortress, 1993.

———. *The Torah's Vision of Worship*. Overtures to Biblical Theology. Minneapolis: Fortress, 1999.

Bar-Efrat, Shimon. *Narrative Art in the Bible*. Journal for the Study of the Old Testament Supplement Series 70. Bible and Literature Series 17. Sheffield: Almond Press, 1989.

Becking, Bob. "'A Divine Spirit is in You': Notes on the Translation of the Phrase *rûªḥ ᵉlahîn* in Dan 5,14 and Related Texts." In *The Book of Daniel in the Light of New Findings*. Edited by A. S. van der Woude. Bibliotheca Ephemeridum Theologicarum Lovaniensium 106. Leuven: Leuven University Press, 1993. 515–19.

"Belshazzar." Editorial staff. In vol. 4 of *Encyclopaedia Judaica*. Edited by Cecil Roth. 16 vols. New York: MacMillan, 1971. 448–50.

Birnbaum, David. *God and Evil: A Unified Theodicy/Theology/Philosophy*. Hoboken NJ: Ktav Publishing House, 1989.

Boda, Mark. "The Priceless Gain of Penitence: From Communal Lament to Penitential Prayer in the 'Exilic' Liturgy of Israel." *Horizons in Biblical Theology* 25 (2003): 51–75.

———. *Praying the Tradition: The Origin and Use of Tradition in Nehemiah 9*. Beihefte zur Zeitschrift für die alttestamentliche Wissenschaft 277. Berlin: Walter de Gruyter, 1999.

Boraas, Roger S. "Purple." In *Harper's Bible Commentary*. Edited by Paul J. Achtemeier. San Francisco: Harper & Row, 1985. 844.

Boyarin, Daniel, and Seymour Siegel. "Resurrection." In vol. 14 of *Encyclopaedia Judaica*. Edited by Cecil Roth. 16 vols. New York: MacMillan, 1971. 95–103.

Boyce, Mary. "Ahura Mazda." In vol. 1 of *The Anchor Bible Dictionary*. Edited by David Noel Freedman. 6 vols. New York: Doubleday & Company, 1992. 124–25.

———. "Persian Religion in the Achemenid Age." In *Introduction; The Persian Period*. Edited by W. D. Davies and Louis Finkelstein. Vol. 1 of The Cambridge History of Judaism. Cambridge: Cambridge University Press, 1984. 279–307.

———. "Zoroaster, Zoroastrianism." In vol. 6 of *The Anchor Bible Dictionary*. Edited by David Noel Freedman. 6 vols. New York: Doubleday & Company, 1992. 1168–74.

Braverman, Jay. *Jerome's Commentary on Daniel: A Study of Comparative Jewish and Christian Interpretation of the Hebrew Bible*. Catholic Biblical Quarterly Monograph Series 7. Washington DC: The Catholic Biblical Association, 1978.

Brenner, Athalya. "Who's Afraid of Feminist Criticism?" In *Prophets and Daniel: A Feminist Companion to the Bible* (Second Series). Edited by Athalya Brenner. London/New York: Sheffield Academic Press, 2001. 228–44.

Brooke, George J. "Susanna and Paradise Regained." In *Women in the Biblical Tradition*. Edited by George J. Brooke. Studies in Women and Religion 31. Lewiston NY: Edwin Mellen Press, 1992. 92–111.

Brown, Francis, S. R. Driver, and Charles A. Briggs, *A Hebrew and English Lexicon of the Old Testament*. Oxford: Clarendon, 1907, repr. 1977.

Brueggemann, Walter. "At the Mercy of Babylon: A Subversive Rereading of the Empire." *Journal of Biblical Literature* 110/1 (1991): 3–22.

Burton, Anne. *Diodorus Siculus, Book I; A Commentary*. Etudes préliminaires aux religions orientales dans l'Empire romain 29. Leiden: Brill, 1972.

Calvin, John. *Commentaries on the Book of the Prophet Daniel*. Translated by Thomas Myers. 2 vols. Grand Rapids MI: Eerdmans, 1948.

Charles, R. H., editor. *The Apocrypha and Pseudepigrapha of the Old Testament in English*. Translated by J. Rendel Harris, Agnes Smith Lewis, and F. C. Conybeare. 2 vols. Oxford: Clarendon Press, 1976.

Clifford, Richard J. "Tammuz." *Harper's Bible Dictionary*. Edited by Paul Achtemeier. San Francisco: Harper & Row, 1985. 1017.

Collins, John J. "4QPrayer of Nabonidus ar." In *Qumran Cave 4. XVIII: Parabiblical Texts, Part 3*. Edited by J. C. VanderKam. Discoveries in the Judaean Desert 22. Oxford: Clarendon Press, 1996. 83–93 + pl. VI.

———. *Daniel: A Commentary on the Book of Daniel*. Hermeneia. Minneapolis: Fortress, 1993.

———. *Daniel, First Maccabees, Second Maccabee: With an Excursus on the Apocalyptic Genre*. Old Testament Message. Wilmington DE: Michael Glazier, 1981.

———. "Introduction: Towards the Morphology of a Genre." In *Apocalypse: The Morphology of a Genre*. Edited by J. J. Collins. *Semeia* 14. Missoula MT: Scholars Press, 1979. 1–20.

Cook, Edward M. "'In the Plain of the Wall' (Dan 3:1)." *Journal of Biblical Literature* 108/1 (1989): 115–16.

Coxon, Peter. "Shadrach, Meshach, Abednego." In vol. 5 of *The Anchor Bible Dictionary*. Edited by David Noel Freedman. 6 vols. New York: Doubleday & Company, 1992. 1150.

Craven, Toni. *Ezekiel, Daniel*. Collegeville Bible Commentary, Old Testament 16. Collegeville MN: Liturgical Press, 1986.

Dahood, Mitchell. *Psalms II: 51–100*. Anchor Bible 17. Garden City NY: Doubleday & Company, 1968.

Dan, Joseph. "Sacrifice." In vol. 14 of *Encyclopaedia Judaica*. Edited by Cecil Roth. 16 vols. New York: MacMillan, 1971. 599–616.

Dandamayev, M. "The Diaspora." In *Introduction; The Persian Period*. Edited by W. D. Davies and Louis Finkelstein. Vol. 1 of The Cambridge History of Judaism. Cambridge: Cambridge University Press, 1984. 326–400.

Davies, P. R. "Reading Daniel Sociologically." In *The Book of Daniel in the Light of New Findings*. Edited by A. S. Van der Woude. Bibliotheca Ephemeridum Theologicarum Lovaniensium 106. Leuven: Leuven University Press, 1993. 352–55.

Deventer, H. J. M. van. "Would the Actually 'Powerful' Please Stand?: The Role of the Queen (mother) in Daniel 5." *Scriptura* 70 (1999): 241–51.

Diodorus, Siculus. *Diodorus of Sicily*. Translated by C. H. Oldfather et al. 12 vols. Loeb Classical Library. Cambridge MA: Harvard University Press, 1933.

Dommershausen, W. "*gôrāl*." In vol. 2 of *Theological Dictionary of the Old Testament*. Edited by Botterweck Ringgren and Helmer Ringgren. Translated by John T. Willis. Revised edition. Grand Rapids MI: Eerdmans, 1975. 450–56.

Donin, Hayim Halevy. *To Pray as a Jew: A Guide to the Prayer Book and the Synagogue Service*. New York: Basic Books, 1980.

Dozeman, Thomas. "The Priestly Vocation." *Interpretation* 59/2 (2005): 117–28.

Efron, Joshua. *Studies on the Hasmonean Period*. Studies in Judaism in Late Antiquity 33. Leiden: Brill, 1987.

Eggler, Jürg. *Influences and Traditions Underlying the Vision of Daniel 7:2-14: the Research History from the End of the 19th Century to the Present*. Orbis biblicus et orientalis 177. Fribourg Switzerland: University Press; Göttingen: Vandenhoeck & Ruprecht, 2000.

Eshel, Esther. "Possible Sources of the Book of Daniel." In vol. 2 of *The Book of Daniel: Composition and Reception*. Edited by John J. Collins and Peter Flint. 2 vols. Supplements to Vetus Testamentum 83. Leiden: Brill, 2001. 387–94.

Feldman, Louis H. *Jew and Gentile in the Ancient World*. Princeton NJ: Princeton University Press, 1993.

———. *Josephus's Interpretation of the Bible*. Berkeley: University of California Press, 1998.

Fewell, Dana Nolan. *Circle of Sovereignty: A Story of Stories in Daniel 1–6*. Journal for the Study of the Old Testament Supplement Series 72. Bible and Literature Series 20. Sheffield: Almond Press, 1988.

———. *Circle of Sovereignty: Plotting Politics in the Book of Daniel*. Nashville: Abingdon Press, 1991.

Fishbane, Michael. *Biblical Interpretation in Ancient Israel*. Oxford: Clarendon Press, 1985.

Flint, Peter W. "The Daniel Tradition at Qumran." In vol. 2 of *The Book of Daniel: Composition and Reception*. Edited by John J. Collins and Peter Flint. 2 vols. Supplements to Vetus Testamentum 83. Leiden: Brill, 2001. 329–67.

Fox, Michael V. *Character and Ideology in the Book of Esther*. 2d edition. Grand Rapids MI: Eerdmans, 2001.

Freedman, H. and Maurice Simon, editors. *Midrash Rabbah*. 10 vols. London/New York: Soncino, 1983.

Frölich, Ida. "Pesher, Apocalyptical Literature and Qumran." In vol. 1 of *The Madrid Qumran Congress: Proceedings of the International Congress on the Dead Sea Scrolls, Madrid, 18–21 March, 1991*. Edited by Julio Trebolle Barrera and Luis Vegas

Montaner. 2 vols. Studies on the Texts of the Desert of Judah 12. Leiden: Brill, 1992. 295–305.

———. *"Time and Times and Half a Time": Historical Consciousness in the Jewish Literature of the Persian and Hellenistic Eras.* Journal for the Study of the Pseudepigrapha Supplement Series 19. Sheffield: Sheffield Academic Press, 1996.

Gammie, John G. "A Journey Through Danielic Spaces" In *Interpreting the Prophets.* Edited by James Luther Mays and Paul J. Achtemeier. Philadelphia: Fortress, 1987. 261–72.

Gilingham, S. E. *The Poems and Psalms of the Hebrew Bible.* The Oxford Bible Series. Oxford: Oxford University Press, 1994.

Ginzberg, Louis. *Legends of the Jews.* Translated by Henrietta Szold. 7 vols. Philadelphia: The Jewish Publication Society, 1968.

Glancy, Jennifer A. "The Accused: Susanna and her Readers." In *A Feminist Companion to Esther, Judith and Susanna.* Feminist Companion to the Bible 7. Edited by Athalya Brenner. Sheffield: Sheffield Academic Press, 1995. 288–302.

Goldingay, John. *Daniel.* Word Biblical Commentary 30. Dallas: Word Books, 1989.

Goldwurm, Hersh. *Daniel: A New Translation with a Commentary Anthologized from Talmudic, Midrashic, and Rabbinic Sources.* The ArtScroll Tanach Series. Brooklyn NY: Mesorah Publications, 1979.

Gottwald, Norman K. *The Hebrew Bible: A Socio-Literary Introduction.* Philadelphia: Fortress, 1985.

Gowan, Donald. *Daniel.* Abingdon Old Testament Commentaries. Nashville: Abingdon Press, 2001.

Grabbe, Lester. "The Belshazzar of Daniel and the Belshazzar of History." *Andrews University Seminary Studies* 26 (Spring 1988): 59–66.

———. *Judaism from Cyrus to Hadrian: The Persian and Greek Periods.* Vol. 1 of Judaism from Cyrus to Hadrian. Minneapolis: Fortress, 1992.

Grayson, Kirk. "History of Mesopotamia (Babylonia)." In vol. 4 of *The Anchor Bible Dictionary.* Edited by David Noel Freedman. 6 vols. New York: Doubleday & Company, 1992. 755–77.

Greenspoon, Leonard. "The Origin of the Idea of Resurrection." In *Traditions in Transformation: Turning Points in Biblical Faith.* Edited by Baruch Halpern and Jon Levenson. Winona Lake IN: Eisenbrauns, 1981. 247–321.

Gruen, Erich. *Heritage and Hellenism: The Reinvention of Jewish Tradition.* Berkeley: University of California Press, 1998.

Gunn, David M. and Danna Nolan Fewell. *Narrative in the Hebrew Bible.* Oxford Bible Series. Oxford: Oxford University Press, 1993.

Haag, Ernst. *Die Errettung Daniels aus der Löwengrub: Untersuchungen zum Ursprung der biblischen Danieltradition.* Stuttgarter Bibelstudien 110. Stuttgart: Verlag Katholisches Bibelwerk, 1983.

Habel, Norman. "The Form and Significance of the Call Narratives." *Zeitschrift für die alttestmentliche Wissenschaft* 77 (1965): 297–323.

Halpern, Baruch and Jon Levenson. *Traditions in Transformation: Turning Points in Biblical Faith.* Winona Lake IN: Eisenbrauns, 1981.

Hammer, Raymond. *The Book of Daniel.* The Cambridge Bible Commentary 41. Cambridge: Cambridge University Press, 1976.

Harrington, Daniel. *Invitation to the Apocrypha*. Grand Rapids MI: Eerdmans, 1999.

Hartman, Louis and Alexander Di Lella. *The Book of Daniel*. Anchor Bible 23. Garden City NY: Doubleday & Company, 1978.

Helfmeyer, J. "*ōth*." In vol. 1 of *Theological Dictionary of the Old Testament*. Revised edition. Edited by G. Johannes Botterweck and Helmer Ringgren. Translated by John T. Willis. Grand Rapids MI: Eerdmans, 1974. 167–88.

Henten, J. W. van. *The Maccabean Martyrs as Saviours of the Jewish People: A Study of 2 and 4 Maccabees*. Supplements to the Journal for the Study of Judaism 57. Leiden: Brill, 1997.

Henze, Matthias. *The Madness of King Nebuchadnezzar: The Ancient Near Eastern Origins and Early History of Interpretation of Daniel 4*. Supplements to the Journal for the Study of Judaism 61. Leiden: Brill, 1999.

Herodotus. *The Histories*. Translated by Robin Waterfield. New York: Oxford University Press, 1998.

Hesiod. *The Homeric Hymns and Homerica*. Translated by Hugh G. Evelyn-White. Loeb Classical Library. New York: G. P. Putnam's Sons, 1926.

———. *Works and Days; Theogony*. Translated by Stanley Lombardo. Indianapolis: Hackett, 1993.

Hiers, Richard. "Kingdom of God." In *Harper's Bible Commentary*. Edited by Paul J. Achtemeier. San Francisco: Harper & Row, 1985. 527–29.

Humphreys, W. Lee. "A Life-Style for Diaspora: A Study of the Tales of Esther and Daniel." *Journal of Biblical Literature* 92/2 (1973): 211–23.

Jagersma, Henk. *A History of Israel from Alexander the Great to Bar Kochba*. Philadelphia: Fortress, 1986.

Japhet, Sara. *I & II Chronicles: A Commentary*. The Old Testament Library. Louisville KY: Westminster/John Knox, 1993.

Jarick, John. *1 Chronicles*. Readings: A New Biblical Commentary. London: Sheffield Academic Press, 2002.

Jastrow, Marcus. *A Dictionary of the Targumim, the Talmud Babli and Yerushalmi, and the Midrashic Literature*. Brooklyn NY: Traditional Press, n.d.

Jones, Ivor. "Music and Musical Instrument." In vol. 4 of *The Anchor Bible Dictionary*. Edited by David Noel Freedman. 6 vols. New York: Doubleday & Company, 1992. 930–39.

Josephus, Flavius. *Josephus*. Translated by H. St. J. Thackeray et al. 10 vols. Loeb Classical Library. Cambridge: Harvard University Press, 1926–1965.

Justin. *Epitome of the Philippic History of Pompeius Trogus*. Translated by J. C. Yardley. Introduction and notes by R. Develin. American Philological Association Classical Resources Series 3. Atlanta: Scholars Press, 1994.

———. *Epitome of the Philippic History of Pompeius Trogus: Books 11–12: Alexander the Great*. Translated by J. C. Yardley. Commentary by Waldemar Heckel. Clarendon Ancient History Series. Oxford: Clarendon, 1997.

Klein, Ralph. *Israel in Exile: A Theological Interpretation*. Overtures to Biblical Theology. Philadelphia: Fortress, 1979.

Kosmala, H. "*gābhar*." In vol. 2 of *Theological Dictionary of the Old Testament*. Edited by G. Johannes Botterweck and Helmer Ringgren. Translated by John T. Willis. Revised edition. Grand Rapids MI: Eerdmans, 1974. 367–82.

Kuhrt, Amélie. "Ancient Mesopotamia in Classical Greek and Hellenistic Thought." In vol. 1 of *Civilizations of the Ancient Near East*. Edited by Jack Sasson. 4 vols. New York: Scribner, 1995. 55–65.

Kugel, James. *The Bible as It Was*. Cambridge MA: The Belknap Press of Harvard University Press, 1997.

LaCocque, André. *Daniel in His Time*. Studies on Personalities of the Old Testament. Columbia: University of South Carolina Press, 1988.

Lattey, Cuthbert. *The Book of Daniel*. Dublin: Browne and Nolan, 1948.

Lawson, Jack. "'The God Who Reveals Secrets': The Mesopotamian Background to Daniel 2:47." *Journal for the Study of the Old Testament* 74 (1997): 61–76.

Levenson, Jon D. *Esther: A Commentary*: The Old Testament Library. Louisville KY: Westminster/John Knox, 1997.

———. "The Jerusalem Temple." In *Jewish Spirituality: From the Bible to the Middle Ages*. Edited by Arthur Green. World Spirituality 13. New York: Crossroad, 1994. 32–61.

———. "The Resurrection of the Dead and the Construction of Personal Identity in Ancient Israel." In *Congress Volume: Basel 2001*. International Organization for the Study of the Old Testament: 17th Congress, 2001, Basel, Switzerland. Edited by André Lemaire. Supplements to Vetus Testamentum 92. Leiden/Boston: Brill, 2002. 305–22.

Levine, Amy-Jill. "'Hemmed in on Every Side': Jews and Women in the Book of Susanna." In *A Feminist Companion to Esther, Judith and Susanna*. Feminist Companion to the Bible 7. Edited by Athalya Brenner. Sheffield: Sheffield Academic Press, 1995. 303–23.

Levine, Barch. *Leviticus*. The JPS Torah Commentary. Philadelphia: The Jewish Publication Society, 1989.

Levine, Lee I. *Judaism and Hellenism in Antiquity: Conflict or Confluence*. The Samuel and Althea Stroum Lectures in Jewish Studies. Seattle: University of Washington Press, 1998.

Mangel, Nissen, translator. *Siddur Tehillat Hashem: According to the Text of Rabbi Schneur Zalman of Liadi*. New York: Merkos L' Inyonei Chinuch, 1988.

Meadowcroft, T. J. *Aramaic Daniel and Greek Daniel: A Literary Comparison*. Journal for the Study of the Old Testament Supplement Series 198. Sheffield: Sheffield Academic Press, 1995.

Mendels, Doron. "Baruch, Book of." In vol. 1 of *The Anchor Bible Dictionary*. Edited by David Noel Freedman. 6 vols. New York: Doubleday & Company, 1992. 618–20.

Mendels, Michal Dayagi. "Susanna, Book of." In vol. 6 of *The Anchor Bible Dictionary*. Edited by David Noel Freedman. 6 vols. New York: Doubleday & Company, 1992. 246–47.

Milik, Jozef, editor. *The Books of Enoch: Aramaic Fragments of Qumran Cave 4*. Oxford: Clarendon Press, 1976.

Milgrom, Jacob. *Numbers*. The JPS Torah Commentary. Philadelphia: The Jewish Publication Society, 1990.

Millard, Alan R. "Daniel and Belshazzar in History." *Biblical Archaeology Review* 11/3 (May 1985): 73–78.

Mitchell, T. C. "The Music of the Old Testament Reconsidered." *Palestinian Exploration Quarterly* 124/2 (1992): 124–43.

Montgomery, James. *A Critical and Exegetical Commentary on the Book of Daniel.* The International Critical Commentary. Edinburgh: T. & T. Clark, 1927.

Moore, Carey. "Daniel, Additions to." In vol. 2 of *The Anchor Bible Dictionary.* Edited by David Noel Freedman. 6 vols. New York: Doubleday & Company, 1992. 18–28.

———. "Susanna: A Case of Sexual Harassment in Ancient Babylon." *Bible Review* 8 (June 1992): 20–29, 52.

Muddiman, John. "Fast, Fasting." In vol. 2 of *The Anchor Bible Dictionary.* Edited by David Noel Freedman. 6 vols. New York: Doubleday & Company, 1992. 773–76.

Müller, H.-P. "*chākham.*" In vol. 4 of *Theological Dictionary of the Old Testament.* Edited by G. Johannes Botterweck and Helmer Ringgren. Translated by David E. Green. Revised Edition. Grand Rapids MI: Eerdmans, 1980. 364–85.

Nicklesburg, George. "Eschatology, Early Jewish." In vol. 2 of *The Anchor Bible Dictionary.* Edited by David Noel Freedman. 6 vols. New York: Doubleday & Company, 1992. 579–93.

Pardee, D., Paul Dion, and Stanley Stowers. "Letters." In vol. 4 of *The Anchor Bible Dictionary.* Edited by David Noel Freedman. 6 vols. New York: Doubleday & Company, 1992. 282–94.

Porter, Paul A. *Metaphors and Monsters: A Literary-Critical Study of Daniel 7 and 8.* Coniectanea Biblica: Old Testament Series 20. Lund: C. W. K. Gleerup, 1983.

Pfandl, Gerhard. "Interpretations of the Kingdom of God in Daniel 2:44." *Andrews University Seminary Studies* 34 (1996): 249–68.

Polybius. *Histories.* Translated by W. R. Paton. 6 vols. Loeb Classical Library. New York: G. P. Putnam's Sons, 1922–1927.

Porteous, Norman. *Daniel: A Commentary.* The Old Testament Library. Philadelphia: Westminster, 1965.

Portier-Young, Anathea. "'Eyes to the Blind': A Dialogue between Tobit and Job." In *Intertextual Studies in Ben Sira and Tobit: Essays in Honor of Alexander Di Lella.* Edited by Jeremy Corley and Vincent Skemp. Catholic Biblical Quarterly Monograph Series 38. Washington DC: The Catholic Biblical Association of America, 2005. 14–27.

Prinsloo, G. T. M. "Two Poems in a Sea of Prose: the Content and Context of Daniel 2.20–23. and 6.27–28." *Journal for the Study of the Old Testament* 59 (1993): 93–108.

Pritchard, James B., editor. *Ancient Near Eastern Texts Relating to the Old Testament.* 3rd edition. Princeton NJ: Princeton University Press, 1969.

Rabinowitz, Louis Isaac. "Idolatry." In vol. 8 of *Encyclopaedia Judaica.* Edited by Cecil Roth. 16 vols. New York: Macmillan, 1971. 1227–38.

Rajak, Tessa. *The Jewish Dialogue with Greece and Rome: Studies in Cultural and Social Interaction.* Arbeiten zur Geschichte des antiken Judentums und des Urchristentums 48. Leiden: Brill, 2001.

Rappaport, Uriel. "Maccabean Revolt." In vol. 4 of *The Anchor Bible Dictionary.* Edited by David Noel Freedman. 6 vols. New York: Doubleday & Company, 1992. 433–39.

Reddish, Mitchell. *Revelation*, The Smyth and Helwys Bible Commentary. Macon GA: Smyth & Helwys, 2001.

Redditt, Paul. *Daniel*. The New Century Bible Commentary. Sheffield: Sheffield Academic Press, 1999.

———. "Daniel 9: Its Structure and Meaning." *Catholic Biblical Quarterly* 62 (2000): 236–49.

Reid, Stephen Breck. *Enoch and Daniel: A Form Critical and Sociological Study of Historical Apocalypses*. Berkeley CA: Bibal Press, 1989.

Rosenberg, A. J. *Daniel; Ezra; Nehemiah: A New English Translation of the Text, Rashi, and a Commentary Digest*. Judaica Books of the Hagiographa—The Holy Writings. New York: Judaica Press, 1991.

Rowland, Christopher. *The Open Heaven: A Study of Apocalyptic in Judaism and Early Christianity*. New York: Crossroad, 1982.

Sacchi, Paolo. *The History of the Second Temple Period*. Journal for the Study of the Old Testament Supplement Series 285. Sheffield: Sheffield Academic Press, 2000.

Schalit, Abraham. "Alexander the Great." In vol. 2 of *Encyclopaedia Judaica*. Edited by Cecil Roth. 16 vols. New York: Macmillan, 1971. 578–79.

Schiffman, Lawrence. "Mourning Rites." In *Harper's Bible Dictionary*. Edited by Paul Achtemeier. San Francisco: Harper & Row, 1985. 661–62.

Schiffman, Lawrence. *Reclaiming the Dead Sea Scrolls*. The Anchor Bible Reference Library. New York: Doubleday & Company, 1995.

Segal, Alan. *Life after Death: A History of the Afterlife in Western Religion*. New York: Doubleday & Company, 2004.

Shahar, Ravi, translator. *The Book of Daniel: Shield of the Spirit: The Commentaries of Rashi and Rabbi Moshe Alshich on Sefer Daniel*. The Alshich Tanach Series. Jerusalem: Feldheim, 1994.

Siegel, Richard, Michael Strassfeld, and Sharon Strassfeld. *The First Jewish Catalog: A Do It Yourself Kit*. Philadelphia: The Jewish Publication Society, 1973.

Slotki, Judah. *Daniel, Ezra, Nehemiah*. Soncino Books of the Bible. Revised 2d edition by Ephraim Oratz. London: Soncino, 1951, rev. 2d ed., 1992.

Smith, Daniel L. "The Politics of Ezra." In *Second Temple Studies: Persian Period*. Edited by Philip R. Davies. Vol. 1 of *Second Temple Studies*. Journal for the Study of the Old Testament Supplement Series 117. Sheffield, England: JSOT Press, 1991. 73–97.

Smith-Christopher, Daniel. "Prayers and Dreams: Power and Diaspora Identities in the Social Setting of the Daniel Tales." In vol. 1 of *The Book of Daniel: Composition and Reception*. Edited by John J. Collins and Peter W. Flint. 2 vols. Supplements to Vetus Testamentum 83. Leiden/Boston: Brill, 2001. 266–90.

Smith, Morton. "Jewish Religious Life." In *Introduction; The Persian Period*. Edited by W. D. Davies and Louis Finkelstein. Vol. 1 of The Cambridge History of Judaism. Cambridge: Cambridge University Press, 1984. 219–78.

Spiegel, Shalom. *The Last Trial*. Translated by Judah Goldin. New York: Schocken, 1969. Repr., Woodstock VT: Jewish Lights, 1993.

Stefanovic, Zdravko. "The Presence of the Three and a Fraction: A Literary Figure in the Book of Daniel." In *To Understand the Scriptures: Essays in Honor of William H. Shea*. Edited by David Merling. Berrien Springs MI: Andrews University Press, 1997. 199–204.

Stern, Ephraim. "The Persian Empire and the Political and Social History of Palestine in the Persian Period." In *Introduction; The Persian Period.* Edited by W. D. Davies and Louis Finkelstein. Vol. 1 of The Cambridge History of Judaism. Cambridge: Cambridge University Press, 1984. 70–87.

Stern, Menahem. "Diaspora." In vol. 6 of *Encyclopaedia Judaica.* Edited by Cecil Roth. 16 vols. New York: Macmillan, 1971. 7–19.

Sullivan, Kevin. *Wrestling with Angels: A Study of the Relationship Between Angels and Humans in Ancient Jewish Literature and the New Testament.* Arbeiten zur Geschichte des antiken Judentums und des Urchristentums 55. Leiden: Brill, 2003.

Talmon, Shemaryahu. "Daniel." In *The Literary Guide to the Bible.* Edited by Robert Alter and Frank Kermode. Cambridge MA: The Belknap Press of Harvard University Press, 1987. 343–56.

Teeple, H. M. "Mystery." In *Harper's Bible Dictionary.* Edited by Paul J. Achtemeier. San Francisco: Harper & Row, 1985. 672–74.

Thompson, Henry O. *The Book of Daniel: An Annotated Bibliography.* Books of the Bible 1. New York: Garland Publishing, 1993.

———. "Dura." In vol. 2 of *The Anchor Bible Dictionary.* Edited by David Noel Freedman. 6 vols. New York: Doubleday & Company, 1992. 241.

Tigay, Jeffrey. *Deuteronomy.* The JPS Torah Commentary. Philadelphia: The Jewish Publication Society, 1996.

Toorn, Karel van der. "In the Lions' Den: The Babylonian Background of a Biblical Motif." *Catholic Biblical Quarterly* 60/4 (1998): 626–40.

Tov, Emanuel. *Textual Criticism of the Hebrew Bible.* Minneapolis: Fortress, 1992.

Towner, W. Sibley. *Daniel.* Interpretation, a Bible Commentary for Teaching and Preaching. Atlanta: John Knox, 1984.

———. "The Poetic Passages of Daniel 1–6." *Catholic Biblical Quarterly* 31/3 (1969): 317–26.

Trepp, Leo. *The Complete Book of Jewish Observance.* New York: Behrman House, 1980.

VanderKam, James. "Prophecy and Apocalyptics in the Ancient Near East" In vol. 3 of *Civilizations of the Ancient Near East.* Edited by Jack Sasson. 4 vols. Peabody, MA: Hendrickson, 2000. 2083–94.

———, editor. *Qumran Cave 4. XVII: Parabiblical Texts, Part 3.* Discoveries in the Judean Desert 22. Oxford: Clarendon Press, 1996. 88–89.

Venter, P. M. "The Function of Poetic Speech in the Narrative in Daniel 2." *Hervormde Teologiese Studies* 49 (1993): 1009–20.

Watts, John D. W. "Babylonian Idolatry in the Prophets as a False Socio-Economic System." In *Israel's Apostasy and Restoration: Essays in Honor of Roland K. Harrison.* Edited by Avraham Gileadi. Grand Rapids MI: Baker, 1988. 115–22.

Weinberg, Joel. "The International Elite of the Achaemenid Empire: Reality and Fiction." *Zeitschrift für die alttestamentliche Wissenschaft* 111/4 (1999): 583–608.

Weinfeld, Moshe. *Social Justice in Ancient Israel and in the Ancient Near East.* Minneapolis: Fortress, 1995.

Wesselius, Jan-Wim. "Discontinuity, Congruence and the Making of the Hebrew Bible." *Scandinavian Journal of the Old Testament* 13 (1999): 24–77.

Wills, Lawrence. *The Jew in the Court of the Foreign King: Ancient Jewish Court Legends.* Harvard Dissertations in Religion 6. Minneapolis: Fortress, 1990.

Wilson, Gerald. "The Prayer of Daniel 9: Reflection on Jeremiah 29." *Journal for the Study of the Old Testament* 48 (1990): 91–99.

Wolters, Al. "An Allusion to Libra in Daniel 5." In *Die Rolle der Astronomie in den Kulturen Mesopotamiens.* Edited by Hannes D. Galter. Graz: rm-Druck- & Verlagsgesellschaft, 1993. 292–306.

———. "The Riddle of the Scales in Daniel 5." *Hebrew Union College Annual* 62 (1991): 155–77.

———. "'Untying the King's Knots': Physiology and Wordplay in Daniel 5." *Journal of Biblical Literature* 110/1 (1991): 117–22.

Wright, N. T. *The New Testament and the People of God.* Vol. 1 of Christian Origins and the Question of God. London: SPCK, 1992.

———. *The Resurrection of the Son of God.* Vol. 3 of Christian Origins and the Question of God. Minneapolis: Fortress, 2003.

Xenophon. *Cyropaedia.* Translated by Walter Miller. 2 vols. Loeb Classical Library. New York: G. P. Putnam's Sons, 1925–1932.

Yamauchi, Edwin M. "Greece and Babylon Revisited." In *To Understand the Scriptures: Essays in Honor of William H. Shea.* Edited by David Merling. Berrien Springs MI: Andrews University Press, 1997. 127–35.

———. *Persia and the Bible.* Grand Rapids MI: BakerBooks, 1996.

Zimmerli, Walther. *Ezekiel: A Commentary on the Book of the Prophet Ezekiel.* Hermeneia. Philadelphia: Fortress, 1983.

INDEX OF MODERN AUTHORS

INDEX OF SIDEBARS AND ILLUSTRATIONS

INDEX OF SCRIPTURES

INDEX OF TOPICS